Curriculum Development
Perspectives From Around the World

Edited by
James D. Kirylo
Southeastern Louisiana University
Hammond, Louisiana

Ann K. Nauman
St. Joseph Seminary College
St. Benedict, Louisiana

Association for
Childhood Education International™

17904 Georgia Ave., Ste. 215
Olney, MD 20832
www.acei.org; 800-423-3563

Views expressed do not necessarily agree with positions taken by the
Association for Childhood Education International.

Bruce Herzig, ACEI Editor
Anne Bauer, ACEI Editor
Deborah Jordan Kravitz, Production

Library of Congress Cataloging-in-Publication Data
Nauman, Ann K. (Ann Keith)
  Curriculum development : perspectives from around the world / James D. Kirylo, Ann K. Nauman,
editors.
      p. cm.
  Includes bibliographical references.
  ISBN 978-0-87173-176-0 (pbk.)
 1. Early childhood education--United States.. 2. Early childhood education--Curricula--United States.
 3. Child development--United States. I. Kirylo, James D.
  LB1139.25.C87 2010
  375'.001--dc22
                              2010001832

To hard-working teachers, curriculum workers, and all those who work for a more just and better world.

Table of Contents

Embracing Commonalities, Celebrating Differences, and Learning From Each Other

James D. Kirylo

Nothing is impossible when we work in solidarity
with love, respect, and justice as our guiding lights.
—Joe Kincheloe, 2004

Without dialogue there is no communication,
and without communication there can be no true education.
—Paulo Freire, 1990

Multiple Voices of Curriculum Work

The term "curriculum" is a verb derived from the Latin infinitive verb *currere*, which is an action, or a journey, to run the course (Pinar, 1994; Pinar & Grumet, 1976). The assumption is that the inner dynamics of a person are inherent, thus becoming intimately involved in the curriculum, facilitating direction. As Slattery (1995) asserts, the curriculum becomes an inward journey, a human question. And while the curriculum becomes that personal inward journey of exploration, negotiation, and reconceptualization, it is naturally linked to a concrete plan of instruction and subject matter that students will learn (Ornstein & Hunkins, 2004). Moreover, theories of human development, the nature of learning, the nature of knowledge, and the influence of cultural and social forces play a big part in the process of understanding the meaning, intent, and action of curriculum (Parkay & Hass, 2000). Ultimately, curriculum work should be developmentally appropriate and designed to positively impact student growth (Longstreet & Shane, 1993). To be sure, curriculum theory, planning, and implementation constitute a complicated, untidy endeavor because of the many voices involved in the process, the inherent political nature of schooling, and the basic questions that conceptually underlie all curriculum work (see *Curriculum for a New Millennium*, by Longstreet and Shane [1993]).

Various groups of people, such as policymakers, teachers, school administrators, parent organizations, university scholars, and religious organizations, all want their point of view to be heard regarding the nature of curriculum and what a school curriculum ought to be. These various groups make up what we call a community. And a major element to fostering the development of any community, wherever that may be in the world, is how its youth are educated. Whether that community is located in the remotest part of Brazil or in a metropolis like Kyoto or in the southern hemisphere or the northern hemisphere; education is always a central concern for its people. Naturally, the question is: What kind of education does that community want for its population and what should the curriculum look like?

When Ann Nauman, my co-editor, and I started on this project, we not only spent a considerable amount of time discussing the various complexities inherent in education, and, in particular, grappling with the ongoing conundrum as to the meaning and intent of curriculum and what it should look like in practice, but we also found ourselves speculating about what other countries are doing to make sense of curriculum and how they go about designing and implementing a developmentally appropriate curriculum. Therefore, we thought a book such as this would make a meaningful contribution to the professional literature, facilitating a more global awareness of curriculum development from countries around the world. Indeed, we can learn from each other.

We are proud to say that we have 26 countries represented in this text. Finally, as an integral part of its mission to promote and support the educational global community, we thought that the Association for Childhood Education International (ACEI) would be a natural fit to publish such a book.

Background of Authors and Writing Style

As a point of disclosure, the variety of authors who have contributed to this text fall into three broad categories. Some authors are from the country they wrote about and still live and work in those countries. Other authors were born and raised in the countries they discuss, but now live and work in the United States. Finally, some authors are from the United States, but have had extended stays and/or studied in the country they wrote about. For most of the latter, these chapters were co-authored with individuals who are from the country of topic. While the authors in the second and third category certainly provide a meaningful insight of curriculum in the country they wrote about, it is worth noting that the likelihood of the most authentic, current context of curriculum would be from authors who are in the first category. For more specific detail about each author, one can read the brief biographical information at the end of each chapter.

While each author naturally wrote in his or her own particular writing style and was given the flexibility to select the most appropriate curricular topics, we made suggestions for including relevant points in each chapter. For instance, we asked the authors to provide a brief history of the development of education of the country, with a special emphasis on curriculum development; an understanding of how curriculum has evolved over the years, leading to a current overview of curricula that are presently being utilized in both elementary and secondary education; the kind of teaching methodologies that have been employed over the years, and the current state of pedagogy in both elementary and secondary education, particularly as it relates to a developmentally appropriate practice; expectations and/or pressures placed on school-age youngsters relative to cultural, gender, and ethnic influences and how these factors have affected curriculum development; and the social, political, economic, religious, and educational dilemmas of curriculum and pedagogy in the context of the cultural realities. In the end, while all the chapters were broadly written relative to the suggestions that were provided, some authors chose to focus more intensely on one particular educational or curriculum area, such as science education in Finland, bilingual education in Paraguay, and special education in Turkey. In short, by design, there is no "uniform" presentation of each chapter.

For most of the authors in the text, English is their second language, which, at times, presented some challenges for us as the editors. To be sure, when we consider anyone who writes in a second or third language, particularly when technical or content-related vocabulary is required, one cannot but admire the skill, time, and commitment that are incumbent upon the writers. Thus, the nature of this book and the multiple nationalities represented will naturally have an impact on the variety of writing styles and syntax from chapter to chapter. We made what we thought were necessary editorial changes, but at the same time were careful to maintain the integrity and individuality of each chapter, particularly when complex, conceptual concepts were explained.

Ultimately, the goal of this text is two-fold: first, to produce a comprehensive book on education and curriculum, representative of various countries from around the world, that would be an informative resource for educators in general, but especially for those specializing in multicultural education. Indeed, this book can be a valuable resource for a variety of venues, such as university undergraduate/graduate courses, Peace Corps workers, and other related international educational agencies. Second, to publish a volume that would highlight, recognize, and celebrate our common interests, shared values, varying dilemmas, cultural influences, and the diverse ways curriculum is viewed. In the final analysis, we think this book will be a powerful teaching tool to assist all of us in our ongoing search for a more global understanding of curriculum development around the world.

Represented Countries

We thought that the most logical way to sequence the chapters would be in alphabetical order by country. The following nations are represented in this book: Australia, Botswana, Brazil, Canada, China, the Czech Republic, Finland, Honduras, India, Italy, Jordan, Kenya, Korea, Lebanon, Malawi, New Zealand, Northern Ireland, Paraguay, Poland, Qatar, Russian Federation, Scotland, Swaziland, Turkey, United Kingdom, and the United States. Clearly, the countries represented in this book are only a small sampling of "curriculum from around the world." However, these glimpses of curriculum from a variety of countries provides a window of opportunity to learn from each other, linking the education community closer together. Indeed, a second volume of this type of book is a great possibility.

The first chapter is a historical overview of curriculum, beginning with pre-historical times, written by Ann Nauman. The chapter provides a snapshot view of how we have progressively moved from the rudimentary elements of education and curriculum to the Reformation, the scientific revolution, the Enlightenment, the Industrial Revolution, and other noteworthy eras. Nauman's discussion highlights various influential educational leaders, along with their contributions to curriculum development.

In Chapter 2, Debra Panizzon discusses curriculum development in Australia, highlighting the influence of state/territory and national agendas. She underscores major historical educational initiatives that have had an impact on curriculum design in Australia. In addition, we learn how teachers are involved in curriculum planning and implementation and the central role of pedagogical practices. Panizzon explores how the school curriculum must be fair and just, thereby facilitating "education for all" in Australia.

Botswana is the focus of Chapter 3. In this chapter, we learn from Cephas David Yandila that Botswana, formally known as Bechuandaland, gained its sovereignty in 1966. Yandila points out that since Botswana gained its independence, its economy has moved from an agricultural base to a mining base and is in the process moving toward a technology economy. The principal focus of this chapter is on science education, due to the fact that science plays a primary role in the country's economic growth.

Ann Nauman and Nelio Bizzo begin Chapter 4 by explaining that in 1500, the Portuguese first laid claim to the territory that we now know as Brazil. The authors concisely discuss the role of commerce and colonization in Brazil's early history. Finally, and within a historical, cultural, and political context, the authors shift the major focus of the chapter from the early developments of Brazilian education to the Pombaline Reforms, to Brazilian independence to the various educational and curricular challenges that Brazil has faced over the years.

Chapter 5 is a discussion of education in Canada. Beginning with the educational foundations of New France (the French colony [1655-1763] that included most of present-day Nova Scotia, New

Brunswick, Ontario, and Quebec, and much of the central eastern United States) up to the present day, Brenda J. Gustafson and Marie-Claire Shanahan begin their chapter by providing a succinct historical context of curriculum development in Canada. Understanding the historical context assists us in realizing that curriculum development in Canada has been challenging, as educators have sought a balance between recognizing and celebrating cultural and linguistic diversity and developing a shared national identity.

Nili Luo and Janet S. Arndt, in Chapter 6, emphasize that the rich Chinese tradition in education philosophy has had a significant impact on education in modern China. Starting with their explanation of the founding of the People's Republic of China in 1949, the authors discuss the influence of ancient traditions upon the shift in the role of education from only serving the elite class to the education of the masses, to explaining the combining of Marxism and Chinese tradition and its overall impact on the education system. Ultimately, as Luo and Arndt point out, Chinese education primarily focuses on why and how children must be shaped to benefit the society and the inculcation of the understanding that acquiring knowledge is fundamental.

Chapter 7, written by Ferdinand Mazal, Jiri Stelzer, and Zuzana Vasickova, is about the Czech Republic. Moving from the 13th century to the present day, the narrative tells the long history of a country that has gone through geographic and political changes, all naturally impacting the education system. It was not until 1993 that the Czech Republic became an independent state, and entered the European Union in 2004. In addition to providing a historical context of the history of curriculum development in the Czech Republic, Mazal, Stelzer, and Vasickova underscore that since becoming a European Union (EU) member, there has been an attempt to reform the education system more in compliance with the EU politics and requirements.

In Chapter 8, Jari Lavonen and Heidi Krzywacki discuss the implementation of Finnish education policy through a national core curriculum. They commence their chapter with a historical overview of education in Finland, discussing the interrelationship between international and national entities, and the significance of the geographical location of Finland. While the thrust of their chapter focuses on the national core curriculum, Lavonen and Krzywacki focus on science education to emphasize the intent of the national core curriculum.

Honduras is the focus of Chapter 9. In this chapter, Cristina P. Valentino makes it clear that in order to understand the education system in Honduras, one has to be aware of the financial and political circumstances and the available resources that affect the educational decision-making process. Indeed, as she makes clear, poverty is a major problem in Honduras, presenting many challenges for the Honduran population. In addition to discussing the implications of poverty and its effect on education, Valentino discusses the history of education and the various school reform efforts impacting curricular decisions.

In Chapter 10, focusing on India, Aradhana Mudambi and Basanti Chakraborty divide their work into two major sections. In the first section, they discuss the demographics of the Indian population, primarily focusing on underprivileged groups, including lower social caste, scheduled caste, and scheduled tribe, rural, Muslim, and female students. In the second part of their chapter, Mudambi and Chakraborty provide a historical context of education and the evolving nature of curriculum work. Finally, they discuss the various reform efforts that have attempted to create a quality education program, particularly for the poor and disenfranchised.

Elisabetta Violi LeJeune begins Chapter 11 on Italy by describing how the Italian educational system has been a long, complex endeavor, particularly with respect to the interfacing of secular politics and the Roman Catholic Church. In explaining a historical context of the term "curriculum," she points out that curriculum ultimately is an instrument of planning to help guide the meeting of prescribed objectives. LeJeune goes on to explain in her chapter how various reform efforts have affected the education system in Italy.

Jordan is the subject of Chapter 12, in which Yousef M. Al-Shaboul, Suheil M. Asassfeh, Yaser A. Al-Tamimi, and Sabri Sh. Alshboul point out that the country is governed by a parliamentary system with a constitutional hereditary monarchy and that Islam is the state religion and Arabic the official language. Finally, Al-Shaboul, Asassfeh, Al-Tamimi, and Alshboul provide an overview of education in Jordan, discussing the various curricular decisions made by leaders, as well as teachers' typical pedagogical strategies.

In Chapter 13, Lydiah Nganga and John Kambutu explore curriculum development in Kenya and changes in education since its independence in 1963. Located on the eastern side of Africa and approximately the size of the state of Texas, Kenya has faced many societal, political, and educational challenges. Nganga and Kambutu describe how education has evolved and how curricular decisions have been reached in Kenya, from the colonial education system to its present-day structure.

The school curriculum in South Korea, discussed in Chapter 14, is typically revised every five to six years, due to political, cultural, and social changes. Guang-Lea Lee and Donald A. Myers begin the chapter by providing a brief description of the country's goals for elementary, middle, and high school education. Within a discussion of South Korea's social, political, and cultural context, the principal thrust of the chapter is the development of the national English curriculum in primary schools and its impact on the population in South Korea.

In Chapter 15, Irma-Kaarina Ghosn begins by pointing out that the Republic of Lebanon is a country fraught with strife; since its independence in 1943, Lebanon has suffered periods of unrest, principally because of violent sectarian and intragroup conflicts. With a population of slightly under 4 million, approximately two-thirds Muslim and one-third Christian, Ghosn states that many officials in Lebanon see education as an ideal potential unifying force. Although the unifying impact has been nominal, this chapter explores the role of education and curriculum reform in Lebanon.

Malawi, which lies in southeastern Africa and forms part of the Sub-Saharan African region, has a population of approximately 12 million, with more than 80% of its citizens living in rural areas. Written by Grace Chiuye and Hartford Mchazime, Chapter 16 starts with a brief overview of the economic, political, and social situation in Malawi. They also reveal that the country is divided into three regions, with 16 different languages spoken across the regions. However, because of its importance to economic and political interaction, English is an official language, along with Chichewa. With respect to curriculum development, Chiuye and Mchazime divide their chapter into three distinct eras: the colonial era (1875-1964), the post-independence era (1964-1994), and the democratic era (1994 to the present).

New Zealand is the subject of Chapter 17, which is written by Alister Jones and Bronwen Cowie. The authors begin their discussion by pointing out that since 1877, educators in New Zealand are primarily under a mandate to implement the national curricula. Thus, beginning from its colonial days up to the present, this chapter is a historical sketch of curriculum development and the various reform efforts that have impacted its development. Jones and Cowie delineate the various stakeholders involved in curriculum-making within a complex political and social context.

Northern Ireland is discussed in Chapter 18, wherein Linda Pickett describes integrated education and a curriculum for peace. In order to understand the objective of integration education, a relatively new phenomenon, she provides a social and political context. Pickett points out that since the partitioning of Ireland in 1921, Northern Ireland has been a divided society, principally between the Catholic and Protestant traditions, resulting in conflict and segregated schools. Viewed as a means for social transformation (although not without controversy), the integrated school movement encourages Catholic and Protestant students to unite in school settings with the mission of promoting understanding, respect, and peace.

Valentina Canese in Chapter 19 provides us with a clear understanding of the socio-historical context of Guaraní and its impact on bilingual education and curriculum development in Paraguay. Recognizing the importance of Guaraní in the history of the country, the chapter begins by explaining that the 1992 Paraguayan Constitution adopted Guaraní, along with Spanish, as the official languages of Paraguay. Canese makes the point that Guaraní and bilingual education, within the country's historical, cultural, religious, and political contexts, are necessarily tied to curriculum reform in Paraguay.

In Chapter 20, Agnieszka Gutthy shares how curriculum development in Poland has been punctuated by challenging times. Gutthy provides a concise history of education and curriculum development in Poland, whether it was fighting to preserve its national identity and language during the Nazi occupation or seeking balance between the influence of the Church and the role of the government.

Qatar is nearly surrounded by the Persian Gulf, and as Allen J. Fromherz and Robin E. Fromherz point out in Chapter 21, it was once primarily populated by fishermen, pearl divers, nomads, and merchants. Today, Qatar is a progressive country, with a per capita gross domestic product nearly equal to that of Switzerland. While Dubai may be most internationally recognized city in Qatar for its glamour, the capital city of Doha is increasingly receiving much attention as a center for world diplomacy and international trade. Moreover, the education system is embracing the notion of constructivism in their curriculum, the primary focus of this chapter.

In Chapter 22, Elizabeth J. Sandell, Olga V. Klippa, and Maria S. Taratukhina provide an overview of curriculum development in the Russian Federation. They begin the chapter by mentioning that, geographically, Russia is the largest nation in the world, spanning more than 11 time zones. Starting with the Pre-Tsarist Period (prior to 1547) and proceeding to the Imperial Period (1547 to 1917), to the Soviet Period (1917 to 1991), to the Reform Period (1991 to 2001), and finally to the present day, Sandell, Klippa, and Taratukhina explain the historical unfolding of education and curriculum development in Russia. In addition, they describe various teaching methodologies within the various grade levels, and discuss the impact of cultural and ethnic influences on schooling.

In Chapter 23, which focuses on Scotland, Kevin Kelman and June Mitchell report that compulsory schooling for elementary school-age children was enacted in 1872, when the core curriculum was the "three Rs." However, the 1872 Act made exceptions, stating that children were not required to attend school if they could demonstrate a grade-appropriate competency in reading, writing, and arithmetic. Prior to the 1872 Act, religious education was the norm in Scottish education. In addition to a variety of various reform efforts, Kelman and Mitchell discuss the five National Priorities (2000) for education in Scotland.

The education system in Swaziland, which is the focus of Chapter 24, had its beginnings with a primal focus on survival, leisure, and safety. Moreover, as Betty T. Dlamini asserts, education was made possible through oral tradition, whereby the elders were considered the sole custodians of knowledge, leaving no written record of curriculum content. Because of colonization, the education system in Swaziland was highly influenced by British thought. Thus, in this chapter, Dlamini discusses the various political, social, cultural, and economic factors that have influenced curriculum development in Swaziland over the last 50 years.

In Chapter 25, Selda Ozdemir writes about curriculum, policy, and practice in Turkey. Beginning with an introduction of the historical context of general and special education, she explores the new curriculum reform effort and examines the challenges and dilemmas. For Ozdemir, the focal point of the chapter is special education, which has been undergoing a needed transformation with respect to perception, practices, and emphasis.

The subject of Chapter 26, written by Martin Braund, is the United Kingdom. Braund discusses the various school curricula trends and challenges. He points out that curriculum development is inseparable from politics and the social climate. Because of the expansive nature of the history of curriculum, Braund's primary focus is confined from the post-1944 period to the present day, as he discusses the various reform efforts that have shaped education in the United Kingdom.

Chapter 27 discusses the history of curriculum development in the United States. Susan P. Santoli, Rebecca McMahon Giles, and Edward L. Shaw, Jr., begin their discussion with curriculum development in colonial America, moving toward what they characterize as the Progressive Era (1900-1950), leading to their examination of present-day education in America. Throughout their chapter, the authors introduce various reform efforts, landmark decisions, and influential figures who have shaped education in the United States.

In the final chapter, Jerry Aldridge, Lois Christensen, and L. Kay Emfinger "tie" all the chapters together, providing an insightful reflection regarding "curriculum from around the world." To encapsulate, they provide three broad lenses from which we can view the complexity of the meaning, intent, and practice of curriculum. These lenses are Fraser's Model of Social Justice (Fraser, 1997), Jungck and Marshall's (1992) curriculum perspectives, and Aldridge, Emfinger, and Martin's (2006) frameworks, approaches, and models ideas concerning curriculum differentiation.

Emerging Themes

As a result of working on this book, three major themes unfolded. First, bringing a project together such as this leads one to step back and reflect, marveling at the wonders of technology and its impact on facilitating the notion of a global education community. Second, whatever the country, education and the making of curriculum are naturally rooted in a historical context, in which decisions are filtered through a blending of complex political, religious, and cultural influences. Yet, despite different geographic locations, histories, and influences, most countries share common education and curricula challenges. Finally, education is a natural tool that can be instrumental in building a global community where tolerance is taught, cultural differences are celebrated and shared, and commonalities are viewed as building blocks to unity.

From the process of extending invitations to the various authors to participate in this project, to the writing of their chapter proposals, to the actual writing of the chapters, to the editing and revising process, and, finally, to an external review, one must consider the technological implications of such an endeavor. First, it is worth reminding readers that the 49 authors/co-authors who contributed chapters to this book are spread out the world over, representing countries from all the settled continents. Second, for most of the authors, English is a second language, but dependence on the common language of technology has become a mainstay for all. Third, although I have met only a few of the authors who have contributed to this project, I have come to know them through electronic and phone communication. Fourth, as one of the editors, I found it remarkable to receive practically instantaneous responses regarding needed clarifications from the authors. For example, it was not uncommon for me to write an author in Botswana, Lebanon, or Scotland, then receive a response within an hour or even just minutes.

In an age of e-mail and document attachments, communicating with people from around the world is as convenient as talking to a colleague in an office right next you. For most of us, we now take for granted the wonders of the speed, efficiency, and convenience of electronic communication. However, it was only a short time ago that the mode of this type of communication was not possible, much less an attempt to edit and revise 27 different manuscripts, with most coming from all parts of the globe. Thus, what has taken a relatively short time to put together, conceivably would have taken 10, 15, or more years to do in times past. Clearly, technology has been an integral tool to conveniently and rapidly circulate information, foster communication, and cultivate relationships. In short, technology use is an empowering tool to the building of a global community.

As one reads this text, it becomes clear that regardless of the country, a complex web of cultural, religious, and political influences has an enormous impact with respect to education and curriculum development. Yet, while each country naturally possesses its own unique perspectives and influences, most share common education and curricula challenges, particularly as they relate to the co-existence of colonial influences and indigenous traditions, the link of language learning and national identity, the national versus local autonomy curriculum debate, preparation of teachers, teacher shortages, social justice concerns, economic development, and war and natural calamities. From reading about what each country desires regarding what educators should teach, how they teach, and what the youth should be learning, it is evident that while we certainly can learn about and appreciate our cultural, religious, and political differences, we also quickly find out about our common challenges.

Thus, the concept of dialogue comes to mind regarding cultivating an appreciation for differences and uniting in addressing common challenges. What may seem obvious, but is seemingly difficult to grasp and put into practice, is that building a global education community must begin with the understanding that different mentalities and ways of looking at the world are important assumptions when engaging in genuine dialogue (Gutierrez, 1990). Appreciation for differences disarms resistance and is an important cornerstone for building relationships. Moreover, the more an effort is made to communicate and understand, the better the possibility that stereotypes, fears, and ignorance are dispelled, and the better our chances are for working together regarding the various common educational and curricula challenges. Indeed, education is about entering into relationships, and dialogue is the important link to make connections from person to person and nation to nation (Freire, 1990, 1996). In the final analysis, education can be a powerful unifying force in the building of a "united nations" where tolerance, respect, and relationships are fostered. The late Joe Kincheloe (2004) is so right when he declares, "Nothing is impossible when we work in solidarity with love, respect, and justice as our guiding lights" (p. 3).

References

Aldridge, J., Emfinger, K., & Martin, K. (2006). Curriculum frameworks, approaches, and models in early childhood education: What's the difference? *Focus on Teacher Education, 7*(2), 3-7.

Fraser, N. (1997). *Justice interruptus: Critical reflections on the "postsocialist" condition.* New York: Routledge.

Freire, P. (1990). *Pedagogy of the oppressed* (M. Ramos, Trans.). New York: Continuum.

Freire, P. (1997). *Pedagogy of the heart* (D. Macedo & A. Oliveira, Trans.). New York: Continuum.

Gutierrez, G. (1990). *The truth shall make you free* (M. O'Connell, Trans.). New York: Orbis Books.

Jungck, S., & Marshall, J. D. (1992). Curricular perspectives on one great debate. In S. Kessler & B. B. Swaderner (Eds.), *Reconceptualizing the early childhood curriculum: Beginning the dialogue* (pp. 19-37). New York: Teachers College Press.

Kincheloe, J. (2004). *Critical pedagogy.* New York: Peter Lang.

Longstreet, W., & Shane, H. G. (1993). *Curriculum for a new millennium.* Boston: Allyn and Bacon.

Ornstein, A. C., & Hunkins, F. P. (2004). *Curriculum: Foundations, principles, and issues.* Boston: Pearson Education.

Parkay, F. W., & Hass, G. (2000). *Curriculum planning: A contemporary approach* (7th ed.). Boston: Allyn and Bacon.

Pinar, W. (1994). *Autobiography, politics, and sexuality: Essays in curriculum theory.* Dubuque, IA: Kendall/Hunt.

Pinar, W., & Grumet, M. R. (1976). *Toward a poor curriculum.* Dubuque, IA: Kendall/Hunt.

Slattery, P. (1995). *Curriculum development in the postmodern era.* New York: Garland Publishing.

A Historical Overview of Curriculum (Prehistory to 1900 CE)

Ann K. Nauman

Thousands of years ago, long before any history was written, Neolithic man and woman began to adapt their environment to their and their family's needs, and to teach children survival and conformity skills. There was little need for writing. "They learned and retained and passed on to their children by recitation what seemed necessary in the way of historical record. It was probably by committing such oral traditions and folk lore to writing that literature began" (Durant, 1963, p. 76).

The teaching method was demonstration and imitation, and their curriculum included the necessary elements of community living, tool making, hunting and food gathering for males and rudimentary child care for females, and defensive and survival techniques, along with clan rituals and taboos. Education was informal; the reward was survival.

Mesopotamia

Long before the concept of curriculum became a field for investigation, people attempted to teach their children specific skills—first, what they needed for simple survival, then what they needed to achieve success in their lives. The Sumerians (ca. 3000 BCE), who lived in southern Mesopotamia (modern-day Iraq), were the first in recorded history to offer a "course of study" in an organized education system. "Schools were attached to most of the temples and clergy instructed boys and girls in writing and arithmetic, formed their habits into patriotism and piety and prepared some of them for the profession of scribe" (Durant, 1963, p. 129). Instruction was based upon memorization of appropriate subject matter and the utilization of cuneiform script. Murphy (2006) writes, "There is considerable evidence that by the time of Hamurabi (1762-1950 BCE), there was an elaborate system of schools for the . . . education of priests, scribes, and civil servants" (p. 3). These schools taught, along with

Overview

17

the rudimentary reading and cuneiform, religious doctrines and civil law. In the lower echelons of society, young people were taught such skills as surveying, farm techniques, and toolmaking (Longstreet & Shane, 1993).

The Babylonians, who lived in the lower portion of Mesopotamia, used cuneiform as the basic curriculum for the scribe, and "scribal education was basic to all careers, whether in the clergy, army or civil service" (Hallo & Simpson, 1998, p. 156). Historians use the school at Nippur as a model for reconstructing the curriculum and other aspects of school life.

> *Instruction began with a list of some 450 cuneiform signs, learned in a fixed order and written out repeatedly one beneath the other, . . . on school tablets, until the pupil's hand approached the master's sample in excellence. . . .*
>
> *Having mastered the writing and pronunciation of the simpler cuneiform signs, the student next embarked on learning by rote and by hand, a long succession of syllabaries and lexical lists. . . . The scribal curriculum was never confined entirely to purely lexical and grammatical texts. Syntax could hardly be learned except from connected prose and poetry. In the elementary curriculum of the Old Babylonian period, the Sumerian proverbs were particularly popular. (Hallo & Simpson, 1998, p. 156)*

The Near East, the Ancient Hebrews

The early *habiru* were a Semitic people who settled, after a long period of migration, in the Arabian peninsula in the third millennium BCE (Lucas, 1972) and established a theocratic community. They very soon saw the need for educating youth in the tenets and rituals of their faith. As early as the sixth and seventh centuries BCE, there were structured places of instruction in Hebrew communities. "Sons of the prophets," as the students were called, gathered in groups of 50 to 400 at the feet of learned men for instruction in religious traditions and practices (Durant, 1963). Lucas (1972) explains, "Subjects taught included music, sacred poetry, theology, prayers, rituals of worship, and means of inducing a state of religious ecstasy" (p. 150). Later, there arose a scribal class, educated men who functioned as lawyers, copyists, and professional teachers. The scribes were self-perpetuating, teaching young men to become scribes in their turn. Scribal students learned the laws, rituals, and taboos of Hebrew culture.

Around 75 BCE, a set of education reforms proposed compulsory education, because a large majority of the Jews could neither read nor write. This ideal was not realized until 64 CE, when the high priest, Josua ben Gamala, made elementary schools obligatory for all males, making the Jews the first ancient people to make some formal schooling compulsory and universal (Lucas, 1972).

Boys began their formal education at the age of 6, devoting themselves to ever-more intensive study of the Torah. The curriculum included reading, writing, arithmetic, ancient Hebrew, and the vernacular language, Aramaic. After the third century CE, the curriculum also included Psalms, the Prophets, the Book of Proverbs, synagogal liturgy, rituals, and Greek (Lucas, 1972).

Some boys, when they reached the age of 15, were sent to the *Beth-hamidrash* (House of Exposition) for study of the *Mishna* or Oral Law. Jerusalem was a center for higher education, with doctoral-level individual instruction and independent research. Students at this level learned to translate Hebrew into Aramaic or Greek, and studied Hellenistic philosophy and literature.

Ancient China

Murphy (2006) states, "There is evidence to suggest that formal schools existed in China during the Hsia and Shang dynasties, perhaps as early as 2000 BCE" (p. 3). By the time of Confucius (551-479 BCE) (and Plato a bit later), philosophers and educators saw the need for organization of the process of schooling. Such organization was culturally based, asking what the student needed to learn and to become in order to find success in life. Confucius placed great emphasis upon ethics and taught only what young men needed in order to prepare them for court positions. The Confucian Ideal was filial piety (Pai & Adler, 2001). His curriculum, according to the historian Gerald Gutek (2005), "emphasized literature, poetry, music, the study of rites and ceremonies, and the practice of civility" (p. 23). In addition, young men in ancient China (formal education was only for males) studied history, government documents, and civil law in order to prepare themselves for careers in government or, failing that, in teaching (Murphy, 2006).

Ancient Greece

During the Homeric period of Greek history, about the 9th century BCE, educational ideals were shaped by the two heroic epics, the *Iliad* and the *Odyssey*. Young men sought to emulate the heroes and perform great deeds of physical strength rather than of mental acuity. Lucas (1972) writes, "Young men of the *aristoi* (aristocrats) were to be educated by their fathers . . . the content of instruction conjoined rhetorical and military training with little or no emphasis upon other areas of development" (p. 51). Education was largely informal, acquired as part of the normal process of growing up (Nagle, 1995).

Between the 8th and the 6th centuries BCE, great social changes took place in Athens and the other city states of Hellas. Common people (the *demos*), through trade and commerce, became wealthy and demanded a part in government. As democracy became stronger, the need for change in educational practices grew. As a result, less emphasis was placed upon the heroic deeds of the past and more upon the practical needs of the present. Writing, arithmetic, geometry, drawing, music, and gymnastics—to maintain the balance between intellectual and physical training—made up the curriculum of most of the schools of the day.

The Sophists (wise men), the first professional teachers, who were worldly men from the metropolitan areas of the littoral of Asia Minor, appeared in the Greek city states in the 5th century, offering the youth the relevant training they were so avidly seeking. The Sophists did not advocate a set curriculum, but rather promised to teach students "everything necessary to the educated man" (Lucas, 1972 p. 69); that is, they would teach them all they needed to know in order to enjoy political advantage. The Sophists' interpretation of *arete*[1] was the accomplishment of political ambition and the ability to influence the thinking and actions of others. The curriculum of the Sophists included logic, grammar, rhetoric, oratory, eristics (disputation), and dialectics. Protagoras of Abdera (481-411 BCE) best typified the Sophists' pragmatic approach when he stated, "Man is the measure of all things." That is, everything studied and learned must be relevant to man's own existence. No longer was he to spend his time solely with esoteric and, to the Sophists, irrelevant contemplation of the meaning and the universality of truth; rather, he would learn those things that would help him to achieve the material things that were important to him. Cicero later said of the Sophists, "[They] brought philosophy down from heaven to the dwellings of men" (Lucas, 1972, p. 71).

There were both philosophic and curricular reactions to the Sophists. The most prominent opponents were Socrates (469-399 BCE), Plato (427-347 BCE), and Aristotle (384-322 BCE). Lucas (1972) states, "Plato aimed to refute the Sophist doctrine of skeptical relativism and to substitute for it a theory of an ordered stable universe in which there are absolute, transcendent standards for ethical conduct" (p. 78). Heavily influenced by his mentor Socrates, Plato saw the need for the study of mathematics and its rationality for his "Philosopher Kings." In his institution of higher learning, the Academy, Plato imposed a preliminary curriculum of arithmetic, geometry, astronomy, philosophy, and harmonics—all needed to prepare students for higher learning through the study of the dialectic—along with music and gymnastics for building a sound body. He believed in and practiced censorship, advocating in his most famous writing, *The Republic,* that children be allowed to read only the classic hero tales and stories designed to uplift and edify.

Aristotle was both a student and a teacher in Plato's Academy. Although he accepted most of Plato's philosophic tenets at first, Aristotle later in his life began to find, with his scientist's mind, areas of disagreement with his mentor's philosophy and curriculum. Aristotle was interested in the natural sciences and had an opportunity, as tutor to the young Alexander of Macedonia, to set forth his ideas in a course of study for the young prince. Aristotle's own school, the Lyceum, established in Athens in 334 BCE, was both a teaching institution and a center for scientific research. The curriculum included the natural sciences, geography, politics, metaphysics, and ethics. His lectures covered logic, arts, psychology, physiology, political science, mathematics, zoology, botany, biology, law, metaphysics, epistemology, astronomy, and ethics (Gutek, 2005), although he did not confine himself to those topics. He wrote and lectured on every area of interest of his times. His writings were "very logical, orderly, and rich in insight" (Murphy, 2006, p. 40).

During what is known as the "Hellenistic period" (323-30 BCE), the process of education became more formalized, with curricula based upon achievement of the "Golden Mean"—a state of balance among the arts, the sciences, and physical training. The educated individual who was a lifelong learner sought "*paideia*, the ideal of personal life enriched and nurtured by the values of classical culture, a precious possession imparted through education" (Lucas, 1972, p. 96). He wanted to achieve perfection in both mind and body. In Athens, philosophy, oratory, music, and physical training were emphasized; in Sparta, only military skills were taught. Women, for the most part, received no formal education at all in Athens, although Plato had admitted a few qualified women to his Academy. In Sparta, women received intensive physical training in order to ensure that they would bear healthy children.

During the third century BCE, gymnastics and music were gradually replaced by the study of language and literature. Oratory remained a central core subject, although its practical applications in the political context had largely disappeared. A greater emphasis was placed upon pedagogy and institutionalization of schools. Children in the third and second centuries BCE were first taught reading and writing. Beyond the primary school stage, they learned literature and grammar and there were *gymnasia* for those who wanted athletic training. At the higher levels, the schools offered philosophy, rhetoric, physical sciences, geography, mathematics, and oratory. Many institutions of higher learning specialized, and offered lectures, in only one or two subjects. There were schools of rhetoric and those offering philosophy, along with "research centers," which offered, in addition to the sciences, history, geometry, medicine, art, and literature.

Early Rome

In 509 BCE, after Roman citizens had overthrown their Etruscan ruler, the city/state of Rome became a republic. The people of the republic were not innovators. Perhaps they were pragmatists, and were willing to accept and adapt the already developed Greek systems of government, religion, and education. In any case, they tended to use whatever cultural elements seemed to meet their immediate needs. However, in one very important way the Romans differed vastly from the Greeks—in child-rearing techniques. The Roman family was strong and the father had power of life and death over his wife and his children, a power that lasted for all their lives. Education became a matter of family responsibility and pride, the wealthy *patricians* being able to give their children extensive and long-term instruction, while the *plebeians* often had to content themselves with basic literacy and vocational skills.

In the days of the early republic, mothers were expected to give their children basic instruction in the home, teaching both boys and girls to read and write. Girls were later taught by their mothers the skills necessary to run a household, the management of a slave-run household, and child care practices. Boys were instructed by their fathers, the tradition mandating that the son would follow the father into trade, government, or a profession.

Formal schools, patterned upon the Hellenic model, appeared in Rome about 300 BCE (Murphy, 2006). The *ludus litterarius,* the elementary school, served children from ages 7 through 12. Boys studied grammar, both Greek and Latin, composition and literature, all taught by the *grammaticus,* usually an educated Greek slave (Kamm, 1995).

Later additions to the curriculum were: all of the liberal arts—grammar, rhetoric, dialectic, arithmetic (rudimentary because the system did not include the zero), use of the abacus, geometry, music, and astronomy. Boys had to learn the civic law code of Rome, The Law of the Twelve Tables—sometimes they used it as a writing exercise, copying long passages—and all males were taught the virtues of fortitude, justice, and prudence (Murphy, 2006). Kamm (1995) stated, "Formal education ceased for girls at the age of 12, but boys who showed promise were sent on to the 'grammar school'," where they studied Greek and Latin literature (p. 117).

With the death of Julius Caesar and the ascendancy of his heir, Octavian (Augustus), the Roman Republic ceased to exist (31 BCE). The Roman Empire was born.

The Roman Empire

Much of the energy and attention of political leaders after the assassination of Julius Caesar (44 BCE) and during the early years of the empire was concentrated upon their struggles to retain power, to put down revolts among subject peoples, and to pacify the unemployed and poverty-stricken citizens of Rome. There was, consequently, little done by the first emperors to deal with problems in education.

For the most part, formal Roman education followed the Greek pattern, with curricular emphasis on Greek and Latin grammar. The school of the rhetor appeared in the last century of the Republic and skilled orators opened private academies where they offered courses in rhetoric. Lucas (1972) wrote, "Romans enrolled in rhetorical schools with the avowed aim of acquiring *humanitas*, of becoming cultured gentlemen. But that ran directly counter to the deeply ingrained Roman concern for practicality, for narrow utilitarianism" (p. 121). Young men wanted to be prepared for the Forum, the marketplace, and the professions.

The Emperor Titus Flavius Vaspasianus (Vespasian) (CE 69-79) made peace with the Senate and re-established constitutional government, after which he gave his attention to cultural matters. Cognizant of the fact that many of those who wanted training in addition to that offered by the rhetors' schools were going abroad to Alexandria, Antioch, Tarsus, or Rhodes, Vespasian opened a library and *Athenaeum* in Rome similar to those of Alexandria, and endowed chairs of rhetoric. According to Lucas, "By endowing chairs of rhetoric and exempting rhetoricians from important civil responsibilities, Vespasian enabled an intellectual class to get its education on 'home territory' " (p. 121). Will Durant (1944) wrote of Vespasian:

> *It remained for this blunt soldier to establish the first system of state education in classical antiquity. He ordered that certain qualified teachers of Latin and Greek literature and rhetoric should thereafter be paid out of public funds and should receive a pension after 20 years of service. (p. 289)*

Marcus Fabius Quintilianus (Quintilian) (35-95 CE) was a well-known teacher of rhetoric in imperial Rome. Born in Spain, the son of a rhetorician, he studied in Rome and was an admirer of Cicero. When Quintilian was 33, he opened a school of oratory in Rome under the patronage of the emperor Vaspasian, who created a chair of Latin rhetoric for him. For his students, Quintilian insisted upon a mastery of all the arts and sciences. Writing in his multi-volume work on pedagogy, *Institutio Oratoria,* Quintilian averred, "He who speaks eloquently must have a firm grounding in all useful knowledge; he should be a true polymath" (Lucas, 1972, p. 130).

Quintilian sought to formalize the curriculum and to eliminate subjects that he thought to be counterproductive or unfit for study. The course of study was to be relative to the students' own lives and appropriate to their developmental levels. The curriculum in the formative years would include moral training, reading, and writing. In later years, literature and poetic interpretation, music, geometry, Greek syntax, linguistics, and composition were added, followed by Latin grammar and literature as the child advanced. Since, at that time, Greek was the language of learning, Quintilian felt that the student needed a firm grounding in that language before perfecting his vernacular. Quintilian advocated shaping the curriculum to meet individual achievement levels, needs, and interests; in other words, having it grow with the student. In his work *The Elements of Oratory* (1.4, 1-5), Quintilian wrote,

> *As soon as a boy has learned to write, it is time for him to study with a grammaticus. . . . I prefer that priority be given to a Greek teacher. But both offer the same curriculum. And this curriculum can be divided very briefly into two main subjects: the art of speaking correctly and the interpretation of poetry. However, the curriculum offers much more in the details of the program than is at first apparent . . . the art of speaking and the art of writing are connected . . . flawless reading precedes interpretation . . . critical judgment is required in all cases. (Shelton, 1998)*

The years CE 14 through 96 are often referred to as the "Silver Age of Latin Letters." According to Durant (1944), "In epigram, in satire, the novel, history and philosophy, the Silver Age marks the zenith of Roman literature" (p. 295).

The Middle Ages

By the seventh century, Rome had fallen to the barbarians and the center of learning had moved eastward to Alexandria in Egypt and Constantinople in the Byzantine Empire. Western Europe was in decline, with ignorance the rule rather than the exception. Even aristocrats and clergyman were often illiterate. In 768, Carolus Magnus, known today as Charlemagne, took the throne of Frankland and very soon began to express great interest in education. He forced the higher clergy to open schools in monasteries and cathedrals and brought in learned men to train teachers and to open a palace school for children of the aristocracy. The most prominent of Charlemagne's imports was Alcuin of York (735-804), who was selected to direct Charlemagne's education reform efforts. Others were set to work copying books, both for use by bishops in the training of clergy, and for teachers in the palace schools. Alcuin arranged the curriculum around the seven liberal arts, the *trivium*, consisting of grammar (mainly Latin), dialectic, and rhetoric, which was used in the lower levels, and the *quadrivium*, arithmetic, geometry, music, and astronomy (Murphy, 2006). More advanced students studied Church doctrine, Latin and Greek poetry, theology, geometry (which could include such topics as natural science and medicine), and history. Because all books had to be hand-copied, Alcuin saw great need to emphasize spelling and orthography. He is credited with the development of a new style of handwriting, called the "Carolingian Minuscule," which became the style for printing (Murphy, 2006).

Early in their development, the monastery schools appear to have been more rigid and narrower in their curricular offerings than the palace schools. Although there are few records to verify the assumption, the main goal of monastery school was to train young men to become part of their institutions, not to give them cultural or life skills. Certainly, reading and writing and probably Church history, along with rituals and practices inherent in the monastic life, constituted their curricula. From the earliest days, the primary secular function of the monks was the copying of manuscripts, so both Latin grammar and orthography were essential components in their curricula.

Lucas (1972) states that, "By the year 1000, the medieval monastic school had evolved a regular course of studies [for its novices and *externi*] . . . organized around the seven liberal arts" (p. 209). The *trivium* consisted of grammar, dialectic, and rhetoric, while the *quadrivium* included geometry, arithmetic, music, and astronomy. All students were extensively drilled in Latin grammar, as by this time, Latin had replaced Greek as the official language of both academia and the Church. Females, at least those whose parents could afford to pay, could attend convent schools, where the curriculum included such subjects as reading, writing, Latin, music, weaving, spinning, and needlework. Some of the more advanced also offered the *trivium* and *quadrivium*.

In the late Middle Ages, "technical-vocational" training was available for the children of merchants and tradesmen through guild apprenticeship. There was no formal curriculum, but the master was expected to provide rudimentary instruction in reading, writing, arithmetic, and religion, while also teaching the apprentice his trade. Those among the upper classes who wanted to enter the professions of law, medicine, and theology attended specialized universities—law and medicine in Italy and theology in northern Europe. The curriculum of the university during the preliminary years of study consisted of the first three subjects of the seven liberal arts, enhanced by study of the works of Aristotle. After a period lasting from four to seven years, the student was ready for specialized instruction, usually in the form of lectures about the works of famous men of the chosen profession (Haskins, 1923; Lucas, 1972).

Renaissance in Europe

The Renaissance, or "rebirth," took place roughly between 1300 and 1600. It had a tremendous impact on European intellectuals and was a time of enthusiasm and renewed effort in all academic and artistic areas. Scholars and artists wanted to return Europe to the "good old days"—the time of the ascendancy of Greece and Rome. Again, man and his needs were the yardstick by which all things, including education, were to be measured. The Renaissance marked a turning away from the asceticism, fatalism, and authoritarianism of the Middle Ages, making man rather than God the center of the universe (Lucas, 1972). In education, emphasis was placed upon "the practical and concrete, on the active rather than contemplative side of life" (Lucas, 1972).

Renaissance education was dominated by the Humanists. As Herrick (2005) explains, "Humanists have taken a great interest in education, both as an area of moral education and as a place where religious bias remains" (p. 91). Such men as Desiderius Erasmus of Rotterdam (1466-1536) saw the ideally educated person as one who epitomized the four qualities of: piety, love of learning, fitness for public life, and personal style. He advocated study of classical languages in order to read great works of literature in the original Greek or Latin, and also put great emphasis upon Bible study in schools in order to encourage moral development and piety. Ethics, the nature of the human, and free will replaced universals and abstracts. Francesco di Petracco (1304-1374), known as Petrarch, immersed himself in the study of classic literature, ancient history, languages, and philosophy, thereby typifying himself as the educated "Renaissance Man." The Humanists were, however, highly elitist. They firmly believed that only some men, and no women, were capable of receiving and using the type of education they advocated. Interestingly enough, it was a religious movement, the Protestant Reformation, that tended to "democratize" education.

The Reformation

When Martin Luther (1483-1546) defied the Roman Catholic Church, he declared that salvation was available to all through faith alone, rather than being dependent upon the intercession of priests, prelates, or saints. He stated that faith was clarified in the pages of the Holy Bible, making it imperative that everyone who sought salvation learn to read. Luther felt that schools should teach young people to read the Bible in their own vernacular and to respect the laws of the state. He also insisted upon religious instruction so that people could defend their beliefs against other sects (Gutek, 2005).

A contemporary of Luther's in the religious upheaval, John Calvin (1509-1564) was concerned with purging any residue of Roman Catholicism. His religious/civic establishment in Geneva required that all children attend school to be inculcated with Calvinist principles as set forth in his masterwork, *Institutes of the Christian Religion* (1536). All had to be literate in order to read the Bible, the force that governed their lives. Children attended the *schola privata* until they were 16. There, they studied elementary reading and writing (from Calvin's catechism), Latin, and French. Later, Greek, music, and logic were added to the curriculum for the higher levels. The next step was the *schola publica*, which later became the University of Geneva, to study theology, Hebrew, Greek, philosophy, mathematics, and rhetoric (Gutek, 2005).

The Scientific Revolution

The next great historical era, like the one before it, did not begin suddenly, but rather was an outgrowth of study, courage, curiosity, and critical inquiry. With the crumbling of the Church's influence and power as a result of the Protestant Reformation, and a change in men's attitudes toward science, along with an expansion of trade, the growth of cities, and the influence of resurrected Hellenistic rationalism, the 1600s witnessed the dramatic Scientific Revolution. Lucas (1972) avers, "Science as a directive force in Western civilization, displacing theology and classical letters, was more than a method of inquiry or even a body of knowledge." It was also an "attitude of mind and creator of a metaphysical world view" (p. 303).

Great discoveries were made in this era and long-repressed scientific theories were verified and published. Invention of the Gutenberg printing press made it possible to record and disseminate new knowledge. An English philosopher, Francis Bacon (1561-1626), provided the first comprehensive statement of scientific method in his works *Advancement of Learning* (1605) and *Novum Organum* (1620). René Descartes (1596-1650), in his *Discourse Upon Method* (1637), outlined a "universal mathematics" that would be a source for all further study. Scholars of the day, the *Encyclopedists*, were boldly outlining plans for acquiring all knowledge and recording it for humankind. Isaac Newton (1642-1727), in his *Principia Matematica* (1687), "showed how a mathematical method of investigation could be applied universally to problems of mechanical motion" (Lucas, 1972, p. 305). These men and many others provided new theories to be investigated and new knowledge to be stored and used.

In the curricula of the schools and universities, utilitarianism was a factor, epitomized by the efforts to replace Latin with the vernacular and to substitute scientific and social studies for study of classical languages and literatures. Educators of the 1600s wanted to organize a curriculum that was an integrated whole, rather than just adding courses to those already in place. They wanted students to recognize the relationships among the subjects and develop the broadest possible knowledge base through an integrated course of studies. Knowledge was to be viewed holistically. German elementary schools introduced geography, civics, and elementary science into their curricula; secular *academies* in France taught French grammar as well as Latin, geography, history, politics, art, and jurisprudence, along with physical sports. In England, where the Puritan influence was strong, writers demanded curricula aimed at occupational preparation, from primary school through tertiary educational institutions (Murphy, 2006).

The English poet and scholar John Milton (1608-1674), in his *Tractate on Education,* proposed a much more comprehensive course of studies for English "nobler and gentler" youth: mathematics, Latin grammar and literature, geometry, Greek literature, agriculture, philosophy, geography, physiology, poetry, modern literature, economics, politics, history, logic, rhetoric, Hebrew, and Italian (Lucas, 1972). After the Stuart Restoration in 1660, nonconformists established schools and offered history, trigonometry, economics, and navigation, in addition to the conventional Latin grammar school curriculum.

Called "the great Pansophist" for his views on universal education, the Moravian Jan Amos Comenius (1592-1670) sought to create a system of universal knowledge as the temporal goal of learning, a kind of basic liberal education that would provide the learner with the essentials of life. Lucas (1972) wrote, "Comenius was asking the question what kind of well-rounded education of mind, body, and spirit would produce the highest type of human wisdom?" (p. 318). Comenius proposed a four-stage system, each stage encompassing six years of instruction. In the first, the *Schola Materna* (Mother School), the infant and small child would be taught "the rudiments of all the knowledge that we wish to give a human being for the needs of life" (Lucas, 1972, p. 319). The second level, the *Schola Vernacula*, would provide classes in reading, writing, arithmetic, history mechanics, religion, ethics, and music. As its name implies, all instruction in the *Schola Vernacula* was to be in the vernacular. In the classical school, the *Schola Latina*, the curriculum was more intensive, including four languages and all the arts and the sciences. At the highest level, the university, students would concentrate upon their selected specializations, all the while working toward the pansophic ideal of an appreciation of the interrelationship of all subjects and fields of study.

The Enlightenment

The 18th century is often called the "Age of the Enlightenment" or the "Age of Reason." This period is characterized by a pervasive indifference to organized religion, to the nay-sayers and pessimists, and to the strictures of superstition-laced educational practices. There was general agreement among intellectuals, led by Montesquieu (1689-1755), Turgot (1721-1781), Diderot (1713-1784), and Voltaire (1694-1778), that established religion and entrenched monarchies were obstacles to social progress (Lucas, 1972). The individual felt a new power to make decisions and chart a course, based upon discoveries and knowledge acquired through exploration and scientific research. Schools were expected to encourage students' ability to reason, to learn through discovery, and to question entrenched ideas.

"The leaders of the Enlightenment were [French] *philosophes*, a new class of literary men, popularizers, and propagandists" (Lucas, 1972, p. 329). Their heaviest criticism fell upon the elementary schools, beyond which few people progressed, and their staid curriculum of reading, writing, and religious indoctrination. Jean Jacques Rousseau (1712-1778), like his *Philosophe* contemporaries, tried to "explain everything." In his opinion, the traditional schools were failing to educate. For Rousseau, the first essential to reform was a change of setting. He thought that society would have a corrupting influence on children and that formal schooling was not necessary until age 15. He also believed that the child is a product of his environment and a natural environment was necessary for effective learning. Rousseau's curriculum at the early stages focused on sensory and physical training, rather than on reading. All emphasis was placed upon "natural learning" and opportunities were provided for varied experiences. Not until the "age of humanity"—between 18 and 20—did the individual under Rousseau's tutelage begin to study history and social sciences (Lucas, 1972).

Across the channel there were English intellectuals who also voiced concern. English schools were characterized in 1795 as "empty walls without scholars and everything neglected but the receipt of salaries and endowments" (Lucas, 1972, p. 332). However, due to the efforts of concerned individuals such as Jan Comenius, and improved communications, more people were aware of the problems. One such man, John Locke (1632-1704), who has been called the "Father of Empirical Realism," had some radical notions about education in general and curriculum in particular (Lucas, 1972, p. 333). In his work *Some Thoughts Concerning Education* (1693), Locke maintained that all knowledge comes from sensations and perceptions. An elitist, he advocated early physical training for the development of the "cultivated man," and his curriculum for the gentleman consisted of reading and writing in the vernacular, French and Latin taught by means of natural conversation, geography, mathematics, geometry, history, religion and ethics, jurisprudence, dancing, fencing, and riding. He rejected the teaching of rhetoric, pure logic, and Greek. He also rejected existing content and methodology in educational institutions of his day, maintaining that "the classic studies they taught were unfit for preparing the sons of cultivated men for their duties in a civilized life" (Lucas, 1972, p. 334).

The French Revolution, which began in 1789, was expected to bring positive political, social, and economic changes (Gutek, 2005). Philosophers, educators, and even the poor tradesmen of the cities, as well as farmers of the rural areas, came to believe that the revolution's slogan of "liberty, equality, and fraternity" would be translated into the "rights of man." One such optimist was Johann Heinrich Pestalozzi (1747-1827), a native of Zurich, who was influenced by the Enlightenment, by its rationalism, and by its promise of a better future for humans and reform through natural law. School reform became his goal. Both in France and in Switzerland, Pestalozzi had observed vernacular schools that stressed basic literacy, writing, singing, and arithmetic, along with religious conformity. Most schools, under the rigid control of religious sects, generally used catechetical methods to inculcate their own rites, rituals, and creeds, along with rudimentary literacy. Secondary schools were no less traditional, with curricula designed to prepare young men for ministerial careers—ancient Greek and Latin literatures provided their main focus. In 1774, Pestalozzi decided to make education, along with farming, his life's work; in an unusual experiment, he turned his property, Neuhof, into a model farm and handicrafts school. He took in 50 children, ages 6 to 18, and clothed and fed them. In addition to teaching them reading, writing, and counting, Pestalozzi taught them to run the farm and to make saleable handicrafts. The venture was not particularly successful, however, due to a number of factors.

Pestalozzi's ideas were more about method and educational environment than curriculum—Rousseau's *Emile* was his model for the education for his own child—and he stated, "The public education of the whole world . . . appeared to me altogether as a crippled thing, which was to find a universal remedy for its present pitiful condition in Rousseau's lofty ideas" (Lucas, 1972, p. 351). Schools, he felt, should be calm, loving extensions of the family, where children would find trusting relationships and emotional security. Pestalozzi was opposed to the catechetical method of inculcating religious doctrine—that is, children memorizing concepts, using words they did not understand. He felt that the method fostered religious intolerance. His own method, according to Gutek (2005), "was based on affective human relationships that led to God" (p. 165). In his *Account of the Method* (1800), Pestalozzi gave the rationale for his pedagogy:

> *I am trying to psychologize the instruction of mankind . . . to bring it into harmony with the nature of the mind. . . . I start from no positive form of teaching, but simply ask what I must do to give a single child all the knowledge and practical skill he needs. . . . In order for the child to develop as a whole—physically, morally, mentally—learning must take account of the individual's readiness at each stage, must begin at the level of direct experience and must be organized around the fundamental elements of sense perception. (Lucas, 1972, p. 355)*

In 1799, Pestalozzi established an educational institution in Burgdorf, in an old castle. The school's curriculum included geography, drawing, singing, history, language, arithmetic, and gymnastics. In 1801, the curriculum was expanded to include teacher training. In that same year, he wrote *How Gertrude Teaches Her Children* in order to publicize his success at Burgdorf.

The education methods practiced at Pestalozzi's school were widely noted and imitated, and he received international recognition and honors. Through the efforts of Charles Mayo (1792-1846), who, with his sister Elizabeth, opened a school on the Pestalozzian model in England, the new pedagogy was spread all over England; also, such outstanding 19th century pedagogues in the United States as William Maclure, Henry Barnard, and Edward Sheldon helped make the Pestalozzian method popular there.

The late 17th and early 18th centuries gave rise to the establishment of new types of schools, many of which were provided for the children of the under-classes through the efforts of philanthropists. In this category were the "Monitor Schools" of Joseph Lancaster (1778-1838) and Robert Owen (1771-1858) in England and America, respectively, which were designed to give the children of the poor a free, secular, rudimentary education that would not interfere with their work in the factories. In the United States, there were the utopian movements in Oswego and New Harmony, which, through the efforts of William Maclure and Joseph Neef (a Pestalozzian brought to the United States by Maclure), incorporated the Pestalozzian methodology into their schools, which were dedicated to communitarian principles and scientific research.

In the German states, the Pietist missionary August Hermann Francke (1663-1727) established a charity school for poor children, supported by public contributions, which was later to become the "burgh" or elementary school. The curriculum of the burgh school consisted of history, geography, counting, reading, writing, and music. At the secondary level, the *gymnasium*, children studied history, geography, music, mathematics, science, Latin, Greek, and Hebrew. In 1763, the King of Prussia, Frederick the Great, issued the *General School Regulations*, which mandated compulsory education for all children between the ages of 5 and 14 (Lucas, 1972). In 1747, a student of Francke, Johann Julius Hecker (1707-1768), opened a vocational secondary school in Berlin, expanding his mentor's curriculum to provide practical subjects, including teacher training.

Friedrich Froebel (1782-1852), who is known as the "Father of the Kindergarten," was very much influenced in his early days by Georg Hegel and later by Pestalozzi. Froebel outlined his ideas on early childhood education in his work *Principles, Aims, and Inner Life of the Universal German Educational Institute in Keilbau* (1826). He opined that every child should be respected as an individual and his needs should be considered when he is educated. Gutek (2005) wrote, "He sought to develop a method of instruction that encompassed both the universal laws of child development, and ways in which each child could express herself or himself creatively" (p. 264). His kindergartens stressed play as a learning activity. Froebel wrote songs and rhymes for 3- and 4-year-olds and made up games for 5-year-olds. Froebel's kindergarten curriculum was represented through "gifts" (objects that represented what Froebel described as "fundamental forms") and "occupations" (items that children could use in construction activities—paper, pencils, clay, etc.), along with organized play, songs, rhymes, and games (Gutek, 2005, p. 269).

America, the New Republic

Thomas Jefferson (1743-1826) was very much a product of the Enlightenment. He felt that educational methodology should follow the scientific method, with "human reason rather than divine revelation . . . the key to understanding" (Gutek, 2005, p. 176). In his opinion, science was the pathway to knowledge, with its rational explanations and patterns, leading to the development of systematic studies of geology, chemistry, botany, zoology, and physics. The scientific curiosity of the *philosophes* led people to wonder about places, things, and people outside their own sphere—thus, the development of such subjects as geography, anthropology, and sociology. Jefferson embodied this curiosity when he sent Lewis and Clark out to explore and map the American west.

Jefferson saw a need for an educated electorate in the republic of free citizens he was working to establish. He believed that civic education was essential, along with academic freedom and an education system free of governmental or religious control, all of which would provide an environment conducive to free discussion and debate. Jefferson's plan for curricular revision and expansion met with considerable opposition from conservatives and traditionalists, especially in the colleges and universities. The idea of people rationally making decisions affecting their own lives was abhorrent to some, who wanted nothing more than to maintain the status quo and the sovereignty of church and state (Lucas, 1972). Monarchs already had the example of both the American and the French revolutions to show what could happen if people began to think seriously about their own conditions through a study of the social sciences, and to use that knowledge to search for remedies. An enlightened electorate was anathema to those who subscribed to the theory of the "Divine Right of Kings."

Traditionalists could not envision a world without classical education—for them, Latin and Greek formed the core of all learning. Jefferson, on the other hand, saw the sciences and social studies as essential to the creation of a new society, one with all people empowered to make intelligent decisions for themselves and to elect those enlightened individuals who would work for the greater good of all (Murphy, 2006).

Early Republican educators, such as Benjamin Rush, Robert Coram, and Samuel Smith, set forth ideals for the creation of a distinctly American Republic. Their educational goals included:

1. The knowledge and values needed for civic participation in a republic
2. The inclusion of scientific knowledge, method, and temperament in curriculum and instruction
3. The creation of a unique and distinctive United States culture. (Gutek, 2005, p. 180)

In 1779, as a member of the Virginia legislature, Jefferson introduced several plans for an equitable education system for the commonwealth. Virginia's counties were to be divided into districts, and each district was to provide and maintain, at public expense, an elementary school. All free children were to be provided with schooling for at least three years. The curriculum was to include reading, writing, and the history of Greece, Rome, Great Britain, and North America. After the first three years, parents could pay for their children's continued instruction (Gutek, 2005). Jefferson's plan for a rather elitist secondary system was not implemented and the Virginia legislature did not support the part of the plan that called for public support.

Thomas Jefferson worked for improvement in the curricula and organization of colleges in Virginia, seeing the English classical models of Cambridge and Oxford as inappropriate for the new Republic. He planned for, and in 1816 the Virginia legislature authorized, the establishment of the "Central College," which was to become the University of Virginia. The mission of the new university was to provide the useful knowledge that the nation required through the promotion of scientific inquiry and instruction. There were to be no required subjects and theology was not part of the curriculum.

Although the Enlightenment and the theories of Thomas Jefferson had great influence on U.S. civic life, education in the early 19th century retained much of its traditionalism and character of evangelical Protestantism. Increased immigration, especially from southern and eastern Europe, brought in people speaking new languages, with differing religious and cultural practices. "Pluralism" began to replace the "melting pot" concept (the idea that everyone should conform to the established customs and mores of his/her country, and use the same language), as those of English ancestry began to be outnumbered by immigrant groups, whose languages and religious beliefs often differed radically from those of the Anglo/Americans. For Protestant evangelicalism, common or public schools, supported by the state and attended by all children, were the most efficient purveyors of essential knowledge. According to Gutek (2005), "Their . . . rationale was that U.S. institutions, including schools, should reflect the beliefs and values of the dominant Protestant culture" (p. 216). Economics, too, played a major part in the development of American education from the middle of the 19th century, when the effects of Europe's industrial revolution began to be felt in the United States, and there was a shift from agrarian to urban economic systems. This shift was to bring about change in both kinds of schools and their curricula.

Horace Mann (1796-1859) was named the first secretary to the Massachusetts State Board of Education in 1837. As part of his job, Mann traveled extensively, compiling data and writing reports on the condition of schools in the state. He developed a formula for education that included such precepts as the purposes of schooling: to create responsible citizens, to provide the basis for economic prosperity, to serve as a social leveler, and to provide moral and ethical leadership. Mann, often called the "Father of American public education," developed a plan for a system of publicly supported and controlled schools—the Common School—in the state of Massachusetts. In this concept, all children, rich and poor, would be educated together, and, in that way, provide a means for bringing social classes together in a non-stressful atmosphere. Mann believed that in order to create a common civic community with diverse social, political, and religious groups, all acting in harmony for the good of the community, the common school "curriculum should provide the same basic knowledge and skills equally to all students" (Gutek, 2005, p. 227)—a broad curriculum, including, along with the basics of reading, writing, spelling, arithmetic, and "common Christianity," history, geography, health, art, and music. With increased immigration from Italy, Ireland, Spain, and Russia, the population of Catholics (Roman and Eastern Rite) and Jews increased. These groups objected strenuously to the imposition of a "common Christianity," which they saw as "common Protestantism."

Mann also was concerned with teacher preparation, and so he worked for a standardization of teacher qualifications and training. The establishment of normal schools, modeled on the French *école normale,* was authorized by the legislature, and minimum admittance requirements established. The curricula were more utilitarian than those of the universities, with Latin and Greek classics being replaced with English composition and grammar, while also offering the essentials of the common school—spelling, geography, arithmetic, health, and history.

The 19th century was a time of economic polarization, with the industrialists of England and the United States dominating social life and politics. Theorists on both sides of the Atlantic rationalized both slavery and socioeconomic and educational imbalances. Herbert Spencer (1820-1903), an Englishman who developed socio-educational theories based upon Charles Darwin's theory of evolution and natural selection, developed the radical "Social Darwinism" theory, which became popular in Great Britain and the United States among men of great wealth, who used the theory to try to rationalize the gap between rich and poor and the essentiality of industrialization.[2]

From the first time he wrote of educational theory, Spencer advocated a more practical and useful course of studies. He advocated a scientific curriculum, with content determined through the identification of important human activities and appropriate subjects designed to build the skills necessary to appropriately perform those activities. His priorities were listed as: physical health; self preservation—earning a living; rearing and educating children; civic education; and leisure activities, such as art, music, drama, poetry, and music. Of Spencer's impact on the future of education, Gutek (2005) writes,

> *The Spencerian concept of unhurried evolutionary development carried immense educational implications. First, it argued for change in the curriculum and methods and challenged the verbalism of schools dominated by rote, routine, and custom. Second, in terms of broad educational policy and social goals, Spencer's evolutionary concept placed the school on the side of the socioeconomic status quo. (p. 307)*

It wasn't until the 20th century that great educational intellects, such as Jane Addams and John Dewey, began to refute the theories of the Spencerians.

Conclusion

This brief overview has perhaps not recognized important instances and individuals, and is admittedly slanted toward Western Civilization as the historical contributor to the concept of educational organization. However, the overview does provide a glimpse into the historical unfolding of the development of curricula and the impact that such curricula have had on the past and in the present. To be sure, in the current information age and given the notion of a global community becoming more prevalent, curriculum work has great possibilities with respect to celebrating diversity and the making of more meaningful connections from nation to nation.

Notes:

[1] Lucas defines *arete* as "the distinctive excellence or virtue that bestows upon an individual superiority, a condition of honor" (p. 51).

[2] For an overview of Spencer's theories, see Spencer, H. (1996). *Essays: Scientific, political and speculative.* London: Routledge/Thoemmes.

References

Durant, W. (1944). *Caesar and Christ: A history of Roman civilization and of Christianity from their beginnings to AD 325.* New York: MJF Books.

Durant, W. (1963). *Our oriental heritage.* New York: MJF Books.

Green, P. (1973). *Ancient Greece: An illustrated history.* London: Thames & Hudson

Gutek, G. L. (2005). *Historical and philosophical foundations of education* (4th ed.). Upper Saddle River, NJ: Pearson Merrill Prentice Hall.

Hallo, W. W., & Simpson, W. K. (1998). *The ancient Near East: A history* (2nd ed.). Fort Worth, TX: Harcourt Brace College Publishers.

Haskins, C. H. (1923). *The rise of universities.* Ithaca, NY: Cornell University Press.

Herrick, J. (2005). *Humanism: An introduction.* Amherst, NY: Prometheus Books.

Kamm, A. (1995). *The Romans: An introduction.* London: Routledge.

Kebric, R. B. (1993). *Roman people.* Mountain View, CA: Mayfield Publishing Co.

Longstreet, W. S., & Shane, H. G. (1993). *Curriculum for a new millennium.* Boston: Allyn & Bacon.

Lucas, C. J. (1972). *Our western educational heritage.* New York: Macmillan.

Murphy, M. M. (2006). *The history and philosophy of education: Voices of educational pioneers.* Upper Saddle River, NJ: Pearson/Merrill Prentice Hall.

Nagle, D. B. (1996). *The ancient world: A social and cultural history* (3rd ed.). Upper Saddle River, NJ: Prentice Hall

Pai, Y., & Adler, S. A. (2001). *Cultural foundations of education* (3rd ed.). Upper Saddle River, NJ: Merrill Prentice Hall.

Shelton, J. (1998). *As the Romans did: A sourcebook in Roman social history* (2nd ed.). New York: Oxford University Press.

About the Author

Ann K. Nauman, Ph.D., is a professor of history and Academic Dean at St. Joseph Seminary College in St. Benedict, Louisiana.

Curriculum Development in Australia: A History of Running the Gauntlet Between State and National Agendas

Debra Panizzon

A single national approach to curriculum development, student assessment and credentialing would provide numerous benefits. The national approach would offer powerful economies of scale. It would create opportunities to enhance teacher professional development offered by universities and other registered providers, as well as opportunities to improve research into teaching and learning. It would create a more open market for employers and more career opportunities for teachers. It would lead to the development of world-class education faculties in Australia. (Riordan, 2006, p. 2)

Curriculum matters always attract a great deal of attention as various stakeholders champion particular issues in education (Marsh & Stafford, 1984; Seddon, 2001). Australia is no exception, with questions currently being raised about the content of courses taught in schools, the pedagogical approaches used by teachers, aspects related to preservice teacher preparation, and the life skills required to create a generation of informed citizens (Kalantzis, 2001) with "the necessary knowledge, understanding, skills and values for a productive and rewarding life in an educated, just and open society" (Ministerial Council on Education, Employment, Training, and Youth Affairs [MCEETYA], 1999, p. 1). Interestingly, many of these issues are not new, but represent age-old concerns for educationalists.

The high value placed on curriculum in Australia is demonstrated by the existence of a national body titled the Australian Curriculum Studies Association (ACSA). This organization, established in 1983, supports professional educators in the area of curriculum at all levels and sectors. It also provides national advocacy

Australia

with a commitment to curriculum reform that embraces respect, social justice, and equity for all citizens. A visit to the website suggests that while Australia has historically borrowed many of our ideas about schooling and curriculum from other countries, we now recognize our own expertise in being able to cater to students within an Australian context.

As is often the case, achieving educational goals generates considerable protracted debate (Gough & Gough, 2003; Seddon, 2001). This is currently the case in Australia, with the introductory quote from Riordan (2006) representing one side of a very contentious issue that has surfaced in Australia on numerous occasions. In reviewing the quote, it would seem that a national focus on curriculum provides many valuable educational outcomes as part of an integrated and coordinated approach. However, of equal significance for educationalists in Australia is the loss of autonomy for individual jurisdictions in terms of being able to develop and implement a curriculum that addresses the needs of students by using an established infrastructure and process that is relevant within a particular educational context (Seddon, 2001). To fully understand this divergence in opinion in Australia, it is necessary to explore curriculum development from a historical perspective, beginning with Australia's colonization by Britain to our current position as a player in the global community.

The following chapter explores curriculum development in Australia by focusing on the unique dichotomy between the influence of state/territory and national agendas. This is achieved within four sections. First, curriculum is defined within an Australian context so as to distinguish it from a syllabus and provide a shared language for the chapter. Second, the process of curriculum evolution is presented by highlighting major historical educational events that have shaped and impacted curriculum design in Australia. Third, the role of teachers in curriculum implementation, and the centrality of pedagogy to this process, are discussed. Finally, I explore the extent to which curriculum is *fair* and *just,* thereby facilitating "education for all" in Australia.

Defining Curriculum in Australia

Curriculum is derived from the Latin word *currere,* meaning "to race" (Costello, 1993, p. 340), which provides an interesting metaphor for considering a school curriculum. This meaning differs greatly from "a group of related courses, often in a special field of study" (Costello, 1993, p. 340), which typifies the views of the majority of teachers and school educators concerning curriculum. In contrast to this rather narrow dictionary definition, ACSA considers curriculum as "the product of social, historical, political and economic forces. It involves the selection, interpretation, representation and assessment of culturally-based knowledge, skills and values" (ACSA, 2005). ACSA further states that a curriculum should:

- Be informed by political, social, economic, and historic analysis
- Involve explicit identification and evaluation of the values on which it is based
- Be a collaborative experience for all participants
- Involve collective critical reflection
- Be resourced to ensure active participation by teachers, students, and parents
- Be based on action at personal, school, community, and system levels
- Acknowledge that individuals will experience the same learning activities in very different ways
- Acknowledge that curriculum should be flexible and responsive to the experience of learners (ACSA, 2005).

In reviewing these statements, very little reference is made to courses of study, content, or pedagogy, although these are implicit in much of what is stated. What is critical is that curriculum is seen as a "strategic plan for learning" (Bruniges, 2005, p. 3) with knowledge, skills, and understandings prioritized in consideration with personal and social values to maximize learning opportunities for all students (Kalantzis, Cope, & Harvey, 2003; Reid, 2005). The major advantage of such a focus in

Australia is that the ACSA framework provides generic principles to guide curriculum development across the country regardless of whether this is at a national, state, or local level. In so doing, a degree of autonomy is provided for educational groups to stipulate *what* is taught, *when* it is taught, and *how* it should be taught within their own particular educational contexts (Bruniges, 2005).

With this broad definition identified, it is important to recognize a number of components of curriculum that become important when considering its implementation at a school and classroom level.

1. Hidden or implicit curriculum: Refers to those things learned by students as a result of the way in which the school is organized or structured, although not overt in the curriculum planning. Examples here may include values and attitudes, which may be demonstrated unconsciously by teachers in the classroom (Gough & Gough, 2003; Kelly, 1999).
2. Planned and received curriculum: Incorporates what is specified in the syllabus as being taught, learned, and assessed, compared with what students actually experience in reality. The gap between the two may be either a deliberate or unconscious oversight by a teacher to influence student learning (Kelly, 1999; Reid, 2005; Williams, 1976).
3. Formal and informal curriculum: Relates to those lessons, learning opportunities, or experiences that are included by the school in the timetable, compared to those activities that occur during lunchtime, after school, or on a weekend (e.g., sporting activities) (Kelly, 1999).

Identification and clarification of these sub-components of curriculum are critical because they can be "controlled" by the teacher and/or the school administration. So, while curriculum designers may have a particular idea or plan in mind, what is learned by students will depend ultimately on how the curriculum is implemented in the classroom (Reid, 2005).

With curriculum defined, it must be differentiated from a *syllabus*, which tends to be the main focus for individual teachers in schools (Marsh & Stafford, 1984). In Australia, a syllabus refers to the content or body of knowledge to be taught, along with the order in which this should be addressed, so that students achieve particular learning outcomes (Bruniges, 2005). Subsequently, little direction is given to the overall aims and objectives, learning experiences provided for students, or the critical role of evaluation as a means of ensuring that students are achieving the designated outcomes (Kelly, 1999). This area highlights an interesting dichotomy within Australia, with New South Wales on one side having specified syllabi for all discipline areas in elementary and secondary education (i.e., Years 1-12), while all other states and territories occupy the opposite position, because they provide a curriculum that allows individuals to develop their own unique syllabi. The following discussion outlines the historical background that helps explain the evolution of this dichotomy over time.

Historical Overview of Curriculum Development
In 1788, more than 1,500 settlers from England arrived in Botany Bay and established a settlement at Port Jackson, which became Sydney, New South Wales. Subsequent colonies arose in Tasmania (1803), Western Australia (1827), South Australia (1836), Victoria (1851), Queensland (1859), and the Northern Territory (1863) to form the Federation of Australia in 1901 (Marsh & Stafford, 1984). As a result of these origins, Australia has developed over time a dual system of government having both Commonwealth (i.e., national) and state representation. Not surprisingly, this has created major issues as the two levels of government deflect financial responsibilities and argue over various policy matters. The complexity of this duality and the effects on educational policy, including curriculum development, are explored in this section.

Establishment of State and Territory Education Systems[1]
The first schools in Australia were established by religious denominations in New South Wales in 1819 as a means of providing basic education for the "lower orders of society . . . to upgrade moral fibre"

(Marsh & Stafford, 1984, p. 92). Public education in schools was to come later with the Education Act of 1848 (Bruniges, 2005). This act resulted in the creation of the Board of National Education (elementary public schools) and Denominational Schools Board (elementary religious schools) in New South Wales. However, this dual system collapsed in 1893 when centralized departments of education, funded by state governments, were established in each of the colonies (Watt, 1996). From this point onward, public and religious schools were administered collectively within each state or territory, and this is still the case.

Throughout this establishment period, the school curriculum was derived from the United Kingdom, with the same curriculum materials being utilized in all schools across Australia. While this universal adoption was due in part to a lack of alternative resources, another major contributing factor was the use of student examination results to determine teachers' salaries and promotions (Watt, 1996). Not surprisingly, teachers tended to adhere to the prescribed syllabi for reading, writing, and arithmetic, using the supplied curriculum materials. Throughout this period, large-scale development in education was constrained by a general lack of resources, poorly trained teachers, and schools that were widely dispersed across the Australian continent (Marsh & Stafford, 1984).

The impact of British educational policies on Australian education continued with the Balfour Act of 1902, resulting in the introduction of secondary education into both countries simultaneously. However, it was the Hadow Report of 1926, with a recommendation that secondary education be for *all* children, that was implemented as policy by every state director of education in the early 1930s (Watt, 1996). Still, it was not until after World War II that a rapid expansion of secondary public education occurred and this was in response to a report in 1957 from a committee chaired by Harold Wyndham, Director General of New South Wales Department of Education (Duffield, 1990). The recommendations identified in this report led to a major reorganization of secondary education and the introduction of comprehensive high schools based on four-years-plus-two-years of education into New South Wales. Students also completed external examinations at the end of each phase of their secondary schooling (Marsh & Stafford, 1984). The first year consisted of core subjects, while subsequent years included a choice of core and elective subjects. Within a few years, the system was adopted by all states in Australia. Clearly, New South Wales played a very prominent role in the majority of educational initiatives, so it is not surprising that it demonstrates a strong culture of leadership in matters of policy and curriculum to the present day.

The massive reorganization of secondary education and the centralized state educational systems established by the late 1950s prompted important changes in the area of curriculum. While curriculum development had been the responsibility of state committees, by the 1960s, each state had established a statutory board to coordinate curriculum and administer state-wide examinations at the completion of secondary education (Watt, 1996). This step ensured a high degree of uniformity in terms of curricula within each state and territory, so that parents could assume that all students received the same basic education (Seddon, 2001).

However, another wave of change was evident by the 1970s, as school-based curriculum development gained momentum across Australia, with some states and territories being particularly proactive. For example, the Australian Capital Territory adopted a school-based approach to curriculum in 1977, followed by Victoria in 1983 (Watt, 1996). Significantly, this movement resulted in decentralized decision-making, allowing schools greater autonomy to develop an individual curriculum based on the needs of their students (Seddon, 2001). Interestingly, New South Wales supported school-based programs while still providing syllabi in all disciplines in elementary and secondary education (McGaw, 1996). Therefore, in reality, schools in this state had little flexibility to modify and alter the content and skills taught (Marsh & Stafford, 1988).

This discussion demonstrates that the states and territories have jealously guarded school education and curriculum in Australia for a considerable period (Reid, 2005). However, in 1963 the dynamic began to alter slowly, with the Commonwealth government providing funding to school education (Seddon, 2001). The last two decades have seen a national push to establish commonality across Australia, with the Commonwealth government seeking to influence state and territory curricula indirectly by funding curriculum and teaching projects (Reid, 2005; Seddon, 2001). The following overview furnishes the various strategies implemented nationally to bring about greater consistency and collaboration across the state and territory boundaries.

Emergence of a National Agenda for Education

As alluded to earlier, education remained within the jurisdiction of the states, even after the Federation's formation in 1901 (Watt, 1996). To ensure that there was some cohesion and a forum for discussing educational issues across the states, the Australian Education Council (AEC) was established in 1936. All Commonwealth and state ministers of education were members of the committee. Almost immediately, this council became a significant policy organization through which educational initiatives were controlled nationally. So successful was the council that, in 1993, it was amalgamated with a number of other prominent bodies to form the Ministerial Council on Education, Employment, Training and Youth Affairs (MCEETYA). Today, this is one of the most powerful national authorities, as it oversees the coordination of strategic policy in all areas of education and training in Australia (Marsh & Stafford, 1984).

Another critical national organization established in the 1930s was the Australian Council for Educational Research (ACER). In the early years, ACER was responsible for correspondence education in Australia, the development of standardized achievement and intelligence tests, undertaking studies of Australian education, and publishing research reports. The focus for ACER changed during WWII, with a move away from correspondence education to a total emphasis on standardized testing procedures.

While AEC and ACER were gaining credibility within the educational community, curriculum development was controlled extensively by the states. However, this position began to change in 1963, when the Commonwealth government began offering funding to states and territories for educational curriculum projects. Overnight, science, social science, and English were targeted as three areas for national collaboration. The first initiative occurred with the Australian Science Education Project (ASEP), developed by ACER, which produced 44 curriculum materials for use in junior secondary science (i.e., Years 7-10). The project operated for five years and was highly successful, with a number of national evaluations undertaken to assess its impact in Australian schools. Piper (1997) recognized this event as the "advent of national curriculum development in Australia" (p. 11).

The success of ASEP and the perceived value of a national collaborative project resulted in the foundation of the Curriculum Development Centre (CDC) in 1973 (Reid, 2005). The main functions of the CDC were to:

- Conduct and support research
- Develop and "seed" projects
- Act as a clearinghouse of education information
- Promote field services
- Provide advisory, technical, and evaluative expertise to schools
- Publish and market curriculum products.

Two important directives emerged from the Curriculum Development Centre, based on curriculum reform projects occurring in the United States at the time. The new projects were the Social Science Materials Project (SSMP) and the Language Development Project (LDP). Both projects involved teams of teachers from each state and territory developing hands-on activities that focused on process skills that could be adapted by teachers across Australia, given that curriculum was still driven by each state and territory.

Significantly, the Curriculum Development Centre was moving toward a core curriculum for Australian schools by 1977. A working party was established to consider various aspects of curriculum, including a definition, identification of the core curriculum, and consideration of the relationship among curriculum, teaching, and learning. However, this initial success in moving toward a national curriculum agenda was tempered by political constraints and funding restrictions, resulting in the closure of the CDC in 1981 (Marsh & Stafford, 1984).

The national education agenda gained momentum again with the election of a Commonwealth Labour government in 1983, with particular focus around stimulating an economic recovery, promoting social equity, and rejuvenating elementary and secondary education (Watt, 1996). A number of commissions held during the next few years recommended consolidating programs around these major areas (Bruniges, 2005).

One of the first initiatives emerging from such a commission was a strategy for national collaboration in curriculum development, led by John Dawkins (1988), then the Commonwealth Minister of Employment, Education and Training. He criticized the duplication of materials across the states and territories, the variation in quality evident in curriculum materials, and the escalating costs associated with design and publication on a small scale (Reid, 2005; Seddon, 2001). This resulted in a "mapping of the curriculum" exercise in mathematics, science, technology, English and literacy, study of society and environment, health, physical education and personal development, the arts, and languages other than English (Watts, 1996). Although limited in its success, the mapping laid the foundations for the development of *National Statements* that described the progression of learning outcomes for students in Years 1 to 10, our compulsory years of schooling in Australia.

The Hobart Declaration of Schooling built upon the work begun by Dawkins. In 1989, the Declaration endorsed the development of a common curriculum framework for all schools with objectives that could be adapted to meet the particular needs of states and territories (Bruniges, 2005). Ten National Goals for Education were developed to support the framework (see Appendix 1).

In considering these goals, it is interesting to reflect upon the inclusive manner in which curriculum is defined. While some of these goals focus on content and/or skills related to schooling (e.g., a consistent handwriting style), the other goals relate to the responsibility of schools to provide equitable opportunities within an ethical context while engendering Australian values. Ultimately, these goals provided a framework for cooperation between the Commonwealth, states, and territories, enabling school systems to develop specific strategies and objectives relevant to their context (Piper, 1997). The Hobart Declaration represented a critical step in the development of a national and collaborative approach to schooling across Australia, as ministers of education in each state and territory indicated their long-term commitment to supporting these goals (Reid, 2005).

To support this national agenda, the Curriculum Corporation was established in 1990. Its main aims were to undertake research for national initiatives, complete commissioned projects, provide advisory services to curriculum-related organizations, and offer advice about the national curriculum framework (Watts, 1996). With a focus initially on mathematics, the Curriculum Corporation developed a National Statement on Mathematics for Australian Schools in 1991, which was followed over the next few years by similar statements for science, technology, English, studies of society and the environment, and the arts (Curriculum Corporation, 1991, 1994). According to Boston (1993), these developments represented one of the most significant collaborative activities in Australia, with the involvement of thousands of teachers, trials with 70,000 students, and consultations with more than 250 organizations across the nation (Watts, 1996).

Not surprisingly, this harmony was not to last, with widespread dispute emanating among respective discipline groups, which criticized the integrity of the National Statements and Profiles (Reid, 2005; Seddon, 2001). In fact, so much dissension was expressed by state government education ministers that a meeting was convened with the ministers from New South Wales, Western Australia, Victoria, Tasmania, and the Northern Territory agreeing to block the adoption of the National Statements (Watt, 1996). As a consequence, Australia was truly divided, with South Australia, Queensland, and the Australian Capital Territory using the National Statements and Profiles to guide their state curricula, while all the remaining states and territories adhered to their own practices without linking to the National Curriculum Framework (Reid, 2005). The only consensus remaining across the states and territories was the endorsement of the National Goals for Schooling at the Adelaide Declaration in 1999 (MCEETYA, 1999) (see Appendix 2). These goals set the broad focus of schooling for the future and surpassed the goals of the Hobart Declaration 10 years earlier.

Interestingly, over the last decade, the idea of a national curriculum has been raised on a number of occasions as a means of ensuring greater standardization across Australia and minimizing the impact of student migration between states. Just to put this in perspective, approximately 80,000 children migrate annually, which is more than the population of Tasmania (Smith, 2005).

Historically, the movement toward a national curriculum has in most cases involved the Commonwealth government indirectly influencing state and territory educational agendas through the use of funding (Reid, 2005; Seddon, 2001). This *modus operandum* changed dramatically several years ago when the Commonwealth Education Minister, Brendan Nelson, made a national curriculum his top priority. This resulted in the Ministerial Council on Education, Employment, Training and Youth Affairs (MCEETYA, 2006) endorsing the development of *National Statements of Learning* for the areas of civics and citizenship, English, mathematics and science, and information and communications technology. This framework now guides all curriculum development in each state and territory.

While the expectations identified by Nelson were similar to those raised by Dawkins 15 years earlier, Nelson broadened his agenda to include a push for common school-starting ages, a consistent Year 12 (i.e., the final year of secondary schooling), testing across Australia, and the most contentious issue: a report system, with 20% of students in every class (regardless of academic level) categorized into five grades, A-E (Department of Education and Training, 2006). States and territories that did not sign an agreement to implement the new reporting regime failed to gain substantial funding from the Commonwealth government. From an academic perspective, the major issue with the proposed assessment and reporting processes specified by Nelson meant that Australia returned to an inequitable style of assessment used 20 years ago. Additionally, Nelson's policy disregarded completely all the accrued research literature outlining assessment practices that enhance and support student learning (Black & Wiliam, 1998a, 1998b).

Role of Teacher and Pedagogy in Curriculum Implementation
The discussion so far has explored curriculum development at a state/territory and national level, with only minor reference to how this has affected teachers and their classroom practice. One example outlined earlier was that even during the establishment period of schooling in Australia (late 1800s to early 1930s), there was a high degree of teacher accountability, as salaries and promotions were determined by student success in examinations (Watt, 1996). Not surprisingly, this resulted in the widespread adoption of syllabi and resources from Britain and later the United States. Clearly, there is a powerful lesson to be learned here that, regardless of what the planned curriculum may be, its implementation in the classroom lies with the discretion of individual teachers (Hattam & Howard, 2003).

> *Teachers have a "make or break" role in any curriculum innovation. Teachers have been known to sabotage attempts at change; certainly it is clear that change can succeed only when the teachers concerned are committed to them and, especially, when they understand, as well as accept, their underlying principles. (Kelly, 1999, p. 9)*

This section focuses on the important role of the teachers and their pedagogy. While curriculum has evolved over time, this has coincided with major changes in teaching practices in the Australian context, particularly in elementary, middle, and junior secondary schooling (i.e., compulsory years).

Moving Toward Constructivism

As with many countries over the last few decades, teaching in Australia has moved from a transmission approach to embracing constructivist views of learning in all discipline areas. From the early colony in New South Wales through to the mid-1960s, the majority of Australian children sat single-file in classrooms, focused on the teacher at the front of the room. During this time, most curriculum documents emphasized the content and facts to be learned, with heavy reliance on recall and memorization. Process skills were gradually included in these documents, but this took some time, even for highly practical disciplines, such as science (Marsh & Stafford, 1988). Interestingly, one of the major advances for science teaching in Australia was the development of the national Australian Science Education Project (ASEP) in the 1960s (Watt, 1996). The curriculum materials developed required a more "hands-on" pedagogical approach for junior secondary science, resulting in major changes for science teachers (Northfield, 1986).

The ASEP approach embraced the notion of constructivism and the view that children "arrive at meaning by actively selecting, and cumulatively constructing, their own knowledge, through both individual and social activity" (Biggs, 1996, p. 348). An important aspect of this view of learning is that children come to the classroom with preconceived ideas and understandings about their world (Osborne & Freyberg, 1985). Hence, before beginning a new unit of work, it was important for teachers to gauge students' scientific conceptions so that teaching could be directed to the appropriate level of the learners (Northfield, 1986). From the 1960s onward, a learner-centered approach to teaching slowly gained momentum in all discipline areas, particularly in elementary and junior high schools (Hattam & Howard, 2003). For example, educators during this era moved toward the use of concrete materials in primary and junior secondary curricula to help students develop understandings of mathematical concepts, as opposed to having them merely "doing the sums."

Encouraging teachers to embrace a constructivist approach in the classroom could not have been easy, as it required a major shift in their philosophical views about pedagogy and the learning process. In fact, we still observe remnants of traditional transmissive practice in Australian schools, particularly at senior levels of secondary school (i.e., Years 11 and 12) (Hattam & Howard, 2003). This is due predominantly to the high-stakes assessment used in the majority of states and/or territories, and because of teacher accountability associated with student achievement at this level of schooling (Swain, 2000). What this anecdote highlights is that while the planned or intended curriculum may outline what is taught, learned, and assessed, the received curriculum will often appear quite different (Gough & Gough, 2003).

Grappling With Constructive Alignment

Within Australia, there has been a move to constructive alignment embracing three arms of curriculum: content, teaching practices, and assessment (Biggs, 1996). In the last decade, assessment has become a critical focus of state and territory curricula, with considerable teacher professional development provided across Australia. Driving this initiative has been a global interest in assessment as a means of raising the standards of learning, using what Black and Wiliam (1998a) refer to as "formative assessment" (p. 139). This type of assessment refers to "all those activities, undertaken by teachers . . . which provide information to be used as feedback to modify the teaching and learning activities" (Black & Harrison, 2000, p. 25). According to research by Black and Wiliam (1998b), use of these assessment strategies in the classroom can result in an effect size of between 0.4 and 0.7. To explain the impact of such a result, an effect size of 0.4 indicates that an average student involved in the intervention demonstrated the same achievement as a student in the top 35% who was not involved.

While education authorities in each of the states and territories have embraced this new approach to assessment to varying degrees, New South Wales has adopted an *assessment for learn-*

ing agenda for Years 1-12 that is embedded within all curriculum and syllabus documents. This approach encapsulates the work of Black and Wiliam (1998a, 1998b) with a focus on teachers providing quality feedback to their students in an ongoing manner (Board of Studies, 2000).

Essentially, this represents "good teaching" because it allows students to monitor their own progress and provides direction for teachers about what should happen in the next lesson. However, this change has caused great anxiety within the teaching profession in New South Wales, given that it is one of the most highly tested jurisdictions in Australia. For example, within this state, all students attending public schools complete the following state-wide examinations:

- Basic skills tests for numeracy and literacy in Years 3 and 5
- English Language and Literacy Assessment, Secondary Numeracy Assessment Program, and Essential Secondary Science Assessment at the completion of Year 8
- School Certificate examinations in English/literacy; mathematics; science; Australian history, geography, civics and citizenship; and computing skills at the completion of Year 10.

Additionally, those students who remain beyond the compulsory years of schooling (i.e., 11 and 12) complete state-wide examinations in all disciplines at the completion of Year 12, with the results used to produce a Tertiary Entrance Ranking score, which is used by universities for student selection.

Clearly, this testing regime places a high degree of accountability on teachers working in the New South Wales public school system. Hence, it is not surprising that these teachers are generally conservative about the kinds of assessment tasks used with their students and the marking process applied in their classrooms. This has been reinforced by the lack of sustained professional development for teachers and the rapidity with which the new assessment regime was implemented. Subsequently, the New South Wales case study demonstrates again the conflict between the planned and received curriculum, with the teacher making the ultimate decisions and judgments based on factors outside of what may be considered "best for the student" (Kelly, 1999).

Education for All in Australian Schools

In 1973, the Commonwealth government endorsed the recommendations of the Karmel Report, which called for the recognition of special groups in the community. It was suggested that financial support be provided to promote equity programs for students disadvantaged by gender, poverty, non-English speaking backgrounds, and indigeneity (Seddon, 2001). To drive this agenda, the Commonwealth Schools Commission was established, which encouraged curriculum and educational developments that supported inclusivity in the classroom (Seddon & Deer, 1992). Also, the Adelaide Declaration (see Appendix 2) ensured that social justice and equity were a major focus of schooling. These moves initiated changes to state and territory curricula to create opportunities for all students.

Australian education has a reputation of resilience and resourcefulness (Caldwell, 2003), and our teachers are generally considered to be some of the most innovative in any education system (Bruniges, 2005). In large-scale international tests, such as the Trends in International Mathematics and Science Study (TIMSS), and the Programme for International Student Assessment (PISA), Australian students achieve highly in the areas of science, mathematics, reading, and problem-solving (Thomson, Cresswell, & De Bortoli, 2004). For example, approximately 12,500 students from 321 schools across Australia took part in the test in 2003 (Thomson et al., 2004). The OECD average score was 500, with only a few countries outperforming Australia in the four areas assessed (see Table 1).

At first glance, the above indicators suggest that "we are doing all right." However, a more detailed investigation of the educational landscape indicates that there are signs of stress and inequities.

Examples include the:

- Widening gap between high-performing and low-performing students
- Massive movement of students from public to private sectors (i.e., independent and Catholic schools) of education
- Attraction and retention of teachers, particularly in rural and regional areas
- Lack of performance of Indigenous students
- Failure to meet the National Goals of Schooling (e.g. the Adelaide Declaration, Appendix 2).

To explore some of these areas in greater detail, this section focuses on the lack of performance of our indigenous students, and the perceived inequity that has emerged recently between student achievement in metropolitan, regional, and rural areas of Australia.

Lack of Performance of Indigenous Students

During colonization, Britain failed to acknowledge the existence of Indigenous peoples (i.e., Australian Aborigines and Torres Strait Islanders) occupying Australia at the time (Seddon, 2001). This position was not to improve in the short term, with the result that Indigenous cultures and languages were not recognized in any curriculum until the 1970s (Beresford, 2001). Given this historical background, it is not surprising that Indigenous people have felt marginalized, resulting in low rates of participation in schooling. To illustrate this point, 71% of Indigenous students attending secondary schools in 1996 dropped out before the completion of Year 12 (the final year of schooling), compared to only 26% for non-Indigenous students (Seddon, 2001).

In addition to the reduced rates of retention, the achievement of Indigenous students has been significantly lower than that of the general population. For example, the publication of PISA data (Thomson et al., 2004) provides within-country comparisons that demonstrate the lower performance of Indigenous 15-year-old students. For 2003 PISA mathematics literacy, Indigenous students performed approximately one standard deviation (i.e., 50 points) below the OECD average of 500 points, while non-Indigenous students achieved one-quarter standard deviation (i.e., 25 points) above the OECD average (Thomson et al., 2004). Similar results emerged for scientific literacy, reading, and problem-solving. Consequently, Indigenous students were overrepresented in the lower categories of proficiency and underrepresented in the higher categories. These results provide evidence that we are not meeting the educational needs of our Indigenous students.

However, Sanderson and Thomson (2003) indicate that some improvements in the retention rates of Indigenous students into tertiary education are emerging (Department of Education, Science, and

Countries Achieving Significantly Higher Results Than Australia for PISA 2003

Science (Aust. *Mean* = 525)	Mathematics (Aust. *Mean* = 524)	Reading (Aust. *Mean* = 525)	Problem-solving (Aust. *Mean* = 530)
Finland	Hong Kong-China	Finland	Korea
Japan	China		Hong Kong-China
Korea	Finland		Finland
	Netherlands		Japan

Table 1

Training, 2002). They suggest this change is due to the combined efforts of teachers and advisers in public schools across Australia who are supporting Indigenous students and their families within their communities. While this is a positive outcome, it is still evident that "significant impediments to Indigenous education remain" (Sanderson & Thomson, 2003, p. 96). Unfortunately, this inequity goes beyond the scope of education, embracing the broader community issues of health, justice, and the way in which resources are allocated and distributed in Australia.

In terms of curriculum and schooling, cultural inclusivity is evident in all major policy documents (e.g., MCEETYA, 1995). However, it is the difficulty of putting this theory into practice that has become extremely complex. Some of the possible reasons for this omission include the lack of priority given to indigeneity in preservice teacher education, the irrelevance of the content of the curriculum to Indigenous needs and interests (MCEETYA, 1995), pedagogy (Christie, 1994), and the lack of availability of in-school work opportunities. Clearly, providing equitable educational experiences for Indigenous students requires the cooperation of teachers and schools working with Indigenous communities and families "to deconstruct the legacies and practices of institutional racism in order to design a public education system for this century" (Sanderson & Thomson, 2003, p. 117).

Inequity in Student Achievement Across Metropolitan, Regional, and Rural Areas

Schools in rural and regional Australia over the last decade have experienced difficulty in:

- Attracting and retaining qualified teaching staff
- Ensuring teacher access to professional development opportunities
- Providing necessary resources. (Roberts, 2005; Vinson, 2002)

Recent data have indicated that these issues are particularly problematic in the areas of mathematics, science, and information and communications technology, causing government concern about the future of Australia's economy (MCEETYA, 2001). Of critical concern is that these factors already appear to be impacting the received curriculum and, ultimately, what students are learning in the classroom. For example, students in metropolitan schools achieve at a higher level than students attending schools in regional and rural areas (Lyons & Panizzon, 2006). While much of this data is derived in specific states or territories, an analysis of PISA 2003 data provides evidence based upon large-scale objective international assessment. Of the 321 participating schools in Australia, approximately 70% of these were in metropolitan areas, 27% in regional areas, and only 3% of schools were located in remote areas of Australia (Thomson et al., 2004). While, overall, Australian students outperformed the majority of countries, major inequities emerged when compared across geographical boundaries (Figure 1).

The standard error bars express the variation about the mean. A lack of overlap between these bars for student achievement scores for the four areas assessed across the three locations indicates that the results are significantly different ($p \leq .05$). Consequently, students attending metropolitan schools achieved significantly higher results than students attending provincial (equating to regional) and remote schools. Similarly, students at provincial schools achieved significantly better than their peers in remote schools. Of particular concern is the realization that with the exception of problem-solving, the achievement of students in remote schools for science, mathematics, and reading literacy was below the OECD mean of 500.

To help address these concerns, the Commonwealth government funded the establishment of the National Centre of Science, ICT and Mathematics Education for Rural and Regional Australia (SiMERR Australia) in 2004 at the University of New England. One of the first priorities of SiMERR Australia was the development of a national survey to identify and compare key characteristics of science, ICT and mathematics education in different parts of the country and to explore the extent of any geographical differences (Lyons, Cooksey, Panizzon, Parnell, & Pegg, 2006). Results from the survey are being used to establish a national agenda for overcoming these inequities in rural and regional Australia.

Conclusion

It is clear from this discussion that curriculum development in Australia has been crafted in response to political, economic, social, and cultural factors. Our historical beginnings have resulted in a dual system of administration, with states and territories overseeing their own educational policy and curricula, while a national agenda emerges periodically to merely "muddy the waters" or provide national organizations that support specific educational endeavors. However, the actions of Commonwealth ministers of education in recent years suggest that the national agenda will become more prominent and that further political decisions will be made to ensure there is greater consistency of educational standards across Australia. Ultimately, this could lead to the implementation of a truly national curriculum. Regardless of what happens, though, it is sure to initiate a great deal of controversy and vigorous debate.

In the absence of a national curriculum, *The Adelaide Declaration on National Goals for Schooling in the Twenty-first Century* (1999) provides a set of goals that guide curriculum reform in every state and territory. The value of these goals is that they embrace a number of critical areas, thereby ensuring that Australian students experience a balanced education and develop an appreciation for "lifelong learning." Broadly, the goals identify the importance of developing fully the talents and capacities of all students; support the attainment of knowledge, skills, and understandings of students in a wide range of discipline areas; and value social justice as a means of providing equitable educational outcomes for all students. As articulated in this chapter, curriculum development in relation to these goals has varied across Australia (Bruniges, 2005), so there is still much work for educationalists to do in collaboration with the local communities in which we work and live. This is a critical step if we are to deal with the current challenges while preparing for those that will emerge in the future.

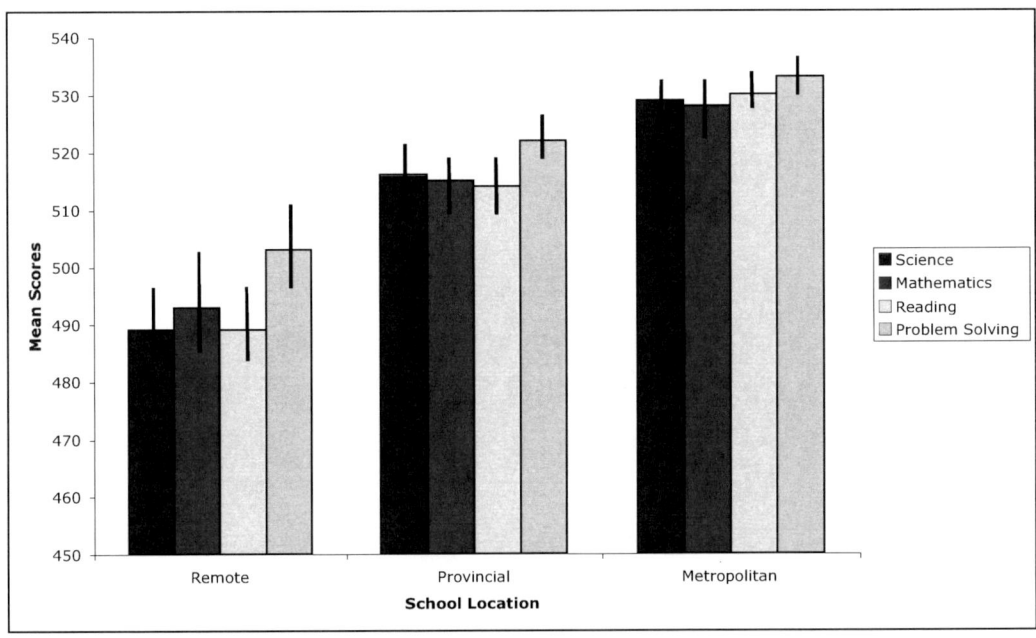

Figure 1

Student Achievement Across MCEETYA Schools Geographic Location Classification (source: Thomson et al., 2004).

Note

[1] A territory is a division of a country that does not have the full rights of a state. Australia has two major territories relevant to this paper, namely the Australian Capital Territory (including Canberra), established in 1911, and the Northern Territory, established in 1911.

Acknowledgment

I am appreciative of the comments and constructive advice provided by Greg McPhan on the content and scope of the chapter.

References

Australian Curriculum Studies Association. (2005). Retrieved November 20, 2006, from www.acsa.edu.au/.

Beresford, Q. (2001). Policy and performance: Aboriginal education in Western Australia in the 1990s. *Australian Journal of Education, 45*(1), 23-35.

Biggs, J. (1996). Enhancing teaching through constructive alignment. *Higher Education, 32*, 347-364.

Black, P., & Harrison, C. (2000). Formative assessment. In M. Monk & J. Osborne (Eds.), *Good practice in science teaching: What research has to say* (pp. 25-40). Buckingham, UK: Open University Press.

Black, P., & Wiliam, D. (1998a). Inside the black box: Raising standards through classroom assessment. *Phi Delta Kappan, 80*(2), 139-148.

Black, P., & Wiliam, D. (1998b). Assessment and classroom learning. *Assessment in Education, 5*(1), 7-71.

Board of Studies NSW. (2000). *Science stage 6 support document, Part 1.* Sydney, Australia: Author.

Boston, K. (1993). What does the AEC decision on national statements and profiles mean for New South Wales? *School Education News, 3*(10), 3-4.

Bruniges, M. (2005, June). *What is driving curriculum reform in Australia?* Paper presented at the Curriculum Corporation 12th National Conference, Brisbane, Queensland. Retrieved December 2, 2006, from http://cmslive.curriculum.edu.au/conference/2005/conference.asp?id=264

Caldwell, B. J. (2003, November). *A new vision for public schools in Australia.* Paper presented at the Economic and Social Outlook Conference, University of Melbourne Institute, Melbourne, Victoria.

Christie, M. (1994). Aboriginalizing the post-primary curriculum. *The Aboriginal Child School, 2*(2), 86-94.

Costello, R. B. (Ed.). (1993). *The American heritage college dictionary.* Boston: Houghton Mifflin.

Curriculum Corporation. (1991). *Mathematics in our schools: A guide for parents and the community.* Carlton, Victoria: Curriculum Corporation.

Curriculum Corporation. (1994). *A statement on science for Australian schools.* Carlton, Victoria: Curriculum Corporation.

Dawkins, J. (1988). *Strengthening Australia's schools: A consideration of the focus and content of schooling.* Canberra, ACT: Australian Government Publishing Service.

Department of Education, Science & Training. (2002). *Achieving equitable and appropriate outcomes, Indigenous Australians in higher education.* Canberra, ACT: Author.

Department of Education and Training. (2006). *Curriculum planning and programming, assessing and reporting to parents K-12: Policy standards.* Retrieved November 20, 2006, from www.curriculumsupport.education.nsw.gov.au/timetoteach

Duffield, J. (1990). The making of the Wyndham scheme in New South Wales. *History of Education Review, 19*(1), 29-42.

Gough, N., & Gough, A. (2003). A new public curriculum or reworking the languages of curriculum. In A. Reid & P. Thomson (Eds.), *Towards a public curriculum* (pp. 1-16). Flaxton, Queensland: Post Pressed.

Hattam, R., & Howard, N. (2003). Engaging lifeworlds: Public curriculum and community building. In A. Reid & P. Thomson (Eds.), *Towards a public curriculum* (pp. 75-94). Flaxton, Queensland: Post Pressed.

Kalantzis, M. (2001). Civic pluralism and total globalization. In B. Buckley & J. Conomos (Eds.), *Republicanism, culture, visual arts* (pp. 110-123). Sydney, NSW: Pluto Press.

Kalantzis, M., Cope, B., & Harvey, A. (2003). A public curriculum. In A. Reid & P. Thomson (Eds.), *Towards a public curriculum* (pp. 33-42). Flaxton, Queensland: Post Pressed.

Karmel, P. C. (1973). *Interim report of the Commonwealth Schools Commission.* Canberra, ACT: Australian Government Publishing Service.

Kelly, A. V. (1999). *The curriculum: Theory and practice.* Thousand Oaks, CA: Sage Publications.

Lyons, T., Cooksey, R. W., Panizzon, D. L., Parnell, A., & Pegg, J. E. (2006). *Science, ICT and mathematics education in rural and regional Australia—The SiMERR national survey.* Retrieved November 20, 2006, from http://simerr.une.edu.au/national_survey/index.html

Lyons, T., & Panizzon, D. (2006, July-August). *The rural-urban divide in Australian science education: Are rural students becoming second-class citizens?* Paper presented for the International Organization for Science and Technology Education, Penang, Malaysia.

Marsh, C., & Stafford, K. (1984). *Curriculum: Australian practices and issues.* Sydney, NSW: McGraw-Hill.

McGaw, B. (1996). *Their future: Options for reform of the Higher School Certificate.* Sydney, NSW: Department of Education and Training.

Ministerial Council on Education, Employment, Training and Youth Affairs. (1989). *The Hobart Declaration on national goals for schooling in the twenty-first century.* Retrieved October 20, 2006, from www.mceetya.edu.au/mceetya/default.asp?id=11577

Ministerial Council on Education, Employment, Training and Youth Affairs. (1995). *National review of Aboriginal and Torres Strait Islander education.* Canberra, ACT: Author.

Ministerial Council on Education, Employment, Training and Youth Affairs. (1999). *The Adelaide declaration on national goals for schooling in the twenty-first century.* Retrieved December 9, 2006, from www.dest.gov.au/sectors/school_education/policy_initiatives

Ministerial Council on Education, Employment, Training and Youth Affairs. (2001, July). *Information statement from the 12th MCEETYA meeting,* Melbourne. Retrieved April 9, 2006 from www.mceetya.edu.au/mceetya/default.asp?id=11558

Ministerial Council on Education, Employment, Training and Youth Affairs. (2006). *National consistency in curriculum outcomes – Statements of learning and professional elaborations in science.* Retrieved November 21, 2006, from www.mceetya.edu.au/mceetya/default.asp?id=11893

Northfield, J. (1986). Increasing curriculum responsibility: Science teachers respond to a new challenge. *Research in Science Education, 16*(1), 119-124.

Osborne, R., & Freyberg, P. (1985). *Learning in science: The implications of children's science.* London: Heinemann.

Piper, K. (1997). *Riders in the chariot: Curriculum reform and the national interest 1965-1995.* Melbourne, Victoria: Australian Council for Educational Research.

Reid, A. (2005). *Rethinking national curriculum collaboration: Towards an Australian curriculum.* Canberra, ACT: Department of Education, Science and Training.

Riordan, G. (2006). A response to the proposal for an Australian Certificate of Education. *Curriculum Leadership, 4*(21). Retrieved October 20, 2006, from http://cmslive.curriculum.edu.au/leader/default.asp?id=15031

Roberts, P. (2005). *Staffing an empty schoolhouse: Attracting and retaining teachers in rural, remote and isolated communities.* Sydney: NSW Teachers Federation.

Sanderson, V., & Thomson, P. (2003). Towards a just Indigenous education: A continuing challenge for state schooling. In A. Reid & P. Thomson (Eds.), *Towards a public curriculum* (pp. 95-120). Flaxton, Queensland: Post Pressed.

Seddon, T. (2001). National curriculum in Australia? A matter of politics, powerful knowledge and the regulation of learning. *Pedagogy, Culture and Society, 9*(3), 307-331.

Seddon, T., & Deer, C. E. (1992). *A curriculum for the senior secondary years.* Hawthorn, Victoria: Australian Council for Educational Research.

Smith, K. (2005, June). *Mind the gap.* Paper presented at the Curriculum Corporation 12th National Conference, Brisbane, Queensland. Retrieved December 2, 2006, from http://cmslive.curriculum.edu.au/conference/2005/conference.asp?id=264

Swain, J. (2000). Summative assessment. In M. Monk & J. Osborne (Eds.), *Good practice in science teaching: What research has to say* (pp. 139-157). Buckingham, UK: Open University Press.

Thomson, S., Cresswell, J., & De Bortoli, L. (2004). *Facing the future: A focus on mathematical literacy among Australian 15-year-old students in PISA 2003.* Camberwell, Victoria: Australian Council for Educational Research.

Vinson, A. (2002). *Inquiry into public education in New South Wales: Second report.* Retrieved August 18, 2005, from www.pub-edinquiry.org/reports/final_reports/03

Watt, M. (1996). Selecting curriculum resources for Australian schools: A review and analysis of current methods and future possibilities. Retrieved November 25, 2006, from http://eric.ed.gov/ERICWebPortal/Home.portal. ERIC Document Reprduction Service No. ED405249

Williams, R. (1976). *The long revolution.* Harmondsworth, UK: Penguin.

Appendix 1

Hobart Declaration 1989:
Ten National Goals of Schooling

1. To provide an excellent education for all young people, being one that develops their talents and capacities to full potential, and is relevant to the social, cultural and economic needs of the nation.
2. To enable all students to achieve high standards of learning and to develop self-confidence, optimism, high self-esteem, respect for others, and achievement of personal excellence.
3. To promote equality of education opportunities, and to provide for groups with special learning requirements.
4. To respond to the current and emerging economic and social needs of the nation, and to provide those skills that will allow students maximum flexibility and adaptability in their future employment and other aspects of life.
5. To provide a foundation for further education and training, in terms of knowledge and skills, respect for learning and positive attitudes for lifelong education.
6. To develop in students:
   a. the skills of English literacy, including skills in listening, speaking, reading, and writing
   b. skills of numeracy, and other mathematical skills
   c. skills of analysis and problem solving
   d. skills of information processing and computing
   e. an understanding of the role of science and technology in society, together with scientific and technological skills
   f. a knowledge and appreciation of Australia's historical and geographic context
   g. a knowledge of languages other than English
   h. an appreciation and understanding of, and confidence to participate in, the creative arts
   i. an understanding of, and concern for, balanced development and the global environment
   j. a capacity to exercise judgment in matters of morality, ethics, and social justice
7. To develop knowledge, skills, attitudes, and values that will enable students to participate as active and informed citizens in our democratic Australian society within an international context.
8. To provide students with an understanding and respect for our cultural heritage, including the particular cultural background of Aboriginal and ethnic groups.
9. To provide for the physical development and personal health and fitness of students, and for the creative use of leisure time.
10. To provide appropriate career education and knowledge of the world of work, including an understanding of the nature and place of work in our society. (MCEETYA, 1989)

Appendix 2

Adelaide Declaration 1999:
National Goals for Schooling in the 21st Century

1. Schooling should develop fully the talents and capacities of all students. In particular, when students leave schools, they should:
- Have the capacity for, and skills in, analysis and problem solving and the ability to communicate ideas and information, to plan and organize activities, and to collaborate with others
- Have qualities of self-confidence, optimism, high self-esteem, and a commitment to personal excellence as a basis for their potential life roles as family, community, and workforce members
- Have the capacity to exercise judgment and responsibility in matters of morality, ethics, and social justice, and the capacity to make sense of their world, to think about how things got to be the way they are, to make rational and informed decisions about their own lives, and to accept responsibility for their own actions
- Be active and informed citizens with an understanding and appreciation of Australia's system of government and civic life
- Have employment-related skills and an understanding of the work environment, career options, and path-

ways as a foundation for, and positive attitudes toward vocational education and training, further education, employment, and lifelong learning

- Be confident, creative and productive users of new technologies, particularly information and communication technologies, and understand the impact of those technologies on society
- Have an understanding of, and concern for, stewardship of the natural environment, and the knowledge and skills to contribute to ecologically sustainable development
- Have the knowledge, skills, and attitudes necessary to establish and maintain a healthy lifestyle, and for the creative and satisfying use of leisure time.

2. In terms of curriculum, students should have:
- Attained high standards of knowledge, skills, and understanding through a comprehensive and balanced curriculum in the compulsory years of schooling encompassing the agreed-upon eight key learning areas:
    - the arts
    - English
    - health and physical education
    - languages other than English
    - mathematics
    - science
    - studies of society and environment
    - technology
    - the interrelationships between them
- Attained the skills of numeracy and English literacy; such that every student should be able to numerate, read, write, spell, and communicate at an appropriate level
- Participated in programs of vocational learning during the compulsory years and have had access to vocational education and training programs as part of their senior secondary studies
- Participated in programs and activities that foster and develop enterprise skills, including those skills that will allow them maximum flexibility and adaptability in the future.

3. Schooling should be socially just, so that:
- Students' outcomes from schooling are free from the effects of negative forms of discrimination based on sex, language, culture and ethnicity, religion or disability; and of differences arising from students' socio-economic background or geographic location
- The learning outcomes of educationally disadvantaged students improve and, over time, match those of other students
- Aboriginal and Torres Strait Islander students have equitable access to, and opportunities in, schooling so that their learning outcomes improve and, over time, match those of other students
- All students understand and acknowledge the value of Aboriginal and Torres Strait Islander cultures to Australian society and possess the knowledge, skills, and understanding to contribute to, and benefit from, reconciliation between Indigenous and non-Indigenous Australians
- All students understand and acknowledge the value of cultural and linguistic diversity, and possess the knowledge, skills, and understanding to contribute to, and benefit from, such diversity in the Australian community and internationally
- All students have access to the high quality education necessary to enable the completion of school education to Year 12 or its vocational equivalent and that provides clear and recognized pathways to employment and further education and training. (MCEETYA, 1999)

About the Author

Debra Panizzon, Ph.D., is an Associate Professor and Deputy Director for the newly established Flinders Centre for Science Education in the 21st Century at Flinders University, Australia. She can be contacted at debra.panizzon@flinders.edu.au

Changes to Science Curricula in Botswana

Cephas David Yandila

Botswana, formerly called Bechuanaland, emerged as an independent sovereign state on September 30, 1966. It had no official pre-primary schools, but had a few primary and vocational schools with relatively small enrollment and nine secondary schools. Of these secondary schools, three offered science subjects (up to the senior level), designed and examined by the University of Cambridge in England. They were called University of Cambridge Overseas School Science Syllabuses.

Description of curricula changes in Botswana is herein confined mainly to science, because of the major roles that science and technology have played in overall resource development. Worldwide, the last century has witnessed a rapid growth and development of science and technology. Almost all walks of life have been influenced by scientific and technological innovations and inventions. Nations are now classified as developed, developing, or underdeveloped on the basis of their societies' use and application of scientific and technological knowledge. Botswana's economy since its independence has been transformed from an agro-economy to a mineral-economy and is currently moving toward becoming a technology-economy. Botswana has visualized a rapid growth in science and technology by ensuring adequate investment in them. The country's Vision 2016 states that:

> *Botswana must recognize the rapid international developments in science and technology that are re-shaping the societies of the world. While much can be borrowed from other countries, we will need to look within our own resources and culture to find the sources of innovation that will allow us to shape our own future. The Vision strategy must ensure adequate investment in the development of technology. . . . Science and technology must be emphasized through the education system. All children with appropriate aptitude, male and female, should be encouraged to study science. (Republic of Botswana-Vision 2016, 1997, pp. 40-41)*

Botswana

Botswana had a great task of training her own people in science, science-related fields, and technology, in order to become self-reliant in all specialized fields. In order to tackle this task, the new state had to consider several areas associated with science education. These were:

- Teacher training programs for primary and secondary schools, colleges, and universities
- Science curricula changes at primary, secondary, and tertiary institutions
- Expansion of educational institutions with all the attendant factors, including buildings, science teachers, etc.

A science and technology policy (S&T Policy, 1998) was established for the country that emphasized the need to increase awareness and appreciation of science and technology in Botswana. For example, Botswana suffers from a shortage of local science and technology teachers and teacher trainers at all levels of the education system, resulting in low output in S&T. Thus, the objective of the science and technology policy is to develop adequate human resource capacity with an optimum mix of capabilities to generate and apply S&T based on the needs of industry and the society, and to cultivate a culture of S&T in all sections of the population (Singh, 2003).

Strategic planners hope to promote science and technology education at all levels, with a view toward producing an enterprising Botswana. The growing popularity of science and technology among secondary students was reported in a ROSE (Relevance of Science and Technology Education) study carried out by Yandila et al. (2006). The study showed that students recognized the relevance of school science to their lives and future careers. Most of them showed some appreciation of the fact that science is a part of their lives and through learning it, they would acquire the knowledge and skills they need to cope with a rapidly changing world. It also brought into light the fact that school syllabi do not cover some topics very well. Two of the recommendations from the ROSE study were that:

- The Department of Curriculum and Evaluation should ensure that science syllabi are relevant to the needs of the learners.
- Schools should ensure that they have relevant equipment and facilities to help students have a true appreciation for what school science encompasses so that they can grow up to apply the learned skills in their everyday situations.

Curricula Changes in Science

As was the case in most new independent African countries in the 1960s and 1970s, Botswana's inherited curricula needed urgent revision at the primary, junior, and senior secondary school levels. The science syllabi were teacher-centered, dominated by teacher talk and lecture, while students were passive and depended on the teachers' verbal information. Observation and investigation were discouraged; instead, students were taught to rely upon the teacher's assistance in drawing conclusions. Changes have been made in science curricula at different educational levels at different times. Major changes were made first in primary and junior secondary science, and finally in senior secondary school science.

Curricula Changes in Primary Science

Primary school science was taught in the 1930s as nature study, which emphasized the study of plants and hygiene. The syllabus stressed the importance of observation, experimentation, and recording by students. In practice, however, the teacher was the most active person in class—giving lectures, carrying out demonstrations, asking questions, and determining how learning should proceed. The students were on the receiving end, listening, copying notes, and committing science knowledge to memory. Teachers were generalists in that they taught all primary school subjects from standard one to four in lower primary, and from standard five to eight in higher primary. At the end of standard four, students sat for a promotion and qualifying examination.

After Botswana gained independence in 1966, the country introduced education reforms. The broad aim of education was to change the syllabus taught in the primary schools to include such subjects as basic agriculture and home economics, which teach young girls and boys how to run a homestead. Independence brought a new look to the primary school curriculum. Subject panels were established to improve the existing curriculum. The curriculum was revised in stages in 1965 and 1969, and finally in 1982. It was introduced in schools in 1982. However, as far back as the new syllabus of 1969, it is alleged that most primary teachers did not know how to teach it. While they were mandated to undertake a two-year inservice course, science in primary schools was still badly taught and poorly learned by students.

In light of this poor performance of the 1969 science syllabus, subject panels were asked to review the entire science curriculum as part of the entire primary school curriculum. The panel examined the content of the curriculum, the learner, teaching methods, facilities available in schools, and the goals for teaching primary science. While this review was in progress, the National Commission for Education also carryied out its own investigation, which resulted in the National Policy on Education called "Education for Kagisano" (1977). Most of its stipulations were implemented, including the establishment of the Curriculum Development Unit (CDU), which developed the new primary school curricula.

The science panel in the CDU constructed a trial syllabus for primary school science, which was implemented in 1982. The syllabus was child-centered, activity-oriented, and process-skill oriented. To achieve this goal, the amount of subject matter and cognitive domain in the syllabus was reduced and both psychomotor and affective domains were emphasized, with the aim of training the learner in the skill of observation. Teachers' guides were written to meet the above-stated course objectives. In order to assist teachers to comfortably teach the new curriculum, the CDU ran periodic inservice workshops in the country. Teachers were given guidelines for using the teaching materials. The CDU also established the Teaching Aid Production Unit (TAPU), whereby teachers were taught how to make various teaching aids for their science lessons.

After further revisions, the final primary school science syllabus was released in 1992-93. According to Molosi (1993), it forms part of the Ten-Year Basic Education Program from the Primary School Level Curriculum to the Junior Secondary Level and reflects a continuous and integrated Nine Years of Basic Education Curriculum. The syllabus is divided into two parts. Part 1 is for Standards 1-4, and Part 2 is for Standards 5-7. The content in each part is presented in the form of modules composed of those elements, which have been grouped together through selection and sequencing, and which students will be required to learn in the time allocated.

In the Standards 1-4 syllabus, the process skills of observation, recording, measuring, comparing, classifying, experimenting, predicting, and interpreting data form the modules. In addition, the syllabus includes modules on Keeping Healthy, Environmental Awareness, Safety, Family Life, and Projects. In the Standards 5-7 Syllabus, the modules are organized around science topics of immediate concern in students' everyday life. Science process skills introduced at the lower levels are integrated with the selected topics of the content. The modules include Weather and Seasons, Plants in Nature, Animals in Nature, Water, Forms of Energy, Keeping Healthy, Environmental Awareness, Safety, and Family Life.

Guidelines for assessing student work are described in the new primary science syllabus. The assessment focuses on three key components of science: scientific process skills, scientific attitudes, and scientific knowledge. Through primary school experience, the students will:

- Develop the skill of finding out information for themselves, using science process skills that underlie the continuing development of scientific knowledge
- Gather knowledge that will enable them to understand science concepts likely to be met in everyday life
- Express awareness of and interest in the natural world surrounding them
- Express awareness of science contributions to the social and economic life of the community

- Express a respect for all life and the desire to maintain the quality of their surroundings
- Develop a positive attitude toward science. (Molosi, 1993, pp. 2-3)

It is unfortunate that the basic principles and concepts of technology are not included in the primary science syllabus. Nonetheless, the syllabus described above is part of the 10 years of basic education and therefore a prerequisite for the three years of junior secondary school science syllabus.

Curricula Changes in Junior Science

Until the mid-1960s, junior secondary science in Botswana was called "introductory science" and consisted of selected topics from biology, chemistry, and physics. Physics was examined in greater depth than the other subjects. The syllabus provided for the course to be taught with the help of science laboratories. However, laboratories in most schools were inadequate and apparatus and chemicals were not available for students to perform experiments. Science teachers themselves were ill-equipped to teach the syllabus. Teachers' guides did not indicate the depth to which topics were to be taught. Through a rote-learning approach, teachers managed to have relatively good results in the introductory science course.

Although the results of junior secondary science looked impressive, the results of the same students on the Cambridge Overseas School Certificate examination science were relatively poor. This could have been caused by a number of factors, including the following:

- Junior science was not the prerequisite for senior science.
- At the junior level, students did not master the science knowledge; rather, they learned it by rote just to pass the junior examinations.
- Science teachers at the senior level were poorly trained, compared to those at junior secondary school level.

In 1977, the Examination Council of Botswana, Lesotho, and Swaziland (ECOBLS) agreed to replace the two introductory science syllabuses with a single one, which was named "Integrated Science." The Council established the outline of the new syllabus and left the science panels of each country to work out details of the course. The Botswanian Ministry of Education stipulated a few principles upon which the new syllabus was to be based. These were:

- It must cover the first three years of secondary education, and the third year must provide for the beginning of some form of specialization
- It must be adequate introduction to school certificate courses in biology, chemistry, and physics
- The syllabus must be terminal for those students who leave school at the end of three years of secondary school
- The course must be teachable by one teacher or by team teaching
- The course must be designed to cover all the stated objectives with relevant materials
- Care must be exercised to have the subject matter graded within any one topic.

In 1972, the Ministry of Education established the Botswana National Science Panel, which eventually prepared a new syllabus and presented it to the science panels of Botswana, Lesotho, and Swaziland for adoption (Letsholo, 1995). The syllabus was aimed at providing students with the knowledge, skills, and attitudes needed for understanding and for responsible participation in society. Extra activities were provided to accommodate faster students. It was supported by students' worksheets and teachers' guides, which adjusted for mixed-ability teaching.

The syllabus was learner-centered, with a large and essential component of practical work in a laboratory or science room, making maximum use of easily available, low-cost materials. It utilized the discovery method to transfer useful skills and knowledge to the students, and was structured around integrated themes and topics, some of which were immediately practical.

The teaching of this syllabus was to be learner-centered rather than teacher-centered. The objective of science teaching in the first two years of science education was to begin teaching what science is and how a scientist works. The course was to be a practical one. Students were to work in science laboratories. However, laboratory examinations were discontinued. The course was designed to serve as terminal for the students (roughly half) who leave formal schooling after completing junior secondary school. It was to serve as an introduction to School Certificate and university qualifying examinations for the other half of the students.

The integrating themes of the new science course were energy, the particle nature of matter, and life. The course consisted of 15 teaching units. Teacher's guides and students' worksheets were produced for each unit. Each unit in the teachers' guide was prefaced with a list of objectives and detailed guidance on how to teach each topic. Details of experiments and lists of necessary equipment and chemicals were given. Worksheets for students included experimental procedures. At the end of each unit, specially designed tests were prepared to help students in their learning process.

The entire integrated science syllabus was being revised in light of teachers' experiences, which they had reported to the panel. A critical comparison between the integrated science and the Cambridge school syllabus showed a lack of logical relationship between the two.

Before the new integrated science syllabus was introduced in junior secondary schools, all science teachers were invited to attend an inservice workshop aimed at preparing them to teach it meaningfully. Finally, in January 1974, the new course was introduced in schools and later renamed Science by Investigation in Botswana.

Since its introduction, Science by Investigation in Botswana has undergone several changes aimed at its improvement. In spite of all these changes, its implementation still faced logistical problems, including:

• Most expatriates were not qualified to teach the syllabus.
• Many local science teachers had been trained to teach only one science subject and yet the new syllabus required that they teach at least two subjects.
• There was still a high turnover rate of expatriate science teachers.
• There was also a significant drift of local science teachers from the teaching profession into industries for greater rewards.
• There was a contradiction between the claim that the syllabus was student-centered and laboratory-based and what actually took place in the classrooms. The teachers did not fully make use of the laboratory facilities, due to a lack of technical staff and motivation. Nor were the new teaching approaches outlined in the teachers' guides being followed closely.

In light of these problems, the new syllabus had to be refined. It was implemented in 1992 and examined for the first time in 1993. Some of the changes included presenting the content in modules composed of elements that had been grouped together through selection and sequencing, and that pupils were required to learn in the allocated time. These modules had been organized on the basis of integrated science topics and themes. Each module emphasized process skills and concepts. It also had been stated that at the end of form two, the Integrated Science test items would assess the students' achievements of the objectives, as stated in the syllabus (Molosi, 1992).

In addition to these changes, the new syllabus was renamed "Basic Science" and presented science topics, such as biology, chemistry, and physics. A new set of teachers' guides and students' textbooks were published. The aims of the new Basic Science courses were based on the aims of the nine-year basic education curriculum, which are to gain:

• Understanding of the methods of science (and mathematics) and their influence on human life in everyday activities

- Ability to observe and record accurately events and activities in life
- Ability to think rationally and logically
- Effective use of skills and instruments in activities connected with later studies or out-of-school work.

The new course was said to be practical-based, and would involve students in learning through investigation. It included tasks that inculcated in the students an inquiring mind that continually strives to establish scientifically tested conclusions. It consisted of topics and/or principles drawn from biology in part one and chemistry and physics in part two.

The syllabus was designed to cater to students who would proceed to senior secondary education or vocational training, as well as those who would leave at the end of form three to the world of work. The syllabus is organized into 10 broad themes called "modules," which are introduced in form one or two, and further developed during the later years. Module one is all presented in form one, because it introduces those basic scientific skills necessary to work properly and safely in science. These skills should be applied right through the three years.

Each module is subdivided into units, which, in turn, are broken down into topics to allow the scientific processes to function and help students acquire knowledge that will enable them to understand some science principles and concepts. For each topic, general objectives that give rise to specific objectives are derived. The specific objectives describe what students are expected to do; this includes applying basic science process skills, interpreting natural phenomena, and understanding and applying scientific principles.

Aims of the Three-year Junior Secondary Science Program

At the end of three years of the Junior Secondary Science Program, students are expected to have developed:

- An understanding of basic principles and concepts of science, as they are experienced in everyday life
- Positive attitudes towards such scientific skills as curiosity, open-mindedness, creativity, objectivity, integrity, and initiative
- An ability to use process skills associated with the practice of science for understanding and exploring natural phenomena, problem-solving, and decision-making
- An awareness and appreciation of the interrelationships among science, technology, and society in the context of science and everyday life
- An awareness, literacy, and an understanding of the significance of computers in science-related careers
- The ability and responsibility to protect the environment and use natural resources on a sustainable basis
- The ability to make informed decisions about further studies and science-based careers and vocations.

Assessment

The assessment for this science syllabus consists of a terminal examination and continuous assessment. The terminal examination consists of three papers, namely:

- Paper 1: Objective type questions; examining pupils' comprehension of scientific principles and concepts, and their application to new situations.
- Paper 2: This is made up of Sections A and B. Section A: Short-answer questions; knowledge and recall of scientific concepts; understanding of scientific knowledge and relationships; translation of information from one form to another; reading information from graphs, tables, and charts;

representing information in the form of graphs, tables, and charts. Section B: Description/essay and problem-solving questions; translation of information from one form to another; reading information from graphs, tables, and charts; representing information in the form of graphs, tables, and charts; application of scientific knowledge and understanding to new situations; explanation, interpretation, and application of information; analysis, synthesis, and evaluation of scientific information; planning of investigations.

- Paper 3: A series of questions to test past experience of practical work; planning of investigations; designing and planning an experimental procedure; use of apparatus and materials; record observations and measurements; interpret and draw conclusions from observations and experimental data. Continuous assessment (CA) for students' progression is undertaken by teachers throughout the three years. These may be made up of the following activities done by the students:
  - Written tests during the three years: Items should match the skills being measured and not the convenience of the teacher.
  - Normal laboratory work: Teachers will have to administer far more individual practical work than ever before. This will entail obtaining and maintaining sufficient equipment, making and keeping to schedules, and creating and maintaining records.
  - Project work: Through project work, the teacher gets to know about the students' learning and attitude. The teacher is expected to put the responsibility for learning on the student and may involve a student's family and community. Several projects could be contemplated during the three years, with expectations for improvement as students gain experience. Students should be encouraged to choose their own project topics in consultation with teachers. (Molosi, 1996, pp. 1-4)

Once again, the junior secondary school science syllabus is a prerequisite for the senior secondary school science syllabus—Pure Science in Biology, Chemistry, Physics; Single Science and Double Science. Based on the school visits that my former students and I have made in several junior secondary schools in the country, the problem of inadequate science laboratories—lack of equipments and resources—continues to negatively affect the effective teaching and learning of science. In some schools, science laboratories are used as base classrooms. Most schools do not have trained laboratory technicians to assist teachers. Students' carrying out practical work is an option rather than mandatory; when they do so, they work in groups of 5-8. The very nature of the practical work is not investigatory, but confirmatory. It is now left to researchers to find ways to effect the implementation of the new syllabus in schools.

Curricula Changes in Senior Secondary Science

Only insignificant changes were made to the science syllabus at the senior secondary school level until 1997. Tailor-made subject syllabuses with course aims assessment objectives and course outlines, summative examinations, and marking of examination scripts were all done at the University of Cambridge in the United Kingdom. Each year, with the increase in the number of examination candidates in Botswana, this dependence upon externally administered syllabus and examination was proving to be an expensive venture. Besides, there was no reason why a country with a booming economy could not complete localization of all her educational programs, as virtually all her neighbors had done. Doing this would significantly ensure the country's full control of educating her people. Thus, in 1991, plans to localize the senior secondary school syllabus and examination by the end of NDP7 (National Development Plan 7 for the period 1991-97) were announced.

The senior secondary curricula was not revised until 1996 (NDP 8, 1998; Yandila, 1999), a process that was not completed until 2003. The Ministry of Education, in partnership with the University of Cambridge Local Examinations Syndicate (UCLES), embarked on a phased program in 1995 to localize the Cambridge Overseas School Certificate Examination with respect to the marking of examination scripts, the curriculum, the examination papers, and the examination processing system. This involved a series of stages: 1) commissioned research; 2) a blueprint that provided the philosophy, rationale, aims, objectives, assessment, and guidelines; 3) assigning the work to the subject taskforces; 4) developing revised syllabuses; 5) consulting with schools and incorporating their views; 6) introducing the new curricula in schools; and 7) running implementation workshops for teachers, school head teachers, and departmental heads. The National Commission on Education (1993) recommended that:

- A fully fledged autonomous National Examinations Council be established
- Markers and examiners in different subject areas should be trained
- Preparation, rewriting, and adaptation of syllabuses, starting with subjects of more local relevance and context, should be done
- Examination papers should be set and a grading system of scripts should be developed with Cambridge moderation
- Provision of physical facilities should be required, and procurement of equipment for printing and processing examination should be made.

The Revised National Policy on Education (1994, p. 23) stipulated that:

- The senior secondary school syllabuses and examinations should be localized and enable the latter to cater to a wider ability group, emphasizing the development of practical and business subjects. The development of curriculum and instructional materials should reflect the world of work by promoting integration across subjects.
- In the future certification system for senior secondary school leavers (graduates or completers), the role of continuous assessment should be fully recognized, with some weighting in the final grading, and teachers should be given adequate training to handle continuous assessment.

The Senior Secondary School Science was to be a two-year program designed for students who successfully completed Junior Secondary education. It was to provide them with scientific knowledge, skills, and attitudes, and to prepare them for tertiary education, vocational training, and employment.

All of the science subjects fall into one optional group called the sciences, consisting of Pure Sciences, Double Science, Single Science, and Human Social Biology. Students are required to choose one of them except the latter, which is only offered to private candidates (Ramatsui, 2000). Pure Science Subject, referred to as Triple Award, is equivalent to three science subjects of biology, chemistry, and physics, which are prerequisites of university or college first-year science programs worldwide.

Each syllabus is organized around broad content areas subdivided into topics. Each topic consists of general objectives that give rise to specific objectives. The specific objectives constitute what learners are expected to demonstrate on each topic. These objectives are divided into core objectives and extended objectives. The extended specific objectives are highlighted in bold italics. All learners are expected to follow the core specific objectives. The extended objectives provide more challenging work for those learners able to benefit from it (Ramatsui, 2000, p. v). Their contents are shown below:

1. Biology Topics
   - Process skills (biological investigations in using and organizing apparatus and materials, applying basic process skills to problem solving, collecting data, and handling experimental observations and data)
   - Living things (cell processes and maintenance and variety of plants and animals)
   - Obtaining essentials of life (nutrition, respiration, transport, and circulation)
   - Control of the internal environment (homeostasis and excretion)
   - Response and coordination (nervous system, hormonal coordination support, movement and locomotion, and the use and abuse of drugs)

- Reproduction (forms of reproduction, sexual reproduction in flowering plants and in mammals)
- Genetics, natural selection, and evolution (inheritance, chromosomes and genes, natural selection and evolution)
- Living things and the environment (ecology and conservation)
- Biotechnology.

2. Chemistry Topics
   - Process skills (chemistry investigations in using and organizing apparatus and materials, applying basic process skills to problem solving, collecting data, and handling experimental observations and data)
   - Matter (4 weeks) (particulate nature of matter, atomic structure, periodic table, chemical bonding)
   - Chemical reactions (9 weeks) (energy changes, rate of reaction, reversible reactions, redox reactions, electrolysis, acids, bases, and salts)
   - Stoichiometry (8 weeks) (chemical formulae and equations, the mole, chemical calculations, quantitative analysis)
   - Metals and non-metals (8 weeks) (properties of metals, extraction of metals, uses of metals and alloys, non-metals, sulfur, carbon and carbonates, nitrogen, chlorine)
   - Chemistry in the environment (7 weeks) (water, air, recycling, sources of energy)
   - Carbon chemistry (5 weeks) (homologous series, alkanes, alkenes, alkanols, alkanoic acids, macromolecules, synthetic condensation polymers, natural macromolecules).

3. Physics Topics
   - Process skills (biological investigations in using and organizing apparatus and materials, applying basic process skills to problem solving, collecting data, and handling experimental observations and data)
   - General physics (length and time; motion; mass; weight and center of mass; density; forces: effects on shape and size, effects on motion, and turning effects of forces; scalars and vectors; energy; work and power; pressure)
   - Thermal physics (simple kinetic molecular model of matter, thermal expansion of matter, measurement of temperature, heat capacity, melting and boiling, transfer of thermal energy)
   - Properties of waves, including light and sound (general wave properties, light, electromagnetic spectrum, sound)
   - Electricity and magnetism (magnetism, electric practical electric circuitry, electromagnetic effects, introductory electronics, electronic systems)
   - Atomic physics (radioactivity).

The Double Science Award consists of two thirds of each of the pure science content and specific objectives of biology, chemistry, and physics, giving it an equivalent of two science subjects. The Single Science Award consists of one-third each of the content and specific objectives of pure biology, chemistry, and physics, giving it an equivalent of one science subject. Pure Science Syllabuses were introduced in school in 1998; the others were introduced in 1999.

Another major change in the new senior secondary school science syllabi was the recommended teaching methods. The syllabi encourage a learner-centered approach, as emphasized in the curriculum blueprint. This involves emphasizing science process skills, problem-solving, and the acquisition of hands-on experience, which should increase the participation and performance of all groups (e.g., groups of different abilities, learners with special needs, boys and girls).

Another new feature of the new syllabus is the combination of the students' two-year Coursework Assessment marks with the Final Examination marks in each subject. In the course of study, pupils are to be assessed in the following practical skills: 1) using and organizing techniques, apparatus, and materials; 2) observing, measuring, and recording; 3) handling experimental observations and data; and 4) planning investigations. This only applies to those who take triple and double award sciences.

The introduction of single and double sciences has caused logistical problems in most schools, because science teachers are either single or double majors in one of the three subjects. For schools to require that each instructor teach all the contents of either single award or double award sciences is professionally stretching them. Curricular implementation studies have shown that in some schools, three teachers are assigned to teach the same class of pupils taking single or double science, thereby increasing their teaching loads and causing conflicts in teaching schedules. In other schools, although each teacher is assigned to teach the entire content of single or double science, they are allowed to make private arrangements for team teaching. This is also not the best solution. The best would be to increase the number of science teachers so that everyone teaches the content for which he/she was trained (Mbengwa, 2002; Yandila, 1999a, 1999b).

Assessment

To ensure that learners attain the set aims, each course is assessed through a variety of continuous assessment techniques, including projects, tests, experiments, and surveys. The outcomes are used to improve instruction and guide progression. At the end of the course, a terminal examination is administered and is weighted 80%. Continuous assessment in the form of coursework contributes 20% to the final grade of the course. The coursework is locally and externally moderated. When it is not possible to offer coursework, alternative papers to examine the same knowledge, skills, and attitudes are used. The examining body developed examination syllabi to provide teachers with guidelines on objectives to be examined. The final examinations are marked by the Botswana Examination Council and moderated by external examiners.

The new syllabi introduced a number of commendable features in the senior secondary school education system. However, several concerns have been expressed by some teachers, schoolchildren, parents, tertiary institutions, and industry. Most of the concerns may have emanated from insufficient information about the nature, scope, rationale, and philosophy of the new curricula. This may be because they were inadequately consulted during the design and construction of the new curricula. But some concerns may be dismissed as purely resistance to change by those concerned, particularly pupils and teachers. However, it is worthwhile to review the process that led to the new curricula, as well as their implementation and assessment, and to solicit the views of all stakeholders about different aspects of the curricula. The information gained from such reviews may assist in the ongoing revision of the new curricula in future, because no curriculum should be sacrosanct.

The implementation of the new senior secondary school science syllabus marked the accomplishment of a revision process of basic education that started in 1965 at the primary school level. Finally, Botswana has its own syllabus and examination at each educational level, including the tertiary. We should all be proud of this sign of progress and look forward to contributing to its success through ongoing evaluation. One could wish that all the Southern African Development Community (SADC) countries could begin to consult with a purpose of designing a regional curriculum, syllabi, and examinations, such as found in other regions of Africa.

Conclusion

In Botswana, as it is for all nations of the world, education, especially in the areas of science and technology, is the cornerstone and foundation upon which civic, economic, and social development is constructed and preserved. It is, therefore, very important that every effort be made to see that students and teachers are motivated to take learning and teaching seriously in order for Botswana and her people to continue to advance in the world community of nations. The successful implementation of the primary and secondary school programs depends heavily on the Ministry of Education's attending to problems that the empirical studies have identified in recent years (Manchisi, 1993; Mbengwa, 2000; Mogapi & Yandila, 2001; Nokaneng & King, 2003; Singh, 2003).

References

Letsholo, D. (1995). *An analysis of process skills in science lessons in Botswana primary schools.* Unpublished Masters Project. University of Botswana.

Manchisi, S. S. (1993). *Certificate course for secondary school science laboratory assistants in Botswana.* Unpublished Discussion Paper Presented at the Science Panel of the Ministry of Education.

Mbengwa, R. (2002). *An assessment of practical skills in biology in four selected senior secondary schools in Botswana.* Unpublished M.Ed. Dissertation. University of Botswana.

Moahi, L. T. (2003, August). Keynote address on translating Vision 2016 into reality through curricular change. In D. Letsholo, T. D. Mogotsi, K. N. Sebina, C. Molelo, R. Solomon, T. A. Kgwefane, B. Matenge, D. D. Yandila, & P. J. Motshidisi (Eds.), *Translating Vision 2016 into reality through curricular change.* Selected papers presented at the 5th Biennial Conference on Teacher Education, Tonota, Gaborone.

Mogapi, M., & Yandila, C. D. (2001). *Assessment in BGCSE science subjects.* Paper presented at the fifth Biennial Conference of the National Council for Teacher Education.

Molosi, P. O. (1992). *Junior secondary school syllabuses for science.* Gaborone: Ministry of Education, Curriculum Development Division. Government Printers.

Molosi, P. O. (1993). *Junior secondary school syllabuses for science.* Gaborone: Ministry of Education, Curriculum Development Division. Government Printers.

Molosi, P. O. (1996). *Nine year basic education syllabuses.* Gaborone: Ministry of Education, Curriculum Development Division. Government Printers.

Nokaneng, J., & King, O. (2003, July). *Primary school in action.* Paper presented at 6th Biennial Conference on Teacher Education: "Towards the Realization of a Developed and Informed Nation-A Challenge for Educators," University of Botswana.

Ramatsui, P. T. (1997). *Botswana general certificate secondary education teaching syllabus: Biology.* Gaborone: Ministry of Education, Curriculum Development Division. Government Printers.

Ramatsui, P. T. (2000). *Botswana general certificate secondary education teaching syllabus: Chemistry.* Gaborone: Ministry of Education, Curriculum Development Division. Government Printers.

Rantabe, D. R. (1992). *Teacher behavior in the classroom: An analysis of primary school science teaching in Botswana.* Unpublished Masters Project. University of Botswana.

Republic of Botswana. (1977). *National Commission on Education.* Gaborone: Government Printers.

Republic of Botswana. (1992). *Primary school syllabuses.* Gaborone: Government Printers.

Republic of Botswana. (1991). *The National Plan 7, 1991-1997.* Gaborone: Government Printers.

Republic of Botswana. (1993). *National Commission on Education.* Gaborone: Government Printers.

Republic of Botswana. (1994). *The revised national policy on education white paper.* Gaborone: Government Printers.

Republic of Botswana. (1997). *Vision 2016: Towards prosperity for all. A long term vision for Botswana.* Gaborone: Government Printers.

Republic of Botswana. (1998). *Science and technology policy for Botswana approved by Parliament, Ministry of Finance and Development Planning, Government of Botswana.* Gaborone: Government Printers.

Republic of Botswana. (1998). *National Development Plan 8, 1998-2005.* Gaborone: Government Printers.

Republic of Botswana. (2000). *Botswana general certificate secondary education teaching syllabus: Science double award.* Gaborone: Ministry of Education, Curriculum Development Division. Government Printers.

Singh, V. P. (2003, July). *Towards an effective science and technology education programme in Botswana.* Paper presented at 6th Biennial Conference on Teacher Education: "Towards the Realization of a Developed and Informed Nation-A Challenge for Educators" held at the University of Botswana.

Yandila, C. D. (1999a). *The implementation hiccups of senior secondary school science syllabus in Botswana.* A paper presented at the ninth symposium of IOSTE held in Durban-Westville.

Yandila, C. D. (1999b). *The new senior secondary school science syllabuses in Botswana.* A paper presented at the 4th National Conference on Teacher Education held at the Sun Hotel, Gaborone.

Yandila, C. D., Komane S., & Moganane, S. (2003). Evidence of hands-on teaching/learning approaches in Botswana's senior secondary school science lessons. In S. P. Loo, A. Aminah, S. Yoong, S. T. S.

Azian, L. W. Lee, & S. C. Toh (Eds.), *Increasing the relevance of science and technology education for all in the 21st century* (pp. 182-193). Penang, Malaysia: SEAMEO RECSAM.

Yandila, C. D., Moganane, S., Bothasitse, S. M., Lekote, L., & Mongweemang, G. G. (2006, July-August). *Perceptions of the relevance of school science held by secondary school students in Botswana.* Paper presented at IOSTE 12th Symposium held in Penang.

About the Author

Cephas David Yandila, Ph.D., is a Zambian who served as science educator at the University of Zambia & University of Botswana (1975-2006) & External Examiner in Kenya, RSA & Namibia. He has been a member of IOSTE since 1982 and a founding Director of Kazungula Christian Academy.

The Development of
Education in Brazil

Ann K. Nauman and Nelio Bizzo

In 1500, the Portuguese first laid claim to territory in the New World when Pedro Alvares Cabral's fleet, bound for the Indies down the coast of West Africa, turned westward and touched upon a land-form jutting into the Atlantic. The Portuguese king, Dom Manuel, named the new land *Vera Cruz* (True Cross), but soon after changed the name to *Santa Cruz* (Holy Cross)[1], and claimed it for the Portuguese crown. Although Cabral's men made contact with the native population, and they noted the commercial value of the dyewood and brazilwood trees in the area, they made no attempt at first to colonize the territory. Historians recognize that the enthusiasm for the new discovery was very low compared with the excitement engendered by Vasco da Gama in the summer of 1499, when he brought the news of having reached India the year before (Fausto, 1995; Loução & Santos, 1998).

In those first years, Portugal signed an agreement with a group of merchants, led by Fernando de Loronha, or Noronha, a new Christian, who would explore the coast, sending at least six ships each year, and exercise a commercial monopoly over the newfound land (Fausto, 1995). At that time, Portugal had a large trade with the East Indies and profitable commercial contacts with Asia. As a result of Spanish and French efforts to pirate the lucrative dye trade, the Portuguese crown authorized a naval commander, Martim Afonso de Sousa, to clear the foreigners from the coast and to explore the area in a first colonizing expedition (1530-1533). The first town in the new colony, São Vicente, was established by Martim Afonso in 1532 (Lockhart & Schwartz, 1983).

Throughout the 16th century, Portugal continued to be preoccupied with her rich possessions in Asia and sought to use the same management methods in the Western Hemisphere that had worked so well in the Azores and Madeira: the system of hereditary seigneury or donatary captaincy (*Capitanias Hereditárias*), with governing authority given to individuals with contracts designed to stimulate settlement and encourage economic development.

Brazil

Between 1533 and 1535, 15 donatary captaincies were created and captains received large strips of territory stretching inland from the coast. Early recipients of the captaincies were minor aristocrats (*fidalgos*) who had little or no expertise, few economic resources, and no political connections; and, as a result, most of their colonization and commercial enterprises failed. The crown offered no support and simply reclaimed the land for reassignment when it no longer produced the required revenue. According to Lockhart and Schwartz (1983), "The gentlemen who received the donations (*donatários*) were given broad powers of jurisdiction, taxation, and other administrative and fiscal privileges" (p. 184). This decentralization of authority led to serious repercussions, as Brazil developed into a loose federation of nation-states, with strong individuals constantly challenging any central authority and striving for wealth and personal power.

The social situation in the Lusitanian (Portuguese) colony repeated what was prevalent in Portugal: aristocrats, both major and minor, controlling wealth and intellectual advancement, while the lower classes and slaves performed the work that made the colony viable. Only the elite had the time and the inclination for educational and leisurely pursuits. It wasn't until the 20th century that there were concerted efforts to remediate the social ills of Brazil.

Early Developments in Brazilian Education

Throughout Brazil's history, there has been a lack of proper awareness of the need for popular education, mainly due to the traditional emphasis placed upon the achievement of wealth through commerce so prevalent in 15th and 16th century Portugal. The aristocratic merchant did not feel the need for education for himself or for his sons; typically, merchants believed that education was a luxury, useful only to settle commercial disputes in courts of law. Early commercial and intellectual development in the colony was severely limited, as education was available only to the members of the elite class and most of the instruction fell in the area of the humanities.

The Catholic Church was a strong force in the development of education in the Portuguese colony; prior to 1759, the Brazilian educational processes depended fundamentally upon the instructional tradition of the Society of Jesus (Jesuits) and its *Ratio Studiorum* (1599 to 1759), which provided rules for the "precise methods of instruction to be followed, how schools were to be organized, how discipline should be maintained, how educational officers' responsibilities should be discharged, and the exact aims to be pursued" (Lucas, 1972, pp. 259-260). Authorized and supported by the crown, usually through *sesmarias* (land grants), Jesuit schools were primarily established in large coastal towns. Lockhart and Schwartz (1983) state, "The Jesuit schools in Salvador, Olinda, and Rio de Janeiro became the centers of learning where most native-born Europeans received their basic education" (p. 240).

At the lowest level (*studia inferiora*), the Jesuit curriculum included grammar, humanities, and rhetoric. At the secondary level (*studia superiora*), boys studied the sciences, mathematics, and philosophy (Lucas, 1972). Girls, for the most part, were home-schooled, if they were educated at all.

While the Jesuits retained control of elementary and secondary education in Brazil, the Portuguese crown held tightly to the reins of both tertiary education and literary production. The Lusitanian tradition differed radically from the Spanish tradition in the matter of the literacy of the elites in her colonies. The Spanish crown had established universities in the colonies in the 16th century, but this did not occur in Lusitanic America throughout the colonial period. In fact, until the 19th century, there was neither university nor printing press in Brazil. The University of Coimbra provided post-secondary instruction for the Brazilian elite. Lockhart and Schwartz (1983) explain, "Any Brazilian who wanted to pursue a university degree, enter the royal magistracy or study canon law or medicine had to travel to Portugal, normally to the university at Coimbra" (p. 240). Given the distance and the expense of travel, the University of Coimbra was never overcrowded with Brazilians. Fausto (1995) said, "In 1787 there were 19 Brazilian students matriculated in the University of Coimbra, 10 of those from Minas Gerais" (p. 114).

The Pombaline Reforms

As may be imagined, there was much resentment of the power of the Jesuits among Brazilians, as in Europe. In addition to their control over the native population, the Jesuits possessed much property and wealth, and enjoyed a protected position in society in that they were exempt from the payment of the royal tithe. Through their control of primary and secondary education in the colonies and tertiary studies in Europe, they exerted significant political and cultural influence. Many complaints against the Society found their way to Portugal; with the accession to power of Sebastião José de Carvalho e Mello, the Marquis of Pombal[2], in 1750, the authority of the crown over all aspects of society was asserted and strengthened. Under the Pombaline Reforms, the power of the Inquisition was curtailed; the Church hierarchy was brought under tighter control, the University of Coimbra was reformed, and the Jesuits were suppressed. In addition, access to titles was smoothed for those who made contributions of money or talent to the crown (Lockhart & Schwartz, 1983).

In 1759, the Jesuits were expelled from Portugal and her territories, creating a vacuum in education that other religious groups (e.g., Franciscans, Oratorians) hastened to fill. The expulsion from Brazil of nearly 600 Jesuit priests made necessary a new explicit orientation of the educational process and the identification of a central power over education. At this point, Portugal introduced a profound change in the manner in which education was viewed by the crown. Schools became secular, whether public or private, and both education and teachers "suffered with the lack of interest, seriousness, and justice that they received from the power of the state" (Freire, 1998, p. 139).

By the middle of the 18th century, education reforms, which were based upon Luis Antonio Verney's pro-scientific *True Method for Study* (1742), were in place, and Pombal levied a new tax—the "literary subsidy"—for support of the schools. As Lockhart and Schwartz (1983) elaborate,

> *Teachers of rhetoric, grammar, and philosophy came on contract from Portugal. Laymen in former Jesuit Indian villages of the backlands instructed children in first letters, lace-making, and weaving. In 1776 the Franciscans of Rio de Janeiro updated their curriculum to include physics, geometry, and natural history. The bishop of Pernambuco established a seminary in Olinda based on the principles of the reform of Coimbra, in which science received strong emphasis. In 1771 public education was placed under the direction of the Royal Board of Censorship, an arrangement reflecting the somewhat uneasy relationship between the new ideas and the traditional order. (p. 397)*

Pombal created a school for the sons of the nobility, both for the Lusitanians and those from the colony, with the express purpose being to instill in them the principles of regalism.[3] By including the colonial elite, he recognized the importance of the great land barons of Brazil to the further expansion and maintenance of Portuguese royal interests and ensured their continued support of the crown's colonial policies.

In many ways, although it was repressive, the Pombaline period was a time of intellectual renewal, with the influences of the Enlightenment being felt in Portugal and in her colonies. Books on philosophy, politics, economy, science, and law from England, France, and Italy found their way into Brazil and were devoured by intellectuals, who often formed study societies to discuss the new ideas and how they could be implemented. During the course of the 18th century, small groups gathered in Salvador, Rio de Janeiro, Minas Gerais, and Pernambuco. Although they accomplished little, the fact that they existed at all indicated a type of intellectual ferment that was to lead to change in education practices.

Brazil as the Seat of an Empire

Between 1807 and 1809, Napoleon Bonaparte controlled almost all the Iberian peninsula; unwilling to tolerate Portugal's commercial relations with Great Britain, he invaded Portugal in 1807, with the result that Regent Prince João VI[4] and his court fled to Rio de Janeiro and set up their capital there. Pandiá Calogeras (1939) tells of the Brazilians' welcome of their monarch: "For the first time in its history the country was governed as an autonomous unit and not merely as a source of revenue to meet the needs of the mother country" (p. 53). In 1808, Dom João and his court brought a new era of development to the country, and he expressed concern for the training of clergy and public servants and the strengthening of military preparedness. Lockhart and Schwartz (1983) tell of the results of that concern: "Brazil quickly acquired a military academy, naval school, printing press, financial institutions, a reorganized judiciary system and more" (p. 414).

However, there was little change in the traditional humanities curriculum in the schools and the crucial role of professionals, such as teachers. Two medical schools were founded in Brazil after the arrival of the royal family—one in Rio de Janeiro and the other in Bahia. However, the students' diplomas were issued by the Chancellery of Portugal in Lisbon by the *Junta do Protomedicato*, which was created in 1782. This situation was not modified until 1822 with independence, when a similar board was created in Brazil.

The reign of Dom João VI was, despite its problems and mistakes, a time of economic progress for Brazil. Nevertheless, the social situation changed little, and political upheaval, along with the imperialistic tendencies of both Spanish and Portuguese royalty, kept attention away from Brazil's domestic concerns. The elevation of Brazil to the status of a kingdom in 1815 was highly unpopular in Lisbon and the residence of the royal family in the former colony was galling to the Portuguese. In Brazil, the winds of revolution were beginning to blow.[5] Constitutionalism was being touted in Portugal. When an ultra-liberal constitution was adopted, it became apparent that Dom João VI had to return to Europe to secure his throne. On April 26, 1821, the royal entourage set sail for Lisbon, leaving the king's son and heir, Dom Pedro, in Brazil as regent.

Brazilian Independence and Teacher Education

As it drew to a close, the year 1821 was a critical time for Brazil, as there was a suspicion that Prince Dom Pedro would join his father in Portugal, leaving the country with no members of the royal family in residence. This would certainly mean returning to the old condition of a dependent colony instead of enjoying equal rights and privileges with the mother country. In addition, people feared that the move would be a preliminary step to removing from Brazil the judiciary system and other benefits enjoyed while the court was in residence.

Maria Graham, the wife of the captain of the *HMS Doris*, in port in Rio de Janeiro, wrote in her journal[6] that the decision of His Royal Highness to remain in Brazil [January 10, 1822] was "greeted with the discharge of artillery, and every mark of public rejoicing" (p. 55). There were fears that Portuguese soldiers, under the command of General Avilez, would take the prince by force and transport him to Lisbon. Maria Graham made note of the Portuguese troops' reputation among the inhabitants and the foreign merchants: [They had] "long been most tyrannically brutal to strangers, to Negroes, and not infrequently to Brazilians" (p. 59).

On September 7, 1822, in response to a demand from the *Cortes*[7] in Lisbon that he return to Portugal, Dom Pedro stated, "From today on, our relations with them [the *Cortes*] are finished. I want nothing more from the Portuguese government and I proclaim Brazil forevermore separated from Portugal" (cited in Levine & Crocitti, 1999, p. 64). Brazil now had its own resident monarchy in the person of the Emperor Dom Pedro I, of the House of Bragança. The new emperor was 26 years old, intelligent, clever, and idealistic. Although he did seem to realize the importance of specialized instruction for the elites, he had received almost no formal education; his wife, however, was very interested in science and became something of a botanist and geologist.

Dom Pedro I promulgated the first General Law of Education in Brazil on October 15, 1827. It was an important landmark in Brazilian history, which stipulated the first national curriculum and other issues—for instance, stipulating that equal wages were to be paid to male and female teachers. This act attributed to the provinces a duty to provide elementary education to Brazilian citizens.

In addition, the legislation provided for the training of teachers in schools located in provincial capitals, although it did not provide for the inclusion of botany or zoology, among the courses specified, and candidates for the teaching profession were expected to pay their own education expenses (which guaranteed that the measure would be unsuccessful). Article 6 mandated:

> *Teachers must teach students to read, write, and perform the four operations of arithmetic, practice of fractions, decimals and proportion and the most general theories of geometric practice, the grammar of the national language, and the principles of moral conduct, and the doctrine of the Roman Catholic faith, proportionally to the comprehension of children and selected readings of the Constitution of the Empire and the history of Brazil. (non-paginated)*

Thus the need for disciplined, formal teacher training in Brazil, which existed long before the founding of the first normal school, was recognized. The plan to establish schools to prepare teachers had to wait for the abdication of Dom Pedro I (April 7, 1831) and was effectively only to be achieved after his death, which occurred in 1834.

It was in the period of the Regency (1831-1840) that the first normal schools (*escolas normais*) were established. Normal schools were opened in Niteroi and Bahia in 1836, and in Pará in 1839. Despite political and social upheavals around the country, training schools were established in Ceará in 1845 and in São Paulo in 1846. The normal school of São Paulo was created upon a very precarious foundation. It was restricted to male candidates and had only one teacher, who also worked on the preparatory course for the school of law. It functioned until 1867, when it was closed due to the retirement of the teacher. In its 21 years of existence, it granted diplomas to only 40 students (Marcílio, 2005).

These institutions followed the Lancastrian Method, which proposed a program of individualized, monitorial education for the teaching of the masses, with the establishment of classes of students, collective activities, "mutual learning," and other educational innovations, including such tools as chalk and the board for simultaneous activities. This method was officially authorized and implemented in Brazil through the General Law of Education of 1827.

General Education

The 19th century saw a great contrast in educational opportunities. On one side was a huge mass of unlettered citizens; on the other side was a political and social elite highly educated in the imperial style, most having achieved the highest level of schooling, with the majority concentrated in the judicial field. Thus, a political elite was constituted around a homogeneous and consistent legal doctrine, in a group that was rather limited, but included significant exchanges among provinces. This produced an understanding among the elites of the importance of education—they were fully aware of their own need for education in order to maintain the stability of their economy, based, as it was, upon slave labor and foreign markets, and upon their social position in the Empire (Fausto, 1995).

The trend for giving increasing autonomy to the provinces was inaugurated in 1824 and gave the provinces public education. The Provincial Assemblies would be responsible for the public and free education that the Constitution of 1824 guaranteed as the right of every citizen, confirmed by the Additional Act of 1834. Therefore, the presidents of the provinces and the Provisional Assemblies had the responsibility for providing a basic education to the entire population. However, implementation depended upon overcoming enormous obstacles.

In 1872, Brazil had nearly nine million people (excluding slaves), only 2 percent of whom attended school. The census of 1872 indicated that 400,000 people, of whom 70,000 were slaves, lived in the city of Rio de Janeiro. There were 12,000 students, half of them attending public primary schools. There were 211 primary schools, with only 116 of them private and 95 public. It was believed that only from the increasing participation of private initiative could they significantly increase the depth and breadth of schooling in the country. Throughout the country, there were 10,911 students in secondary schools, with three-fourths of them attending private institutions (Schwartzman, 2003, p. 7).

A German immigrant, who was a teacher at the Provincial Lyceum of Desterro (now Florianópolis) in the years 1862-1865, stated that there were four subjects taught at the secondary level: mathematics, Latin, French, and English. He added,

> To someone accustomed to the German educational system, this school is interesting. There are no compulsory classes, not even a defined curriculum. Parents can enroll their sons in the discipline they like, as in our German universities. . . . It is extremely difficult to organize a scheme which made it possible to offer all the subjects chosen by each student. (Glick, 2003, p. 181)

Government supported public secondary schools hardly existed in municipal centers such as São Paulo in 1870. In the words of the inspector of schools in the province, "You can say that, for secondary education, there are only those of preparatory classes attached to the Faculty of Law, held by the general coffers, and the two chairs of Latin and French in Itu[8], which was closed in 1882" (Marcílio, 2005, p. 78). In 1890, there were no public secondary schools in the province of São Paulo. Secondary education was restricted to an elite group in São Paulo—those who were prepared by the Faculty of Law. It excluded women, Indians, slaves, and nearly all the poor. The mission statement for one of the secondary schools read:

> In this secondary school the male students will at least be exposed to all disciplines that are the basis of morality and instruction; those required for enrollment in the juridical course: Christian religion, reading, writing, grammar of the Portuguese language, Latin, French, Spanish, arithmetic and geometry, rhetoric, philosophy, history and geography, and music.
> The girls, in addition to the Christian religion, reading, writing, English grammar, arithmetic, French, geography and music, will be taught to sew, embroider, draw and write decoratively. (cited in Marcílio, 2005, p. 79)

Educational advisers suggested that students under 14 years of age, those belonging to "decent families," board at the schools they attended. One explained, "[The student] will be examined in the presence of his father or correspondent, and his qualifications listed[;] for the future they [school administrators] can assess his progress through bulletins" (in Marcílio, 2005, p. 78).

Rui Barbosa, the great Brazilian liberator, gave a portrait of secondary education and its curriculum at the end of the Empire and the beginning of the Republic:

> This corruption of procedures practiced in secondary education is inevitably the result of the lack of scientific spirit, which can only be instilled by returning to science its leading position in the education of human generations. . . . Perceive the phenomena, discern relations, comparing the similarities and differences, classify the realities, and induce the laws, as a science; this is, therefore, the target that education should take into its sights. Search out the intelligent source in the faculties whose tender care is required in these cases to discover and assimilate the truth, it is that which should care for programs and methods of teaching. Instead of educating students in the skills of discovery, learning and thinking, the student and the school, between them, occupy themselves exclusively in creating and developing the mechanical habits of decorating and repeating. (Lourenço-Filho, 2001, p. 132)

Into the 20th Century

The Republic of Brazil was established in 1889, soon after slavery was abolished. The new republic did not change the general trend toward decentralization of public administration, including education. The first Republican Constitution (1891) was silent on the topic of public instruction, leaving to the provinces the responsibility of dealing with the matter. Many provinces, in their turn, passed on to municipalities educational concerns, which were actually not addressed until recently. The first Republican Constitutional Assembly deputies were deeply liberal and they argued that citizens should be free to choose whether or not to pursue education. In fact, free basic education, in the 19th century in Brazil, survived only legislatively, not as a general practice, and even so only from 1824 (the first Imperial Constitution) until 1891 (the first Republican Constitution) (Cury, 2000).

In the years 1913 and 1914, which were a period of depression and general uncertainty due to the situation in Europe, the government of Brazil negotiated huge loans and printed money in a futile effort to salvage the country's failing economy. Minister Rivadavia Correia of the Department of the Interior and Justice sought educational reforms, possibly as a diversionary tactic, to free education from bureaucratic oversight and interference. Bello (1968) states, "He decreed a general educational reform based on the Comtist philosophy. The secondary schools were given complete didactic and administrative autonomy and the humanities ceased to be simply preparatory courses" (p. 228). The result of this action was a proliferation of secondary schools, "aggravating the old problem of a superabundance of degree-holders who were wretchedly educated and inevitably wanted public jobs" (Bello, 1968, p. 228).

In the Old Republic (1889-1930), there were several educational movements worthy of note, including those in São Paulo, seeking to modernize education, integrate immigrants, and reduce illiteracy. The 1920 São Paulo legislation, following the reform known as *Sampãio Doria,* responded to the nativist pressure to force cultural assimilation by providing government schools to supplant private, foreign language-oriented ones. The study of Portuguese became a regular part of the curriculum, and Brazilian history and geography were mandated subjects.

In the 1930s, the nativists became more demanding and the government passed more restrictive school-based legislation. "In 1935, São Paulo designated Portuguese as the only permissible language of instruction in grades 1 through 4; in the higher grades only one hour of instruction in a foreign language was allowed per day" (Luebke, 1987, p. 212).

The Getulista Movement (1930-1935) and the Estado Novo (1937-1945)

One of the most colorful individuals in Brazil's history was Gertúlio Vargas, who came to power as a result of an abortive revolution in 1930. It was especially during the *Getulista* movement that national dimensions changed the educational scene. In some ways, it reversed the trend of 1824, as it inaugurated the decentralization of educational activities, delegating normative and executive powers to the provinces for decisions relating to basic education and the establishment of standards for the opening of universities. In fact, one of the first acts of the insurgents, after their victory in the revolutionary movement in October 1930, was the creation of the Ministry of Education and Public Health, accomplished through Decree 19402 of 14 November, 1930.

The platform of the Liberal Alliance, Vargas' political party, included, "instructional measures, applied to both [urban and rural] to address their respective needs. These measures should include instruction, education, hygiene, diet, housing, protection of women and children" (cited in Levine & Crocitti, 1999, p. 156).

The first government of Getúlio Vargas is seen as a modernizing one, which brought an end to the Old Republic, inaugurating what is known as the "New Republic." A new constitution, in 1934, provided not only the right of basic education, but also provided the means as it established fixed sources for the financing of basic schooling for the first time in Brazil's history (Cury, 2000).

During the period 1937 to 1945, called the *Estado Novo* (New State), a new Constitution was issued, inspired by Mussolini's Fascist model. Getúlio Vargas was the dictatorial head of state until 1945 and was elected President in 1950, remaining in that position until his suicide in 1954. Vargas was, in every way, a pragmatist. He claimed that he advocated for change; however, he held firmly to the status quo in most decisions. He continued to favor the rich and ignore the poor. His National Educational Plan called for free and semi-mandatory public education, and was made part of the 1934 Constitution. In criticizing Vargas' actual accomplishments, Levine and Crocitti (1999) state, "Vargas lauded public schoolteachers as the 'little, over-shadowed heroes of daily life,' but he did little to improve their pitiful wages" (p. 153). He had very definite ideas about educational license and academic freedom. In 1937, during the dictatorial period, a North American visitor to education facilities wrote,

> There is no liberty of teaching in Brazil. In fact, the idea of liberty of speech in the classroom is so alien to the thought of the Brazilian teachers that I found it impossible to explain what it signified in the United States. "We can teach anything we want to in Brazil; that is, anything that is not against the government," was the consensus of opinion of the teachers. (cited in Levine & Crocitti, 1999, p. 201)

It was said by some apologists that in the 1930s, Gertúlio Vargas was "cleansing" the schools, purging them of undesirable elements, cleaning out all "liberal" literature from the libraries, and revising the school texts so that students would learn only what was approved for them. His *Estado Novo* legislation promised change, but remained underfunded.

Education was, in this period, immersed in a debate between opposing views. On the one side were the liberal reformers, who preached public education, free and secular, irrespective of gender, with modern methods of teaching. Some questioned the involvement of the Catholic Church in education.[9] People expressed additional concerns about academic freedom and the need for constraints on profits in private schools. The liberals' position took shape in the Manifesto of the Pioneers of Education of 1932, as well as the tax reform movement of the 1920s. These two reform movements highlighted the opinions of such prominent educators as Fernando de Azevedo, M. S. Lourenço-Filho, and Anísio Teixeira. On the other side were the conservatives, the traditional and ultramontane Catholic[10] thinkers, advocates of confessional (sectarian) education with centralized and equal standards throughout the country, and opposed to a single school for boys and girls between the ages of 7 and 15 years, which was state-supported, free, and open to all; moreover, they certainly opposed any school that enjoyed great autonomy.

Young politicians, such as the conservative Francisco Campos, who was minister between 1930 and 1932, and Gustavo Capanema, fomented this confrontation. The conservatives remained very loyal to Catholic doctrine and were able to prevent the action of more liberal reformers. The newly created Ministry of Education and Public Health set its priorities for secondary and higher education, with most of its attention directed at the tertiary level. A series of decrees were issued establishing the National Council of Education (Decree 19.850/31); the Status of Brazilian Universities (Decree 19.851/31), whose base is formed by the Faculties of Law, Medicine, and Engineering; and the University of Rio de Janeiro (Decree 19.852/31). All were approved on April 11, 1931. The latter decree created the Faculty of Education, Sciences, and Letters, whose function would be to promote and facilitate the practice of original research, and develop any specialized knowledge necessary to the practice of teaching. This model for teacher preparation became known as "3+1," and persisted through the year 2006 in public universities.[11] In 1939, in the period of the *Estado Novo*, the Faculty of Education was reduced to two sections of the National School of Philosophy, one of them responsible for awarding the bachelor's degree in pedagogy, and the other responsible for courses in didactics. The first bachelor's degree was awarded in 1941 (Pereira, 2000, p. 39).

Under the provision of the reform laws of 1933/34, the Federal Education Ministry began to oversee the training of teachers and establish the criteria for their certification. Teachers had to pass competitive examinations in order to be eligible for jobs, which they often secured only through political influence. In order to provide training for potential teachers, the University of São Paulo and its School of

Teachers was founded in January 1934, by Decree 6283/34. Article 5 of its charter states:

> *§1. The license for secondary teaching will be sent by the University only to the candidates who, having been licensed in any of the sections which specializes in the Faculty of Philosophy, Science and Letters, have completed the course of education at the Institute of Education.*
>
> *§2. The candidate for the teaching side, choosing the section of knowledge in which one wants to specialize in the Faculty of Philosophy, Science and Letters, one can do both in the 3rd year in the course of training for teaching in the Institute of Education. (cited in Souza Campos, 2004, p. 67)*

While *Estado Novo* public schools suffered from political manipulation, underpaid teachers, and a lack of professional supervision, private schools proliferated for those who had sufficient funds and ambitions reaching higher than secondary school. Most middle-class parents were aware that private schools in Brazil were superior to those provided by the State. Attendance at the private intermediary school was important, because the university entrance examinations (*vestibular*) were based upon the curriculum of the secondary school.

The curriculum in a typical private school in the 1930s included Portuguese grammar, arithmetic, history, geography, science, sewing (for girls), singing, and gymnastics. Classes met four hours a day, from 8:00 a.m. until noon. From a student in a military school (secondary and post-secondary levels) in Rio de Janeiro in the late 1930s and early 1940s, we learn that the curriculum there was highly specialized: "We studied ballistics, military strategy, topography, military history, mathematics up to integral and differential calculus. We also received a general education, learning about health, the exact sciences, the humanities" (Levine & Crocitti, 1999, p. 208).

Toward the Dark Years

The 1946 Constitution (upheld by directives in 1961 – Law 4.024/61) set standards for national education and divided responsibility among federal, state, and municipal governments. Public elementary and secondary instruction was considered almost entirely the responsibility of the municipalities and the states, while tertiary education came under the aegis of the federal Ministry of Education. Public education was to be free at all levels, and nonprofit private schools could receive public funding. The Federal Council of Education was established in 1961 to coordinate implementation of constitutional and directive provisions.

In 1948, Anísio Teixeira[12], an advocate of free public education, did a study in his native state of Bahia. He found that the reform laws of Vargas were being enforced in a way prejudicial to the needs of ordinary people. Following is an excerpt from a speech Teixeira made in Salvador that year:

> *Things are worse now than twenty years ago. . . . Primary schools have been reduced to being inefficient places for teaching reading and writing, and suffer a corresponding loss of social prestige. Middle schools have to perform the functions of elementary schools, and, as a result, they are stigmatized. Secondary schools do little more than teach what primary schools should have done, and they serve mostly as gateways for the ornamental classes [elites] of the country to become public functionaries. (Levine & Crocitti, 1999, pp. 204-205)*

The years after the death of Vargas (1954) were filled with administrative changes, *coups d'état*, protests, and a shift from populism to military dictatorship from 1964 to 1979. The military mandated that the schools teach *civismo* (citizenship), and the government let it be known that it required unconditional loyalty to the country and its military leaders.

In 1961, during the initial year of João Goulart's presidency, new legislation was adopted (*Lei de*

Diretrizes e Bases, or the Law of Guidelines and Bases), which was to have a profound effect upon education. Fundamental schooling was to be mandatory and the federal government was to contribute at least 12 percent of its tax revenues to education, while state and local governments were required to set aside 20 percent of their annual revenues for education (Article 92).

During the era of military dictatorship (1964-1985), the education law was amended and a new constitution was issued (1967). In general terms, it meant not only the end of the short period wherein the financing of education was ensured, but also a considerable reduction of resources and significant transfers of public funds to private institutions. State subsidies to private institutions became significant and the First Constitutional Amendment (1969) reintroduced a fixed percentage of taxes for education, but only in municipalities, which meant a dramatic shortfall, especially in the poorer areas of the country (Cortes, 1989).

One of the most outspoken and liberal voices for the poor and marginalized was the late Paulo Freire (1921-1997), who is also touted in many quarters as the "most important educator of the second half of this [20th] century" (Martin Carnoy, in his foreword to Freire's *Pedagogy of the Heart,* 1998, p. 7). In 1963, Freire was invited by President João Goulart to head a national commission on popular culture (Bartlett, 2003). A military coup put a stop to Freire's efforts to improve adult literacy and teacher training; and, according to Bartlett (2003), "The accession to the state apparatus of a politicized education dedicated to the redistribution of social power was nullified before it could even begin to make, much less fulfill, promises" (p. 183).

About the same time, a controversial partnership was established between the Brazilian Ministry of Education and Culture (MEC) and the U.S. Agency for International Development (USAID). Teachers were sent to the United States to develop skills for writing textbooks, and several links were forged that eventually led to major changes, including a new law of higher education, a reactionary process called *Reforma Universitária* (University Reform), defined by Law 5540/1968. It was approved after street rioting and huge demonstrations, as protestors demanded more placements in the universities. Public institutions became sites for resistance against the government, and therefore were targeted in the reform. The law also provided for rapid teacher preparation, a process tailored to private institutions, which soon were spreading throughout the country. Short-term courses were created, mainly by private institutions of higher learning, after the new law (Law 5.692/1971) was approved. It was then possible to become a school teacher after completing a two-year course. This step opened the profession to a wider social range, a process referred to as "proletarianization of the teaching profession," not only due to the economic erosion, but also for the downgrading of the intellectual preparation (Ferreira & Bittar, 2006).

After the Dark Years

Paulo Freire returned to Brazil from exile in 1979, and in 1988 he was appointed Secretary of Education for the city of São Paulo. During his tenure as Secretary, Freire advocated social awareness, change, openness to the world, and education that "works effectively to keep poor children in school and learning, . . . with the focus upon critical thinking, the development of self- and collective-identity, democratic participation, and cooperation" (Freire, 1998, p. 17). Freire's method sought to involve as many people as possible in the educational decision-making process. The First Municipal Seminar on Education, held from October 1 to 4, 1991, attracted over 6,000 participants. The stated objectives of the meetings were:

> to broaden discussions around the political-educational principles of the Department of Education, discuss basic topics associated with national education, create another opportunity in the process of permanent development of educators, record and publicize the advances of pedagogical action in local schools, foster discussion on the diverse experiences within the different areas of public education, and the [on] impact in the local schools. (Freire, 1998, p. 8)

Freire (1998) continued his description of the seminars:

> *They also discussed the educator's commitment and the national policy on the education of children and adults, elementary and basic education, interdisciplinary integration, urban planning and education, evaluation and the issue of women as education workers, literacy and early childhood education, curriculum, mathematics, informatics (computers), along with art, music and theater. (p. 120)*

Freire worked to improve professional development for teachers, in close contact with professors from the major universities in the state. He stated, "The urgently needed improvement in the quality of our education is linked to increased respect for educators, through significant improvement of their salaries . . . and through reform of teaching preparation programs" (Freire, 1998, p. 61). Reform efforts involved linguists, mathematicians, computer specialists, philosophers, and curriculum specialists.

After the end of the era of military dictatorship, a new Federal Constitution was approved in Brazil (1988), and brought with it some new directions incorporating regulations for compulsory education from the age of 7 to 15, in eight grades, and with specific instructions aimed at improving public expenditure on education. The constitution mandates that not less than 25 percent of states' and municipalities' budgets and not less than 18 percent of federal budgets should be directed to education.

The new light of democracy brought new concern for education. The 1988 Federal Constitution specifies a fundamental curriculum as a common core, along with a diversified part. The common core, defined by the Federal Council of Education, is compulsory in the entire country and consists of Portuguese; social studies, including history and geography; physics; biology; and mathematics. "The diversified part is defined by the needs of each educational system and of each school, taking into account regional and local characteristics, the schools' plans as well as individual differences and aptitudes of students" ("Brazil. Education." Retrieved from www.un.int/brazil/brazil.brazil-education.htm).

The Brazilian government established major action programs targeting education following the recommendations of the world conferences at Jomtien, Thailand (1990) and New Delhi, India (1993). The most important was the "Decennial Plan: Education for All" (1993-2003) conference, with the promise to extend education to all children, adolescents, and adults by the year 2003. During the period 1990-1993, a series of conferences and public meetings were held to call attention to the need for sharing responsibilities to improve educational standards in the country.

On September 2, 1994, a national agreement was approved and submitted to the federal government for signature. The document was called *Pacto Nacional de Valorização do Magistério e Qualidade da Educação* and was a statement of a compromise designed to raise educational standards and teachers' wages, providing careers with professional dignity and social validity, and was intended to be a cross-government action plan (Bizzo & Mattos, 2004).

After the elimination of the Federal Council of Education in 1994, accusations of improper links with private institutions and corruption led to the 1961 education legislation being replaced with a new Law of Guidelines and Bases (Law 9394/1996). The new law described a fundamental four-level structure for educational efforts:

1. *Educação Infantil* (Infant Education)—an optional provision for children under 7. Its purpose is to develop motor, cognitive, and social skills, while getting the child ready for the acquisition of more knowledge.

2. *Ensino Fundamental* (Fundamental Education)—mandatory for children ages 6 to 14. The objective of this level is for the child to achieve literacy. For this level, the Federal Council of Education (*Conselho Federal de Educação*) sets a core curriculum of Portuguese, history, geography, science, mathematics, arts, and physical education. More advanced students take one or two foreign languages (usually English or Spanish). Each system supplements the core curriculum with a diversified cur-

riculum defined by the needs of the region and the abilities of individual students.

3. *Ensino Medio* (Secondary Education)—three years of instruction. The core curriculum includes Portuguese (including Portuguese language, and Brazilian and Portuguese literatures), foreign language (usually English or Spanish; very rarely French), history, geography, mathematics, physics, chemistry, and biology. Recently added were philosophy and sociology, which were banned during the era of military dictatorship (1964-1985). Professional training (including that for teachers) is also available, along with regular secondary core courses. Two years are usually required to complete professional coursework.

4. *Ensino Superior* (Higher Education). The standard Brazilian undergraduate four-year bachelor's degree (*graduação*) is taken in arts, humanities, social sciences, mathematics, or natural sciences. Teaching and other professional careers require five-year specialized programs. (Moura Castro. *Educação.* Retrieved from www.mre.gov.br/cdbrazil/itamaraty/web/port/polsoc/educa/apresent/apresent.htm)

Soon after the approval of the new Law of Guidelines and Bases for Education (Law 9394//1996), the Brazilian Congress passed an amendment to the constitution (*Emenda Constitucional no. 14,* Law 9424/1997, and Decree 2264/1997) called *Fundo de Manutenção e Desenvolvimento do Ensino Fundamental e de Valorização do Magistério* (FUNDEF). This law set forth strict regulations regarding public expenditure for education. A long-standing problem relative to the financing of public education was not the amount of resources devoted to education, but rather the way in which money was spent at the local level. In some rich municipalities, there were plenty of resources for education, following constitutional constraints, but few students (or even no students) at the elementary level; therefore, it was impossible to spend the whole amount prescribed by law. The education budget was supposed to be spent only for compulsory education; if there were insufficient numbers of students, the money was to be redistributed to places lacking resources. Some municipalities provided schools with nonessential materials, and sometimes expenditures were not directed to strictly educational ends. Rich municipalities could not objectively spend on education as much as the constitution required; consequently, some of these cities established municipal universities in areas where there was a lack of basic education, arguing that the state (and not the country) should provide free primary and secondary education. The new law also sought to improve teachers' salaries within a 10-year period.

Statistical studies indicate that Brazil has made substantial progress in educating her children during the last two decades. Enrollment of children 7 to 14 years increased from 80.9 percent in 1980 to 96.4 percent in 2000. Among 15- to 17-year-olds, in the same time period, the rate rose from 49.7 percent to 83 percent (Secretaria de Educação Fundamental, 2002). According to the Federal Census, in 1990 there were 37.6 million students. Of that total, 3.9 million were in preschool, 29.4 million in elementary school, 3.7 million in secondary school, and 1.7 million in university. Despite these high figures, less than 40 percent of the high school-age population was enrolled in school, and it was estimated that 19 percent were illiterate (based upon the ability to sign one's own name) ("Brazil. Education." Retrieved from www.photius.com/countries/brazil/society/brazil.society.education.html).

By 1998, there were 35,838,372 children in elementary schools, 6,967,905 at the secondary level, and 1,868,529 in universities. In 1999, 96 percent of children of primary school age were enrolled in school and 69 percent of those eligible attended secondary schools. The pupil-teacher ratio was 27 to 1.

Brazil has made efforts to address the problem of adult illiteracy through federal and state campaigns and programs. UNESCO figures for the year 2000 indicate that, while there has been progress, adult illiteracy stood at 14.7 percent (males, 14.9 percent; females, 14.6 percent) at the beginning of the 21st century (Brazil. Education. Retrieved from: www.nationsencyclopedia.com/Americas/Brazil-EDU-CATION.html). Brazil spends about 5 percent of its GNP on education. The greater portion of that expenditure goes to higher education, where higher salaries, full-pay retirement, and teaching hospitals take a large bite out of the federal budget, leaving less for secondary and pre-secondary educational needs (Brazil. Education. Retrieved from: www.un.int/brazil/brazil/brazil-education.htm).

On January 1, 1995, Fernando Henrique Cardoso took the oath of office as president of Brazil. In his inaugural address, Cardoso expressed his concern for education:

> *The school must be the heart of the teaching process once again. . . . A school is a gathering place where the actions of parents, the solidarity of the social medium, the participation of students and teacher and proper administration are added together to train properly prepared citizens. . . . We can no longer exist with massive levels of illiteracy or functional illiteracy. . . . We have had enough of a situation in which we built ridiculously monumental schools, and then filled them with badly paid and badly trained teachers, as well as unmotivated students who were not materially or psychologically ready to take full advantage of their education. (cited in Levine & Crocitti, 1999, p. 286)*

In the latter years of the 20th century, Brazil was still a land of social and economic contrasts and, according to Simon Schwartzman (2003), "known for having one of the world's highest levels of income inequality" (p. 9). Many parents are too poor to afford the cost of sending their children to school and many send the children out to work to help support the family. Schwartzman (2003) further states, "As a rule, public schools in poor regions, municipalities and neighborhoods tend to be of worse quality, and school achievement depends heavily on the family's economic, social and cultural background" (p. 10). The populations in these poorer areas tend to be marginalized in all aspects and their children receive only the bare minimum in the way of educational facilities, materials, and instruction. Schwartzman sums up the Brazilian educational dilemma as follows:

> *the system as a whole is under severe strain, financially and institutionally, and needs to change and adjust, for more quality, efficiency and relevance. . . . The amount of resources already committed to education is substantial; we know much more about education than we did in the past; society is more concerned with education than it has been until recently; and there are important segments of the academic and teaching professions that can participate and eventually lead. . . . In the meantime, it is necessary to put the existing resources to better use, by adjusting the system's size to the actual need, and introducing better managerial and accounting practices. (p. 33)*

Into the 21st Century

In 2003, a new president, Luiz Inácio Lula da Silva, was elected. His government adopted a pragmatic approach to education. This proved to be a disappointment to the radical left, which expected a ban on private education as well as private property. However, one of the first acts of the new government was to provide places for poor students in private universities through a huge program of scholarships, which opened opportunities for some 100,000 students per year. This had a tremendous impact upon the secondary schools, a level of education that was not traditionally seen by the poorer families as a target for their sons and daughters. Critics saw it as a huge transfer of public resources to private institutions. New teacher training opportunities were offered, along with new university curricula.

A new law for financing public education was approved, creating a larger fund that covers a wider range of schooling than before. The old fund covered only the eight years of compulsory education, while the new one will pay for preschool through secondary levels. There has been a considerable controversy over the choice of taxes included in the new fund, and many argue that there will not be enough resources for all levels of education. There is no doubt that great changes are under way; however, there is still some concern about their impact on the quality of Brazilian education, now and in the future.

Notes

[1] The name was soon changed to "Brazil" in 1503, some say to reflect the presence of the large quantities of brazilwood trees that were found on the coast.

[2] The Marquis of Pombal was Prime Minister of Portugal between 1750 and 1777.

[3] The doctrine of royal prerogative or supremacy.

[4] João was the son of Maria I and Pedro III. João was named Regent in 1792, after the death of his father because his mother, Maria, was mentally unstable. Upon the death of Maria (9 March, 1816), he became King of Portugal, Brazil, and Algarve.

[5] In 1817 in Pernambuco, a revolutionary uprising led to the proclamation of a republic.

[6] Published in 1993 as *The Captain's Wife* (Mavor, 1993).

[7] The Parliament in Portugal.

[8] A town about 60 miles from São Paulo.

[9] In the Empire period, the Catholic faith was the official religion of the Brazilian state. The Republic had changed this situation, and had forbidden religious instruction in public schools. The 1931 decree of Vargas reintroduced the possibility of religious education in public schools (Cury, 2000).

[10] Schwartzman (2003) explains, "Part of the conflict had to do with the pact signed between Vargas and the conservative Catholic Church, according to which Brazilian education would be reorganized under the Church's guidance and direction" (p. 18).

[11] It has been proposed that the long persistence of this model, which attributed an overwhelming importance to the bachelor's degree, could have been explained as a resistance to the dictatorship of 1964-1985, which targeted universities and intellectuals. Changes advocated by the Ministry of Education were seen as a strategy to undermine the participation of university students in political affairs (Bizzo, 2005).

[12] Born in Bahia in 1900, Teixeira was a leading educational reformer. He held a doctorate from Columbia University and was an apostle of John Dewey.

References

Anderson, J. B. (2005). Improving Latin America's school quality: Which special interventions work? *Comparative Education Review, 49*, 205-229, 295.

Bartlett, L. (2003). World culture or transnational project? Competing educational projects in Brazil. In K. Anderson-Levitt (Ed.), *Local meanings, global schooling: Anthropology and world culture theory.* New York: Palgrave/Macmillan.

Bello, J. M. (1968). *A history of modern Brazil, 1889-1964* (4th ed.). Stanford, CA: Stanford University Press.

Bizzo, N. (2005). Formação de professores de ciências no Brasil: Uma cronologia de improvisos. In R. Durand (Org.), *Ciências e cidadania: Seminário internacional ciência de qualidade para todos* (pp. 127-147). Brasilia: UNESCO.

Bizzo, N. M. V., & Mattos, M. M. F. (2004). Educational systems: Case studies and educational indices in South America. In N. Pavlovna (Ed.), *Quality of human resources: Education.* Oxford, UK: Eolss Publishers.

Calogeras, J. P. (1939). *A history of Brazil.* Chapel Hill, NC: University of North Carolina Press.

Cortes, C. R. J. (1989). Financiamento na educação: Salário-educação e suas dimensões privatizantes. *Cad. Saúde Pública, 5*(4), 408-423.

Cury, C. R. J. (2000). A educação como desafio jurídico. In E.M.T. Lopes et al. (Eds.), *500 anos de educação no Brasil* (pp. 567-584). Belo Horizonte: Autêntica.

Fausto, B. (1995). *História do Brasil.* São Paulo: EDUSP.

Ferreira, Jr., A., & Bittar, M. (2006). A ditadura militar e a proletarização dos professores. *Educ. Soc. Campinas, 27*(97), 1159-1179.

Freire, P. (1998). *Pedagogy of the heart.* New York: Continuum Publishing.

Glick, T. (2003). Oposivismo brasileiro na sombra do darwinismo: O grupo Idéia Nova em Desterro. In H. M. B. Domingues et al. (Eds.), *A recepção do darwinismo no Brasil* (pp. 181-189). Rio de Janeiro: Fiocruz.

Levine, R. M., & Crocitti, J. J. (Eds.). (1999). *The Brazil reader: History, culture, politics.* Durham, NC: Duke University Press.

Lockhart, J., & Schwartz, S. B. (1983). *Early Latin America: A history of colonial Spanish America and Brazil.* Cambridge, UK: Cambridge University Press.

Loução, P. A., & Santos, C. A. (1998). *A viagem de Vasco da Gama.* Lisboa: Ésquilo.

Lourenço-Filho, M. B. (2001). *A formação de professores: Da escola normal à escola de educação.* Brasilia: INEP.

Lucas, C. J. (1972). *Our western educational heritage.* New York: Macmillan.

Luebke, F. C. (1987). *Germans in Brazil: A comparative history of cultural conflict during World War I.* Baton Rouge, LA: Louisiana State University Press.

Marcílio, M. L. (2005). *História da escola em São Paulo e no Brazil.* São Paulo: Instituto Braude & Impresa Oficial.

Mavor, E. (Ed.). (1993). *The captain's wife: The South American journals of Maria Graham, 1821-1823.* London: Weidenfeld & Nicolson, Ltd.

Moura Castro, C. de. *Educação.* Retrieved April 3, 2008, from www.mre.gov.br/cdbrasil/itamaraty/web/port/polsoc/educa/apresent/apresent.htm

Pereira, W. C. (2000). *Educação de professors na era da globalização: Subsídios para uma proposta humanista.* Rio de Janeiro: Nau Editora.

Schwartzman, S. (2003). *The challenges of education in Brazil.* Oxford, UK: University of Oxford Centre for Brazilian Studies. (Working paper CBS-38-2003.)

Secretaria de Educação Fundamental. (2002). *Politicas de melhora da qualidade da educação: Um balanço institucional.* Brasilia: Ministério da Educação.

Souza Campos, E. (2004). *História da Universidade de São Paulo.* São Paulo: EDUSP.

www.nationsencyclopedia.com/Americas/Brazil-EDUCATION.html

www.photius.com/countries/brazil_society_education.html

www.un.int/brazil/brazil/brazil-education.htm

About the Authors

Ann K. Nauman, Ph.D., is a professor of history and Academic Dean at St. Joseph Seminary College in St. Benedict, Louisiana.

Nelio Bizzo, Ph.D., is a professor of science methodology on the Faculdade de Educação da Universdidade de São Paulo.

Curriculum Development in Canada

Brenda J. Gustafson and Marie-Claire Shanahan

The ongoing narrative of Canadian curriculum development includes regional, cultural, and linguistic diversity, balanced with a shared national priority to develop an educated citizenry. Questions about Canadian curriculum development continue to surround issues of balancing diversity with unity—how can we provide consistent, high-quality education for all students while respecting and responding to local needs and realities in a country that is expansive and diverse? For example, how can a focus on outcomes-based learning (e.g., provincial and international examination programs) be balanced with curriculum intended to include local cultural realities (e.g., Aboriginal language and culture courses)? This tension has existed in Canadian education from the earliest days of the country's history, when school systems attempted to meet the needs of at least three distinct communities of students (British-Canadian, French-Canadian, and Aboriginal). These realities were also interwoven with the challenges of setting and implementing curricula that meet the needs of students in both urban and rural communities.

The importance of culture to Canadian education also has been a consistent force in curriculum development since the time of the earliest settlers. Cultural survival, in particular, was a dominant force during the transition from informal to formal schooling in both English and French Canada. The earliest schools and school systems in Canada all served as a major vehicle for cultural survival—for French Canadians in New France and after the British conquest of 1763, and for British Loyalists arriving in Canada after the American Revolution (Tomkins, 1986). The importance of including diverse cultural perspectives continues to influence curriculum frameworks in all 10 provinces and 3 northern territories. Including these perspectives is viewed as a vehicle for engaging all children in the curriculum and for preserving cultural traditions and languages.

Canada

Historical View of Canadian Curriculum Development

Educational Foundations of New France (1655-1763)

No united school system existed in New France (the French colony that included most of present-day Nova Scotia, New Brunswick, Ontario, and Quebec, as well as much of the central eastern United States) prior to the English conquest in 1763. Some sporadic public funding was earmarked for education, but the initiative for starting and maintaining schools rested primarily with the Catholic Church and private, church-related groups (Titley, 1982; Tomkins, 1986). The first formal schools (*les petites écoles*—the little schools) were run by individual parishes, taught by parish priests, and focused on a curriculum of catechism and introduction to reading, writing, and arithmetic (Audet, 1970). Only about half of the parishes in New France had such schools, and informal schooling—conducted by notaries and other educated laypeople in their homes—was also common (Tomkins, 1986).

The first move toward school and curriculum control in New France was precipitated by concerns over the moral content of books being used in informal school contexts. A 1729 ordinance ordered that no one could teach reading and writing or keep any manner of school without the permission of the bishop of Quebec. After this declaration, all educational control of schooling rested with church-sanctioned organizations (Tomkins, 1986).

Within this context, one of the key influences on education in New France was the Jesuit religious order; Jesuit priests became the leaders of the first organized school system in Canada. They implemented the highly structured and centralized *Ratio Studiorum*—the official plan of studies for Jesuit education (Titley, 1982). They also innovated and foreshadowed future efforts to create a specifically Canadian education experience, by teaching in the local French language rather than in Latin, as was still done in European Jesuit schools (Audet, 1970).

The aim of all of the church-controlled schools, Jesuit and parish-run *petites écoles* alike, was transmission and indoctrination of core French and Catholic values. The goal of schooling was to make children "good servants of the King . . . and of God" (Clark, 1962, cited in Tomkins, 1986). These aims were seen as necessary for the survival of French culture in this new and foreign land. The curriculum—focused on catechism, reading, and writing—reflected this aim.

Following the British Conquest, themes of cultural survival of the French under British rule became ever more urgent (Titley, 1982). French Canadians vigorously resisted English attempts to establish a state system of elementary and secondary schools, viewing the plan as a step toward Anglicization and secularization (Tomkins, 1986). The Quebec Act (1774) confirmed the Church's right to control education in Lower Canada (now Quebec)—control that was maintained until the 1960s.

Education in Early English-Canadian Settlements (1763-1840s)

In a similar vein, schooling in the earliest English-Canadian settlements (present-day Nova Scotia, New Brunswick, and Ontario) was largely organized around maintaining British and Protestant social values. These settlers perceived the need to fight for the cultural survival of British values in a new and, in some cases, largely French milieu. The Society for the Propagation of the Gospel played a role similar to that of the Jesuits in New France. They organized the first system of schools in the eastern Canadian settlements of present-day Nova Scotia and New Brunswick with the goals of "doctrinal soundness and a regard for British institutions" (Society for the Propagation of the Gospel, 1896, p. 844, cited in Hamilton, 1970). The curriculum included catechism, scripture reading, and learning to write "in a plain and legible hand" (Society for the Propagation of the Gospel, 1896, p. 844, cited in Tomkins, 1986).

Western Canadian schooling and curriculum (in what is now Manitoba, Saskatchewan, British Columbia, Yukon, and the Northwest Territories) and that of Northern Ontario and Quebec had their foundations particularly in the missionary efforts of both Catholic and Protestant orders. Additionally, the Hudson's Bay Company, which was rooted in the fur trade industry of the west and north, provided a network of local schools for the children of its officers. These schools served practical needs by training youngsters to work in the company as well as providing a comforting British influence for families living in remote communities (Tomkins, 1986). The company took pride in providing a classical education equivalent to that available in any city (McLean, 1849). At first, these schools were available only to the high-ranking officers; lower ranking families were left to create and support their own schools (McLean, 1849). Later, however, the schools expanded to welcome all school-age children living in the vicinity of the forts and trading areas. They became important community gathering places and were among the first schools to integrate and welcome Métis students (students of mixed Aboriginal and European ancestry). In addition, they were among the first truly non-denominational schools in Canada (Pollard, 2003).

Following the influx of English loyalists (mostly to Eastern Canada) after the American revolution of 1776, the emphasis on educating for "Britishness" became increasingly strong (Hamilton, 1970). Tomkins (1986) argues that the efforts of loyalists to justify their cause and celebrate their triumphs over adversity created a "loyalist cult" (p. 17) whose influence still permeates social studies curricula in English Canada. As a result of the loyalist influence, many of the school building and curriculum development efforts at this time aimed to counter American influences and revolutionary ideals. It was argued that a publically controlled Canadian school program was necessary to maintain order and preserve British values (Hamilton, 1970; McDonald, 1982).

In English-Canadian provinces (i.e., all provinces other than Quebec), the move toward publically controlled schools began in the early 19th century. In Upper Canada (present-day Ontario), the Common Schools Act of 1816 created the first government-supported elementary schools. These locally controlled but publicly funded schools laid the foundation for creating a fully centralized government-run system of public schools, beginning under the leadership of Egerton Ryerson in 1846 (Carney, 1990; Wilson, 1982). The impetus for creating this system rested on the desire to curb American influences and on the Victorian notion that education was necessary for control of criminality, alcohol abuse, and other anti-social behavior (Baldus & Kassam, 1996; Carney, 1990; Wilson, 1982).

The tension between providing a practical industrial education and preparing students for further study through a classical education permeated curricular decision-making in this new school system. In addition, following the Constitution Act of 1867 (which united several provinces and created the Dominion of Canada), efforts to inculcate the students with a Canadian identity began in earnest (Tomkins, 1977). This became a recurrent curricular theme that remains to this day.

Early Canadian Curriculum Development (1840s-1920s)

In the nascent provincial school systems, mandated curricula consisted primarily of lists of desirable subjects to be addressed in schools (e.g., grammar, geography, linear drawing, and natural history). The enacted curriculum, however, focused almost entirely on reading, writing, and preliminary mathematics (Tomkins, 1986).

Concerns for standardization and resistance to American influences believed to be found in textbooks prompted Ryerson to advocate the adoption of the *Irish National Readers* as required texts for Ontario schools in 1846. They were followed the next year by the *Canadian Series of Reading Books* (a Canadianized version of the Irish Readers). These highly prescriptive graded readers quickly became the de facto curriculum in Ontario schools and were rapidly adopted in English schools across the country (Brummelen, 1986; Carney, 1990). The use of text-as-curriculum served the powerful function of regulating and standardizing instruction in rural and urban schools and was a key tool for assimilation and inculcation of British-Canadian morality across the country (Baldus & Kassam, 1996; Brummelen, 1986; McDonald, 1982). For example, the standardized grammar approved for use in British Columbia in 1872 included mostly Protestant biblical texts for reading exercises, and the sentences provided for analysis were predominantly moral maxims, such as, "Were they wise, they would read the Scriptures daily" (Brummelen, 1986, p. 20). These standardized texts were implemented with little consideration of the realities and diversities of school contexts in Canada. Texts exemplifying and advocating the values and morals of city-dwelling students and families were used in equal measure in urban schools in Ontario and schools in the northern territories (in present-day Yukon, Northwest Territories, and Nunavut), where most of the references were irrelevant and some were incomprehensible (Chambers, 1999).

In addition to the powerful influence of the text-as-curriculum, test-as-curriculum became an important theme after 1870, when secondary school enrollments boomed. The boom was precipitated, at least in part, by the new requirement that students have one to two years of secondary schooling for entrance into Ontario normal schools (teacher training schools). Similar requirements were implemented in other provinces (Tomkins, 1986). Elementary schools began to focus on preparing students for secondary school entrance examinations, and secondary schools began preparing growing numbers of students for university entrance exams. The content covered in these examinations, in conjunction with the authorized graded texts now approved for all subjects, became the de facto curriculum in Canadian schools (Tomkins, 1986). This system remained intact and relatively unchanged through the early 20th century.

The Maturing Canadian Curriculum (1920s-1950s)

As the 20th century began, reformist voices from the United States and Britain were being heard in Canada, and movements for the creation of child-centered curricula gained momentum. New subjects, such as domestic science, physical and health education, and commercial studies, entered the curriculum. Tomkins (1986) argues, however, that the general trend in Canada was really one of "curriculum development by accretion" (p. 116), in that new subjects were added, but little was removed or truly reformed.

The trend in curriculum writing at this time was toward more detailed and prescriptive curriculum outlines that included accompanying materials for both students and teachers. The form of the written curricula moved away from being merely lists of topics to be covered toward an outline of what the teacher should be doing in class. For example, in the 1924 Alberta *Programme of Studies for the Elementary School*, considerable text space was devoted to suggested teaching practices and example scripts of teacher talk. The introduction stated that the document was written to "be a definite handbook and guide to the teacher in interpreting the various subjects" (Department of Education, Alberta, 1924, p. 3). As with the earlier introduction of readers, the aim of this more detailed curriculum was to provide guidance to and accountability for teachers, especially those in rural communities (Tomkins, 1986).

These efforts toward more detailed curricula did not, however, diminish the influence of the text-as-curriculum. Approved and required texts that were mandated or written by provincial education departments were the norm in all regions of Canada. In 1936, however, Ontario experienced a power shift toward independent authors when the government relinquished control of textbook writing and began to select texts from lists submitted by publishers. Text contracts were generally for seven-year periods, during which the written and enacted curricula were essentially frozen (Tomkins, 1986).

The continued focus on structure, standardization, and testing led to considerable criticism of the Canadian school system during this time. The system was accused of being too formalized, exam obsessed, and having curricula that had changed little since the turn of the century (e.g., Kirkconnel, 1920; Sandiford, 1930; Thomson, 1941, cited in Tomkins, 1986).

In the 1920s and 1930s, however, more Canadian educators began to study abroad, most notably at Columbia University and the University of Chicago, both considered major centers of progressivist thought (Lemisko & Clausen, 2006). In addition, the Great Depression of the 1930s added urgency to calls for social and economic reform and school curricula were viewed as promising vehicles for such change. These two factors led to a critical mass of Canadian educators advocating for child-centered approaches that connected school and teaching to children's lives. These reforms were taken up most enthusiastically in Alberta, where an integrated enterprise approach became the central organizing feature of the curriculum, beginning in 1936. These reforms were implemented gradually and with caution, however, and the 1936 Alberta *Programme of Studies* warned that "the teacher will not find it desirable to follow exclusively either the enterprise procedure or that of formal teaching" (Department of Education, Alberta, 1936, p. 5). The height of the enterprise approach in Canada can be found in the 1940 Alberta curriculum, in which social studies, science, and health were subsumed under "The Integrated Programme" in which "No attempt [was] made to differentiate between the various subjects throughout the programme. They appear as they contribute to a better understanding of the particular concept of study involved" (Department of Education, Alberta, 1940, p. 47). Most other provinces added at least some mention of "projects" or "enterprises," meant to ground the curriculum in children's experience, but no other curriculum attempted such large-scale integration of subject matter (Tomkins, 1986). Despite this example of extreme integration, even in Alberta, the curriculum recommended teaching methods for reading, writing, and mathematics that remained traditional and unchanged (Department of Education, Alberta, 1940; Tomkins, 1986).

Canadian Curriculum: Post-War to the 1990s

In the post-war boom of the 1950s, enthusiasm for project methods and progressivism waned and a feeling grew among parents and politicians that children ought to be educated for participation in the vigorous new economy. This led to a return to subject-centered approaches and to curriculum standardization and control (Lemisko & Clausen, 2006). Reflecting the emphasis on standardization and control, the form of the written curriculum shifted again—this time away from describing what the teacher should do and toward describing what students should learn. Many post-war curricula contained lists of facts that students should be taught. For example, the 1964 New Brunswick *Elementary Programme of Studies* lists in the Grade 3 natural science curriculum such facts as "The sun seems to move across the sky each day" and "Shadows are made by things that light will not go through" (Government of the Province of New Brunswick, 1964, p. 15).

As the 1960s progressed, however, parents and educators again became frustrated with the heavy emphasis on testing and rote learning. Discipline-oriented theories of learning also began to emerge from the United States and the United Kingdom. These trends are often related to Jerome Bruner and his early arguments that disciplines had their own internal structure, and that this structure could form the basis of teaching the seminal ideas and patterns of thought associated with each discipline. Child-centered (often called neo-progressivist) discovery methods, modeled after the professional practice, became the dominant ideal (Tomkins, 1986). In science, for example, teachers were encouraged to give their students ample opportunities to emulate the habits of mind (such as rationality and objectivity) purportedly possessed by scientists (Gauld & Hukins, 1980). It was also at this time that scholars in the fields associated with school subjects became actively involved in making curricular recommendations (Tomkins, 1986).

These trends, and such influential documents as the Hall-Dennis report (Hall & Dennis, 1968), led to new curricula that were open and broad, rather than prescriptive. The Hall-Dennis report (formally titled *Living and Learning*) argued that

> *the modern curriculum must be flexible, not only by providing options for pupils with different interests at more senior levels but by providing learning experiences to meet the needs of individual young people at every level. . . . Although many classes under many different teachers may share one course of study, every class, every group within a class, and every pupil may have a unique curriculum. (p. 75).*

The new and open approach gave considerable power to classroom teachers and local curriculum developers and was a significant departure from earlier curricula aimed at standardizing the experience of students across provinces and across the country.

Following the trends set in the late 1960s, written curricula of the 1970s, 1980s, and early 1990s exemplified this open approach by prescribing very little required content. There were short descriptions of recommended subject matter, often only 5 to 10 sentences per topic, and a focus on local elective topics. The biggest changes from previous curricula were: 1) a heavy emphasis on developing attitudes and skills and 2) a focus in the language of the curricula on what the students should be *doing* rather than what they should be *taught*. In science, for example, units of study often consisted of one or two key concepts (e.g., "electricity is a form of energy" and "electrical energy can be changed to heat energy and light energy"), supported by activities in which students should engage (e.g., "observe how a switch affects an electrical circuit") (Manitoba Department of Education, 1979, p. 52). These activities were organized around scientific processes (e.g., observing, classifying, and inferring) that were meant to represent, and help students emulate, the work of scientists. This type of curriculum dominated Canadian education until the mid- to late 1990s.

Current Curriculum Documents

As in many other Western countries, the mid-1990s brought a return to ideals of accountability and efficiency in government and education. Since this time, curricula in Canada have again become increasingly prescriptive so that curricular decision-making power rests solely with provincial and territorial authorities rather than being shared with teachers and local school districts (Heydon & Wang, 2006). The effects of this movement were felt acutely in Ontario, where the "Common Sense Revolution" swept through the provincial parliament and the education system with the election of a new Conservative government in 1995. *The Common Curriculum* (Ontario Ministry of Education, 1995), implemented by the New Democrats earlier in 1995, and based mainly on the inquiry and neo-progressivist ideals of earlier curricular movements, was swiftly replaced by a new curriculum in 1997 (Ontario Ministry of Education and Training, 1997). *The Common Curriculum* emphasized the integration of subjects as well as teacher, student, and district autonomy in finding ways to help students achieve the essential outcomes outlined by the curriculum (Wien & Dudley-Marling, 1998). It highlighted student-directed and student-centered inquiry and recommended a "shift in curriculum emphasis to more integrated programming and active, inquiry-oriented learning" (Ontario Ministry of Education, 1995, p. 7).

In contrast, the 1997 *Ontario Curriculum* marked a drastic turn toward accountability and prescriptively stated curricula (Wien & Dudley-Marling, 1998). The shift in the form of the curriculum was this time away from what students should *do* and back to what they should *learn*: "The required knowledge and skills for each grade set high standards and identify what parents and the public can expect children to learn in the schools of Ontario" (Ontario Ministry of Education and Training, 1997, p. 2). The document is prescriptive and detailed and sets clear standards for learning and achievement at each grade level. For example, from the science and technology curriculum: "By the end of Grade 6 students will explain why formal classification systems are usually based on structural characteristics" (p. 25). The drive for standardization is especially evident in the inclusion of a prescriptive kindergarten curriculum—the first one in Ontario in over 50 years (Heydon & Wang, 2006).

It should be noted, however, that despite the emphasis of prescriptive outcomes-based language in the current curriculum, an effort also is underway to include elements of previous reforms. In the science curriculum, the content expectations are central, but there is also a considerable emphasis on inquiry, design, and communication skills, an emphasis not unlike that found in the neo-progressivist curricula. Also included in the science curriculum is a third emphasis on the connections between science, technology, society, and the environment—an integrative perspective also consistent with neo-progressivist reforms. The overall trend at this point in Canadian curriculum development appears to be the effort to address societal needs for accountability, efficiency, and standardization, while also maintaining the important influences of integrationist and inquiry-based teaching practices.

Curriculum and Schooling History of Aboriginal Students

Alongside this system of provincial and northern territorial school systems, however, the Constitution Act (1867) put responsibility for all Aboriginal community affairs in the hands of the federal government. This meant that education for Aboriginal students was administered in a manner that was separate and different from that for other Canadian students (Titley, 1986). Aboriginal students were expected to attend schools created and administered by the federal Department of Indian Affairs. In order to accomplish this, most of the curriculum and teaching responsibility was given over to Catholic, Anglican, Methodist, and Presbyterian missionaries willing to operate schools for Aboriginal students in remote areas. These schools set their own curricula and placed a heavy emphasis on imposing and inculcating European religious and social values (Schissel & Wotherspoon, 2003). Initially, there were both day schools and boarding schools (residential schools). It soon became apparent, however, that socialization and assimilation were difficult in day schools where students returned home each day (Titley, 1986). Residential schools, situated on property held by the religious orders, became the preferred model of student education. The curricular aims of these schools were based on the view that "the 'savage' was to be made 'civilized,' made fit to take up the privileges and responsibilities of citizenship" (Royal Commission on Aboriginal Peoples, 1996, p. 335). Residential school course curricula centered on Euro-Canadian settlement and history and often portrayed Aboriginal people as the enemy of the civilized settlers (Schissel & Wotherspoon, 2003). The same standardized texts used in provincial schools were also implemented in residential schools, despite being culturally and pedagogically unsuitable. Little attention was paid to developing curricula that were tailored to the language and sociological needs of the students or their communities (Titley, 1986).

During the post-war period, many communities began to recognize that these schools were not working. From the government's perspective, they were not cost-effective and students were ill-prepared for life in Euro-Canadian society as well as for traditional Aboriginal life (Schissel & Wotherspoon, 2003; Titley, 1986). From an Aboriginal perspective, they were often cruel environments with a single goal—assimilation and destruction of Aboriginal culture (Schissel & Wotherspoon, 2003). As a result, the residential schools began to close in the 1940s, although the last one did not shut its doors until 1996. The scars of children's experiences in these schools continue to have a strong impact on Aboriginal people and communities.

Following the closing of the residential schools, students were gradually moved into mainstream, provincially run schools, noted for a conspicuous absence of courses and content that incorporated Aboriginal perspectives. Through the 1960s and 1970s, evidence mounted that provincial curricula were inappropriate and often offensive to many Aboriginal students. It was within this context that the first community-controlled schools began to open with the goal of providing locally developed and appropriate curricula for students. This movement was exemplified by the document *Indian Control of Indian Education*, published by the National Indian Brotherhood (now the Assembly of First Nations) (1972). Since that time, the theme of culturally appropriate, locally developed curricula has become a major theme in Canadian education.

CURRENT PERSPECTIVES OF CANADIAN CURRICULUM DEVELOPMENT

Curriculum Development Leadership

The Constitution Act of 1867 conferred responsibility for education and curriculum development on what are now 10 provinces and three northern territories. This decision recognized the importance of having local politicians and citizenry designing programs responsive to local needs and acknowledged the existing school systems in each of the provinces and northern territories.

Currently, each provincial and northern territorial governments has a department or ministry of education that provides leadership for K-12 curriculum development. Departments or ministries develop philosophy statements, assist in designing standards-based learning outcomes (what students should know and do), and set policies for student assessment. They also may be involved in distance learning initiatives, student support services, curriculum implementation, and career services. Some northern territorial departments and ministries, while officially responsible for curricular decisions, have fulfilled this responsibility by using curricula developed in other provinces (e.g., Nunavut currently uses some curriculum approved in Alberta and Saskatchewan; the British Columbia curriculum forms the basis of the Yukon curriculum). Increasingly, however, northern territories are moving toward developing their own curricula (e.g., Nunavut is currently building capacity for an Inuit-led curriculum development process).

Although the responsibility for curriculum development lies with the provinces and northern territories, publicly elected ministers of education recognize that regions do share some common expectations and that a degree of curriculum alignment among the regions would benefit students, teachers, parents, publishers, and, quite possibly, address pressure for increased accountability. The Council of Ministers of Education, Canada (CMEC) was established in 1967 to provide a forum for discussing common educational policies and issues, including curriculum development. CMEC has collaborated to produce the *Pan-Canadian Protocol for Collaboration on School Curriculum* (CMEC, 1997a) and a *Common Framework of Science Learning Outcomes K-12* (CMEC, 1997b). The science learning outcomes document has been particularly influential on science programs across Canada.

A second consortium active in curriculum development involves western provinces and some northern areas of Canada (Yukon, Northwest Territories, British Columbia, Alberta, Saskatchewan, Manitoba). These regions form the Western and Northern Canadian Protocol (WNCP), whose partners meet to explore common educational issues. WNCP partners have developed common curriculum frameworks for mathematics (1995, 1996, and 2006), English language arts (1998), social studies (2002), bilingual programming in international languages K-12 (1999), international languages K-12 (2000), and Aboriginal language and culture programs K-12 (2000). These frameworks have been used to inform provincial and northern territorial curriculum development in western and some northern regions.

A final curriculum consortium, the Council of Atlantic Ministers of Education and Training (including ministers from New Brunswick, Newfoundland and Labrador, Nova Scotia, and Prince Edward Island), has developed the Atlantic Framework for Essential Graduation Learnings in Schools. This outcomes framework anchors curriculum development in the Atlantic provinces for core courses. It has become the basis for shared English language curricula in core courses, such as science, mathematics, and social studies, at both the elementary and secondary levels.

Curriculum Development and Revision Processes

Provincial and northern territorial ministries or departments of education have designed inclusive curriculum development and revision processes that involve collaboration with educators (teachers, principals), other relevant government ministries, stakeholders (post-secondary institutions, teacher associations, school trustees, parent advisory councils), the general public, and nongovernmental organizations (environmental, business). Curriculum development commonly includes reviewing international and circumpolar curriculum standards documents and studies (e.g., National Science Education Standards, NRC, 1996; TIMSS—The Trends in International Mathematics and Science Study, 2000, Martin; Greenland curricula in the case of northern territories); international delivery approaches (e.g., technology-based approaches); current educational research; Canadian reports (e.g., *Science Council of Canada* reports); other provincial and territorial programs; CMEC-developed curriculum frameworks; and a variety of Canadian common curriculum frameworks documents (e.g., those produced by WNCP and the Atlantic provinces).

Curriculum development is governed by a variety of guidelines designed by the provinces and northern territories to ensure a fair, equitable, and inclusive process. In general, curriculum development begins with soliciting feedback on the current curriculum (e.g., what needs to be re-thought or included), forming a team to work on the revision, using ongoing feedback from a wide range of people and groups to write multiple drafts of the new curriculum, field testing a final draft, and distributing the new curriculum for mandated use within the province or northern territory. Ongoing feedback (much of this feedback is now done online) is solicited from diverse groups of people, who may be asked to comment on alignment with provincial or northern territorial education philosophy statements, the inclusion of key skills, attitudes, and knowledge, the sensitivity to the local context, and resource availability. Curriculum development processes reflect a belief in a systematic approach involving knowledgeable people who represent diverse interests and yet are able to make decisions for the common good.

Notable within Canada are current efforts by northern territories to develop curricula that feature northern cultures and languages and include Aboriginal communities in planning and revising curriculum. In Nunavut, Elders Committees have been struck to develop foundational principles and concepts critical to including a strong language and cultural component in early years curricula. Partnerships have been formed with the Inuit Heritage Trust to develop courses based on local needs and interests. For example, Elders, educators, and the Nunavut Department of Education are working together to design a Nunavut curriculum focused on Inuit Quajimajatuqangit (I.Q.). I.Q. is a mix of Inuit tradition, wisdom, and perspective on the world that includes three strands:

- Nunavusiutit: the relationships that Nunavut peoples have with each other and with the land.
- Inuktitut Ukausiliriniq: the study of Inuit languages.
- Inuuqatigiiniq: personal roles, responsibilities, and relationships.

Curricula are being developed to incorporate these three strands and allow students to explore Inuit customs, values, and everyday experiences.

In the Yukon, an Education Reform Process (in partnership with the Council of Yukon First Nations) has been launched to develop local curriculum. The Northwest Territories also has worked to include northern cultures in the curriculum (e.g., Dene Kede: A Dene Perspective; NWT K-6 Science and Technology Curriculum).

The intent of all these groups is to develop curriculum more relevant to northern students, especially Aboriginal students, and to ensure that cultural and linguistic traditions are passed on to future generations. The important aims of these groups are summed up by Chambers (1999), here describing the Dene curriculum development project in the Northwest Territories: "The team struggled with the age-old curriculum question: 'What knowledge is of most worth' with the addendum 'of most worth *here*, for the Dene' " (p. 141).

Common Themes and Regional Differences

An overview of Canadian curricula shows a common trend toward identifying important knowledge, skills, and attitudes, and incorporating these into learning outcomes statements. There is a consistent emphasis on wording written curriculum in the form of testable student outcomes. These are reflective of a theme of consistency and cohesiveness across the provinces, which has been a major goal of the Council of Ministers of Education and an important rationale supporting the development of WNCP and Atlantic Canada curriculum framework documents.

Alongside this move toward cohesiveness, however, remains a history of regional differences based primarily on language and religion. Prior to the Ontario Common Schools Act of 1816, all schools in Canada were religiously affiliated and governed by local church and community groups. The early 19th century saw many provinces moving toward single, more centralized non-denominational school systems, but many churches and church groups remained active in providing and governing schools. When the first four provinces joined under the Constitution Act (1867), provisions guaranteed the rights of communities to maintain the schooling structure that had been in place prior to unification, including a guarantee of education rights for Roman Catholics. In Ontario, this led to the creation of two parallel systems, one public (although largely Protestant) and the other Catholic. (In the United

States, Australia, and Canada, a public school is funded from tax revenue and most commonly administered to some degree by government or local government agencies. This usage is synonymous with the British English equivalent of "state school.") The decision to fund a separate Catholic school system was made with the provision that all control of curriculum and textbooks, with the exception of those for religious instruction, would reside with the province. This has resulted in two parallel systems that follow the same provincial curriculum in all core subjects. The situation is similar in Alberta, Saskatchewan, and most of the Atlantic Provinces.

In Quebec, policies have been much different. The early provincial governments left the responsibility for education, including curriculum development, to Protestant and Catholic religious organizations. Until 1964, the churches maintained complete control over teacher training, certification, textbooks, and curricula, and the two school systems existed in almost complete isolation (Foster, Smith, & Donahue, 2000). It was not until that year that a provincial ministry of education was created and that curriculum became consistent across the Catholic and Protestant school boards. The most recent change in Quebec education has been the shift, implemented in 1998, to a language-based organization of schools. Quebec now maintains a consistent curriculum between the two boards and religious education is overseen separately within the two language-based systems.

A second major regional difference is the provision of French language education and curriculum for francophones living outside of Quebec. The 1982 Canadian Charter of Rights and Freedoms guaranteed official language minorities (i.e., French speakers living in English provinces and English speakers living in Quebec) the right to first language education in their mother tongue. In the *Pan-Canadian Protocol for Collaboration on School Curriculum*, the Council of Ministers of Education "recognize[s] and respect[s] the distinct character of francophone and anglophone education" (CMEC, 1997a). Despite this commitment, in all parts of the country, a struggle continues to exist between implementing a consistent and cohesive program for all students while also acknowledging the differences between francophone and anglophone contexts, as well as the important role that francophone schools play in community and identity development for French language students and their families (Behiels, 2004). Given this tension, the approaches to French and English first language curricula vary considerably by province.

New Brunswick, Canada's only officially bilingual province, allows the separate development of francophone and anglophone curriculum documents. The school system is governed by the same Minister of Education, who has curricular veto power, but there are separate francophone and anglophone curricular advisory committees (Office of the Commissioner of Official Languages, 1998). In core subject areas, the anglophone curriculum follows the common curriculum created by the Council of Atlantic Ministers of Education and Training (e.g., New Brunswick Department of Education, 2002). French immersion schools (for anglophone students learning French) follow a translated version of this curriculum. The francophone schools, however, follow a curriculum specifically created for francophone education in the province (e.g., Ministère de l'Éducation, Nouveau Brunswick, 2003). The arrangement is similar in Prince Edward Island, where anglophone schools follow the Atlantic curriculum, but both French immersion and francophone schools follow a curriculum developed specifically for French language education (e.g., Ministère de l'Éducation, Île-du-Prince-Édouard, 2003). In Alberta, the curriculum is developed in English and translated for use in francophone schools, but the governing bodies of the francophone schools, *les Conseils Scolaires*, may amend the learning expectations to create a more locally appropriate program (Office of the Commissioner of Official Languages, 1998). The situation is similar in Ontario, where the core subject curricula are the same but the entire francophone program is overlaid with an additional French language development policy, which allows for flexibility in the implementation of subject curricula to encourage a greater focus on language and identity development (French-Language Strategy Task Force, 2004). Given these differences, and the Charter guarantee of minority language control over schooling, many francophone communities continue to lobby for greater curriculum and governance power over French language schools (Behiels, 2004).

PEDAGOGICAL PRACTICES IN CANADIAN SCHOOLS

Despite the prominence of outcomes-based curricula, the enacted curricula continue to be influenced by trends toward integrated education, the importance of inquiry, and the development of skills and attitudes in all subject areas. This is evident from a policy standpoint given the theoretical introductions of most curriculum documents. For example, science documents stress the importance of making science learning relevant to students' lives; connecting science, technology, society; and aiming to foster positive attitudes toward science (e.g., Ministry of Education and Training, Ontario, 1997). These documents also emphasize the key role that teachers play in implementing the written curriculum. Ministries and departments in all provinces and northern territories have placed considerable emphasis on professional development, with the aim of helping teachers to implement the curriculum in a way that is consistent with aims and outcomes addressed in the curricula. These pedagogical approaches, such as an emphasis on inquiry, are consistent across K-6 and 7-12 settings.

Pedagogical Practice in K-6 Schools

Provincial and northern territorial curricula include ideas about the delivery of prescribed learning outcomes. These ideas emphasize the critical role teachers play in guiding students' development and learning and the responsibility students have to take an active role in their own learning. In general, K-6 teachers are advised to consider the whole child and help students develop intellectually, socially, and physically by:

- Implementing a variety of instructional strategies (e.g., direct instruction, inquiry learning) to address student diversity and different learning styles, and to promote literacy
- Establishing a supportive learning environment (e.g., teaching for success) to enable students to reach their full potential and create a positive future for themselves and their communities
- Practicing ongoing assessment and evaluation (e.g., formative and summative assessment) to diagnose learning difficulties, design early and appropriate interventions, and improve teaching and learning
- Using a variety of technologies (e.g., computer technology integrated into all subject areas) to provide educational opportunities for all students.

These suggestions recognize that although teachers work with mandated curricula, they still need to engage in pedagogical decision-making and practice a flexible approach to instruction and assessment in order to create classroom environments that support diverse learners. Quebec summarizes a message in many curriculum programs that teaching requires autonomy, creativity, and personal expertise.

Some provinces and northern territories make explicit reference to the idea that teachers, students, and parents have complementary responsibilities. Ontario and Quebec outline the idea that students must make the effort to apply themselves to educational tasks and take an active role in learning—a stance other provinces relate to constructivist learning theory. Parents also are viewed as playing a critical role in supporting students' learning. Through including these references, the development of the whole child in K-6 school is viewed as contingent upon a collaboration between the school and the home. Schools should design learning contexts that connect to children's everyday lives and parents should support teachers' efforts to help children grow toward becoming productive citizens.

Pedagogical Practice in 7-12 Schools

Just as in the K-6 schools, the teaching practices in 7-12 schools recognize the importance of educating the whole student and encourage personal and intellectual growth to prepare students for life outside of school. Across all subjects there is an emphasis on promoting literacy—as defined in both the traditional sense and the broader context of, for example, scientific literacy, mathematical literacy, and technological literacy (e.g., English-language Expert Panel on Student Success in Ontario, 2004). This emphasis on broadly defined subject literacy has led to a movement toward teaching skills and attitudes in conjunction with the concept-based outcomes. This emphasis on literacy is also connected to the prominence, in all subject areas, of inquiry methods that link learning to real-world problems and engage students in complex decision-making. Teachers are encouraged, and have been moving progressively toward, engaging students in rich tasks that will require students to think in the complex ways that they will use in life—outside of and after school. The aim is for teachers to choose practices that reflect a view of inquiry not as an add-on to a traditional program but rather as an organizational framework for all pedagogical practices (Alberta Learning, 2004).

There also has been a recent trend toward choosing pedagogical practices that better reflect and address the needs of adolescent learners. This is being achieved through a greater emphasis on attitudes and the affective domain of learning—as seen in teaching practices that encourage confidence and positive self-efficacy in students (English-language Expert Panel on Student Success in Ontario, 2004). Additionally, Canadian educators have placed a greater emphasis on grounding teaching practices in emerging neuroscience research. There is now recognition that even the older adolescent brain is still working within a growth and transition framework and that many of the learner expectations in the curricula require a complex use of symbolic and abstract representations (English-language Expert Panel on Student Success in Ontario, 2004). Teaching practices that recognize this challenge and attempt to teach students to move between representation systems and manage abstract ideas have been increasingly encouraged in 7-12 classes across all subject areas. Similarly, in recognition of the needs of the adolescent brain, many 7-12 schools advocate practices that promote student responsibility for and ownership of learning. The practices generally begin gradually in the middle grades (7-9), with students taking increasing responsibility as they reach the senior grades (10-12) (e.g., Department of Education, Prince Edward Island, 2007).

FUTURE TRENDS IN CANADIAN CURRICULUM DEVELOPMENT

Many of the issues and trends that have persisted in the history of Canadian education are still at the forefront of efforts to develop and improve curricula. Since the time of the first organized Canadian school systems, tension has existed between 1) providing standardized curricula that can give students a consistent foundation, regardless of geographical location, and 2) providing locally appropriate curricula that meet the cultural and economic needs of students and their communities. Currently, there is a strong recognition that a "one-size-fits-all" approach to curriculum is not appropriate for many Canadian students.

The CMEC (2005a) has recognized that "existing curricula and teaching delivery methods do not sufficiently reflect Aboriginal needs and values" (p. 1). Currently, the Aboriginal Educational Action Plan describes aims to not only engage community members in the North, as described above, but also bring together all provinces and northern territories, along with the federal government and Aboriginal leaders and educators, to create a curricular framework for Aboriginal education that will be available to and valuable for students in all parts of Canada—including those not educated in a specifically Aboriginal context.

Similarly, there is continued recognition that francophone students in minority language settings (i.e., living in English provinces) are not well-served by the current teaching methods and curricula. Their performance on standardized tests as a part of the Pan-Canadian School Achievement Program shows the achievement of francophone 13- and 16-year-olds in minority language settings to be significantly lower than that of anglophone students in the same districts and significantly lower than that of francophone students in Quebec. The CMEC is currently in Phase II of its Pan-Canadian French as a First Language Project (CMEC, 2005b), with the aim of creating resources for francophone schools, as well as a framework for curricular development. Together, this project and the Aboriginal Educational Action Plan exemplify a current trend toward culturally specific and appropriate curricula.

This trend also is related to the recognition that the school environment plays a key role in a student's education experience. Many provinces have begun to highlight the importance of safe and healthy schools and recognized that the development and implementation of all curricula take place within the context of providing this environment for students (Safe Schools Action Team, 2006). British Columbia has become a national leader in implementing curricular programs that encourage student health, safety, and recreation, including mandated physical activity for all students K-12. In implementing this plan, curriculum leaders argue for strong connections between physical well-being, learning, and the achievement of curricular goals (Ministry of Education, British Columbia, 2007).

In summary, early efforts to formalize Canadian curricula and pedagogical practice were critically influenced by a theme of cultural survival—the survival of French Catholic and English Protestant cultures and languages. This same theme remains for historically marginalized Aboriginal peoples. With increasing support from departments and ministries from across Canada, curricula are being transformed to help all students understand the essential worth of Aboriginal perspectives.

Canadian conversations about current curriculum developments are also increasingly focusing on the need to educate a healthy future citizenry that has the knowledge, skills, and attitudes needed to make informed decisions about issues related to their lives. Canadian curriculum, therefore, is moving toward providing increasing room for students to engage in debates, participate in diverse decision-making tasks, and reflect on the consequences of those decisions. Curriculum development is a creative human activity and, as such, is always a work in progress. A primary recurring goal is to provide learning contexts that will help students to live productively within the Canadian milieu.

References

Alberta Learning. (2004). *Focus on inquiry: A teacher's guide to implementing inquiry-based learning*. Edmonton, AB: Author.

Audet, L.-P. (1970). Society and education in New France. In J. D. Wilson, R. M. Stamp, & L.-P. Audet (Eds.), *Canadian education: A history* (pp. 70-85). Scarborough, ON: Prentice-Hall.

Baldus, B., & Kassam, M. (1996). "Make me truthful, good, and mild": Values in nineteenth-century Ontario schoolbooks. *Canadian Journal of Sociology, 21*, 327-358.

Behiels, M. D. (2004). *Canada's francophone minority communities: Constitutional renewal and the winning of school governance*. Montreal, QC: McGill-Queen's University Press.

Brummelen, H. V. (1986). Shifting perspectives: Early British Columbia textbooks from 1872 to 1925. In N. M. Sheehan, J. D. Wilson, & D. C. Jones (Eds.), *Schools in the West: Essays in Canadian educational history* (pp. 17-38). Calgary, AB: Detselig Enterprises.

Carney, R. J. (1990). Going to school in Upper Canada. In E. B. Titley (Ed.), *Canadian education: Historical themes and contemporary issues* (pp. 9-44). Calgary, AB: Detselig Enterprises.

Chambers, C. (1999). A topography for Canadian curriculum theory. *Canadian Journal of Education, 24*, 137-150.

Council of Ministers of Education, Canada. (1997a). *Pan-Canadian protocol for collaboration on school curriculum*. Toronto, ON: CMEC Secretariat.

Council of Ministers of Education, Canada. (1997b). *Common framework of science learning outcomes, K-12*. Toronto, ON: CMEC Secretariat.

Council of Ministers of Education, Canada. (2005a). *Aboriginal educational action plan*. Toronto, ON: CMEC Secretariat.

Council of Ministers of Education, Canada. (2005b). *Pan-Canadian French as a first language project*. Toronto, ON: CMEC Secretariat.

Department of Education, Alberta. (1924). *Programme of studies for the elementary schools grades I to VIII*. Edmonton, AB: King's Printers.

Department of Education, Alberta. (1936). *Programme of studies for the elementary schools grades I to VI*. Edmonton, AB: King's Printers.

Department of Education, Alberta. (1940). *Program of studies for the elementary schools grades I to VI*. Edmonton, AB: King's Printers.

Department of Education, Prince Edward Island. (2007). *Intermediate program of studies and authorized materials 2007-2008*. Charlottetown, PE: Department of Education.

English-Language Expert Panel on Student Success in Ontario. (2004). *Leading math success: Mathematical literacy grades 7-12*. Toronto, ON: Ontario Minister of Education.

French-Language Education Strategy Task Force. (2004). *Report presented to the Honourable Gerard Kennedy*. Toronto, ON: Ontario Minister of Education.

Foster, W., Smith, W., & Donahue, H. M. (2000). Systemic education reform in Quebec: How far have we come? Where are we headed? *EAF Journal, 15*, 12-34.

Gauld, C. F., & Hukins, A. A. (1980). Scientific attitudes: A review. *Studies in Science Education, 7*, 129-161.

Government of the Province of New Brunswick. (1964). *Elementary programme of studies: For New Brunswick schools*. Fredericton, NB: Author.

Hall, E. M., & Dennis, L. A. (1968). *Living and learning*. Toronto, ON: Department of Education, Ontario.

Hamilton, W. G. (1970). Society and schools in Nova Scotia. In J. D. Wilson, R. M. Stamp, & L.-P. Audet (Eds.), *Canadian education: A history* (pp. 86-105). Scarborough, ON: Prentice-Hall.

Heydon, R. M., & Wang, P. (2006). Curricular ethics in early childhood education programming: A challenge to the Ontario kindergarten program. *McGill Journal of Education, 41*, 29-47.

Lemisko, L. S., & Clausen, K. W. (2006). Connections, contrarieties, and convolutions: Curriculum and pedagogic reform in Alberta and Ontario, 1930-1955. *Canadian Journal of Education, 29*, 1097-1126.

Manitoba Department of Education. (1979). *K-6 science*. Winnipeg, MB: Manitoba Department of Education.

Martin, M.O. (2000). *TIMSS 1999 International Science Report: Findings from IEA's Repeat of the Third International Mathematics and Science Study at the Eighth Grade*. Chestnut Hill, MA: International Association for the Evaluation of Educational Achievement.

McDonald, N. (1982). Canadianization and the curriculum: Setting the stage, 1867-1890. In E. B. Titley & P. J. Miller (Eds.), *Education in Canada* (pp. 93-110). Calgary, AB: Detselig Enterprises.

McLean, J. (1849). *Notes of a twenty-five years' service in Hudson's Bay Territory, Volume II.* London: Richard Bentley.

Ministère de l'Éducation, Île-du-Prince-Édouard. (2003). *Sciences: Programme d'études 5ᵉ année.* Charlottetown, PE: Author.

Ministère de l'Éducation, Nouveau Brunswick. (2003). *Science de la nature: Cinquième année, Plan d'études.* Fredericton, NB: Author.

Ministry of Education, British Columbia. (2007). *B.C. sets national standard in promoting student health.* Ministry of Education Press Release, retrieved September 24, 2007, from www2.news.gov. bc.ca/news_releases_2005-2009/2007EDU0113-001078.htm#

National Indian Brotherhood. (1972). *Indian control of Indian education: A position paper.* Ottawa, ON: National Indian Brotherhood.

National Research Council. (1996). *National Science Education Standards.* Washington, DC: National Academy Press.

New Brunswick Department of Education. (2002). *Science grade 5.* Fredericton, NB: Author.

Office of the Commissioner of Official Languages. (1998). *School governance: The implementation of Section 23 of the Charter.* Ottawa, ON: Author.

Ontario Ministry of Education. (1995). *The common curriculum, grades 1 to 9.* Toronto, ON: Author.

Ontario Ministry of Education and Training. (1997). *The Ontario curriculum, grades 1-8.* Toronto, ON: Queen's Printer.

Pollard, R. (2003). The instance and legacy of residential schools, 1938-1949. In N. Janovicek & J. Parr (Eds.), *Histories of Canadian children and youth* (pp. 57-70). Don Mills, ON: Oxford University Press, Canada.

Royal Commission on Aboriginal Peoples. (1996). *Report of the royal commission on Aboriginal peoples.* Ottawa, ON: Minister of Supply and Services Canada.

Safe Schools Action Team. (2006). *Safe schools policy and practice: An agenda for action.* Toronto, ON: Ministry of Education.

Schissel, B., & Wotherspoon, T. (2003). *The legacy of school for Aboriginal people.* Don Mills, ON: Oxford University Press, Canada.

Titley, E. B. (1982). Tradition, change and education in French Canada. In E. B. Titley & P. J. Miller (Eds.), *Education in Canada* (pp. 45-60). Calgary, AB: Detselig Enterprises.

Titley, E. B. (1986). Indian industrial schools in Western Canada. In N. M. Sheehan, J. D. Wilson, & D. C. Jones (Eds.), *Schools in the West: Essays in Canadian educational history* (pp. 133-154). Calgary, AB: Detselig Enterprises.

Tomkins, G. S. (1977). Canadian education and the development of a national consciousness: Historical and contemporary perspectives. In A. Chaiton & N. McDonald (Eds.), *Canadian schools and Canadian identity* (pp. 6-28). Toronto, ON: Gage Educational.

Tomkins, G. S. (1986). *A common countenance: Stability and change in the Canadian curriculum.* Scarborough, ON: Prentice-Hall, Canada.

Western and Northern Canadian Protocol. (1995). *The common curriculum framework for k-9 mathematics: Western Canadian protocol for collaboration in basic education.* Edmonton, AB: Alberta Education

Western and Northern Canadian Protocol. (1996). *The common curriculum framework for grades 10-12 mathematics: Western Canadian protocol for collaboration in basic education.* Edmonton, AB: Alberta Education.

Western and Northern Canadian Protocol. (1998). *The common curriculum framework for English language arts, kindergarten to grade 12: Western Canadian protocol for collaboration in basic education.* Edmonton, AB: Alberta Education.

Western and Northern Canadian Protocol. (1999). *The common framework for bilingual programming in international languages, kindergarten to grade 12: Western Canadian protocol for collaboration in basic education.* Edmonton, AB: Alberta Education.

Western and Northern Canadian Protocol. (2000). *The common curriculum framework for international languages, kindergarten to grade 12: Western Canadian protocol for collaboration in basic education.* Edmonton, AB: Alberta Education.

Western and Northern Canadian Protocol. (2002). *The common curriculum framework for social studies, kindergarten to grade 9: Western Canadian protocol for collaboration in basic education.* Edmonton, AB: Western Canadian Protocol for Collaboration in Basic Education.

Western and Northern Canadian Protocol. (2006). *The common curriculum framework for k-9 mathematics: Western and Northern Canadian protocol.* Edmonton, AB: Alberta Education.

Wien, C. A., & Dudley-Marling, C. (1998). Limited vision: The Ontario curriculum and outcomes-based learning. *Canadian Journal of Education, 23,* 405-420.

Wilson, J. D. (1982). The Ryerson years in Canada West. In E. B. Titley & P. J. Miller (Eds.), *Education in Canada* (pp. 61-92). Calgary, AB: Detselig Enterprises.

About the Authors

Brenda J. Gustafson, Ph.D., is a professor of elementary education in the Faculty of Education, University of Alberta, Edmonton, Alberta, Canada.

Marie-Claire Shanahan, Ph.D., is an assistant professor of elementary education in the Faculty of Education, University of Alberta, Edmonton, Alberta, Canada.

Curriculum Development
in Modern Mainland China

Nili Luo and Janet S. Arndt

A rich tradition of philosophy has impacted China's education throughout its long history. The focus of this chapter will examine the historical transformation and main characteristics that began with the founding of the People's Republic of China in 1949. As China struggled to become a modern country in the last half of the 20th century, the role of education shifted from serving an elite class, whose task was to rule the country through a privileged bureaucracy, to serving the masses in order to prepare them for a modern world.

Background of Chinese Education

China is a country with over 5,000 years of history and ancient traditions, with an emphasis on a select group of educated scholars to serve the national interests. The Chinese education system produced thinkers and scholars who produced many amazing advances in science and technology not duplicated in the West. Several essential products were first invented in China: the compass, paper, anesthesia, and gunpowder. Various wars and invasions during the last few hundred years, however, contributed to a stagnation of education in China, preventing fulfillment of the promise to further advances in science and modernize the country. With the establishment of the People's Republic of China in 1949, especially with the combination of Marxism and Chinese traditional education, many new ideas were tried in order to develop a more modern Chinese education system.

Presently, Chinese society honors the unique characteristics and fine traditions from the older Chinese education system. The People's Republic of China launched a recommitment to the high calling of education that began in ancient China under Confucius. The Confucian doctrine of *"Wan Ban Jie Xia Pin, Wei You Du Shu Gao"* ("Reading books is more valuable than anything else") was disseminated throughout people's daily life and thoughts.

Chinese education has two major themes. First, children must be shaped into people who are beneficial to society and who are obedient to their

China

parents, respectful of elders, responsible, honest, benevolent, and charitable in their communities. Second, children must acquire knowledge (Si Shu Wu Jing, 2004). These values continued as goals for the entire education system when the new regime took power in 1949.

Another important goal of the new regime was to adopt the use of only one language and handwriting system throughout the national education system. The purpose of this decision was to initiate the concept of a national identity. While there are more than 50 minorities in China, only Mandarin Chinese is taught and used officially. The hope was that this practice would promote national unity among the general population.

A review of the history of Chinese educational practice shows a variety of options on how to obtain an education. Families could choose home schooling, known as *Si Shu*, a tradition dating back over 2,000 years. Home schooling has held an important status in China. Starting with the Sui and Tang dynasties, preliminary examinations testing the content of Confucianism classics began for scholars taught at home. Wealthy and influential upper-class families often sponsored an edition of home schooling that focused on Confucianism's several decrees and regulations (Wang, 1999). Families hired private teachers to teach their children at home.

Another kind of private school, akin to today's charter schools, was sponsored by a group of community people or several families in a community. Children entered those schools at the age of 6. Later on, the government initiated Guan Xue, the first charter school in the Chinese education system. The curricula among different schools were similar. Some specialized schools focused on professions, much like technical/vocational schools in the United States that educate students for a specific occupation, such as electrician or plumber.

According to Chinese culture, the parents' primary childrearing duty is to ensure that their male child is well educated (San Zi Jing, 2005). One common saying reflecting this idea is *"Yang Bu Jiao, Fu Zi Guo"* ("It is the parent's fault, if they only give birth to the child instead of educating him") (San Zi Jing, 2004). Not only must parents make sure that their male children are educated according to the virtues of filial piety (*Xiao*), heavily emphasized by Confucianism, but male children also must honor their families and ancestors (Zhou, 2004). If children do not succeed in society, they will lose face in front of their families and ancestors.

Studying is another important principle of education in China. The belief is that those who nurture their minds by paying attention to their teachers and studying diligently will learn. Chinese society continues to place great emphasis on the relationship between students and teachers. Students are expected to show respect for their teachers. Traditionally, teaching was held to be a position of honor. Confucius taught that education means finding a good teacher and imitating his words and deeds (*Lun Yu*). While many ancient philosophies influenced Chinese society and its view of education, Confucianism continues to have great sway. An exception to this is the traditional bias against women. Confucianism proclaimed that "the best virtue of women is illiteracy." Women and morally corrupt men were considered to be "not educable." In 1949, the new government moved away from this traditional bias, giving women equal rights with men. It was then said that "women can hold up the half-sky," indicating that there is no difference between the genders.

Religion has had little or no impact on traditional Chinese education. Since the era of ancient China, around 500 BCE, the government always provided the most important influence on the education system. Scholarship was the major path to political power. Well-known scholars often became the famous politicians of their day. The rulers of society determined what was important for the citizens and provided direction on how people should conduct their lives. The tradition of politics and education working hand in hand is also reflected in current educational practices of modern China.

CHANGES IN EDUCATION BASED ON STAGES OF HISTORY

Since the communist revolution of 1949, we can point to four stages that have influenced curriculum in China. Within each stage, questions were raised about the tasks of curriculum development, teaching methodology, goals, and cultural issues. All of these stages affected the Chinese education system and changed the way students were taught.

First Stage: 1949-1965. Overemphasis on Political Development in the Education Curriculum

In October 1949, when the People's Republic of China was established, Chairman Mao announced to the whole world, "Chinese are standing up now" (Mao, 1997). During this time period, China followed the example of the former Soviet Union in creating its government, economy, and education policies.

The *Common Program (Gong Tong Gang Ling)*, developed by the Chinese People's Political Consultative Conference, provided a temporary constitution for the People's Republic of China. This policy stated that the People's Republic of China's education policy now provided democratic, ethical, scientific, and general cultural education for the common people. The government's educational goal sought to improve the intellectual level of individuals, foster leaders for the country, clean up feudalism, and eliminate *mai bang, fa xi Shism*. The latter phrase refers to individuals who rely on foreign capitalists' support in order to control the Chinese people. The Chinese government's goal is to have Chinese people in control of their own lives.

Chairman Mao believed that the main task of education is to serve the people. The *Common Program* also stated that theory and practice need to be the same. The People's government planned to reform the old education system's curriculum and methods, step by step. The policy sought to strengthen middle school education, higher education, professional education, and current leaders' education, while also focusing on technology. The purpose of change was to give both young and old intellectuals the political education to serve the needs of the new country, and to create new jobs. The new education policy also set up moral education standards promoting love of country, people, labor, science, and public property. This policy continues today.

On October 19, 1949, the government appointed new administrators for a Central Education Bureau. On November 1st, the Central Educational Bureau was created; it remains the highest administrative organization in China's education system to this day. The first national educators' conference was held in December of that year.

Four major tasks were to be completed from 1949 to 1957. The first task was to redesign the curriculum to reflect a change in philosophy from capitalism to socialism. The second task was to administer over all schools, including higher education. Third, the administration was to abolish the old education system entirely. Finally, the fourth task was to establish the socialist education system (Li & Wang, 1999).

The wars of this period drained Chinese financial resources, which meant that money to complete reform was insufficient. Schools were in poor condition and there were not enough trained teachers. The overall educational level of the population remained very low. A cultural leader was named to encourage towns to eliminate illiteracy and rally the citizens to embrace education. The educational charge for the towns was to foster cultural knowledge, and to love the communist party and its political ideals.

The Soviet Union aided the Chinese government and supported the development of the Chinese education system. Once the education system was developed throughout China, it was expected that people would popularize the importance of education. In new China, the government took over public and private schools, requiring them to embrace the new philosophy, educational policy, and curriculum. The private school became private in name only. Foreigners had managed large numbers of church schools, which were taken over by the government and forced to adopt the state school policies and curriculum. From November 1949 to 1951, there continued to be changes in all schools' curricula from elementary education through higher education. The Central Education Bureau studied, unified, and formulated the nationwide curriculum standard (Li & Wang, 1999; Mao & Shen, 2006).

In October 1951, there appeared a new initiative titled "Reform Educational System Decision." This plan divided the school system into five sections: kindergarten, primary education, middle education, higher education, and various political training centers (for various age groups and for the professional fields). Each section was considered a type of political training class. The Soviet model influenced the Chinese education system, from the specialized focus of political training to the program of instruction. A program to develop political leaders was also built within the system. The education structure provided a uniform teaching standard and a uniform plan of instruction for each grade level. The Central Education Bureau decided that this format provided integrity of instruction, as it was systematic for all learners, required specific teaching material, and determined the teacher's role in the education process. New curriculum plans were established in collaboration with scholars from the Soviet Union. Many teachers were sent to the Soviet Union for training in universal education policies.

In order to help eliminate illiteracy in the population, the government set up adult classes simultaneously in primary and middle schools. The peasants, farmers, and working class were expected to accelerate their learning by going to education classes during their non-working hours. The political appointees in each town rallied the townspeople to go to school for an education. The intensive training required three to four years to reach the middle school level. Upon completion of middle school, the individual then could go to university. The goal of this training was to provide foundational cultural knowledge, and to instill a deep love for the party and socialism. This educational goal was known as *Ren Ming Zheng Zhi*, which means a common political education that promotes the love of work and physical education. During the last half of the 1950s, all schools were set up for political education to study Mao Zedong philosophy.

In 1951, the first systematic academic year, cities who had enough resources were required to set up kindergarten education for children age 3-7, as well as primary education for children, youth, and some adults. The adults were those individuals, including factory workers and peasants, who did not know how to read and write. Primary education took five years. If children did not go to kindergarten, they would need one year of "preschool" before entering elementary education. Middle schools educated average youth and provided a more fast-paced educational setting for factory workers and peasants. In addition, there were professional technology schools similar to high schools, including fundamental normal schools, medical schools, and trade and business schools. An educational experience would take 12 years, including primary, middle school, and high school. Until 1958, this system was also called "6-3-3."

Higher education included college/university education, professional academy, and some technology colleges. This was a 3- to 5-year process. Besides these schools, political training schools and centers were also established for those intellectuals who received education prior to the establishment of the new government. This new academic focus emphasized primary and middle education for peasants, factory workers, and professional students' education (Li & Wang, 1999).

In 1951 to 1952, the Bureau of Central Education stated that the goals and principles of primary and middle school education were "to raise new generations who will be well developed in intelligence (cognitive), moral, physical, and aesthetic education, building the foundation for over all development" (Yao & Wang, 2005, p. 21).

In 1957, Chairman Mao stated, "Our education policy must ensure that students should become well developed morally, intelligently and physically, to make sure they understand socialism and are a well-educated and skilled labor force for the new country" (Yao & Wang, 2005, p. 22). In 1958, Mao initiated *Liang Ge Bi Xu* (Two Shoulds), which was the educational policy and philosophy of the communist party, which stated that education should serve proletariat politics and should unify productive labor and education (Yao & Wang, 2005). The previous two statements impacted the Chinese education profoundly for over 20 years.

By 1957, it was evident that a strict imitation of the Soviet Union's education model led to many problems. One major problem was that education instruction was theoretical and did not focus on real-world experiences. Thus, students were not able to adapt their knowledge to the professions. The Central Governing Committee of China, the Communist Party Committee, and the State Council, which were the highest authorities in China, sent out a directive called "Educational Work Instruction." This decree explicitly stated that education led by the communist party needed to serve proletariat politics and unify productive labor.

Many different kinds of educational ideas arose, some of which violated the established ideas of education. That same year, the *Fan-You* (anti-rightist) drive started. The "rightist" referred to those who were against socialism and who believed in capitalism. Before 1957, teachers, scholars, and professional intellectuals had been categorized as working class people. This anti-rightist drive expanded and claimed that all intellectuals believed in capitalism and so were targets for revolutionists. Many teachers were fired. The government sent "fired" teachers to "retraining classes" to help them rethink their philosophy in favor of the working class struggle.

In 1958, another political event happened in China, called "The Great Leap Forward." This event was aimed at accomplishing economic and technical development of the country at a faster pace and with greater results. The shift to the left that the new "General Line" represented was brought on by a combination of domestic and external factors. Chairman Mao and other party leaders were pleased with the First Five-Year Plan; however, they felt that, with the Second Five-Year Plan, more could be achieved if people were encouraged to be more efficient in their work in agriculture and industry. Improved ideological programming and an intensified mobilization of people, they believed, would help to develop a more responsive political system.

During this period, China attempted to break out of the limitations of the Soviet Union model. The government established a new socialist education system, which more readily blended with Chinese society by trying to link labor skills and education together. Education played a part in that movement because so many individuals followed the party plan and became literate. After touring China, Chairman Mao felt that Chinese people could accomplish anything. He believed that China should increase its economy, especially in areas of industry and agriculture. In order to do that, China was arranged in communes of approximately 5,000 people each. Nurseries and schools were formed within the communes, allowing adults to work and produce. The new focus became the factory farm and productive labor. The goals for adults' education fell by the wayside. Children continued to participate in nationalized elementary and middle school education; however, the quality of education declined during this period. The length of academic training changed to 10 years: five years for elementary education, three years for middle school, and two years for high school. The entry age for elementary education changed to 6 years old, instead of 7. The aim was for all children reaching the age of 16 or 17 to have received a 10-year education, and have the knowledge level necessary for a college education (Ye, 2006).

Chairman Mao's new thoughts challenged the learned scholars. His actions lessened the scholars' teaching authority. He also ended the replication of the Soviet Union's model. The change, however, overemphasized practical field experience and failed to provide the theory that was needed for a successful integration of theory and practice. This lack of theory interfered with the order of teaching dramatically. The school experience became chaotic and educational quality took a downward turn.

Overview of the Curriculum in the First Stage. During this first stage, four different curricula were implemented. The first curriculum started in September 1950. The government formed the People's Publishing House by the fall of 1951, which printed a curriculum that covered grades 1-12. The second curriculum was prepared in 1954-1955. This curriculum mainly adopted much of its content from the Soviet Union. The content proved too theoretical and too difficult to blend with the ideals of Chinese culture. The third curriculum was published in 1960 for grades 1-10. The Chinese government attempted to reduce the number of years for an education from 12 to 10 years. In 1961, the government began to edit another curriculum. This time, the emphasis was on language, math, and foreign language education. Unfortunately, these curricula were never formally used, due to the difficulty of content.

The Second Stage: 1966-1976. Politics Only

The 10-year Great Cultural Revolution occurred in China from May 1966 to October 1976. The entire nation was in chaos. The movement deeply hurt the economic development of China, which was a disaster for the Chinese people. The effect on education was very detrimental. In order to understand the effects on education, one must review the impact of the political factors.

In May of 1966, Chairman Mao wrote a letter to Lin Biao, stating that all professionals must excel in their profession; study politics, economics, culture, and work; and criticize capitalism. Students were taught this philosophy in the universities so they could, in turn, train future workers to embrace communism for a socialist society. The Chinese government started the Great Cultural Revolution to prevent capitalism from making inroads into the socialist system and to magnify the class struggle. On August 8, 1966, the Communist Party of China passed "The Great Proletarian Cultural Revolution's Decision." This document proposed reformation of the old education policies, system, and methods. Other goals were to reduce the academic year and totally reform the curriculum. It was decided that the curriculum needed to be simplified. Students not only needed to study culture, how to read and write, *Gong* (engineering, how to work as a factory worker), *Nong* (agriculture, how to be a farmer), and *Jun* (military training, how to be a soldier), they also needed to participate in the critique of the bourgeoisie as a necessary part of the Cultural Revolution (Li & Wang, 1999).

On August 1st of that year, Chairman Mao wrote a letter to the Red Guards (middle school students) in Qinghua University Lab School to support their behavior in destroying the bourgeoisie. On August 18th, Chairman Mao met with thousands of Red Guards. These students came from various places all over the country and they helped fan the flames of the Cultural Revolution. On August 19th, with the innocence, ignorance, curiosity, and excitement of youth, the first "Break the Four" happened in Beijing. This statement refers to the eradication of old thought, old culture, old customs, and out-of-date habits. The central governors did not explain how to "Break the Four." In late August, Beijing's Red Guards ran into the community and destroyed cultural and historical sites. They burned art, handicrafts, and other valuable mementos. The Red Guard imprisoned and even tortured to death the so-called class enemies and reactionary gang members. Lin Biao gave a speech at the rostrum of Tian An Men Square representing Mao Zedong and gave high praise to the Red Guards' actions. On August 22, the *People's Daily* carried two articles highly complimenting the students' actions. The government wanted the general population to support and follow the students.

After the "Great Cultural Revolution," the Red Guard was associated with horrible scenes of bloodshed and fighting. From August until the end of November, Chairman Mao met with 1,300,000 teachers and Red Guard members. Voices of opposition arose from all over the country. Even within the Red Guard, there was dissension, as not all agreed with the way the Cultural Revolution was going. At the end of 1966, almost all schools in the nation stopped educating due to the revolution. The government decided that students should experience work in factories. The placement of students in factories allowed time for workers to talk with the students. Production was interrupted and confusion abounded in society. In addition, other students were sent to the countryside to work with peasants. The use of students as workers helped convey the message of the Cultural Revolution throughout the country. The role of the teacher was repudiated during this time. There was a total critique of all that had been done for education over the past 17 years.

Teachers who objected to the Cultural Revolution suffered serious persecution. During the end of the 1960s and beginning of the 1970s, efforts were made to "clear up the class group." For example, about one-third of all teachers were fired and put into work camps. In Si Chuan province, 1,822 out of 31,193 teachers died, some of whom committed suicide, and 4,866 were fired from teaching. The majority of these teachers were considered excellent, experienced teachers. In 1965, there were 7,800 rank professors and associate professors in China. In 1977, only 5,800 teachers were left (Mao

& Sheng, 2006).

The massive cultural curriculum was reduced to "the class struggle," which became the main topic of learning. The principles of education were thoroughly changed. There were no differences between the engineering major and the agricultural major. All were taught about class struggle. Although elementary and middle schools still taught some basic language and mathematics, the quality of the education was deemed unimportant. The political struggle emerged as the most important topic. Every day in school, teachers and students were involved in the political struggle. The movement left this entire generation of China uncultured and in need of education.

After middle school students in the city graduated, they needed to involve themselves in the life of the country; they were sent to hard labor for their physical and mental well-being. Students who graduated from the middle school and whose political thinking was correct would be the only ones recommended for university. The length of a college education was reduced to three years instead of four. There were no college admission exams. A recommendation from a party member in authority was all that was necessary to enroll in college. Students went to college not to study culture, but mainly to learn from Mao Zedong's writings. From 1966, at the start of the "Great Cultural Revolution," colleges stopped recruiting students for six years. The graduate schools stopped recruiting students for 12 years and also stopped accepting foreign graduate students for seven years. The Ministry of Education was paralyzed for more than 8 years, causing an enormous hole in the education of Chinese people (Li & Wang, 1999).

Another tragedy during this time was that many urban middle school students were sent to work in the countryside, far away from home, into very remote areas. This hardship traumatized these students and affected their emotional well-being. The students experienced social and psychological problems.

Overall, the main character of elementary and middle school curriculum during this time emphasized the political class struggles due to the Cultural Revolution until the end of 1976. None of the schools had any curriculum as such to teach. In February 1967, the central government called students back to class. The curricula became as follows: 1st- through 4th-grade students were to study Chairman Mao's words, learn how to read, write some characters, and memorize revolutionary songs, as well as master some basic math and science. Fifth- and 6th-grade students were to memorize Chairman Mao's words as well as his articles that were published before 1949 (Mao & Shen, 2006), along with many revolutionary songs.

During farming seasons, all teachers and students were expected to go to the countryside to work. Later in 1967, soldiers were sent to schools to organize the students as soldiers. Time for school was reduced. Elementary school was five years; middle school and high school were two years each. Later on, elementary school curriculum included political language, math, revolutionary music, military physical education, and labor education. The curriculum for middle school consisted of Chairman Mao's educational theory, basic agriculture, revolutionary music, military physical education, and labor education. All curricula for middle school and high school education, and even for early childhood education, were required to recognize the pitfalls of capitalism and to struggle against them.

Third Stage: 1977-2000. Recovering Education

In 1976, Mao Zedong died. The death of this powerful Chinese leader and the overthrow of the "Gang of Four" ended the Great Cultural Revolution. China started to gradually reform and develop an open policy. This is when education began to revive and reorganize. Classes resumed in school buildings, additional schools were built, and teachers were rehabilitated and returned to classrooms. Teachers once again were honored and revered. Their salaries improved and social conditions for them changed. The following changes occurred:

Elementary and Middle School Education. In the late 1970s, elementary and middle schools began to teach new material for nine years of compulsory education. Classroom instruction and tests became standardized. The government developed two kinds of schools for the high school level. One school was for general studies, which allowed students to pursue advanced coursework. The other type of school was developed for vocational and technical jobs.

In January 1978, the Chinese Ministry of Education issued the "Full-time Ten-Year System Elementary and Middle Schools Plan of Instruction Implementation Draft." The unification document stipulated that the curricula for elementary and middle schools had to be full time. The breakdown of the 10 years of schooling were: elementary school for 5 years, middle school for 5 years (further broken down into 3 years of junior middle school), and high school for 2 years.

In December 1980, the Central Committee of the Chinese Communist Party and the State Council sent out the "Popularization of Primary Education Certain Question Decision," which changed the education system. It proposed that the elementary and middle schools program would gradually change to a 12-year system. The education system changed quickly. Elementary school went to six years, the junior middle school changed to three years, and the high school changed to three years. The school year started in September instead of the spring.

The Ministry of Education organized experts in various disciplines to enrich the school instruction. The Ministry compiled the national general elementary and middle school programs of instruction and textbooks. Certain aspects of foreign elementary and middle school teaching materials also were adopted (Mao & Shen, 2006). Classroom instruction and tests were standardized. The teaching in elementary and middle schools focused more on the results of learning. Competition among schools arose, as schools wanted to recruit better quality students so they could prepare those students to get into colleges at a competitively higher rate.

For 20 years, the college entrance examination system trained large numbers of talented people to teach in the elementary and middle schools. This action gave China a big advantage. Now, the Chinese government pays for nine years of universal compulsory education (6 years of elementary school and 3 years of middle school). Students who need more years have to pay on their own after nine years, unless they are peasants. The primary school-age matriculation rate is now 99.7%. The middle school pupil matriculation rate is above 88.6%. The illiteracy rate for 15-year-olds dropped to 8.72%. The country realized its two goals of popularizing the compulsory education plan and reducing illiteracy among youth. At the same time, preschool and high school education became a new focus for reform (Li & Wang, 1999).

Changes in Elementary School Curriculum. The elementary school curriculum has benefited from a strengthening of the relationship between math, the Chinese language, and foreign languages with other curriculum areas. The fundamental curriculum in China is dependent upon a strong curriculum in language, mathematics, and foreign language. Foreign language class starts at the lower grades instead of at middle school. If students have difficulty and fail one of these subjects at their grade level, they remain at that grade until they pass.

The study of general science begins with 1st-grade students. Calligraphy classes begin in elementary school. At the junior middle school level, students are introduced to labor technology classes. In elementary school, junior middle school, and high school, the curriculum includes computer science, logic, economics, cooking, environmental science, sewing, and household management and other life skills.

Reforms were enacted to teach using methods that support students' abilities. More time has been given to the students for self-study, instead of direct lectures. In the elementary and middle schools, various teaching methods were adopted emphasizing the slogan "take the teacher as the leadership, take the student as the main body" (Mao & Shen, 2006, p. 316). The purpose of these reforms and new teaching methods was to inspire students' self-motivation and independent study. The belief is that these reforms will produce students, starting from the lower grades, who will be quick to learn and develop into excellent scholars. The idea is similar to developmentally appropriate practices, emphasizing student-centered classroom teaching and problem-solving skills.

Although the government is the primary manager of elementary and middle schools, it has allowed industry and mining businesses to become involved. This action has opened China to private schools once again. The businesses pay for needs of the elementary and middle schools. This structure permits schools to exist based on a market economy.

Higher Education. In 1977, the test for entrance admission into college was restored after being stopped for six years, and enrollment in higher education increased rapidly. From 1977 to 1981, there was an increase in college enrollment from 625,000 to 1,279,000 students. In China in 2000, there were 1,041 national ordinary universities and 772 professional universities. In 1977, the Ministry of Education restored and established various branches of colleges and teaching materials became more available.

The following curricula were reinstated by 1979: science subjects, engineering, agricultural curriculum, and medical curriculum. Part-time education opportunities also were restored. In 1981, the country authorized China's first batch of doctoral and master's degree awards (Mao & Shen, 2006). Along with developments in higher education, many other new educational questions appeared, compelling the Chinese government to quickly reform.

The usual close relationship between education and politics changed to a more important relationship of education and economics. In the fall of 1983, the Chinese leader Deng Xiaoping spoke to the Beijing Jingshan School during his inspection visit. He offered words of encouragement about the new educational movement. He commented, *"Jiao Yu Bi Xu Mian Xiang Xian Dai, Mian Xiang Shi Jie, Mian Xiang Wei Lai,"* which means that education curriculum must involve how to solve problems the country faces. The country's challenges are modernization, current world issues, and the future. This idea became known as the "three Mian Xiang's in education." Later on, Deng Xiaoping published "three Mian Xiang's" ideas, which became the policy of education (Mao & Shen, 2006, p. 266). This policy indicated the direction for China's education curriculum development and had a significant influence upon it. The policy encouraged people to be open minded, to rethink educational ideas that would reform education in a deeper direction, and to promote educational reform for all-around development. Deng Xiaoping's thoughts played a historic and strategic role in the current education system in China (Xin Hua Wang, 2003).

The Communist Party of China made it clear from 1978 that China must shift its emphasis from the national work of political struggle to economic development and education. China also desired to become part of the new technological revolution that was beginning in 1984. The Chinese government's hope was to make education special and make the curriculum increase the knowledge base of students, encourage technology development, and make China a force in the world market.

Another goal of reform was the emphasis on fostering students' problem-solving abilities. Although reform has changed curriculum, teaching methodology in China lacks creativity. Memorization of material is still considered extremely important. Time for independent study has increased while teaching time has been reduced. The link between theory and practice moved to the forefront requiring more of a balance. Students must take foreign language and computer training. Students are expected to study and be able to demonstrate increased knowledge and ability in each course. Students are also expected to engage in extracurricular activities so their college experience will be enriched and they will have the opportunity to develop socially.

Government funding was no longer the sole source of education funding; foreign private individuals, local associations, and businesses contributed funds to run schools. College students receive stipends from the government and do not have to pay tuition. Elementary and middle school students pay only a little tuition along with some other miscellaneous expenses. Slowly, China began to look to other countries, especially the United States, for ideas in education.

Changing Pattern of Higher Education. Typically, higher education students would go to school full-time. However, the majority of people in China did not have the economic means to do so. In addition, it was difficult to educate the massive population of potential college students and to accommodate them at a university. Since the Great Cultural Revolution, the government struggled with how to educate the population. In 1980, the government developed broadcast television education, started correspondence courses, and evening university. These new avenues established a part-time education system for the first time in higher education. More of the population was able to take advantage of higher education at less cost and regardless of their job.

College Admission Reform. Beginning in 1977, with the adjustment of college admission practices, the method was now to have national exams on assigned dates, once a year. Students were divided into two groups—social science and natural science majors—according to the students' overall scores. Enrollment in the colleges was filled strictly by the score achieved by the individual student. Most thought the method was rigid, yet fair.

Starting in 1984, China allowed those with lower scores greater opportunity to fill places available at colleges. In 1985, there were 72 colleges that waived the college entrance exam and accepted the top students recommended by their current schools. Although the recommended students did not need to participate in the college entrance exams, they had to show evidence of being morally sound, physically fit, and well-prepared intellectually. All students must pass an interview by the college representatives.

Changes in Graduate Job Assignment. After 1983, the government changed its practice of assigning jobs to college graduates. Instead, the government began to allow the supply and demand of the market to determine job availability. Students began to choose their jobs, which were based more on their interests, and schools and employers developed a mutual understanding of what was needed in order to meet the concerns of the market.

In China, the prospect of a college education deeply impacts K-12 education. Even today, kindergarten children's activities are preparing them for college entrance. Such extracurricular activities as piano lessons and Ping-Pong have national standards. Children attaining the highest rank of the program receive 10 extra points for college admission.

During 1980-1990, college students were viewed as "sons of heaven." They received government subsidies for living expenses until they found a job. The belief was that these students would bring glory to the community, school, and family. College students receive many privileges in society, reflecting the traditional thoughts of China. It does not matter what kind of socio-economic class you belonged to, as long as you pass the test. The educated child is thought to be in a position next to a king. This is why the Chinese put a lot of importance on education. The revival of educational standards has sped China's movement toward becoming a modern nation.

Fourth Stage: 2001-Present
Conforming to Educational Trends of the Modern World (Europe/America)

During the past 20 years, the education system in China recovered and developed dramatically. By the year 2000, nine sets of different curricula were used with children ages 6 to 18 years (www.moe. edu.cn/edoas/website18/72/info7072.htm). Up to that point, the curriculum raised serious challenges because it focused on content of subject areas, but neglected the students' socio-emotional development. Teachers and students could not freely exchange ideas. There was a lack of cooperation and no opportunity for the student to develop individually. Common learning standards were stressed while individual differences were ignored.

Overall, the curriculum structure overemphasized a single standard for each subject area. Not all students were able to demonstrate strengths in all areas, such as mechanics or machinery training. Since only one standard was set for all the students in each area, individual students' needs or abilities were ignored. Student assessments focused on academic achievement, to the neglect of full-scale development. Many educators believed this curriculum lacked creativity and effectiveness.

In 1999, the Third National Educational Work Conference was held at Beijing, hosted by the Central Committee of the Chinese Communist Party and the State Council. At the meeting, the Comprehensive Advancement Education for All-Around Development was introduced. On June 13, 1999, the Chinese Communist Party and State Council announced Policy No. 9, 1999, called "The decision of in-depth reform of overall education." It stated that the curriculum implemented education for all-around development in order to make China a partner in the world education system. The curriculum sought to prepare students to be citizens of the world and was appropriate with respect to age, local areas, and social-emotional differences. The curriculum changed the content of the courses so that the courses reflected more practical applications (Education Department Policy www.chinalawedu.com/news/1200/22598/22615/22793/2006/3/he7396032197360029150-0.htm).

In June 2001, the National Elementary Education workshop convened in Beijing. Prior to the meeting, "The State Council Decision of Elementary Education Reform" and the "Reform of the Elementary Education Curriculum (Draft)" were promulgated, which proposed the new comprehensive curriculum reform emphasizing the humanist spirit. In addition to course content, attention would now be paid to students' interests, experiences, and physical well-being. The teacher became the organizer, mentor, and facilitator of instruction. The detailed curriculum content of the compulsory nine-year education suggested by the Central Education Department consisted of moral education (7-9%); history/social studies (3-4%); science (7-9%); Chinese language (20-22%); math (13-15%); physical education (10-11%); foreign language (6-8%); art, including music, art appreciation (9-11%); and local curriculum—field experience (16-20%) (Jiao Ji, 2001, No. 28).

By 2005, the government opened more schools with the reformed curriculum until 27 provinces within the country had complied with the changes. The new curriculum pays significant attention to the humanist spirit in course content. Children's emotional development is recognized as important to learning. The curriculum highlights innovation and provides more time for practice of skills. Science, humanities, and environmental awareness are all part of the curriculum. Teachers recognize the importance of students becoming lifelong learners, having vigorous, healthy bodies and spirit. They foster aesthetics and a healthy lifestyle. The curriculum focuses on children's developmental level, practical skills, and students' interests and experiences (Yao & Wang, 2005, p. 42-48).

The new curriculum also focuses on content instruction. It requires the acquisition of information that directly correlates with the student's life experience and its relationship to society. The curriculum emphasizes the need for students to actively participate in their own learning. It encourages students to develop problem-solving and analyzing skills in order to gain new knowledge. The curriculum stresses the importance of cooperative learning and caring about each other as students prepare to be successful citizens in a global society.

Conclusion

The positive impact of curriculum change is evident for today's students and teachers in China. Since 1977, the Chinese government has emphasized education, including elementary and middle school levels. This progress in education is an important symbol of China's development. China has developed into the world's fourth largest economy. Whether or not China continues to prosper, a sustainable foundation has been constructed and is rooted in the development of the education system and a well-educated Chinese citizen.

References

Education Department Policy. (2006). Retrieved December 12, 2008, frp, www.chinalawedu.com/news/12 00/22598/22615/22793/2006/3/he7396032197360029150-0.htm)

Jiao Ji 2001. No. 28 (2004). Retrieved December 12, 2008, from www.moe.edu.cn/edoas18/level3,jsp?tabl ename=32&infoid=417

Li, G., & Wang, B. (1999). *The history of Chinese education*. Shangdong, P.R. China: Shandong Education Press.

Lu, D. (2000). The people's publishing house. Retrieved December 14, 2008, from www.moe.edu.cn/edoas/ website18/72/info7072.htm

Mao, L., & Shen, G. (2006). *General history of Chinese education*. Shangdong, P.R. China: Shandong Education Press.

Mao, Z. (1997). *Selected works of Mao Zedong* (Vol. 5). People's Publishing Agency.

San Zi Jing. (2005). Retrieved May 6, 2008, from http://blog.china.alibaba.com/blog/gzzengweihua/article/ b0-i1107785.html

Si Shu Wu Jing. (2004). Retrieved June 12, 2004, from www.sunpride.com.cn/backup/myweb/si/lunyu005. html.

Wang, L. (1999). *The study of early childhood education*. Chang Chun, China: Northeastern Normal University Press.

Wang, X. H. (2003). Retrieved August 2, 2007, from http://news.xinhuanet.com/edu/2003-09/16/content_ 1082526 & http://acc6.its.brooklyn.cuny.edu/~phalsall/chinbib.html.

Yao, D., & Wang, M. (2005). *The changes among the fundamental education*. Anhui, China: Hefei Industry University Press.

Ye, L. (2006). *Xin Ji Chu JiaoYu Lun*. Beijing, P.R. China: Science and Education Press.

Zhou, D. (2004). *The moral education of confusionsim*. Retreived October 8, 2004, from http://course33. gzedu.com/A1006/text/t03005039.doc/

About the Authors

Nili Luo, Ed.D., was born in China. She studied at East Normal University, Shanghai, China, in the school of education and did her doctoral work at University of Massachusetts, Amherst. She was a middle school teacher in China and served as assistant professor, lecturer, and associate professor in one of the key universities in Anhui Province for over 10 years. Luo continues to supervise curriculum development in the Welfare Institute in China. Currently, she serves as professor and director of Early Childhood Education at Southwestern College, Winfield, Kansas. For the past three summers, she conducted research, lectured, and taught many educational workshops in China. nili.luo@sckans.edu

Janet S. Arndt, Ed.D., is an assistant professor of education at Gordon College, Wenham, Massachusetts. She has researched and written with Luo on such topics as social-emotional well-being in Chinese schools and Chinese nutrition and physical health. In February 2008, she was awarded a faculty initiative grant to conduct a cross-cultural study of early childhood programs in China and the United States. janet.arndt@gordon.edu

Curriculum Development in the Czech Republic

Ferdinand Mazal, Jiri Stelzer, and Zuzana Vasickova

The Czech Republic has only existed as an independent state since 1993, but the history of the country, including that concerning the development of its educational pedagogy and curricula, is long and rich. The two are closely linked and a full appreciation of the latter requires an understanding of the country's historical development. The emergence of educational institutions in what were at the time the Czech Lands (Bohemia, Moravia, and Czech Silesia) began during the 10th century as a part of the Holy Roman Empire and continued under the influence of many different totalitarian systems until 1989. These early schools were religiously affiliated with such organizations as the Jesuits, Unity of the Brethren, and local churches, staffed by clergy, housed at monasteries and cathedrals, and served as the sole means of formal education until municipally financed schools made an appearance in the 13th century. At that time, the Czech Lands expanded to Moravia, Silesia, Lusatia, Brandenburg, New Bohemia, and Luxembourg. The curriculum in the early public schools focused on training clerks and other municipal employees, and the programs were initially taught by clergymen. Later on, teachers were drawn from the ranks of graduates of the faculty of arts from Charles University.

Charles University, the first university in the Czech lands, was established in Prague in 1348 by the Czech king and reigning Roman emperor Charles IV. Originally, the university consisted of four faculties, or colleges: arts, medicine, law, and theology. Because Charles University was one of the older higher education institutions in Europe, it maintained a strong positive influence on both the Czech territories and surrounding European countries for several centuries. The Czech Lands were considered to be the most educated countries in all of Europe, a position they held for several centuries (Chaloupecky, 1948). In 1573, the second oldest university, Olomouc, was founded with two faculties: liberal arts and theology. Today, Olomouc is known as Palacky University.

Czech Republic

The Czech Lands existed in different variations until the end of World War I (1918), when the country of Czechoslovakia was formed. Czechoslovakia combined Bohemia, Moravia, Silesia, Slovakia, and Carpathian Ruthenia (formally known as Ukraine). Until the beginning of World War II, Czechoslovakia was a prosperous and moderate democratic republic. During World War II, most of Czechoslovakia was occupied by Nazi Germany and Slovakia became a client state of Nazi Germany. After World War II (1945), Czechoslovakia was re-established and from 1948 until 1989 was under the influence of the Union of Soviet Socialist Republics (the USSR).

During the 20th century, Czech school curricula reflected a combination of the ethos of the country; the many social, political, and economic factors that influenced decisions over time; and, most important, the philosophical changes that occurred since the country moved from a closed, totalitarian system into an open, democratic society in 1989. This transformation caused a break from the past and closer alignment with the current thinking of other European Union member states.

The 17th Century

Widespread access to education for the general population of the Czech Lands began in the 17th century. The emphasis for this movement is attributed to the noted philosopher Jan Amos Comenius (1592-1670), who is known as "the teacher of nations." Comenius advocated the view that education should be a lifelong opportunity available to all citizens regardless of social status or gender, and promoted the concepts of precise age-based levels of learning and a coeducational classroom format. His translated works were circulated and applied across Europe and eventually, following European migration, in North America.

The 18th Century

The Age of Enlightenment spawned numerous philosophical, social, and economic changes throughout Europe in the 18th century, including major reforms in education. The impetus for these changes stemmed primarily from recognition by the nobility and ruling classes that an illiterate population produced an illiterate labor pool, and this shortfall was an obstacle to economic growth and development. Schools, teachers, curricula, and teaching methods of education underwent a major evolution during this roughly 100-year period.

Maria Theresa (1741-1780), the queen of Hungary, Croatia, and Bohemia, issued a new Universal School Regulation act in 1774, which established three types of compulsory schools: 1) trivial–1 year, 2) principal–3 years, and 3) normal–6 years (see Appendix 1). The trivial schools could be taught in Czech rather than in German; the other two types were taught in German. The trivial schools covered reading, writing, arithmetic, religious training, and the basics of economy and industry, and were taught in parsonages. The principal schools covered social studies, Latin, stylistics, drawing, and geometry, and were taught in towns. The normal schools were located only in major cities and covered the same content as the trivial and principal schools but, as a consequence of a longer time period, the content was covered in greater detail. These three types of schools were not connected and did not constitute a system of schools as we know it in the present structure; however, these schools provided fundamental education to all children, regardless of their social status. The trivial schools were funded locally; the principal and normal schools were funded by the state (Vesela, 1992).

Although the act in 1774 introduced "six years of compulsory education" (trivial, principal, and normal), the term cannot be understood as a compulsory school attendance regulation; it just required mastering the content of knowledge, not the obligation to attend school on a daily basis throughout the whole year. This was especially true for children living in the country, who attended school, for the most part, only in winter. It was incumbent upon them and on their teachers to master everything they needed to pass their final examinations, which were attended by a church supervisor.

After the act was passed in 1774, the number of schools in the Czech Lands grew extensively. In 1780, there were 1,891 trivial schools and 12 principal schools. In 1790, there were 2,168 trivial and several other types of schools and 20 principal schools educating 142,000 children out of the total 239,000 children of school age. This system of elementary education operated until 1869.

This period is also marked by the emergence of secondary schools—gymnasiums. Gymnasiums became the centers of liberal scholarship and facilitated the inclusion of other subjects into education. Most of the students who studied at secondary schools were from the wealthy classes and were preparing for university studies. However, the state did not consider universities places of liberal scholarship, but rather institutions preparing young people, most of all, for life practice. Despite that, the quality of university education grew quickly in the fields of medicine, natural science, history, literature, and law.

At the same time, along with the new school regulations, a new institution for teachers' education emerged. These preparatory schools were usually a separate part of secondary schools, and they concentrated on preparing teachers with the educational content of normal or principal schools and lessons of pedagogy and didactics. The preparatory schools became an institutional platform for the education of teachers and gave support to establishing the field of education as a social profession.

The 19th Century

In the 19th century, nations within the multi-national empire sought to establish national education systems, including teaching in the national languages. However, Austria-Hungary strove to keep its central control and preserved German as the official language. The effort of the individual nations to establish their independence within the empire led to revolution in 1848, which was suppressed by the government.

An act issued in 1868 meant an important turning point concerning the education system, since it established strictly secular education for the first time in history. It covered the basic principles of the relationship between schools and church and introduced the non-confessional schools for the first time. The administration of the schools was turned over to local, district, and state school councils. From that time, the Church retained only the organization of school religious education and could establish private schools for children of a particular confession.

One year later, in 1869, an Education Act that modified education in the Austro-Hungarian Empire passed, which introduced compulsory general schooling for eight years (Váňa, 1963). Compulsory school attendance was required when a child reached the age of 6 and continued until the end of his or her 13th year (see Appendix 2). A child could legally avoid the schooling obligation if he or she proved mastery of the needed competences prescribed for general schools (i.e., reading, writing, and counting). Children could be exempted from general school attendance if they attended schools of a higher level, if they were mentally or physically disabled, or if they were educated privately. The act significantly extended the content of education to be learned by students, and it also specified the requirement of university education for teachers of compulsory education.

The act restricted compulsory education to general and municipal schools (see Appendix 2). Principally, the curriculum of general schools stressed developing children's morality, piety, and knowledge. The content of education involved religious studies, language, counting, cultural studies, writing, geometry, singing, and physical training. Girls were educated in handwork and housekeeping.

Municipal schools were intended to provide better education than the one offered by general schools. The curriculum contained such subjects as religious studies, language and writing, geography, history, natural science, biology, arithmetic, geometry, bookkeeping, drafting and drawing, neat handwriting, singing, and physical education. Similar to the practice at general schools, girls were taught handwork and housekeeping. German lessons were recommended at non-German municipal schools. The act allowed lessons in other foreign languages as well. Neither of these two types of school prepared pupils purposely for further studies, as most of those who left school sought employment. Those aiming for universities had to enter secondary schools, which were not great in number, and charged tuition.

The duration of secondary grammar schools changed from 5 years to 8 years. At the end of the 8th year, every student had to take an examination. Passing the examination was a mandatory requirement for entering a university. Latin and Greek occupied 58% of school time. Nevertheless, the share taken up by mathematics, natural science, humanities, and languages gradually increased (Váňa, 1963; Veselá, 1992).

At the same time, a new type of secondary school—vocational school, or so-called "real schools"— emerged. Natural science and technical subjects formed the core of education and, in contrast to grammar schools, the students were prepared for studies at technical universities (see Appendix 2). The development of technology and industry in Europe as well as in the Czech Lands led to the establishment of the first Czech technical university. After 1867, the more practically oriented secondary schools expended more on their education programs, and started to provide general courses rather than only technically oriented subjects. The schooling became structured into seven years and finished with a school-exit examination, enabling the students to pursue tertiary education at all universities, not just technical universities.

Secondary schools for girls were established at the end of the 19th century. Up to that point, there had been no such schools. They were the result of the women's fight for emancipation and equality in education. The first grammar school for girls was founded in 1890 in Prague and bore the name "Minerva." Societal mores meant that girls were required to attend separate schools. Minerva was the real beginning of higher education for girls in Central Europe. Universities opened to girls later; graduates of girls' gymnasium (grammar) schools could enter faculties of arts beginning in 1896 and medical faculties starting in 1900. That same year, the demand from girls for education urged the state to establish six-year secondary schools called "girls' lyceum" (see Appendix 2). The course consisted of religious studies, Czech, German, and French languages, history, geography, mathematics, natural science, biology, drawing, handwriting, and physical training.

Of great importance in the system of education was the creation of the first Czech nursery school in 1869, which marked the beginning of world-class quality in this field in the Czech Lands. The nursery schools were educating little children who were not yet eligible for school attendance, thus introducing preschool education.

The 20th Century

The establishment of an independent Czechoslovakia in 1918 after WWI did not cause an immediate change of the education law. The school system had to be transformed gradually and procedurally. The principles of civil republican upbringing had been deeply rooted in the people of the Czech lands. It formed a matrix for following these principles: democratic policies in education, offering equal chances to all children, a free education, and secular schools.

The 1919 minority school act defined the grounds for national minority schools in regions where a population of different nationalities prevailed. These schools were established in every community with at least 40 children of different nationalities, based on a three-year average. The aim was not participation but support of Czech interests in regions with a population majority of German and other nationalities. The act ensured eight-year school attendance throughout Czechoslovakia. It introduced two new subjects for boys—civics and handwork—and restored the obligation of physical training for girls. In addition, it recommended parity between male and female teachers and a decrease in the pupil-teacher ratio to 60 pupils to one teacher (Kadner, 1929).

The influence of so-called experimental schools during the 1920s and then the introduction of reform designed by Vaclav Příhoda (1931) were of significant importance in compulsory education. Příhoda studied at Columbia University's Teachers College and the University of Chicago, the two great springs of modern educational ideas in the United States. He was an enthusiastic supporter of the educational theories of philosopher John Dewey. When Příhoda returned to Czechoslovakia, he was appointed as a head of a national school reform committee by Socialist Education Minister Ivan Dérer. Under Příhoda's leadership, the reform committee started a few progressive schools;

by 1933, the Ministry of Education officially ordered a revision of the curriculum for the entire country, permitting progressive methods in all schools.

These schools, which, for their time, used quite progressive methods, were intended to attest to principles of reformation pedagogy. The new ideas emphasized artistic and working training, lessons without the school bell, individualized education, self-study, group lessons, decrease in number of subjects taught at the same time, pupils' progress structured according to subjects, no grades, retake of only the subjects that a pupil had failed (not the entire grade), new education principles (natural situation and reaction, lesson dynamism, globalization), new education methods (problem-based, project-based), new types of assessment (didactic tests, classification), etc. Příhoda (1930) also criticized the contemporary school system, indicating that it was undemocratic because it preferred children of rich parents and it limited equal chances of all children. He proposed a modification of the school system based on unified but internally differentiated schools. Although the reforms were not understood at that time, for the first time they documented the limited validity of some principles of pedagogy and contributed to the re-opening of the debates concerning the purpose of schools and education (Vanova, 1995, 2000). Deprived of the support of both the theoreticians and the public, the experiments dissolved during the 1920s.

Education plans of the general and municipal schools were modified in 1933 so that the difference between the two types of schools decreased. Secondary schools continued to provide comprehensive education in both the gymnasia (grammar) and real schools. Language competence was necessary for education at that time, and all secondary schools devoted half of the school time to language learning. Secondary education was completed with a school-exit examination *maturita,* which entitled the graduates to enter a university. However, all attempts to systematically reform the education system were cut off by the Munich Treaty in 1938, and then by the war (1939-1945).

The End of WWII

The war and its bloodshed left Europe and its schooling system in ruins. Social ideology changed in Czechoslovakia, along with the shift in political influence. Czechoslovakia had been liberated from Hitler's Germany, only to have Soviet troops stationed there. Understandably, the ideology and social missions and goals of the curricula and schools changed as well. The act establishing unified schools was issued in April 1948, after the 1948 revolution in which the Communist Party of Czechoslovakia took power (Váňa, 1963). Comprehensive general education was introduced for youth from 6 to 14 years of age. Compulsory school attendance increased to a total of nine years. From that time on, the education system was divided into nursery schools (for children ages 3-6), general schools—1st level (5 years), and general schools—2nd level (4 years). Secondary education, which consisted of gymnasia (grammar) and technical schools (4 years) were preparatory schools for the universities. Finally, the vocational schools (3 years) prepared students for manufacturing jobs (see Appendix 3).

These organizational transformations brought about changes in the content, too. Schools were interlinked with society; they had to comply with the overall politics of the Communist party. Their goal was to bring up "politically conscious citizens of a people's democratic state." The new subject of civics (originally, political education) was designed to support conscious upbringing; nevertheless, religious studies were taught at the same time at both levels of the compulsory education (Dejiny skolstvi v Ceskoslovensku, 1982). All the transformations were formally supplied with new educational objectives, plans, curricula, and textbooks. The act was implemented for only four years. The continuity of Czech education was interrupted, apparently due to economic problems and political pressure.

A New Act in 1953

The act in 1953 introduced some changes (Zákon o školské soustavě a vzdělávání učitelů, 1953). The length of compulsory education decreased to eight years and secondary education—gymnasia (grammar) and vocational schools—decreased to three years. Only the technical secondary education lasted for four years (see Appendix 4).

The one-year shortening of general education significantly increased the requirements for pupils. Such subjects as history, geography, and biology started as early as in the 4th grade, replacing traditional subjects, including introduction to science, homeland study, and writing. Pupils failed more often. On the other hand, the quality of polytechnic, physical, and aesthetic training increased (Váňa, 1963).

Nevertheless, the overall drop in the quality of education was dealt with at the Eleventh Communist Party of Czechoslovakia Convention in 1958; these meetings always set plans for further political, economic, and social development. The main idea of schooling was set: schooling should create a close connection between the school and life. For example, a student of a secondary school was to master not only the fundamentals of sciences but also of manufacturing. A graduate of such a school had to learn skills for a working career (Váňa, 1963).

The New Act From 1960

This act again extended the compulsory school attendance to nine years (Zákon o soustavě výchovy a vzdělávání, 1960). Specialized classes were introduced (i.e., music, physical training), and a foreign language (Russian) was taught. Secondary education went back to gymnasium and technical schools (4 years) and vocational schools (three years). Vocational schools were intended to increase the qualification of employed people and the working class as the leading power in society. They were put on the same level as comprehensive secondary schools and in the form of boarding schools, and were designed to provide a complete secondary education, with a school-exit certificate after successful termination of studies. The practice, however, did not fulfill these expectations; companies did not have enough capacity for accepting students in practical training. Practical training in manufacturing was canceled as a subject after several years.

Education and Curricula After 1989

The remarkable political-societal and socio-economic changes that took place in Czechoslovakia after the fall of communism in November 1989, have logically resulted in fundamental legal, educational, organizational, and, in particular, ideological-pedagogical changes in the field of education and training and their management. This kind of transformation of the concepts of content, organization, and management has also brought about changes in the respective education acts and related binding regulations, as well as in the creation of new legal standards, especially considering the current international documents and recommendations in the field of education and training. However, many experts claim that the present-day school system remains, from a structural perspective, very similar to the Unified School Act of 1948 (Walterova, 2006). The curriculum changes that were to be implemented immediately after 1989 were:

- Diversify education as a result of abolishing the state monopoly on education, establish private schools and schools with alternative concepts, and consider the possibility of school and class profiling
- Remove the communist ideological concepts observed in civics, history, and literature; introduce the possibility of choosing a foreign language; and introduce previously taboo topics, such as sex education, works in literature, and arts by authors who had been banned by the communists
- Liberalize curricular policy by loosening the central standards and partially decentralizing and giving more control to schools in the development of curriculum (by loosening the education plan standardized by the state, widening the choice of optional and non-compulsory subjects offered at a given school, loosening the time schedule of the subjects, and increasing the flexibility for the teacher to devote up to 30% of the class to the topics of his or her choice)
- Stress the curriculum toward humanistic and anthropological directions (i.e., areas that were poorly covered in the communist era), which meant giving more attention to arts and humanities in the education plan and enhancing students' critical thinking in these areas

- Reduce factual learning and emphasizing more critical thinking in students, including ideas and activities that enhance creative thinking, etc.
- Allow teachers to choose methods and forms of instruction.

Most of the above changes have been implemented; some of them are still in the process of being implemented (Walterova, 2006). Walterova (2006) believes that the main reasons why some of the recommendations have not yet been implemented is because there are unskilled and untrained school administrators and unprepared teachers who don't know how to implement the new curricular changes.

The present education system (see Appendix 5) of the Czech Republic consists of kindergartens (nursery schools), compulsory education, secondary education (gymnasia, technical schools, vocational schools, apprenticeships, and conservatories), and universities.

Pupils attend school from Monday to Friday. There are no classes on weekends. In addition to morning classes, afternoon classes are held once or twice a week. The school year begins on September 1, and ends on August 31 of the following year. The main summer holidays (two months) are in July and August. There is a one-week holiday in spring, with other short holidays in the fall, at Christmas, and at Easter.

Kindergartens strive to develop children's emotional, cognitive, and physical domains, and to build life values and interpersonal relationships. The parents are charged a small fee to enroll their children in a kindergarten.

Compulsory education has two levels: the first level covers 1st to 5th grade, and the second level covers 6th to 9th grade. In the first level, all subjects are usually taught by a generalist teacher; at the second level, subjects are taught by teachers specializing in two subjects or, exceptionally, in one subject. Classes are coeducational. Since 1990, compulsory education has been established by municipalities. People have the right to a basic education, free of charge. The number of contact hours per week is as follows (The Ministry of Education, Youth and Sports, 2001):

First Stage	**Second Stage**
Year 1 – 20 lessons	Year 6 – 28 lessons
Year 2 – 22 lessons	Year 7 – 29 lessons
Year 3 – 23 lessons	Year 8 – 31 lessons
Year 4 – 24 lessons	Year 9 – 31 lessons
Year 5 – 25 lessons	

Every lesson lasts 45 minutes. The maximum number of pupils per class is 30. If a class integrates pupils with special educational needs, the number is reduced (Education Act, No. 561/2004).

In September 1998, home education on an experimental basis was approved. At the beginning of the experiment, about 60 pupils of the first level were participating. Since 2005, this type of education was made official by a new Education Act as individual education; in the same year, 339 pupils were educated at home (Education Act, No. 561/2004).

The system of secondary education (see Appendix 5) in the Czech Republic is very diverse and extensive. The goal of secondary education is to develop knowledge, skills, and values attained within basic education in either broader general education or vocational education connected with general education. Secondary education creates conditions for fair personal, civilian, and professional life, continuing education, independent acquisition of information, and lifelong learning. It consists primarily of four-year gymnasia, technical and vocational schools, three-year apprenticeship schools, and specialized schools. The length of the study corresponds to full-time study programs. The same level of education also can be attained through other part-time forms of education (evening, distance, combined). In this case, however, the study may be one year longer.

The aim of study at gymnasia is to provide pupils with broad educational background and key competences, which they will further cultivate in a lifelong learning process. It prepares students for study at higher education institutions or, possibly, for some professions that require a wider cultural basis. In addition to general courses, there are 12 fields of study (e.g., languages, humanities, natural sciences, mathematics, and physical education), with special focus on these subjects in the curriculum. However, generally oriented gymnasia prevail. Gymnasia may offer 4-year courses for pupils at the age of 15 (after completing the compulsory school attendance), 6-year courses for pupils at the age of 13 (after pupils complete the 7th grade), or 8-year courses for pupils at the age of 11 (after completing the 5th grade), often within the same school.

Secondary technical schools started in the 19th century and traditionally offered a four-year degree, providing pupils with secondary education, similar to that of the gymnasia. The secondary schools stressed three components:

• General education—common subjects relating to the socio-cultural function of education
• Key competences—communication, problem-solving skills, information, and communication technology usage
• Basic technical education.

Curricula include general subjects (the Czech language and literature, a foreign language, mathematics, natural sciences, civic education, history, and physical education), and vocational subjects, the selection of which depends upon the relevant field of study. The vocational subjects include various practical or laboratory tasks. The curriculum also includes work placement in companies or various other institutions, the duration of which depends on the relevant field of study. The ratio of general to vocational subjects varies according to the study field and the year of study.

Under current legislation, there are two types of vocational schools. The first type of school lasts two or three years and ends with a final examination. Such schools train pupils for a vocational qualification in professions where attaining an apprenticeship certificate is prescribed. Pupils are admitted to the first year of study upon completion of compulsory school attendance (15-year-olds). The second type of vocational schools is authorized to train pupils in four-year courses, provided these are recorded in the Register of Schools and School Facilities. In such cases, the four-year training leads to a graduate examination and entitles the pupil to enter a higher education institution.

Conservatory schools are one example of a specialized school that prepares students for demanding careers in fine arts and art pedagogy in music, dancing, singing, and performing arts. Two types of conservatory schools exist in the current system. The first offers a secondary education completed with a graduation examination and higher professional education completed with a performance examination (see Appendix 5). The courses last between four and eight years. The other popular specialized schools offer nursing and foreign languages.

Higher education is regulated by the same Education Act (No. 561/2004) as compulsory and secondary education. Higher education consists of two types: a university type, providing all levels of degrees, and a lower university type, usually offering only bachelor's degrees. Bachelor's degrees are focused on professional training and provide a basis for studies in master's study programs. The study lasts 3 to 4 years.

Master's study programs are aimed at providing theoretical knowledge based on the latest scientific findings, research, and development; mastering their applications; and developing creative skills. Their standard length is 1 to 3 years. It is possible to have a study program accredited that will have bachelor's and master's programs together. In such cases, the study would be from 4 to 6 years long.

A doctoral study program can follow after the completion of a master's program. It is aimed at scientific work, independent creative activity in the area of research and development, or at independent theoretical and creative skills in art. It is offered solely at the university level. It lasts between three and four years. The higher education of Czech citizens is mostly free of charge, as fees involved are small.

The New Curricular System

In 2004, the Czech Republic became a member of the European Union, which had an impact on the country's education goals. There has been an attempt to reform the education system more in compliance with the EU politics and requirements. The new Education Act in 2004 (No. 561/2004), which included preschool education, compulsory education, and secondary education, introduces a new system of curricular documents for schooling of pupils ages 3 to 19.

The goal of the new curricular system is to adjust the objectives and content of education to the needs of personal, professional, and civil life, as well as to the different pupils' and students' abilities, so that the school provides not only a broad knowledge base and practical skills, but also tools that would be universally applicable in everyday life. School should thus teach students the so-called key competencies. These include the ability to communicate, process information and numerical data, work in teams, and apply all learned information in real-life situations (Act No. 561/2004).

There are two levels of Czech curricular documents: the national one and the school one. The *national level* of the curricular system is represented by The Framework Educational Programs (see Appendix 6). The Framework Educational Programs specify the obligatory frames for individual stages of education—preschool, compulsory, and secondary education at the national level. It defines nine educational spheres formed by one or more educational areas, cross-section subjects, and additional educational areas. Mother tongue, mathematics, and physical education are taught in all years. Foreign language teaching starts in year 3 (it can also start in year 1); the second foreign language is optional and is introduced in year 8 at the latest.

The *school level* is represented by the School Educational Programs, which are the basis for actual instruction delivered at individual schools. The aim of the school level is to provide a set of key competencies for each pupil on the individually accessible level and to prepare pupils for further education and integration within the society (Belz & Siegrist, 2001). Developing the key competences is a long-term and complicated process that begins in preschool education, proceeds in compulsory and secondary education, and finishes gradually during the lifetime of the student. The School Educational Program breaks the subject matter distribution into individual years and is laid out into subjects and curriculum. The objectives are to:

- Encourage pupils' creative thinking, logical reasoning, and problem solving
- Guide pupils to general, effective, and overt communication
- Develop pupils' ability to cooperate and to respect the work and success of both themselves and other people
- Prepare pupils for interacting as independent, free, and responsible personalities, and for demanding their rights and fulfilling their duties
- Create pupils' need for expressing positive emotions while behaving, acting, and experiencing different life situations; to develop sensibility and empathy for other people, the environment, and nature
- Teach pupils how to develop actively and to protect physical, mental, and social health, and how to be responsible for it
- Guide pupils toward toleration and consideration toward other people and respect for their cultural and religious values, and to teach them the way to live among other people
- Help pupils define and develop their own abilities with respect to their actual potentiality, and to assist them in connecting their acquired knowledge and abilities with deciding about their own personal and professional future
- Enable pupils to develop the learning strategies and to motivate them for lifelong learning.
The process of replacing the old curricula in compulsory education already has started. The plan

is to finish replacing completely the old curricula in compulsory education by the 2011/12 academic year and start replacing the secondary curricula in the year 2012.

It is obvious that the curriculum in the Czech Republic is currently undergoing profound transformation, and it seems fated to develop into a long-term process. Deeper change of the curricular concept is connected with the development of society in Europe. The goal is to find relevant proportions between implementation of national, European, and global dimensions in the content of education and provision of an educational standard, which is important for integration of the Czech Republic and other EU members. Preparation of a more loosely defined curriculum for respective levels of education will bring a substantial change in the course of several years. It will apparently modify the functions, objectives, and inter-subject relations. The required integrated topics connected with the key competences should be natural byproducts of schoolwork. They will be related not only to the needs of pupils, schools, and the region, but also to the competencies necessary for success in the labor market. Unfortunately, the current situation of giving priority to solving financial problems, legislative framework, and institutional status of school education pushes the issues of curricular reform to the background.

References

Belz, H., & Siegrist, M. (2001). *Klíčové kompetence a jejich rozvíjení.* Praha: Portál.

Cach, J. (1984). Vznik a vývoj středního školství v českých zemích. *Acta Universitatis Carolinae Philosophica et Historica, 5,* 15-74.

Chaloupecký, V. (1948). Charles University, Prague. pp. 117-119

Education Act No. 561/2004. *Zakon o předškolním, základním, středním, vyšším odborném a jiném vzdělávání.* Vláda ČR, dodatek 9/2/2007.

Kadner, O. (1929). *Vývoj a dnešní soustava školství.* Praha: B. Janda.

The Ministry of Education, Youth and Sports. (2001). *Národní program rozvoje vzdělávání v České republice: Bílá kniha.* Praha: UIV Tauris.

Prihoda, V. (1930). *Racionalizace skolstvi.* Praha: Orbis.

Prihoda, V. (1931). *Skolska reforma.* Praha: Orbis.

Váňa, J. a kol. (1963). *Dějiny pedagogiky pro pedagogické školy, vyšší pedagogické školy a vyšší školy pedagogické.* 2. Vydání. Praha: SPN

Váňová, R. (1995). *Československé školství ve 30. letech: Příhodovská reforma.* Praha: Univerzita Karlova.

Váňová, R. (2000). České gymnázium v 70. a 80. letech 20. století. In *Minulost, současnost a budoucnost gymnazijního vzdělávání* (pp. 101-414). Semily: Státní okresní archiv.

Veselá , Z. (1992). *Vývoj české školy a učitelského vzdělání.* Brno: Masarykova univerzita.

Walterová, E. (1994). *Kurikulum: Proměny a trendy v mezinárodní perspektivě.* Brno: Masarykova univerzita.

Walterová, E. (2006). Proměny paradigmatu kurikulárního diskurzu. In *Problémy kurikula základní školy* (pp. 11-22). Brno: Masarykova Univerzita.

Zacatek noveho skolniho roku: Statisticke informace k novemu skolnimu roku. (2006). Praha, Czech Republic: Ministerstvo školství mládeže a tělovýchovy.

Zákon o školské soustavě a vzdělávání učitelů, Národní shromáždění ČR, 23. duben. 1953, Praha

Zákon o soustavě výchovy a vzdělávání, Národní shromáždění ČR, 1960, Praha.

Appendix 1

*All appendices are used with permission by the original authors.

1774 – Universal School Regulation Act

Age

Age				
21 20 19 18 17			**Tertiary Education** Universities	
16 15 14			**Secondary Education** Grammar school (liberal and grammar)	
13 12				Preparation for teachers
11 10 9 8 7 6	Compulsory education	Trivial school (villages) 1 grade Reading, writing, arithmetic, religious training and the basics of economy and industry	Principal schools (towns) 3 grades Social studies, Latin, stylistics, drawing and geometry	Normal schools (main cities) 6 grades Same as principal schools, just in more detail

Kovaricek, V. (1970). *Materialy k dejinam pedagogiky.* Olomouc, Czech Republic: Pedagogicka Faculta, Palacky University.

Appendix 2

1869 – Education Act

Age

Age						
21		Universities				
20						
19						
18		Secondary education		Grammar school	Real schools	Lyceum (girls)
17						
16						
15						
14						
13	Education 2nd level	General schools	Municipal schools			
12						
11						
10	Compulsory 1st level	General schools				
9						
8						
7						
6						
5	Preschools (kindergarten)					
4						
3						

Kovaricek, V. (1970). *Materialy k dejinam pedagogiky.* Olomouc, Czech Republic: Pedagogicka Faculta, Palacky University.

Appendix 3

1948 – Unified Schools Act

Age

Age				
21		Universities		
20				
19				
18		Technical schools		Grammar schools
17	Vocational schools			
16				
15				
14	Compulsory education	General schools -2nd level		
13				
12				
11				
10		General schools – 1st level		
9				
8				
7				
6	Preschools	Kindergarten		
5				
4				
3				

Kovaricek, V. (1970). *Materialy k dejinam pedagogiky.* Olomouc, Czech Republic: Pedagogicka Faculta, Palacky University.

Appendix 4

1953 – New School Act

Age					
21			Universities		
20					
19					
18					
17					
16	Secondary education	Vocational schools	Technical schools	Grammar school – 11 years	
15					
14					
13	Compulsory education	General schools			
12					
11					
10					
9					
8					
7					
6	Preschools	Kindergarten			
5					
4					
3					

Kovaricek, V. (1970). *Materialy k dejinam pedagogiky.* Olomouc, Czech Republic: Pedagogicka Faculta, Palacky University.

Appendix 5

2007 - The Present Education System

Age

Age							
27	University	Doctoral program					
26							
25							
24		Master's program					
23							
22		Bachelor's program					
21							
20							
19							
19	Secondary education	Grammar school Graduate Exams	Technical School Graduate Exams	Vocational School Graduate Exams	Apprentice-ships Final Examination	Conservatory Performance	Conservatory Graduate Exams
18							
17							
16							
15	Compulsory education		Second level				
14							
13							
12							
11							
10		First level					
9							
8							
7							
6	Preschools	Kindergarten					
5							
4							
3							

Vzdělávací systém České republiky. Vydáno s podporou Ministerstva školství, mládeže a tělovýchovy. (2006). Praha.

Appendix 6

The System of Curricular Documents

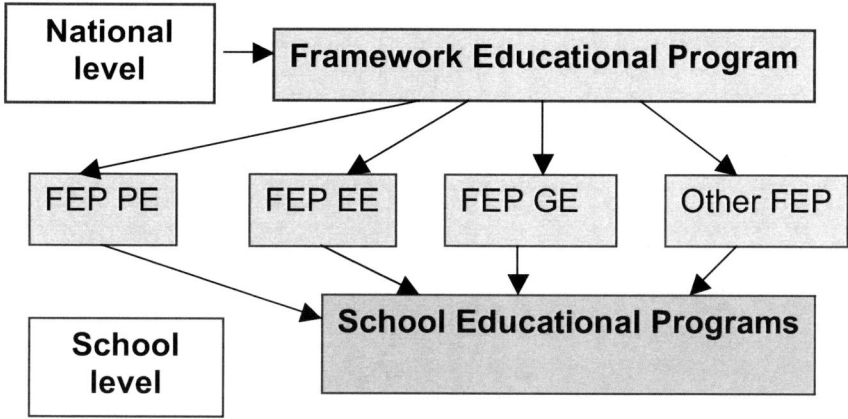

Glossary:
FEP PE – Framework Educational Program for Preschool Education
FEP BE – Framework Educational Program for Elementary Education
FEP GE – Framework Educational Program for Grammar School Education

About the Authors

Ferdinand Mazal is the head of the Department of Sports in the College of Physical Culture, Palacky University, Olomouc, Czech Republic. Mazal specializes in professional teacher development and he is a leading expert on "teaching games for learning" in the Czech Republic. Mazal can be reached at ferdinand.mazal@upol.cz

Jiri Stelzer received his Ph.D. in health, PE, and recreation at the University of New Mexico in 2000. Since then, he has taught at Valdosta State University, Georgia. He is interested in multicultural and interdisciplinary approaches in teaching. He had made many presentations on teaching and learning using online approaches in the Czech Republic, Russia, Slovak Republic, Canada, and Poland. Stelzer can be reached at jstelzer@valdosta.edu

Zuzana Vasickova graduated with a master's degree in English at the Palacky University, Olomouc, in the Czech Republic, and is working as a research assistant in the Kinantropology Department.

Implementation of Finnish Education Policy Through National Core Curriculum: Science as an Example

Jari Lavonen and Heidi Krzywacki

In order to understand the background of the Finnish education system, the authors present an overview of education policy and the broader framework of basic education. It is not only current education policy and the social picture that affects the way basic education is implemented, but also historical and cultural factors as well. Traditions have an effect on general attitudes and the ways and mannerisms of politics. This chapter will begin with a brief outline of the education history of Finland and continue with curriculum concepts, explain current education policy and practices, and give a description of the school system in Finland.

A Brief History of Finnish Education

The history of Finnish education is characterized by interaction between international and national stimuli, wherein Finnish language and culture, in addition to the country's geographical position, have been significant (Kuikka, 1997). Finland was under Swedish rule for some 600 years, up to 1809. In the 16th century, literacy culture in Finland was affected by the democratic spirit of the Reformation, and it seems that attitudes toward education became more favorable than before. In 1809, Finland was attached to the Russian empire, and remained so for just over a century until 1917, when the final formation of the concept of a national state in Finland was realized. The national epic *Kalevala* was published in 1835, and the Finnish language reached an equal position with Swedish, which was Finland's only official language besides Russian before then. Local government now had a stronger position in administrative models; yet political tension existed at the end of the Russian era, which was reflected in education. Most especially, the position of the Russian language's supremacy was an issue and a cultural concern in education.

Finland

One of the greatest steps taken in Finland toward democratizing society was the establishment of the unicameral parliament in 1906. This extension of democracy caused a large increase in the numbers of the enfranchised, including women, who received the vote. Thus, Finland became the first country in Europe, and the second in the world, to allow women the right to vote.

Finland declared its independence in 1917. Education was an essential part of the final implementation of the nation state, even if it was made compulsory for everyone rather late, in 1921 (Simola, 2002). Educational enthusiasm seized Finns and developmental guidelines for the society seemed to be clear. The idea of a civilized state concerned with education for all was truly becoming a reality. However, according to Simola (2002), schooling was principally legitimized by the needs of society, of the nation (or the fatherland). After enjoying independence for 23 years, Finland was attacked by the Red Army in 1930; during World War II, the Finnish ideology constructed in the 1920s and 1940s was put to the test. Afterward, between 1946-50, a new education system became a focus of discussion and it was only then that schools for everyone emerged all over the country (Simola, 2002). Attempts were made to modernize the curricula of schools, and it was declared that the function of school was to raise the competence level of all members of society and to develop their personality. From the 1950s onward, Finnish schools were more and more influenced by Anglo-Saxon didactics; meaning, among other things, emphasis on the learning of pupils, outcomes, and personal development using learner-centered methods. The foundation of a new school system was accomplished at the end of the 1960s: comprehensive schools were established, whereby educational equality and continuing education were basic ideals and special needs education was included.

After the Second World War, Finnish society passed through an economic and cultural transition, moving from a monocultural, agrarian, and peripheral society to a multicultural, high-tech knowledge economy with an active role in shaping the present-day European economic and political environment. During the first decade of the 21st century, Finland has been ranked three out of four times as the most competitive economy in the world by the World Economic Forum (Porter, Schwab, & Lopez-Claros, 2005). The nation can boast a very high level of human capital, widespread use of information and communication technologies, and education and research institutions that have been redesigned to foster innovation and cutting-edge research and development (Routti & Ylä-Anttila, 2006).

This "high tech" atmosphere also affects students and it has had an effect on their interest in studying science and technology and in finding related job openings. The Finnish education system has become an attractive and internationally examined example of a high-performing system that successfully combines high quality with wide-spread equity and social cohesion through reasonable public financing. Finnish 15-year-old students have achieved the highest score in the PISA (Programme for International Student Assessment) scientific literacy assessment twice, in 2000 and 2003 (Organisation for Economic Cooperation and Development [OECD], 2004). This success has been explained by education policy cornerstones, which will be described in the next section, and by a relatively homogeneous society (Sahlberg, 2004; Simola, 2005). Välijärvi, Linnakylä, Kupari, Reinikainen, and Arffman (2002) have suggested various reasons for the Finnish students' success in PISA: for example, pedagogical philosophy and practice. Simola (2005) also has emphasized the significance of the historical framework as a reason for success, emphasizing the motivation provided by hardships suffered during the First and Second World Wars.

Education Policy in Finland

Education policy is controlled by the Finnish Ministry of Education (ME). The Basic Education Act 628/1998 presents general national educational objectives, distribution of lesson hours, and education goals, in addition to guidance to municipalities. In the act, for example, a vision of the "good" individual is presented. The Finnish National Board of Education (NBE), which implements this education policy, is responsible for development of education, preparation of the National Core Curriculum for Basic Education (NCCBE, 2004), and the organization of national evaluations based on samples. The policy guidelines are described in national strategies. Figure 1 summarizes the implementation of education policy, based on descriptions in this chapter.

According to the education policy documents, the most important features of the policy is a broad commitment to *a vision of a knowledge-based society.* This vision is widely shared and accepted by employers and labor organizations as well as by industry and their interest groups. Representatives of these organizations also have been participants on the advisory board of the national curriculum development projects. Furthermore, parents have respected education, school, and teachers for a long time, as described above in the historical overview.

Another long-term objective of Finnish education policy has been to raise the general standard of education and to promote *educational equality.* In practice, all Finnish young people complete the same nine-year comprehensive school education, which is provided free of charge (including such learning materials as schoolbooks, meals, transport, and health care). Education in science, mathematics, the mother tongue (Swedish or Finnish), another national language (Swedish or Finnish), and foreign languages is provided for everybody. Special needs teachers help those with special educational requirements, and guidance counselors give advice relating to studies and careers. Moreover, one of the features characterizing basic education is that there are only a few private schools in the whole country, meaning that practically everybody attends public school.

A third general education policy principle in Finland is *devolution of decision power and responsibility at the local level.* Local municipalities allocate tax revenue for social services and education to each school, with a separate budget. The local education providers (local authority or municipalities) plan the local curriculum with teachers, based on the National Core Curriculum for Basic Education (NCCBE, 2004). Teaching might be focused according to local needs, which helps decide elective subjects. The local education providers also are responsible for organizing general assessment of the schools. They use the data to evaluate how well the goals have been achieved and education policy is working in practice. The role of headmasters or principals is important in school development and evaluation, and in implementing education policy at the local level, including budgetary authority, which encompasses decisions on class size and purchasing of learning materials.

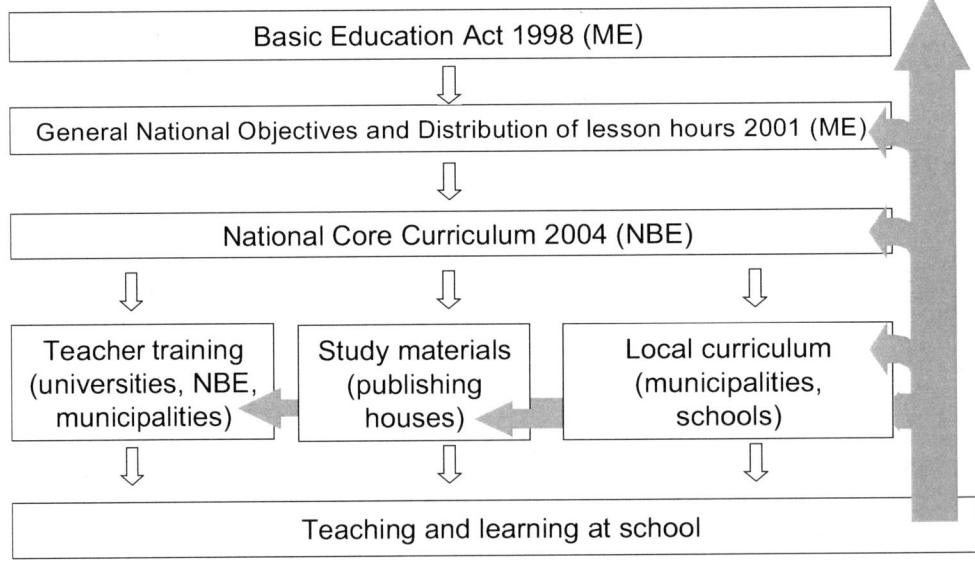

Education policy, its implementation and feedback loop through assessment in Finland.

Figure 1

Essential Role of Professionally Educated Teachers

There are special demands for Finnish teachers, who have an essential role in developing and implementing school level curriculum, in addition to assessing outcomes. The Finnish comprehensive school system is very challenging to teachers, because they need versatile professional skills to manage classes consisting of low- and high-achieving students. Therefore, separate teacher education colleges and teacher training schools were united to become a part of the universities in 1974. All class teachers (at grades 1-6 in elementary school) and subject teachers (at the lower and upper secondary school, grades 7-12), are educated in master's level programs, requiring 300 credit points (cp.), which are offered by eight universities in Finland (KATU-project, 1978). Master's level programs ensure that teachers play a central role in preparing each new generation and actively participating in the curricula process.

Teachers who are teaching science in grades 7-9 specialize in subject area instruction. Typically, they teach two subjects, like mathematics and physics, and have at least two years of university-level studies (60 ECTS credits) in that particular school subject. A research-based approach, emphasizing the teacher's pedagogical thinking, is integrated into all teacher education programs in Finland (Kansanen et al., 2000). The local education provider (local authority or municipalities) and NBE are responsible for teachers' inservice training in order to update teachers' knowledge and skills as professionals.

According to the general national education strategy Education and Research 2003-2008 (2004), education at the university shall be based on scientific research and professional practices in the field. In particular, the study program should provide the students with the knowledge and skills needed for operating independently as experts in and developers of their field. In addition, other strategies describe goals for teacher education, such as Education, Training and Research in the Information Society (1999) and Teacher Education Development Programme (2002). According to these, teacher education programs should help students to acquire:

- High-level subject knowledge and pedagogical content knowledge, and knowledge about how knowledge is constructed
- Academic skills, like research skills; ability to use pedagogical information and communication technology; and the skills needed to develop a curricula
- Social skills, such as communication skills and ability to cooperate with other teachers
- Knowledge about school as an institution and its connections to society (school community and partners, local contexts, and stakeholders)
- Moral knowledge and skills, such as the social and moral code of the teaching profession
- Skills needed in developing one's own teaching and the teaching profession.

It is teachers' responsibility to choose appropriate learning materials and such teaching methods that objectives of curriculum may be achieved in the best possible way. There are several pathways by which to achieve the goals and the role of a teacher as a competent academically trained professional. There are neither approval procedures for learning materials nor school inspectors on the national or local school level. Teachers are valued as experts in curriculum development, teaching, and assessment at all levels (NCCBE, 2004). The local curriculum is regarded as more of a process than a product and has a central role in school improvement. Consequently, there is good and flexible interaction among national, municipal, and school levels. *The culture of trust* means that education authorities and national level education policymakers believe that teachers, in cooperation with principals, head teachers, and parents, know how to provide the best possible education for children and youth at a certain level. National level assessment (based on samples) is used for guiding developers of NCCB. Assessment is not based on national-level centralized tests; however, teachers on the school level are obligated to assess student progress. Assessment data is used by teachers and students on the local level.

The government defines broad national objectives and decides how to allocate instructional time in different subjects. The main objective of education in comprehensive schools is to support students' growth toward humanity and ethically responsible membership in society, and to provide them with the knowledge and skills necessary in life. Moreover, the instruction should promote equality in society and the students' abilities to participate in education and otherwise develop themselves (Basic Education Act 628/1998).

The Finnish Education System

This chapter focuses on education at grades 5-9 in Finnish comprehensive schools. The overview of the education system provides an understanding of the framework of basic education. The Finnish system consists of basic education, post-comprehensive general (upper secondary school) and vocational education, higher education, and adult education. Comprehensive school (grades 1-9, ages 7-16) was earlier divided into elementary (grades 1-6) and lower secondary (grades 7-9) school; today, however, education policymakers are emphasizing a common comprehensive school without any clear division into two different levels. Moreover, an official preschool education for 6-year-old children was organized some years ago. Even though teachers are educated separately for elementary and lower secondary school teaching, class teachers (equivalent in the United States to elementary teachers who give instruction in all subject areas) teach almost all subjects in elementary school in grades 1-6, including mathematics and science. Subject teachers typically teach two subjects each in grades 7-9 in lower secondary school and at upper secondary school.

In 2006, there were 3,393 comprehensive schools and 578,918 comprehensive school pupils in Finland. At the same time, there were 44,623 comprehensive school teachers. About 60% of the students continue their studies in upper secondary school (Tilastokeskus, 2007). Typically, Finnish schools have fewer than 300 pupils in each school, with class sizes ranging from 20-30 students. Therefore, schools often forge close educational communities of teachers and pupils, and enjoy parental support and involvement.

Structure of the Comprehensive School Curriculum

The National Core Curriculum for Basic Education (NCCBE, 2004) is the national framework on the basis of which the local curriculum is formulated. Besides general and subject specific goals, NCCBE addresses basic concepts in each subject (syllabus), integration and cross-curricular themes, and final assessment criteria (standards). All school subjects are emphasized, giving equal value to all aspects of an individual's growth of personality, morals, creativity, knowledge, and skills. The goals described in the National Core Curriculum are, from the point of view of legislation, standards (as opposed to law) that the municipalities and the teachers should follow. The government determines subject-specific minimum number of lesson hours (comprehensive school) and courses (upper secondary education).

The education provider, typically a municipality, is responsible for the preparation and development of local curriculum. Local curriculum should be formulated regarding the educational and teaching task of comprehensive school or basic education, and the objectives and contents specified in the core curriculum, as well as other factors bearing on the provision of education, also are specified (NCCBE, 2004). The core curriculum also allows pupils' parents and guardians to influence the local curriculum's educational objectives. Pupils also may be involved in the curriculum work. As it concerns pupil welfare and home-school cooperation, the local curriculum also should be drafted in collaboration with authorities charged with tasks that are part of the implementation of the local authority's social and health services.

General Aims in the Core Curriculum

The general part of the National Core Curriculum structure describes the underlying values and mission of basic education. For example, the core curriculum describes national values as follows:

The underlying values of basic education are human rights, equality, democracy, natural diversity, preservation of environmental viability, and the endorsement of multiculturalism. Basic education promotes responsibility, a sense of community, and respect for the rights and freedoms of the individual. (NCCBE, 2004, p. 14)

Moreover, the core curriculum also discusses learning, learning environments, operational cultures, and teaching methods. The properties of good learning are described as follows:

In addition to new knowledge and skills, both learning and work habits are to be learned that will serve as tools of lifelong learning. . . . Learning results from the pupils' active and purposeful activity, in which they process and interpret the material to be learned on the basis of their existing structure of knowledge. Although the general principles of learning are the same for everyone, learning depends on the learner's previously constructed knowledge, motivation, and learning and work habits. . . . In all its forms, learning is an active and goal-oriented process that includes independent or collective problem-solving. Learning is situational, so special attention must be given to the diversity of the learning environment. In learning, new possibilities open up for understanding culture and the meanings that culture contains, and for participating in social activity. (NCCBE, 2004, p. 18)

According to the Core Curriculum (NCCBE, 2004), the teaching methods used in the comprehensive school should help, support, and guide the pupil's learning. The methods also should develop social,

Allocation of Science Subjects to Grades in Comprehensive School

Grade	1	2	3	4	5	6	7	8	9	10	11	12
Students' age	7	8	9	10	11	12	13	14	15	16	17	18
Level (unofficial)	elementary school						lower secondary school			upper secondary school (high school)		
	Comprehensive school, Basic education											
Science subjects	*Integrated* environmental and natural studies is a subject group comprising the fields of biology, geography, physics, chemistry, and health education. *Altogether, 9 hours/ week/4 years = 2.25 hours/ week/1 year*			*Integrated* Biology and geography *1.5 hours/week/1 year* Physics and chemistry *1 hour/week/1 year*			*Separate:* Biology *3.5 hours* Geography *3.5 hours* Physics *3.5 hours /week/3 years* Chemistry *3.5 hours/week/3 years* Health education *3 hours/week/3 years*			*Separate:* Biology *2+3 courses* Geography *2+2 courses* Physics *1+7 courses* Chemistry *1+4 courses* Health education *(1 course = 1 hour/week/2 years)*		
Compulsory/ Optional	C									C+O	O	

Figure 2

learning, thinking, working, and problem-solving skills, and foster active participation, creativity, and use of information and communication technologies. In addition to previous general principles, some more concrete hints about versatile teaching methods are given in the core curriculum. Teachers are expected to make decisions on methods used in the classroom.

Science Education in the Core Curriculum

In several countries (including the United Kingdom, the United States, and Sweden), it is common to teach science in grades 7 to 9 as an integrated subject by science teachers who have specialized in all science subjects or, in some cases, only in one subject. In Finland, science is divided into separate disciplines: physics, chemistry, and biology starting at grade 5, with a school subject called "Chemistry and Physics." Allocation of science-related subjects to grades in the Finnish curriculum is described in Figure 2.

In the core curriculum, the nature of the teaching/learning process in science is emphasized:

> *The starting points for physics and chemistry instruction are the students' prior knowledge, skills, and experiences, and their observations and investigations of objects, substances, and phenomena in the nature. From these, the instruction progresses towards the laws and fundamental principles of physics and chemistry. The purpose of the experimental orientation is to help the students both (i) to perceive the nature of science and (ii) to learn new scientific concepts, principles, and models; (iii) to develop skills in experimental work and (iv) cooperation; and (v) to stimulate the students to study physics and chemistry (interest). (NCCBE, 2004, p. 188)*

"Experimental orientation" here means physical (hands-on) and mental activity ("mind-on") of the student, emphasizing empirical meanings of the concepts (see, for example, Lavonen et al., 2004). Of course, the role of a teacher is important in this process.

The National Core Curriculum does not allocate goals and contents to a certain grade but rather between grades (e.g., grades 7-9). The goals for science education can be classified as described below (NCCBE, 2004). The goals and contents are classified by the authors of this chapter into the categories that typically can be seen in science education literature (e.g., Hodson, 1996; Millar, Le Maréchal, & Tiberghien, 1999). The authors also underscore how a specific goal belongs to a specific category.

Examples of goals for *learning science subject matter*:
- In grades 5-6, progress is made toward the basic concepts and principles of physics and chemistry
- The tasks of chemistry instruction in the 7th through 9th grades are to guide the pupil in acquiring knowledge and in applying that knowledge in different life situations
- In grades 7-9, pupils will learn in physics to use appropriate concepts, quantities, and units in describing physical phenomena and technological questions.

Examples of goals for *learning scientific methods*:
The pupils will learn in physics and chemistry in grades 5-6
- To make observations and measurements, and to look for information on the subject of study
- To carry out simple scientific experiments clarifying the properties of phenomena.
The core task of physics instruction in the 7th through 9th grades is to strengthen pupils' skills in the experimental acquisition of information. In grade 7-9 physics classes, pupils will learn:
- Scientific skills, such as the formulation of questions and the perception of problems
- To make, compare, and classify observations, measurements, and conclusions; to present and test a hypothesis; and to process, present, and interpret results
- To plan and carry out a scientific investigation in which variables affecting natural phenomena are held constant and varied and correlations among the variables are revealed

- To use various graphs and algebraic models in explaining natural phenomena, making predictions, and solving problems.

In grade 7-9 chemistry classes, pupils will learn:

- To use research methods that are typical from the standpoint of acquiring scientific knowledge, and to evaluate the reliability and importance of the knowledge
- To carry out scientific investigation and to interpret and present the results.

Examples of goals for *learning the nature of science*:
- In grades 7-9, the core task of physics instruction in the 7th through 9th grades is to broaden pupils' conception of the nature of physics. The instruction guides the pupil in thinking in a manner characteristic of science, in acquiring and using knowledge, and in evaluating the reliability and importance of knowledge in different life situations. The purpose of the experimental orientation is to help pupils to perceive the nature of science.

Examples of goals for *affecting the pupils' interest in the study of science*:
- In grades 5-6, the instruction must stimulate the pupils to study science
- In grades 7-9, the purpose of the experimental orientation is to stimulate the pupils to study physics and chemistry.

Examples of goals for *stimulating the pupils to become familiar with society*:
- In grades 5-6, the instruction must stimulate the pupils to take care of their environment and act responsibly in it
- In grades 7-9, physics instruction helps the pupil understand the importance of physics and technology in everyday life, the living environment, and society. It also provides capabilities for making everyday choices, especially in matters related to environmental protection and the use of energy resources.

Examples of goals for *cooperative skills development*:
- In grades 7-9, the purpose of the experimental orientation is to help pupils to learn cooperation skills. Pupils in physics classes will learn to work and investigate natural phenomena safely, together with others.

Standards as a Part of the National Core Curriculum

The role of the assessment is to take the measure of how well the goals have been reached. There are actually two kinds of standards in the Finnish curriculum—goals and final assessment criteria, known as "real standards." The subject-specific goals described in the previous section are viewed more as standards (compared to law), and they are the guidelines that municipalities and teachers have to follow. These goals describe what pupils are expected to learn in general and in each subject during their studies at comprehensive school. Thus, the National Core Curriculum states that "The assessment is to address the pupil's learning and progress in the different areas of learning" (NCCBE, 2004, p. 260). In summary, the goals for science education are the most important guiding principles for planning both teaching and assessment at the local level.

The fact that the education system is based on broad guidelines and trust in the teacher's professionalism has raised some challenges. The need for real standards that would guide assessment in the final phase of the studies in the comprehensive school was recognized soon after the implementation of the Framework Curriculum for Comprehensive School Guidelines in 1994 (FCCS, 1994). The basic idea of the FCCS was to continuously take into account the changes in the environment and the information obtained through assessment. It was planned that the objectives given in the curriculum framework should not restrict teaching and the development of teaching, as well as participation of the teachers in the preparation of the school curriculum and other school-level development activities. This 1994 framework curriculum has been the most decentralized curriculum document in Finland until now.

Unfortunately, the ideas described in the 1994 framework curriculum were not completely realized in school practice, leading to variations in the assessment of pupils among schools and among teachers in a specific school. Authorities were especially worried about pupils' equality and comparison of pupil assessment at the end of their comprehensive school education. Therefore, it was decided to develop final-assessment criteria (real standards) for the end of the 9th grade and, consequently, the pendulum swung from decentralization toward centralization. These criteria were introduced in 1999 (Final-assesssment Criteria for the End of Comprehensive School [FACEC], 1999), and the document describes what pupils should understand and be able to do, but not the manner in which pupils will achieve the outcomes. In practice, the criteria described knowledge and skills required for grade 8, which is in the middle of the grading scale (4-10) used in Finland.

Consequently, by introducing the final-assessment criteria, it was hoped that teachers would use an absolute (criterion-referenced) assessment system at the end of the comprehensive school course and that teachers would compare students' performances with a described standard performance. The second aim was to help teachers calibrate their assessment tools and to evaluate their own scale. The validity of this grading system depends, of course, on the teacher's ability to devise valid and reliable measurements of student performance.

When planning the National Core Curriculum for Basic Education (NCCBE, 2004), it was decided that goals, core contents (syllabus), and final-assessment criteria at the end of 9th grade and descriptions of good performance at the end of 4th and 6th grade should be produced for each subject. Therefore, both goals of science education and final-assessment criteria are discussed here as standards. The description of good performance at the end of 4th and 6th grade and the final assessment criteria at the end of 9th grade specify, on a national basis, the knowledge and skill levels that constitute the basis of pupil assessment. The final assessment criteria determine knowledge and skill levels for a grade of 8, on a scale of 4-10. The criteria outline what a pupil should know, understand, and be able to do in science and are, therefore, a complete set of outcomes for pupils—they do not prescribe a curriculum.

The *description of good performance* in environmental and natural science at the end of 4th grade is classified according to the following themes:
• Science activities (scientific method and nature of science)
• Organisms and environments
• Natural phenomena and substances around us
• The individual and health
• Safety.

The *description of good performance* in physics and chemistry at the end of 6th grade is classified as follows:
• Science activities (scientific method and nature of science)
• Energy and electricity
• Scales and structures
• Substances around us.

The *final assessment criteria* at the end of 9th grade for physics are classified as follows:
• Science activities (scientific method and nature of science)
• Motion and force
• Vibrations and wave motion
• Heat

- Electricity
- Structure of matter and universe.

The *final assessment criteria* at the end of 9th grade for chemistry can be classified as follows:
- Science activities (scientific method and nature of science)
- Chemical processes and their models
- Properties of substances
- Structure of matter
- Chemical applications, the environment, and the chemical industry.

Conclusion

This paper has described and discussed the Finnish National Core Curriculum for Basic Education and education policy behind the curriculum. The authors have focused on science education in the comprehensive school in order to expose the structure and implementation of national curriculum within basic education. In summary, we claim that Finnish curriculum is actually a tool for professional teachers to implement national education policy. Even if the framework curriculum is given, teachers have an essential role in planning and specifying local level curriculum.

Finnish decisions dealing with the national curriculum and standards are different from those in many other countries. To summarize, the Finnish system for implementing educational policy reveals an absence of detailed descriptions of goals and content. Goals and contents are described in more detail on the local level, but individual teachers have the freedom and responsibility to implement the curricula the best possible way they know. Besides, the role of teachers on the school level is essential when formulating local level curricula. The curriculum can be understood only as a part of a whole education policy, as a tool for professional teachers to implement certain educational direction within the given framework.

Several opposing trends can be recognized when Finnish education policy and its implementation are compared to the education movements in other countries. The well-known outcome-based education movement became popular in the 1980s, followed in the 1990s by standards-based education policies, including centrally prescribed performance standards for schools, teachers, and students that were so favored in Anglo-Saxon countries (Hargreaves, Earl, Shawn, & Manning, 2001; Sahlberg, 2004). On the contrary, in Finland, flexibility and diversity have been the main guides in implementing the national framework curriculum and assessment at the school level. Especially important in Finland has been the devolution of decision power, preparation of local curriculum, assessment, and responsibility at the local level. It is obvious that teachers are not only more committed to the planning process of the local curriculum and single lessons, but also that they have become aware of contents and standards described in the curricula. Master's-level teacher education also inculcates knowledge and readiness for this work. The aim of the master's thesis is to train students to find and analyze problems that they will face in their future work. This small-scale research training improves teachers' competence to plan, teach, and evaluate.

One global trend in education has been consequential accountability systems for schools. Success or failure of schools and their teachers is often determined by standardized tests, school inspectors, and external evaluations that only devote attention to limited aspects of schooling, such as student achievement in mathematical studies, science, and reading literacy. In Finland, another direction has been chosen: *trust through professionalism.* The culture of trust within the education system values teachers' and head teachers' professionalism in judging what is best for students and in reporting on progress of their learning.

There are also several differences in our example subject, science curriculum, when it is compared to science curricula in other countries. A global trend in science education is integrated science. In contrast, separate science subjects—biology, geography, physics, chemistry, and health education—are taught in grades 5-9 in Finland. Science in grades 7-9 is taught by highly specialized subject teachers.

These subject studies also give teachers readiness to teach epistemological and ontological aspects of the subject and to discuss the subject knowledge in various contexts.

The Finnish decision to have "standards without non-centralized assessment" is, of course, not an easy one for teachers and local authorities. Therefore, this decision is taken seriously in teacher education programs and student teachers are trained for organizing assessment. Moreover, the National Board of Education is organizing inservice training for teachers and giving support for local level pedagogical decision-making and local authorities and head teachers.

References

Basic Education Act 628/1998. Retrieved September 1, 2007, from www.finlex.fi/en/laki/kaannokset/1998/en19980628.pdf

Education and Research 2003-2008; Development Plan. (2004). *Publications of the Ministry of Education, Finland 2004:8.* Retrieved September 1, 2007, from www.minedu.fi/OPM/Julkaisut/2004/koulutuksen_ja_tutkimuksen_kehittamissuunnitelma_2003-2008?lang=fi&extra_locale=en

Education, training and research in the information society: A national strategy for 2000-2004. (1999). Helsinki: Ministry of Education. Retrieved September 1, 2007, from www.minedu.fi/OPM/Julkaisut/1999/koulutuksen_ja_tutkimuksen_tietostrategia_2000_-_2004?lang=fi&extra_locale=en.

FACEC. (1999). *Final-assessment criteria for the end of comprehensive school (in Finland).* Helsinki: National Board of Education.

FCCS. (1994). *Framework curriculum for the comprehensive school (in Finland).* Helsinki: State Printing Press and National Board of Education

Hargreaves, A., Earl, L., Shawn, M., & Manning, S. (2001). *Learning to change. Teaching beyond subjects and standards.* San Francisco: Jossey-Bass.

Hodson, D. (1996). Laboratory work as scientific method: Three decades of confusion and distortion. *Journal of Curriculum Studies, 28,* 115-135.

Kansanen, P., Tirri, K., Meri, M., Krokfors, L., Husu, J., & Jyrhämä, R. (2000). *Teachers' pedagogical thinking. Theoretical landscapes, practical challenges. American University studies xiv 47.* New York: Peter Lang Publishing.

KATU-project. (1978). *Luokanopettajan koulutusohjelman yleinen rakenne. Kasvatusalan tutkinnonuudistuksen ohjaus- ja seurantaryhmän raportti. [General Structure of the Class Teacher's Education. Report of the steering and follow-up group of the curriculum reform.]* Opetusministeriö. Korkeakoulu- ja tiedeosaston julkaisusarja n:o 27.

Kuikka, M. T. (1997). *A history of Finnish education.* Helsinki: Otava Publishing.

Lavonen, J., Jauhiainen, J., Koponen, I., & Kurki-Suonio, K. (2004). Effect of a long term in-service training program on teachers' beliefs about the role of experiments in physics education. *International Journal of Science Education, 26*(3), 309-328.

Millar, R., Le Maréchal, J.-F., & Tiberghien, A. (1999). "Mapping" the domain: Varieties of practical work. In J. Leach & A. C. Paulsen (Eds.), *Practical work in science education* (pp. 33-59). Roskilde, Finland: Roskilde University Press.

National Board of Education. (2004). *National Core Curriculum for Basic Education 2004.* Helsinki: Author.

National Research Council. (1996). *National science education standards.* Washington, DC: National Academy Press. [ED 391 690]

Organisation for Economic Cooperation and Development. (2004). *Learning for tomorrow's world: First results from PISA 2003.* Paris: Author. Retrieved January 15, 2007, from www.oecd.org/dataoecd/1/63/34002454.pdf

Porter, M. E., Schwab, K., & Lopez-Claros, A. (2005). *Global competitiveness report 2005-2006.* New York: Palgrave Macmillan.

Rajakorpi, A. (Ed.). (1999). *Peruskoulun 9. luokkalaisten luonnontieteiden oppimistulosten arviointi. Keväällä 1998 pidetyn kokeen tulokset [Evaluation of the learning results in natural sciences of the 9th grade comprehensive school students. Results of the test that has been organised in the spring 1998].* Oppimistulosten arviointi 2/1999. Helsinki: Opetushallitus.

Rinne, R., Kivirauma, J., & Simola, H. (2002). Shoots of revisionist education policy or just slow readjustment? The Finnish case of educational reconstruction. *Journal of Education Policy, 17*(6), 643-658.

Routti, J., & Ylä-Anttila, P. (2006). *Finland as a knowledge economy. Elements of success and lessons learned.* Washington, DC: World Bank.

Sahlberg, P. (2004). Teaching and globalization. *Managing Global Transitions, 2*(1), 65-83.

Simola, H. (2002). The Finnish miracle of PISA: Historical and sociological remarks on teaching and teacher education. *Comparative Education, 41*(4), 455-470.

Simola, H. (2005). The Finnish miracle of PISA: Historical and sociological remarks on teaching and teacher education. *Comparative Education, 41*(4), 455-470.

Teacher Education Development Programme. (2002). Helsinki: Ministry of Education, Department for Education and Research Policy. Retrieved Sept. 1, 2007, from www.minedu.fi/OPM/Julkaisut/2001/opettajankoulutuksen_kehittamisohjelma?lang=fi&extra_locale=en.

Tilastokeskus. (2007). *Esi- ja peruskouluopetus.* Retrieved Sept. 1, 2007, from www.stat.fi/til/pop/index.html

Välijärvi, J., Linnakylä, P., Kupari, P., Reinikainen, P., & Arffman, I. (2002). *The Finnish success in PISA-and some reasons behind it.* Jyväskylä: Kirjapaino Oma Oy. Retrieved Sept. 1, 2007, from http://ktl.jyu.fi/arkisto/publications/ierpd056.htm

Appendix 1

Examples of Descriptions of Good Performance at the End of the 6th Grade

Science Activities

The pupils will:

- Know how to make observations and measurements with different senses and measuring instruments, and how to direct their observation at the target's essential features, such as motion or temperature, and at changes in those features.
- Know how to perform simple experiments—for example, to investigate what factors affect the dissolving of a solid.
- Know how to use concepts, quantities, and their units in describing, comparing, and classifying the properties of substances, objects, and phenomena.

Energy and Electricity

The pupils will:

- Know about different voltage supplies, such as a battery and an accumulator, and know how to do experiments in which electricity is used to produce light, heat, and motion.
- Know that electricity and heat can be generated from various natural resources, and know how to classify natural resources as renewable or non-renewable.

Scales and Structures

The pupils will:

- Know how to investigate forces, such as gravity, friction, and air and water resistance, and how to recognize different types of motion.
- Recognize phenomena caused by the motion of the earth and moon, such as times of the day, seasons, phases of the moon, and eclipses; know about the structure of the solar system; and be able to make observations of the night sky.

Substances Around Us

The pupils will :

- Know how to investigate the various properties of water and know how water is purified.
- Know how to classify substances from the soil, know the chemical symbols for elements in the soil, and know how to use various methods of separation, such as filtering, crystallization, and sifting.

Appendix 1 (cont'd)

Examples of Final-Assessment Criteria for a Grade of 8 in Physics

Science Activities

The pupils will:

- Know how to work safely and follow directions, alone and with others.
- Know how to perform a science investigation according to the instructions given, to plan simple experiments, to agree on tasks and the allocation of tasks, and to set objectives or goals together with other pupils.
- Know how to prepare small-scale research reports, to present results with the help of tables and graphs, for example, and to interpret those results.
- Know how to perform a controlled experiment and to evaluate the functionality of the experimental arrangement and the reliability, precision, and meaningfulness of the results.

Motion and Force

The pupils will:

- Know how to investigate various phenomena connected with interactions and motion and to use such quantities as time, distance, velocity, acceleration, and force in describing them.
- Know how to make graphic presentations, for example about the results of measuring uniform and accelerating motion; to interpret those results; to use a model of uniform (rectilinear) motion to make predictions concerning motion; and to employ the equation of average velocity to estimate and calculate distance or time.
- Know the relationship between work and energy.
- Understand the physical basis of rules concerning traffic safety.

Vibrations and Wave Motion

The pupils will:

- Recognize wave motions and the phenomena characteristic of them, including for example the production, progression, detection, reflection, and refraction of wave motion.
- Know how to investigate the reflection and refraction of light and to explain, using a ray of light as a model, various vision-related phenomena and the functioning of mirrors and lenses.
- Understand the importance of sound and light to the individual and the community, as in the case of noise, protection from noise, or light in data transmission.

Heat

The pupils will:

- Recognize phenomena related to the flow and storage of heat in nature and know how to interpret those phenomena.
- Know how to use the laws of heating, changes of state, and thermal expansion when examining and explaining thermal phenomena in nature.

Electricity

The pupils will:

- Know the principles of using electrical and heat-producing devices safely and economically, and know how to estimate and calculate the costs of utilizing electrical devices of various power levels.
- Know about applications, such as electrical devices and electronic communication.
- Know about the processes associated with production and transmission of electricity, such as the functioning of a transformer, and know how to explain the conversion of energy at a power plant and evaluate the advantages and disadvantages of different types of power plants.

Structure of Matter and Universe

The pupils will:

- Know the types and effects of radiation, be able to distinguish between harmful and harmless types, and know how to protect themselves against radiation.

Examples of Final-Assessment Criteria for a Grade of 8 in Chemistry

The pupils will:

- Know how to work safely, individually and in a group, according to the instructions given.
- Know how to carry out simple science experiments—for example, to investigate the combustion of a substance, the dissolving of a combustion product in water, or the acidity of the aqueous solution formed.
- Know about different industrial sectors, such as the metal and wood-processing industries, and about their products and importance to everyday life.
- Know how to interpret product descriptions, to explain the life cycle of a product, and to make choices as a consumer.
- Know how to describe an atom, chemical bonds, and compounds, using the proper models.
- Know how to draw conclusions about a substance's reactivity on the basis of electronic structure of the atom or an element's location in the periodic table.

About the Authors

Jari Lavonen, Ph.D., is a professor of physics and chemistry education and a Director of the Subject Teacher Education Section at the Department. He is also a Director of the Finnish Graduate School for Research in science and mathematics education. Address: Department of Applied Sciences of Education, University of Helsinki; P.O. Box 9; FIN-00014 University of Helsinki; Finland; Jari. Lavonen@Helsinki.fi

Heidi Krzywacki, Ph.D., is a researcher at the Department of Teacher Education, University of Helsinki. Her doctoral thesis focused on teacher identity formation in preservice mathematics teacher education. Her current research is focusing on the use of ICT in teaching and learning science and mathematics. She also is involved with research projects related to teacher professional identity and research-based development of teacher education.

Education in Honduras

Cristina P. Valentino

In order to understand the Honduran education system, it is first necessary to know something of the country's financial and political circumstances and the resources available to its citizens. Located in the middle of Central America, Honduras covers an area of 112,492 square kilometers (*Foro Nacional de Convergencia*), or 43,278 square miles—about the size of the U.S. state of Tennessee (InfoPlease, 2007). One of the poorest countries in the western hemisphere, Honduras has a population of roughly 7 million and an annual population growth of 2.24%. While Spanish is the national language of Honduras, other languages are spoken in isolated places on the northern coast and in heavily forested places, such as Lenca, Misquito, Pech, Chorti, and Garifuna. Most of the Honduran people (90%) are descended from multiple ethnicities (*mestizo*), 7% are native Indian, 2% are African, and 1% are white (USAID, 2004). The majority of the people in Honduras (97%) are Roman Catholic. Forty-seven percent of Honduras's population is concentrated in two cities: Tegucigalpa and San Pedro Sula.

After gaining its independence from Spain in 1821, Honduras went through more than 300 internal rebellions, civil wars, and changes in government. Most of these government changes occurred in the latter half of the 20th century. The government of Honduras has been a democracy since the early 1980s, after decades of military rule. However, while democratic rule has been better, needed change is hard to come by in Honduras—as are jobs. Not only are jobs hard to find, an education does not guarantee better employment. The best way to get a decent job in Honduras is to make friends with government employees or officials, which could at least guarantee a job for up to four years, so long as you maintain your connections. The reason a job is only considered relatively stable for that period of time is because that is the length of time between Honduran elections. By the

Honduras

time an existing party has outlined and put in place some mechanisms for change, a new party comes in, "sweeps" all of the old party members out—along with their studies, policies, and the rest of the work they have done—and replaces them with new people, who have their own ideas about what should be changed, and a burning desire to see their own names on those changes.

HURRICANE MITCH

By the late 1990s, Honduras had actually begun to have some success with changing government services to the people and enacting some needed policies. However, on October 26-31, 1998, Hurricane Mitch (called Hurricane Witch by Hondurans in honor of its concurrent timing with the Halloween holiday) pounded Honduras, devastating the country. Only now, more than a decade later, is the rebuilding taking off. Because Honduras is a third-world country without many resources, a disaster has much more impact there than in the United States. For instance, when Hurricane Katrina hit the U.S. Gulf Coast, emergency personnel from around the country responded very quickly in comparison. Within a few days to a week at most, housing, food, medical care, etc., were being provided. Moreover, contractors, electricians, engineers, and construction workers flocked to New Orleans, to help rebuild the city. Trailers were purchased by FEMA and given to families who had no homes. Conversely, the Honduran government had no such resources; thus, its people were dependent upon whatever help could be garnered from other countries and international aid agencies. There was no one to rebuild Honduras other than the Hondurans themselves—and what few resources they had, including many of their government and historic papers, were buried in the mountainsides and swept into the sea by Mitch. According to Carlos Flores Facusse, then-president of Honduras, "The storm destroyed 50 years of progress" (National Oceanic and Atmospheric Administration [NOAA], 2006, ¶1). According to NOAA,

> [Due to] orographic effects by the volcanic peaks of Central America and Mitch's slow movement, rain fell at the rate of a foot or two per day in many of the mountainous regions. Total rainfall has been reported as high as 75 inches for the entire storm. The resulting floods and mud slides virtually destroyed the entire infrastructure of Honduras . . . whole villages and their inhabitants were swept away in the torrents of flood waters and deep mud that came rushing down the mountainsides. Hundreds of thousands of homes were destroyed. (¶4)

This huge event brought about an economic depression that is still going on today. In fact, NOAA cited estimates that recovery efforts from Mitch could take as long as 20 years.

POVERTY IN HONDURAS

Today, 73% of the country's population is poor and more than half of that number is extremely poor (*Foro Nacional de Convergencia,* 2000). The average annual income for Hondurans is $927 U.S. Approximately a third of children under the age of 3 are chronically undernourished. Some do not live in homes with electricity or running water. Life expectancy from birth for Hondurans is 66.2 years, compared to 77.8 in the United States (Centers for Disease Control and Prevention, 2007), and the median age is 16, compared to 35.3 years in the United States (U.S. Census Bureau, 2001); young people between the ages of 15 and 24 represent just under a third (about 2 million) of the population (USAID, 2002). While this information has significance for the discussion of education in Honduras for many reasons, including the effects of poor nutrition on learning, one main reason to highlight Honduran poverty is to explain that it propels children to begin working often as early as age 3, typically by asking for money or selling fruit or newspapers. Children may be taken out of the school system entirely at any age between 3 and 12 or 13 to work full-time to help support their families. The official age at which Hondurans are to enter the workforce is 12 or 13.

History of Education in Honduras

Due to the infrastructure damage caused by Hurricane Mitch, it is difficult to find much historical information about anything in Honduras, including education. The information gathered for this section of this chapter was obtained from the Honduras Department of Education, unless otherwise noted. The earliest reference found to education in Honduras states that preschool education in Honduras actually began in 1907, although it was not formally recognized until 1953, when it appeared for the first time in a presidential memorandum. The Honduran Code of Administrative Procedures was established in the mid-1930s. Special education in the form of a school for the deaf was created in 1938. The National Music School came into being in 1953. Essentially, however,

> *Honduras lacked a national education system until the late 1950s. Before the reforms of 1957, education was the exclusive privilege of those who could afford to send their children to private institutions. The government of Ramón Villeda Morales (1957-63) introduced reforms that led to the establishment of a national public education system and began a school construction program. (Merrill, 1995, ¶1)*

On December 19, 1957, Honduras's 14th constitution was created and included a passage giving the *Universidad Nacional Autónoma de Honduras* (UNAH; National Autonomous University of Honduras) the right to govern itself and to coordinate and evaluate higher education (Article 146). In 1958, students were given participatory rights to UNAH's administrative decisions. The constitution of 1965 kept Article 146 and repeated the commission in Article 160.

Legislation Affecting Teacher Preparation

Initially, educators were prepared to teach elementary school over a six-year span, called *educacion normal,* after middle school. Then, in 1959, it changed to three years of preparation (the equivalent of high school) after middle school. *Educación normal* was taught in private and public schools. If an educator wished to teach in either preschool or higher education, an additional two to four years of training was required. A curriculum program for elementary was adopted in 1967. In 1972, four public schools, known as *escuelas normales,* were established to prepare teachers to teach elementary education, although this legislation was abandoned in 1977 under President Suazo Cordova as more schools were created across the country. In 1974, the National School of Music opened the door to training and certifying music teachers.

Structural Changes in the 1970s and 1980s

An office for preschool education was established in 1976, although a hierarchal link to the elementary school office was not established until 1983. Also in 1976, specific areas for vocational study were delineated, such as tailoring, dressmaking, and sewing; mechanics, carpentry, and electricity; radio, television, and woodworking; and cosmetology and hair styling/beauty. Laws were passed in 1978 allowing for the establishment of private universities and created the first office of investigation and research under the Department of Education to further data collection through an education census.

In 1982, UNAH was established as the authority over higher education, and the executive branch under the Secretary of Education was assigned oversight for preschool and elementary education. It should be noted that for Honduras, the Secretary of Education is actually an office rather than a person. That same year saw the formal establishment of education as the responsibility of the government. In 1987, the National Congress established a law for the handicapped. The National Council of Education was created in 1989. Headed by the Honduran president or the president's designee, other members of the council were the head of the Department of Education (as a vice president); the president of UNAH (as a second vice president); the head of the Department of Culture and Tourism;

the head of the Department of Planning, Coordination, and Budget; and two representatives from the Higher Education Council (one from the public sector and another from the private). The purpose of the national council was to supervise and coordinate the system, create proposals to further Honduran education, and create rules and regulations as necessary to guide the system.

Further Structuring in the 1990s

Comparatively speaking, there was considerable legislation in the 1990s. Beginning in 1990, the Centros Communitarios de Iniciacion Escolar (CCIE) enabled children 6 1/2 years old to attend pre-school—most of these children previously had not had such an opportunity. The first Honduran law related to employment of handicapped people appeared in 1991, although it was never implemented. Also in 1991, students were permitted to attend the national music school in order to pursue music as a vocational career. In 1992, *El Agricultor* (*The Agricultor*, a rural newspaper read by 30% of the rural population) was used as a means for educating people living in rural areas, specifically by providing teachers with lesson plans for their curriculum (Schuh, 2004).

The need for adult education was finally recognized in 1995 as part of the new school reform with implementation of the *EDUCATODOS* (Education for All) school reform (USAID, 2004). Among these changes was the replacement of the National Council with a new structure under the Department of Education and the restructuring of the new governing entity so that it was supported by the national, state, and county governments, as well as by the schools themselves. *EDUCATODOS* was retained but abruptly discontinued in 1998 as a result of Hurricane Mitch. In 1999, Honduras emerged from the wreckage and renewed the urgent call for and pursuit of school reform. Since 1999, Honduras has worked hard to bring about national school reform, partnering with the United States through USAID to come up with a workable and forward-moving system. The creation of new education standards, discussed later in this chapter, is an aligned goal that the government of Honduras is pursuing separately from the work with its international partners.

The Case for Reform

Honduras currently spends 7.2% of its gross domestic product (GDP) on education, most of it on salaries, indicating a serious weakness in resource allocation (Document HO-0202 from the Inter-American Development Bank). The education system serves about 1.6 million students in 17,367 public and private schools with 44,566 teachers. According to USAID, the literacy rate for Hondurans age 15 and older was 81.5% in 2004, up from a literacy rate of 72.7% in 1990. About 20% of the Honduran population over the age of 10 has never completed Grade 3, and Honduras's economic sectors are among the lowest producers in Latin America, due to the lack of trained professionals to work in them (USAID, 2004). However, school reform has had an effect. For instance, the percentage of eligible children enrolled in preschool education increased from 52.8% in 1990 to 78% in 2003 (USAID, 2004).

Obstacles to education reform have taken many forms—lack of resources, teacher training, qualified teachers, supervision, evaluation, and support, as well as natural disasters such as Hurricane Mitch and the high incidence of poverty. Approximately 400,000 children between the ages of 12 and 17 live in urban areas fraught with serious economic problems (HO-0202 Document of the Inter-American Development Bank). According to Merrill (1995, citing the Ministry of Education),

> *Honduras suffers from widespread illiteracy (more than 40% of the total population and more than 80% in rural areas). A significant percentage of children do not receive formal education. Especially in rural areas, schools are not readily accessible. When they are accessible, they often consist of joint-grade instruction through only the third grade. Schools are so understaffed that some teachers have up to 80 children in one classroom. Only 43% of children enrolled in public schools complete the primary level. Of all children entering the first grade, only 30% go on to secondary school. (¶3)*

In the decades following WWII, governments in Latin America, including that of Honduras, generally have undertaken the responsibility for providing formal education to their constituents. However, education in Honduras has suffered in the aftermath of the last decade's financial crisis as a result of Hurricane Mitch and the ensuing depression, and also due to technological changes around the world. Statistics also show that education in Honduras is not widely available: 40% of Honduras's children never finish grade school, and 10% never go to school at all, because their families cannot afford and/or do not have access to public education (USAID, 2004).

The call for education reform in Honduras has been heavily impacted by globalization, as expanding businesses and global corporations migrating to Latin America require multiple skills, including foreign language skills. The strength of the education system in Honduras is critical to improving the country's ability to compete in the global market as well as to help better the lives of its citizens. The current government has realized the need to address the country's failing education system. Due to its lack of resources, Honduras has been forced to seek outside assistance from international organizations and is currently working with USAID to develop a workable education system. However, there is no guarantee that the solutions undertaken by the present government will necessarily be taken up by the next one.

The Current Honduran Education System

The Honduran education system is divided into two sections: formal education and non-schooling. Formal education is a permanent and systematic process divided into grade levels and requiring teaching personnel as well as pedagogical space designed and equipped for that function. Informal education, or non-schooling, is a flexible and diverse process used to satisfy professional needs in particular areas and is given by professional educators and/or experts in the field in a format similar to a training workshop.

Formal Education

Formal education in Honduras is divided into four phases: 1) preschool education, 2) elementary education, 3) secondary education (middle and high school), and 4) higher education. These entities function under the responsibility of the Secretary of Education. They can be public or private; if private, it is under the auspices of the National Federation of Private Educational Institutions (FNIEP). Classes in Honduras begin on February 1 and run until November 30. The vacation months in Honduras are December and January. The school year consists of 200 school days (Monday through Friday), requiring a total of 30 hours of class time per week for Grades 1 through 4 and 31 hours for Grades 5 and 6. Classes are a minimum of 40 minutes long, with a recess of 20 minutes. According to the constitution of Honduras, private schools also are required to follow these guidelines.

Private Schools. Private schools operate on the funds charged for tuition and whatever donations they can garner, while public schools are supported by the government. In discussing the deficiencies of the Honduran school system, particularly with regard to the private schools, Merrill (1995) noted:

> *Because of the deficiencies of public education, the years since 1970 have seen the proliferation of private schools. With few exceptions, however, private education is popularly viewed as a profit-making enterprise. Great skepticism remains regarding the quality of the education that private schools offer. (¶6)*

It is important to note that any person may establish an elementary school as long as the Honduran laws are followed; private schools are approved and supervised under the department of education (in the same manner as public schools). Though they are not necessarily well-regarded, it is a mark of prestige and wealth to attend or to have one's children attend private school. One benefit to the education system offered by the private schools is that they are required to support the public schools to some degree, either through monetary donations—rarely given in Honduras, due to the fact that such donations often do not reach their intended recipients—or through donations of such supplies as textbooks or services, such as tutoring. Students in private schools must do some kind of service work for the public school as part of their educational requirements.

Bilingual Education. Honduran law requires that native Honduran citizens teach certain courses, such as the constitution, civic education, Spanish, and Honduras's history and geography. Specifically, Honduras's education law (Chapter VI, Article 64) states:

> *In order to teach at any level in the educational system, one is required by law to have an education certificate/diploma and to be a Honduran citizen; except in those cases where there is a lack of specialized personnel to teach specific areas at the various grade levels (elementary, middle, and high school). These teachers are considered "out of field." (p. 14)*

This law particularly affects bilingual education, for which there is a great push in Honduras as part of making it competitive in the global economy. The requirements for teaching in bilingual education are teacher certification, fluency in English, and/or Honduran citizenship. Teachers who are not Honduran citizens would be considered out of field, as mentioned above. However, finding qualified teachers is difficult and the professional development necessary to prepare teachers to teach a bilingual education curriculum is also expensive. The curriculum used in many bilingual schools in Honduras is based on the Honduran educational requirements. Classes are offered in Spanish and English. The homeroom teacher, who must be fluent in English, teaches math, science, health, reading, language (grammar), and spelling in English. Specialized Honduran teachers teach Spanish (grammar), social studies, music, arts, dance, computers, and physical education in Spanish. Because it is so expensive to establish a bilingual curriculum, all the bilingual schools in Honduras are private. As so many private schools teach most of their curriculum in English, however, Honduran law states that at least one year's education (10 months or 200 days) must be taught in Spanish. The law also requires that curriculum include issues related to democracy and civics as part of developing the virtue of patriotism.

Honduran Curriculum

Preschool. Preschool or early education is the initial step in the education system. It guides the child's first experiences, with an aim of socialization and of helping to develop the child's self-esteem. This period is up to three years of education prior to reaching the elementary level at age 6 1/2 (Honduran Education Law, Art. 19 & 20). Preschool curriculum is primarily concerned with 1) psychomotor development: increasing motor skills; 2) socio-affective development: the child's adaptation to the school environment; 3) intellectual development: introduction to math, pre-reading, and pre-writing skills, as well as an introduction to natural sciences; and 4) language development: acquisition of syntax, verbal, and conversational structure through the enrichment of vocabulary. Preschool programs must have the following classroom centers: drama, building, arts, science, and library. The same is true for elementary schools. The three years of preschool are pre-kindergarten, kindergarten, and *preparatoria* (preparation for Grade 1). Children begin preschool at 3 1/2 years old.

Elementary Education. Elementary education, which extends from kindergarten through Grade 6, is the government's responsibility and every child's right, unless that child has a disability that will stop him/her from learning (Honduras Education Laws, Articles 21-26). In order to enroll a student in elementary education, a parent or legal guardian must be present, the student must be at least 6 1/2 years old and no older than 13, and must have a birth certificate and grades from the previous year.

Elementary education focuses on five core areas: 1) health: physical education; 2) intellectual:

Spanish, social studies, math, and science; 3) visual and performing arts: music, singing, drawing, calligraphy, orthography, and decoration; 4) technical education: industrial arts, home economics, and agriculture; and 5) orientation: counseling (students take a class in which a family orientation is given). Elementary education is also geared toward helping children develop self-esteem. Curriculum is focused on developing good manners, critical thinking, scientific understanding, civic responsibility, family values, respect for the country, healthy habits, and appreciation for the arts through such courses as natural science and social studies. Religion is taught if parents request it.

Due to the high illiteracy rate, adult education for those older than 14 is also offered at the elementary level and is known as *extraescolar* (extra-schooling education). Enrollment in adult education also requires a birth certificate and grade transcripts from the previous year. If the student is age 12 or 13, verification of the reason for enrollment is required, usually in the form of current employment verification. Specialized schools, such as the Institute of Professional Development or the Council for the Development of Human Resources in Honduras, offer this type of adult education. Class time for these centers is limited to about five hours per week, so courses are offered in only five basic areas: math, social studies, Spanish, science, and human development. Their programs are structured according to four levels with the following goals:

1. Level 1, the equivalent of Grade 1, teaches reading and writing
2. In Level 2, equivalent to Grades 2 and 3, learning is more cultural and humanistic
3. Level 3, the equivalent of Grades 4 and 5, is also focused on cultural and humanistic learning
4. Level 4, the equivalent of Grade 6, attempts to establish a bridge between elementary and secondary education.

Secondary Education. Secondary education depends upon the student's area of study and follows the curricula in the elementary grades. It is divided into two areas: middle school and high school. Middle school lasts up to three years (Grades 7 through 9) and the time students spend in high school varies depending upon the program, but is usually less than two years.

Middle school (*educación media*) is integral education good for either entering higher education or obtaining employment. Those planning on earning a higher education degree spend two years in middle school, culminating in a bachelor's degree, while those going into technical areas, agriculture, industry, elementary education, or services in arts or sports, spend three years in middle school. Demand in these areas depends on the needs of the country at the time they graduate. Middle school offers instruction in the following areas: math, social studies, science, Spanish literature and language arts, civics and moral education, physical education, health, and visual and performing arts (music and drawing).

Based on the Honduran educational laws (Articles 19-43), the programs offered at the high school level are:

- College prep: a bachelor in science and language arts degree (*Bachiller en Ciencias y Letras*)
- Vocational schooling: agriculture, pottery, accounting, secretarial education, home economics, technicians (mainly two: mechanical technicians and electrical technicians), culinary education, etc. (i.e., professions considered important to developing the country)
- Visual and performing arts schooling: two programs confer a degree related to the area or program of study
- Elementary education: a three-year program conferring a degree in elementary education, which students are allowed to enroll in after middle school.

Higher Education. Higher education includes universities, schools, institutes, academies, and specialized centers. Undergraduate programs are short degrees (*carrera corta*, similar to an associate's degree), bachelor's degrees, or pre-med degrees. Graduate degrees, known as *especialities*, are the

Honduran equivalent of a master's degree. Honduras has very few doctoral degrees. The National University of Honduras (UNAH) is the only entity of higher education that has a direct connection with the government. It is public and therefore free to all Honduran citizens. The government has given UNAH the right to accredit other universities and/or authorize any degree conferred by another higher education entity to a Honduran citizen. All other universities must go through UNAH to open their doors; they can only receive government authorization if UNAH agrees with their regulations.

UNAH is relieved from any taxes and the government supports the university by giving 3% of the national revenue. The government offers scholarships and grants, as well as financial aid, to qualifying students who have earned such assistance by vocation, grades, or recommendations from the organizations where they work. These types of assistance enable students to purchase school supplies and textbooks, as the tuition is free.

As mentioned previously, there are few graduate degrees in Honduras. However, a graduate degree is required to teach either preschool or secondary education. In order to seek such a graduate degree for preschool, the student must first serve as an elementary teacher, and in order to obtain a degree in secondary education, the student must have a degree in secondary education in any of the areas mentioned above. These degrees are an additional two to four years after high school.

School Reform

National Forum of Convergence

Current school reform in Honduras primarily stems from the National Forum of Convergence, held in 2000 in Honduras, to address the many issues of the Honduran education system. The National Forum of Convergence proposed the following general objectives and principles for the new school reform program:

New School Reform Objectives
- Develop critical thinking
- Create responsible citizens
- Strengthen and promote family and national values
- Transmit knowledge of democracy
- Develop scientific knowledge
- Promote a strong work ethic and self-esteem
- Develop healthy habits
- Promote tolerance.

New School Reform Principles
- Academic freedom
- Equity and quality of life
- High-quality and free education
- Education as a right
- Innovation and dynamic education
- Identity
- Universal vision.

The National Forum on Convergence renamed preschool as "pre-basic education" and grades one through nine as "basic education," and mandated communication between the community, private entities, the secretary of education, and other organizations as a requirement of the government and the Honduras Department of Education. Basic education is obligatory and free and emphasizes reflective, creative, constructivist, and preventive (critical) thinking, and it incorporates three essential elements as part of the basic education curriculum: 1) foreign language (currently English),

2) technology, and 3) ethnic languages and culture, particularly native Honduran languages and culture, but also other foreign languages and cultures that might advance Honduras in the global marketplace. This element (ethnic languages and culture) is still being developed. It should be noted that one of the major components of the new school reform proposal from the National Forum for Convergence is bilingual education, which includes the possibility of languages other than English as also integral to the global economy.

Basic education includes elementary and middle school. The curriculum for elementary school is organized in three phases of three academic years each, a total of nine years, from grades 1 through 9. Phase 1, 1st through 3rd grade, emphasizes communication skills (reading and writing), math, and socialization. The second phase, grades 4 through 6, continues education in reading, writing, and math, introduces technology, analyzes the socio-economic realities and politics of Honduras, and focuses on the development of skills that will promote scientific investigation. Phase three, grades 7 through 9, is geared toward developing scientific and critical thinking and furthering knowledge and skills related to technology. This phase reinforces abilities and skills related to the different vocational areas as well, serving as a pre-vocational phase targeted to developing students' potential and an orientation to work that will align with their middle school education.

The new school reform proposal also outlined some points related to non-schooling/non-formal education, such as meeting the needs of participant organizations through activities aimed at developing necessary skills to help improve performance, and integrating higher education projects with the projects done in non-formal schools. Some of the activities that might be promulgated include workshops or training for professional groups, cooperatives, or managerial personnel; agricultural and forestry training; language or preschool training; workshops about health, housing, environment, family, or special education; and training and workshops about unions, community education, and citizenship.

Although special education has not yet been addressed, it was discussed as part of the new school reforms, and methods for implementing some type of program are currently under investigation.

Education Reform Programs

The Honduras Department of Education has developed intensive alternative educational programs to improve the education offered by the public school system. The United States has partnered with Honduras in this effort and these programs are funded in part by foreign grants, primarily from the U.S. Agency for International Development (USAID), and operated by non-governmental organizations (NGOs) and private entities. The Inter-American Development Plan specifically mentioned four programs:

1. *EDUCATODOS* (Education for All), financed by USAID
2. *Sistema de Aprendizaje Tutorial* (SAT; tutorial-based program), financed by the Honduran Department of Education
3. Honduran Radio-Education Institute (IHER), *Maestro en Casa*, which is self-financed: virtually all funding comes from students and sales of educational materials
4. *Telebasica,* funded by the Honduras Department of Education.

SAT. Based on similar programs in other countries, the target population for this program is youth who have completed their primary education. It is a secondary education program aimed at youth in rural areas with content based on community issues. A tutor coordinator meets with the students at agreed-upon locations and times. Students learn at their own pace and according to their abilities. The estimated cost per student is $240 US, and it has been supported by the association known as BAYAN (approximate translation: The Socio-Economic Association for the Honduran Native American Development) since 1996. The association helps with training tutors and resource teachers and with the adaptation and publication of textbooks. SAT has not been evaluated in Honduras, but there is high demand for it.

Maestro en Casa. For this program, the target population is youth and adults in rural areas who have dropped out of the conventional system prior to completing their education. Covering Grades 1 through 12, the program offers an accelerated primary educational program, an academic lower secondary program (*Ciclo Comun*), and an upper secondary program (*bachillerato*—regular high school level in science and humanities). Materials are presented to students in simplified forms, such as radio broadcasts and weekly tutorials. Classes are held in centers assisted by an outreach volunteer. Students pay no fees for these classes.

Telebasica. The target population of this program is youth and adults still attending school. The equivalent of grades 7 through 9, the program is based on the Mexican Education Ministry's *Telesecundaria* program. The classroom method combines classroom instruction by a school teacher with supporting textbooks and television programs. The cost per student is $303 US, and is funded by the Honduran Education Department. The program serves 35 centers in semi-urban and rural areas and, in comparison with the conventional school system, has shown positive results.

EDUCATODOS. The main program for improving education currently underway in Honduras is *EDUCATODOS*, which is based on an effort to provide infrastructure, a major concern in Honduras, as well as materials for expanding middle school to better address the needs of the country (Siri, Mendez, & Diaz, 2001). Schuh (2004) states that it was not until 1990 that USAID and the Honduran Department of Education started looking for different alternatives for ensuring that youth and adults completed an education through the 6th grade. In 1996, an option was presented that would offer an accelerated program covering grades 1 through 6 in three years. The precursor to the current *EDUCATODOS* program began in 1995 in the states of Choluteca and Valle and eventually was adopted in 13 states: Choluteca, Valle, La Paz, Intibuca, Lempira, Ocotepeque, Copan, Santa Barbara, Cortes, Francisco Morazan, Comyagua, and Yoro y Atlantida. The second phase began in July 2005 with the addition of two more states: Olancho and el Paraiso. The program was to have been instituted in the last three states (Colón, Gracias a Dios, and Bay Islands) by the end of 2006. The program has a technical coordinator, an administrative and financial administrator, and a technical committee (consisting of two project implementation unit coordinators, the office of human resources, two auditors, and representatives from three of the 15 state departments).

The goal of *EDUCATODOS* is to encourage youth and adults who have not finished school to participate in integrated learning combined with community action. The program offers quality and relevant learning that is accessible to those who wish to improve their living conditions and teaches quality education as the basis of a democratic society. According to Siri, Mendez, and Diaz (2001), the program is taught by about 5,600 volunteer facilitators in an available setting close to home or the workplace. It is sponsored by private business, NGOs, local government entities, and schools. *EDUCATODOS* uses radio broadcasts and other technology to facilitate learning. It has curriculum covering four basic areas of knowledge: math, science and technology, communication, and social studies, with an emphasis on the individual, values, ethics, and global society. Performance standards derived from these four basic areas focus on concepts and content pertinent to the participants' daily lives in five specific themes: population, environment, health, national identity, and citizenship and democracy. All learning is student centered, and important characteristics of the program are the flexibility and functionality of its curriculum.

More than 6,000 centers around the country have been opened to teach the program, which has reached more than 600,000 participants. The program has an impressive record of volunteer recruitment: more than 6,000 volunteers are involved in the program, providing oversight and assistance. *EDUCATODOS* has excelled in the establishment of collaborative linkage and partnerships, obtaining bonuses and incentive payments for facilitators. Its success also has been remarkable: 85% of the participants have obtained a certificate. The program is very close to surpassing its original goal target of $50 million in lifetime earning from the participants, ably demonstrating the program's potential to reduce poverty. USAID is gradually decreasing its funding as the Honduran government increases its part. There are 90,000 students in grades 1 through 9—80,000 of whom are receiving passing grades. The program has an efficiency rate of 70%.

There are a number of advantages to the program. It costs much less than the traditional education system. English instruction is included as an important tool for competing in the global market. The program relies on a network of coordinators and uses existing local and federal infrastructure. It offers nine years of basic education in just five years and is implemented by volunteers from diverse backgrounds. The program uses an integrated curriculum utilizing audio and printed materials to effectively meet the needs of the students. Of particular benefit to the students, the program has a flexible schedule of 2.5 hours a day of group work, complemented by homework. Multiple age groups are included and participants are able to enroll in the regular school once they pass grades 6 through 9.

According to Schuh (2001), data from 2001 showed that about 310,000 children ages 12 through 18 did not complete grade 6, and about 230,000 students between the ages of 15 and 18 who had completed grade 6 did not finish grade 9. These are the target populations for *EDUCATODOS*. Participants who enroll in the program have different levels of education. Many adults who enter the program are there just to learn to read and write.

In a study conducted by the Universidad Pedagógica Nacional (UPN) under the department of Unidad Externa de Medición de la Calidad de Educación (UMCE) in October and November of 2001, which examined the program's effectiveness and compared it to the traditional system, *EDUCATODOS* students showed similar or better performance in Spanish and math. In Spanish, 67% of 7th-graders achieved full mastery of the competencies for at least up to grade 4, and 46% of the 6th-graders had achieved full mastery of 7th-grade skills. The mathematics results were slightly lower.

New Performance Standards

New performance standards also have been set that include several indicators that the elementary students (Grades 1 through 6) must follow each year. These standards encompass the concepts of knowledge comprehension, skills, and attitudes in the areas of Spanish (listening, speaking, reading, and writing), math, science (particularly natural), and social studies (targeted to creating respectful citizens and family members). These performance standards are considered a basic tool to evaluate knowledge and skills and include indicators to allow teachers to plan according to student performance (i.e., classroom activities are linked to the objectives, materials, and school resources). The performance standards and their indicators apply to both general and specific areas. Under this curricular strategy, learners are given the opportunity to acquire concepts and develop learning processes that encourage democratic attitudes and behaviors. Some of the activities are designed for the promotion of tolerance, justice, equity, and recognition of the values and achievements of classmates and other members of the community. The curriculum encourages the students to analyze their rights and responsibilities in a democratic society. Development of these standards has been a long process, incorporating ideas from teachers, parents, consultants, and education specialists.

CONCLUSION

As has been discussed, there are a number of limitations that Honduras's education system must overcome, including insufficient funding, the lack of K-12 standards, insufficient training for teachers and administrators, a fragmented vocational system, and an unstable system overall, due to the unstable political infrastructure in Honduras. The government of Honduras continues to try to overcome these challenges in order to improve the system and provide effective and high-quality education. Clearly, poverty will not be reduced in Honduras without substantial improvement in the education system. Honduras must make more effective investments to reach the goals of quality, efficiency, and equity in education by closing these gaps and developing a more educated and skilled workforce that could better enable Honduras to compete in the global market.

References

Centers for Disease Control and Prevention. (2007). *Life expectancy.* Retrieved from www.cdc.gov/nchs/fastats/lifexpec.htm

Colegio de Professores de Educacion Media en Honduras (COPEMH). (1947). *Honduran education laws.* Tegucigalpa, M.D.C., Honduras, C.A.: Author.

Foro Nacional de Convergencia (National Forum of Convergence). (2000). *Proposal from the Honduran society to transform national education.* Tegucigalpa, M.D.C., Honduras, C.A.: Author.

Honduras Department of Education. (1993). *New performance standards.* Tegucigalpa, M.D.C., Honduras, Central America: Author.

InfoPlease. (n.d.). *Honduras.* Retrieved from www.infoplease.com/ipa/A0107616.html

Inter-American Development Bank. (n.d.). *Honduras: Secondary education and job training program.* Retrieved from www.iadb.org/exr/doc98/apr/ho1552e.pdf

Merrill, T. (Ed.). (1995). *Honduras: A country study.* Washington, DC: U.S. Government Printing Office for the Library of Congress. Retrieved from http://countrystudies.us/honduras/58.htm

National Oceanic and Atmospheric Administration. (NOAA). (2006). *Hurricane Mitch.* Retrieved from http://lwf.ncdc.noaa.gov/oa/reports/mitch/mitch.html

Schuh, A. M. (2004). *Honduras case study: EDUCATODOS.* Washington, DC: Academy for Educational Development.

Siri, C., Mendez, V. R., & Diaz, R. (2001, March). *Strengthening democracy through education.* Paper presented at the annual meeting of the Comparative and International Education Society, Washington, DC. USAID document no. PN-ACL-070.

USAID. (2002). *Honduras activity data sheet.* Retrieved from www.usaid.gov/pubs/cbj2002/lac/hn/522-006.html

USAID. (2004). *Improving the quality, efficiency, and equity of basic education in Honduras: Honduras at a glance.* Honduras, Central America: Author.

U.S. Census Bureau. (2001). *Nation's median age highest ever.* Retrieved from www.census.gov/Press-Release/www/2001/cb01cn67.html

About the Author

Cristina P. Valentino, Ed.D., graduated from the University of North Florida with a degree in educational leadership with a concentration in ESOL/language acquisition. She is the ESOL coordinator and an assistant professor at Jacksonville University. cvalent@ju.edu; 904-256-7218.

CHAPTER
10

Curriculum in India:
The Struggle of Caste, Creed, Gender, and Humanity

Aradhana Mudambi and Basanti Chakraborty

In 1947, when the red denoting a British colony that had colored India on world maps for 200 years finally disappeared, India held a unique position in the world. It was an ancient entity, an old culture, but a new country. This paradox brought about an interesting challenge in the development and transmittance of educational curriculum in India.

This chapter reviews the Indian curriculum and its development, and swings through history and its current problems, trying throughout to understand why formal education has not become a ubiquitous phenomenon in this ancient land. In doing so, this chapter uses John Bobbit's definition of curriculum as the backdrop to the understanding of curricular development in India. According to Bobbit, a curriculum is the "series of deeds" experienced by children that transform them into adults. Included in this series may be training and "participation in community life" (Bobbit, 1918, p. 42). Hence, every child, including those who do not attend school, is subject to some sort of curriculum, formal or otherwise. It is through formal education, however, that a greater control over this curriculum—one that hopefully leads to literacy, prosperity, and success—can be attained.

In order to contemplate curricular development, this chapter is divided into two major sections. The first section looks at curriculum for the Indian population as a whole and especially for under-privileged groups, including lower social caste, scheduled caste and scheduled tribe, rural, Muslim, and female students. This section provides a historical backdrop to education, demonstrating the transformation of curriculum, from a values-based education that followed Bobbit's definition of curriculum into an education system that demonstrated the hierarchy of people by excluding various groups. It then explores various attempts and proposed solutions to eradicate unequal curricula, including the use of foreign aid in creating educational programs and legal reform initiatives. Finally, it analyzes various problems prohibiting universal education, such as the lack of qualified teachers and the manner in which the curriculum is transmitted.

India

The second section attempts to understand why, in spite of the measures discussed in the first section, a fair and equal curriculum, amounting to not only universal education but also equal education for underprivileged groups, has not been achieved. It takes the curricular developments for girls since ancient times as a quintessential example of the difficulties in achieving both universal, formal education and a fair curriculum that encourages the prosperity of the underprivileged. This section also focuses on the historical aspects of the formal, female curriculum, demonstrating how foreign influences have degraded girls. Furthermore, it discusses additional steps taken to improve female education and the constant vacillation between curricular improvements for girls and a return to a biased, unequal curriculum, proving that reform only can be successful when it occurs within the hearts of the Indian people, rather than through formal measures.

UNIVERSAL EDUCATION

Historical Perspective

During Vedic times[1], the ancient Gurukul system required students during secondary schooling to live in their teachers' homes, where teachers took near-familial interest in their students, providing children with food and clothing. Testing was obviously not a strong component of the system, so teachers could concentrate on helping the children develop as people rather than as test takers. In line with developing the whole person, the curriculum included two important aspects, academics and morals. It required instruction under four major subject headings: *Anyikshaki,* or sciences derived from focused introspection; *Trayi,* or three of the Vedas constituting the religious literature; *Varta,* or agriculture; and *Dandanti,* or government and civics. Sanskrit was also very important to the learning process. Equally important to this academic training, teachers were expected to shape students' personalities, enabling them to face challenges and serve society (Dogra & Gulati, 2006). Hence, the traditional Indian approach to education focused on both the academic and moral development of students.

By the medieval era (1000 AD), a sense of caste hierarchy and gender inequalities had crept into Hindu society, alongside many superstitions. These evils could be seen in the school system. In response, Buddhists created their own education system, thus reforming the existing structure. They made no caste or gender distinction, although all teachers were monks. The curriculum was conveyed in vernacular languages rather than the traditional Sanskrit, thus helping make education more universal. Furthermore, the curriculum purged unscientific, arguably evil elements that had crept into the Vedic education system. Such elements included witchcraft, certain spells and incantations, omens, incantations, and astrology. The Buddhist curriculum focused on yoga, arithmetic, medicine, poetry, and the study of the four Vedas, among other similar subjects. Furthermore, as done in the *Gurukula* system, teachers and students were expected to have a close bond; thus, each one would have a stake in the well-being of the other. Also, as in the *Gurukula* system, students were expected to renounce the outside world during their studies (Dogra & Gulati, 2006; Mookerji, 2003; Sgharfe, 2002). The development of the Buddhist education system was not an attempt to eradicate all elements of the existing Hindu system, but it worked as a reform movement to streamline the curriculum and make universal formal education.

Both the Vedic *Gurukula* system and the Buddhist education system followed the idea of curriculum that Bobbit endorses. Curriculum was not simply the written prescription of texts and math problems that students were expected to absorb. Since students lived in a community with their teachers, their education also included their daily, social lives within a community. Chores and socialization automatically became an integral part of their formal education.

The British, after colonizing India in 1757, introduced their own system of education. Their system, unlike that of ancient India, had little to do with such lofty ideals of moral and character development. Students generally attended school by day and learned typical western academic subjects, such as math, reading, and sciences. More important was learning the English language, particularly for students who aspired to attend the university. Stressing the importance of the "British" aspect of the curriculum, those elite young men whose families could afford it traveled all the way to Britain in order to finish their higher education. Although there is nothing ostensibly wrong with the curriculum at a purely academic level (there was, however, the erosion of culture, depicted by the change in language and the lack of Indian religious instruction), the British curriculum was only available to elite men, as the British tried to create an Anglo-friendly upper strata of Indians who would, in the name of the paramount power, control the people. Overall, lower-class/caste children, the rural population, poor Muslims, and girls were left out of the superior British schools (Cohn, 1996). Instead, their educational curriculum, in accord with Bobbit's definition, involved only working in the fields or performing housework. Hence, not only did the British schools teach academic subjects, they also taught that there is an inherent hierarchy among people according to gender, caste, and economic status. This lesson, which the British taught through their formal schools, did not reach just those who attended school but, by virtue of exclusion, also reached those who did not have the opportunity for formal education.

During the 1930s, the Government of India, although still under the British Raj, adopted Mahatma Gandhi's scheme of basic education to initiate reform. Gandhi's educational philosophy, known as *Nai Talim*, intended to provide general education through the life and work of the village community. Gandhi was inspired by the ancient classical texts of India as well as by Tolstoy, Ruskin, Thoreau, Bondaref, Besant, Carlyle, and other western thinkers. Mahatma Gandhi valued children and their holistic development; hence, he wanted to ensure that irrespective of class, caste, creed, and socio-economic status, all children would receive true education in the early years. Gandhi believed that education is a lifelong process and should cover the whole life from conception to death. In December 1944, in Sevagram, Gandhi said that education was not limited to school-age children, but had to reach all beings from conception to the moment of death.

Gandhi's system of education was, schematically, the following:

- Adult education of the whole community, including the parents of newborns
- Pre-basic schooling from 2 to 7 years
- Basic schooling from 7 to 14 years
- Post-basic schooling from 14 to 18 years
- University and teacher training institute education (Palmer, 2001).

In regard to education for children, Gandhi believed that education should bring out the best in all the domains of a child's life: physical, intellectual, and spiritual. According to Gandhi, education should cultivate the hearts of young people. Gandhi's *Nai Talim* emphasized the use of the theoretical and practical knowledge of the culture of the society; education was imparted to build competence and scientific understanding through spinning, weaving, animal husbandry, and other rural crafts. Gandhi truly believed that children benefit by learning through craft. Active work and craft create interest and naturally make the educative process easy and simple. As for adults, Gandhi strongly advocated self-discipline of people through the establishment of small and decentralized communities or villages. In a sense, his *Nai Talim* was a silent social revolution and intended to provide a healthy relationship between the city and the village. It was nationalist in setting, idealist in nature, and pragmatic in social purpose (Marlow-Ferguson, 2002; Palmer, 2001).

Upon India's birth as an independent nation, the country's founders, like Gandhi, wanted to provide formal education for all children, regardless of caste, creed, or gender. Article 45 of the Indian Constitution, which was signed into effect in 1949, promised to "Endeavor [sic] to provide, within a period of ten years from the commencement of this Constitution, for free and *compulsory* education for all children until they complete the age of 14 years." Nevertheless, great disparities continue to exist in formal educational attainments among upper caste, urban males and other subsets of the population, such as Scheduled Caste/Scheduled Tribe, rural, Muslim, and female children (Bajpai, 2003).[2] What accounts for these differences 60 years after independence? This chapter will explore various possible explanations to try to explain the unequal education system in India.

Economic Difficulties

First, through mercantilism and high taxation, the British left many in the Indian community impoverished (Stokes, 1973). Until American president Lyndon Johnson's assistance through the green revolution, through which farming techniques were industrialized, many rural Indians went hungry (Wu & Butz, 2000). Given these dire circumstances, it was only logical that the Indian government would concentrate its efforts on making food available to its people rather than on reforming education.

Nevertheless, the excuse of financial hardship cannot completely explain why India has been unsuccessful in equalizing education. The world responded favorably to India's need for assistance in developing education. For instance, the Indian government has accepted external funding from the World Bank, the Swedish International Development Agency (SIDA), UNICEF, the European Commission (EC), and others (*External Funding for Education*, n.d.). In turn, this money has been used for a variety of programs, such as the District Primary Education Programme (DPEP), Shiksha Karmi Program, and the Sarva Shiksha Programme (District Primary, n.d.; SSA Focus on Improvement, n.d.). Hence, financial hardship cannot entirely explain away the inequalities that still exist in Indian education.

Analysis of Various Programs

If financial difficulties for the government have not been the absolute problem for making education universal in India, what has continued to hold back the various, underprivileged Indian subsets? To further explore the topic, one must analyze the programs developed with the international funds set aside for education to determine if their goals and initiatives have been appropriate for equalizing the curriculum.

First, the District Primary Education Program (DPEP), funded by the European Commission, was launched in 1994, with its main objective being the universal attainment of primary education. Special emphasis was placed on women, but the program embraced all rural area subgroups. Its main goals were universal access, retention, and achievement. DPEP tried to accomplish these goals by constructing new schools, opening up non-formal school centers, setting up early childhood education centers, and providing instruction to disabled students. While the program had many successes (helping to open more than 100,000 schools), the enrollment of female students in the program still lags behind that of male students (District Primary, n.d.). Hence, DPEP cannot claim to have been totally successful in achieving universal education or even in helping to provide equality in education to girls.

Furthermore, the Shiksha Karmi Program (SKP), funded by SIDA, has been instrumental in reforming education in Rajasthan by helping girls, as well as by providing for schools in backward areas and targeting backward classes. As with other institutions, the program lists making universal education one of its primary aims (*India*, n.d.). Nevertheless, the Census of 2001 demonstrates that the literacy rate for girls still hovers around 40% while it is 70% for boys. Why the failure? The SKP itself has identified the lack of qualified teachers in Rajasthan as an obstacle. For male education, men with 8th-grade education are chosen and trained; for female education, women with at least 5th-grade education are trained (*India*, n.d). Although also prompted by necessity, the disparity in educational levels of teachers according to gender works through the "hidden curriculum" to keep female students suppressed, thereby at least partially explaining the gender gap in literacy.

Finally, the Sarva Shiksha Abhiyan (SSA) serves the whole country, with a special emphasis on girls, schedule caste, and schedule tribe children, as well as on children with special needs. Along with the recruitment and training of teachers, the provision of free textbooks for all schedule caste, schedule tribe, and female students, and the opening of schools where educational facilities are not easily accessible, the SSA also attempts to catalyze uniformity in education by providing for curricular reform. Grant money is provided to fund the development of curricular materials that emphasize local context (*Basic Features*, n.d.; *SSA Focus on Improvement*, n.d.). The hope is that if learning is more authentic and relevant, rural students will be more likely to learn and want to remain in school.

In order to further push SSA's ability to reach the female population, the Indian government of 1993 launched the National Program for Education of Girls at Elementary Level. Its main goal is to impact the "hardest to reach" girls, especially those currently not enrolled in schools. The National Program for Education of Girls at Elementary Level focuses on enhancing the education of girls who live in rural areas where levels of female literacy are lower than the national average and the gender gap in education is above the national average; the government labels these areas as educationally backward blocs (EBB). A strong curricular component exists among traditional reform measures (such as the provision of school supplies). The program attempts to develop gender-sensitive curricular material and to train teachers in the equal treatment of genders. As a result, teachers will conceivably not be imparting the curriculum with any preconceived biases that inadvertently discourage female students from pursuing their education (*Guidelines for Implementation*, n.d.). However, between the training of equal treatment and the eradication of actual bias exists a large gulf.

The full effects of the program cannot yet be analyzed as of the writing of this chapter, since one of the stated goals focuses on the future. They include that all children, 6-11 years of age, should have completed primary education by the year 2007 (a goal that a mere walk through an Indian village or city proves unaccomplished), and that all children ages 6-14 should complete eight years of schooling by 2010 (*Basic Features*, n.d.; *SSA Focus on Improvement*, n.d.).

Of course, other similar programs have been developed to reach all children, regardless of caste, creed, or gender, such as Operation Blackboard and National Bal Bhavan. Each has tried to improve education in similar ways; however, a unique technique is the National Bal Bhavan's attempts to use singing and the exploration of instruments to enhance learning (Singh, 1999). Unfortunately, Bal Bhavan has also failed to universalize education. Overall, the programs have not provided the reform necessary for universal education.

Legal Reform Initiatives

Alongside various government and internationally funded programs, the Indian government has passed a variety of legal reform initiatives to emphasize its commitment to universal education, encompassing girls, minorities, all religious groups, and underprivileged classes. The most important of these emphasized the use of curriculum to attract and retain students; these legal initiatives were the National Policy of Education (1986) and the National Policy of Education (1992). Together, these reform statements emphasized various curricular reforms. For example, they stressed the need for a common curriculum throughout the country. Furthermore, although most state boards offer education in local, mainstream languages, tribal populations are often excluded because of language barriers. Hence, in order to reach this group, the reform statements called for the transmission of education in tribal languages. In addition, as the National Program for Education of Girls at Elementary Level took to heart, the reforms called for the use of education and textbooks to teach equality. As a unique balance among society's needs, the reforms also demanded an improvement in the teaching of the sciences and the exposure of students to the various roles that each of the core subjects—sciences, humanities, and social sciences—have in society. The latter emphasizes, in a test-driven society that values only science, that all students, regardless of interests, should continue schooling. Moreover, one of the most important curriculum reform suggestions is the development of adult education, turning influential adults in young students' lives into models of lifetime learning. Finally, the legal statements emphasized the reduction of test-driven curricula and memorization, thereby eliminating one of the strongest enemies of education, as discussed briefly.

Other Difficulties

In spite of such reform programs and legal initiatives, why has India not succeeded in universalizing education? Do parents of rural, SC/ST, and female children not want their children attending school? According to the Public Report on Basic Education in India (PROBE) survey, an overwhelming majority of parents want their children, regardless of caste, creed, or gender, at school. Of course, there are exceptions (later discussed). However, statistics provided by PROBE demonstrate that parents are not exclusively to blame for students not attending school (Public Report on Basic Education, n.d.). Among the other reasons include overcrowded classrooms, scanty supplies, inadequate teacher training, indifference of the community, and the lack of quality education. Furthermore, according to District Information System for Education (2006), over 9% of schools remain a single classroom and over 10% do not even have classrooms. How are students supposed to learn in such environments? Furthermore, the average student-teacher ratio for the country is 36:1, demonstrating that classes are too large for successful learning to occur. Worse yet, over 5% have more than 100 students! (DISE, 2006).

Further dampening efforts toward universal education are lack of transportation to distant schools, unattractive school environments, and fixed school hours. Since rural, SC/ST, and especially female students are responsible for working for household maintenance, students should be able to attend school when it is convenient to them. Furthermore, one of the worst obstacles to universal schooling is the lack of teacher motivation. Teachers not only impart the overt curriculum, but they also teach children to value or despise learning through their own attitudes. Thus, teacher attitude becomes part of the "hidden curriculum." In spite of reform movements designed to train teachers and enhance their status, Indian society fails to value educators. Primary school teachers are burdened with trivial tasks. Hence, very little time is left for actual teaching. Besides, in rural schools, teacher absenteeism is a common phenomenon, because teachers often live in nearby villages from which they have to take public transportation. The money that teachers must spend on taking public transportation often eats up their salary. Many teachers who remain absent from their schools can appoint village residents as replacements, typically high school dropouts who take over the primary class without a basic knowledge of pedagogy. Hence, not only are trained teachers unmotivated, they also are often replaced by untrained, uneducated villagers (Ramachandran et al., 2005).

The most challenging setbacks to universal education are poverty and the overt curriculum. First, only rich students receive early childhood education. Preprimary education is not a fundamental right provided for by India's constitution. However, well-to-do students are able to start school at age 3 or 4 in lower kindergarten (LKG) and continue through upper kindergarten (UKG). These classes often teach such school-related skills as socialization and such basic literacy elements as letters and sight words. Since these students have a greater knowledge base when they start primary school, they are more likely to be successful and, therefore, stay in school, unlike their poorer, often lower caste counterparts. This factor partially explains the educational achievement gaps among various socioeconomic groups. Second, students from all backgrounds drop out prior to finishing school because school supplies become prohibitively expensive for parents. Furthermore, many interested students leave school in order to take up gainful employment to help family expenditures or, if they are female, to marry, thereby ridding their parents of a financial burden (*Universal Primary Education*, 1997).

Third, the methodology of imparting the Indian curriculum is perhaps one of the greatest setbacks to education. Classes are highly "teacher-centered, passive, and unnecessarily repetitive" ("Classroom," 2001, ¶1). Teacher-student relationships rest on reverence and unreciprocated respect towards teachers (Mudambi, 1999). Hence, students not only fail to learn to think critically or to question what they are being told, they also have very little opportunity to enjoy a class when rote memorization and drill are the norm. Further worsening the system is India's test-based education system, which places undue pressure on students, who, upon failure or threat of failure, may choose to drop out. Furthermore, rural students with other home-related responsibilities may not be able to handle the additional stress of exams. Finally, in needing to teach to the test, teachers use repetition and copying from the textbooks as their teaching tools (Nambissan, 2004). Such boring activities as rote memorization cannot be expected to keep the interest of young minds, who may be more attracted by other pursuits.

A Cultural Issue

In spite of the vast number of obstacles to the ultimate goal of universal education, one must note that the aforementioned education reform programs and legal initiatives have addressed most of these difficulties in attaining universal education. From teacher training to free textbooks, nearly every problem is covered. Why have these issues not been resolved? Why does a wide disparity continue to exist among various groups within India? Regardless of government intention, does the Indian culture prohibit the advancement of lower socio-economic castes, Muslims, and women?

In order to further explore this suggestion, it can be helpful to consider the curricular history and development of education in regard to any one group in particular as an example in order to attain a more in-depth perception. This section explores the evolution of female education.

FEMALE EDUCATION

Current Disparities

In spite of the aforementioned programs and legislation designed to provide equal education, girls, especially in rural and strongly patriarchal societies within the nation, have received the short end of the stick when it comes to education. According to the Indian Census of 2001, after more than 50 years of independence, India's average female literacy rate is 54.28%, which is still very low compared to India's average male literacy rate of 75.96%. Why is there such a large disparity between literacy rates? Primarily, not all Indians recognize the importance of education for girls. For instance, as one man in a Rajasthani village asserted, "A man is one who earns," and a girl is expected to become a homemaker (Kumar, Gupta, & Abraham, 2002, p. 8). This foreordained career thereby eliminates her need to attend school. Also, even girls who begin school are often withdrawn to help care for younger siblings or to protect their honor when they hit puberty (Velkoff, 1998).

Additionally inhibiting the growth of female literacy are the strong, patriarchal systems ubiquitous in many parts of India, especially in the rural areas. These systems are set in place to function without consideration given to women's needs. For example, in Rajasthan, not only have women been consistently denied opportunities for learning, they also have been denied proper health care and independence. More than 80% of Rajasthani women need permission even to visit relatives or to go to the market (Kumar et al., 2002). Even in states such as Gujarat, where the gender ratio is slowly declining, a strong patriarchal system continues to be set in place (Nagar et al., 2002; Visaria, 2005). This system helps keep the gender gap in literacy high in Gujarat.

Such societal factors can mistakenly suggest an inherent flaw within Indian culture prohibiting the development of education for girls; however, it is not the Indian culture per se, but foreign influences that have played the strongest part in prohibiting the proper development of female education. Although those girls who are not allowed to attend school are affected the most, even girls who graduate from high school (upon completion of the 10th standard) often receive an unequal education in spite of the various well-intentioned education reform movements. To fully understand the tug of war between progress towards gender equity in education and the maintenance of the status quo, one must understand the history of curricular development for girls in India.

Vedic Education for Women

Ancient Indians believed in the equality of the genders and thus provided for the education of women. Girls could choose between two paths, the first to become *sadyovadus*, or students, until the age of 16, when they married, or they could become *brahmavadinis*, or lifetime scholars. Regardless, all girls were expected to read and study the *Vedas*, the ancient texts of the Hindu religion, and eventually participate in a religious thread ceremony that served as a rite of passage (Haddad & Findly, 1985). The importance of female education was so great that in the ancient text of the *Brihadaranyaka Upanishad*, a meal is prescribed for parents who want to beget a daughter who will become highly educated. Hence, for parents, it was important that their daughters were successful in their schooling. In the same holy book, there are female *Brahmavidyas*, or those who are familiar with the highest knowledge. Women such as Gargi engage in high-quality intellectual conversations with their male counterparts, demonstrating recognition of intellectual parity between the sexes (Krishnananda, n.d.; Thorner & Raj, 2000). Further suggesting that early Vedic Indians recognized intellectual parity, students participated in co-educational, outdoor classrooms. Finally, not only were there female students, but there were also many female teachers, providing young girls with models of successful, learned women. These female teachers were able to sustain themselves economically and attracted students of both genders (Haddad & Findly, 1985).

Medieval Education

During medieval times, the quality of education for women decreased. The thread ceremony, a rite of passage for Hindus, became exclusively for upper caste men (Haddad & Findly, 1985). This loss eliminated the need for girls to read and study the *Vedas*. Various theories have been proposed to explain this societal decay, including that women were required to marry earlier and therefore did not have enough time to complete their Vedic studies (Scharfe, 2002). However, this explanation fails to demonstrate why women were marrying earlier. Why were changes occurring leading to the meltdown of equal education?

The Hindu culture, for better or for worse, has historically been malleable, absorbing and bending to incorporate various cultures under its own canopy of beliefs (Michaels, 2004). Greek, Roman, and other near-western influences penetrated Indian minds, and women were gradually excluded from Vedic studies. Since many ancient cultures believed in the inferiority of women, the influences of foreign cultures easily marked upon Indian society a sense of patriarchy.

The process of change in Indian attitudes can be seen in Vatsyayana's *Kama Sutra* (1962). Although Vatsyayana urges the wife to satisfy the whims of her husband (such as to wash his feet upon his arrival home and to allow him to add wives if he tires of her), he also outlines a rigorous curriculum for female education. Alongside what is now considered the stereotypically female roles of cooking and sewing, he also includes the fine arts, such as "playing on musical instruments" and "dancing," as well as literacy pursuits, such as "reading," "drawing inferences," and "study of sentences" (Vatsyayana, 1962, pp. 69-71). He even includes the sciences of chemistry, geology, warfare, and medicine. Vatsyayana suggests that women who are separated from their husbands, "even in a foreign country," can be self-sufficient if they know these arts (Vatsyayana, 1962, pp. 69-72). The idea of women standing on their own two feet suggests a semblance of the then-disappearing Vedic equality between genders; however, he qualifies his position on gender equality, stating that women who are well-versed in these arts will "make their husbands favourable [sic] to them, even though these may have thousands of other wives" (Vatsyayana, 1962, p. 72). Hence, the primary purpose of learning the arts is to become a better housewife. Furthermore, unlike during the early Vedic times, Vatsyayana did not suggest that formal, female teachers instruct young girls; rather, he suggested that married female friends and relatives should guide female students (Vatsyayana, 1962). This assignation demonstrates not only that women were no longer considered worthy of positions of employment but also that the woman's place was now confined to the home and that her primary role was that of a wife.

Colonial Influences

As time progressed, the amalgamation of Indian culture with various foreign cultures further relegated women from their once equal position to a subservient position in society, thus making any system of education for women nearly defunct. When the British colonized India, the paramount rulers no doubt brought their own gender biases with them. Such gender biases included Victorian ideas of female frailty, Protestant depictions of the ideal woman as stolid, and beliefs that upon female morality rests the survival of society. In fact, the British not only believed in the inferiority of women and their intellectual capacity, but also by the second half of the 19th century, presented quasi-scientific proof to back their views. According to the British and other Europeans, the frontal lobes of the brain were the seat of intelligence. Scientists reasoned that since men had bigger frontal lobes, they were the more intelligent sex (Karlekar, 1989). Hence, British influence did not present an alternative to the well-established Indian biases against women. Instead, British society supported and further encouraged them.

During the mid-1800s, foreign Christian missionaries brought about the first formal attempts to return Indian women to an educated state. By this time, many Indian women who were active in the independence movement and/or social reform already recognized their need for formal education and thus welcomed the opportunity for young girls to learn. Missionaries opened day schools and *zenanas,* or home schools, in order to instruct girls. Education for girls and boys were nearly on par with one another; however, the missionaries had an underlying aim to proselytize students (Mukhopadhyay & Seymour, 1994). Upon realizing this intent, nationalists feared yet another erosion of their Indian identity.

Although nationalist men found themselves in need of British education in order to survive economically, they looked upon their female counterparts as embodiments of an Indian identity that they wished to preserve. There was, however, no denying that many girls wanted an education and would turn to the missionaries. Hence, Hindu and Muslim nationalist schools for girls in India were opened during the mid-1850s. These schools, in turn, cultivated supposedly "traditional" Indian values, such as spirituality, so that girls could embody a traditional *Bharat* in an amorphous, colonial India. Girls learned to read and write vernacular languages, leaving the foreign yet more progressive English language to their male contemporaries. Furthermore, they prepared for their vocation as wives and mothers rather than as active members of the public sphere (Karlekar, 1989; Mukhopadhyay & Seymour, 1994; Sangari & Vaid, 1999).

While it is easy to see this step backward in gender equity as a result of culture, nationalist reaction was a result of colonialism. Indians were trying to maintain a distinct identity from their colonizers. They mistrusted missionaries, recognizing the missionaries' intent to convert Indian children. Facing an even greater challenge, Muslims, as minorities, feared the erosion of their religious identity by not only the British, but also by the Hindu *shuddi* movement, which was started by the Arya Samaj to convert non-Hindus (Mukhopadhyay & Seymour, 1994). Many nationalists also mistakenly labeled progress and social reforms regarding gender equality as British and imperial rather than as a feminist movement that was emerging in sovereign nations worldwide. Although this feminist movement existed in India, it could have conceivably emerged more strongly in the absence of colonialism.

Furthermore, the British, as earlier noted, still struggled with their own stereotypes; thus, in spite of missionary efforts to provide equal education, they supported the notion that women were to be educated for the purpose of maintaining family values. According to Wood's Educational Despatch of 1854, "The importance of female education in India cannot be over-rated" because of its impact on "the moral tone of the people" (Karlekar, 1989, p. 12). Hence, the British also reinforced the idea that women were not learning for employment or critical thinking purposes, but rather for the betterment of family and, consequently, society. Without a doubt, such views negatively impacted the curriculum for women.

Steps To Improve Female Education

Immediately following independence, in order to remedy the low attendance of girls in schools, the Indian government began to address education for girls in a series of five-year plans. In 1950, it proposed eliminating single-sex schooling in order to increase female attendance in schools. However, centuries of separate male and female spheres rendered this attempt unsuccessful, as parental fears could not be allayed. In response, the next five-year plan recommended alternatives to co-educational schooling and encouraged the training of more female teachers (*Universal Primary Education,* 1987). The current five-year plan suggests building more dorms near schools for girls and better toilet facilities (*Working Group Report,* 2007). These suggestions, however, echo unfulfilled suggestions by the National Committee on Women's Education, which was created by the Indian government in 1958 (*Universal Primary Education,* 1987). The repetition of suggestions to improve education for girls, after nearly 50 years, demonstrates the futility of these efforts.

The government also worked toward curricular equalization. For example, two government-sponsored committees, The National Committee of Women's Education in 1959 and The Committee on the Differentiation of Curricula for Boys and Girls in 1964, recommended that boys and girls be educated through the same curriculum. For example, their suggestions included that both boys and girls study home sciences (*Universal Primary Education*, 1987). The Government of India, through the Department of School, Education, and Literacy, currently posts its intent to provide girls with "gender-sensitive teaching-learning materials including textbooks" on its website (*Girls' Education*, n.d.). Hence, a continuous movement has existed to provide an equal education for both genders.

Such efforts have resulted in a gradual equalization of educational opportunities for girls in school. First, the number of girls educated has increased. In fact, the total enrollment of girls in primary school increased at a faster rate than the total enrollment of students in general between 1950 and 2003. Second, the percentage of total students in primary and secondary schools who are girls more than doubled during the same period (*Working Group Report*, 2007). Middle-class, urban girls generally attend school (Karlekar, 1989).

Furthermore, there has been a change in the curricular offerings for girls. For example, in 1968, the 10+2 system (10 grades and pre-university) was adopted, requiring all students to take sciences through the 10th standard. This requirement replaced the arts and home economics classes offered to girls (Karlekar, 1989). Hence, it is more common for girls, especially in urban areas, to become doctors, lawyers, teachers, and other professionals (Karlekar, 1989).

Continued Struggle for Equalized Education

In spite of the ostensible improvements aimed toward gender equity in education, a struggle between antiquated notions of gender and modern attempts at social reform has continued throughout the post-independence era. As aforementioned, many rural societies and economically disadvantaged families still deny their girls an education. Furthermore, various "committees" have echoed ideals from the 1850s that women must be educated for the sake of family, demonstrating the difficulty in destroying old beliefs (*Universal Primary Education*, 1987). As recently as 1984, the Commission for Planning of Higher Education in West Bengal proposed to increase the offerings of home sciences courses to girls in order to "teach to create an atmosphere of peace, happiness and moral and spiritual well-being in the family" (Karlekar, 1989, p. 12). Hence, the Commission once again relegated the purpose of female education to preparing the ideal wife and mother.

In addition, in spite of the fact that the curriculum offered to both genders is ostensibly the same, when girls choose their proposed course of study, more girls than boys choose to go into the arts or into a vocational program, in spite of having similar or superior scores (Karlekar, 1989). Therefore, at the university level, girls, on their own, appear to create a differentiated curriculum for themselves. This disparity is one of the most difficult enigmas to understand. Considering the high status Indian society places on the sciences, why do fewer girls choose to pursue the sciences even when they have been provided equal education?

First and foremost, family and social pressures play a role. As previously noted, many Indians believe that a girl's primary vocation is to marry. By the time a girl reaches university level, she is of age to marry and, therefore, parents may choose for her to take an easier educational path and concentrate her efforts in getting married. Furthermore, to maintain that the education provided for both sexes is equal just because the same courses exist ignores the existence of a "hidden curriculum" that continues to teach male superiority.

Schools provide students with unwritten lessons that impart values that translate into social function. For instance, various studies demonstrate that girls, unlike their male counterparts, are expected to be less vocal during whole-group learning, to give up their seats to the boys, and to perform housekeeping chores, such as tidying the room (Nambissan, 2004). As a consequence, girls are taught to take on an inferior role when dealing with boys. Furthermore, having girls, in particular, perform housekeeping chores in their classes clearly brings the purpose of school back to preparing girls to become good housewives.

In addition, there is a paucity of women teachers in schools (Karlekar, 1989; Nambissan, 2004). This inadequacy not only keeps some female children out of the school system when parents fear the idea of placing their daughters in the care of male adults, but also keeps female students from having adequate female role models who can demonstrate that women, too, can be gainfully employed and can pursue all levels of education.

Pupils also absorb hidden social messages through their schoolbooks. In spite of the government's various mandates to purge textbooks of gender inequality, various studies have demonstrated that such biases still exist. According to Nambissan (2004), textbooks continue to depict women as paragons of "warmth, affection, love, nurture, and needing [male] protection" (p. 6), unlike the male characters, who possessed characteristics imputed to more rational people, such as "strong, brave, independent, and determined" (p. 6). Hence, students are taught that men are rational, whereas women are weak and emotional. Such a lesson directly correlates with the entrance of more male students than female into the rational sciences.

Similarly, a review of the National Council of Educational Research and Training (NCERT) books between February and April of 2007 demonstrates that a recent improvement of textbooks did, in fact, eliminate various illustrations containing gender biases. Nevertheless, women are still depicted as weak, frivolous, and angelic, whereas men were shown to be intelligent and strong (Mudambi, 2007). NCERT's efforts to eliminate various stereotypical illustrations—while still managing to include other illustrations with the very same biases—epitomizes the struggle between reform and status quo. With such an entrenched tradition of teaching that men and women are not equal, it is hard to let go of biases even when one so desires. Whether it is the Rajasthani man who denies his daughter education because her future is in the home, the teacher who makes the girls clean up in class instead of the boys, or the NCERT book that continues to depict women as angelic embodiments of Indian identity, centuries of bias still hold back the advancement of Indian education for girls. It is not enough to blindly encourage reform; instead, the biases within the hearts of those who control education, from parents to teachers to textbook publishers, must be addressed.

CONCLUSION

Although there were times when equal education existed that encouraged both academic and moral achievement in India, the curriculum had fallen to an all-time low by the time of independence. The recognizably best education system was reserved for the upper-class men, leaving women and lower caste/class men out of the picture. The latter groups experienced a curriculum that involved housework or menial labor—chores they would have to master for adult survival. Nevertheless, with the help of various programs, the formal education system has steadily encompassed more students from various underprivileged subgroups and has begun to change its curriculum in order to provide a more equal education for all. However, the change has not been sufficient for over 60 years of reform efforts.

A careful study of the history of women's education, and the vacillation between reform and status quo in regard to female education, demonstrates that true curricular reform is difficult because of very strong biases that foreign powers have inculcated into the minds of Indians. Although this lesson results from an in-depth look at female education, the same idea easily can be applied to other subgroups, since the British created a sense of bias by denying education to the majority of Indians. Therefore, when dealing with suppressed groups, making provisions for more facilities, better teachers, etc., is not enough. Curricular improvements, such as blind attempts to improve textbooks or the elimination of home sciences, also are not sufficient. To achieve true curricular reform, the government and outside benefactors should concentrate on truly changing people's attitudes and biases. Only when the equality once accepted in ancient India is fully accepted by all Indians will equal education and a truly uniform curriculum become reality.

Notes:

[1] The Vedic Period or Vedic Age refers to the period when the Vedas, the oldest texts of the Hindu people, were composed. While scholars are unsure of the exact dates these texts were composed, Indologists typically place the Vedic Age between 1300 BC and 500 BC (Kulke & Rothermund, 2004).

[2] Scheduled Caste and Scheduled Tribe are terms reserved for Indian communities that have traditionally been denied opportunities in India. They represent a fifth class in a traditionally four-class system. The Scheduled Caste/Scheduled Tribe communities were known to be without caste and, therefore, genetically impure for both dignified occupations and participation in mainstream Hindu religious rites. The Indian Constitution affords these communities protection. Other terms often used for Scheduled Caste/Scheduled Tribes include Depressed Caste, Dalits, and "Harijans" by Gandhi, meaning "children of God" (Ghurye, 1961).

References

Bajpai, N. (2003). *India: Towards the Millennium Development Goals.* Retrieved September 15, 2007, from United Nations Development Programme website: http://hdr.undp.org/docs/publications/background_papers/2003/India/India_2003.pdf

Basic Features of Sarva Shiksha Abhiyan. (n.d.). Retrieved September 15, 2007, from Ministry of Human Resource Development website: http://ssa.nic.in/ssaframework/ssafram.asp#1.0

Bobbit, J. (1918). *The curriculum.* Boston: Houghton Mifflin.

Brihadaranyaka Upanishad. (Krishnananda, Trans.) (n.d.). Retrieved September 4, 2007, from Swami Krishnananda□The Divine Life Society□Sivananda Ashram website: www.swami-krishnananda.org/brhad_00.html

Classroom Teaching in India. (2001). *Janshala, 5.* Retrieved March 5, 2007, from www.un.org.in/JAN-SHALA/aprjun01/clsteach.htm

Cohn, B. (1996). *Colonialism and its forms of knowledge: The British in India.* Princeton, NJ: Princeton University Press.

Constitution of India. (n.d.). Retrieved August 5, 2007, from http://indiacode.nic.in/coiweb/welcome.html

District Information System for Education. (2006). Retrieved on July 15, 2007, from www.dpepmis.org/

District Primary Education Programme. (n.d.). Retrieved on September 16, 2007, from The European Commission's Delegation website: www.delind.cec.eu.int/en/dev/education/dpep.htm

Dogra, S., & Gulati, A. (2006). Learning traditions and teachers' roles. An Indian perspective. *Educational Research and Reviews, 1,* 165-169. Retrieved on September 5, 2007, from cademicjournals.org/ERR/PDF/Pdf2006/Sep/Dogra%20and%20Gulati.pdf.

External Funding for Education for All. (n.d.). Retrieved September 4, 2007, from Ministry of Human Resource Development website: http://education.nic.in/cd50years/g/T/HB/0THB0K01.htm

Ghurye, G. S. (1961). *Caste, class, and occupation* (4th ed.). Bombay: Popular Book Depot.

Girls' Education at Elementary Level. Retrieved March 3, 2007, from Ministry of Human Resource Development website: http://ssa.nic.in/girlseducation/Girls%20Education.pdf

Guidelines for Implementation of "The National Programme for Education of Girls at Elementary Level" as a Component of the Scheme of Sarva Shiksha Abhiyan. (n.d.). Retrieved from Department of School Education and Literacy website: http://education.nic.in/npegl.pdf

Haddad, Y. Y., & Findly, E. B. (Eds.). (1985). *Women, religion, and social change.* Albany, NY: State University of New York Press.

India. (2005). Retrieved September 15, 2007, from International Council for Science website: www.icsu.org/8_teachscience/icsu-iap/pays.php4?lang=en&choixpays=12

Karlekar, M. (1989). *The slow transition from womanhood to personhood: Can education help?* Retrieved March 3, 2007, from International Centre for Research on Women website www.cwds.org/OCPaper/SlowTransitionMK.pdf, ibid

Kulke, H., & Rothermund, D. (2004). *A history of India.* New York: Routledge.

Kumar, S., Gupta, S. D., & Abraham, G. (2002). *Masculinity and violence against women: An exploratory study in Rajasthan.* Retrieved March 3, 2007, from International Centre for Research on Women website www.icrw.org/docs/DV_India_Report4_52002.pdf

Literacy Rate—India Part 3. (2001). Retrieved August 14, 2007, from Census of India website: www.censusindia.net/results/provindia3.html

Marlow-Ferguson, R. (2002). *World education encyclopedia: A survey of educational systems worldwide.* Farmington Hill, MI: The Gale Group.

Michaels, A. (2004). *Hinduism: Past & present* (Harshav, B., Trans.). Princeton, NJ: Princeton University Press.

Mookerji, R. (2003). *Ancient Indian education; Brahmanical and Buddhist.* Delhi, IN: Motilal Banarsidass Publishers.

Mudambi, A. (1999, September 18). Discipline, American style. *Deccan Herald* (Bangalore), NP.

Mudambi, A. (2007). *Relationship between gender-based domestic violence and education in India.* Manuscript submitted for publication.

Mukhopadhyay, C. C., & Seymour, S. (Eds.). (1994). *Women, education, and family structure in India.* Boulder, CO: Westview Press.

Nagar, U., Padiyar, M., Patel, R., Jaiswal, J., Rathwa, L., Premila Rathwa, et al. (2002). Women initiated response to domestic violence in Gujarat: A study of Nari Adalat and Mahila Panch. In *Women—Initiated community level responses to domestic violence.* Retrieved March 15, 2007, from International Centre for Research on Women website: www.icrw.org/docs/DVIndia_Report5_702.pdf

Nambissan, G. (2004). Integrating gender concerns. *Seminar Web Edition.* Retrieved March 5, 2007, from www.india-seminar.com/2004/536/536%geetha%20b.%20nambissan.htm

National Policy on Education, The. (1986). Retrieved March 15, 2007, from Ministry of Human Resources website: http://education.nic.in/cd50years/g/T/49/toc.htm

National Policy on Education as Modified in 1992, The. (1992). Retrieved March 15, 2007, from Ministry of Human Resources Web site: http://education.nic.in/policy/npe86-mod92.pdf

Palmer, J. A. (2001). *Fifty major thinkers on education.* New York: Routeledge.

Public Report on Basic Education. (n.d.). Retrieved March 15, 2007, from Asha for Education website: www.ashanet.org/stats/PROBE.html

Ramachandran, V., Pal, M., Jain, S., Shekar, S., & Sharma, J. (2005). *Teacher motivation in India.* Retrieved on September 15, 2007, from Azim Premji Foundation website: www.azimpremjifoundation.org/downloads/tech_motiva.pdf

Sangari, K., & Vaid, S. (Eds.). (1999). *Recasting women: Essays in Indian colonial history.* New Brunswick, NJ: Rutgers University Press.

Scharfe, H. (2002). *Education in ancient India.* Boston: Brill.

Singh, A. (1999, February 7). The appeal of rhythm and movement. *The Hindu.* Retrieved September 15, 2007, from www.hinduonnet.com/folio/fo9902/99020200.htm

SSA Focus on Improvement in Quality of Elementary Education. (n.d.). Retrieved on September 15, 2007, from Ministry of Human Resource Development website: http://ssa.nic.in/qualityedu/Updated%20Quality%20Brief%208[1].6.2007.pdf

Stokes, E. (1973). The first century of British colonial rule in India: Social revolution or social stagnation? *Past and Present, 58*, 136-160.

Subash & Lourdes. (2000). *Educational endeavours in Auroville Tamil schools and their relevance to Indian mainstream schools.* Paper presented at the 2000 Asha Conference, Tamil Nadu. Paper retrieved April 5, 2007, from www.ashanet.org/projects-new/documents/596/whitepaperPrimaryedu.pdf

Thorner, A., & Raj, M. K. (2001). *Ideals, images, and real lives: Women in literature and history.* Bombay: Sameeksha Trust.

Universal Primary Education for Girls: India. (1987). United Nations Educational Scientific and Cultural Organization Principal Regional Office for Asia and the Pacific. (ERIC Document Reproduction Service No. ED325436)

Vatsyayana. (1962). *The Kama Sutra of Vatsyayana: The classic Hindu treatise on love and social conduct* (Burton, R. F., Trans.) (1st ed.). New York: E. P. Dutton.

Velkoff, V. (1998). *Women's education in India.* Retrieved March 14, 2007, from U.S. Census Bureau website: www.census.gov/ipc/prod/wid-9801.pdf

Visaria, L. (2005, July). *Sex selective abortion in India: Some empirical evidence from Gujarat & Haryana states.* Paper presented at the XXV International Population Conference Tours. Retrieved March 12, 2007, from http://iussp2005.princeton.edu/download.aspx?submissionid=51652

Working group report of the development of education of SC/ST/Minorities/Girls and Other Disadvantaged Groups for 11th Five Year Plan. 2007-2012. (2007). Retrieved on July 1, 2007, from Government of India

Planning Commission website: http://planningcommission.nic.in/aboutus/committee/wrkgrp11/wg11_scst. pdf

Wu, F., & Butz, W. (2004). *The future of genetically modified crops: Lessons from the Green Revolution.* Santa Monica, CA: Rand Science and Technology.

About the Authors

Aradhana Mudambi is a bilingual teacher at José de Escandón, a Texas-Mexico border elementary school. For the last 10 years, Mudambi has worked as a teacher in four different countries, including in India, where the *Mysore Star* honored her for her efforts at SOS Children's Village, a local orphanage. Mudambi writes for the children's supplement and the education section of the *Deccan Herald*, one of India's largest English-language newspapers. She has an M.Ed. in educational leadership and cultural studies from the University of Houston and a B.A. in economics and managerial studies from Rice University. She is interested in gender issues in multicultural education, including the relationship between education and domestic violence.

Basanti D. Chakraborty is a faculty member of the Early Childhood Education Department at New Jersey City University. She received a Ph.D. in education from Utkal University, India. Her book *Education of the Creative Children,* containing research findings on the effectiveness of the National Rural Talent Scholarship scheme of the government of India, was published by the Indian Council of Social Sciences Research (ICSSR). She conducted postdoctoral research on giftedness and creativity at Teachers College, Columbia University, and Mississippi State University, respectively. She served as a teacher educator in the government colleges of teacher education in Orissa, India.

Curriculum Development
in Italy

Elisabetta Violi LeJeune

The history of the education system in Italy is long and complex, always dictated by the changes in the political leadership and by the relationship between the leading political party and the Roman Catholic Church. With the unification of Italy in 1871, the Kingdom of Italy gained political control of Rome, the political center of the Catholic Church. The Church, which had been the carrier of learning and keeper of knowledge since the Middle Ages, did not easily give up control over education to the secular power of the monarchy. The difficult relations between the Italian and Vatican leaders lasted until Mussolini came to power and enacted education reforms that, ultimately, lasted from 1923 to 1963.

During the ascendancy of fascism, education often became propagandized in order to shape the minds of the youth into compliance with the regime. Since the end of the Second World War, the control of education has been in the hands of the politically driven Ministry of Public Instruction, which changes often with the course of Italian politics. In 1963, a major restructuring of the middle school curriculum allowed more flexibility and gave more opportunities and choices to all students, regardless of social class, gender, or disability. As more changes took place in the 1980s and the 1990s, the system gave more independent choices to teachers, local administrators, parents, and students. However, the reforms came at a fast pace and replaced each other as quickly as they were adopted, leaving a sense of uncertainty. In September 2007, the Ministry of Public Instruction issued a new plan, which allows for the autonomy of schools in the determination of curriculum. Thus, the power struggle for the control of education has been eliminated with the independent choices that are now given to local educational entities.

Curricolo

To better understand the terminology of Italian education laws, it is pertinent to know that in Italy the Latin term "curriculum," as it is used in the U.S.

educational context, has changed to *curricolo,* and as such it is mentioned in the documents of the Ministry of Education. In Italian the Latin term "curriculum" is used exclusively as in *curriculum vitae,* while the Italian *curricolo* is used exclusively in the context of education. As explained by Professor Fiorino Tessaro of the European University Association (2007), "F. Bobbit, in 1918, with the text *The curriculum,* has introduced the definition of 'curricolo,' in a scholastic setting, in reference to the analysis, the reflections, and the actions (didactic and pedagogic) of the second half of the twentieth century" (www.univirtual.it/). This definition, which seems to be accepted and applicable in Italy in an educational context, specifies that *curricolo* is an "intentionally structured succession of the didactic or formative actions which the school explicitly adopts to complete and to perfect the development of the abilities of a subject" (Tessaro, 2007, www.univirtual.it/). Therefore, in the context of Italian education, the word *curricolo* is used to define an instrument of planning that allows analysis of efficiency to verify if proposed objectives have been reached. The reforms that have impacted the educational program in Italy are referred to as *ordinamento,* which translates into more than "order." It also defines the relationships between the parts of the plan and their reliance on each other to function properly.

The first *curricolo* of the state-controlled school system was determined in 1859 when the Casati Law, which had regulated education in the region of Piemonte, was extended to the entire country in an effort to reduce illiteracy (Coppa, 1995). The *legge* (law) created a ministry of public instruction whose task was to "regulate and inspect education throughout the kingdom" (Coppa, 1995). It also gave the state the supervision of all schools, leaving the local municipalities responsible for the administration of elementary schools. In addition, a complex system of authoritarian bureaucracy had the task of making sure that the orders from the minister were executed. The scholastic system was divided into elementary education, which consisted of two parts of two years each, the first being compulsory; and secondary education, which allowed two choices in unconnected branches of studies: the classical school and the technical. Only the classical school, which was articulated into two parts (the gymnasium of five years and the lyceum of three years), allowed enrollment in university studies. On the other hand, the program of technical instruction, which was divided into two levels of three years each, prepared students for the workforce. Another course of studies was the *scuola normale* of three years which prepared students to become elementary school teachers (Coppa, 1995). The rigid *ordinamento degli studi,* or ranking of educational options, forced the students as young as 10 to decide if university studies or work would be their future choice in another six or eight years. This system remained in effect with few modifications until the fascists took control of the country in 1922.

Over the last four decades of the 19th century, the government tried to lower the rates of illiteracy, which were particularly high, especially in the south. It also tried to maintain diplomatic relationships with the Catholic Church. From 1824 to 1861, during the Resurgence, which defines the military process of the political unification of the Italian peninsula, the Liberal party joined with the nationalist movement in an attempt to create a civic spirit in citizens of various principalities that found themselves subjected to the control of a single political power. In the academic institutions, it became important to focus on rhetoric and linguistic traditions to mold the Italian language into the language that "defined the national identity" (di Luzio, 1999, p. 12). In this context, humanities became the privileged field of study that opened all avenues and could help identify those who distinguished themselves as future leaders.

In gaining control over the Italian territory, the newly formed Kingdom of Italy deprived the Papacy of its temporal power (Coppa, 1995). In reaction, the Roman Catholic Church forbade Italians to participate in political life, therefore keeping them away from any input in decisions concerning education. So, the Coppino Law of 1877, which made education of children from 6 to 9 compulsory and eliminated the teaching of religion in elementary schools, faced no opposition. In place of religion, students were required to study civic education with the intent of increasing the citizens' sense of civic duty. The study of civic education has remained in place until today;

however, the subject has never been given serious consideration, its teaching being delegated to the history professor.

At the beginning of the 20th century, before the First World War, Giovanni Giolitti, leader of the Liberal-Democratic party, promoted several changes that impacted education. He tried to compromise with the Catholic Church on the subject of education. As Prime Minister, Giolitti felt that freedom of choice was the better option in order to satisfy the wishes of those who desired religious education for their children (Decollanz, 2003). Giolitti also believed that the low level of education was damaging to the economy of the country and that "the school was an indispensable instrument for the economic, moral and intellectual improvement of the people" (Decollanz, 2003, p. 40). Because of Giolitti's reforms in 1911, the state became responsible, for the first time, for elementary schools with more than 40 students (Decollanz, 2003). Assistance for needy students was provided, the conditions of schools improved, and teachers benefited from better working conditions. Another important landmark was raising compulsory education to the age of 12. These changes led to a significant reduction in the rate of illiteracy during the years from 1911 to 1921.

The Gentile Reform

As the Fascist party came into power, the school system was still unable to find solutions or compromises to some pressing issues: the state's direct responsibility for elementary education, the teaching of religion, and the unification of middle school *curricolo*. Despite attempts to balance the control of education between the State and the Church, the struggle between the Pope and the Italian government for the control of education continued. The division of church and state over educational issues lasted until Mussolini took power and the enactment of the Gentile Reform of 1923 (named after Giovanni Gentile, Mussolini's first minister of education). In fact, allowing the image of a crucifix in the classrooms was Mussolini's first step in his attempt to reconcile the relations between the state and church. As Richard Wolff (1980) points out, "The question of the training of Italian youth, especially during the Fascist period, became a central bone of contention between the Church and the Party" (p. 4). The Gentile Reform was well received by Catholics, who were pleased to see "compulsory religious instruction in the state elementary schools" (Coppa, 1995, p. 142). However, the application of the Gentile Reform did not pose any danger to the ideology of the regime. Gentile himself believed that the student would outgrow the "puerile conception of religion that had been taught him (sic) in the primary schools and to transcend it by his (sic) own thought" (cited in Wolff, 1980, p. 6). These intentions were noted by Pope Pius XI, who, in 1928, accused the regime of endorsing a "plan which tends toward monopoly in the education of youth, not only in physical matters, but in moral and spiritual matters, as well" (cited in Wolff, 1980, p. 9). The strained relations continued until the dialogue between Mussolini and Vatican representatives resulted in the Lateran Agreement of 1929, which included the Concordat. According to Coppa (1995), "The Concordat, which defined the Church in Italy, aroused controversy. It recognized Catholicism as the religion of the state and made religious instruction compulsory, in secondary as well as primary schools" (p. 143). The resistance of the Papacy, which never relented on the idea that education was the prerogative of parents and of the Catholic Church, moderated the influence of the Fascist educational program. As the network of Catholic organizations became more widespread, religious instruction also was imposed in both primary and secondary schools, and students had to demonstrate proficiency in the subject to advance to the next grade.

However, the Gentile reform did more than address the issue of religious education: it set the structure of elementary and secondary education that would last for the next 40 years, until 1963 when the *scuola media unica* (unified middle school) eliminated the divisions that had controlled the choices of students and their families. The structure of the new educational program shaped by Giovanni Gentile was designed to separate and direct the youth into choices of careers often predetermined by social and economic status. This change brought about by the reform created long-lasting consequences in the design of curriculum in elementary and secondary schools. Gentile was a philosopher who considered pedagogy a philosophical science. His program's ideological foundation is explained in his writings, *Summary of Didactic* (1922). The opening sentence states: "There is no school without discipline." Subsequently, it points out that the authority of those who teach has to be recognized (*Sommario*, 1922, p. 32). This guiding principle served well the military style of education later instituted by the Fascist regime.

When Gentile became the Minister of Education in Mussolini's first government, in 1923, he changed the *ordinamento* (or organization) that had been in effect for the past 70 years. He issued the *Regio Decreto Maggio 6* 1923 № 1054 *Ordinamento della Istruzione Media e di Convitti Nazionali* (Royal Decree May 6th 1923 Number 1054 Organization of Middle Instruction and National Boarding Schools). Under his direction, the five years of the elementary school were divided into lower and higher levels; then the lower secondary education and the higher secondary education were reorganized into several types. With Gentile's intervention, secondary education became a system that directed students toward specific channels that were not in communication. Some of the available options gave students the opportunity of attending college, while other options simply aimed to offer professional education and precluded the choice of further studies. Casati had set the path for the rigid division, and now Gentile added more choices with access to university studies. However, young students and their families were still forced to make a decision that was not easily reversible. If the students decided to continue their studies after the 8th grade, in some cases they had to repeat the three years of middle school from 6th to 8th grade following another *curricolo*. In addition, it was necessary to study Latin and to attend the classic lyceum to be eligible to attend university studies with no restriction of fields. Any other choice limited the future opportunities of young students.

After the first five years of elementary education, whose *curricolo* was the same for all, students could enroll in the "complementary school of professional preparation," or *avviamento professionale*. The aim of the three-year program was to complete the education of youth who did not intend to pursue further education. It was a "dead end" channel, since it did not allow students to continue their studies in any other programs. However, since the age of compulsory education was raised to 14, it gave students the option to complete their eight years of studies with a terminal diploma. For those who wished to continue their studies after age 14, the choices included several programs that were structured into two levels with different *curricoli* for each course of study: the gymnasium of five years for those who planned to attend the lyceums, or four years in the lower levels of programs for those interested in enrolling in technical institutes or the *magistrali*, which prepared elementary school teachers (Gentile, 1923, *Royal Decree*).

The *liceo classico* (classical lyceum) challenged those who attended and successfully completed its requirements of a longer course of studies with more examinations to pass in order to continue to the next level. First, students had to pass an admission exam given at the end of elementary school to be able to enter the gymnasium, the completion of which was a requirement to enter the classical lyceum. The rigorous *curricolo* of the gymnasium included two levels of studies: five years divided into the first three with an exit exam, and two more years followed by another exam. The first three years included Italian, Latin, history, geography, mathematics, and a foreign language. At the second level of the gymnasium, Greek language and literature were added to the list of subjects. After the gymnasium, the *curricolo* of the three years of lyceum included the same subjects as the gymnasium, with the addition of philosophy, political science, physics, chemistry, and art history (Gentile, 1923, *Royal Decree*).

Although the *liceo classico* did not provide any practical skills for the workplace, it prepared the students for the rigor of higher academic studies. Furthermore, it was the only secondary school that gave the freedom of unlimited career choices to 19-year-old students who had persevered through the demanding *curricolo*. It also was the school more adept at educating the future *classe dirigente* (ruling class).

Another option was the *liceo scientifico* (scientific lyceum), which prepared students for university studies in medicine and science during the course of a four-year program. The subjects included

Italian, Latin, philosophy, finances, mathematics and physics, natural sciences, chemistry and geography, foreign language and literature, and drawing (Gentile, 1923, *Royal Decree*). The subject missing in the scientific lyceum was the study of classical Greek.

The challenging programs of the lyceums culminated with an *esame di stato*, an exit exam administered by the state and not by the local teachers. The exam was established in 1923 when "schooling was elitist and limited to fewer students. The traditional exam was considered so difficult that it became a recurring nightmare in the dreams of those who took it" (Nardi, 2001, p. 339). This selective system prepared students for university studies, since all branches of studies in higher education with no restrictions were available to those who possessed a diploma from the *liceo classico*. Those who had earned a diploma from the scientific lyceum could not, however, enroll in the department of *Lettere* (Literatures).

The *liceo femminile* (lyceum for women) was exclusively devoted to the education of young women who wished to gain a general culture, but had no intention of attending a university or obtaining a professional degree. The three-year curriculum included home economics, music, art, and dance. A separate institute, called *Magistrali*, prepared those who wished to teach; its purpose was to prepare elementary school teachers, or *maestri*. It replaced the *scuola normale* (normal school) of Casati. The new course of studies lasted seven years and was divided into two levels: the lower level, of four years, with such subjects as Italian, Latin, history, geography, foreign language, drawing, and music; and the higher level, with the addition of philosophy and pedagogy, math, physics, natural science, and art (Gentile, 1923, *Royal Decree*). The new, longer program aimed at giving a general knowledge of culture to those who attended (Gentile, 1923, *Royal Decree*).

Two different technical institutes could be attended after completing the four years of lower technical education. They prepared young professionals in the field of accounting and land surveying. Also included in the new *ordinamento* were art institutes and music conservatories. Special programs were formed to give handicapped students an opportunity to receive an education; however, the students attended special institutes that served their needs, and they were not mainstreamed into the school system (Gentile, 1923, *Royal Decree*).

The complex structure created by Gentile was difficult to modify. Each sector was articulated with its specific function according to a rigid and compartmentalized hierarchy (Decollanz, 2003, p. 67). To ensure that his plan would be carried through, Gentile centralized the minister's power into a pyramid of hierarchical bureaucracy and administration. In fact, Gentile served the Fascist regime in giving it the power of enforcing the fascist agenda of education while taking control and autonomy away from the local educational entities. To introduce the Fascist ideology into the minds of youth, the party used military models of training in the schools, it made educators "faithful servants of the State," and it forced students into youth organizations whose purpose was to indoctrinate their minds for compliance.

Ministry of National Education

The Ministry of Public Instruction was renamed the Ministry of National Education. Elementary and secondary school educators were required to swear a loyalty oath to the Fascist party. All forms of academic freedom were eliminated when every university professor was included in this requirement. Specific prescriptive programs were adopted that took all autonomy and didactic freedom away from educators. And to ensure uniformity and a consistent point of view in teaching the values of the system, a "textbook of state" was used in all elementary schools. These new modifications, while they did not alter the structure of Gentile's education plan, undermined the pedagogic values that were at the base of his reform.

A youth organization, called *Opera Nazionale Balilla*, served the task of providing paramilitary training to young boys and girls from 8 to 18 years of age. Its purpose was to prepare "tomorrow's fascists." By instilling the values of nationalism and fascism, the program directed the young students to become faithful servants of the state. The focus of the training was physical education, military training, home economics for female students, and moral education, which was joined with religious education. The members also received assistance, if needed, with health, economic, or educational problems.

With this plan in place, under the direction of Giuseppe Bottai from 1936 to 1943, education served the state. Bottai was the creator of the *Carta della Scuola* (or School Protocol), which defined a radical reform of the scholastic system to integrate it more fully within the regime. The system also experienced "cleansing" when, after removing those who refused to obey, Bottai also ordered Jewish teachers and students removed from Italy's schools and universities (Decollantz, 2003, p. 79). However, the legacy of his service as Minister of National Education was the *ordinamento* of the new middle school. In an attempt to unify the *curricoli* of the three years after elementary education, the plan called for a *scuola media unificata* (or unified middle school). It was supposed to become the school for those who wished to continue their studies after eight grades of instruction, while the *scuola di avviamento professionale* remained for those who were going to end their education at age 14 after fulfilling their obligation to education. The new middle school included the study of Latin, which became the instrument of selection for those who wished to attend the classical lyceum. According to Bottai, "Latin will be the stone of comparison (the measuring stick) of intelligence, because nothing like Latin, even in its basic elements, has the ability of coloring/tinting the minds and making it easier to evaluate them" (as cited in Decollanz, 2003, p. 81). The institution of *Centri Didattici* (Learning Centers) was also another important addition to the system. Their purpose was to support the minister and the educational boards in "the development of pedagogical and didactic activities," thereby substituting the functions of the dreaded inspectors (Decollanz, 2003, p. 84).

After the Second World War, the American occupation designated Carleton Washburne to direct the Commission for Education, whose task it was to eliminate any remains of the Fascist ideology from scholastic programs while focusing on democratic values of peace and collaboration. According to Decollanz (2003), "The program of Washburne aimed to spread in Italy the new pedagogical theories . . . which had produced positive results in America and which were considered suitable to the needs of the democratic reeducation of the [Italian] people" (p. 91).

In 1948, the Constitution of the new Republic of Italy included article 34, which promised eight years of free education for all citizens to the age of 14 to complete their obligation. Article 7 of the new constitution required that "the relationships between the legal systems of Italy and the Roman Catholic Church should be regulated by the Lateran Treaty, which can therefore override any piece of Italian legislation" (www.quirinale.it/costituzione/costituzione.htm). It also added that only the state could issue a degree or diploma with legal validity. For the next two decades after the war, the Christian Democrats and the Socialist Party dominated the political field. In the Republic of Italy, the relations between the government and the Papacy changed. Religious (Catholic) education was offered as an elective subject in all public schools in all grades. However, in a country predominantly Catholic at that time, almost all students attended catechism at churches of their parish, where rote memorization was used to indoctrinate children in the Catholic Credo values.

Therefore, little attention needed to be given in the elementary classroom to religious education, which was already so ingrained in the social structure of the society. Then, in 1985, the revison to the application of the Lateran Treaty removed Catholicism as the state religion, and established an agreement stating that "the Italian Republic, recognizing the value of religious culture and taking into account that the principles of Catholicism are part of the historical patrimony of the Italian people, will continue to ensure . . . the teaching of Catholic religion in public schools of any order and rank, excluding universities," according to the Law of March 25, 1985 *(Legge 25 marzo 1985)*. Therefore, the teaching of the Catholic religion was and still is a subject offered in the public schools, and students can opt to enroll or not. Some compromises were made in 1995 to accommodate other religious denominations and to ensure religious freedom to ethnic minorities immigrating into Italy.

Preschool Edcation

Another change during the second part of the 20th century impacted the preschool programs. Until the 1960s, the care of preschool children had been the charge of private institutions, whose main purpose was to attend to economically deprived or orphaned preschoolers in facilities called *asilo d' infanzia* (school for infants or orphans). In 1968, the *scuola materna statale* (public maternity school or kindergarten) was instituted to provide free and optional care for children ages 3 to 6. After the new directives issued in 1991, the preschool program focused exclusively on educating and preparing children for their entrance into elementary school, eliminating the public assistance motivation, which, until then, had been the core of the program (Dei, 2000). The preschool program was now called *scuola dell' infanzia* (school for infants), which referred to pre-elementary education. Many innovative programs in early childhood education have received international recognition, such as the *Reggio Emilia* approach, named after the Italian city that pioneered the concept. Rebecca New (2003), in her article "Reggio Emilia: New Ways To Think About Schooling," defines the program this way: "Embedded in the Reggio Emilia approach to education is an image of children, families, and teachers working together to make schools dynamic and democratic learning environments" (p. 34). Because of the changing needs of the society (e.g., with more mothers joining the workforce), enrollment in preschool programs grew rapidly during the last decades of the 20th century.

Elementary Education

After the Second World War, the aim in the development of *curricoli* was to unify the cycles and eliminate those knots that had separated and divided the system into branches that could not meet. The process of unification of the educational programs was slow, often contradictory, and not completely resolved. Many hurdles were difficult to remove because they were so deeply ingrained into the system. Among them were the many exams required to pass to the next level: exit exams and admission exams marked the student's educational process.

In 1955, the elementary school was reorganized into two cycles: the first cycle, which included the first two grades, and the second cycle, which included the next three grades. An exam separated the 2nd from the 3rd grade. Students were also required to pass another comprehensive exam at the end of 5th grade to continue into the second cycle, and then another one at the end of the 8th grade to be admitted into the secondary education level. The constant pressure of evaluation was a recurring nightmare for many students who, every three years, had to perform well enough on those exams to continue their studies. However, another kind of exam was dreaded even more: the *esame di riparazione* (exam of remediation), commonly called the *esame di settembre* (September exam), after the month when the exams were administered. If, at the end of the school year, a student failed to meet the passing criteria for one or two subjects, but was otherwise proficient in other subjects, he/she was given the opportunity to remedy those deficiencies during the summer and then take exams on the failing subjects a few weeks before the beginning of the following school year. The student had to pass the exams in order to advance to the next level. While the exams gave students a second chance, they also motivated them to study during the school year, since having to take the September exams meant no summer vacation. Failing the exam of *riparazione*, on the other hand, meant having to repeat the entire grade. With a sequence of reforms, gradually the exams were abolished to facilitate the passage to the next grade and to unify the first cycle of education.

Middle School

The reform of 1955 was supposed to include a third cycle, which, eight years later, became the *scuola media unica* (unified middle school). In 1963, the new middle school was formed with the elimination of the three-year program of *avviamento professionale* and the merging of the three years of schooling following the five years of elementary education into one system. The plan fulfilled the promise of free education to the age of 14 with the possibility of continuation of studies, and it underlined the rights of all citizens to equal educational advantages. Some variations within the program still existed, however. Such subjects as music and technical applications (separated by gender into home economics and mechanics) were optional in the second and third year. On the other hand, the classic studies started to change when Latin was eliminated in the first year of middle school. It was now introduced in the second year of middle school as a required subject for all students, but it was optional in the last year of middle school. According to Giorgio Bini (1986), the reform of the middle school was a very political issue that separated the proponents of the unified school, represented by the progressive parties, from those who wanted a system that separated students on the basis of their choice to study Latin as an elective subject. The separation was in fact not only academic, but also social, and could be used as an "instrument for selection and class discrimination. Those who wanted the two schools, with Latin as the discriminating agent, wanted a school which separated the students on the basis of scholastic merit that would correspond to social placement" (Bini, 1986, p. 85). However, the study of Latin was still the requirement for those who wished to attend the classic lyceum. The changes in the *curricolo* of middle school backfired at the secondary school level when, for example, the exam at the end of the gymnasium to continue in the classic lyceum was abolished in 1968. To make education truly equal, the study of Latin in middle school was altogether eliminated in 1977, while technical education, which did not separate students by gender anymore, became mandatory in all three grades. More important, the new law guaranteed that "the *licenza* (diploma) gives access to all schools and institutes of higher instruction" (Codignola, 1986, p. 147).

The completion of the programs that led to a terminal diploma was regulated by a sequence of exams that culminated in the *esame di stato* (state exam). As the name implies, the exam was designed and administered by the state or Ministry of Instruction to ensure uniformity of standards across the country. The exam, formerly called *esame di maturità* (exam of maturity), was revised in 1969 when, instead of being a comprehensive exam that tested students' knowledge in all subjects, it tested the students only on two randomly selected subjects (and one selected by the students). The grade or ranking acquired from passing the exam was not a requirement in the application to higher education, since having a diploma was the only admission criterion and no other exams were required.

Secondary Education

The decisions that attempted to modify the system created by Gentile 50 years earlier were dictated by political views rather than pedagogical choices. Therefore, the challenges of the last three decades of the 20th century were the divisions of the political leadership and the need of rising to the standards of the European Community. Starting in 1970, proposals to modify the structure of secondary education were examined; however, the lack of agreement on a new reform led to a phenomenon that can be defined as *sperimentazione* (experimentation). In 1977, the elementary school curriculum experienced several modifications: the abolition of the exam between 2nd and 3rd grade and the introduction of the study of a foreign language in the 2nd grade (Dei, 2000, p. 48). Also, instead of their academic performance being evaluated with numeric grades, students now received a *scheda personale* (personal file) outlining the student's development, personality, and motivation toward studies. The *esami di riparazione* (exams of remediation) were also eliminated, as they were seen as an obstacle to achieving the goal of mandatory education. However, passing the exit exam at the end of 5th grade was still a prerequisite to enroll in middle school. In secondary school, students who were not meeting the criteria to be promoted to the next level in a subject contracted a *debito formativo* (formative debt), which meant that during the following academic year, they needed to remedy the lacking subject in order to be promoted to the next grade. While in the past the debt had to be "paid" by passing the *esame di riparazione*, starting in 1995, the debt could be carried on and accumulated.

A Period of Restructuring

New programs were adopted in the 1990s. To manage problems of organization and administration, the *Legge Finanziaria* (Budget) of 1994 gave the schools autonomy to make independent choices. By 2000, schools become *personalità giuridica* (corporations), independent of the state from which they are still getting funding. With this approach, new concepts were formed to define the operation of the independent systems. As explained on the website of the Ministry of Public Instruction, *Piano dell' Offerta Formativa* (Plan of the Formative Offer) is the school's identification card, which "illustrates distinguishing features of the institution, the cultural and pedagogical inspiration that moves it, the curricular, extracurricular, didactic and organizational planning of its activities" (Autonomia, 2007, ¶1).

In 1996, when Luigi Berlinguer became the Minister of Public Instruction, a period of restructuring started with the intent of adjusting education to the needs of a society that was changed by globalization and technology. Then, a new law, the *Riordini dei Cicli Scolastici* (Reorganization of Scholastic Cycles), reformed the structure of mandatory education:

> *In six articles [it] replaced the structure created by Giovanni Gentile to place the Italian system on the same level as those of other European countries, to reduce the rate of dropouts, and to increase retention. The compulsory grades are divided into scuola di base (base school) or primary cycle of seven years inclusive of elementary and middle school. Then the secondary school of five years is divided into two-year and three-year cycles according to the model 2+3 and it is articulated into five branches: humanities, sciences, technology, arts, and music. (Dei, 2000, p. 14)*

In addition, the plan guarantees that after the second year of the secondary cycle, a student can transfer to any of the other curricula after adequate preparation, if required.

The reform shortens the cycles from 13 years to 12 years, also lowering the age of completion of upper secondary from 19 to 18 years of age. Most European countries conclude the cycle of education required to prepare for university studies by the age of 18. The rationale of the new plan takes into account the fact that preschools (or *scuole per l' infanzia*) have become the norm and not the exception, as they once were. In 2001, when Luigi Berlinguer wrote *La Scuola Nuova* to explain his new program, he pointed out that, "today the preschool is attended by 94% of children" (p. 7).

Berliguer's reform is a *legge quadro* (frameset statute) and, as such, its application hinges on the many variables of regional administrations that have the task of applying and enforcing the procedures. The *legge quadro* attempts to coordinate how regional governments should apply some national mandates. It is a confusing procedure that can be overruled; therefore, an existing plan can be replaced suddenly without much preparation. Raffaele Ladu (2001), of the University of Padova, described the *legge quadro* by

> *comparing it to a tune a class of organists or jazz players is asked to improvise on: everybody can play their [sic] melody, to the extent that it can be music legally derived from the tune (and if the players go beyond the rules of musical variation, the master is allowed to scrap their tunes, reproach the players or even punish them). (¶ 5)*

The precarious application of the reform puts a lot of pressure on local administations.

In 2003, with Minister Letizia Moratti, more changes altered the structure of the base cycle. The new program incorporated preschool in the cycle of mandatory education by lowering the age for children to start attending school. As outlined in the Legislative Decree of 19 February 2004, available on the website of the Minister of Instruction, the existing structure of elementary cycle followed by middle school was merged the following way:

> *The first cycle of eight years, which constitutes the first segment in which the right and duty of instruction and formation is realized. Primary school, which lasts*

five years, is articulated in a first year connected with the scuola dell' infanzia (preschool) and in two biennial periods. Then the secondary school of first level, which lasts three years, is articulated in a didactic period of two years and one third year, which completes the preceding course of studies and ensures the orientation and the connection with the second cycle. (Ministero della Pubblica Istruzione, 2007, ¶3)

The exam that separated the 5th grade from the middle school was eliminated. English and computer literacy were introduced in 1st grade, while a European foreign language was required starting in the first year of middle school. This plan was to be implemented gradually to ensure a smooth transition in anticipating the age of mandatory attendance. However, within two years, the new proposal of reform was eliminated by Giuseppe Fioroni, the Minister who replaced Moratti in 2006.

In September of 2007, the website of the Ministry of Public Instruction began outlining and describing the curricula of the *scuola secondaria di secondo grado* (high school), which comprises the years following middle school for students ages 14 to 18. The choices are between the lyceums, classical or scientific, the Institutes of Art, Technical Institutes, or Professional Institute ("Ordinamenti," 2007, ¶ 1-3). A new reform is brewing, coming from Minister Fioroni's new plan, which has been adopted as law in an experimental phase for two academic years until 2009. The plan implemented at the beginning of the 2007 academic year requires uninterrupted education for 10 years until the student reaches the age of 16. It also modified the *curriculo* of the first cycle of secondary education or middle school. A previous reform by Minister Moratti had already raised the age of education to 18 years as a right and duty of civic responsibility. According to one newspaper article (Illiano, 2007), Minister Fioroni's proposal identifies four cultural axes that will organize the first two years of secondary education. The first two years of secondary education were affected by the reform of 1963, which left the last two years of gymnasium, while the first three were absorbed by the *scuola media unificata.* So students would attend the 4th and 5th gymnasium, while the 1st, 2nd, and 3rd gymnasium no longer existed. In an interview, Vice Minister Mariangela Bastico explained that the purpose of the reform was to "raise the level of general instruction, just like it happened 1962 with the institution of the *scuola media unificata*" [italics added] (Illiano, 2007). In fact, after the third and last year of middle school, students will still have the choices of lyceum, technical institutes, professional, or three-year programs. However, they will be assured that during the first two years of secondary school, they will follow a plan of studies that can facilitate the passage from one course of studies to another, depending on the credits earned (Illiano, 2007). Students can decide to switch into other courses of studies even after the fifth year of secondary education and choose, if they wish, to pursue university studies.

The daily newspaper *Il Corriere della Sera* points out that a step back in time brings forth more multiplication tables, syntax, and grammar for middle school students. In the 8th grade, the history of the 20th century will be the exclusive topic of the history class. On the other hand, computer technology, English as a foreign language, and business courses will be set in the background, erasing some of the changes of the Moratti reform (Benedetti, 2007). In general, the trend of the new reforms tends to return to a stricter and less forgiving system. According to the new program, the passage from grade to grade will be monitored more closely in an effort to eliminate accumulation of large "formative debts." The *debito formativo* allowed large deficiencies to go unchecked and let students continue to the next grade. An article published in the daily newspaper *La Repubblica* reports Minister Fioroni stating that, "Forty-two students out of one hundred are admitted to the next grade with a debt, and only one out of four will repay it, but the rest continue anyway" (Intravaia, 2007). An article in the *Corriere della Sera* explains that the

schools must organize . . . didactic-educational intervention of remediation for students who have insufficiencies; after the remediation courses, which are of-

fered during the academic year, students must be tested to demonstrate that they have recovered from the debt accrued. At the end of the academic year, schools will organize more remediation courses for students who have failed one or more subjects. (Fioroni: Tornano gli Esami di Riparazione, 2007)

Secondary school students have until August 31 before the beginning of each academic year to "repay" the debt. The outcome is passing to the following grade or failing and having to repeat the grade, without "forgiveness" for insufficient performance in some areas. Overall, it appears that the goal of the last reforms attempts to bring back higher standards.

Conclusion

During the relatively brief span of 150 years, which marks the management of education in Italy by the state, the gradual process of raising the age of compulsory education has corresponded to relative reforms in the *curricolo*. At first, reforms have sorted students by directing them into academic programs that run parallel to each other without any communication or exchange between them. The *curricoli* also divided the educational process into segments separated by exams, such as the exams at the end of the second and fifth years of elementary education, the exam after middle school, and finally the *esame di stato*. As the age of compulsory education has been raised, the exams, including the remediation exams, have been perceived as roadblocks in the progress toward the next step. Progressively, these exams have been eliminated as the age of compulsory education has been raised to 16. Also, the goals of the last reforms have been the merging of the *curricoli* for the years of mandatory education into one uniform and large avenue that allows all students to continue their studies in any field of their choice. The system still divides the *curricolo* into three cycles. At the same time, the trend of the education reforms of the last 10 years of the 20th century has been to allow more independent choices, to give more responsibility to the local communities, and less control by the Ministry of Education, which still provides funding. Now, with the last reforms of the first decade of the 21st century, education is not seen anymore as primarily an obligation to fulfill the civic duty toward the betterment of the country, but also as a right offered and guaranteed by the state and the community.

References

Benedetti, G. (2007). Scuola, Tornano Tabelline e Grammatica. *Corriere della Sera.* Retrieved September 14, 2007, from http://archivio.corriere.it

Berlinguer, L. (2001). *La scuola nuova.* Bologna: Laterza.

Bini, G. (1986). La riforma della scuola dell' obbligo. In M. Gattullo & A. Visalberghi (Eds.), *La scuola Italiana dal 1945 al 1983* (pp. 80-95). Firenze: La Nuova Italia.

Codignola, T. (1986). La guerra dei trent'anni. In M. Gattullo & A. Visalberghi (Eds.), *La scuola Italiana dal 1945 al 1983* (pp. 120-148). Firenze: La Nuova Italia.

Coppa, F. J. (1995). From liberalism to fascism: The church-state conflict over Italy's schools. *The History Teacher, 28*(2), 135-148.

Decollanz, G. (2003). *Storia della scuola e delle instituzione educative.* Bari, Italy: Laterza.

Dei, M. (2000). *La scuola in Italia.* Bologna: Il Mulino.

Di Luzio, A. (1999). *Il liceo classico.* Bologna: Il Mulino.

Fioroni: Tornano gli esami di riparazione. (2007). *Il Corriere della Sera.* Retrieved October 23, 2007, from www.corriere.it/cronache/07_ottobre_03/fioroni_esami_settembre.shtml

Gentile, G. (1922). *Sommario di didattica.* Bari, Italy: Laterza.

Gentile, G. (1923). Regio Decreto 6 Maggio 1923, n° 1054. *Ordinamento della istruzionemedia e dei convitti nazionali Gazzetta ufficiale 2 Giugno 1923 n° 129.* Retrieved September 21, 2007, from www.territorioscuola.com/download/Regio_Decreto_6_Maggio_1923_n_1054_(Riforma_Gentile).pdf

Illiano, L. (2007). Scuola, obbligo lungo in 4 percorsi. *24 Ore.* Retrieved September 29, 2007, from www.pubblica.istruzione.it/dg_post_secondaria/rassegna/070607/ilsole24ore.pdf

Intravaia, S. (2007). Scuola, gli esami di riparazione torneranno già da quest'anno. *La Repubblica.* Retrieved October 22, 2007, from www.repubblica.it/2007/10/sezioni/scuola_e_universita/servizi/scuola-2007-sette/scuola-2007-sette/scuola-2007-sette.html

Ladu, R. (March 19, 2001). *Overview of the sources of Italian law.* Retrieved October 9, 2007, from www.llrx.com/features/ladu2.htm

Legge 25 marzo 1985, n. 121. Published in the Supplement of the *Gazzetta Ufficiale* 10 aprile 1985, n. 85. *Centro per la Riforma del Diritto di Famiglia.* Retrieved October 15, 2007, from www.crdf.it/legge_25_marzo_1985_n._121.pdf>

Ministero della Pubblica Istruzione. (2007). *Autonomia scolastica.* Retrieved October 10, 2007, from www.pubblica.istruzione.it/argomenti/autonomia/pof/default.shtml

Ministero della Pubblica Istruzione. (2007). *Decreto legislativo.* Retrieved October 5, 2007, from www.pubblica.istruzione.it/riforma/allegati/dl190204.pdf

Ministero della Pubblica Istruzione. (2007). *Ordinamento.* Retireved October 10, 2007, from www.pubblica.istruzione.it/news/2006/ordinamenti/ordinamenti.shtml#2

Nardi, E. (2001). The transition from school to university in Italy: Examination reform and outstanding issues. *Assessment in Education, 8*(3), 339-351.

New, R. (2003). Reggio Emilia: New ways to think about schooling. *Educational Leadership, 60*(7), 34-38.

Tessaro, F. "Che cosa è il curricolo?" European University Association. Retrieved September 16, 2007, from www.univirtual.it/

Wolff, R. J. (1980). Catholicism, Fascism, and Italian education from the Riforma Gentile to the Carta della Scuola. *History of Education Quarterly, 20*(1), 3-26.

Dedication

To Randy

About the Author

Elisabetta Violi LeJeune was born in Italy. After earning a Laurea in Foreign Languages and Literatures from the University of Rome, she moved to Louisiana, where she pursued an M.A. in English from Southeastern Louisiana University and an M.A.T. from Tulane University. She has been teaching English and Italian at Southeastern Louisiana University.

Curriculum Development in Jordan: Continuous Improvement Toward Excellence

Yousef M. Al-Shaboul, Suheil M. Asassfeh,
Yaser A. Al-Tamimi, and Sabri Sh. Alshboul

At the outset of writing this chapter, it was evident to us that the research literature pertinent to curriculum development in the Hashemite Kingdom of Jordan, Jordan henceforth, is meager. Indeed, it was a challenge to trace curriculum development in Jordan and articulate its educational, social, and economical impacts. Thus, this chapter represents a serious attempt to enrich this line of research by taking it one step forward. It unfolds by introducing general background about the setting of Jordan, followed by an introduction to curriculum development, an overview of education in Jordan (past and present), the realm of curricula in Jordan, and teaching methods adopted. The chapter ends by describing the current challenges facing the education system in Jordan.

The Setting: Jordan

Jordan is located on the eastern coast of the Mediterranean. Most of the 92,300 square kilometers is desert (75%). It is bordered by Syria on the north, the Kingdom of Saudi Arabia to the south and the southeast, Iraq to the east, and Palestine (Israel) to the west. According to 2002 statistics, the average Jordanian family includes 5.7 members (Ministry of Education [MOE], 2004). Jordan is governed by a parliamentary system with a constitutional hereditary monarchy. The state religion is Islam and the official language is Arabic. Its population follows an Islamic Arab tradition.

Unlike most of its surrounding countries, Jordan lacks such natural resources as water and oil; therefore, its economy is shaded by poverty and unemployment as basic constraints in the path of economic development. Nonetheless, Jordan's record of educational development has been impressive, including a literacy rate of 89 percent (USAID, 2007). Jordan invests 13 percent of public expenditure on basic and secondary education, for which the enrollment rates are 90 percent and 70 percent, respectively. Male enrollment is nominally higher in basic education, whereas female students make up 55 percent of the secondary education population (USAID, 2007).

Jordan

Curriculum Development: What Does It Mean?

Traditionally, curriculum was associated with the content of taught subjects, or such "permanent" subjects as grammar, reading, logic, rhetoric, mathematics, and literature, all making up essential knowledge. More recently, the meaning of the concept has expanded to include all planned learning for which the school is responsible, or all the experiences learners have under the guidance of the school (Marsh & Willis, 2003). Despite the various definitions of curriculum, there seems to be a universal agreement that all curricula incorporate: 1) conscious planning, 2) formalized courses of study, and 3) some form of structure with the intention of facilitating students' learning (Murray, 1998). Curriculum development, therefore, means re-creating or modifying what is taught to students by making a number of decisions whose outcomes aggregate as a curriculum design. This process does not start from scratch, "because most 'new' curricula represent revisions of those in existence" (Sowell, 2000, p. 9). It takes into account philosophical, social, and psychological foundations and embodies planning for objectives, content, teaching and presentation models, and evaluation and assessment strategies. The process of planned development of curriculum, therefore, describes all the ways in which a training or teaching organization plans and guides learning that can take place in groups or with individual learners, as well as what can take place inside or outside a classroom (Rogers & Taylor, 1998).

Unlike curriculum change, which may lead to negative consequences, there is a consensus among most educators that curriculum development is transformation, through a well-organized and guided process, from the status quo toward the most excellent, with the intention of arriving at new and distinguished educational outcomes (Jaradat, 1992). Therefore, the springboard should be an immense review for the curricula, including all of the inputs, processes, and outputs of the education system, followed by a massive evaluation and assessment process. On the other hand, curriculum development needs constant follow-up in order to ensure that all recommendations are taken seriously and that all problems and solutions are given attention. Jordan made the change possible by extending the chance to all stakeholders to participate in, contribute to, and enrich the process of reform.

Education in Jordan: An Overview

Since the establishment of the country, the leadership in Jordan has assigned great importance to education. This has been reflected at the constitutional level and translated through the keenness of consecutive governments to provide equal educational opportunities to citizens, regardless of ethnic, sexual, linguistic, religious, or regional differences.

The fundamentals of Jordan's education system go back to the First National Teachers Conference (1923) and to the Education Council and Education Act (1933), prior to Jordan's independence from British rule in 1946. After assuming the kingdom's throne in 1953, the late King Hussein started the education development process by forming the Royal Education Commission in 1954. One year later, an education law was passed introducing free and compulsory education for the first six grades. In 1964, the Education Act expanded compulsory education to nine years (six elementary and three preparatory), and introduced secondary education, with academic and vocational streams, in order to meet domestic and regional demands. In 1962, Jordan established its first university, the University of Jordan.

Notwithstanding the fact that some educational, political, and regional factors emerged in the 1960s and 1970s requiring education reform at the national level, the efforts made then were not comprehensive enough, as they were limited to a few subjects and on an individual basis. In the early 1970s, the Board of Education (BOE) was founded to assist with the process of reform. Between 1973 and 1975, the Education Development Plan was developed, recommending: 1) diversifying the secondary cycle into academic and vocational streams, 2) introducing prevocational education in the preparatory school grades (7-9), 3) expanding teacher training and certification, and 4) developing schools' infrastructure. By the mid-1970s, a modern education system was firmly established, despite the rapid quantitative expansion that occurred at the expense of equality of access and quality of output. While the 1950s and 1960s denoted a period of quantitative expansion, the early 1970s represented a shift toward qualitative improvement of the education system. Yet, the resulting reforms were modest, so the education system had to continue confronting problems until the mid-1980s (MOE, 2003).

In 1985, due to the severe economic recession that marked the entire decade, His Majesty Late King Hussein, in his speech addressing the parliament, called for comprehensive education reform. In it, he emphasized the role of quality education in sustained national development and in improving the quality of life for all people. He also emphasized the necessity of linking education with national social and economic development needs to more effectively respond to the challenges of the 21st century (see entire speech in MOE, 1988, pp. 9-10). His Late Majesty entrusted His Royal Highness Crown Prince Hassan with following up on the reform program.

The education reform unfolded as a two-year process of critical review and assessment between 1985 and 1987 and commenced with the establishment of a Commission on Education Policy. The Commission was responsible for preparing a comprehensive study of the education system, which was submitted to the government one year later. The two-year assessment process culminated in the First National Conference on Educational Development, September 6-7, 1987, under the patronage of His Majesty King Hussein, who provided the opening address (MOE, 2003).

A major result of the First National Conference was a report examining weaknesses in the curricula and acknowledging the following points: 1) the goals of the curricula are not clearly defined, 2) the curricula neither reflect nor endorse the learners' needs or the values and attitudes of the Jordanian society, and 3) the curricula focus on discrete subject matters. On the other hand, the First National Conference, using the King's address as a foundation for education policy, established the basic principles for the Educational Reform Plan (ERP) to be implemented in seven phases over 10 years (1989-98). Among its many recommendations, the plan focused on curriculum development and outlined the following goals (Risalat Almuallim, 1989): 1) endorse educational potentials and stress the objective of scientific thinking, 2) reinforce the functional and applied curriculum, 3) endorse and deepen the values and attitudes toward productivity, 4) enhance national and human patriotism, and 5) extend the obligatory level to 10 years instead of nine and reduce the secondary to two years instead of three.

To ensure that the reform would be instituted, the National Center for Human Resources Development (NCHRD) was created under the umbrella of the Higher Council for Science and Technology. The 1988 Temporary Education Law (since replaced by the 1994 Education Law): 1) restructured the general education system; 2) introduced curricula for the new grade structure; 3) revised the examination system (including the General Secondary School Certificate Examination); 4) completed basic cycle texts; 5) upgraded school administrators' qualifications and school facilities; 6) built and equipped new schools; 7) established Educational Management Information System (EMIS); and 8) opened several private universities (MOE, 2003).

The new curriculum in Jordan provides teachers with detailed "units," which outline objectives and teaching methods in a very structured way. The new curriculum asks teachers to model the qualities they need to develop in their students and show greater innovation and creativity in their lesson activities, more varied methods of assessment to match the new vision of the learner, and a wider range of classroom resources.

The education system in Jordan strives to prepare and empower youth through a range of educational and social experiences. As stated in the Jordanian National Report on the development of education (2004),

> *The education system of Jordan must continually strive to provide sound and proper environments for learning and growth and contribute fully to the required nurturing and caring for youth. Our rewards will be young citizens who are well-qualified and trained, multi-talented, capable of self-learning and lifelong learning, flexible and open to other cultures, and entirely comfortable in coexisting and integrating within their environment. (p. 3)*

Congruent with this vision, the MOE launched Education Reform for the Knowledge Economy (ERfKE), a two-phase comprehensive project with five years for each phase, supported by the domestic sectors and foreign donors (MOE, 2004). ERFKE represents a landmark step in the progress of change in education in Jordan, since it sets out in detail the intentions for reform of early, basic, and secondary schooling, including the following areas: learner, teacher, curriculum, evaluation methods, management and decision-making, and information and communications systems. The impetus to create this type of education reform came from the recent Vision Forum for the Future of Education, held in September 2002. The four distinct coherent components to the project are: 1) reorienting the educational policy, objectives, and strategy through governmental and administrative reform; 2) changing the educational programs and practices to achieve learning outputs in harmony with knowledge economy; 3) providing support for a good quality learning environment; and 4) developing complete readiness for learning through education from early childhood.

General Outcomes of (Basic and Secondary) Education

It has been stated earlier that the structure of the educational school system includes KG (kindergarten, 2 years), basic education (10 years), and secondary education (2 years). The last has a comprehensive track that is based on a common base of knowledge as well as specialized vocational or academic knowledge, and an applied track that is based on vocational preparation and training.

According to Tyler (1949), the four elements of any curriculum are: objectives, content or subject matter, methods or procedures, and evaluation. The first two concern what to achieve using what content, whereas the last two concern how to present the content and how to ensure the accomplishment of desired objectives. Relevant to these elements and pertinent to the Jordanian setting, the Central Department of Curricula and Textbooks highlights, in one of its most recent publications, the *General Framework and General and Specific Outcomes for Basic and Secondary Education* (2006), the major foci of the Jordanian school system. This framework states the general outcomes and their specifications for each school subject at each grade level. It also specifies, as explained below, the content of textbooks in the form of themes that are expanded in a spiral model of curriculum as the student progresses to higher grade levels. In addition, the general framework lists a plethora of teaching methods, along with the advantages and constraints associated with each method. Finally, it suggests a variety of assessment strategies, techniques, and procedures.

KG Education

As stated on its website, MOE started KG education in Jordan in the private sector in the early 1860s. In 1999, reflecting the increasing awareness of the importance of early childhood education, the MOE began establishing public kindergartens providing education to 375 children taught by 15 teachers. In the scholastic year of 2006-07, however, the number of children increased to 7,700, taught by 403 teachers. This number is low compared to the number of children served by the private sector where, today, we have a total of 1,281 kindergartens serving 91,984 children, distributed over 4,285 classes all over the kingdom.

In 2006, work on the development of the curriculum of KG has been well-documented and systematized. Thus, the Department of Curricula and School Textbooks articulated its General Framework and General Outcomes for the KG Curriculum (2006) that specifies, as its title suggests, the philosophy behind and the intended outcomes of KG education. This goes in harmony with the national general outcomes of the Jordanian school education, considering recent research findings pertinent to childhood education. A major target of KG education, therefore, is to prepare children for the type of education that depends on innovation, creativity, and putting knowledge into practice, as implied by the principles of Education Reform for the Knowledge Economy (ERfKE).

Toward this end, it is essential that KG education develops the child's multiple intelligences—verbal, analytical, arithmetic, psychomotor, spatial, social, and moral—and physical well-being. Based on this, the following six dimensions have been identified as fundamental for KG education to carefully address: 1) moral (religious), through focusing on the relationship between the child and his/her creator, the Almighty Allah; 2) socio-psychological, by developing the child's ability to understand, appreciate, control, and express him/herself through initiating and maintaining productive relationships with others; 3) verbal (linguistic), by developing the child's ability to construct and verbally communicate meaning with others; 4) physical (health), by enhancing the child's physical growth and acquainting him/her with appropriate habits; 5) cognitive (knowledge), by developing the child's ability to think and enhancing his/her enthusiasm to learn and think creatively; and 6) artistic, by developing the aesthetic appreciation.

Each of these dimensions is split into more specific dimensions. The first, for example, is subdivided into the three components of the child's understanding of his/her relationship with the Creator (Allah), the relationship with Prophet Mohammad (Peace Be upon Him, PBUH), as well as understanding and applying the Islamic ethics, morals, and guidelines. At a more specific level, the child is required, with concern to the first subdivision, to know the Names and Attributes of Allah (the Merciful, the Curer, the Generous, etc.), realize that Allah is the Creator, mention some of Allah's blessings, know some prayers, thank Allah, mention the Pillars of Islam, and memorize "I bear witness that there is no deity worthy of worship except Allah and that Muhammad is Allah's Prophet and messenger." (This expression is a translation for the first of the five pillars of Islam. It indicates faith or belief in the Oneness of God and the finality of the prophethood of Muhammad.)

The above example extends to other dimensions as well. And to acquaint the reader with the level of objectives that KG children are expected to accomplish, we provide this example, as pointed out in the General Framework and General Outcomes for the Curriculum of KG (MOE, 2006, p. 44), which addresses listening, speaking, reading readiness, and writing readiness. In listening, the child is expected to show interest in what s/he learns, demonstrate understanding of simple spoken English, and develop auditory perception of sound and word patterns s/he learns. As for speaking, the child should use simple and basic vocabulary appropriately, make appropriate responses to what s/he listens to, express his/her ideas and feelings in phrases, describe objects in simple English, and communicate with others in simple English. Pertinent to reading readiness, s/he should read the pictures of objects s/he knows, recognize the sounds of English letters, recognize the shapes of selected letters of the alphabets that represent children's names or familiar words, and read selected letters and words from left to right. Relevant to writing readiness, s/he should understand that the direction of written English letters is from left to right, trace and copy the selected letters of the alphabet from left to right, and dictate selected word/phrase to an adult.

Basic and Secondary Levels

At the broadest level, the Jordanian school curriculum calls for students to accomplish the following at the basic and secondary school levels: adopting Islamic beliefs, developing personal and societal values, fulfilling the obligations of good citizenship, developing positive attitudes toward learning, and acquiring technological competencies, as well as acquiring some fundamental skills pertinent to learning, communication, teamwork, and thinking. Toward this end, students are expected to demonstrate faith and a commitment to Islamic values, exercise their rights and duties as citizens, and contribute to the improvement of their community and country. Furthermore, they should apply an awareness of regional, national, and international events and issues in order to strive for peace and human rights. Additionally, they should demonstrate a commitment to lifelong learning and be responsible, self-confident, independent, and innovative researchers of new ideas. Moreover, they should communicate effectively with others in a variety of ways and work effectively with them in groups and teams. Relevant to information and communication technologies, they should locate, manage, analyze, and communicate information and generate and apply knowledge. This cannot be achieved without using critical thinking, problem solving, and decision-making skills in a creative and effective way.

Each of these general outcomes is translated in the form of targets. With regard to the first outcome (adopting Islamic beliefs), as an example, students are expected to 1) demonstrate a commitment to faith in Allah and religious values; 2) demonstrate honesty, integrity, and similar values from religion; 3) respect the beliefs, religions, and rights of others; and 4) behave according to religious and cultural traditions. These targets are articulated in the form of subsequent goals. Thus, for example, in Islamic studies, 1st-grade students are to accomplish the following goals: 1) acquire the basic concepts, facts, and principles related to *Qur'anic* sciences and the purpose behind them; and 2) develop awareness of the greatness of *Qur'an* and to interact with it in recitation, explanation, memorization, and application to behavior. At a more specific (yet not a behavioral) level of objectives, students should be able to: 1) show some understanding of topics related to the *Holy Qur'an*, 2) memorize some verses and understand their general meaning, and 3) recite some verses from the *Holy Qur'an*. At a specific (behavioral) level, 1st-graders, as an example, are expected to: 1) mention the source of the *Holy Qur'an*, to whom it was revealed and by whom; 2) mention some etiquette rules to apply when reading from, listening to, or reciting the *Holy Qur'an*; 3) mention some names of the *Holy Qur'an*; 4) memorize 10 verses of the *Holy Qur'an* (basically, these are all short ones that consist of 3-4 lines); 5) provide the meanings of some of the words that appear in the to-be-memorized verses; and 6) imitate the teacher's way of reciting the *Holy Qur'an*. Additionally, students are to accomplish some objectives pertinent to the affective domain. Thus, for example, they are expected to love the *Holy Qur'an* and show willingness and desire to learn, memorize, and recite parts of it.

According to the curriculum development policy adopted in the Jordanian education system, upon the endorsement of a general outline set by the Education Council, the Directorate of Curricula and School Textbooks selects a panel of textbook authors and forms a Supervision and Guidance Committee. The authors and supervisors in the two committees work in a systematically sequenced process to ensure the development of textbooks that abide to the general outline, on the one hand, and meet standards of high-quality textbooks. The content of a given textbook, therefore, is selected or developed by a panel of authors who work under the guidance of the supervisory committee.

In terms of content, the curriculum has major topics/themes, for each subject at each grade level. For example, the major foci of Islamic studies at the basic level are the *Holy Qur'an* and its sciences, the Holy Sayings (*Hadeeth*) of Prophet Muhammad (PBUH), Islamic faith, the life of Prophet Muhammad (PBUH), Islamic *fiqh*, and Islamic system and ethics. At the secondary level, these same foci are expanded, in addition to topics in Islamic civilization and the current status of the Islamic world.

In history, as another example, the major topics addressed at the basic school level are 1) Islamic history, 2) the role of the Hashemite leadership throughout history, 3) the history of Arabs and Muslims, 4) the history of ancient civilizations, 5) the history of Europe during both the middle ages as well as at present time, and 6) modern Arab history and contemporary issues. At the secondary level, core topics are modern history and contemporary issues in/of Jordan and Arab and world contemporary issues. Notably, the earliest grade level at which students are exposed to topics pertinent to international issues comes at the 7th grade, when they learn about ancient civilizations in the Arab region (Syria, Jordan, Iraq, etc.). And later, in the 8th grade, they learn about other civilizations (e.g., Greek and Romans), revolutions (e.g., American and French), and unity movements (Italian and German). They also learn about the Industrial Revolution.

In exploring historical events, the curriculum links the history of old civilizations to the history of the Arab world and the ancient places we have in the students' native country. It is also linked to the use of technology in instruction by requiring students to conduct further research using the Internet.

Jordan follows a centralized system in curriculum development, which entails adopting the same textbooks all over the world. Yet, especially in the English language, almost all private schools use a supporting textbook—in addition, of course, to the regular one enforced by law. These supporting textbooks have to be approved by the MOE following careful review and analysis of their content. Thus, the MOE posts on its website the results of an evaluation of some of these textbooks for private schools to consider when selecting a particular book as a textbook. For instance, in a textbook published by Harcourt Publishing Company, the MOE requires that the word "Ham" and the word "holy," describing the Crusaders' war, be removed. These reservations, it can be inferred, are based on religious and cultural considerations. Anyway, the point to be made here is that the MOE does censor the content to which students are exposed, even in private schools.

The Syllabus of Basic and Secondary Education

At the basic school level, some subjects are taught to all students throughout all grades. These include Islamic education, Arabic language, English language, mathematics, social and national education, science, physical education, art, music, and vocational education. Other subjects are studied at particular grade levels. For example, computer science is studied from the 7th grade through the 10th, and French is optional, starting from the 8th grade through the 10th.

The time (measured by the number of 45-minute sessions) devoted for each subject per week does, in a sense, reflect the weight the education system assigns for each subject. At the basic school level, as Table 1 shows, some subjects have a fixed number of sessions regardless of the grade. This is true for mathematics (5 sessions), Islamic education (3), art (1), and vocational education (1). The variability in the number of sessions for each subject across grades of the basic level is reflected in Table 1 (Adapted from Table 1: *The Syllabus for Basic and Secondary Education*, 2006, p. 11).

A glance at the above table indicates that the 3 Rs receive ample attention, for a student has two sessions of Arabic language almost daily. The number of sessions decreases as the student progresses in the grade level. Noticeably, the number of English language sessions increases as the student progresses in the grade level, whereas it decreases for Arabic language sessions. Math, with five sessions, is also assigned importance, and the number of science sessions increases as the student progresses to higher grade levels.

Vocational Education (VE)

After successful completion of the 10th grade, students are distributed over academic and vocational streams. The decisive factors in distributing students over different streams include the student's desire, grades in the 8th, 9th, and 10th grades, and physical health conditions. The branches include

Syllabus for Basic Education

Grade/ Subject	Arabic Language	English	Social and National Education	Science	Physical Education	Vocational Education	Computer Science	French
1st	9	4	2	3	2	1	0	0
2nd	9	4	2	3	2	1	0	0
3rd	9	4	2	4	2	1	0	0
4th	9	4	2	4	2	1	0	0
5th	7	5	3	4	2	2	0	0
6th	7	6	3	4	2	2	0	0
7th	7	6	3	4	2	2	2	0
8th	7	5	3	5	1	2	2	3*
9th	7	5	3	7	1	2	2	3*
10th	6	5	3	7	1	2	2	3*

* French is an optional subject added to the sessions of a student selecting it.

Table 1

home economics, agriculture, industry, nursing, and hotel management. The first of these, home economics, is mainly for females. It has the subspecialties of cosmetics, production of clothes, childhood education, home industry, and traditional handcrafts.

In an attempt to improve VE, MOE revised its policy and programs in 2004 to meet the requirements of a knowledge-economy society. Since then, several committees have been established to implement over three years the following recommendations: 1) developing a new structure for VE, 2) setting national standards to control VE outcomes, 3) improving VE inputs and outputs, 4) reconsidering VE syllabi, 5) ensuring the principle of equal opportunities for enrollment in VE to both genders, 6) decentralizing VE, 7) consolidating the reciprocal relationship between the private and the public sector, 8) adapting the legislations towards a productive policy of VE, and 9) reducing the number of vocational education subspecialties so that agriculture and home economics become one (main) branch and industrial education comprises nine families made up of 19 subspecialties. But one result of the efforts of these committees is that a year ago, nursing was removed from vocational schools and hosted by academic schools under the label of "Health Sciences."

In 2005, the ratio of students enrolled in vocational education to the total number of 11th-graders was 29% and 17% for males and females, respectively. These ratios may partially reflect an increase in male students' awareness of the importance of VE, compared to academic education, as a shortcut to joining the workforce in the society. The low ratio of female enrollment in applied education can be associated, according to the Director of Curricula Directorate (F. Jaradat, personal communication, November 29, 2007), with several possible reasons. These include the cultural understanding implying that applied education is associated with males more than with females, the relatively long distance between the homes of applied education students and the applied schools themselves, and the nature or content of applied education that requires physical practice. It also may reflect females' tendency in an increasingly competitive Jordanian society to pursue undergraduate and graduate education, rather than being content with only a high school qualification.

The general outcomes of VE pertinent to the curriculum for the basic and secondary levels are being developed at the moment of writing this chapter. The under-process general outcomes for vocation education, however, aim at equipping the student with the basic skills and values in order to develop positive attitudes toward work, colleagues, and the society, and to be able to absorb and use the new inventions in technology. Those skills and values are of great importance to the student in order to develop the self-efficacy necessary for selecting the job or profession that matches his or her skills and fulfills his or her needs.

Teaching Methods

Due to the latest reports and the results of evaluations carried out by some Jordanian researchers, it became very clear that teaching methods in use were traditional, focusing on the teacher at the expense of the learner (MOE, 2004). Therefore, increasing voices started calling for more roles for the learner as an independent partner in the teaching-learning process and for the teacher to become more of an organizer, facilitator, and evaluator. Thus, it became urgent to equip teachers with state-of-the-art teaching strategies and methods that include direct instruction, problem solving and investigation, group learning, activity-based learning, and critical thinking.

While each instructional approach has its own unique explanation, we provide, as an example, what is involved with the application of a direct instructional approach. This example serves not only to draw parallels with the other instructional approaches, but also to underscore the interfacing of the variety of approaches.

Direct instruction controls the focus of attention, especially when there are time constraints. The learning material is often presented through questioning and statements that allow for student feedback. The student responses guide the teacher to adjust the lesson as necessary. Some examples of direct instruction (that meets needs of auditory learners) are: lecture, demonstration, guest speaker, seminar, question-and-answer lesson, working from a textbook, workbook, worksheets, practice-and-drill, directed reading activities, and flashcards.

Using direct instruction, students are expected to listen actively, ask questions to ensure understanding, contribute to the lesson by offering comments to add information, ideas, and opinions, practice skills learned under the direction of the teacher and independently, and use self-assessment skills to monitor learning. On the other hand, teachers have to identify the key knowledge and skills that students will need understand the lesson, organize and plan the delivery in a logical sequence, check often for student understanding (e.g., by direct questioning during the lesson), model a skill and provide opportunities for students to practice, monitor student progress (formative assessment) during the practice portion of the lesson, support students who are having difficulty, and plan the next steps in learning based on answers to the questions (adapted from MOE, 2003).

The instructional practices adopted are student-centered. That is, they are designed to meet the students' individual needs, challenge them, and support their accomplishment of set objectives. These practices are guided by the following four principles (MOE, 2003), which take into consideration psychological, environmental, developmental, and cognitive factors that affect the student's ability to learn (MOE, 2003).

The first principle is that active learning deepens understanding. Active learning tasks have a clear purpose and require students to create knowledge from new experiences that make connections to their prior knowledge. Active participation is likely to occur when, for example, students work with materials or develop new ideas or products; when students respond to higher order questions (e.g., analysis, application, synthesis, evaluation) instead of lower order questions (e.g., restate facts; recall a procedure; state what, when, where); or when they spend more time in discussion activities that allow them to become involved and respond to ideas.

The second principle is that the different students' learning needs can be met by using a variety of teaching methods. In response to this, the teacher has to have a variety of teaching methods and literacy strategies at his/her disposal in order to meet the students' different learning styles. The teacher should help students to benefit from the range of learning styles. They can do so by using Information Communication Technology (ICT) and concrete materials to facilitate comprehension of new concepts, using hands-on activities to promote learning by doing, adopting different assessments to show the students' potentials, and using group activities to develop teamwork and interpersonal skills.

Third, learner-centered activities enable students to achieve and apply their learning to life. As a result, when applying learner-centered policies, the teacher increases the amount of attention per learner. Teachers' criteria for success should not only concern how much of the textbook is covered, but also focus on approximating students' potentials as much as they can. Teachers should help students reach their potentials through challenging their skills and meeting the standards they have set for them.

The fourth and last principle holds that real-life situations encourage students to ask questions and make connections. Teachers should work hard to build authentic activities that reflect the world outside the classroom. When teaching involves real-life tasks and authentic materials, students become more motivated. Teachers should be keen to include materials of interest to the learner, because that will help learners to make connections with their background knowledge, facilitate understanding, and enable learners to update, modify, and/or change their understanding (Barlett, 1932; Rosenblatt, 1978). Students will become better problem-solvers, applying what they learn to real-life situations. Teachers should help students to make connections between what school offers and what awaits them outside the school. Students need to see how their learning fits within the family, the community, and the world to which they belong. By using a variety of teaching methods that acknowledge the aforementioned principles, it is hoped that the quality of teaching is taking a step toward excellence.

In the final analysis, effective teaching addresses not only "what to teach," but also "how to teach" (Ornstein, Pajak, & Ornstein, 2006). Accordingly, students are no longer viewed as passive recipients for information but rather as partners in the teaching-learning process. Consequently, teachers should not dominate all the time; rather, they should gradually release and plausibly share their authority with the students. Teachers need to think of the many roles to play and the results they want to achieve. They must obtain a repertoire of strategies with which they are comfortable.

Current Challenges

At the outset of the new millennium, Jordan faces many challenges: political, economical, social, and educational challenges. Whether explicitly or implicitly stated, some universal, regional, and domestic challenges are acknowledged by the MOE in Jordan. To begin with, the rapid renewal of knowledge demands further and greater care and responsibility in determining the type of knowledge worth including in the content of the school curriculum. In addition, the construct of terrorism, a vague buzz concept in today's world, needs to be redefined and carefully dealt with to achieve global mutual understanding and toleration. The rights and responsibilities of individuals and nations in a context of clear definition of what is legitimate and what is not are worth wise reconsideration and careful treatment. Ethical issues with respect to individual persons and a collective consciousness regarding such concepts as honesty, productivity, and devotion to one's mission require that curricula stress the importance of these values.

At a narrower level, curriculum decisions need to shift from following a centralized system in which responsibilities are hardly delegated to a less centralized system, in which responsibility and participation are shared with as many stakeholders as possible. In addition, curricula need to bridge the gap between the skills taught in schools and workplace needs, and the skills required for a knowledge economy, especially given the fact that the current curricula focus more on content than on skills.

Furthermore, outdated teaching methodologies that focus on rote learning and passive retention of information need to be replaced by teaching practices that promote the development of critical thinking and acquisition of problem-solving skills. It is our impression that there is clear variability between the formal and the actual curriculum, for many teachers have expressed their struggle with the new curricula adopted by our education system. The point these teachers make is that putting into practice a variety of teaching methods is time-consuming. According to them, a comparison between inquiry learning and direct instruction in teaching science indicates that direct instruction is much easier and less time-consuming. Therefore, coverage of the content of school textbooks using innovative teaching methods becomes a heavy burden on those teachers and steers their instruction. This situation, we believe, requires modifying teachers' and supervisors' beliefs about the importance of flexibility as a requisite for designing experiences that help in creating personal meaning to the new content in the learner's own life. Simultaneously, curriculum developers are invited to carefully consider the variability in students' abilities and the amount of content in each subject at each grade level.

It is also our impression that there are teachers who are not sufficiently willing or enthusiastic to modify their attitudes and instructional practices. This could be attributed to some teachers' belief that the policy of decision-making is top-down, and innovative practices are insufficiently justified. This also could be attributed to another problem relating to paperwork. Some teachers, for example, are preoccupied with the belief that the lesson plans they are required to write add nothing beneficial to their instruction. These lesson plans, from their view, do not go beyond being a means for showing to administrators that the job (teaching) is being done. This is not divorced from the need for institutionalized preservice and inservice teacher-training process that advocates reflective, technology-assisted, task-based team learning that goes beyond the traditional methods of content delivery. As a consequence, the current system of preservice and inservice training, necessary for improving and standardizing teaching methods and sector-specific expertise, does not fully meet the challenges of preparing students for the modern workplace.

In addition to the above challenges, social issues need careful consideration in the curriculum to ensure both equal and fair opportunities for both males and females. Despite the fact that Jordan has one of the highest female literacy rates in the region, females are often directed into generalist streams, which deprives them of opportunities to take part in the type of learning beneficial for them in the workforce and creates significant gaps in future employment and income as compared with male peers. Financial hardships may lead families to put pressure on their daughters to drop out of school very early—in many cases to care for younger siblings—despite the fact that the parents value education. This practice negatively affects female participation rates and ensures a life of economic and social challenges for affected women (USAID, 2007).

Jordan's financial situation also means that the country has sometimes inadequate school buildings. This challenge is manifested in the crowded classes of, in some directorates, 60 students in each classroom. What adds to the complexity of this challenge is the increasing number of students enrolling. Despite serious efforts by MOE to solve this problem, some buildings are still rented and two-shift (morning and evening) classes exist. One can hardly claim fairness when students are assessed based on the same standards, despite these regional and socioeconomic differences.

The Jordanian society is considered very young (about 55% of the population is under 18) (Twal, 2002). This is a strong indication that the Jordanian society is, and will continue to be, young, energetic, and dynamic. However, there is a need for increasingly rational, targeted, and directed investments to provide services for youth. This poses a challenge to appropriately prepare and empower them as change agents for future national growth. This goes in line with His Majesty King Abdullah II's vision of Jordan becoming a regional role model for human resource development in the knowledge economy global society. This means that education must be a major investment and a vital contributor toward real change.

Conclusion

In 2003, Jordan launched a four-year initiative to rewrite the curriculum for Basic and Secondary Education. This initiative was aimed at providing new definitions that specify what students will need to know, be able to do, and understand. Toward this end, the first step has been taken by carefully developing and precisely stating the curriculum framework that articulates the distinct features of the new curriculum: emphasis on knowledge economy competencies, integration of information and communications technologies, identification of new roles for both students and teachers, and implementing alternative assessment techniques.

The new curriculum views a knowledge economy society as one that prospers because it uses the creativity of its people as fully as possible. Thus, it requires citizens to locate, analyze, and communicate information; cooperatively support development of new ideas, new services, and new products that benefit citizens at home and that can be marketed globally; and create a prosperous knowledge economy for all. Moreover, the new curriculum acknowledges that the computer is one of the foremost indispensable tools for acquiring information; therefore, the new curriculum will encourage teachers to use this tool to broaden and deepen student learning. Many e-learning resources will be developed to support the curriculum in every subject. Using the new technology will enable students to access information, do research, and communicate effectively around the world in the ways required by knowledge economy.

The new curriculum emphasizes that students should learn how to innovate by setting goals and using their talents and creativity to follow their interests. The new curriculum will provide more opportunities for students to define their own ways of reaching the desired outcomes. There will be more encouragement to go beyond the textbook to explore what is personally meaningful. Focusing on the outcomes will make teachers more responsible for demonstrating creativity and variety in their teaching and allow more freedom to select resources and vary the order in which they introduce topics. The new curriculum also will provide teachers with opportunities to assess learning in many new ways. In addition to taking tests and examinations, students will need to be credited for teamwork, presentations, research, and other innovative skills they acquire.

Finally, developing a shared vision among curriculum stakeholders is a must if shared responsibility, commitment, and success are sought. Thus, the new curriculum will be written by teams of educators from across the country. Teachers and supervisors from different school districts will join other specialists. Teachers across the country will be consulted as curriculum is being written.

References

Barlett, F. (1932). *Remembering.* New York: Cambridge University Press.

Good, C. V. (Ed.). (1973). *Dictionary of education.* New York: McGraw-Hill.

Jaradat, I. (1992). Philosophy and directions of educational reform in Jordan. *Risalat Al Muallim, 33*(1&2), 5-61.

Marsh, C. J., & Willis, G. (2003). *Curriculum: Alternative approaches, ongoing issues* (3rd ed.). Upper Saddle River, NJ: Merrill Prentice Hall.

Ministry of Education. (1988). A special issue on the First Conference of Educational Reform. *Risalat Al-muallim, 29*(3&4).

Ministry of Education. (2003). *General framework: Curriculum and assessment.* Unreleased Document.

Ministry of Education. (2004). *The development of education: National report of the Hashemite Kingdom of Jordan.* Presented to the 47th Session of the International Conference on Education, Geneva, 2004.

Ministry of Education/Department of Curricula and School Textbooks. (2006). *The syllabus for basic and secondary education* (in Arabic).

Ministry of Education/Department of Curricula and School Textbooks. (2006). *General framework and general outcomes for the curriculum of KG* (in Arabic).

Murray, P. (1998). *Curriculum development* (2nd ed.). Sydney, Australia: Allen & Unwin.

Ornstein, A., Pajak, E., & Ornstein, S. (2006). *Contemporary issues in curriculum* (4th ed.). Boston: Allyn & Bacon.

Rogers, A., & Taylor, P. (1998). *Participatory curriculum development in agricultural education: A training guide.* Rome: FAO .

Rosenblatt, L. (1978). *The reader, the text, and the poem.* Carbondale, IL: Southern Illinois University Press.

Sowell, E. J. (2000). Overview of curriculum processes and products. In D. Stollenwerk, P. Burleson, & L. Bayma (Eds.), *Curriculum: An integrative introduction.* Upper Saddle River, NJ: Prentice-Hall.

Twal, N. (2002). *Jordan to take part in Youth Employment Summit: Participants to emphasize private sector's role in reducing unemployment.* Retrieved October 28, 2007, from www.jordanembassyus.org/09062002003.htm.

Tyler, R. W. (1949). *Basic principles of curriculum and instruction.* Chicago: University of Chicago Press.

USAID. (2007). Retrieved October 20, 2007, from www.usaidjordan.org/sectors.cfm?inSector=17

Acknowledgment

Many thanks are due to Dr. Fawaz Jaradat, General Director of Curricula Directorate, and his colleagues for their valuable help.

About the Authors

Yousef M. Al-Shaboul, Ph.D., is an assistant professor at the Hashemite University. His major research interests include teaching English as a second/foreign language, family literacy, reading, language arts, and qualitative research methodology. yosouf@yahoo.com; yshbool@hu.edu.jo

Suheil M. Asassfeh, Ph.D., is an assistant professor at the Hashemite University. His major research interests include curriculum design, academic writing, and teaching English as a second/foreign language. suhail_habashneh@yahoo.com

Yasser A. Al-Tamimi, Ph.D, is an assistant professor at Hashemite University. His major research interests include phonetics and phonology, and language acquisition. ytamimi@hu.edu.jo

Sabri Sh. Alshboul, Ph.D., is an assistant professor at the Hashemite University. His major research focuses on morphology, grammaticalization, and second language acquisition. sabri@hu.edu.jo; sshboul@yahoo.com

Curriculum Development in Kenya: Exploring Changes in Public Education Since Independence

Lydiah Nganga and John Kambutu

Kenya is located on the eastern side of the African continent. To the north is the country of Ethiopia, Somalia is on the northeast border, Sudan is to the northwest, and Uganda is to the west. The country of Tanzania is to the south, and the Indian Ocean runs along the southeast coastline. Roughly the size of the U.S. state of Texas, Kenya has a population of approximately 33 million people, representing 42 different ethnic groups. Taking advantage of the natural resources of the region, different groups of people have lived in Kenya for over 2 million years (Shillington, 1995). Archeological evidence indicates a number of ethnic groups have lived in different parts of Kenya during various epochs. These groups developed unique cultural practices.

Prior to the British occupation in the early 1800s, for example, ethnic groups in Kenya adopted curricula for survival that were unique to each group. An abundance of natural resources along with variances in geographical conditions (i.e., wet to dry, highlands to plains and forests to grasslands) shaped these curricula tremendously. The imperialists, however, altered dramatically the structure of ethnic-based curricula (Njiro, 1989). Curricula for survival were replaced with colonial ideologies intended to create space for foreign occupation. To pacify local communities, religious institutions assumed the responsibility of transforming Africans from "superstitious heathens" to morally and spiritually "saved" souls (Shillington, 1995). In addition to condemning African cultural practices, the colonizers required an adoption of European cultures. European education was the engine to propel that intended cultural transformation (Ngugi, 1965).

To an extent, the colonizers created a compliant public, but unrelenting armed resistances from different groups nearly halted colonial occupation. The Kikuyu of central Kenya are especially famous for the Mau Mau rebellion, which forced the British government to leave Kenya in 1963 (Njiro, 1989). The departure of British colonizers enabled Kenyans to create an independent nation governed by indigenous people. In spite of gaining political freedom, however, education issues remained an area of contention as Kenyans struggled to establish a curriculum that served the national needs and interests. This chapter

Kenya

explores the history, challenges, and success stories of Kenya's primary through secondary school curricula since independence in 1963.

Education in Colonial Kenya

Generally, Kenya's education history can be divided into three distinct periods: pre-colonial, colonial, and post-colonial. As stated earlier, pre-colonial education was ethnic in design and practice. Different groups enacted unique informal curricula to address their needs (Ominde, 1964). Generally, the focus was on acquiring knowledge, skills, and dispositions critical to each group. As a result, cultural indoctrination in such areas as traditional organizations, values, languages, beliefs, and worship were studied. Instruction was delivered orally, but hands-on strategies were used to teach practical skills, such as hunting, gathering, and warfare. African curricula existed until the arrival of British imperialists in the early 1800s, when the British colonizers introduced western-based curricula (Shillington, 1995).

The colonial curricula were different in many ways. For example, instead of adopting need-based instructional themes, the colonizers introduced a new teaching approach known as "Asomi" (Gachathi, 1976). The Asomi approach required Africans to emulate western cultures. Indigenous cultural practices, such as languages, ethics, morals, and religions, were downgraded. African children learned to be suspicious of their traditions, including family structure and authority (Ngugi, 1977). Extra negative scrutiny was placed on traditional ways of knowing. Kenyans were systemically introduced to the notion of British cultural superiority. The colonizers popularized European cultures as superior alternatives to African ways. As a result, English became the national language. Gradually, the government proscribed the use of all indigenous languages in government facilities. Boarding schools were introduced to isolate children from their cultural practices. A "monitor" system that used selected children to spy and report to school authorities all violators of the English-only requirement was introduced. Children caught speaking indigenous languages were punished severely. Other government systems facilitated Kenya's cultural transformation.

British citadels coerced Kenyans, albeit insidiously, to relinquish African names in favor of English ones. The Anglicization of African names created an identity crisis that still lingers. In addition to preferring English names because they are inherently Christian, Kenyans believe, consciously and otherwise, that English names confer status. This internalization of oppression is obvious in Kenyan's pride in adopting such English names as John, Joseph, Mary, and Jane. Other names, such as Victoria, Elizabeth, Charles, Alexander, and Philip, associated commonly with English heroes, confer heightened status. Because language and names are crucial in identity development, Kenyans usually have two identities (i.e., European and African), but African cultural practices that appeared "heathen" in nature and "superstitions" in practice have been eliminated (Gachathi, 1976). Colonial schools played a central role in this deconstruction of Kenyans' identity.

The intention of colonial schools was to teach basic literacy. The colonial government preferred schools to teach only limited skills to enable indigenous people to read religious literature. Other curricula models that prepared Kenyans for colonization were acceptable (Ominde, 1964). However, a curriculum that taught Kenyans the skills needed in white-collar jobs was generally forbidden. Because it was easier to colonize a divided people than a united one, schools were segregated along racial lines. As a result, the government established racially segregated schools. Different races (Africans, Asians, Arabs, and Europeans) attended separate schools until 1960, when the colonial government abandoned all school segregation policies due to increased resistance from indigenous people (Sheffield, 1973). The emergence of a Christian group sympathetic to the African course provided additional impetus to stop all divisive, oppressive, and meaningless educational practices (Anderson, 1965). Upon gaining political independence in 1963, the new government, headed by indigenous Kenyans, completed the school desegregation process, thus marking the beginning of a new education era.

Post-colonial Education

After gaining political independence in 1963, the new government provided free primary education for all children in grades 1 through 7 (Abagi & Odipo, 1997). Provision of free basic education was recommended by the 1965 Ominde Commission. The government considered the attainment of basic education central to Kenya's economic development. Consequently, in the 1964-69 economic development plan, the role of education was positioned in the context of relieving the shortage of skilled manpower and equalizing economic opportunities among all citizens. Lacking in this five-year plan, however, was an agenda to cultivate acceptable national social values. This critical omission plagued most of post-colonial education (Mackay, 1981).

Unlike colonial curricula, which offered only the basic skills needed in blue-collar jobs (Ominde, 1964), post-colonial curriculum prepared Kenyans for white-collar professions as well. Upon gaining its independence, Kenya lacked enough trained indigenous people to occupy the various professional positions vacated by British colonialists. This deficit in qualified personnel required immediate solutions. Consequently, the new Kenyan government introduced an elitist education system tailored after the old colonial curricula (Mackay, 1981). An academic system involving seven years of primary education, four years of secondary education, two years of advanced high school, and three years of university training was adopted. In addition to preparing an effective workforce, the government also intended to build nationalism. While the adopted colonial curriculum was effective at preparing a skilled workforce, Kenyans continued to lack essential skills, knowledge, and dispositions in local cultures. To address the issue, the colonial curriculum was modified in 1969 to create an education that could prepare Kenyans to function in Africa's social and economic landscape.

The task of developing and implementing national curricula was a daunting one. Perhaps because humans are creatures of habit and association (Kambutu & Nganga, 2008), Kenyans were not receptive to a new curriculum. Instead, they preferred British-based curricula that prepared people for white-collar jobs. By 1986, however, the country had a surplus of qualified indigenous people and the level of unemployment was high. For example, out of the 20 million people in the country, only 1.2 million had formal employment. To address the high unemployment rate, the government charged the Mackay Commission with the task of designing a curriculum relevant to the needs of the country (Mackay, 1981). Among other recommendations, the commission approved a practical education plan with an emphasis on technical and science subjects (Kamunge, 1988). A new education system, the 8-4-4 pattern, replaced the previous 7-4-2-3 British setup (the 7-4-2-3 education system involved seven years of primary education, four years of secondary education, two years of advanced high school, and three years of university training. The 8-4-4 pattern required eight years of primary education, four years of high school, and four years of university training).

The aim of the 8-4-4 education system was to provide a curriculum based on national interests. An education that focused on national needs was mentioned first in the 1965 Ominde Report. In a later extrapolation, Kay (1975) recommended an education that could foster a sense of nationhood, promote national unity, meet the economic and social needs for national development, provide opportunities for the fullest development of individual talents and personality, promote social equality, and develop Kenya's rich culture. The 8-4-4 curriculum addresses these goals through the teaching of regular academic subjects, such as languages, mathematics, sciences, and social studies. Also included in the 8-4-4 curriculum is an education that promotes practical skills. At the primary level, for example, children are introduced to skills in various crafts. The secondary education curriculum covers careers (vocational) and trades. Academic subjects that address social, political, economic, religious, and cultural dilemmas are offered as well. Because the 8-4-4 education curriculum has a wide scope, both in nature and practice, it has the potential to address the needs of the country.

The 8-4-4 Education System

The 8-4-4 curriculum is designed to promote self-reliance and survival. The Kenya Institute of Education (K.I.E.) is charged with the responsibility of designing and implementing it. K.I.E. was organized in 1968 by the Ministry of Education to develop and coordinate the implementation of all curricula in Kenya (Ojwang, 1993). A collaboration effort between K.I.E. and the Ministry of Education developed the 8-4-4 curricula. Along with increasing the total number of years that children spent at the primary education level from seven to eight, the 8-4-4 system supports practical-based learning, a possible solution to the growing problem of unemployment. Due to the knowledge, skills, and dispositions required, a broadened 8-4-4 curriculum, both in structure and scope, was necessary. Thus, the 8-4-4 curricula incorporate both academics and training in technical skills at all levels of schooling.

Primary education curricula are responsible for educating children from birth to 14 years old. For efficiency, primary education is divided into two groups—early childhood care and development (ECDE), which runs from birth to age 5, and primary education, which runs from age 6 to 14. Before entering secondary school, students complete the Kenya Certificate of Primary Education (KCPE) standardized test. Successful students enroll in four years of secondary education before completing the Kenya Certificate of Secondary Education (KCSE), a standardized test that is required for college entrance. University education lasts for four years, but students who fail to garner enough points for university admission enroll in technical, industrial, vocational, and entrepreneurship training (TIVET) institutions. A practical curriculum is available that prepares learners for careers requiring hands-on skills. Students are prepared for both academics and hands-on curricula at other levels of schooling, as well.

Pre-primary Education

Pre-primary education (i.e., preschool, nursery, and kindergarten) admits children from ages 3 to 5. Although pre-primary education prepares children to enter formal education, its goal is to help children to develop: 1) physical and language skills; 2) temporal and spatial relationships; 3) concept of numbers and problem solving skills; 4) knowledge of the physical, biological, and social worlds around them; and 5) an appreciation of other people's needs and views. Commenting on the importance of a solid early childhood curriculum, Kamunge (1988) theorized that

> *The need to develop a national and culturally oriented curriculum for pre-primary education cannot be over-emphasized. There is need to socialize children, to acquaint them with culture and to link experiences gained at home with those at school. The curriculum should be flexible enough to allow for local variations arising from different environments, cultures and languages. (p. 18)*

Pre-primary education was managed initially by the Ministry of Social Services. The Ministry of Education has since assumed administrative responsibilities by providing policy guidelines, licensure, curriculum development, teacher training, supervision, and school inspection. Such ministerial supervision ensures quality and relevance within and between programs. However, the National Center for Early Childhood Education (NCECE), an auxiliary of K.I.E., has the responsibility of coordinating early childhood education throughout the country.

Primary Education Curriculum

Primary education has been an area of scrutiny since independence in 1963. The government has, therefore, formed numerous commissions to study its purpose and structure. Different commissions have made different recommendations. For example, the 1976 Gachathi Commission recommended a curriculum that focused on numeracy, literacy, and scientific and social understanding. Later, the 1988 Kamunge Commission recommended a primary education that was both academic and practical. Consequently, while academic subjects in lower primary grades (i.e., grades 1 through 3) were increased to eight, children in upper primary studied 14 subjects. Although these recommendations laid the foundation for the 8-4-4 education system, which increased subjects of study exponentially, it was the 1999 Koech Commission that provided the needed direction.

The 1999 Koech Commission recommended a total revision of the existing 8-4-4 education system. At the pre-primary level, a number of new competencies were added, such as communication, writing, reading, listening, and speaking. Other skills, such as numeracy and number manipulation, social skills, understanding the environment, and free play, were introduced. At the lower primary level (i.e., standard one through three), skills in number work and languages (including Kiswahili, English, and indigenous languages) were recommended. Additional skills in environmental science, religious education, and physical education were introduced as well (Ministry of Education, 2002, Volume 1 & 2 primary syllabus). The Koech Commission also modified the upper primary curriculum (i.e., grades 4 through 8) (Koech, 1999).

At the upper-primary level, the curriculum was broadened to include several new academic subjects, such as music, art, craft, home science, physical education, and pastoral programs, but these new areas were not examinable at the Kenya Certificate of Primary Education (KCPE) level. In addition to increasing curriculum content at different levels, the Koech Commission specified the language(s) of instruction. For example, indigenous languages would be used at the lower primary level. Exempt from this requirement are urban schools, due to their diverse student population. Kiswahili, a national language, is used for instruction in all urban and other multiethnic schools. At the upper primary level, English is recommended as the medium of instruction. The most significant recommendation associated with the 1999 Koech Commission, however, is its recognition of primary education as a right for all Kenyans.

Recognizing primary education as the minimum basic education in Kenya, the Koech Commission attached the following objectives to it: 1) imparting literacy, numeracy, and manipulative skills; 2) developing self-expression and utilization of the senses; 3) developing a measure of logical thought and critical judgment; 4) laying a foundation for further education, training, and work; 5) developing awareness and understanding of the environment; 6) developing the whole person, including physical, mental, and spiritual capacities; 7) appreciating and respecting the dignity of labor; and 8) developing positive attitudes and values toward society. The commission's recommendations impacted secondary education curriculum, as well.

Secondary Education Curriculum

The goal of secondary education is to prepare students for adult life. The 1999 Koech Commission, therefore, mandated secondary education with the task of "providing equal opportunities to every individual up to a minimum of 12 years so that every individual is exposed to essential education for future life choices" (Koech, 1999, p. 285). At the secondary education level, a broad curriculum that teaches the following academic and applied life skills is followed: 1) acquiring knowledge, skills, and attitudes for development of the self and the nation; 2) promoting love and loyalty to the nation; 3) promoting harmonious co-existence among the peoples of Kenya; 4) developing mentally, socially, morally, physically, and spiritually; 5) enhancing understanding and respect for one's own and other people's cultures and places in contemporary society; 6) enhancing understanding and appreciation of inter-relationships among nations; 7) promoting positive environmental health practices; 8) building a firm foundation for further education and training; 9) developing an ability for equity, critical thinking, and rational judgment; 10) developing into a responsibly and socially well-adjusted person; 11) promoting acceptance and respect for all persons; 12) enhancing enjoyment in learning; 13) identifying and developing individual talents; 14) building a foundation for technological and industrial development; and 15) developing into a self-disciplined individual who appreciates work and manages time properly (Ministry of Education, Science & Technology [MOES&T], 2002, Vol. 1).

To teach to these different objectives, the secondary education curriculum is split into five broad categories. Category one requires all students to complete academic such subjects as English, Kiswahili, and mathematics (MOES&T, 2002, Volumes 1, 3, & 4 secondary syllabus). In the second category, students choose two subjects out of the four selections for science-oriented subjects, such as physics, chemistry, or physical science, and biology or biological science. Subjects with a social studies focus, including history and government, geography, business education, social education, ethics, and religions (i.e., Christianity, Islam, and Hindu), are carried in the third category. Students take at least one of these subjects. Students are required to take only one subject from group four, which includes subjects with a practical orientation, such as agriculture, home science, art and design, metal work, building construction, power mechanics, electricity, drawing and design, aviation technology, and computer studies. In group five, students enroll in one of the offered foreign languages, such as French, Arabic, or German.

Secondary schooling is completed either in government-aided or Harambee-aided (community-aided) schools. These two tracks of secondary education differ in many ways. For example, the top level consists of students with the highest scores on the Kenya Certificate of Primary Education (KCPE) examination; they are admitted to government-aided schools. Due to high academic competition, roughly one in four students is admitted to government schools. Students with an average score, and those who can afford it, attend Harambee schools. Harambee schools make up the bulk—75 percent of all secondary schools. Admission to Harambee schools is usually less competitive. Due to limited teaching and learning resources, few students seek admission. By contrast, however, there is a high demand for admission to government-aided schools.

Government-aided secondary schools are well funded. An abundance of funds allows government schools the luxury of providing multiple benefits, including qualified educators and adequate learning and boarding facilities. Many educators in government schools are also involved in the setting and grading of the Kenya Certificate of Secondary Education (KCSE), a university entrance examination. Along with other privileges, educators' prior knowledge of test items is a possible cause for the large proportion of students in government schools who qualify for university education. Educational inequalities at the secondary education level, however, are not the only problems plaguing the 8-4-4 education system.

Challenges

Since its inception in 1985, the 8-4-4 education system has had numerous problems, largely because of initial poor planning. For example, the Mackay Commission, which recommended the introduction of the 8-4-4 system, based its recommendations on data generated from a small sample of 400 people in a country that had over 20 million inhabitants at the time (Mackay, 1981). Data from such a small sample provided a potentially faulty picture of the country's needs and interests. But the Mackay Commission also succumbed to political pressure. The decision to introduce the 8-4-4 education system was a political one (Abagi & Odipo, 1997). The government was interested more in building a historical legacy than in solving the country's unemployment rate, which was then at 70 percent. In essence, the Mackay Commission was a government "smoke screen" designed to provide an appearance of formality and purpose. The government was prepared to implement a new education system with or without national support. Consequently, important stakeholders, such as parents and educators, were not included in the initial planning. The decision to exclude educators was a mistake that continues to impact curricula structure. In addition to lacking knowledge about purpose, teachers generally lack the knowledge and skills to implement the new curricula. Lack of teaching resources, which were supposedly to be provided by unwilling parents, was an additional issue. Because the government was in such a hurry to implement the 8-4-4 curricula, an ideal transition period from the old to the new education system was not considered, either.

The transition process from colonial curricula to the new 8-4-4 education was hurried, haphazard, and abrupt. In 1985, for example, a government order required all primary schools to adopt the 8-4-4 curriculum. That was contrary to Fullan's (1991) recommendations on effective strategies to implement curriculum change. For change to succeed, it should be implemented in small segments. A few changes made sequentially over a period of time are less upsetting than big ones implemented at once (Hall & Hord, 1987). Other problems were debilitating, such as the lack of trained change agents and programs to educate the public about the upcoming educational changes. Additionally, the government failed to provide enough money to support the planned change. The 8-4-4 system proved expensive to implement (Kiptoon, 2007). The cost of providing new teaching resources, such as science facilities, technology, workshops, teaching methods, and curricula, raised the education budget by 10%, a dramatically high increase for a country with meager resources.

The government's inability to fund the 8-4-4 education system resulted in unintended negative consequences. For example, an achievement gap emerged between schools sponsored by poor parents and schools supported by affluent families. While most schools in rural settings are poor, schools in major cities are supported by wealthy parents. Poor schools lack basic teaching resources, but affluent schools usually have excess resources, including enough qualified educators. The economic imbalance between the poor and wealthy schools was vividly apparent in the 1990 national examinations results. At both the primary and secondary levels, children from poor schools performed poorly compared to their peers in affluent schools.

Disproportionate educational performance is a crisis that continues to plague the 8-4-4 education system. Although the problem was first noted in 1986, the performance gap has widened. For example, out of the 200,000 students who completed the Kenya Certificate of Secondary Education (K.C.S.E.) in 1990, only 10,000 qualified for college education (Abagi & Odipo, 1997; Nafula, 2002). An overwhelming majority of qualifying students came from rich schools. This national disaster, largely caused by lack of trained teachers, teaching resources, and science facilities in poor schools, is a national trend. Additionally, subject overload and strict grading requirements exacerbate the problem.

The 8-4-4 system requires children to study 13 instead of the seven academic subjects previously studied (Abagi, 1997). On grading, students are expected to pass 10 subjects (five compulsory) with a minimum of a "B" per academic subject needed to qualify for university admission. Commenting on this seemingly inhumane educational practice, the Minister for Health labeled the practice "unhealthy" for students because they had little time left for play (Abagi & Odipo, 1997). As the nation continued to reel from unprecedented failures in national examinations, the number of student riots at all levels of schooling skyrocketed.

Schools riots became a normal phenomenon during the initial stages of the 8-4-4 implementation. For example, there were more than 20 serious school riots in 1991. In one riot at St. Kizito's, a mixed secondary school in the Meru district, the school was destroyed completely, 19 girls were killed and 72 were raped (Siringi, 2000). The Minister for Health once again attributed the students' irresponsible behavior to excessive overload in schoolwork, which left little room and time for play. The extensive destruction at St. Kizito convinced the government to overhaul the 8-4-4 education system. The 1999 Keoch Commission was charged with this critical task.

The Koech Commission started by building a national consensus around the 8-4-4 education system. Unlike the 1985 Mackay Commission, whose recommendations were influenced largely by the government, the Koech Commission was immune from such influence and was, therefore, able to solicit input from all Kenyans. Among other findings, the commission identified an urgent need to overhaul all technical subjects. Technical subjects were expensive to implement, due to high personnel and equipment costs. Other issues were evident, including the lack of credible data to support curricula change and the best ways to implement that change. Consequently, the 8-4-4 education system was experiencing a wide range of challenges, such as lack of educators' support.

Issues of subject overload caused educators, parents, and students to develop a negative judgment regarding the new education system. Additionally, the high costs involved in the daily running of 8-4-4 education, coupled with limited learning and teaching materials, were other areas of contention (Nafula, 2002). Evidently, due to poor funding, facilities were overstretched, the schools were overcrowded, and the teacher-pupil ratio was high in the rural and poor schools. Lack of community support was rampant, due to a perception that the government was responsible for providing free primary education. But in addition to overlooking both the disadvantaged and children with special needs, the 8-4-4 education system was unable to address effectively the needs of a growing number of children orphaned by HIV/AIDS (MOES&T, 2005). Building an understanding of the challenges plaguing the 8-4-4 system enabled the Koech Commission to design a new philosophy for the beleaguered curricula.

Philosophy of Education

Education for social cohesion and human and economic development guides the structure, management, and delivery of the new 8-4-4 education philosophy (MOES & T, 2005). The role of education is, therefore, considered broadly as that of transforming people to become productive and civil citizens. In specific terms, however, the 8-4-4 education philosophy has an emphasis on practical and lifelong learning skills. A holistic education that promotes both cognitive and affective domains is thus recommended. An education that helps learners to acquire such values as patriotism, equality, peace, security, honesty, humility, love, respect, tolerance, cooperation, and democracy is embraced. Additionally, a practical education that addresses emerging challenges, such as lack of respect for human rights, increased drug and substance abuse, corruption, violence, and social exclusion, is embraced. The following seven principles guide the new 8-4-4 education philosophy.

Principle One. National Unity: To achieve national unity, basic education was declared a Kenyan right. As a result, access to free primary education to all Kenya became a national goal. This goal was achieved in 2005. The use of tribal languages or mother tongues as media of instruction during the early years of schooling is required. Kiswahili and English, the national and business languages, respectively, are media of instruction in the upper primary levels and beyond. Urban and multiethnic schools are exempt from tribal language requirement.

Principle Two. Unity of Purpose: The use of instructional strategies that promote teamwork is required. Additionally, various educational objectives that address issues of the common good are applied.

Principle Three. Social Responsibility: Education and training integrate principles of social responsibility, gender equity, and care for vulnerable groups and cultural practices.

Principle Four. Moral and Ethical Values: Such topics as peace, integrity, hard work, honesty, and equity are included in the curricula.

Principle Five. Lifelong Learning: Education and training that teach the importance of learning throughout life are included at all levels of schooling.

Principle Six. Science and Technology: A curriculum that involves research, innovations, and use of technology and information processing is required.

Principle Seven. Environment: Education and training that equip people with the skills necessary to conserve and harvest environmental resources in a sustainable manner are implemented. (MOE&T, 2005)

The Ministry of Education has the responsibility of not only implementing the new 8-4-4 education philosophy, but also ensuring educational access.

Educational Access

In 1963, the new Kenya government promised free primary education to all Kenyans. Although free education was available for a while, the high costs of running the 8-4-4 curricula caused the government to gradually desert the promise of free education. Parents assumed the burden of educating children, but the poor ones were unable generally to raise funds. While children of poverty were excluded, children from wealthy families enjoyed full access to education. In 2001, however, a new government headed by President Mwai Kibaki came to power. The government renewed the promise for free primary education. Several registrations were passed, such as the Children's Act of 2001, which made primary education a right. The government provided free primary education in 2005. The intent now is to institute free secondary education as well. The responsibility of ensuring equal educational access at all levels, however, belongs to the Ministry of Education.

To promote educational access at the primary level, for example, the Ministry of Education is supporting low-cost boarding schools in arid and semi-arid areas. Without such support, children in hardship areas could not attend. The ministry has grants for special needs students. Children in city ghettos or slums qualify for educational aid that helps in the purchase of curriculum and instructional materials. To improve children's health, a collaborative nutrition program with the Ministry of Health has been started. Non-governmental agencies with an educational focus are included. Meanwhile, the government has mainstreamed education for children suffering from, or affected by, the HIV/AIDS epidemic. Previously, because of negative stereotypes, affected children had been discouraged from attending school. Gender discrimination is now illegal and other affirmative action measures have increased the participation of female students. Educators participate in regularly scheduled professional development activities in pertinent areas. Additionally, frequent curricula reviews ensure relevance, but primary education is charged with the task of preparing children for secondary education.

As discussed earlier, the implementation of 8-4-4 secondary education curricula was problematic. Perhaps because of the many problems plaguing secondary education, enrollment declined dramatically. Faced with a 30% drop-out rate, the government revised the curriculum to reduce subject load, both for students and teachers. Rehabilitation programs to improve school environments also are in place. Support of poor and disadvantaged children through bursaries has been enacted. Other measures are helpful, such as the development of educational partnerships among the government, parents, communities, private sectors, and other stakeholders. While the government seeks to provide education that is guided by local needs, other relevant international events inform educational policies.

The government of Kenya supports various international educational initiatives, declarations, protocols, and conventions. Of particular importance is the 2000 Dakar, Senegal, declaration that challenges education systems to ensure access, equity, quality, and relevance of curriculum materials. As a result, Kenya is now supporting early childhood education (for children birth to 3 years old) and pre-primary education (for children 4 to 5 years old). Additionally, gender inclusion is added to the curricula at different levels of schooling. Specifically, educators are required to use gender-inclusive resources; existing instructional materials, however, are still gender unbalanced. An analysis of the social studies textbooks recommended by the Kenya Institute of Education (KIE), for example, has numerous gender stereotypes.

Osler (1993) exposed numerous gender-biases in 8th-grade textbooks. In one review, a social studies book contained nine pictures with women, four of which illustrated a section on "The Family." In this section, there were twice as many women as men and all, with the exception of an elderly woman, a bride, and her attendant, were carrying babies. Of the remaining pictures, only three showed women at work or pursuing other activities unrelated to children. By contrast, the men were presented in a wide variety of roles, such as addressing political rallies, driving lorries, fishing, and sailing.

While teaching resources display men playing key, expert roles, women are either invisible or portrayed in traditional family roles, such as cooking, cleaning, and giving birth. Women's roles are low in status. For example, a home science and music curriculum describes men as performing the important task of providing food for the family. Women are described in the context of being housewives. Curriculum materials that present women in non-stereotypic roles are missing at all levels of schooling (Harber, 1989). Because the government is committed to gender equity, however, there is hope for curricula that will transform all Kenyans into responsible and skillful citizens.

Conclusion

Several conclusions are obvious. The first conclusion concerns the process of implementing curriculum change. After considering the history, challenges, and successes of implementing the 8-4-4 education system, it is certain that developing an effective curriculum change is a process, not an event. To be successful, the process should pay attention to the various factors involved. For example, a change that is driven by a community's needs is likely to succeed. Conversely, a change that is driven by external forces, such as political pressure, might not be supported by other stakeholders. A curriculum change that lacks the support of administrators, educators, students, parents, and the general community is likely to fail. A consensus is not necessary, however, in cases where a curriculum change serves the common good (Quinn & Meiners, 2007). For example, the government of Kenya implemented a social justice curriculum that was not necessarily popular, but it was needed for the common good. A successful change is, however, possible when the government is supportive, but change that is considered a government "project" with little public input will fail (Morrison, 2007).

The second conclusion from the above analysis is that to implement successful curricular changes, it is essential to consider all stakeholders' needs. Curriculum developers are likely to succeed when they allow societal needs to drive change. An objective study that solicits input from stakeholders is likely to illuminate fully a community's desires, needs, and interests. The task of developing and implementing curricular changes in diverse communities could be daunting, because diverse communities have diverse needs. This third conclusion reminds curriculum developers to always seek common ground (i.e., themes or issues that are shared across the community) in order to implement widely acceptable changes. A consideration of broad, inclusive, and holistic curricula schemes will ease the process of developing shared curriculum goals. A narrowly focused change that addresses the needs of one group will only be rejected by other groups. Implementing curricular change, however, is overwhelming in terms of both time and resources.

Curriculum developers need to appreciate the fact that implementing change takes time and resources. This fourth conclusion weaves through the history of the 8-4-4 curricular changes. The lesson from this conclusion calls for clear understanding of the factors involved before initiating change. First is the issue of change itself. Because people are creatures of habit and association, they are less likely to embrace new habits. Implementing change takes time, because people need enough time to build new habits. The needed time is significantly reduced when stakeholders are involved and, therefore, agreeable to the impeding change. The lesson for curriculum developers, then, delves into the benefits of securing consensus before actually implementing curricular change. The available media—print and electronic—are helpful, but conducting public forums where people can express their agreements, struggles, apprehensions, and concerns is helpful. Change also is impacted by resource availability.

Implementing curricular change requires additional resources. This fifth and final conclusion reminds us that due to a lack of critical resources, the initial 8-4-4 curricular change faced a myriad of challenges. After careful planning, however, a revised 8-4-4 system, supported broadly by various stakeholders, was implemented successfully.

References

Abagi, O., & Odipo, G. (1997). *Efficiency of primary education in Kenya: Situational analysis and implications for education reform.* Discussion paper No. DP 004/97, Institute of Policy Analysis and Research, University Way, Nairobi, Kenya.

Anderson, J. E. (1965). The Kenya Education Commission Report: An African view of educational planning. *Comparative Education Review, 9*(2), 201-207.

Fullan, M. (1991). *The new meaning of educational change.* New York: Teachers College Press.

Gacathi, P. J. (1976). *Report of the National Committee on Education Objectives and Policies.* Nairobi, Kenya: Government Printer.

Hall, E., & Hord, S. M. (1987). *Change in schools: Facilitating the process.* Albany, NJ: SUNY Press.

Harber, H. (1989). *Politics in African education.* London: Macmillan.

Kambutu, J., & Nganga, L. (2008). In these uncertain times: Educators build cultural awareness through planned international experiences. *Teaching and Teacher Education, 24*(4), 939-951.

Kamunge, J. M. (1988). *Report of the presidential working party on education and manpower training for the next decade and beyond.* Presented to His Excellency Daniel T. arap Moi, President and Commander-in-chief of the Armed Forces of the Republic of Kenya.

Kay, S. (1975). Curriculum innovations and traditional culture: A case history of Kenya. *Comparative Education, 11*(3), 183-191.

Kiptoon, J. (2007). *Kenya.* Retrieved on September 29, 2007, from www.ibe.unesco.org/curriculum/Africapdf/.

Koech, D. K. (1999). *Totally Integrated Quality Education and Training-TIQET.* Report of the Commission of Inquiry into the Education Systems of Kenya. Presented to His Excellency Daniel T. arap Moi, President and Commander-in-chief of the Armed Forces of the Republic of Kenya.

Mackay, C. B. (1981). *Second university: Report of presidential working party.* Presented to His Excellency the President Hon. Daniel T. arap Moi, Republic of Kenya.

Ministry of Education, Science & Technology. (2002). *Secondary education syllabus* (Vol. 1). Kenya Institute of Education.

Ministry of Education, Science & Technology. (2002). *Secondary education syllabus* (Vol. 3). Kenya Institute of Education.

Ministry of Education, Science & Technology. (2002). *Secondary education syllabus* (Vol. 4). Kenya Institute of Education.

Ministry of Education, Science & Technology. (2005). *A policy framework for education, training and research* (Session 1, Paper No. 1). Nairobi, Kenya: Government Printer.

Ministry of Education. (2002). *Primary education syllabus* (Vol. 1). Kenya Institute of Education. Republic of Kenya.

Ministry of Education. (2002). *Primary education syllabus* (Vol. 2). Kenya Institute of Education. Republic of Kenya.

Morrison, K. (2007). Shaking the foundations: Education professors fight Virginia's proposed changes to teacher preparation. *Rethinking Schools, 21*(4), 23-24.

Nafula, N. N. (2002). Achieving sustainable universal primary education through debt relief. *Kenya Institute for Public Policy and Analysis, Nairobi, Kenya.* Discussion Pare No. 2002/66 United Nations University, World Institute for Development Economic Research.

Ngugi, T. (1965). *The river between.* Great Britain: Cox & Wyman, Ltd.

Ngugi, T. (1977). *Petals of blood.* Nairobi: Heinemann.

Njiro, E. I. (1989). *A history of Africa in the 19th century.* Nairobi, Kenya: Kenya Literature Bureau.

Ojwang, A. (1993). Pied crow magazine in Kenya: A development education spice. In A. Osler (Ed.), *Development education: Global perspectives in the curriculum.* London: Cassell.

Ominde, S. H. (1965). *Kenya Education Commission report, Part II.* Republic of Kenya.

Ominde, S. H. (1964). *Kenya Education Commission report, Part 1.* Republic of Kenya.

Osler, A. (1993). Education for development and democracy in Kenya: A case study. *Education Review, 45*(2), 165-173.

Quinn, T., & Meiners, E. (2007). Do ask, do tell: What's professional about taking social justice and sexual orientation out of classrooms? *Rethinking Schools, 21*(4), 25-26.

Sheffield, J. R. (1973). *Education in Kenya. A historical study.* New York: Teachers College Press.

Shillington, K. (1995). *History of Africa.* New York: St. Martin's Press.

Siringi, S. (2000). Alarm over attacks on girls' schools. *Daily Nation* on the web. Retrieved August 5, 2007, from www.nationaudio.com/News/Daily.

About the Authors

Lydiah Nganga is an assistant professor of Elementary and Early Childhood Education at the University of Wyoming/Casper College Center. Her research work is in social justice, cultural diversity, global education and teacher education.

John Kambutu is an assistant professor of Educational Studies at the University of Wyoming/Casper College Center. His research work is in cultural diversity, international cultural immersion, transformative learning, and adult education.

Curriculum Development in Korea: English Language Instruction

Guang-Lea Lee and Donald A. Myers

The educational curriculum of schools in Korea is normally revised every five or six years in response to new political, cultural, and social changes. When the leadership of the government changes, it is customary for it to apply its own doctrines and political views in what is a highly centralized national curriculum. There have been seven revisions since the first Korean national curriculum was established in 1955, two years after the end of the Korean War. The latest national curriculum, which was revised in 2007, will be implemented in 2009.

This chapter will focus primarily on the history and development of the national English curriculum in primary schools. By understanding in-depth how the English curriculum has evolved to its current state of educational policy, a parallel can be drawn to all subjects in the grade 1 through 12 curriculum to gain a general understanding of all curriculum development in Korea. The subject of English *per se* was selected for review, because the majority of those involved in education, such as policymakers, publishers, education suppliers, and families, regard efficient English ability as an ultimate academic goal that Korean students should achieve before graduating from high school.

To improve students' English language ability, the Korean government, for the first time in its history, mandated in 1997 that English be taught to 3rd-grade students in all primary schools, with an emphasis on the spoken language. Requiring English language education in earlier grades was deemed necessary for Korean children to become successful dual language speakers of Korean and English. This step was required because many Korean students, even after studying English from middle school to the end of university training, were unable to communicate with foreigners in the global society's preferred language of English.

As improving English ability became a major mission of Korean education, English as a foreign language was given greater weight in academic achievement tests. The Korean government, employers, and higher education institutions consistently require that young people possess a high level of competency in English knowledge and speaking skills. Also, the 2007 policy of the Ministry of Education and Human Resources, referred to by Koreans as MOEHR, recommended providing English language

Korea

curriculum for the 1st-grade students in 50 selected elementary schools. As of 2010, schools are required to provide one hour longer English instruction—2 hours a week in 3rd and 4th grade and 3 hours a week in 5th and 6th—and to hire a native English-speaking teacher to collaborate with English teachers who are required to use only English without giving Korean translations in English class.

This chapter begins with a brief description of the goals for elementary, middle, and high school education, followed by a discussion of the political, social, and cultural factors impacting the national English curriculum. This is followed by an overview of the national English curriculum. A historical analysis begins with a review of English curriculum during the last emperor's rule, from 1883 to 1910, through subsequent periods—the Japanese colonial period (1910-1945), the American military era (1945-1955), and the 1st through 7th Korean national curricula (1955-current). In addition, we explore teacher training procedures for English education in primary school, as well as future directions for teaching young children English as a foreign language. Further, we investigate educational dilemmas concerning linguistic difficulties of learning English and the psychological struggles of young children becoming dual language speakers.

Curriculum for Elementary, Middle, and High School Education

The Ministry of Education and Human Resources (MOEHR) is responsible for setting educational guidelines for learning standards and curriculum content. The national curriculum for elementary, middle, and high school education states that the objectives of Korea's education system are to assist in perfecting individual character, to develop the ability to achieve an independent life and be democratic citizens, and to promote prosperity of all humankind (Korea Institute of Curriculum and Evaluation [KICE], 2006).

Korean people value education very highly, because they believe it will foster the development of what they see as the ideal person. An ideal person possesses creative ability, seeks promising career paths, demonstrates moral values, has a well-rounded individuality, and contributes to the development of the community. To educate students who possess these ideal personal profiles, Korea's education curriculum specifies specific educational goals for elementary, middle, and high school.

The goals of elementary school education emphasize helping students acquire basic skills, cultural traditions, and habits essential for learning and daily life; middle school education emphasizes developing well-rounded personalities, fostering individual potential, building problem-solving abilities and career paths, valuing cultural traditions, and cultivating the democratic way of life; high school education emphasizes acquiring abilities essential for progressing along chosen career paths and developing the qualifications of world citizens.

To achieve the primary, middle, and high school education goals, Korea's education curriculum requires a common basic curriculum. The common basic curriculum for grades 1 and 2 takes place in five classes—Korean language, mathematics, disciplined life, intelligent life, and pleasant life. The "We Are the 1st-graders" program teaches students about appropriate behaviors, such as respecting teachers and school facilities. The common basic curriculum for grades 3 to 10 includes 10 classes, which are Korean language, moral education, social studies, mathematics, science, practical arts (technology, home economics), physical education, music, fine arts, and foreign language (English).

Korea has an elective-centered curriculum for grades 11 and 12, which allows students to choose classes from specialized fields in addition to taking the general classes. Specialized fields include courses in agriculture, industry, commerce, fishery and marine transportation, home economics and vocational education, science, physical education, the arts, foreign languages, and international affairs. General classes consist of Korean language, moral education, social studies, mathematics, science, technology and home economics, physical education, music, fine arts, foreign languages, Chinese characters and classics, and military training.

The number of instructional hours in schools is increased as students progress to higher grades.

For grade 1, the standard number of school weeks is 30 per year and 34 weeks for other grades. All students in grades 1 and 2 attend Saturday school every other week. Currently, English is not a required subject for grades 1 and 2, except in some schools selected as trial schools for early English education. English is taught 34 hours for grades 3 and 4, 68 hours for grades 5 and 6, 102 hours for grades 7 and 8, and 136 for grades 9 and 10.

Political, Social, and Cultural Factors That Impact the National English Curriculum

English language education in Korea historically has been linked closely to the political climate and is tightly controlled by the government (Choi, 2006). In 1945, for example, when Korea was liberated from Japan, the American military administration began, and the involvement of Americans in the governing of the nation required more emphasis on English language education. The U.S. military administration between 1945 and 1955 stressed the necessity for intense English language instruction because of the government's belief that fluent English was necessary to acquire Western knowledge, advance technology, and gain aid for the country's industrial development (Jeong, 2001). The Korean government believed that fluency in English was essential to build a strong government and to protect it from communism. As a result, English became a required subject in the college entrance examination (Kim, 1991).

In addition to the historical and political changes that influenced English education, social, economic, and cultural factors also affected English curriculum. An understanding of those influences on English curriculum development provides insight as to why the government and many Korean parents are so eager to teach their children English. Korea needed more people speaking English, because the nation's economic development was achieved through external trade, which increased the number of foreign tourists, investments, and industry. Since fluent English ability offered more opportunities and a higher chance of securing lucrative positions in government and industry, English education became especially important, leading to a change in the national English curriculum.

Culturally, Koreans regard education not only as a means of success, but also as a measure of one's self-worth and a representation of high socioeconomic achievement. This cultural belief has influenced Korean parents and their children. Most parents instill in their children the idea that the family's acceptance is contingent upon high academic performance. In the same manner, Korean children feel obligated to receive high grades and are imbued with the notion that their academic success is linked to the family's reputation (Lee, 2002). This cultural factor of respecting academic success motivates children to study English harder and parents to support them, since the ability to speak and write English is a significant measure of success in Korea.

In addition, Koreans generally possess an intense sense of extended family and community. They believe strongly that each generation should advance and become more successful than the previous ones. This sentiment is not only a consideration of the happiness and well-being of Korean children; it is also a function of the Korean cultural belief that grown children are responsible for the care of elderly parents. A strong command of the English language helps to guarantee both a happy and successful life for those in the job market as well as the ability to provide care for the elderly. To achieve this goal, parents not only have high academic expectations, but also instill the importance of academic success in their children's minds. Parents also are willing to sacrifice their own retirement finances to support their children's educational needs.

HISTORIC OVERVIEW OF THE NATIONAL ENGLISH CURRICULUM

A brief overview of the history of English language curriculum in Korea can be divided into three periods: the last Korean Monarchy (1883-1910), the Japanese colony (1910-1945), and the 1st through 7th national curricula (1955-current). Table 1 provides the history of national English curricula, time, content characteristics, and teaching methods. Since 1945, Korea's independence from Japan, the national curriculum for English has been changed eight times.

Initiation of English Education in Korea

English education in Korea was first introduced in 1883 in the "Hermit Kingdom" (so named for the policy of refusing any entry of Western culture), which started to open its doors to foreign countries. English instruction took place at Tongmunhak (Tongmun School) by the order of Emperor Kojong in 1883, in order to provide official interpreters for the royal court (Kim, 1991).

The students were mostly government officials who had a thorough knowledge of Chinese characters, which was required of all government officials. The teachers were T. E. Halifax, a British telegraph technician, and two Chinese who had been educated in United States universities. Since the teachers did not speak Korean, English was taught in a direct method using concrete objects and actions, such as hand gestures (Moon, 1976).

Tongmunhak was closed after three years and a more modernized institution, Yugyoung Gongwon, began teaching English in 1886. All subjects were taught in English and students were expected to have mastered 3,000 English words in 10 months. Considering the fact that high school graduates

Chronology of English Curriculum in Korea

Historic Period	English Curriculum	Years	Instructional Methods	Instructional Emphasis
Korean Monarchy	Initiation of English Education	1883-1910	Bodily kinesthetic and multi-sensory approach	Memorization of vocabulary words
Japanese Colony	Darkness of English Education	1910-1945	Grammar-translation method	Grammar rules
U.S. Military Administration	Transition of English Education	1945-1954	Grammar-translation method	Grammar, composition, and reading basic patterns of sentences
National English Curriculum	The 1st English Curriculum	1955-1963	Grammar-translation method	Standard American English usage
	The 2nd English Curriculum	1963-1973	Audio-lingual approach	Speaking, listening, and practical dialogues
	The 3rd English Curriculum	1974-1981	Audio-visual approach in laboratory booths	Speaking, grammar, and vocabulary
	The 4th English Curriculum	1982-1988	Phonics approach	English language structure and phonics
	The 5th English Curriculum	1989-1994	Eclectic approach	Speaking and grammar
	The 6th English Curriculum	1995-2001	Communicative approach	Communicative expressions
	The 7th English Curriculum	2001-2008	Communicative and flexible instructional approach	Communicative expressions
	Revised English Curriculum	2009-	Learner-centered approach	Communicative expressions and English fluency

Table 1

today are expected to master about 3,000 words, the instructor's standards were much higher than in the past.

The Japanese colonial period (1910-1945) was a dark period for English education in Korea because the Japanese closed the foreign language schools. English was taught two hours a week in junior colleges and high schools, but Japanese was taught 4 hours a week (Moon, 1976). The Japanese teachers used the grammar-translation method in teaching English and Japanese terminology for teaching grammar. During World War II, English education was forbidden in all schools, because Japan regarded English as the enemy's language. After Korea's liberation from Japanese colonial control in 1945, the American influence on Korean society and education grew, and English education was revived. Its importance and support have grown steadily ever since (Choe, 1995; Kim-Rivera, 2002).

During the years of U.S. military administration (1945-1954), after independence from the Japanese imperial rule, English language education experienced a transition period until the first national curriculum was established in 1955. It was quite natural for American democratic education to become the dominant model for Koreans to follow (Yun, 1975). During this period, Korean education closely followed the education system of the United States. The fact that Americans trained or influenced Korean educators had a strong impact on educational policymaking and administration.

The primary goal of education during the U.S. military administration was to replace the previous imperial education system and to foster a democratic mind-set similar to that of American society. The goals for the national English curriculum during the U.S. military administration were for effective communication among Koreans and the enhancement of Korea's presence in the international community. Regardless of the government's emphasis on communication skills in English education, classroom instruction focused mainly upon the understanding of English linguistic rules rather than its application and use. Instruction was based primarily on grammar-oriented and translation methods. Specifically, English curriculum focused on learning and teaching written English grammar, composition, reading practice, and pronunciation. Students memorized patterns of sentences, writing (through dictation, copying, penmanship, and free writing), reading (through translation exercises), pronunciation (through choral reading), spelling, and vocabulary (through studying word lists) (Choi, 2006).

Eight Revisions of the National English Curriculum

The national English curriculum in Korea refers to mandatory guidelines for English education. It establishes curriculum goals, specifies English textbooks, sets teacher qualifications, and determines course content, materials, scheduling, and teaching syllabi for English instruction. It designates who teaches, who learns, what they learn, how it is taught, which materials to use, how it is assessed, and in what language. There is little consideration of individual differences. The following provides an overview of changes of the Korean national curriculum for English, from the establishment of the first national curriculum in 1955 to the present.

The First National Curriculum (1955-1963)

The Korean War (1950-1953) severely damaged the nation's economy and people suffered from the destruction caused by the war. After losing so much in the war, Koreans understandably yearned to obtain materialistic possessions, which represented higher economic status. They saw successful education as a means for regaining possessions. The first curriculum was established to support people's optimistic outlook for the future and to enhance students' skills and knowledge needed in rebuilding the destroyed society.

The most important purpose of the national curriculum during this time, however, was to confront the ideological conflict between democracy and communism with a view of infusing anticommunism into the people's minds and to train skilled workers (Kim, 2004). The English curriculum was very important for communication with the American military, and focused on teaching standard American English and helping students acquire practical English.

The Second National Curriculum (1963-1973)

The second national curriculum, which was actually a slightly revised first national curriculum, appeared after a military coup in 1960, which resulted in the removal of the first president of the Republic of Korea, Rhee Syng Man, and his associates. General Pak Chung-Hee became president and was in power for the next 18 years. Sensing a need to justify its power, the new military administration designed a policy that emphasized the establishment of a national identity, the modernization of the state, and the non-communist unification of North and South Korea. These were automatically accepted as educational objectives.

During the second period of national curriculum, the English curriculum focused on teaching four skills of English—listening, speaking, reading, and writing—as tools of communication based on the audio-lingual approach. Teaching methods in this period emphasized the teaching of speaking and listening before reading and writing, used dialogues and drills, and discouraged the use of the mother tongue in the classroom, because the predominant use of the first language typically interferes with learning a new language.

The Third National Curriculum (1974-1981)

The third national curriculum was accompanied by an amendment to the national constitution, which was needed to maintain the long-term rule of president Pak Chung-Hee. The president justified this action in order to protect the nation from communist North Korea, as Korea was not yet free from the ideological dispute between democracy and communism. Korea also faced various social problems caused by rapid economic growth and the discord between the government and the people, who longed for democracy. The objectives of this curriculum were to enhance the quality of life, create a stronger national identity, decrease public sentiment for communism, and advance knowledge and technical education.

During this period, a new approach in the English language curriculum was teaching through audiovisual methods. Students practiced speaking and listening in laboratory booths before reading and writing. This curriculum discouraged the use of the Korean language in the classroom, used recorded dialogues with film-strip picture sequences to present language items, used drills to teach basic grammar and vocabulary, and implemented a more integrated experience for students to memorize grammatical points.

The Fourth National Curriculum (1982-1988)

The fourth national curriculum took place after Pak Chung-Hee was assassinated and a new military officer came to power through a coup d'état. The new military administration carried out two objectives designed to overcome its lack of political justness. One objective was to suppress people who voiced opinions against the government's coup and encouraged greater freedom of press and democracy. The second objective was to reform educational policies to gain the people's support.

The curriculum during this period added various new ideas. It demonstrated the public demand for creating a Korean curriculum in place of one that simply mimicked that of the United States. The revised curriculum was produced by a research institute, the Korean Educational Development Institute, not by the central government. The idea of curriculum integration appeared for the first time. In addition, private companies could produce textbooks. This opened up the possibility of localization of the curriculum.

The purpose of this curriculum was to establish a well-organized educational program emphasizing national spirit, science and technology, and education for the whole person. During this period, the English curriculum focused on teaching English language structures based on phonics, thus recognizing the relationship between letters and sounds. The focus of English instruction was to build up to the pronunciation skills of a new or familiar word by saying it one sound at a time.

The Fifth National Curriculum (1989-1994)

The curriculum during this era was not significantly different from the fourth. The new president, a former general, ordered only ceremonial reform of the national curriculum, because he wanted to maintain the framework of the fourth national curriculum implemented by his predecessor. The goals of this curriculum were to help educate people, and to attain subjectivity, autonomy, creativity, and morality.

The English curriculum during this period focused on the eclectic approach to teaching English with audio pronunciations, thesaurus, word of the day, and word games (Cha, 2000). The instructional approach was building a natural language using transformational grammar or transformational-generative grammar developed by Chomsky (1969), who believed that language is a mirror of the mind and is rule-governed. This approach was a method of language instruction that emphasized the teaching of grammatical rules while learning language naturally (Han, 1992).

The Sixth National Curriculum (1995-2001)

In 1993, a new democratic government came to power through a peaceful transition, the first transition of its kind in the history of Korea. The new democratic government initiated the sixth national curriculum. This government introduced the idea of globalization and a free-market system, which could be achieved through school reforms and would strengthen the nation's competitive power in an internationalized world. The government aimed at the total reformation of the Korean school system, especially with respect to the teaching of English, in an effort to better prepare students for lives in the 21st century. The major objectives of the sixth national curriculum were:

> to improve basic abilities, skills and attitudes, to develop language ability and civic morality needed to live in society, to increase the spirit of cooperation, to foster basic arithmetic skills and scientific observation skills, and to promote the understanding of a healthy life and the harmonious development of body and mind. (Ministry of Education, 1995, p. 2)

> The curriculum for elementary schools consisted of nine principal subjects: moral education, Korean language, social studies, mathematics, science, physical education, music, fine arts, and practical arts until English is required in 1997. (Ministry of Education, 1995, p. 3)

Perhaps the most significant innovation in the history of English language teaching in Korea was the introduction, in 1997, of English as a regular subject in elementary schools, beginning in the 3rd grade, for two hours a week (Ministry of Education, 1995). This curriculum emphasized the importance of communication of meaning and function and more effective and productive language teaching, rather than simply learning grammar (Kwon, 2000). Teachers used a communicative approach to help students express and understand different kinds of functions, such as using exemplary sentences to greet, thank, and express likes and dislikes for social interaction with other people (Lee et al., 1995). For example, in a chapter of "apologizing" sentences, students learn the following sentences: "Sorry (about that)! Excuse me. That's all right. Oh, I see. It's nothing. No problem! Sorry, I'm late." Students were expected to listen to and comprehend these key expressions, which were listed at the beginning of each chapter, before studying. Students were taught to acquire language fluency and speedy information processing before giving their attention to pronunciation and grammar accuracy. English teacher training emphasized developing teachers' communicative competence.

The Seventh National Curriculum (2000-2008)

The seventh national curriculum, which was implemented in 2000, updated many elements of the curriculum to reflect changes in Korean society and gave high priority to the development of creativity in elementary, middle, and high school (i.e., the importance of required subjects was diminished and that of electives stressed). Also, the curriculum was organized according to individual students' achievement levels rather than by grade and year.

The basic philosophy of the seventh English curriculum was not much different from that of the sixth. Still, the English curriculum focused on learner-centered, activity- and skill-based instruction, critical/creative thinking, and the communicative approach for acquiring practical language (Kim, 2000). These approaches were adopted to help students become competent English speakers. In this way, the nation would be one step closer to Korea's globalization, a process that would contribute to its national development.

This curriculum aimed to teach students English based on hands-on activities, providing useful functional expressions (such as saying the right thing at the right time), and grouping arrangements to match instructional needs and proficiency-based levels. Individual teachers were encouraged, for the first time, to adjust the national curriculum to fit their schools, and if necessary, develop school curriculum appropriate for the level of their students and their needs (Lee, 1998). This was a dramatic change. Prior to the seventh curriculum, every student was taught the same content through uniform teaching methods and textbooks in one large group, using identical lessons, irrespective of differences in students' abilities, schools, and regions.

To enhance hands-on learning activities and active student participation, the government recommended the following teaching and learning methods in the seventh national English curriculum for elementary school students (Ministry of Education, 2000, pp. 29-31):

- Use chants and songs in order to increase students' interest in English
- Use games, role plays, and plays based on task-based activities
- Teach English through various techniques according to a proficiency-based program
- Utilize different kinds of teaching materials according to individual differences
- Teach English through group practices and individual drills
- Encourage students to master English by using self-initiated practices
- Use various multimedia materials, such as CD-ROM, audio, video, Internet, etc.
- Improve students' communicative abilities and fluency by talking more
- Speak English in the classroom.

The English textbooks are designed to accompany the above recommended teaching and learning methods, and intended to promote students' oral language. The most significant difference is in its total exclusion of written language in the first year of instruction. During first-year English class, only spoken English is taught. In the second year, reading is limited to identifying letters of the alphabet. Reading on the word level and phonetic writing are taught in the third year of instruction, which begins in the 5th grade. Writing on the short sentence level is taught in the 6th grade (Chang, 2002). For example, a unit of the textbook for 3rd grade, developed by Kwon, Ko, Lee, Shim, and Procter (1997), contains several activities to enhance students' spoken language: look and listen / listen and repeat / chant / listen and do / speak / sing / play / role play / review, encourage students to use English.

Unlike the sixth curriculum, which provided two hours a week for elementary school English, the seventh English curriculum sets aside only one hour a week for 3rd- and 4th-grade English, and two hours a week for 5th- and 6th-grade English. As the instruction time was reduced, the suggested vocabulary for elementary school also was reduced. The sixth curriculum required that 500 words of elementary school English be taught over four years. In the seventh curriculum, 450 words were required for elementary English, 80-120 for 3rd and 4th grades, and 90-130 each for 5th and 6th grades. This meant that although the number of words to be taught in a certain grade could be flexible, the total number for the four years should not exceed 450 (Kwon, 2000).

Revised National Curriculum (2009-)

The latest revision of the national curriculum will be adopted gradually by 2009 for 1st and 2nd grade in primary schools, by 2010 for 3rd and 4th, and by 2011 for 5th and 6th grades (Ministry of Education and Human Resources, 2007a, 2007b). Unlike the previous national curricula, this latest revision, proposed in 2007, will limit major curriculum reforms, maintain current educational philosophy and systems, and minimize drastic changes. It allows for the gradual phasing in of changes and supplements to the current curriculum, which was implemented in 2000. Beginning with this revision, periodic curriculum changes will be made only as needed in order to meet new educational demands, such as a rapidly changing society and workforce. These demand-based revisions will hopefully avoid Korea's historic trend of launching a new national curriculum each time a new political leader comes to power. Under this latest revision, the government will promote curriculum and administrative decision making at the local level, thereby reducing the central government's control (Ministry of Education and Human Resources, 2007a).

The 2007 revision is profound, as it will be the first time in Korean history that English is officially required in the 1st grade. The MOEHR, along with the Korean government as a whole, recognizes that English is a critical medium for promoting Korea's national interests in international markets where policy and trade negotiations are conducted, and that agreements increasingly are documented in English. The revised curriculum continues to echo the emphasis of the seventh national curriculum, with its focus clearly on English fluency in listening, speaking, reading, and writing. English fluency in each of these areas is critical for Korean people to enjoy success in school and work, as well as an enhanced quality of life in general. Nevertheless, the recommended English education policy for 1st and 2nd grade in primary schools was not implemented in 2009 because of the unsettled controversy among educators, parents, and politicians over the critical periods and means of teaching English to young children. While the parental and societal demands for early English instruction in 1st and 2nd grade in primary schools continue to rise, many influential education policymakers and child psychologists had to stop the implementation of the new educational policy of teaching English to the 1st-grade children in 2009, due to their concern with the current trends of parents trying to teach English too soon using developmentally inappropriate approaches. Although early childhood language experts realize that the introduction of English when children are young is extremely important in successfully learning a foreign language, they also believe that when the learning of a second language is a burden and a stressful process, it will diminish young children's interest and harm their motivation to learn.

English Teacher Training for Elementary Schools

Korea's rapid economic growth has transformed the country from agricultural villages to an industrialized urban society where the use of English, in schools and in the workforce, is required more than ever before. The demand for English competency is extremely high in business sectors, as well as in education. Therefore, schools at all levels, from primary to university, must try to improve students' competence in practical English.

In an effort to strengthen teacher candidates' English ability, teacher education departments in universities have modified existing English courses. Since 1997, when English became a required subject in elementary school, teacher education programs have required increased courses in language skills and English language teaching pedagogy. They now require preservice teachers to complete six to seven English courses in order to prepare future teachers who are competent in English teaching (Lee, M. J., 1997).

It is extremely important for preservice teachers to acquire fluency in English, because they will be expected to teach English in self-contained classrooms in primary schools. Although their major is education, they are required to teach a foreign language, such as English, upon graduation (Kwon, 1997). To help preservice teachers with this requirement, teacher education programs provide English classes that focus less on linguistic knowledge and more on practical English instruction to improve communication. Preservice teachers are trained effectively and efficiently in English language ability prior to receiving their teaching positions. However, inservice teachers often struggle with teaching English, because they did not receive the college training currently offered to preservice teachers. This lack of ability to conduct active communicative teaching is considered a major obstacle to achieving the purported goals of English curriculum in primary school (Kim, 2001).

Although English had been offered as an extracurricular subject in elementary school in the past, very few teachers taught it. The vast majority of inservice teachers, therefore, were not prepared to teach English as a regular subject when, in 1997, it became a requirement. Although teachers had completed required English courses in university, most did not possess adequate listening and speaking abilities. To combat this, the MOEHR designed and implemented inservice English training programs in all cities and provinces in 1996 (MOE, 1996). This inservice training focused more on useful conversation than it did on linguistics and literature. Unfortunately, after receiving this intensive inservice training, many teachers still felt they lacked the necessary language ability to teach English, preferring that it be taught by a qualified English-subject-only teacher (Lee, 1999).

Currently, the MOEHR is committed to increasing the number of English-subject-only teachers with the knowledge of elementary education, and to hiring at least one native speaker of English (referred to as NS in Korea) in all primary schools. In the 1990s, the NS teachers came through the Fulbright ETA (English Teaching Assistant) program and taught English in secondary schools. Inspired by the success of the Fulbright ETA program, the MOEHR started the EPIK (English Program in Korea) in 1996, a project to import and assign NS teachers to secondary schools. NS teachers were recruited from throughout the English-speaking world, including the United States, the United Kingdom, Canada, Australia, New Zealand, and South Africa. In addition to EPIK, which was designed to supply NS teachers only to secondary schools, universities and colleges began hiring NS instructors on their own, and NS instructors were hired by the dozen for enhanced college English programs (Kwon, 2000). The private education sectors that offer English classes to preschool and school-age children in afterschool programs also imported a great number of NS teachers by offering lucrative wages, and compensating for travel expenses and room and board (Park, 1997). Exposure to the NS teachers is a very effective way of learning English, and NS instructors brought more developmentally appropriate teaching ideas, which influenced a change in English curriculum from grammar-based to a focus on communicative competence.

Korea's Future Directions for English as Foreign Language Curriculum

Korea, one of the smallest nations in the world geographically, has amazingly emerged as the 11th largest economy in the world, with its GDP reaching $803 billion, its GPD per capita of $16,400, and its $546 billion trade in 2005. To continue this prosperity, the people's ability to read and speak English is essential. To this end, the future curriculum for English education in primary schools will have the following emphases, which are more developmentally appropriate for children's English instruction than those of the past:

- *Encourage Interactive Language Learning*: Students participate in a small group or a paired group to practice their oral language exercises.
- *Periodic Study Abroad Experiences*: Students are exposed to an environment where English is the only language used to communicate.
- *Promote Speaking and Writing Ability:* Focus will be on the spoken language, yet written language will not be neglected.
- *Emphasis on Authentic Learning and Teaching:* Focus will be on students' communication competence and natural language interactions in English.
- *More Authentic Language Assessment:* The assessment will match the instructional style and measure students' authentic ability to listen, speak, and write in English.

- *Consider Individual Differences:* Teachers will modify lessons based on learners' individual needs.
- *More Use of Technology:* Use multimedia lessons that are available on the Internet, DVDs, satellite TV programs, English websites, Internet chat sites, and English e-mails.
- *English in Content Areas:* Teachers use English immersion in mathematics and science.
- *Native English Teachers:* English classes should be taught exclusively in English by teachers fluent in English or by native-speaking teachers.

Educational Dilemmas in Early English Language Education

MOEHR has found that parents spend massive amounts of money sending their children to English study programs overseas. In 2006, roughly 40,000 minor students transferred to schools in English-speaking countries to learn English. This exodus for a better English education cost parents about 50 million dollars nationally. To reduce the education exodus, increase the number of English-speaking Koreans in the workforce, and promote the country's international presence, the government changed the required age for English education, and started a pilot program teaching English to 1st- and 2nd-graders for one hour a week at 50 elementary schools around the country in 2007. By offering English class from 1st grade as part of the national curriculum or in English immersion schools, the government expects that fewer students will leave the country for better English education elsewhere.

In a further attempt to carry out this mission, MOEHR selected two major provinces to invest in for improved English competency. In these two selected areas, the Jeju province and the "special free economic area" of Incheon, mathematics and science will be taught using the English language beginning in 2008. These changes were designed, in part, to provide better educational opportunities and life success for children from low-income brackets by reducing a widening gap between children living in cities and those in provincial areas. However, the government's decision caused several societal problems. The new policy shows that the outcome of the "earlier English" policy produces the opposite results from its intentions. Many children living in large cities and from prominent families receive more private tutoring in preparation for regular English classes, while children living in remote areas and/or in poverty cannot afford this extra tutoring, thus leading to a further widening of the gap between rich and poor.

Since the government emphasized the critical nature of learning English during early childhood, many parents have become more eager than ever to expose their young children to the English language. Korean parents are paying an amazing 20 billion dollars per year for out-of-school learning (referred to as OL in Korea). This is close to Korea's educational expenditure for the entire school system for one year, which was 29 billion dollars in 2006 (Korea Education Development Institute, 2006). In one case, a young father, whom one of the authors interviewed in 2006 in Korea, of two children, age 5 and age 3, spent $1,130 monthly, 50% of his income, for his two children's OL. The first child attended three different schools (a half-day kindergarten, English, and math OL in the evening) at a cost of $950 a month. The second attends piano and reading class at a cost of $180 a month.

Many parents decide to have their children learn English at a young age because they believe that young children acquire foreign sounds much more easily then; however, the question of whether young children should be exposed to a foreign language prior to acquiring concepts of letters and words in their native language is quite controversial, with some early childhood specialists in favor and others vigorously opposed. Those opposed believe that early exposure to multiple languages may be deleterious to children's cognitive, psychological, and physical development. This is especially true for those Korean parents who pressure toddlers to sit and watch English DVDs for hours, or go to the extreme of having their child's tongue surgically altered to aid in the pronunciation of certain English consonant and consonant digraphs, such as the r, l, f, b, v, ch, th, and ph sounds.

Those who support early English education claim that it is much easier to learn speech sounds of foreign languages at an early age and that it is impossible to achieve true fluency if children miss this critical period's opportunity (Kim, 2000). This is a hypothesis that has yet to be verified. To begin with, linguists say there have been almost no studies that adequately analyze whether early foreign language education is effective. As many language specialists believe, children need to be exposed to both oral and written language during the "critical period" of learning their first language. However, the "critical period" is not what is most important in acquiring a second language.

Opponents of early English education claim that the government does not offer guidelines or a curriculum necessary to properly teach young children English. They believe what is needed is further research into what teaching methods would be effective for emergent learners of English. In addition, they are concerned that the current policy of English education in the 1st grade will affect the psychological and even physical development of young students, who suffer from Korean society's pressure to learn English.

According to a recent study, eight out of 10 children attending 1st and 2nd grade are receiving private English instruction. Among the respondents, 38% of children said that they learned English at kindergarten or an English-only preschool. As such, many Korean students feel enormous pressure, and see studying as their primary duty in life (Diem, Levy, & VanSickle, 2001). They accept that attending private learning centers for long hours each day after school is just a part of their daily routine. Early childhood educators are concerned that the government's change to earlier English education might worsen the pressure on students and increase the demand for private English tutoring of preschool children. They believe it will accelerate private tutoring more than ever.

The authors believe that this policy will not be as successful as the government planned. It may actually create more psychological pressure for children and a financial burden on parents and ultimately increase the education exodus. Will learning English one hour a week in school truly help struggling learners to catch up and be successful in this highly competitive country? The new policy of teaching one hour of English instruction, given mostly in Korean by Korean teachers, is not going to satisfy families willing to send their young children overseas to study. Koreans have a burning desire to learn English, and more effective English instruction will have to be provided in primary schools in order to reduce the pressure placed on young children to master this language.

Conclusion

Helping Korean children become effective English speakers has been a major goal of the national English curriculum because of its importance in the advancement of the nation. As the significance of English has continuously grown throughout Korean businesses and schools, the national English curriculum had to be revised to improve the communicative competence of the Korean workforce. Each revision was necessary to address social and political demands for English usage, as well as to reflect research findings in more effective English instruction.

Ironically, while the government emphasizes the importance of English usage, elementary schools require a mere one or two hours per week of English instruction, and English is not widely spoken in daily conversation. The government should continue to search for ways to increase teaching hours, and stress the importance of the utilization of practical English for Korea to remain competitive in an increasingly globalized world.

The government's high priority in English education and its effort to continuously improve communicative competency serve to illustrate the importance of English language to Korean parents. As parents become more eager to help their children learn English, the government should provide accurate information on the most effective instructional methods and encourage them to support their children's English education, without creating an undue burden.

References

Cha, J. G. (2000). Historical perspectives of English curricular innovations in Korea. *Modern English Education, 1*, 225-239.

Chang, B. M. (2002). The development of English education materials based on the 7th national curriculum of Korea. *Journal of Pan-Pacific Association of Applied Linguistics, 6*(1), 15-28. (ERIC Document Reproduction Service No. EJ 657556)

Choe, Y. (1995). Characteristics of the Japanization policy of Koreans at the end of Japanese rule. *Studies of Korea's Modern and Contemporary History, 2*, 234-259.

Choi, Y. H. (2006). Impact of political situations on the early history of English language education in Korea. *School Subject Education Study, 10*(1), 235-259. Seoul: Ewha Women's University.

Chomsky, N. (1969). Should traditional grammar be ended or mended? *Educational Review, 22*(1), 5-17. Birmingham, England: School of Education.

Diem, R., Levy, T., & VanSickle, R. (2001). *South Korean education focusing on the future.* Retrieved on September 17, 2007, from www.askasia.org/teachers/essays/essay.php?no=68

Han, I. S. (1992). Functional grammar and transformational grammar at the early stage of language teaching. *The Journal of Studies in Language, 8*(1), 191-204.

Jeong, D. B. (2001). Teaching English based on the 7th national English curriculum. *English Linguistic Science, 7*(1), 1-26.

Kim, H. J. (2000). Curriculum development for open English education. *Journal of Pan-Pacific Association of Applied Linguistics, 4*(1), 73-86. (ERIC Document Reproduction Service No. EJ 619893)

Kim, H. J. (2004). National identity in Korean curriculum. *Canadian Social Studies, 38*(3). Retrieved on September 17, 2007, from www.quasar.ualberta.ca/css/Css_38_3/ARkim_national_identity_korean.htm

Kim, J. H. (2001). The effects of elementary English teacher training. *Korean Elementary Education Association, 7*(1), 103-132.

Kim, O. S. (1991). A study on the history of English education in Korea (1876~1945). *History, Society, Philosophy, 5*(1), 69-98. Published by the International Cultural Association, Korea.

Kim-Rivera, E. G. (2002). English language education in Korea under Japanese colonial rule. *Language Policy, 1*, 261-281.

Kim, Y. J. (2000). A study of the immersion program in English education of children. *English Linguistic Science, 5*, 535-548. Published by The English Linguistic Science Association of Korea.

Korea Education Development Institute. (2006). *Korean Government Expenditures vs. Ministry of Education & Human Resources Development Budget.* Educational Statistic Year Book. FY 2006. Seoul, Korea:

Korea Institute of Curriculum and Evaluation [KICE]. (2006). *National vurriculum.* Retrieved on September 17, 2007, from www.kice.re.kr/kice/eng/info/info_2.jsp.

Kwon, O. (1997). Korea's English teacher training and retraining: A new history in the making. *English Teaching, 52*(4), 155-183.

Kwon, O. (2000). Korea's English education policy changes in the 1990s: Innovations to gear the nation for the 21st century. *English Teaching, 55*(1), 47-91.

Kwon, O., Ko, K.-S., Lee, W.-K., Shim, K.-N., & Procter, S. (1997). *Elementary school English 3.* Seoul, Korea: Kyohaksa Publisher.

Lee, G. L. (2002). Six buckets of tears: Korean Americans' school experiences. In G. Boutte (Ed.), *Resounding voices: School experiences of people from diverse ethnic backgrounds* (pp. 63-90). Boston: Allyn & Bacon.

Lee, H. B., Kwon, O., Kim, I. D., Boo, K. S., Lee, W., Choi, Y. H., & Huh, K. C. (1995). *A draft of the elementary school English curriculum.* Seoul, Korea: The Elementary School English Curriculum Development Committee, Sogang University.

Lee, J. H. (1998, April). *The debate over the organization of English textbooks contents appropriate to a proficiency-based curriculum 2.* A seminar on the organization of English textbooks appropriate to a proficiency-based curriculum. Ducksung Women's University, Open Education Council.

Lee, M. J. (1997). Teacher training program for elementary English teachers. *English and English Literature Department Theses Collection of the University of Suwon, 15*, 53-63

Lee, Y. J. (1999). The effects of in-service training on the sense of efficacy of the primary English teacher. *The Journal of Humanities, 29*, 227-250

Ministry of Education. (1995). *The curricula of elementary school: General and the English subject.* Ministry of Education Notification Number 1995-7. Seoul, Korea: Author. Retrieved on May 19, 2008, from http://cutis.mest.go.kr/main.jsp?idx=040301.

Ministry of Education. (1996). *The supply plan of elementary English teachers.* Seoul, Korea: Author.

Ministry of Education. (2000). *The curricula of elementary school: General and the English subject.* Ministry of Education Notification Number 1997-15. Seoul, Korea: Author. Retrieved on May 19, 2008, from www.kice.re.kr/kice/article/m301/view?searchtype=stored&hitadd=1&articleid=60436

Ministry of Education and Human Resources. (2007a). *The documents associated with the notification of primary and middle school curricula revision.* Office of School Policy. Seoul, Korea: Author.

Ministry of Education and Human Resources. (2007b). Ministry of Education and Human Resources Notification Number 2007-79: English Education Curriculum. Seoul, Korea: Author. Retrieved on May 19, 2007, from www.kice.re.kr/kice/article/m302/view?searchtype=stored&hitadd=1&articleid=64473.

Moon, Y. (1976). A historical evaluation of our country's English education. *Applied Linguistics, 14,* 203-222.

Park, D. S. (1997, April 16). [Population of] Illegal American workers explodes thanks to the Korean's English education fever. *The Chosun-Ilbo* [newspaper], pp. 20.

Yun, P. J. (1975). An analytical study on the development of curriculum research in Korea. *Seoul National University of Education, 8,* 411-444.

About the Authors

Guang Lea Lee teaches in the Department of Curriculum and Instruction at Old Dominion University. Her area of expertise includes the Korean education system, diversity, and reading instruction.

Donald Myers teaches in the Department of Curriculum and Instruction at Old Dominion University. His area of expertise includes foundations of education and teacher empowerment.

Quest for National Unity: The Rhetoric and Reality of School Curricula in Lebanon

Irma-Kaarina Ghosn

The Republic of Lebanon, a country of 3,900 square miles, has a population of slightly less than four million, constituting 18 different confessional communities (Lebanon is a parliamentary democracy in which the highest offices are proportionately reserved for representatives from certain religious communities, the "confessional" communities). It is estimated that approximately two thirds of the current population are Muslim and one third are Christian, a reversal of the situation prevailing in the first half of the 20th century, when Christians formed the majority. The country's history is fraught with strife; since its independence in 1943, Lebanon has witnessed several periods of unrest and violent sectarian, as well as intragroup, clashes. In the two decade-long civil war that ended in 1991, an estimated 150,000 people were killed, with material losses amounting to billions of dollars. A survey of the national curricula reveals that throughout the 20th century, authorities have looked to education as a potentially unifying force. The official curricula of the independence era all express the desire to bring together the various confessional factions for a cohesive nation through civic education, but apparently with little success.

The school system is made up of three types of schools: public, private, and private subsidized schools. The public schools, called "official schools," which are under the direct supervision of the Ministry of Education, enroll approximately half of the total student population (Ministry of Education and Higher Education [MEHE], 2007). The other half is enrolled in private schools, some of which are government subsidized and accommodate children from disadvantaged backgrounds. The subsidized schools are typically affiliated with various confessional communities. Other private schools are either international schools (e.g., American Community School; Lycée Française) or proprietary schools operated for profit by individuals or groups. Annual tuition fees in the private sector average $1,300 U.S. (Ministry of National Education, Youth and Sports [MNEYS], 1998), but can reach $8,000 U.S. in the elite international schools. The minimum wage in Lebanon at the time of this writing is $200 U.S. per month. Although the Lebanese parliament promulgated a law for mandatory, free education at

Lebanon

the primary cycle, it presently cannot be enforced, due to a serious lack of resources.

In the private sector, approximately 60% of the schools use French as the instructional language, while the figure in the public sector is 70% (MEHE, 2007). However, the demand for English-medium instruction has steadily increased in the wake of the establishment of several private English-medium universities and colleges. The foreign instructional language has deep roots in the country, traceable to the 16th century.

Foreign Legacy in the Curriculum

Foreign Missionary Schools of the Ottoman Era

Lebanon's strategic location on the Eastern Mediterranean, at the cross-roads of Europe, Asia, and Africa, has fundamentally influenced the national culture, as well as its education system. The history of education in the country can be traced to the 3rd century A.D., when the famous Roman Law School was established in Berytus (Beirut). During the Arab era (700-1250) and the Mamluk rule (1250-1516), basic education for boys was provided by the clergy in churches and mosques, with the primary aim of transmitting religious values and community mores (Kurani, 1949). Formal schooling in what is now Lebanon was established by the Ottomans (early 1500s to 1918), who designed a curriculum consisting of primarily of basic reading, writing, and arithmetic skills. These schools eventually formed the nucleus of the Lebanese public school system (Frayha, 1985).

In the 17th century, Druze Emir (prince) Fakhreddine encouraged Catholic missionaries to establish private schools. The first official education policy was expressed in resolutions of the Maronite Synod of 1736, which called for establishment of schools in all major communities and for a provision of semi-free education for all, with the poor and orphans to be educated at the expense of the church. The resolution further stated that children need to be taught to "behave in fear of God"; be guided to "piety and worship at an early age"; be "educated in virtue"; and be instructed in reading, writing, the Psalms, the Book of Mass, and the New Testament (Atiyeh, 1969). In the 18th and 19th centuries, a number of Catholic missionaries opened schools in the country. In the schools operated by religious orders, boys learned reading, writing, and grammar in Syriac and Arabic, music, and the church calendar. Capable students also received instruction in rhetoric, philosophy, and astronomy. Textbooks were translated from Latin by monks who had received their own education in Rome (Atiyeh, 1969).

With Ottoman permission, British protestant missionaries—and American missionaries traveling with British passports—established several schools around the country in the 19th century. Soon, the various foreign missions competed with each other to establish more and better schools (Atiyeh, 1969). In 1866, the American Presbyterian mission founded what is now the American University of Beirut. Soon after, the Jesuits established St. Joseph University. What was probably the first school for girls in the Ottoman Empire was opened by the American Presbyterian Mission in Beirut in 1834. This school eventually became the American Junior College for Women, the predecessor of the Lebanese American University (Ghosn, 1995).

The education efforts of the foreign missionaries did not please everyone, however. Many Lebanese resented what they perceived as the political ambitions of the governments of the missionaries' native countries, and began opening their own schools. By the end of the 19th century, all major confessional communities had established their own schools or school systems (Atiyeh, 1969). Since then, the private school sector has been a significant force in the country, with the Lebanese gradually establishing their own private schools, the majority of which were modeled after the French system.

Francophone Lebanon

In the aftermath of World War I, Lebanon was placed under the French mandate in 1920, and France took responsibility for public education. Instruction in Ottoman Turkish was replaced by mandatory instruction in French and Arabic.

During the mandate, the public primary school comprised six years of lower primary and four years of upper primary education. The lower primary was divided into three levels. According to the *Bulletin de l'Enseignement* (Haut Commissariat, 1923-1924), children under 8 were taught in the infant section (*la division enfantine*), where the curriculum included vocabulary, language, reading, writing, dictation, and arithmetic in French; Arabic reading and writing; morals, drawing and crafts, gardening, and playing. The lower primary curriculum of four years (*le cours élémentaire* and *le cours moyen*) comprised religious education, Arabic reading, writing, vocabulary and recitation, French, general knowledge, arithmetic, history and geography, morals, and physical education and "practical work." In the higher primary program of two years (*le premier cours* and *le deuxieme cours*), Arabic literature was added to the curriculum, while hours of mathematics and general knowledge were increased. In 1928, when Lebanese officials gained the decision-making authority, primary education was reorganized and the upper primary program was renamed as "complementary course," consisting of religious studies, moral and civic education, language, mathematics, history and geography in Arabic; language and sciences in French; drawing, socialization, music and singing, physical education, and recreation.

Although no public secondary schools existed at the time, a secondary course of study was established, heavily modeled after the French curriculum, but with the addition of Arabic, Arabic philosophy, and local history and geography. In year 10, students had to choose whether to follow a scientific or literary track. The secondary curriculum served as the basis for the Lebanese matriculation examinations taken at the end of years 11 and 12, Baccalaureate I and II, respectively. The secondary school curriculum included only the subjects required in the matriculation examination (Frayha, 1985). The absence of public secondary education, while offering exit examinations to private school students, reveals the perception of both French and Lebanese authorities that higher education was the prerogative of the elite who could afford private schooling.

During the mandate, about 80% of the schools were French, and as Kurani (1949) notes, French educators were convinced that the best way to provide quality education to the Lebanese was to inculcate them in French culture, logic, and French scientific thought. Anglo-Saxon schools, and local Lebanese-owned schools affiliated with them, were outside the French influence—with the exception of mandatory instruction in French—using their own textbooks and preparing their students either for entry to the American University of Beirut or for British public examinations.

CURRICULA OF THE INDEPENDENCE ERA

The Quest for National Identity

World War II created conditions that enabled independent Lebanon to emerge "in the context of Franco-British competition over the destinies of the peoples of the Near East" (Traboulsi, 2007, p. 104). The National Pact of 1943, which was an unwritten agreement among community leaders, based the government structure on religious sects, guaranteeing Christians political primacy. Maronite Christians, being the single largest community, were allocated the presidency, Sunni Muslims the prime minister position, and Shi'a Muslims the speaker of the parliament. All government positions were similarly distributed on a confessional basis. The National Pact also defined Lebanon as a "country with an Arab profile that assimilates all that is beneficial and useful in Western civilization" (Traboulsi, 2007, p. 110). This was a compromise aiming to satisfy those Christians and Muslims who identified with the Arab culture and envisioned an independent Lebanon, with Christians and Muslims living in harmonious coexistence and having close ties with Syria and the rest of the Arab world. At the same time, the approach attempted to alleviate the "Arabization" fears of Christians identifying with Mediterranean culture. Rather than unifying the country, however, this communal power sharing formula turned out to be a divisive force, a force that has played a role in every violent conflict the country has witnessed since then.

In an effort to minimize the Christian-Muslim division and to create a sense of Lebanese identity, the first government of independence legislated Arabic as the instructional language in the curriculum. However, French and English remained the instructional languages in the private sector. Emphasis was put on the importance of citizenship education. The curriculum of 1946 had as its goal to educate "the Lebanese citizen as a participating and knowledgeable member of his [sic] society" (Ministry of Education [ME], 1946, p. 3). In addition,

> *The government puts great emphasis on physical, moral, social and citizenship education. The Lebanese student would know his [sic] country's history, making him [sic] proud of its past, understand its present, and be ready for the future. . . . He [sic] would also appreciate his [sic] country's position vis-à-vis the Arab World and the West. (ME, 1946, p. 3)*

In an attempt to secularize the public schools and unify students' social and political orientation, religious education was kept to one hour per week.

A number of legislative decrees were issued to achieve the goal of national unity. In 1950, the Ministry of Education issued Decree No. 1436, section 13 of which stipulated that "the curriculum in the private, national and foreign schools should be the national one," but added that "directors of these schools can choose techniques of teaching and add subject matters not included in the national curriculum as they see fit" (quoted in Abouchedid, Nasser, & Van Blommestein, 2002, p. 63). In teaching Lebanese history, geography, moral, and civic education, schools could use only textbooks that were approved by the Minister of Education. Private schools were forbidden to use textbooks

Distribution of Subject Matter in Primary Education, 1946 and 1971

Subject	Grade levels and number of hours per week									
	1		2		3		4		5	
	1946	1971	1946	1971	1946	1971	1946	1971	1946	1971
Religious education	1	-	1	-	1	-	1	-	1	-
Moral & civic ed.	1.5	-	1	-	1	-	1	-	1	-
Arabic	6	8	6.5	8	6.5	8	5	7	6	7
Object lessons/ Sciences	2	2	1.5	2	1.5	2	2	3	2	3
Arithmetic	5	5	5	5	5	5	5	5	5	5
Drawing	2	-	2	-	2	-	2	-	2	-
Music & Singing	2	-	1	-	1	-	1	-	1	-
Art activities	-	4		3		3		2		2
Physical ed.	2.5	2	2	2	2	2	2	2	1	2
History & geography	-	-	2	-	2	-	2	-	1	-
Social Studies	-	2		2		2		3		3
Foreign language	5	8	5	8	5	8	5	8	5	8
Total	27	30	27	30	27	30	27	30	27	30

Based on Ministry of Education data (1946, 1971).

Figure 1

containing subjects banned by the government (Frayha, 1985). Interestingly, private schools could use any history books to teach history of foreign countries.

Schooling was now organized into two levels: primary school, which consisted of two pre-primary grades for ages 3 to 5, and five primary grades; and complementary school of four grades (6-9). The pre-primary curriculum comprised singing, playing, and introduction to reading, writing, and arithmetic. Moral stories were also part of the curriculum (ME, 1946). Figures 1 and 2 show the subject matter taught at primary and complementary grades. In grade 4, students began learning scientific terms in English or French, depending on the school in which they were enrolled. In the complementary grades, mathematics and sciences were taught in a foreign language, primarily French or English.

Government regulated the official baccalaureate and detailed the secondary level program. The program had three levels (grades 10, 11, and 12), and was divided into two tracks, literary and sci-entific. Public secondary schools were finally established in 1951. Figure 3 shows the subjects in the secondary program.

In the 1960s, Lebanon witnessed rapid economic growth, and the strong position of the Lebanese pound encouraged middle-class families to send their children to universities in Europe. Subse-quently, curriculum reviews were again undertaken, and in 1968 an experimental sciences track was added to the 12th-grade program. Boys received military training, while girls were assigned home economics. "Religions and civics" replaced "religion and morals" (see Figure 3). In 1970, a revised curriculum for the complementary level was issued in which "moral and civic education" became

Distribution of Subject Matter in Complementary Education, 1946 and 1970

Subject	Grade levels and number of hours per week							
	6		7		8		9	
	1946	1970	1946	1970	1946	1970	1946	1970
Religious education	1	1	1	1	1	1	1	1
Moral & civic ed.	1.5		1.5		1.5		1.5	
Civic education		1		1		1		1
Arabic language	6	7	6	7	5	7	5	6
Drawing & crafts	2	-	2	-	3	-	3	-
Music & singing	1	-	1	-	1	-	1	
Physical ed.	2	2	2	2	2	2	2	2
History & geography	2.5	3	2.5	3	2.5	3	2.5	3
Foreign language	6	7	6	7	5	7	5	6
Sciences	4	3	4	3	4	3	4	5
Mathematics	4	5	4	5	5	5	5	5
Art activities	-	1		1		1		1
Total	30	30	30	30	30	30	30	30

Based on Ministry of Education data (1946, 1970)

Figure 2

"civic education," and Arabic and foreign language instruction were increased by one weekly hour each, as were mathematics and sciences. Music and singing were deleted, and art activities reduced to one hour a week (see Figure 2). A revised primary school curriculum was issued in 1971, when religion, moral, and civic education were removed from the program in order to allow increased hours for Arabic and foreign language instruction (see Figure 1).

Distribution of Subject Matter in Secondary Education, 1946 and 1968

Subject	Grade levels and number of hours per week								
	Grades 10 & 11				Grade 12				
	Literary		Scientific		Philosophy		Math		Exp. Sci.
	1946	1968	1946	1968	1946	1968	1946	1968	1968
Religious ed & morals	2		2		2		2	1	1
Religions & civics		2		2		1			
Drawing	1		1						
Arabic language & literature	8	7	5	5					
Music & singing	1		1						
Physical ed.	2		2		2		2		
History & geography	4		3		4		3		
History		2		1		2		1	1
Geography		2		2		2		1	1
Physics & chemistry	3		6		5		9		
Physics		2		4		3		6	6
Chemistry		1		3				4	4
Biology						4			5
Foreign language & literature	6	7	5						
Mathematics	3	3	5		2		8	12	7
Philosophy (in Arabic)					7	6	3		
Philosophy (in foreign language					8	11	3		2
Arabic history of sciences								2	2
Translation		2						2	
Military training/ Home econ.		3		3		1		1	1
Total	30	31	30	31	30	30	30	30	30

Based on Ministry of Education data (1946, 1968)

Figure 3

Frayha (1985), who studied the relationship between the religious conflict and social studies education in Lebanon, concludes that,

> *Also, the social studies curricula and textbooks have lacked an important theme in educating students about their society, that is, pluralism. This deficiency has resulted in the students' confusion about their culture. Students have been led to think of Lebanon as a homogeneous society, yet on all sides, they have been confronted with deep differences and conflicts. They have been taught that Lebanon is a sovereign and independent country with an Arab face, yet they could not be sure that this meant they were Lebanese, Arab, or Lebanese-Arab. (pp. 349-350)*

The existing differences became evident in the early 1970s when three documents were released by the three major confessional communities calling for defining the role of education. On the one hand, the Congress of Superiors General of Monastic Maronite Orders proposed a new educational model of liberal education supporting cultural pluralism. By contrast, the Supreme Muslim Shi'a Council's and the Sunni Muslims' working papers requested a standardized system of education that would emphasize the Arab heritage and culture, and establish Arabism in Lebanon (Abouchedid et al., 2002).

However, the debates about a viable educational model were interrupted in 1975, when a civil war broke out, showing once again the failure of schooling to promote cooperation and unity. While intermittent periods of relative calm prevailed, hostilities escalated and the war did not end until 1990. During the bloody period of these 15 years, over 800,000 people were displaced from their communities in sectarian "cleansing" (Traboulsi, 2007). Previously heterogeneous communities became homogeneous, and a generation of children grew up with little contact with "the other," thus further deepening the cleavage between the rival confessional communities.

The New Framework for Education

The war formally ended with the 1989 National Reconciliation Accord, known as the *Ta'if* agreement. Once again, authorities looked to education as a tool to forge social cohesion. The agreement called for schooling that would socialize children into national unity within the framework of Lebanon's Arab identity. Regarding the curriculum, the agreement stipulated the need to standardize history and civic education textbooks so that they would promote national unity (Abouchedid et al., 2002).

Subsequently, a Plan for Educational Reform was issued, which emphasized national integration through mandatory instruction of standardized history and civics in all schools. Immediately, all the confessional communities united to vehemently oppose the plan, which was eventually annulled in 1994. After the aborted attempt, a New Framework for Education in Lebanon was developed by a committee representing educational policymakers, academics, and public and private school authorities. Abouchedid et al. (2002) refer to the new 1997 plan as representing "a tectonic shifting" from the political objectives of the initial plan to "structure, content and styles of pedagogy" (¶ 15).

The development of *Manāhij at-T'alīm al-'Āam wa ahdāfūha* (education curricula and their objectives) was overseen by the Center for Educational Research and Development (NCERD), a semi-autonomous agency under the Ministry of National Education, Youth and Sport. The curriculum document, referring to the Constitution, affirms first and foremost that Lebanon is an independent sovereign nation with a distinct Arab identity. The two broad aims of the curriculum can be summarized as follows:

• Development of individuals capable of self-actualization, with a sense of responsibility and ethical commitment and able to deal with others in a spirit of responsible, cooperative citizens.

- Development of citizens to build a unified, cohesive Lebanese society able to play its role in the global community in general and the Arab society in particular. More specifically, the curriculum aims to develop citizens who are moral, law-abiding, patriotic, and proud of their Arab identity; citizens willing to put the common good ahead of personal interests; citizens aware of their spiritual legacies and national history. The curriculum further aims to foster commitment to Arabic language as the national and official language and mastery of at least one foreign language. (pp. 3-4)

The new National Curriculum organizes the 12 years of schooling into two levels:
- Basic Education
  o First Cycle (grades 1-3)
  o Second Cycle (grades 4-6)
  o Intermediate Cycle (grades 7-9)
- Secondary Education
  o First Secondary
  o Second Secondary: Humanities; Sciences
  o Third Secondary: Literature and Humanities (previously Philosophy); Life Science; General Sciences; Sociology and Economics

Figure 4 presents the subject matter and instructional hours in the new program. At the end of year 9 of Basic Education, students still sit for a Brevet examination, which is a requirement for entry to secondary school. Passing the baccalaureate examination at the end of year 12 qualifies students for higher education.

The school week comprises 30 hours in grades 1 through 6, 35 hours in grades 7 to 9, and 31-35 hours in the secondary grades. The unspecified arts and drama hours allow schools leeway to use additional time for academics while remaining within a 35-hour week. As shown in Figure 4, languages, math, and sciences consume a significant portion of the school day, even in the lower primary grades. Detailed curriculum goals and instructional objectives for core subjects can be retrieved from www.executive.com.lb/cnrdp/currang.html.

Foreign Language and Foreign Instructional Language. The most significant change in the new curriculum is that students must now learn two foreign languages, with the first introduced at the onset of schooling (in the private sector, often as early as age 3 and 4) and the second in grade 7 at the latest. The first foreign language serves as the instructional language in the general curriculum in mathematics, sciences, information technology, and "technology." Although schools can still use Arabic as the instructional language in the primary school, the great majority of schools introduce French- or English-medium instruction from the beginning of schooling. Moreover, in the increasingly competitive private sector, the second foreign language is often introduced in primary school, meaning that children are learning two foreign languages—while still developing literacy in their mother tongue—and also learning school subjects in a foreign language.

The goal is to bring up "a citizen who is proficient in at least one foreign language in order to promote openness to and interaction with other cultures" (MNEYS, 1997, p. 146). The first foreign language curriculum has three broad aims: social interaction, academic achievement, and cultural enrichment. Seven general objectives are identified: communicative competence; effective communication in subject matter areas in general, and mathematics and sciences in particular; linguistic skills for pursuing university education; critical thinking; intercultural understanding; positive attitude toward the target language culture; and ability to work with others. Emphasis is laid on language for academic purposes from the beginning. The national textbooks for both first and second language are text-heavy, with reading and writing introduced from the onset. Private schools generally adopt foreign textbooks.

Arabic Language and Literature. The Arabic curriculum emphasizes spiritual and moral values and Arab heritage. Arabic language and literature instruction focuses on developing students' loyalty for the homeland and commitment to harmonious coexistence with their fellow citizens; facilitating communication and cooperation with the Arab people; and promoting the Arab culture. The role of Lebanese in the Arab renaissance and achievements of the Lebanese internationally also are emphasized.

Because the variety of spoken Arabic used by most Lebanese in their everyday communication differs significantly from *fusha*, the modern classical Arabic, children entering school must learn to read a variety of Arabic they do not speak. The curriculum promotes the use of *fusha* in daily communication in order to link the language to everyday life and thus make it come alive. The curriculum also aims to enable students to access Arabic language media.

Distribution of Subject Matter Hours in the Curriculum, 1997

	Basic Education									Secondary Education						
	Elementary Level						Intermediate Level						12			
	First			Second						10	11					
Grade	1	2	3	4	5	6	7	8	9		Hum.	Sci.	Lit./ Hum.	Sociol./ Econ.	Gen'l Sci.	Life Sci.
Arabic	7	7	7	6	6	6	6	6	6	5	6	3	4	2	2	2
1st Foreign Language	7	7	7	6	6	6	6	6	6	5	6	3	6	4	2	2
Mathematics	5	5	5	5	5	5	5	5	5	5	4	6	2	4	10	5
Sciences	2	2	3	4	4	5	6	6	6	7	3	10	3	4	11	16
Civic Ed.	1	1	1	1	1	1	1	1	1	1	1	1	1	1	1	1
Geography	1	1	1	1	1	1	2	2	2	2	2	1	1	1	1	1
IT	-	-	-	-	-	-	1	1	1	1	1	1	1	1	1	1
Technology	1	1	-	1	1	1	1	1	1	1	1	1	1	1	1	1
Art	1	1	1	1	1	1	1	1	1	Extra-Curricular						
Dramatics	1	1	1	1	1	1	1	1	1	Extra-Curricular						
Plastic Arts	1	1	1	1	1	1	1	1	1	Extra-Curricular						
2nd Foreign Language	-	-	-	-	-	-	2	2	2	2	2	2	2	2	2	2
Philosophy & Civilizations	-	-	-	-	-	-	-	-	-	-	3	2	9	3	2	2
Sociology and Economic	-	-	-	-	-	-	-	-	-	2	3	2	-	8	-	-
Physical Education	2	2	2	2	2	2	2	2	2	2	1	1	1	1	1	1
Total	29	29	29	29	29	30	35	35	35	33	33	33	31	32	34	34

Ministry of National Education, Youth and Sports (MNEYS), 1997

Figure 4

Mathematics. The new mathematics curriculum views mathematics as a subject that "can no longer remain the property of a specialized elite, but many of its results and means must be acquired by a more considerable number of citizens" (MNEYS, 1997, p. 288). Although the statement reflects a shift from the elitist view of education prevailing during the French mandate, it does not seem to make a forceful enough argument for the vital importance of mathematics education for *all* citizens.

The core objectives of the curriculum are mathematical reasoning, solving mathematical problems, mathematical communication, and practical application of mathematics. In addition, the curriculum

> *gives the student a chance to value mathematics by helping him [sic] to acquire confidence in mathematical methods, to appreciate precision, rigor, order and harmony of mathematical theories, to develop intuition, imagination and creativity, to find pleasure in intellectual activities and persevere at work. (MNEYS, 1997, p. 288)*

The curriculum is ambitious in its scope, particularly considering that children are learning mathematics in a foreign language. Six-year-old 1st-graders work on addition and subtraction; by grade 5, children add, subtract, divide, and multiply fractions, measure area, and calculate the diameter of circles and degrees of angles. In the secondary school general science track, the mathematics program is very rigorous, with 10 weekly periods dedicated to the subject.

Science Curriculum. The new science curriculum promotes "a global approach based on the understanding of scientific principles and its relation to everyday life in the domains of health, environment, technology, and ethics" (MNEYS, 1997, p. 458). It aims to develop lifelong learners of science who will continue to learn science beyond the school years.

The primary grades' science curriculum covers six themes: plants, animals, human health, environment, matter and energy, earth and the universe. These themes are spirally repeated over the six primary grades. Intermediate grades' curriculum includes life and earth sciences, chemistry, and physics. Secondary level science curriculum for students in the non-scientific tracks aims "at the development of scientific literacy as it relates to today's world" (MNEYS, 1997, p. 458). The curriculum includes topics in biology, chemistry, and physics, selected to enable students "to engage intelligently in public discourse and debate in matters of technical and scientific concern, interact positively with the environment, and address health problems and consumer concerns" (MNEYS, 1997, p. 458).

Students in general science and life science tracks practice scientific processes of problem solving, and hone their skills of scientific observation, scientific precision, and critical thinking. The curriculum aims at developing individual responsibility with respect to health, environment, technology, and protection of natural resources.

In addition, the science curriculum purports to foster "the development of autonomy and responsibility of personal behavior in learners that are characteristics of a free citizen" (MNEYS, 1997, p. 470). However, it is not clear from the curriculum guide how to accomplish this goal in the context of science classes.

Philosophy and Civilizations. This subject, for grades 11 and 12, replaces the previous philosophy curriculum. In an effort to emphasize the Arab identity of Lebanon, one of its aims is to revive the Arabic philosophic heritage, while also introducing students to diverse civilizations and "their geographic, historical and cultural frameworks" (MNEYS, 1997, p. 668). The curriculum covers the Mesopotamian, ancient Egyptian, Phoenician, Indian, Persian, Greek, and Roman civilizations, but the overwhelming emphasis is on Arab heritage.

Civic Education. Civic education is provided from grade 1 through 12 with one weekly period. From the beginning, there is an emphasis on attachment to the homeland, which is a recurring theme throughout the program. Patriotism is fostered by celebrating national festivals, such as Army Day.

Another recurring theme is the position of Lebanon within the Arab world. Cooperation and team work are emphasized. While some of the other subject curricula also claim to foster the skills of citizenship, very little of that is evident in the instructional objectives and/or textbooks adopted. (The language teaching texts are a notable exception, incorporating issues of heritage, environment, conservation, security, gender and heritage, and promoting cooperative learning strategies.)

History. Although the new curriculum was issued in 1997, and the first new national textbooks were published in 1998, the new national history curriculum and textbook have yet to see the light of day. The reason is that community leaders of all the 18 confessional groups must agree on the text, and while there is little disagreement about ancient history, recent history is a subject of much controversy. Atrocities were committed by all sides during the civil war, and arriving at a representation agreeable to everyone continues to be a thorny issue. The unspoken fear appears to be that recounting what really happened will fuel hatred and spark wars of revenge. If and when an agreement about the curriculum is reached, the resulting outcome is likely to be so watered-down as to be useless in enabling students to make sense of what happened and why.

Consequently, schools teach whatever history they see fit. A number of different Ministry-approved history textbooks from the 1960s and 1970s are used (Abouchedid et al., 2002), many of which present contradictory concepts. As Fattah (2007) notes,

> *In one textbook, the students get to know the Ottomans as occupiers; in another, they read about them as administrators. In some, they study the French as colonialists; in others they study them as examples to emulate. In some Christian schools, history starts with the ancient Phoenicians, who many Christians believe are their original ancestors, and the dawn of Christianity. In many Muslim schools, the Phoenicians are glossed over and emphasis is placed on the Arab history and the arrival of Islam. (¶ 9-10)*

When Fattah interviewed students in one private school in Beirut, he encountered frustrated students, who are well aware that they are not getting an accurate presentation of the events. As one 9th-grader put it, "We keep asking them when we're going to learn the real history." She continues: "The history just suddenly stops. You get this feeling they think that if history is going to create a problem, then just forget the history" (Fattah, 2007, ¶ 8).

Information Technology. IT, referred to as "Informatics" in the curriculum guide, is a new subject and is introduced into the curriculum in grade 7. One weekly period is stipulated through grade 12. The curriculum aims at developing basic computer skills, applying word processing skills, and teaching spreadsheet techniques. Students are also expected to learn to search and retrieve data and practice simple programming. In the private sector, most students are introduced to information technology in the primary school.

Technology. This is another new subject, for which one period a week is allocated. Its aim is to provide students with "the opportunity to understand, study and carefully use technical products" (MNEYS, 1997, p. 614). The themes in the primary grades include food and agronomy, electricity and magnetism, mechanics, means of transport, etc. Students make recycled paper, pottery, and a pinhole camera, grow crystals, construct bridges with different materials, and so on. In the middle grades, students explore materials in common use, tools and simple machines, measuring instruments, electrical mechanisms, and learn techniques of conserving collections such as plant collections. Secondary level themes cover systems and techniques (e.g., acoustics; medical technology), electronics, communication and media, and "economics management" (monetary systems; documents of purchase and sale) (MNEYS, 1997, p. 614).

Geography. The curriculum aims to help students understand geography as a result of interaction of diverse human and natural elements. It develops skills of field study, scientific discovery, and map reading. It fosters awareness of the importance of conserving natural resources and protecting the environment. Students are also expected to become accustomed to organized teamwork. Their sense of national belonging is strengthened through study of Lebanon's rich human and natural resources. Learners' awareness of Lebanon's relation with the Arab world is emphasized, but they are also expected to develop a comprehensive view about the interrelatedness of the world's regions (MNEYS, 1997).

Other Subjects. Physical education, arts, and drama are also allocated time in the curriculum. However, observations and interviews the author has conducted during the past 10 years reveal that in the intermediate grades, arts and drama are often sacrificed in favor of academic subjects, particularly when students begin preparing for the official examinations. In the secondary schools, art and drama activities are extracurricular or available through school clubs. In many schools, however, lack of human and material resources makes education in the arts difficult.

The New Framework for Education further calls for global education, sex education, and integration of environmental, health, and demographic education with the other subjects. All references to religion and religious education were removed from the national curriculum, attesting to the sensitivity of the issue in the country. However, private schools have the freedom to add subjects to their program, and religious education is mandatory in many of the private schools operated by different confessional groups, both Christian and Muslim.

TEXTBOOK AND EXAMS AS THE PERCEIVED CURRICULUM

Public schools use locally produced national textbooks, whereas private schools have the freedom to choose their own books and typically adopt foreign mathematics and science textbooks in the primary and middle school. In secondary school, many private schools supplement the foreign books with the national textbooks in preparation for the baccalaureate.

The author's personal experiences with national textbook development, teacher training, and research indicate that the term "curriculum" in Lebanon is nearly synonymous with the textbook, particularly in primary school. Although detailed goals and learning objectives exist for each subject matter and grade level, most teachers have not seen them. Only the national textbook authors and educators involved in training the teaching force in the new curriculum methods were privy to the full scope and sequence of their subjects. In general, the textbook functions as *the* curriculum for classroom teachers, having almost a personified authority. Observations in primary school show that teachers frequently use the pronoun "they" when referring to the textbook:

> Teacher 1: *They want us to practice conversation here.*
> Teacher 2: *Let's see what they want us to do today.*
> Teacher 3: *They always give us problems to solve.*
> Teacher 4: *They want us to circle the answers here. (Ghosn, 2001, p. 220)*

When a group of primary and middle school science teachers were asked in a workshop to identify the core concepts and learning objectives of their particular grade levels, they provided the workshop facilitator a list of headings from their science books (Ghosn, 2008). In the intermediate and secondary levels, the official examination content drives instruction. As Frayha wrote in 1985:

> *Passing examinations and earning the official diplomas have become the aim of the students and the end of teachers' and schools' activities. Students have not paid much attention to studies that are not included in the official examinations. . . . Students, teachers, schools and even parents have grown to regard French, Arabic, mathematics, and sciences as superior and social studies, arts, music, and physical education as inferior. (p. 348)*

Frayha's comments resonate with the observed reality 20 years later, the difference being only that mathematics and sciences are now the superior subjects, ahead of language. The top occupational choices of secondary school graduates are medicine, engineering, computer sciences, and pharmacy. Furthermore, English has become the first foreign language of choice for a large number of students in the wake of Internet technology and the establishment of several English-medium colleges and universities in the country.

PEDAGOGY

Pedagogy in the 1960s

The first pedagogical guide in the country was published in 1966 by the Ministry of National Education [MNE] as "a message of confidence and a call for modernization" (p. 155). The contents are presented in two languages, French and English—but not in Arabic—and suggestions are offered for teaching a foreign language, mathematics, and sciences. References to foreign child psychologists' work suggest the guide was Western society-inspired.

Referring to developments in the field of child psychology at the time, the guide recommends early teaching of foreign language, with the child's immediate environment and interests as the starting point. Reading instruction was introduced from the beginning, with both phonics and sight word instruction. Throughout the grade levels, the following approach to reading instruction was recommended: The teacher should first read the passage with clear intonation and precise articulation, after which "the best students should read" (MNE, 1966, p. 209), followed by others in a familiar round-robin approach. The passage would be read as many times as necessary for the class to read it correctly. Mistakes were to be corrected immediately as they occurred. Choral reading was not to be permitted, because "individual is real reading, that which the teacher can follow, control, and correct" (MNE, 1966, p. 211). After reading and comprehension questions, books were to be closed and the passage summarized. Older students were invited to discuss the text. The process does not reflect the recommendation to begin with and relate learning to children's experience and interests. A reason for this contradiction will be explored later.

Mathematics, taught in the foreign language in the intermediate and secondary levels, was to be related to real-life exercises taken from the learner's experience, and mathematical reasoning employed to find solutions to everyday problems. Use of visual aids and concrete manipulatives was recommended in algebra and geometry instruction, and the guide provides a variety of suggestions to accomplish this.

The guide warns that science instruction should not consist of "communicating the knowledge of an adult, but of making the child able to get by himself [sic] that knowledge which conforms to his [sic] intellectual maturity" (MNE, 1966, p. 273). Experimental method is promoted, "dogmatic" or "dictated" lessons were forbidden in favor of active methods, and instruction was to proceed from the concrete to the abstract. The dictated lessons, the guide notes, "have created in our classes torpor and intellectual indifference" (MNE, 1966, p. 279). In life and earth sciences, the skills of observation are emphasized, and many suggestions are given for hands-on exploration of terrariums, aquariums, herbariums, and other collections. The guide specifically states that "the book is an auxiliary and not an objective, and one must use it only to consult figures and drawings" (MNE, 1966, p. 290). However, as seen above, teachers are not heeding this advice, at least not in the primary school.

Culture and the New Pedagogy

Developers of the new curriculum clearly borrowed pedagogical approaches from the West, promoting learner-centered instruction, cooperative learning, and development of critical thinking. However, because the classroom is a microcosm of the culture within which it is situated, the communication patterns of the culture are reflected in the classroom discourse (Holliday, 1994) and pedagogy (Ghosn, 2004). Two key aspects of culture are particularly important when trying to understand what can—or cannot—happen in the classroom.

First, where hierarchy and formality guide social interactions, teachers and pupils have clearly defined roles to which they are expected to conform. Lebanon, as most Middle Eastern countries (Israel being an exception), is a hierarchical society. In the classroom, the teacher is the authority who directs the lesson. Curriculum in hierarchical cultures tends to involve a great deal of rote learning, and students may be discouraged from asking questions, because questions might pose a threat to teacher autonomy (Lustig & Koester, 2006).

Second, there is the level of tolerance people have for uncertainty. In societies with low tolerance for uncertainty or ambiguity, classrooms tend to have fixed routines and insist on correct answers (Lustig & Koester, 2006). Arab societies typically have low tolerance for ambiguity, as the following quote from a teacher in Egypt reflects:

> *When I present a reading text to the class, the students expect me to go through it word by word and explain every point of vocabulary or grammar. They would be uncomfortable if I left it for them to work it out on their own or ask them just to try to understand the main ideas. (Richards & Lockhart, 1994, p. 108)*

Needless to say, individuals differ in these two dimensions to varying degrees, even within the same culture. However, classroom observations and interviews with teachers in Lebanese schools suggest that these two aspects do, indeed, influence classroom pedagogy. A study involving over 200 hours of systematic observation in grades K-6 in 14 different private schools around the country shows that the majority of the classes were teacher-fronted and textbook-oriented, often even in the kindergarten (Ghosn, 2008). Teachers identified their most common mode of instruction to be "explaining the lesson," and observations show this to be true, regardless of the subject matter. Teachers' insistence on correct answers, which was observed to be very common, discourages students' experimentation and creative and critical thinking. In a language class, it can result in artificial and personally meaningless discourse and loss of motivation (Ghosn, 2001, 2004).

Even the child-centered teachers favoring active, participatory learning are facing difficulties because of time constraints and the full curriculum. Because in most schools, with the exception of a handful of elite schools, the day is organized around 45- to 50-minute lesson periods, teachers have little opportunity to structure in-depth, uninterrupted exploration of concepts or plan for in-class project work. The textbook has taken over the role of the curriculum, especially in the primary school, the expectation often being that all lessons in the book must be covered. In the upper grades, the official curriculum is extremely ambitious and examination-focused. The result is an instructional cycle with little time for guided practice; teachers present the content, assign homework, and test students.

CHALLENGES

Foreign Instructional Language

The new curriculum poses many challenges for students. One is the foreign instructional language, which typically is introduced at the onset of schooling. Although children in affluent families typically have parents who themselves have received foreign language education in the private schools and universities, and the instructional language is often spoken at home, this is not the case with the great majority of the children. Rural children and children from lower socioeconomic classes are especially disadvantaged in this regard. Educated parents, mainly mothers, spend hours every week teaching their children and helping them with schoolwork, and children in affluent families enjoy the services of private tutors. Parents in lower socioeconomic families can rarely provide such support. Unsatisfactory achievement or failure in the instructional language also will result in low achievement or failure in the academic subjects taught in the foreign language.

The Curriculum Orientation and Drop-Out Phenomenon

Another challenge is the curriculum itself. Besides being overloaded with content, the curriculum goals address specifically the needs of students bound for secondary and tertiary education, ignoring the needs of students heading for vocational or technical education or the job market. It is, therefore, not surprising that over 10% of the children drop out before finishing grade 5 (UNESCO, 2002). A report by the International Labour Organization, *Gender, Education and Child Labour in Lebanon* (ILO, 2004), shows that in 2000, 14% of primary school students and 25.6% of intermediate students were more than one year behind, and that most of the students who fail once or twice end up dropping out of school. In the 2003 academic year, nearly 20% of the 4th-graders and 12-18% of middle graders were retained (Ministry of Education and Higher Education [MEHE], 2004), meaning that if the ILO prediction is accurate, many of these children are at risk of dropping out.

The following quote from the primary school mathematics curriculum reflects the sad reality facing many children in the country:

> *[Primary school curriculum] assures the students who finish this cycle a necessary and durable formation, so that if they have to leave school at 12 years of age to take part in production, they would have enough aptitude not to return to the state of mathematical illiteracy. (MNEYS, 1997, p. 298)*

Although a law exists about mandatory schooling until age 12, it cannot be enforced due to the serious financial constraints facing the post-war public school system.

In 1995, 71% of school leavers surveyed stated academic failure as a reason for dropping out. ILO's Deputy Director Taleb Rifai asserts that the education system is failing to make learning and staying in school meaningful to students (Haddad, 1997). A survey of annual statistics of the Ministry of Education between the early 1990s and 2006 reveals that, in fact, only one half of a cohort entering grade 1 actually can be expected to matriculate from secondary school.

Teacher Qualifications

Teacher qualifications are a third challenge. According to the annual statistics of 2003-04, less than half of the teaching force (42% in private and 44% in public sector) hold university degrees (MEHE, 2004). UNESCO's *Education for All Global Monitoring Report* (2005) further reveals that in 2001, only about a quarter of all primary school teachers held formal teaching credentials, with the figure dropping to 12.5% when pre-primary teachers were included. Consequently, it is not surprising that the drop-out rate in Lebanon is rather high.

Disparity in Academic Achievement

The foreign instructional language and an ambitious academic curriculum, coupled with inadequate teacher qualifications, are a serious problem in Lebanon. A country that has traditionally prided itself on high standards of education, Lebanon is clearly falling behind in this respect. Not only are drop-out figures alarming, but so are the results of the 2003 Trends in International Mathematics and Science Standards (TIMSS)[1] study. Lebanese 8th-graders scored among the bottom five countries out of the 46 participating in the study, and well below the international average. A total of 1,300 students were tested in Lebanon and 4,200 completed a survey. In sciences, Lebanon ranked last of the nine Arab countries in the study. In mathematics, they were among the bottom dozen, but did outscore students in the other Arab countries.

A World Bank analysis (2006) of the TIMSS results concludes that children from poor, unilingual rural families, where parents were uneducated or had only primary education, were at the biggest disadvantage, scoring the lowest. In contrast, children from families with educated parents, where the instructional language was often spoken at home, scored the highest. In other words, education seems to benefit the already advantaged children the most.

CONCLUSION

In conclusion, the recent curriculum reform in Lebanon seems to cater primarily to the middle and upper socioeconomic classes and students aiming for higher education in particular. The program is demanding, and little if any provision is evident in the curriculum for students who do not have the aptitude or inclination for higher education. The result is the alienation of a significant segment of the student population from the curriculum, their failure, and subsequent dropping out. One must question what will become of the students who drop out at age 12 or 13; to what kind of quality of life can they aspire, what contributions can they make to society, and what level of civic commitment can be expected of them? In the absence of serious political will to improve the public sector education, a positive change in this regard is unlikely to happen any time soon.

It is also very unlikely that the new curriculum will be any more successful in unifying the multi-confessional Lebanese society than the previous ones, despite the lofty rhetoric. As Crow (1980) rightly points out, "Functionally, for the Lebanese, the religious community is his [sic] nation; that is the people to whom he [sic] belongs and with whom he [sic] identifies" (p. 154). Strong intergroup identification has the potential to breed hostility toward "the other," particularly in the presence of competition for social status or political power (Brewer, 2001), such as is the case in the Lebanese confessional power-sharing formula. In fact, at the time of this writing, sectarian tensions run high in the wake of a string of political assassinations, and the country teeters on the brink of yet another war. There is fear among the educators that because no consensus about a common version of the recent history has been reached and taught in schools, the youth are doomed to repeat the past, "with most of them learning contemporary history from their families, on the streets or from political leaders who may have their own agendas" (Fattah, ¶ 6). Should that happen, the poor, undereducated youth will be the first to be recruited to protect the interests of their confessional communities, whereas the educated youth from middle and upper classes have the option of emigrating to continue their education or to pursue their professional interests.

What is now urgently needed is a curriculum reform that will meet the needs and aspirations of *all* learners, not only the college-bound. This will reduce the drop-out rates and result in a better educated workforce, one that is able to meet the challenges of the increasingly sophisticated workplace technology. Social studies curricula should socialize children for life in a pluralistic society such as Lebanon. Rather than paying lip service to patriotism and national unity, the curriculum should explicitly address the country's rich diversity, both religious and cultural, as well as its history. Teacher qualifications also need to be improved, so as to enable teachers to engage all students in the learning process.

Finally, a strong public school system would encourage more parents to enroll their children in public schools. This would increase diversity within the school and the classroom, with children having more contact with "the other," especially in the still-heterogeneous communities and urban areas. Daily contact, coupled with sensitive, unbiased instruction about the beliefs and values of the country's diverse communities, would have the potential to foster more positive attitudes toward differences. Of essential importance is for youth to have knowledge of their history, as well as to understand the human and material costs of war.

Note:

[1] TIMSS is a research project sponsored by the International Association for Evaluation of Educational Achievement. It is directed by the International Study Center in the Lynch School of Education at Boston College.

References

Abouchedid, K., Nasser, R., & Van Blommestein, J. V. (2002). The limitations of inter-group learning in confessional school systems: The case of Lebanon [Electronic version]. *Arab Studies Quarterly, 24*(4), 61.

Atiyeh, N. (1969). The development of education in Lebanon. In Beirut College for Women (Ed.), *Cultural resources in Lebanon* (pp. 198-215). Beirut: Libraire du Liban.

Brewer, M. B. (2001). Ingroup identification intergroup conflict: When does ingroup love become outgroup hate? In R. D. Ashmore, L. Jussim, & D. Wilder (Eds.), *Social identity, intergroup conflict, and conflict resolution* (pp. 17-41). New York: Oxford University Press.

Crow, R. E. (1980). Electoral issues: Lebanon. In J. M. Landau, F. Ozbudun, & F. Tachau (Eds.), *Electoral politics in the Middle East: Issues, voters, and elites* (pp. 153-87). London: Croom Helm.

Fattah, H. (2007, January 10). Lebanon's history textbooks sidestep its civil war. *International Herald Tribune.* Retrieved March 27, 2007, from www.iht.com/articles/2007/01/10/news/Beirut.php

Frayha, N. (1985). *Religious conflict and the role of social studies for citizenship education in the Lebanese schools between 1920 and 1983.* Unpublished doctoral dissertation, Stanford University, California.

Ghosn, G. (1995). We dared to venture. *Aramco World, 46*(6), 2-7.

Ghosn, I.-K. (2001). Teachers and students interacting around the textbook: An exploratory study of children developing academic second language literacy in primary school English classes in Lebanon. *Dissertation Abstracts International, 63*/04, 1232 (UMI No. 3049590).

Ghosn, I.-K. (2004). Story as culturally appropriate social context for young ELT learners. *Language, Culture and Curriculum, 17*(2), 109-126.

Ghosn, I.-K. (2008). *Quality of K-6 schooling in Lebanese private schools.* Manuscript in preparation.

Haddad, R. (1997, Oct. 29). "Failures" of school system blamed for child labor crisis. *The Daily Star* [Beirut], p. 4.

Haut-Commissariat de la République Francaise en Syrie et au Liban. (1923-1924). *Bulletin de l'Enseignement, Vol. I.* Beirut: Publication du Service de l'Instruction Publique.

Holliday, A. (1994). *Appropriate methodology and social context.* Cambridge, UK: Cambridge University Press.

International Labour Organization. (2004). *Gender, education and child labour in Lebanon.* Retrieved June 16, 2006, from www.ilo.org/ipecinfo/product/viewProduct.do?productID=341

Kurani, H. (1949). Lebanon: Educational reform. *The yearbook of education, 1949.* London: Evans Brothers.

Lustig, M., & Koester, J. (2006). *Intercultural competence.* New York: HarperCollins.

Ministry of Education. (1946). *Manāhij at-T'alīm* [The curricula]. Beirut: Author.

Ministry of Education. (1968). *Manāhij at-T'alīm* [The curricula]. Beirut: Author.

Ministry of Education. (1971). *Manāhij at-T'alīm* [The curricula]. Beirut: Author.

Ministry of Education and Higher Education. (2007). *Annual statistics 2003-2004.* Beirut: Author.

Ministry of National Education. (1966). *Educational instructions.* Beirut: Author.

Ministry of National Education, Youth and Sports. (1998). *Preliminary statistics for the school year 1996-1997.* Dekwaneh, Lebanon: Office of Educational Research Statics.

Ministry of National Education, Youth and Sports. (1997). *Manāhij at-T'alīm al-'Āam wa ahdāfūha* [The curricula and objectives]. Beirut: Author.

Ministry of National Education, Youth and Sports. (1997). *Annual statistics 1996-1997.* Beirut: Author.

Richards, J., & Lockhart, C. (1994). *Reflective teaching in second language classroom.* Cambridge, UK: Cambridge University Press.

Traboulsi, F. (2007). *A history of modern Lebanon.* London: Pluto Press.

UNESCO. (2005). *Education for all global monitoring report.* Paris: Author.

World Bank Group, The. (2006). *Republic of Lebanon update. First quarter 2006.* Beirut: Author.

About the Author

Irma-Kaarina Ghosn is Associate Professor and Chairperson of the Department of Humanities and Social Sciences at the Lebanese American University Byblos campus, where she also directs the Institute for Peace and Justice Education. She received her Ph.D. from the University of Leicester, UK, and her M.Ed. from University of Virginia in Charlottesville. She can be contacted at ighosn@lau.edu.lb

Curriculum Development and Implementation in Malawi: Issues and Evidence

Grace Chiuye and Hartford Mchazime

Malawi lies in southeastern Africa and forms part of the sub-Saharan Africa region. Its population is estimated at 12 million, of which close to 51% are women (National Statistical Office, 1998). Approximately 83% of the population resides in rural areas, while only 17% makes up the urban population. As of 2001, the United Nations reported that 54% of Malawians live below the national poverty line, and the Human Poverty Index for the country stood at just 42.5 (UNAIDS, 2002), while the life expectancy has dropped from 44 to 39 years. The economy is largely dependent on agriculture, with tobacco, tea, and sugar as the major trade crops. Economic growth has been limited by numerous factors, such as soaring energy prices, unreliable and irregular free trade market regulations, increased numbers of refugees, persistent droughts that trigger widespread hunger and famine, and low agricultural production levels.

The recent globalization policies have negatively impacted the domestic industry and threaten its expansion. The much-heralded effects of increasing macroeconomic sectors in developing countries have not been positive (Wagner, 2001). Many of such countries have put their own economies "at a significant risk" (Johnston, 2002; Prasad, Rogoff, Wei, & Kose, 2003). Liberalization has allowed foreign markets to flourish in Malawi. Backed by a strong capital base and mass production capability, and an abundance of foreign products, liberalization makes it difficult for the local industry to compete favorably. Finally, the HIV/AIDS epidemic, declining donor support (exacerbated by imposed monetary restrictions), and ineffective projections of manpower requirements contribute further to the deteriorating economic base (Creative Associates, Inc., 1999; Keller, 2005; National Statistical Office, 1998; World Bank, 1994).

For many families, this state of affairs means that life is a daily struggle for survival. As Maslow's hierarchy of needs points out (www.business-balls/maslow.htm), lower level needs must be satisfied before meeting those in the upper levels. The lower level needs include those of food, shelter, and

Malawi

clothing. Education is positioned at a much higher level and, therefore, may not be a priority in poor families. Subsequently, the situation impacts greatly on accessing and participating in educational services. Parents and children who are preoccupied with surviving for the day may place education as a secondary consideration. In addition, economic levels impact the curriculum in terms of what content is taught and how it is delivered.

The Language Situation in Malawi

There are about 13 languages for as many tribes that are spoken across the three regions of Malawi. A recent language mapping exercise conducted by the Center for Language Studies found three more languages in the north. These additions were a result of deliberate efforts to make fine distinctions among the existing languages in the northern region (Center for Language Studies, 2006). Chichewa and English are the national and official languages, respectively. English plays a significant role in many circles in Malawi. It is the language of power and a passport to economic success. A lack of English skills and knowledge translates into a lack of, or limited opportunities for, employment and avenues for simply surviving. In essence, the possession of English language knowledge and skills largely determines sustenance of life. Furthermore, English is the language of policy in all government sectors and is highly regarded by many Malawians, who equate it with a Western image.

In the commercial sector, documents and business transactions are conducted in English. Parliament, government, and almost all political positions require proficiency in English. Parliamentary proceedings, official meetings, and transactions are in English. Even in the media, English is the most visible language of communication. Television Malawi is the country's only television network and broadcasts its programs in English and Chichewa. However, more programs are aired in English than in Chichewa. Similarly, radio broadcasts are mainly in English and Chichewa. In addition, the use of other local languages, such as Lomwe, Tonga, Tumbuka, Sena, and Yao, is limited to newscasts and brief programs. A similar pattern may be observed for newspaper publications. For example, editions of the nation's top two newspapers, *The Daily Times* and *The Nation,* are in English, with Chichewa articles carried only on Saturday editions (*Malawi News* and *The Weekend Nation*, respectively). Other papers predominantly publish in English, and yet others use both English and Chichewa. There are publications exclusively in Chichewa. Despite the liberal use of English in Malawi's public and private sectors, the majority of people possess minimal English proficiency levels and only speak English at school. English is, however, spoken in affluent homes (their children often attend private schools).

The Place of English in the Curriculum

Chichewa is the medium of instruction in the lower grades and offered as a subject from Standard 5, when English takes over as the medium of instruction. In 1996, a policy directive required teaching in the predominant local language of each area (Center for Language Studies, 2001; Ministry of Education Science, and Technology, 2001). However, this directive was heavily opposed by the public. One of the reasons was that this mandate required teachers to possess knowledge and fluency in several local languages, which most teachers did not possess. Teachers often are not fluent in the predominant language of the community where they teach. While English is offered as a subject of study from 1st grade, by the 5th grade, it is the currency of instruction in the classroom. All instructional materials are in English (except the pupils' class readers in Chichewa subjects). Students must obtain a passing grade in English to be eligible for promotion to the next grade in primary schools.

In secondary school, students must attain a pass in English for the award of both the Junior Certificate of Education (JCE) and the Malawi School Certificate of Education (MSCE) (Malawi National Examinations Board, 1989). Pilot studies on comparing pupil performance found that pupils learning in their own vernacular language outperformed those who did not belong to the ethnic group of the language of instruction (Chilora, 2007). With this situation in the country, one sees why Malawians would support English-language training, even though education experts argue that children should at least be given an opportunity to be literate in a language that is most familiar to them—in other words, the children's language of play. In 1998, only 4% of the population claimed that they used English in their homes, while the rest used either Chichewa or one of the other local languages. It is against this background that curriculum development in Malawi can be examined and discussed.

Curriculum Development

Curriculum development and implementation in Malawi largely follows the dictates of political, economic, and, to some extent, religious ideologies. In fact, education has followed the tides of these forces throughout the history of Malawi. The political history of the country could be divided into three eras—Colonial, Post-Independence, and Democracy/Multiparty Era.

Colonial Era (1875-1964). The Colonial Era dates back to the 1800s. British missionaries, who came to Malawi to introduce Christianity, began formal education in Malawi in 1875. The purpose was to teach reading and writing skills to help spread the gospel. It was believed that for Christianity to take root and flourish, Malawians needed to know how to read the Bible. Therefore, the curriculum consisted largely of reading, writing, arithmetic, and handwork. In 1931, the Department of Education, which was set up in 1927, provided a curriculum for schools in the country, and it asked schools to offer the following subjects:

Subject	Class 1	Class 2	Class 3	Class 4	Class 5
Religious and Moral Education	5	5	5	5	5
Vernacular	10	10	5	5	5
Historical Geography	1	1	2	2	2
Hygiene	1	1	1	1	1
Nature Study/Gardening	1	1	1	1	1
Arithmetic	5	5	6	6	6
Handwork/Gardening	6	6	5	5	5
Singing	1	1	1	1	1
Number of periods	30	30	30	30	30

All schools were advised to include 10-minute physical drills daily in their teaching, and each school was expected to play two games each week (Lacey, 1931). Due to a reduced teaching force, Pachai (1973) recommended that classes be combined when possible, such as in the case of historical geography and nature study. The syllabus from that time recommended that in class one, children should be taught syllables and short words from reading charts or the chalkboard. In class two, children should be exposed to their class reader and pay attention to pronunciation and punctuation. Simple grammar—such as parts of speech and proper use of words—was to be included with an approved reader. The syllabus for subsequent classes included reading and simple analysis and lessons on syntax. Writing began with copying words and dictation; then, children were introduced to composition writing, including translation of texts from English to the vernacular.

In arithmetic lessons, children were first introduced to counting and then moved on to multiplication tables, division, weights, time and money, reading the clock, problems relating to marketing and trade, taxes, and fractions. The method for teaching was as much as possible relating the subject to everyday life. For example, teaching could be related to hygiene or gardening. Children would be given problems relating to the number of people suffering from a particular disease, how many were healed and how many died. It must be known that because the missionaries were not fully bound by the government, most of the said curriculum was, at most, a framework of intentions into which individual mission institutions fitted what they considered to be "approved" textbooks or materials.

However, missionaries saw most of the government interventions as interference in their work in education. This was exacerbated by the fact that the government's financial contribution to the education budget was very minimal, although it was much higher than was the case before 1927 (Banda, 1982). Some missionaries did not hide their feelings about the regulatory rules the government put forward, especially in the establishment of schools; yet, it was believed that the government's contribution to the education budget was very minimal. The Bishop of Nyasaland had this to say in connection with the fears missionaries had:

> *The main criticism of the present scheme, which I think everyone who knows the facts must accept, is that the Government is taking a very complete control of Education, and, on paper at any rate, dictating terms and limitations of the most drastic character while still taking it for granted that Missions will continue to pay for the greater part of the cost. . . . Where the Government controls anything like this extent, the Government pays. (Malawi National Archives, 1927, Minute S2/2/38)*

In 1940, the Government introduced the Primary School Exit Certificate Examination. Out of the 145 candidates who sat for the examination, only 35 passed (Banda, 1982, p. 73). With these disappointing results, the missionaries asked for a common syllabus from the government. Thus, although the missionaries were uncomfortable with the increasing number of government rules and regulations, this request was, in principle, a sign of succumbing to the government's control. From this period on, the curriculum was therefore largely controlled by the government. A further development happened in April 1941, when the government opened the first secondary school in Blantyre. The subjects for secondary education were dictated by the examinations syndicate of the University of Cambridge in the United Kingdom and it included the following subjects:

Mathematics	*Geography*
General Science	*History*
English Language	*Religious Knowledge*
English Literature	*Chichewa (then Chinyanja) and Latin*

Clearly missing in the curriculum were the industrial subjects that the missionaries had introduced. This change from industrial training to the training in preparation for white collar jobs meant that the curriculum also had to change. Even the primary school curriculum had to change to an academic one in order for it to conform to the secondary school curriculum, because students from primary school would be selected for secondary school education. The change also meant that teachers were now teaching to the requirements directed by external examinations. Instead of teaching what the Malawian society considered to be useful and relevant to their culture, the international examining body dictated what they perceived as crucial. For example, in geography, the curriculum included the study of the Americas, the British Isles, and the Commonwealth countries. According to Banda (1982), although Africa was mentioned in the curriculum, most teachers preferred to teach about other countries, such as Australia, New Zealand, the Americas, and the British Isles. This was understandable. Almost all secondary school teachers were British and they felt more comfortable teaching about these countries rather than teaching about Africa. The books for study in English literature were alien to the students, yet they were supposed to internalize and stretch their imaginations in order to appreciate the great works of western skill in weaving together man's experiences in life.

In summing up the efforts of both missionaries and the Malawi government in education during the colonial era, it can be said that missionary education developed on the principle of winning the hearts of the indigenous Africans to Christianity. In doing so, they emphasized the ability to read so that they could help in spreading the Word of God. However, the government did not become fully involved in education until 1927, when the Phelps-Stokes Commission reported to the British Government about the situation in the country. The Commission stated that:

> *the condition of Nyasaland is in the failure of Government to organize and correlate the splendid educational work of the missions with various phases of colonial life. Missions have been permitted to struggle alone in their respective fields. Latterly a negligible appropriation has been given to them, but there has been no Department nor Director of Education to confer with the Missions, to encourage them in their work, or to help them relate their influences to each other or to colonial needs. (Pachai, 1973, pp. 173-174)*

The government then took steps and its subvention education increased in subsequent years and set in motion supervision of schools to set up common standards. With the opening of the first secondary school, the government started to offer a curriculum for white collar jobs, a contradiction to the industrial curriculum established by the missionaries.

It is pertinent to say that both the government and the missionaries conceptualized curriculum as a change agent, as educators incorporated society's changing needs and expectations for schooling—for the missionaries, the need to Christianize the Africans, and for the government, the imaging of various types of white collar jobs on the market. The teaching methods followed traditional practices at the time—lecture, repetition, imitation, memorization, and, at times, mimicry, particularly in language learning, for which the direct method was used until the 1950s, when the audio-lingual method replaced it. In some cases, the methodology was a reflection of how missionaries were teaching learners in their Bible and moral education lessons. It should, however, be pointed out that teaching in this way was based on habit formation and on behaviorist psychology, whereby stimulus and response were the norm.

The Post-Independence Era (1964-1994). When Malawi became independent in 1964, the ministry of education had only existed for three years. The government saw that there was a great shortage of trained personnel required to take up positions in both the civil service and the private sector. In 1965, the Ministry of Education decided to reduce the number of years for primary education from eight to seven years while increasing the number of secondary school education from four to five years. Furthermore, the Junior Certificate Examinations were suspended for a few years, so that learners were only required to sit for the Primary School Exit Certificate Examinations and the Cambridge School Certificate Examinations. However, although these changes were implemented, the curriculum essentially remained the same. For example, the 1966 primary school English syllabus emphasized the same audio-lingual approach to language teaching when it said:

> *first, it must be remembered that successful language learning depends on successful habit formation. The only way to form a habit is by constant repetition. Accordingly, the Teachers' guide is built on the principle of constant practice and repetition of the sentence patterns to be learned. (Ministry of Education, 1966, p. 106)*

This emphasis on the old structural approach to language teaching and learning was reflected in the materials that were written for the courses in school. The emphasis was made even more forceful when the then-president of Malawi Dr. Hastings Kamuzu Banda (not a teacher himself, but a medical doctor) spoke very strongly about how the subject of English should be taught. On December 10, 1968, Banda argued that:

> *if English is to be learnt properly, Grammar and Composition have to be taught. Grammar, the very foundation of English, has to be taught; simply and with patience. At whatever level you start teaching a child Grammar, he has to be taught the very foundation on which English or any other language is based. Parts of Speech, Noun,*

Pronoun, Adjective, Verb, Adverb, Preposition, Conjunction, Interjection. Let the child know thoroughly what they are. I do not mind if you make them repeat them but they must know. (1968, p. 4)

This public statement became almost the broad framework for the language curriculum, and later the government also discredited the approach to modern mathematics introduced in the country during the independence period. The government said it wanted teachers to go back to traditional mathematics because it taught learners to be more systematic and logical as they developed critical thinking in their academic faculties. Indeed, the post-independence period was a period of many changes in order to address the acute shortage of manpower that was required to Africanize the civil and other social services.

One of the major changes in the education sector was the realization that the country needed a trained workforce that possessed appropriate technical and commercial skills. The Malawi Congress Party, in its Manifesto of 1961, said that, once in power, it would take immediate steps "to provide increased opportunities for commercial and technical education for post-primary as well as post-secondary children up to recognized standards as soon as practicable" (Banda, 1982, p. 104). The government then established the University of Malawi in 1965 and created a college within the university (the Polytechnic) to produce engineers, business managers, and other service providers.

In 1985, the government produced its second education development plan since independence from Britain in 1964. It was a 10-year development plan (Ministry of Education and Culture, 1985), with the objectives to:

- Support and encourage the entry of pupils into primary education at the age of 6
- Seek to reduce, wherever possible, the incidence of repetition (especially in Standard 8) and dropout
- Provide as soon as possible places and resources in schools for 85% of the primary school-age population
- Re-orient the primary school curriculum in the later years of the program toward the community life, which most pupils will enter, given the fact that secondary education will be available for only a limited number of pupils.

At a wider scale, its broad social and political objectives included achievement of permanent literacy, food self-sufficiency, and provision of ethical and socioeconomic knowledge and skills.

The education plan was passed on to the Malawi Institute of Education to develop a curriculum for primary school and later for secondary school. The institute started by examining the existing curriculum with a view toward realigning it to the newly produced education development plan. The institute identified major weaknesses with it. First, it was observed that the curriculum was overloaded—too many subjects (13 different subjects) for 6- and 10-year-old children; too much content within individual subjects; and too many overlaps across subject boundaries (e.g., in agriculture and home economics and geography and agriculture).

Further, the curriculum was too examination-oriented. Consequently, the government divided the school subjects into examinable and non-examinable subjects. Bradbury (1992) observed that:

Pupils, parents and teachers insist on studying only those things which are known to be tested in the examination. The consequence is that aspects of examined subjects which are not in the examination are ignored and other parts of the curriculum which are not examined at all, such as physical education and religious education and art, are simply dropped in the last few years of primary education. (1992, p. 2)

This situation was deleterious to the learners, since they could not enjoy music, physical education, moral lessons from religious education, and creative arts.

Even with the examinable subjects, learners were not taught critical thinking and analytical skills. Since the examinations were mostly of the recall type, learners usually resorted to memorization of facts. A study by the World Bank (1980) reported that the reading comprehension ability of learners in the final year of primary school in Malawi was only 34%, while it was 54% in India and 61% in Chile. The World Bank study also showed that at sentence-level comprehension, Malawi's performance (61%) was much higher than both India's (27%) and Chile's (42%). This in itself may mean that getting factual information at the sentence level was perhaps much easier than what comprehension involves.

Another observed weakness was that the curriculum generally had become irrelevant; in 1987, the government produced a policy document known as Statement of Development Policies 1987-1996. The document stated that:

> The broad policy objective of the sector is to develop an efficient and high quality system of education of a type and size appropriate both to available resources and political, social and economic aspirations of the nation. . . . The role of education as a catalyst is recognized, both in the medium term through specific skills in short supply, and in the longer term through the impact of improved general standards of education; however, the emphasis is increasingly toward equipping the nation's youth with skill and desire for self-employment and entrepreneurship rather than conventional employment. (1987, p. 104)

The shifting of attention to a more practical approach to the envisioned curriculum change rendered the existing curriculum somewhat irrelevant to the expressed needs of the society. The curriculum was academically oriented and it did not favor learners with a slant for practical work. The document stated or acknowledged that very few children (4%) would be absorbed into secondary school education, and that the rest would return to their communities after primary school. Hence, the desire to change the curriculum was imperative. It also was observed that some topics in some subjects had become out of date. Principally, the curriculum had remained the same for quite a long time—since 1966. Although some efforts were made to re-examine the curriculum in 1982, this did not yield any significant changes to fit with emerging issues, such as population explosion, environmental degradation, gender equity, and HIV/AIDS (although HIV was not yet an epidemic at the time).

These weaknesses, together with inadequate instructional materials, shortage of qualified teachers, and the general internal inefficiency of the system, were uncovered and deliberated on before the review started.

The curriculum review then started in earnest in October-November 1987, by training people with potential expertise in curriculum matters at the Malawi Institute of Education, the curriculum nerve center in the country. The training course lasted for a period of six weeks. Immediately after the course, the Ministry of Education and the Malawi Institute of Education called for a curriculum policy formulation workshop, which different stakeholders, including the ministry itself, were invited to attend. The workshop made a number of recommendations, one of which was a proposal for the number of subjects to be offered. The proposed subjects were more than expected, although they were accepted by the government. The workshop also recommended that some subjects should be taught only during the first four years of school because they would be sub-divided into two different subjects, such as general studies, which would be sub-divided into geography and history from Standard 5 up to Standard 8. Another recommendation was that English should be introduced in Standard 3 in order to allow children sufficient time to master literacy skills in the national language—Chichewa. However, the government rejected it and directed that English should be introduced in Standard 1 together with Chichewa, as was the case in the curriculum that was phasing out.

All the recommendations were accepted. At the same workshop, draft objectives of primary education were presented, discussed, and critically examined. Amendments were made and additions or deletions were proposed. These were later accepted and they became part of the curriculum. Subject panels were appointed and were trained in instructional materials writing. When all was in place, the process of writing started in 1990. Twenty-one schools were selected from all the three regions of the country for trial-testing the materials, and the schools were selected from rural, semi-urban, and urban schools in order to allow for a variety of settings. The implementation of the new curriculum started in October 1991 and was implemented, class by class, until 1998.

Orientation of implementers to the new curriculum followed the cascade model. Standard 1 as well as Standard 2 teachers were involved, because instructional materials were already available for these classes. Over 2,750 teachers were trained in 1991 and 1992. One of the challenges during the orientation workshops was that all the teachers taught all the subjects in their respective classrooms. This meant that they were expected to absorb all the new content and approaches in all the eight subjects that were offered in the 10 days devoted to the workshops. In the subsequent years, it was apparent that the energies devoted to the implementation processes were waning. By 1998, organizations and other stakeholders had started to talk of another review of the curriculum, because many issues were already suggesting changes to the new curriculum.

The Democratic Era (1994 to the present). In 1994, the country held its first multiparty elections since 1961. After the 1961 elections, the country was run by a single party without any opposition. It was a totalitarian government wherein people with dissenting views were not tolerated. The 1994 elections ushered in several parties into parliament; the winning party, the United Democratic Front (UDF), declared the introduction of free primary education so that by September of that year, primary school enrollment rose from 1.9 to 3.2 million. In its manifesto, the party stated that once in power it would allow children to be taught in their mother tongue. In 1996, the new government issued a statement that:

> With immediate effect, all Standard 1, 2, 3 and 4 classes in all our schools be taught in their own mother tongue or vernacular language as medium of instruction. English and Chichewa will, however, continue . . . as examinable subjects in the primary curricula. In the past, Chichewa was used as both a medium of instruction and a subject, making it difficult for beginners to grasp ideas. However, English will be used as a medium of instruction beginning in Standard 5. (letter Ref. No. IN/2/14, March, 28, 1996)

The policy was vehemently attacked by both the public and politicians, particularly those in opposition parties. As a result, the policy was shelved and it has not been debated as yet in parliament. Meanwhile, Malawi continues to teach children in English and Chichewa, although there are other local languages that children could be using for learning as well, particularly in literacy. However, the shelving of the policy meant that it could not include the proposed policy on the new curriculum, which was about to start.

Hardly a year after the 1990 curriculum was implemented in Standard 8, the Ministry of Education recommended that the curriculum should be reformed in line with a document that the government was producing, known as the Policy and Investment Framework for Education in Malawi (2000). In 2001, the Ministry of Education launched the process of developing the first curriculum in the democratic era. The reform was necessitated by political, social, economic, and educational issues. In its introduction, the Malawi Primary Education Curriculum and Assessment Framework points out that the issues raised in the reform include:

> the change from a single to a multiparty system of government; rapid population growth; HIV/AIDS pandemic; gender disparity; environmental degradation; an

overloaded curriculum of 14 subjects with overlaps, topic duplication and redun-
dancy both within and across the subjects; and an examination-driven curriculum
which results into concentrating only the teaching of examinable subjects and
neglect of non-examinable ones. (Ministry of Education, 2006, p. 1)

The process started with extensive consultations of different stakeholders, such as parents, chiefs, and others interested in education, in order to assess the needs that could be addressed in the reform. A strategy for communicating findings from the various groups that were consulted was established (see Appendix 2), and discussions were held regularly to integrate the findings with those collected earlier in the process.

The Malawi Institute of Education, in collaboration with the Ministry of Education, commissioned three different studies, namely, the national literature review, a study on pupil literacy levels in the first two years of primary school education in Malawi, and another literature review on curricula in southern African countries, including Uganda and Kenya. Some people were sent to neighboring countries to learn about their curriculum practices. Information gathered from these countries was presented to stakeholders and examined for its possible integration in the process. The national study included reading inspection reports and examining what they portrayed about children's academic performance.

The information from the two literature reviews, inspection reports, the visits to other countries, and consultation meetings led to the conceptualization of the curriculum. Then, the curriculum team proceeded to developing the curriculum and assessment framework, which led to the development of syllabi and instructional materials. It should be pointed out that the new curriculum is different from the one it has replaced. For example, the previous curriculum used the objectives model, while the present one is outcomes-based. As an outcomes-based curriculum, the current curriculum has adopted a broad-fields approach, particularly in the first few years of schooling. The curriculum has six learning areas: literacy and languages; numeracy and mathematics; life skills; social and environmental sciences; expressive arts; and agriculture, science, and technology.

These broad learning areas became specific subject areas in the senior section of primary education. For instance, literacy and languages became English and Chichewa, respectively, and agriculture was separated from science and technology. The implementation of the curriculum started with Standard 1 in 2007; Standards 2, 5, and 6 were implemented in 2008. This approach was different from the year-by-year implementation adopted in the previous objectives model. Instead of taking eight years, it will take only four to five years to implement. Consequently, it will avoid the risk of being overtaken by other curricular developments that may emerge in the course of the implementation, as was the case with the one being replaced now.

Although the language issue was one of the factors that contributed to the decision to change the curriculum, the situation is the same as it was during the post-independence era. Chichewa is still the only local language that has been maintained as a subject of learning. There is also a strong possibility that more subjects may become examinable as the curriculum gets grounded. Anecdotal reports seem to point out that teachers feel that such subjects as life skills cannot receive the attention they deserve if the government does not make them examinable.

It may be said here that the period following the democratic elections witnessed one of the most demanding education reforms. For example, the government introduced free primary education, leading to phenomenal increases in enrollment, without matching the resources required for its smooth implementation. The increased enrollments in primary school triggered the need for expanding secondary school places. As a result, the government opened new day secondary schools, known as community day secondary schools, without qualified teachers. Most of the secondary schools were deplorably understaffed and abysmally under-resourced. Furthermore, the much talked-about language policy was shelved for reasons best known to the authorities, although a language task force was created in 1999 (Center for Language Studies, 2001), and it is still functioning.

Some Issues and Evidence

The education system in Malawi has faced a number of challenging issues since the advent of missionary education. First, each mission had its own standard of education and teacher education standards were different from one mission to another. There was no standardization of either teacher training or pupil learning until the colonial government came in and established the Jeanes College. Each mission had its own curriculum for its schools until 1931, when the Department of Education standardized a code of education. While the purported focus of the curriculum was on the three Rs of reading, writing, and arithmetic, the real focus was on moral education. Other times, there were some disagreements between the Department of Education and the missionaries, because the latter felt that the department was not making sufficient financial contributions to the education sector. However, the department was asking for more changes in mission education in the curriculum. In addition, the department had more control of the establishment of new schools.

One of the issues during the Independence Era was the introduction of examinations in the 1940s. This did not please the missionaries, because the examination results showed how much missionaries were focusing on academic subjects. The examinations influenced changes in the approach to teaching; as a result, schools began to teach only those subjects that they knew were going to be examined. Consequently, the industrial subjects, which missionaries had introduced before, were no longer offered. Only subjects that were preparing students for white collar jobs were offered. Furthermore, the subjects offered were those that the University of Cambridge offered for secondary school, which meant it was difficult to adjust to the needs of the country, as perceived by Africans. Furthermore, the curriculum in primary education has never changed in the past 26 years. The approach to teaching the curriculum is the same: rote learning through memorization and mimicry. There was also the issue of underqualified and insufficient numbers of teachers to handle the overloaded curriculum. Furthermore, the period was dogged with a persistent shortage of instructional materials.

Under the democratic era, most of the challenges in the post-independence period persisted. For example, the curriculum was still regarded as overloaded, and subjects like life skills are now being taught, but are not examinable. The issues of teacher shortages and insufficient instructional materials continue to plague the education system. Despite multiple teacher education reform programs, there is still a shortage of teachers, as evidenced by the large class sizes. These challenges were exacerbated by the advent of free primary education in 1994. Pupil achievement also has been low across various grades. Together, these challenges have contributed to a generally poor quality of education for primary school children in Malawi.

Way Forward

Recent advancements in technology have revolutionalized education, learning, and access. For Malawi, these developments are just coming in and will require a different mindset among education professionals. It will also require the government to support the technological innovations. In the development and delivery of the curriculum, there is a need to have access to multiple sources, including the Internet, to give more support to a logical and comprehensive conceptualization. We still need the presence of the teacher. Instead of teaching, the teacher should take on the role of the facilitator and motivator of learners to actively engage them in meaningful learning experiences. The current practice of segmenting content areas into subject-specific disciplines does not provide enough grounding for children to advance their understanding. This practice also results in the overloading and redundancies of the curriculum.

References

Banda, H. K. (1968). *Speech made by His Excellency the President of Malawi at Kwacha International Conference Center.* Blantyre, Malawi: Malawi Department of Information.

Banda, K. N. (1982). *A brief history of education in Malawi.* Blantyre, Malawi: Dzuka Publishing Company.

Bradbury, R. (1992). *Malawi German primary science project: Occasional Papers No. 1.* Domasi, Malawi:

Malawi Institute of Education.

Center for Language Studies. (2001). *Language mapping survey for the Northern Region of Malawi Report.* Zomba, Malawi: Author.

Chilora, H. G. (2007). *A longitudinal study on a learner's language of play as medium of instruction and as the language of initial literacy development.* Domasi, Malawi: Malawi Institute of Education and GTZ.

Creative Associates International. (1999). *Gable II: Malawi social mobilization campaign for HIV/AIDS awareness.* Lilongwe, Malawi: United States Agency for International Development (USAID).

Johnston, O. (2002, June). *Financial risk: Stability and globalization.* Paper presented at IMF Aids Center Banking Seminar, Washington, DC.

Keller, B. (2005). AIDS infects education systems in Africa. *Education Week, 24*(27), 1, 22-23.

Lacey, A. T. (1931). *Code and syllabus of instruction.* Zomba, Malawi: Department of Education.

Malawi Government. (1987). *Statement of development policies 1987-1996.* Lilongwe, Milawi: Author.

Malawi National Archives. (1927). *Minutes 2/2/38.*

Malawi National Educations Board. (1989). *Malawi school certificate of education regulations and syllabuses.* Zomba, Milawi: Author.

Ministry of Education. (1966). *Primary school syllabus.* Zomba, Milawi: Author.

Ministry of Education, Science and Technology. (2001). *Policy and investment framework for education in Malawi.* Lilongwe, Milawi: Author.

Ministry of Education and Culture. (1985). *Education development plan 1985-1995 summary.* Domasi, Milawi: Malawi Institute of Education.

Ministry of Education. (2006). *Malawi primary education curriculum and assessment framework.* Domasi, Malawi: Malawi Institute of Education.

National Statistical Office. (1998). *Malawi population and housing census 1998.* Zomba, Malawi: Author.

Pachai, B. (1973). *Malawi: History of the nation.* New York: Longman.

Prasad, E., Rogoff, K., Wei, S., & Kose, A. (2003). *Effects of financial globalization in development countries: Some empirical evidence.* Occasional Papers No. 220.

United Nations Program for HIV/AIDS. (2002). *Report on the global HIV/AIDS epidemic.* New York: Author.

Wagner, H. (2001). *Implications of globalization for monetary policy.* Working Paper No. 01/184.

World Bank. (1994). *Malawi education sector policy analysis.* Lilongwe: Author.

Appendix 1

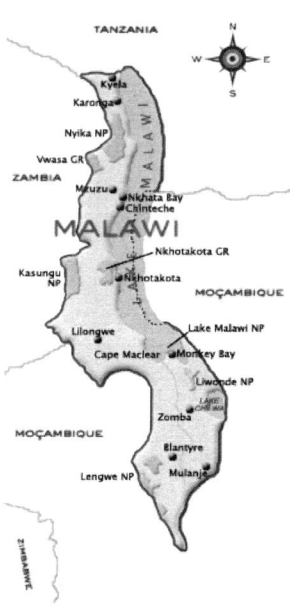

Appendix 2

MODEL OF PRIMARY CURRICULUM & ASSESSMENT REFORM

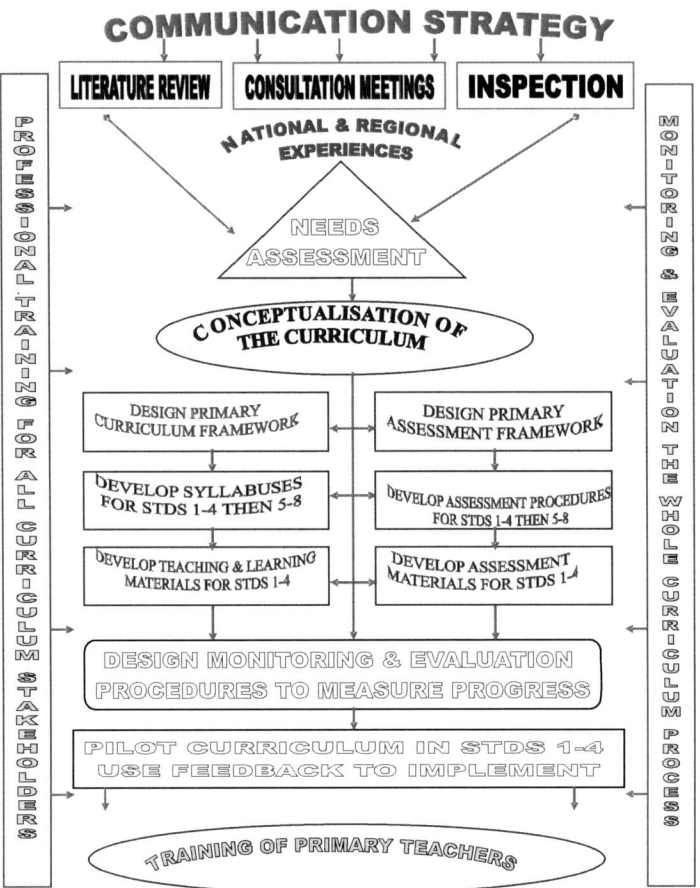

About the Authors

Grace Mwinimudzi Chiuye graduated from the University of Malawi in 1988 with a bachelor of education degree. She received her M.Ed. and doctoral degrees from the University of Akron in Ohio in 1998 and 2005, respectively. Grace worked as a classroom teacher at both elementary and secondary schools before joining the Centre for Educational Research and Training (CERT) at the University of Malawi in 1993. She was appointed Deputy Director in September 2007. Her works include teacher education, girls and women's education, policy analysis, literacy development, nonformal education, and assessment of pupil learning. Her contact address is Centre for Educational Research and Training (CERT), Chancellor College, P.O. Box 280, Zomba, Malawi. E-mail: gchiuye@ chanco.unima. mw; gracechiuye@yahoo.com

Hartford Mchazime holds a B. Phil. (Ed.) from Birmingham University, an M.A. from the University of Warwick (both in the United Kingdom), and a Ph.D. from the University of South Africa. He has 37 years of rich experience in education. He worked as an elementary school teacher, an inspector of schools, an education administrator, a teacher educator, a lecturer at the University of Malawi, a curriculum specialist and an education consultant. Currently, he is working for the American Institutes for Research in Malawi as Deputy Chief of Party. He has co-authored several textbooks for both elementary and secondary schools in Malawi. He has also contributed articles in various journals in southern Africa. As a reading specialist, his interest is in reading and in curriculum matters.

The History and Influences on Curriculum Development in New Zealand

Alister Jones and Bronwen Cowie

New Zealand has a long history of establishing national curriculum and schooling policy. Since 1877, New Zealand teachers have been required to implement national curricula in various guises. This chapter traces the history of curriculum development in a country that began as a colonial outpost and has developed into a country seeking to prepare its students to take an active role on the global level. Influences on the significant curriculum reforms will be highlighted and placed within a broader cultural, political, and economic framework. Issues related to learning and achievement, the development of school programs, social justice (such as the Treaty of Waitangi and the unique place of Maori), multiculturalism, and equal opportunities will be discussed. The interrelationship among curriculum, assessment, and pedagogy will be explicated against the evolving curriculum framework and the changing social context.

The New Zealand School Context

The implementation of any national policy and its associated evaluation needs to be considered in the context in which schools are situated, and in relation to the broader social context of the relationship between government policy and the way that schools are governed and managed. Notable for its geographic isolation, New Zealand has a population of approximately 4.3 million, mostly of European descent, with the indigenous Maori being the largest minority. Polynesian and Asian people also are significant minorities, especially in the cities. New Zealand was granted limited self-government in the 1850s and by the late nineteenth century was fully self-governing, becoming an independent dominion in 1907 and a fully independent nation in 1947. In practice, Britain had long ceased playing any real role in the government of New Zealand.

Education in New Zealand is compulsory for all children between the ages of 6 and 16; most children enroll at school on their fifth birthday. Primary schools are the first level of compulsory schooling. They cater to children from the age of 5 (Year 1) to the end of their 8th year of schooling. Children in Years 7 and 8 may either be in a separate intermediate school or part of a full primary, secondary, or composite/area school. Secondary schools usually provide for students from Year 9 until the end of Year 13. In 2006, there were 2,577 schools in New Zealand; of these, around 20% were secondary schools. There are currently 110 private schools in New Zealand.

A Tradition of National Curricula: From Colony to Global Participant

As would be expected of a British colony, the early New Zealand curriculum was influenced by curriculum development in England. The initial national curriculum, established in 1877, was based on the English Codes and signaled the formal separation of church and state. It. The Native Schools Act of 1867 provided for the establishment of Maori village schools and confirmed the government's acceptance of the need to educate Maori children. The thinking at the time was that "it is absolutely the duty of the State to provide that primary education which is the key to knowledge for every child in the community" (Bowen, cited in Ewing, 1970, p. 277). As such, the national curriculum was intended to guide all classroom activity and was accepted by the community as providing this guidance. Even at this time, there were issues around whether New Zealand had the number of teachers needed to implement the curriculum as well as teacher knowledge to cover a wide range of subjects. The 1880s teaching methods were based on notions that learning related to attention, judgment, reasoning, observation, and memory could be developed through training. That is, they were based on a view that facts should be presented to students. New Zealand, at that time and still today, had a very mobile population, and so it was expected that a national curriculum would allow for a smoother transition as students move from school to school.

In 1904, a new syllabus was introduced that consisted of compulsory subjects and additional subjects. The compulsory subjects comprised English, arithmetic, drawing, singing, physical instruction, moral instruction, nature study, and health. The 1920s and 1930s saw a range of progressive influences in terms of ideas to be considered, but these had little impact on the curriculum. However, beginning in the 1920s, influences from the United States affected educational practices in New Zealand, particularly the views of Thorndike and in relation to arithmetic, science, and social studies (Ewing, 1970). This influence also affected student project work. The introduction of the national assessment of teachers in the 1920s made it more difficult to use flexible teaching approaches, and led to standardization and less responsiveness to mixed-ability classes. Teachers were often assessed on student test results, and this reinforced the conformity of teaching approaches. Ultimately, national assessments narrowed an originally broad curriculum. The removal of the proficiency examinations in 1936 and a revision of syllabi in 1943 to recognize variability of students represented significant changes in curriculum development and implementation. These changes reinforced the professionalism of teachers and signaled the beginning of school-based curriculum development. Individual school schemes were officially introduced in the 1960s, and a Curriculum Development Unit within the Department of Education was charged with ensuring that school-based innovations were more widely disseminated. It needs to be noted, however, that New Zealand elements have long had an influence in the curriculum since the *School Journal* began publishing in 1907. The *School Journal* is a resource distributed to schools that aims to present stories and materials relevant to a New Zealand way of life and to be of interest to and readable by New Zealand students. Since 1939, the journal has included work from local authors, poets, and artists.

In 1944, the Thomas Report stated that all secondary students should receive a generous and well-balanced education. New regulations made a core of general subjects compulsory for all students and legalized a broad range of options and prescriptions for School Certificate, the national external examination for Year 11 students.

From the 1940s to the 1980s, curriculum review was carried out as a form of rolling revision. Each subject syllabus was revised independently of the others. The primary curriculum was essentially a set of suggestions for teachers, while secondary school prescriptions were based on the external national examinations. Until the 1960s, New Zealand was perceived as a stable and wealthy nation, and there was a liberal influence on curriculum with a move to equality of education and social justice for all. In the 1970s, with increasing economic and social upheaval, questions were raised about wealth and power differences across social groupings. The 1980s saw greater attention to equality, excellence, and high standards. The emphasis was on a core curriculum for primary schools and the redevelopment of the secondary curriculum.

Many New Zealanders felt a growing dissatisfaction with the curriculum, assessment, and qualifications during the 1970s and 1980s. In the 30 years following World War II, New Zealand moved from being a British farm to become a post-industrial, independent trading nation operating in most parts of the world. The school curriculum was considered to be slow in responding to these changes. Calls were being made for the curriculum to be responsive to the country's needs for people highly skilled in science and technology, and with the languages and cultural sensitivity needed to maintain international economic competitiveness. In addition, the curriculum was viewed as not being relevant for many students and not maximizing learning for many Maori and Pacific Islander students, or for girls. By the 1980s, the direction and purpose of the school curriculum was a topic for public debate and a target of lobbyists for change.

The Curriculum Review (1984-1987)

In 1984, a Labour government was elected to power, largely in reaction to the economic interventionist policies of the previous national government and the country's near state of bankruptcy. The incoming Minister of Education in this newly elected fourth Labour government set up a review of the curriculum for schools in 1984 (Department of Education, 1987). The terms of reference for the review committee were:

- Review the curriculum in schools, in association with the *Inquiry Into Curriculum and Assessment*, and qualifications in Forms 5 to 7
- Take into account the earlier reviews of the core curriculum carried out in 1983-84, and the responses received by the department to the report *A Review of the Core Curriculum for Schools*
- Prepare material for public discussion, which may include a range of options for consideration
- Provide advice to the Minister and the department on any steps to be undertaken arising from the review. (Department of Education, 1987, p. 5)

The review committee consisted of representatives from the main educational groups (including the Curriculum Development Division of the Department of Education), Maori and Pacific Islander groups, and the Youth Council. No representatives from business, industry, or professions other than education were included. In hindsight, this omission seems out of step with the free-market policies being implemented at the time by other Ministers of the Crown in finance and the state services. Nevertheless, public discussion and consultation was considerable—21,500 submissions initially, and 10,000 submissions to the draft report (from a total population of approximately 3 million). This reaction reflected the extensive consultation process and the extent of public concern about the existing curriculum and education.

The review committee interpreted "the curriculum to be all the activities, events, and experiences that take place in the school's learning programme" (Department of Education, 1987, p. 6). This statement was a departure from the notion of a syllabus or examination prescription that defines the content to be learned and examined. The report contained advice to the Minister on the basis for curriculum design, including the development of a curriculum for schools. In terms of the design of the curriculum, the committee recommended that there be a national common curriculum for all schools, from new entrants to form 5 (year 11), and that the national common curriculum provide for a broad and general education and consist of national curriculum principles and the three inter-related aspects of learning—knowledge, skills, and attitudes and values. It was proposed that the national common curriculum be given status by regulation and that each school have the responsibility to develop a curriculum consistent with the national common curriculum. The report suggested that responsibility be placed on all those involved (students, teachers, administrators, parents, and the community) to ensure that each school's curriculum was not deficient in any of the stated principles and aspects of learning (Bell, Jones, & Carr, 1995). Programs for forms 6 and 7 (Years 12 and 13, ages 16-17) were to be developed from the national common curriculum (Department of Education, 1987).

The review committee report identified the major concerns expressed in the consultation responses as learning, teaching, and evaluating the curriculum; Maori students and communities and the curriculum; sexism, equality, and the curriculum; and greater community involvement and the curriculum. The report also highlighted the concern that the learner be the central focus for schools and identified 15 principles as basic to the curriculum of every school in New Zealand. According to these principles, the curriculum should be: common to all schools, accessible to every student, non-racist, non-sexist, designed so that all students enjoy significant success, reflective of the fact that education is a continuous and lifelong process, whole, balanced, of the highest quality, planned, cooperatively designed, responsive, inclusive, enabling, and providing learning that is enjoyable for all students (Department of Education, 1987). The call for the development of an overview document that stated the direction and purpose of the curriculum for schools was a response to the lack of such a document. Instead, there were numerous separate syllabus documents in the different subject areas, such as English, mathematics, science, social studies, economics, physical education, health, and music. The report described knowledge that is central to the New Zealand curriculum as that which:

- Helps students to understand and be confident in their own culture and in the culture of Aotearoa/New Zealand, and to be sensitive to that of others
- Develops students' confidence and ability in mathematics
- Develops students' creative and expressive confidence and ability
- Develops students' confidence in handling the day-to-day practicalities of their own lives
- Develops students' understanding of how individuals and groups relate to each other and work together in social, political, and economic ways
- Develops students' understanding of the physical, biological, and technological world, and how people interact with and influence their environment
- Develops students' understanding of their own and others' growth
- Develops students' confidence and ability in language.

The skills described as important were those of thinking, expressing, relating to others, and carrying out practical activities and studies (Department of Education, 1987). A Draft National Curriculum Statement (Department of Education, 1988), written in response to the recommendation calling for a national common curriculum for schools, promoted the following principles to guide curriculum planning: focusing on the learner, promoting a sense of cultural identity, promoting equity, achieving balance and coherence, and providing for accountability. The suggested areas of the curriculum, called the curriculum aspects, were: culture and heritage; language; creative and aesthetic development; mathematics; practical abilities; living in society; science, technology, and the environment; and health and well-being (Department of Education, 1988).

While the education community largely favored these developments as heralding a major education reform (Codd, 1993), the Curriculum Review and the Draft National Curriculum Statement were criticized on two main counts. First, while the educationalists involved in the developments emphasised the individual needs of the learner as a focus for teaching and curriculum development at the national, school, and classroom level, others viewed the emphasis on individuality and personal growth as a problem. Levett and Lankshear (1990) argued that the Draft Curriculum Statement did not recognize the opinion that education also should contribute to the material well-being and needs of society. They acknowledged the strengths in the progressive education thinking underlying the developments in its emphasis on egalitarianism, flexibility, tolerance, active learning approaches, and students taking more responsibility for their learning, but they were concerned at the lack of "clear, valid knowledge claims" (Levett & Lankshear, 1990, p. 40). Second, the New Zealand Treasury argued that the documents were not a suitable blueprint for developing school education, claiming that the documents contained unstated and narrow assumptions as to the nature and sources of education; overlooked such issues as community and educational values and benefits, the relationship between education and the economy, and the nature of government assistance; and did not tackle issues of management and consumer choice (Memorandum to Minister of Finance, May 19, 1987, as cited in Codd, 1993). As mentioned previously, these criticisms were made in the context of the immense social and economic changes being implemented by the fourth Labour government in its attempts to improve the economy—the balance of payments and international economic competitiveness.

Two significant events in 1987 overtook the implementation of the Curriculum Review in its original form. One was the establishment of a task force to review education administration. The other was the general election in August 1987, which returned Labour to government but saw a change of Education Minister, with the Prime Minister taking over the education portfolio. This resulted in educational administration becoming the focus of the reform process.

The "Tomorrow's Schools" reforms legislated in the Education Act (1989) created what are known as "self-managing" schools; self-managing schools have substantial autonomy over finances and resources, including human resources, and also over teaching programs. The goal here was to increase parental involvement in education and allow for more parental choice of school for their children. The act established for each school a board of trustees that is responsible for setting the direction of a school, within the parameters of regulation; responsible for appointing the school principal; and accountable to the Education Review Office (an independent audit agency) and to the Ministry of Education for the school's performance. Boards consist of elected members of the school community, the principal, a staff representative and, in the case of secondary schools, a student representative. Boards provide strategic guidance, and a monitoring framework through which to assess the progress toward strategic directions. School management, under the leadership of the principal, accountable to the board for the performance of the school. Thus, since 1989, principalship has been conceptualized as having two dimensions. The principal is responsible for teaching and learning programs to deliver the national curriculum and for the management of all human, financial, and other resources. While this move ensured greater parental involvement, it was not clear in the framing documents whether, and how, parents and communities might be involved in curriculum decision-making. Interestingly, a national survey indicated that parents considered their involvement in schools had decreased from 1989 to 1999 (Wylie, 1999). A national survey of secondary schools in 2003 found that just over two-thirds of parents had no involvement with their children's school (Hipkins & Hodgen, 2004).

Curriculum Development in the 1990s

In November 1989, a National Party government (based on "New Right" philosophies) was elected in New Zealand, and the incoming Minister of Education embarked on a project to revise the curriculum in primary and secondary schools, under the banner of "The Achievement Initiative" (Ministry of Education, 1991). His rationale, mode of operation, and curriculum ideas were heavily influenced by those of the governments in England, Wales, and Northern Ireland. The previous New Zealand Labour government had changed the administration of education in New Zealand (Middleton, Codd, & Jones, 1990), based on New Right philosophies. Now it was the turn of the curriculum to undergo change.

In England, Wales, and Northern Ireland, the core of curriculum debates in the late 1980s centered on the establishment of national curricula, something that had not existed before. Previously, local authorities, examination boards, curriculum development projects, and schoolteachers had been free to determine the curriculum for students. With wide support, legislation was passed for a curriculum that all students would undertake in state schools. The rationale for this decision included the raising of standards and the need to update the curriculum to ensure economic recovery. It was also in line with other government policies to decrease the power of the teachers' unions and to de-professionalize the teaching profession. These policies, passed by the New Zealand government in 1989, essentially imported a solution to a problem New Zealand never had. New Zealand had had national curricula since the early 1950s. Although the mandate to develop the curriculum for schools had already been given in the curriculum review report, and a decade of curriculum development carried out by the Curriculum Development Division of the former Department of Education, the process and the shape of the curriculum development in the 1990s was to bear little resemblance to that of the 1980s.

Claims were made that education was not fostering equity, in terms of participation and achievements, and was marked by middle class capture; that education was characterized by falling standards, and "inputs" were not producing corresponding "outputs"; that it was overly bureaucratic, inefficient, and not responsive to "users" and "consumers" of education, locally and nationally; that it was not giving choice to parents on schooling; and that parents were excluded from decision-making in education. Education also was seen as failing to provide students with skills for future employment and failing to provide the changing economy with a highly skilled workforce to compete and survive economically (Bell, Jones, & Carr, 1995).

In education (as in other sectors of the state), the implementation of policies based on free-market notions has resulted in advisory, regulatory, and delivery functions being separated and undertaken by different agencies to prevent bureaucratic capture; state educational monopolies being reduced to a minimum, with decreased budgets; services provided by the state being privatized or contracted out to private sector providers; management skills, rather than professional and technical skills, being emphasized (and valued); management being devolved; and the quest for greater efficiency, with outputs and outcomes specified and audited (Mitchell, McGee, Moltzen, & Oliver, 1993). With respect to the curriculum, the policies being advocated were vocationalism; entrepeneurship and competition; raising standards (Ministry of Education, 1990); the levels of attainment and the notion of progression linked to accountability; and contracting out the development process.

At this time, the Ministerial Task Group Reviewing Science and Technology Education was influential in shaping this curriculum. This group was set up jointly by the Minister of Education and the Minister of Research, Science and Technology in June 1991, and its findings were reported in 1992 in the document *Charting the Course*. Membership of the task group came from commerce and from those directly involved in science and technology education at the secondary and tertiary levels. The task group's report is significant in hindsight, in that it gives voice to the views of business people who, as a group, were largely absent in the curriculum review of the 1980s. The task group was charged with assessing "the effectiveness of science and technology education in delivering the skills and knowledge required by society and the workplace" (Ministry of Research, Science and Technology, 1992, p. 8), reflecting the criticism leveled at the previous decade of curriculum developments. The terms of reference included consideration of new initiatives that would assist in this process, and of the curriculum changes being sought at that time by the Minister of Education.

Early on, the task group addressed the concern that students viewed education as providing information that was often of little relevance to their lives and, therefore, considered it as important only for passing examinations. Problem-solving skills and communication skills were seen as being neglected in favor of acquiring knowledge. The task group conducted some research consisting of a series of in-depth interviews with representatives of 36 enterprises with reputations for innovation and/or the successful application of technological processes. These top executives in successful businesses provided strong reinforcement for the task group's view that there had been too great a concentration on content knowledge and its transmission, to the neglect of other skills that were crucially important. Those skills frequently mentioned were communication skills, problem-solving skills, and the ability to work in teams rather than as individuals. In addition, the research revealed a strong desire for learning in science and technology to occur in contexts that were significant to the variety of New Zealand activities in these areas, including agriculture and horticulture. Key conclusions documented in the *Charting the Course* (1992) report were:

- Employers believed that the education system provided students with the basic theoretical knowledge necessary to meet present requirements
- Employees are, however, seen to be lacking in computing and information management skills, thereby limiting their ability to meet future challenges
- Shortcomings in employees' practical, commercial, and broader personal skills were attributed in part to the over-emphasis placed on the theoretical aspects of science and technology education. (p. 17)

Some of the relevant recommendations to the curriculum were:

- The need for the national curriculum to teach and assess interpersonal, communication, and broadly based practical skills
- The curriculum should define a broad range of knowledge and skills that should be recognized by assessment procedures
- A general science curriculum suitable for all students up to Form 7 (year 13) should be developed, and specialist science courses should be restricted to Form 6 (Year 12) and beyond.

The recommendations also gave support for consideration of gender issues in science education, the need for vocabulary development in Maori relating to science education, and teaching of science in Maori.

Previous curriculum developments at the senior school level had been largely decided by university educators through the university entrance board, which set the national examinations for entry into university (the Universities Entrance Examination and the Bursary and Scholarship examinations). This board was eliminated under the restructuring of educational administration in 1989; consequently, the New Zealand Qualifications Authority was established.

In the subject curriculum development process, the New Zealand Curriculum Framework (Ministry of Education, 1993a) provided an overarching framework. This framework specified seven essential learning areas that describe, in broad terms, the knowledge and understandings needed by all students. The seven essential learning areas are: health and well-being, the arts, social sciences, technology, science, mathematics, and arts and languages. Schools are required to ensure that all students undertake continued study in each of the learning areas in the first 10 years of schooling, but they have flexibility in how to achieve this goal, and are responsible for making implementation decisions. The New Zealand Curriculum Framework requires that national curriculum statements in each of the essential learning areas specify clear learning outcomes against which student achievement can be assessed. These learning outcomes or objectives must be defined over eight progressive levels and are grouped in a number of strands. The New

Zealand Curriculum Framework also requires the development of essential skills across each of the learning areas. These are stated as communication, numeracy information, problem solving, self-management and competitive, social and co-operative, physical, and work and study skills. In addition, the New Zealand Curriculum Framework requires that its principles be reflected in the learning area documents. These principles relate to learning and achievement, development of school programs, aspects of social justice (such as the Treaty of Waitangi and the unique place of Maori), multicultural aspects, and equal opportunities. This commitment places a huge curriculum responsibility upon schools. The commitment also has been reinforced by the strategy of writing Maori versions of some of the new curriculum statements. The new curriculum framework also reflects attempts to design curriculum that includes Maori perspectives. The framework incorporates the principle "the New Zealand Curriculum recognises the significance of the Treaty of Waitangi" (Ministry of Education, 1993b, p. 7). The Treaty of Waitangi was signed in 1840 by representatives of various Maori tribes and the British Crown and set out rights and responsibilities inherent in the signatories' partnership. The framework principle goes on to say that recognition will be given to the "unique position of Maori in New Zealand society" (p. 7), that Maori children will have access to Maori language, and the curriculum, generally, will include Maori history and values.

The New Zealand Curriculum Framework (Ministry of Education, 1993c) makes a clear distinction between the national curriculum and the school curriculum. The national curriculum is a set of statements that define learning principles and achievement aims that all schools are required to follow. The school curriculum refers to the ways in which a school takes account of local needs, priorities, and resources to implement this curriculum.

The 1980s and 1990s saw a renewed interest in the potential of good-quality early childhood education, which, coupled with the development of the *Te Kohanga Reo* (Maori language) movement and concerns with the provision of early childhood education for Maori *whanau*, provided a platform for the development of a New Zealand early childhood curriculum (Nuttall, 2005). In a bold innovation, the government established a working party to develop a curriculum that would/could be used for all early years children. In 1993, Te Whariki was circulated for comment. The curriculum was revolutionary, in that it focused on the development of learner dispositions and is strongly bicultural. In 1995, the government funded rounds of professional development to support the implementation. In addition, a new assessment approach of "learning stories" was developed to support the sociocultural focus of the curriculum (Carr, 2001), which utilizes a narrative format contributed to by the teacher, the child, and parents/members of the community to represent, with the intention of building on, children's learning. The implementation of the curriculum also was supported by the development of assessment exemplars—*Kei tua o te pae* (Ministry of Education, 2004)—aimed at helping teachers and family better understand and support children's learning.

The curriculum reforms in New Zealand in the 1990s represented an ideological re-emphasis of a set of beliefs that schools should produce citizens who have the necessary skills to enhance the country's global competitiveness (McGee, 1997). The 1990s reflected an international trend toward more detailed specifications of achievement objectives, content, and processes organized in levels of expected standards of achievement, and assessment strategies to check on learning. As McGee (1997) notes, there was a growing tension between central and school-based authorities over the control of the curriculum. The model of contracting out curriculum development over a short time frame can make the process somewhat mysterious to the classroom teacher and, in fact, alienate the teacher. There was a continuing trend for central domination of the development of curriculum in schools. This is called a center-periphery model of curriculum development; that is, the center decides what is good for the periphery (school/community) (McGee, 1997). However given the broadness of the curriculum statement, power (in terms of implementation) rests with the school and the teachers. For curriculum innovation to occur successfully, teachers need to be convinced that such a change is required. As McGee (1997) summarizes, teachers need to perceive a need for them to change, and when change is imposed from the outside, it is not their change or their need—therefore, sustained change is unlikely to occur.

Curriculum Revision 2001-2007

The NZ Curriculum Framework and associated curriculum area documents were constructed and introduced during the 1990s. In response to feedback about their implementation in schools, the Ministry of Education began a Curriculum Stocktake in 2001. A small national group analyzed the documents and sought evidence of schools' and teachers' experiences when using them, including evidence from the large National Schools Sampling Study, which surveyed 10% of New Zealand teachers. This work led to a report to the Minister of Education (Jones, McGee, & Cowie, 2002). The report recommended changes to the New Zealand Curriculum Framework (NZCF), including changes that would reduce the crowded nature of the curriculum and revise the rationale, objective, and content for each curriculum area, and revise statements on vision, principles, values, essential skills, and assessment. In 2003, the Cabinet agreed to the Ministry of Education undertaking redevelopment of the curriculum to focus on high-quality teaching and empowering schools to meet the needs of *all* students. While the Curriculum Stocktake Report highlighted the fact that current curriculum statements were sound and coherent, it recommended modifications to ensure a clearer focus on high expectations for all students and more flexibility for teachers and schools to help students to achieve these expectations. The Minister accepted the recommendations and agreed to the establishment of the Curriculum Project 2004-2007, which undertook to redevelop the curriculum with as much sector involvement as possible. This new project undertook to review the NZCF, and update it according to the recommendations of the Curriculum Stocktake Report. The immediate work of the project was to review the various components of the 1993 NZCF, including the principles and values, and to shape new generic content—for example, in the area of key competencies. The Reference Group for the Curriculum Project was large, with representation from the education sector and community groups.

Concurrent with this, a subject reference group and writing team were set up for each learning area to rewrite the framework statement, and to review and streamline the achievement objectives (AOs) to address concerns that the curriculum was overcrowded, and that teachers did not understand some AOs. The writing teams drafted new statements and the reference groups provided initial feedback on this work. Wider feedback was sought via a dedicated website, to which any interested teachers could subscribe.

In addition, various components of work were contracted to individuals and groups to provide background information on particular aspects of curriculum, such as values in the community, principles, and key competencies. All of this information was used by the Reference Group and Ministry to construct a revised draft document. The draft was widely disseminated for consultation and feedback by the end of 2006. Independent consultants reviewed the feedback, which was then considered by the Curriculum Reference Group, and a final New Zealand Curriculum was completed by mid-2007. It was then launched in November 2007.

Some components of the curriculum statement were retained with little change. They included the design of objectives and content for eight levels over 13 years of schooling. Some major changes also emerged from all this activity, however. They include:

- A shift from "essential skills" to "key competencies" that integrate knowledge, skills, attitudes, and values
- Expanded statements on values in the curriculum
- Inclusion of five future-focused themes: sustainability, citizenship, enterprise, globalization, and critical literacies
- Guidelines on school-based curriculum design

- A clearer vision statement
- Advice on pedagogy and on assessment
- A reduction in the achievement objectives in all learning areas and the inclusion of these in one streamlined document, rather than in separate documents
- Increased emphasis on the teaching of languages other than English.

The curriculum statement (Ministry of Education, 2007) makes it explicit that the competencies are not synonymous with skills and are conceptually fuller than abilities. They are performance-based, needed by everyone across different life contexts. The new curriculum will be a slimmed-down version that highlights the desired key learning outcomes for students while also advocating for schools having greater flexibility to shape curricula that meet their own needs and circumstances. Notwithstanding the involvement of as many people as possible in the Curriculum Project, the scope of these changes will be challenging for many teachers and schools. Considerable support will be needed as each school's staff works to understand how all the changes might come together in their school setting. Inevitably, some school leaders have been, and will continue to be, ahead of others in adopting the curriculum innovations and adapting them to meet their specific needs.

Emerging Themes

A number of cross-cutting themes are evident in the curriculum development processes outlined above. These both reflect and contribute to the unique flavor and nature of the curriculum development in New Zealand. First, there is a strong emphasis on school- and teacher-based responsibility for curriculum development. New Zealand schools and teachers are expected, and expect, to take responsibility for the translation of the official curriculum (as embodied in mandated curriculum documents) into the implemented and experienced curriculum: New Zealand teachers are the ultimate curriculum developers (McGee, 1997). Second, in New Zealand there is evidence of a broadening of the notion of who is, and should be, a stakeholder in the curriculum and the curriculum development process. Third, the New Zealand curriculum documents suggest a view of learning and learners that has shifted from behaviorism to neobehaviorism to constuctivism to community and socially oriented views of learning. Fourth, there is an expressed wish to prepare people for a global marketplace and, at the same time, to prepare them to live more harmoniously in the unique New Zealand cultural, social, and physical environment as a way of addressing and valuing diversity.

New Zealand has a strong tradition of school- and teacher-based curriculum development. The emphasis in New Zealand always has been on the school-based curriculum translation/transformation of official curriculum documents into school and classroom programs. The system has relied on teachers, individually and in groups, to undertake this process. Many primary schools have a bank of teaching units that are taught each year to a particular year level. These units often include parental and wider community involvement, and so they build on and sustain a community expectation of involvement in children's learning around particular ideas and skills. Beginning in the early 20th century, schools in New Zealand had a very strong link between the national curriculum and school practice. Once these national standards and examinations ended in the 1930s, the curriculum in New Zealand was national syllabi, which were interpreted at the school level. The curriculum reforms in the 1990s focused on broad national achievement targets with an emphasis on teacher professional judgments at the school level. School curriculum had to demonstrate how they were linked to the national curriculum. This audit process was undertaken by the Educational Review Office. Student achievement against the national curriculum is undertaken by the National Education Monitoring Project (NEMP), which undertakes national light sampling of multiple types of assessment across curriculum areas. The new curriculum (2007) reinforces the notion of school-based curriculum development against a national curriculum.

In this chapter, we have attempted to trace how views of learning have been apparent in the national curricula over the last 100 years. The early days of the curriculum focused on basic literacy and numeracy, which often were taught in very structured ways. Starting in the 1920s, then, behaviorists' notions of learning dominated New Zealand curriculum for the next 60 years. In the 1980s and 1990s, individual views of learning did still dominate, but constructive approaches to teaching and learning were recommended, although the achievement objectives in the curricula of the 1990s could be seen as new neobehaviorist. The early childhood curriculum at the time began to introduce more sociocultural and social views of learning. The curriculum from 2007 emphasizes social views of learning but still strongly adheres to achievement objects.

Although New Zealand has seen itself as a global entity since early in the 20th century, it is only since the curriculum reviews that began in the 1980s that New Zealand has reflected its place globally, regionally, and as a country with its own unique characteristics. The education of the indigenous Maori population of New Zealand (*Aotearoa* in Maori) is important in the broader national context of curriculum (McGee, 1997). The administrative reforms of Tomorrow's Schools (1988) opened the way for new initiatives in Maori education, which were overdue in a system of low Maori achievement rates, decline in te reo Maori (Maori language) usage, and controversy over separate and mainstream provisions for Maori children. The reforms have resulted in an expansion in the number of Maori language immersion schools and bilingual classrooms in mainstream schools. A Ministry of Education 10-point plan for Maori Education in 1991 included the removal of learning barriers, resources development to support Maori language initiatives, more Maori teachers, and improved home-school relationships. These curriculum goals have been developed into policies in various forms, such as Maori language funding for schools with a commitment to the teaching of Maori, as well as attempts to develop Maori-oriented teacher education programs.

New Zealand has had a long history of national- and school-based curriculum development. The curriculum has reflected the development of the nation from a British colony to a unique country taking its place on the global stage.

References

Bell, B., Jones A., & Carr, M. (1995). The development of the recent national New Zealand science curriculum. *Studies in Science Education, 26*, 73-105.

Bolstad, R. (2005). School-based curriculum development: Is it coming back into fashion? *Curriculum Matters*, *1*, 186-208.

Carr, M. (2001). *Assessment in early childhood settings: Learning stories.* London: Paul Chapman.

Codd, J. (1993). Equity and choice: The paradox of New Zealand educational reform. *Curriculum Studies, 1*, 1.

Department of Education. (1987). *The curriculum review. Report of the Committee to Review the Curriculum for Schools.* Wellington: Government Printer.

Department of Education. (1988). *Draft national curriculum statement: A discussion document for primary and secondary schools.* Wellington: Department of Education.

Ewing, J. L. (1970). *Development of the New Zealand primary school curriculum, 1877-1970.* Wellington: New Zealand Council for Educational Research.

Hipkins, R., & Hodgen, E. (2004). *National survey of secondary schools 2003.* Wellington: New Zealand Council for Educational Research.

Jones, A., McGee, C., & Cowie, B. (2002). *National school sampling study.* Hamilton: University of Waikato.

Levett, A., & Lankshear, C. (1990). *Going for gold.* Wellington: Daphne Brassall.

Middleton, S., Codd, J., & Jones, A. (Eds). (1990). *New Zealand education policy today: Critical perspectives.* Wellington: Allen and Unwin.

McGee, C. (1997). *Teachers and curriculum decision-making.* Palmerston North, New Zealand: Dunmore.

Ministry of Education. (1990). *Tomorrow's standards. The report of the Ministerial Working Party on Assessment for Better Learning.* Wellington: Learning Media

Ministry of Education. (1991). The achievement initiative. *Education Gazette, 70*(7), 1-2, 16 April.

Ministry of Education. (1993a). *New Zealand curriculum framework.* Wellington: Learning Media.

Ministry of Education. (1993b). *Science in the New Zealand curriculum.* Wellington: Learning Media.

Ministry of Education. (1993c). *The New Zealand curriculum framework: Te Anga Marautanga o Aotearoa.* Wellington: Learning Media.

Ministry of Education. (2004). *Assessment exemplars—Kei tua o te pae.* Wellington: Learning Media.

Ministry of Education. (2007). *The New Zealand curriculum.* Wellington: Learning Media.

Ministry of Research, Science and Technology. (1992). *Charting the course: The report of the Ministerial Task Group Into Science and Technology Education.* Wellington: Government Printer.

Mitchell, D., with McGee, C., Moltzen, R., & Oliver, D. (1993). *Hear our voices. Final report of the Monitoring Today's Schools Research Project.* Hamilton: University of Waikato.

Nuttall, J. (2005). Looking back, looking forward: Three decades of early childhood curriculum development in Aotearoa New Zealand. *Curriculum Matters, 1*, 12-28.

Wylie, C. (1999). *Ten years on: How schools view educational reform.* Wellington: New Zealand Council for Educational Research.

About the Authors

Professor **Alister Jones** is Dean of the School of Education at the University of Waikato, New Zealand. He is the former Director of the Wilf Malcolm Institute of Educational Research. He has been extensively involved in science and technology education research since 1980 and has been director of a number of science and technology education contracts, including policy adviser to the Ministry of Education, science and technology curriculum development, and research into student and teacher learning and assessment. His e-mail address is ajones@waikato.ac.nz

Associate Professor **Bronwen Cowie** is Director of the Wilf Malcolm Institute of Educational Research, University of Waikato and former Director of the Centre for Science and Technology Education Research. Her research interests are in the areas of curriculum development, assessment for learning, and science and technology education. Her e-mail address is bcowie@waikato.ac.nz

Integrated Education in Northern Ireland: Curriculum for Peace

Linda Pickett

> *"The core aim of integrated schools is to provide the child with a caring self-fulfilling educational experience which will enable him / her to become a fulfilled and caring adult."*
> —*Northern Ireland Council for Integrated Education (NICIE, 1991, p. 1)*

Integrated education is a relatively new phenomenon in Northern Ireland, where segregation has long been the norm. Rather than being constrained and defined by social problems, integrated education, which celebrated its 25th anniversary in 2006, demonstrates the potential for education as a means of social transformation. This chapter presents background information about the social context in which the integrated movement began, discusses the mission and philosophical base that guides practice in integrated schools, and describes the manifestation of that philosophy through thoughtful curriculum and respectful relationships. Lessons learned from the integrated education experience may well inspire and inform those who would like to see schools become places that are not defined by what is, but instead places that aspire to what could be.

Conflict and Separation

Since the partitioning of Ireland in 1921, Northern Ireland has been a society divided along lines that are primarily defined according to Catholic and Protestant traditions (Fraser & Morgan, 1999). (While Northern Ireland is a part of the United Kingdom, it has its own unique curricular needs and challenges. For more information on the United Kingdom, please see chapter 26.) O'Connor (2002) explains the segregated nature of

Northern Ireland

Northern Ireland as "separate because of history and politics, and the main two communities remain divided in political culture: Catholics who are mainly nationalist and Irish in their political identity, Protestants who are chiefly unionist and British" (p. 7). The division extends to schools, which are highly segregated, with an estimated 95% of students attending schools that are either Catholic-only or Protestant-only (NICIE, 2007a). This chapter discusses the creation and development of integrated schools, where groups of Catholic and Protestant students come together in settings that promote mutual understanding and respect as a core aim and focus of the educational experience. Although integrated education remains controversial and the numbers of integrated schools make up only roughly 5% of the total number of schools in Northern Ireland, the successes of integrated schools in overcoming fear and hatred to create positive and effective learning environments make them a useful model to inform schools across the globe that face similar challenges with diversity and conflict.

Background and Social Context

With the establishment of Northern Ireland in 1921, a Ministry of Education was set up to create a National System of Education. This system was intended to provide non-denominational public education that would be acceptable to both Catholics and Protestants (Fraser & Morgan, 1999). However, in spite of the Northern Ireland Education Act of 1923, Northern Ireland remained a contested society and a dual system of education evolved as the major churches pressed for a system of education that would be managed by churches, with the government retaining some control in return for funding.

The national schools that had been controlled by Protestant churches were transferred to the state (these were known as Controlled Schools) as legally non-denominational and open to all students; they were, however, de facto Protestant and Unionist in ethos. Because this transfer was unacceptable to Catholics, the Church began operating independent (Maintained) schools that were funded by a combination of contributions from the Catholic population and a partial grant from government. Initially, both provided elementary education through age 14, with a limited provision of voluntary secondary education through either Protestant or Catholic traditional grammar schools (Fraser & Morgan, 1999). Virtually all children in Northern Ireland attended schools that were segregated according to religious identity.

The social impact of maintaining separate schools became a focus of study during the "Troubles," a period of civil unrest and violence that took place from 1969 through the Good Friday Agreement of 1998. It was a time in which virtually every family in Northern Ireland was touched by violence, and those experiences reinforced a legacy of distrust and separation between the Protestant and Catholic sectors (McGonigle, 2000; McKittrick, Kelters, Feeney, & Thornton, 1999). Researchers responded to the rising tensions by investigating the role of schools in fostering separation and feelings of distrust. From the studies, two distinct lines of thinking emerged that would have a significant impact on legislation and approaches to educating children. On one hand, it was proposed that schools merely reflected the divisions in society but had no hand in perpetuating division, while others maintained that educating children separately along sectarian lines promoted and reinforced bias and mistrust between groups (Fraser & Morgan, 1999).

Beginnings of Integrated Education

Believing that separate education within a segregated society contributed to ignorance, mistrust, and hatred of the "other," a group of parents formed All Children Together (ACT) in 1974 (O'Connor, 2002; Wardlow, 2006). ACT lobbied for nearly a decade to promote the creation of schools that would educate Catholic and Protestant pupils together as a means to break the cycle of separateness and animosity.

In spite of these lobbying efforts, the government had made no progress toward establishing integrated schools, so a small group of determined parents, assisted by ACT, founded the first integrated school, independent of government funding. Supported by second mortgages and other loans, personal funds, charitable donations, and volunteer efforts, Lagan College opened in Belfast in 1981 (Montgomery, Fraser, McGlynn, Smith, & Gallagher, 2003; O'Connor, 2002). The number of integrated schools grew slowly during the first years, with parent groups receiving support from the Northern Ireland Council for Integrated Education (NICIE), a coordinating body that was formed to develop integrated education and assist parent groups in opening new schools. NICIE (1991) defines integrated education as:

> *Education together in schools of pupils drawn in approximately equal numbers from the two major traditions with the aim of providing for them an effective education that gives equal recognition to and promotes equal expression of the two major traditions. The integrated school is essentially Christian in character, democratic and open in procedures and promotes the worth and self-esteem of all individuals within the school community. The school as an institution seeks to develop mutual respect and consideration of other institutions within the educational community. The core aim is to provide the child with a caring self-fulfilling educational experience which will enable him/her to become a fulfilled and caring adult. (p. 1)*

After years of reliance on donations, statutory changes through the Education Reform (Northern Ireland) Order 1989 gave support for integrated education by providing funds to NICIE and enabling integrated schools to receive government funding for operation. Today, there are 61 primary and second level schools, along with 19 nursery schools, that are associated with integrated schools. While only 6% of schools in Northern Ireland are integrated, enrollment increased by 5% during 2006, a year when enrollment decreased in both the Catholic and Protestant sectors. Although applications for admission each year far exceed the numbers of spaces available for students in integrated schools, authorization for new schools lags far behind demand, due to controversy and pressure from the Protestant and Catholic sectors to limit competition for a decreasing school-age population (NICIE, 2007a; Wardlow, 2006).

The Core Aim of Integrated Education

Fundamental to, and woven throughout, the integrated approach is a commitment to cherish and nurture each child. With regard to promoting positive intergroup relations and non-violence, NICIE affirms: respect for difference and the necessity of educating pupils to know, understand, respect, and appreciate both difference and commonalities; the ability to identify with those less fortunate; and learning to use and trust non-violent means of resolving conflict. Articulated principles recognize self-respect and confidence as necessary prerequisites for the ability to respect difference in others. Integrated schools manifest these principles through practices that support family identity and involvement, value and nurture all children, protect from the segregated tendencies of a divided society, and maintain open relationships with both Catholic and Protestant schools.

The integrated ethos can be described as a child-centered approach that nurtures all abilities, using positive discipline and an anti-bias curriculum (NICIE, 2002). Integrated schools espouse a child-centered approach that values each child as an individual and focuses on the needs of each through respect and encouragement.

Even very young children are deeply influenced by conflict and social divisions (Connolly, Smith, & Kelly, 2002), so from the early years, integrated schools offer "deliberate and structured integration" (Fraser & Morgan, 1999, p. 4) and endeavor to ensure equality of status within the schools and to promote learning of shared and specific culture, beliefs, and traditions. Moreover, the integrated approach to peace and reconciliation is fundamental and comprehensive in maintaining the core aim to enable children to become fulfilled and caring adults. This aim places the importance of attending to the social and emotional realms at the foreground of the educational experience, even as the rigorous standards of the Northern Ireland Curriculum are met. Developing an appreciation of diversity, prosocial skills, and non-violent problem-solving are overarching aspects of a rich comprehensive educational experience. Within fully inclusive and anti-bias programs, students learn to avoid and respond to bullying through explicit curriculum that is embedded in day-to-day teaching and interactions.

A basic premise of integrated education is that children should be "brought up to respect those who differ from them in creed, culture, race or class" and that the educational context should foster an understanding of difference and the ability to recognize commonalities (NICIE, 2007b, p. 1). But, bringing together groups with an "age-old community relations dilemma" (NICIE, 2005, p. 14) was no simple task and required careful planning of environments (Fraser & Morgan, 1999) that would ensure equality of status within the schools. Along with bringing members of segregated groups together in physical spaces, care was taken from the beginning to ensure that those environments would be places where all would feel valued and respected, as well as to promote learning of shared and specific culture, beliefs, and traditions. The right of families to have their children nurtured in their own traditions and culture is deeply respected, along with fostering knowledge and respect for the traditions of others. While a core aim is to improve understanding of difference, the goal of enriching personal convictions also is addressed through the process of sharing.

Equality in Representation

Creating schools that would be equitable and valuing of both major traditions began with ensuring equal and fair representation in numbers of students, teachers, administrators, and in the board of governors. A formula requiring 40% Catholic, 40% Protestant, and 20% other traditions is used to guide pupil admissions, hiring decisions, and curriculum and policy development. Equally important, schools take care to represent both traditions in the curriculum (such as when inviting guests to speak), and they endeavor to maintain an environment free from expressions of prejudice.

Celebrating Diversity and Addressing Controversy

Along with ensuring equal representation, partners in integrated schools faced the daunting challenge of crossing traditional sectarian boundaries and learning to work together. In contrast to silence about the "elephant in the living room" that is the norm in "polite society," they met in homes and meeting halls to engage in dialogue about difficult and controversial issues (O'Connor, 2002). The process of sharing perspectives, experiences, and goals, however difficult, was essential to the process of developing respect and a degree of mutual understanding.

A commitment to openness in social relationships continues to be a theme that runs throughout the curriculum, which teaches children to discuss issues related to creed, culture, race, class, gender, and ability. Diversity is celebrated through meaningful study of world cultures, languages, and religions. Even as knowledge and appreciation of difference is fostered and sources of conflict identified, educators provide opportunities to recognize that which is common across groups. Rather than avoiding controversial issues, those issues are used as opportunities to learn about the experiences and perspectives of others. Conflict is viewed as natural, offering a range of opinion, and pupils learn vital skills for responding to conflict in ways that move toward tolerance and acceptance. Teachers facilitate according to age, maturity, and the difficulty of the issue, using a variety of strategies that may include dialogue and debate, drama, and exploration of symbols, assemblies, workshops, cultural events, or workshops.

Addressing conflict through non-violent, prosocial means is further supported by developing conflict resolution skills and programs that are reinforced by child-centered classroom management strategies that demonstrate positive problem-solving skills. Fostering positive relationships between teachers and pupils is key to developing the trust and confidence that is necessary to examine beliefs and biases. Likewise, personal, social, and emotional development are addressed throughout the curriculum.

Anti-bias and community relations training for parents, teachers, and staff support the curriculum that is used with pupils. Schools engage with community groups, such as those affiliated with Education for Mutual Understanding, to help pupils examine social bias and controversial symbols and terms. Recently, *Joined-Up: Developing Good Relations in the School Community* (Lynagh & Potter, 2005) was developed with the assistance of members of NICIE, integrated schools, the Department of Education, and higher education communities. This resource provides invaluable theoretical and practical information to practitioners who work to develop peaceful, inclusive schools. Strategies continue to be developed to confront sources of fear, mistrust, and bias while promoting the skills needed to communicate effectively, think critically, and solve problems together. As children and adults learn strategies for confronting difficult issues positively, they also learn to trust non-violent methods of resolving conflict.

Child-Centered Approach

Instructional strategies are designed to nurture self-esteem and respect for others, to promote responsibility, problem-solving, communication, and validation of efforts. For example, circle time (Mosley, 2004) is implemented in classrooms where children and adults join together to talk, play games, explore feelings, develop social skills, and solve problems. In the upper grades, pupils who are elected as class representatives facilitate class council meetings where all are able to express concerns and ideas for their classes and the school. Representatives then meet with other class representatives as the school's Pupil Council, who then make recommendations to the head teacher and Board of Governors. The Ecology Council (ECO) identifies environmental issues and organizes school projects to effect change.

Individual self-knowledge and self-esteem are prerequisites for the ability to accept and respect difference in others. Integrated schools have made a commitment to maintaining supportive relationships, and to using a child-centered approach to teaching, positive assessment, and non-punitive methods of discipline.

Childhood is considered an important and unique stage of life, a time when children should be valued as individuals, respected, and encouraged. The child-centered approach is described as placing the child at the center of the curriculum, and, regardless of ability, supporting each child in reaching his or her full potential, according to individual development. Similarly, different aspects of ability and talent are identified and nurtured, with special provisions for children who have learning difficulties or exceptional abilities. Expert teachers work with individual students and the regular classroom teacher to make accommodations, individualize instruction, and utilize methodologies and practice, such as Reading Recovery and Primary Movement.

To be able to effectively meet the needs of a wide range of abilities and interests, assessments are carefully planned and detailed, using a developmental perspective that serves to inform ways of supporting each student's success rather than simply to assign grades. It is approached positively, and framed by goals for each child to reach full potential within his or her own stage of development, rather than by the expectations that all should achieve specific standards at the same time, and that success should be gauged by comparing children to each other.

Attending to physical, emotional, spiritual, and social realms is deemed essential for learning, rather than as "specials" or add-ons to "real" learning. Children are motivated by many opportunities to be successful in a curriculum that is organized by themes integrating mathematics, literacy, science, social studies, technology, social skills, health, movement, and the arts. Teachers use developmentally appropriate strategies and curriculum to challenge students at a level that makes success achievable according to individual stages and abilities (Vygotsky, 1978). Experiential learning experiences that involve creative personal responses through various modes allow students to capitalize on personal strengths and connect to new information in meaningful ways (Gardner, 1993).

In this way, children are able to construct and represent knowledge through a range of modalities during real experiences that are designed to be responsive to individual needs and stages of development. Learning is social, with children and adults talking and sharing ideas and information as they explore and create. Social skills are as highly valued as academic achievement and children are encouraged to work and play together. Significantly, play is recognized as a prime mode of learning and development and has an honored and integral place in the curriculum. It is expected that children should not only learn, but also enjoy learning.

Positive Discipline

Conflict resolution and an anti-bias approach are woven throughout the curriculum and in the daily life of the schools, supporting the positive, non-punitive approach to discipline that characterizes integrated education. As children engage in learning experiences that are appropriate to their development and interests, discipline is approached through positive interactions and sharing of responsibility.

Although specific practices vary among individual schools, this approach to discipline encourages positive pupil-teacher relations and is consistent with the stated goal of developing responsible adults. Adults model respect in their relationships with pupils and other adults as they visibly engage in dialogue and negotiation. Positive relationships between pupils and teachers are important for achieving the basic goals of mutual understanding and respect; such relationships also encourage greater cooperation and limit damaging confrontations that could undermine self-esteem. Constructive dialogue and problem-solving accompany pupil-generated behavior codes.

Positive discipline also encompasses a belief that children will understand and observe rules that they have had a hand in creating. Equally important, pupils' appreciation for those rules is further enhanced when teachers model expectations and adherence to guidelines. Significantly, rules and guidelines for behavior have greater credibility, because they apply to everyone in the school community, adults and children alike. Rather than using punishment to coerce children, educators in integrated schools rely primarily on validation and rewards to motivate positive behaviors, with expectations that are based upon development and ability.

Mistaken behaviors are approached as learning opportunities through constructive dialogue and solution-oriented problem solving. Sanctions are designed to help children take responsibility for actions and develop positive alternatives, rather than to punish through shame or humiliation.

While pupils are held to high standards for behavior, they are also provided with learning opportunities and supports to help them develop those prosocial behaviors. When problems do arise, children are not embarrassed or humiliated; rather they are helped to take responsibility for their actions.

Parent Involvement

Consistent with the history of schools that came into existence as the result of parent efforts, parent involvement remains a central feature of integrated schools; the respectful, reciprocal relationships between families and educators contribute to the democratic nature of the schools. Teachers are expected to respect and work with parents as partners and to affirm the integrated ethos by working together in a manner consistent with the affirmation that each child is important and valued. In each school, parents are represented on the Board of Governors and Parents' Council; all parents are encouraged to participate in policy and curriculum decisions, as well as by helping with activities, raising funds, and attending school functions.

Communication is a key to maintaining reciprocal relationships; parents and children are greeted by principals and teachers as they arrive at and depart from school. These are valuable opportunities to communicate important information, develop relationships, and make the transition from home to school smooth and enjoyable. Many schools offer regular workshops to help parents understand the instructional strategies and the kind of learning that happens in classrooms. These workshops help parents learn techniques for working with children and develop positive relationships with teachers. Parents also participate in assessment activities that facilitate dialogue and collaboration on subsequent teaching and learning.

Each of these approaches to parent involvement would be important in any school, but parents in the integrated sector face additional challenges when they choose to cross sectarian lines and join with an unfamiliar "other" to educate their children. The NICIE organization and individual schools provide resources and offer programs, activities, and events to help parents, as well as staff, understand the integrated approach, support mutual understanding, and enhance positive relationships throughout the school community.

Leadership and Staff

Creating environments that reflect the integrated ethos and promote positive relationships is complex and multifaceted, requiring a knowledgeable and committed staff, parent involvement, relevant and engaging curriculum, and the ability to address conflict in constructive ways.

Clearly, the self-imposed and external demands of integrated schools could not be met without well-qualified and highly professional leadership and staff. At the most basic level, integrated schools require teachers who are prepared to provide an effective education to all pupils. The additional challenges of educating for peace are compounded by the prior segregated educational and life experiences of staff. Integrated schools provide support for adults, as well as for children, in developing knowledge of the "other" as well as the skills needed to develop positive cross-group relationships. Schools maintain collaborative relationships with the NICIE organization in a variety of ways, not only to promote the interests of integrated schools, but also by having teachers serve on NICIE committees. In addition, NICIE provides support for ongoing professional development. Teachers are encouraged and supported in learning about best practices globally through studying abroad, attending conferences, and engaging in research. Along with receiving formal professional development, staff members are encouraged to learn from each other and to express their own cultural identities in respectful dialogue.

Effective school leadership is essential to the success of integrated schools, with successful leaders "walking the talk" of the integrated approach through modeling and implementing democratic approaches with respect to school governance. Principals not only have their traditional duties, they also must maintain an equitable balance of representation, collaborate with NICIE and community relations groups, perform public relations work to promote the integrated sector, negotiate and collaborate with traditional Catholic and Protestant schools and churches, participate in legislative policymaking to ensure that the interests of integrated schools are represented, foster positive relationships with families and community, and ensure that adequate support is provided for staff to be able to meet the unique needs of children and families in integrated settings. The demands on professionals in integrated schools are great, but rather than "burning out," they seem to be energized by the work (Pickett, 2006).

Significance

It is important to note that avenues for developing self-esteem and positive social relations are critically needed throughout the world today, yet educational practice is far too often narrowly constrained by demands for "excellence" in academic performance. While the validity of those demands—and even the definition of excellence—can be debated, for the purposes of this chapter it suffices to say that the integrated education approach is a promising model for developing more peaceful social relationships *and* fostering academic success.

While developing understanding, trust, and respect is the foundation of integrated education, at the same time, schools are required to effectively deliver the statutory Northern Ireland Curriculum. These demands are not approached as competing goals in integrated schools; rather, the integrated ethos and goals are approached through child-centered practice that is informed by ongoing study of current literature and best practices in education. Indeed, practice in integrated schools exemplifies much of what current research suggests is the basis for effective education. It makes sense that these schools are academically successful when we consider the conditions that foster or inhibit learning.

The importance of caring relationships and positive interactions with peers and adults in promoting student learning and development is supported by research across a range of disciplines. Research suggests that safe, supportive environments in which self-esteem, trust, and respect for others are nurtured, along with a challenging and engaging curriculum, are essential for optimal learning and development (Learning First Alliance, 2001). In contrast, focusing on narrowly defined learning goals not only neglects the basic psychological and physical needs of students, it may actually interfere with learning (Bredekamp & Copple, 1997; Comer, 2001; Klem & Connell, 2004; Learning First Alliance, 2001; Maslow, 1970; Resnick et al., 1997). Supportive relationships and a sense of community within the school foster positive outcomes with improved attitudes and achievement among students, along with fewer at-risk behaviors (e.g., Elias, Zins, Graczyk, & Weissberg, 2003).

Current research in neuroscience has further informed our understanding of the physiological effects of stress, especially in terms of negative influences on learning and behavior, providing an additional basis for promoting safe and nurturing learning environments (Hannaford, 2002; Shonkoff & Phillips, 2000). The same research suggests that brain development and learning are complex, non-linear processes that are enhanced by rich experiences, positive social interactions, and language engagements. Learning involves the mind, body, and spirit.

Current research validates the theoretical and practical foundations for the educational experiences provided in integrated schools as academic preparation. But they do so much more than simply teach traditional academic content and skills. Integrated schools were born from the desire to create a better world for children than the one experienced by their parents; they were designed and continue to be crafted with attention to the question of what kind of society they want children to experience, and to help create. And it seems to be working, as the school environments themselves certainly appear to be harmonious and joyful places (Pickett, 2006). After 25 years, research suggests that pupils' experiences in integrated schools do have a positive impact on community relations, including long-term impact on students who feel more positive about diversity and better prepared to address conflict as they continue to engage in cross-group relationships (McGlynn, Niens, Cairns, & Hewstone, 2004; Schubotz & Robinson, 2006). In addition to teaching academic knowledge, integrated schools prepare children with the knowledge and skills needed to make a life and live peacefully with others.

Like the proponents of integrated education, Nel Noddings (1995) claims that "we should want more from our academic efforts than adequate academic achievement and . . . we will not achieve even that meager success unless our children believe that they themselves are cared for and learn to care for others" (p. 675). Indeed, the children, parents, and educators in these schools have shown that it is possible for schools to contribute to "a political ideal of building a more equal and democratic society than the one that now exists" (Featherstone, 1988, p. 4). When faced with challenging conditions, participants in integrated schools do not make excuses, nor do they stray from doing what they believe in; instead, in the words of Principal Olwin Frost, "We just do what needs to be done" (Frost, personal communication, January 15, 2007).

The integrated approach to education offers an alternative to narrow curriculum and "zero tolerance" policies that have no regard for the lives of individual children. By embracing all aspects of development and nurturing positive relationships in an environment of respect for all, integrated schools have demonstrated that it is possible to address social issues, attend to social and emotional development, and provide a high-quality academic education at the same time. This model is a beacon at a time when many schools are pressed to achieve more with less, focus on success as measured only through standardized testing, and spend so much "time on task" that there seems to be little room to explore the human experience. This validation of holistic and reflective practice inspires hope that with collective will and determination, teachers and parents can together envision the kind of world they want for their children and create the kinds of schools that will help make that world a reality. With the vision in place, it's only a matter of "Doing what needs to be done."

References

Bredekamp, S., & Copple, C. (1997). *Developmentally appropriate practice in early childhood programs* (rev. ed.). Washington, DC: National Association for the Education of Young Children.

Comer, J. (2001). Schools that develop children. *The American Prospect, 12*(7), 30-35.

Connolly, P., Smith, A., & Kelly, B. (2002). *Too young to notice?: The cultural and political awareness of 3-6 year olds in Northern Ireland.* Belfast: Community Relations Council.

Elias, M. J., Zins, J. E., Graczyk, P. A., & Weissberg, R. P. (2003). Implementations, sustainability, and scaling up of social-emotional and academic innovations in public schools. *School Psychology Review, 32*, 303-319.

Featherstone, J. (1988). Notes on liberal learning. *NCRTE Colloquy, 2*, 1, 1-8.

Fraser, G., & Morgan, V. (1999). *In the frame: Integrated education in Northern Ireland: The implications of expansion.* Coleraine, Northern Ireland: University of Ulster Centre for the Study of Conflict.

Gardner, H. (1993). *Frames of mind: The theory of multiple intelligences.* New York: Basic Books.

Hannaford, C. (2002). *Awakening the child heart.* Captain Hook, HI: Jamilla Nur Publishing.

Klem, A. M., &Connell, J. P. (2004). Relationships matter: Linking teacher support to student engagement and achievement. *Journal of School Health, 74*(7), 262-273.

Learning First Alliance. (2001). *Every child learning: Safe, supportive schools.* Baltimore: Author.

Lynagh, N., & Potter, M. (2005). *Joined-up: Developing good relations in the school community.* Belfast: The Corrymeela Press.

Maslow, A. H. (1970). *Toward a theory of motivation* (2nd ed.). New York: Harper & Row.

McGlynn, C., Niens, U., Cairns, E., & Hewstone, M. (2004). Moving out of conflict: The contribution of integrated schools in Northern Ireland to identity, attitudes, forgiveness and reconciliation. *Journal of Peace Education, 1*, 147-163.

McGonigle, J. (2000, April). *Improving integrating education in N[orthern] Ireland: Teachers' experiences of the process of "transformation."* Paper presented at the Annual Meeting of the American Educational Research Association, New Orleans, LA.

McKittrick, D., Kelters, S., Feeney, B., & Thornton, C. (1999). *Lost lives: The stories of the men, women, and children who died as a result of the Northern Ireland troubles.* Edinburgh: Mainstream Publishing Company.

Montgomery, A., Fraser, G., McGlynn, C., Smith, A., & Gallagher, T. (2003). *Integrated education in Northern Ireland: Integration in practice.* Coleraine, Northern Ireland: UNESCO Center, University of Ulster at Coleraine.

Mosley, J. (2004). *Quality circle time in the primary classroom.* London: LDA-A Division of McGraw-Hill Children's Books.

Noddings, N. (1995). Teaching themes of care. *Phi Delta Kappan, 76*, 675-681.

Northern Ireland Council for Integrated Education. (1991). *NICIE statement of principles.* Belfast, Northern Ireland: Author.

Northern Ireland Council for Integrated Education. (2001). *What's what in integrated education: A guide for teachers.* Belfast, Northern Ireland: Author.

Northern Ireland Council for Integrated Education. (2002). *Antibias curriculum.* Belfast, Northern Ireland: Author.

Northern Ireland Council for Integrated Education. (2005). *Annual report 2004 2005.* Belfast, Northern Ireland: Author.

Northern Ireland Council for Integrated Education. (2007a). *What is integrated education?* Belfast, Northern Ireland: Author. Retrieved July 20, 2007, from www.nicie.org/aboutus/default.asp?id=20

Northern Ireland Council for Integrated Education. (2007b). *Aims and objectives.* Belfast, Northern Ireland: Author. Retrieved May 9, 2008, from www.nicie.org/aboutus/default.asp?id=27

O'Connor, F. (2002). *A shared childhood: The story of the integrated schools in Northern Ireland.* Belfast: The Blackstaff Press.

Pickett, L. (2006). A cross-border examination of peace education in an integrated primary school of Northern

Ireland. *Journal of Stellar Peacemaking, 1*(1). Retrieved June 10, 2006, from www.jsp.st.

Resnick, M. D., Bearman, P. S., Blum, R. W., Bauman, K. E., Harris, K. M., Jones, J., Tabor, J., Beuhring, T., Sieving, R. E., Shew, M., Ireland, M., Bearinger, L. H, & Udry, J. R. (1997). Protecting adolescents from harm: Findings from the National Longitudinal Study on Adolescent Health. *Journal of the American Medical Association, 278*(10), 823-832.

Schubotz, D., & Robinson, G. (2006). Cross-community integrating and mixing: Does it make a difference? *ARK Research Update, 43*, 1. Belfast: ARK. www.ark.ac.uk/publications/updates/update43.pdf

Shonkoff, J. P., & Phillips, D. A. (Eds.). (2000). *Neurons to neighborhoods: The science of early childhood development.* Washington, DC: National Academy Press.

Vygotsky, L. (1978). Mind in society: The development of higher psychological processes. Cambridge, MA: Harvard University Press.

Wardlow, M. (2006). *Sharing, not separation.* NICIE Reports. Retrieved July 20, 2007, from http://hdl.handle.net/2428/5507

About the Author

Linda Pickett, Ph.D., is an Associate Professor and Chair of the Early Childhood Department at the University of Michigan-Flint. Her research interests include peace education, diversity, and international approaches to early education. Contact her at lpickett@umflint.edu or 810-424-5538.

The Socio-historical Context of Guaraní and Its Impact on Bilingual Education and Curriculum Development in Paraguay

Valentina Canese

The 1992 Constitution adopted Guaraní, along with Spanish, as the official languages of Paraguay, recognizing the importance of Guaraní in the history of the country. Many socio-historical factors have contributed to the survival and vitality of Guaraní as the national language of Paraguay, despite the long history of Spanish colonization and dominance. According to the 2002 census, nearly 4 out of 5 million inhabitants of Paraguay speak Guaraní, either monolingually or bilingually. Some of the factors underlying this circumstance include the peculiarity of the colonizing experience in Paraguay, Paraguay's history of political isolation, and the Catholic church's use of Guaraní for the evangelization of indigenous peoples (Krivoshein de Canese, 2001; Melià, 2004; Steckbauer, 2000). Indeed, the history of Guaraní not only is closely linked to the unfolding history of Paraguay, but also has had an enormous consequence on education. To that end, this chapter explores the historical, social, and political factors of Guaraní and its impact on bilingual education and curriculum development in Paraguay. (Throughout the chapter, "Guaraní" is used to refer to the language, and "the Guaraní" is used to refer to the people who inhabit the region.)

Sociolinguistic Profile

According to census data, there were just over 5 million people living in Paraguay in 2002. Paraguayan Guaraní, the second official language of Paraguay, belongs to the Tupí-Guaraní family of languages and it is the country's most widely spoken language, with nearly 4 million (3,946,904) either monolingual or bilingual speakers. Spanish is the second most widely spoken language in Paraguay, with about 3 million (3,170,812) speakers, most of whom are bilingual. Therefore, more people speak Guaraní than Spanish and over half of the total population (2,655,423) is bilingual in Guaraní and Spanish. On the other

Paraguay

hand, only about 90,000 people (less than 2%) identify themselves as indigenous, making Paraguay one of the most homogeneous countries in South America, with nearly 95% of the population being of Mestizo heritage (U.S. Department of State, 2005).

The language distribution in Paraguay varies greatly between urban and rural areas, where about half of the population lives. Monolingual Guaraní speakers make up over 80% of the population in rural areas; at the same time, monolingual Spanish speakers, most of whom are located in urban areas, represent only slightly over 5%. Bilinguals live primarily in urban areas as well (75%). Table 1 illustrates this urban/rural difference in the way that languages are distributed in Paraguay. One way the 2002 Paraguayan Census gathered language information was by asking what languages are spoken in the homes. Reportedly, Guaraní is the language spoken in the majority of homes, with a total of 59% of these being Guaraní dominant speaking. In 35.8% of the homes, Spanish is the predominant language. In urban areas, Spanish is usually spoken in the home in 54.9% of the cases, while a large number of these homes also use Guaraní on a regular basis. Conversely, rural areas are close to being monolingual, as Guaraní is the dominant language in 82.5% of the homes.

This census data confirms previous observations (Rubin, 1968; Solé, 1995) that Guaraní-Spanish bilingualism is higher in urban and border areas, whereas high rates of Guaraní monolingualism in the home tend to be limited to the rural interior. Gynan (2001) points out that language and gender also interact in the context of Paraguayan bilingualism. Women show a tendency to use Spanish and men tend to use Guaraní. Gynan notes, however, that the Paraguayan linguistic situation, rather than being a dichotomized reality, is better described as a communicative continuum, at each end of which are located cases of absolute monolingualism representing an extremely small number of individuals. At the same time, there is a clear tendency toward disappearance (in the case of Guaraní monolingualism) and, conversely, of increase (in the case of Spanish monolingualism) (Centro Paraguayo de Estudios Sociologicos, cited in Gynan, 2001). Furthermore, a distinction is usually

Language of Individuals According to Area or Residence					
Language	Total	Urban	Rural	Urban %	Rural %
Guaraní	3,946,904	2,165,630	1,781,274	54.9	45.1
Spanish	3,170,812	2,285,301	885,511	72.1	27.9
Portuguese	326,496	205,977	120,519	63.1	36.9
English	91,573	87,503	4,070	95.6	4.4
German	59,166	22,758	36,408	38.5	61.5
Other	31,673	26,344	5,329	83.2	16.8
Indigenous	59,125	5,964	53,161	10.1	89.9
Guaraní and Spanish	2,655,423	1,862,561	792,862	70.1	29.9
Spanish and Portuguese	264,706	191,338	73,368	72.3	27.7
Guaraní and Portuguese	196,716	157,830	38,886	80.2	19.8
Not reported	9,574	5,345	4,229	55.8	44.2

Source: 2002 Paraguayan Census

Table 1

made between Paraguayan Guaraní (which is spoken by the majority of the population), Classic (or Missionary) Guaraní, and Indigenous (or Tribal) Guaraní (de Granda, 1988). Therefore, even though Paraguay is frequently referred to as an exemplary case of stable bilingualism at the national level or as a "truly" bilingual country, the Paraguayan linguistic reality is much more complex than it may first appear (Choi, 2003).

History of Guaraní in Paraguay: Why Did It Prevail as the Language of the Majority?

Despite almost 500 years of Spanish dominance, Guaraní is still alive and well in Paraguay. "Guaraní not only survived in Paraguay and surrounding regions in neighboring countries, but it became the language spoken by almost all of the population in a modern South American country" (Krivoshein de Canese, 2001, p. 13)[1]. Speakers of the language are not the original indigenous people, but those of Mestizo heritage, who make up the majority of the population in the country. However, Melià (2004) warns that in the case of Paraguay, it is important to separate the linguistic process from the process of inter-ethnic or racial mixing.

The forthcoming sections will discuss how the reasons for Guaraní becoming the language spoken by the majority of the population in Paraguay are complexly rooted in Paraguayan history, probably starting even before the period of colonization. According to the same author (Melià, 2004), the history of Guaraní is the history of Paraguay. He calls for the decolonization of history in Paraguay, arguing that it is possible to consider that this country has two histories, as it has two languages. "The fact that the history of the State has been privileged should not discourage the investigation of a new understanding of our historical reality. The history of Guaraní is a path to a broader history of Paraguay" (Melià, 1997, p. 39).

Guaraní Before the Spanish Conquest

Guaraní was used prior to the Spanish conquest as a lingua franca in the South American Atlantic region (Romero, 1998; Steckbauer, 2000). Even though it was not part of an imperial project, Guaraní and the variety of dialects of the Tupí-Guaraní family were the most widely used languages in South America. It was "so universal geographically and demographically before the arrival of Europeans to this continent that it was the most general language used in the La Plata River region" (Melià, 1995, p. 15). Romero (1998) noted that Guaraní was the language that represented the autonomy of the Cari'o Guaraní of Paraguay and it was used as an expansion tool, serving as the language of trade and inter-tribal communication from the region of Paraguay all the way to the Amazon in northeast Brazil. The Guaraní were aware of this linguistic unity and used it for their travels, and Europeans took advantage of this knowledge for their expeditions. Such is the case of Alejo Garcia, who reached the Andes traveling the roads using one language—Guaraní (Melià, 1995).

For the Guaraní, "the word is everything" (Melià, 1995). For this reason, Villagra-Batoux (2002) refers to the Guaraní as the "Civilization of the Word" (p. 66). In these authors' opinions, language and the soul are synonymous, yet the soul/word is never definitive as it evolves in the process of being said and lived. In this way, "the history of the Guaraní is the history of their language, a series of words that form their life's hymn" (Melià, 1995, p. 105). Moreover, as Villagra-Batoux (2002) points out,

> *The Tupi-Guaraní were, from the beginning of the conquest, objects of the colonizers' attention, historians and the record keepers. In fact, their world, object of a simple "discovery," surprised the Europeans, revealing an astonishing cultural universe, expressed above all through their amazing cult of the word. (p. 49)*

Early Colonial Period

At the time of the Spanish arrival in the early 16th century (1524), the Guaraní were undergoing a transition in their social structure from subsisting mainly as hunter-gatherers in a nomadic society to developing as a more agricultural-based, sedentary society. This transition produced a crisis in their social structure and hierarchy, which led the different communities to prepare for the great migration in search of the "Land Without Evil," for which they only needed the arrival of the Karai (prophets). Since the Spanish also were engaged in a quest to find "El Dorado" (the land of gold), the Guaraní saw their desire for migration as a sign and allied with them to follow their respective searches (Steckbauer, 2000; Villagra-Batoux, 2002). This early alliance is what motivated the idealization of the encounter of the Spanish with the Guaraní as peaceful and extraordinary. However, it is now known not to have been as idyllic as portrayed in many historical texts. The Spanish were just as racist in Paraguay as they were in other places, and the Guaraní felt compelled to defend their lands and autonomy. As a result, countless individuals lost their lives (Melià, 2004; Romero, 1998; Roulet, 1993; Villagra-Batoux, 2002).

The colonial situation in Paraguay was different than in other regions of the Latin American continent, such as Mexico or Peru, where pre-Colombian empires existed. Because there was no empire to take over, or precious metals in the region, very few Spanish settled. Because there were no Spanish women, the men initially took advantage of the Guaraní custom of offering their women to allies and would take several Guaraní as wives and concubines. From this union was born the new Paraguayan race, that of the Mestizo. These children spoke the language of their mother, and it represented a form of resistance to the Spanish, who in turn learned Guaraní, which soon became the main language of the colony (Romero, 1998; Villagra-Batoux, 2002).

The process of *encomienda* (the taking of land and natives to work it) took longer to be established in Paraguay, as the Spanish initial intention was not to stay but rather to find a way to Peruvian gold. Once they realized that other colonizers had gotten there first, they had to find other ways to make a profit. One reason why hostile encounters did not occur until later in the colonizing process was that both parties were skeptical that the Spanish intended to stay (Routlet, 1993). Also, the strategy used by the Spanish in Paraguay was not to suppress the traditions and customs of the Guaraní, but rather to modify them by slowly assimilating the practices that were favorable to them, such as the social organization of work, in which the women played a key role as those in charge of agriculture and family economy. Hence, when the women acted as concubines of the Spanish during the *encomienda*, and took control of the education of the children, they transmitted their language to the next generation (Gynan, 2001; Villagra-Batoux, 2002).

In the early 17th century, the first American governor, Hernandarias (1564-1634), ordered that all acts, or laws, would be announced in both Spanish and Guaraní (Romero, 1998). Education during these times was in two languages—Spanish for the children of Spanish and Guaraní for indigenous children. However, Melià (2004) observes that

> *from historic documentation it is possible to infer that during colonial times as well as the first century after independence, Guaraní was of common and everyday use as the colloquial language at home and on the streets, when the Spanish language, while official for government administration, did not have the means to be perpetuated and least to be developed. (par. 8)*

Furthermore, language policy in the Spanish colonies, despite being inconsistent, was respectful of the so-called "general languages," especially during the time of Felipe II (Melià, 2003, 2004; Villagra-Batoux, 2002). Geographical and political isolation are also thought to have influenced the linguistic situation of Paraguay, especially after 1617, when the province of Paraguay was separated from the La Plata province, with the capital in Buenos Aires (Villagra-Batoux, 2002). During colonial times, "the difficulty the settlers faced when traveling in and out of the province, and their failure to discover precious metals, were definitely important factors" (Choi, 2003, p. 84).

The Missions

After the *encomiendas* were established in 1556, the Guaraní realized that the initial alliance had been broken and began to fight for what they saw as their inherent right. The only other option was escaping to the forest, where they could lead a different life. "The relations between the Guaraní and the Spanish had deteriorated and by 1575 had reached the point of crisis. Weapons were no longer enough to impose order. It was then that the specialists were called: Franciscans first and Jesuits later" (Villagra-Batoux, 2002, p. 221). At the missions, or *reducciones,* Guaraní became the language of indoctrination and evangelization. There, the language was "reduced" to written form by missionaries in order to teach reading and writing to a select number of natives, and to spread the teachings of the Bible to all.

The first Guaraní catechism was translated by Fray Luis Bolaños in the 1590s in coincidence with Hernandarias' ordinances in Guaraní (Melià, 2003; Villagra-Batoux, 2002). In their missions, the Jesuits tried to build a Christian utopia (Reiter, 1995) on earth and for nearly two centuries they had an arrangement with the Spanish Crown in which they were the sole administrators of around 30 towns. In these, the social and language policy was the exclusive use of Guaraní and isolation from the Mestizo population (Gynan, 2001; Melià, 1997). "The Jesuits tried to conquer the Guaraní language, but they were also conquered by it" (Melià, 1995, p. 38). The Jesuits were the first to standardize Guaraní by compiling the first Guaraní dictionary and grammar. Some scholars argue that even after the Jesuits' expulsion in 1767, their linguistic contribution, the widespread acceptance of the Guaraní language, became very important in post-colonial Paraguay (Choi, 2003; Romero, 1998; Steckbauer, 2000). Conversely, the role of this "classic" or "missionary" Guaraní in the development and maintenance of Paraguayan Guaraní is a debated issue (Melià, 2003; Villagra-Batoux, 2002) and one that deserves more research, according to Gynan (2001).

The Independent Years

At the end of the 17th century, Paraguay was predominantly Guaraní-speaking and this continued to be the case at the dawn of independence, despite attempts to impose Spanish (Melià, 2004; Romero, 1998; Villagra-Batoux, 2002). Independence was declared on May 15, 1811, and Guaraní prevailed as the language of Paraguay throughout the 19th century (Melià, 2003). Romero (1998) notes that diplomatic correspondence from Argentina to the recently created Paraguayan government was written in Guaraní rather than Spanish. Soon after independence, in 1814, José Gaspar Rodriguez de Francia became dictator; during his term of nearly three decades, the country was isolated from the rest of the world and Guaraní became the language of the republic (Romero, 1998; Villagra-Batoux, 2002). His policies strengthened the hold of Guaraní while weakening that of Spanish, as there was nearly no spread of Spanish in schools or in the media, because the Spanish-speaking elite went into exile (Gynan, 2001). Although Guaraní as an oral language was strengthened and encouraged during this time, the few schools that operated were exclusively in Spanish (Villagra-Batoux, 2002).

After Francia's death in 1840, Carlos Antonio López succeeded him in power, making it his goal to shape Paraguay into a modern nation. Consequently, he opened the borders and made Spanish the official language as a symbol of progress. Some of his decrees included the exclusive use of Spanish in education, the obligation to know Spanish in order to access public office, and the requirement to print reading materials in Spanish only. It was during this time that the much discussed and debated Paraguayan diglossia was established (Melià, 1992; Romero, 1998; Villagra-Batoux, 2002). However, the Paraguayan people, and especially the women, remained primarily Guaraní-speaking (Melià, 2004; Villagra-Batoux, 2002). After his death in 1862, Lopez was succeeded by his son, Francisco Solano, who, in light of imminent conflict with surrounding countries, encouraged the use of Guaraní as a symbol of national unity and patriotism (Romero, 1998; Villagra-Batoux, 2002).

The Two Wars

Guaraní became the language of national defense during the War of the Triple Alliance against Brazil, Argentina, and Uruguay between 1865 and 1870. Patriotic newsletters, as well as poetry and music, were published in Guaraní (Gynan, 2001; Romero, 1998; Steckbauer, 2000; Villagra-Batoux, 2002). The war annihilated the male population and left the country in ruins. Consequently, the population scattered to rural areas, where the remaining women, children, and elders communicated primarily in Guaraní (Melià, 2004; Romero, 1998).

The period after the "Great War" was characterized by a neocolonial liberal land policy and language policy, which involved the banning of Guaraní from schools and from official business. Guaraní was chastised as the enemy of cultural development and those who spoke it were stigmatized as *guarangos* (uncivilized); thus, Spanish was once again viewed as the language of progress. The people of Paraguay, however, remained loyal to the language, which they viewed as a resource to preserve national unity and identity. It was not long until Paraguay was involved in another international conflict, the Chaco War against Bolivia between 1932-35. Much like the previous war, this one contributed to the strengthening of Guaraní as a national symbol as well as a patriotic, cohesive, and strategic device (Gynan, 2001; Melià, 2004; Romero, 1998; Villagra-Batoux, 2002). According to Corvalán (1981), however, the use Guaraní did not achieve prestige, especially in urban areas.

The Post-War and Stroessner Years

The years after the Chaco War brought conflict between the liberals and the nationalists, associated with Spanish and Guaraní, respectively, which ended in civil war and the exile of a great number of Spanish-speaking Paraguayans (Gynan, 2001). After a period of nearly 20 years of instability, a coup brought General Alfredo Stroessner to power in 1954. During the 35 years of Stroessner's dictatorship, he empowered and co-opted the support of the rural Guaraní-speaking sector in return for their political loyalty. This policy could explain the persistence of Guaraní in Paraguay. However, Guaraní was maintained mainly as an oral language (Villagra-Batoux, 2002). Additionally, Stroessner launched an agrarian reform that dramatically increased the population in certain rural areas in the 1970s, thus strengthening Guaraní monolingualism and decreasing bilingualism. At the same time, spending on education, which was conducted in Spanish, amounted to only 1.6% of the Paraguayan gross domestic product in 1972, one of the lowest rates in Latin America (Gynan, 2001).

In 1967, Guaraní was recognized for the first time by the National Constitution in Article 5 as one of the national languages, with Spanish being of official use (Choi, 2003; Gynan, 2001; Romero, 1998; Steckbauer, 2000). Gynan (2001) takes note of a decree by Stroessner in 1972 that, according to the author, "reveals the emerging political discourse of bilingualism in the country" (p. 101). This decree declared Guaraní as "the most highly valued cultural patrimony of our country and it is the duty of every Paraguayan to learn it, disseminate it, and enrich it since it is the vernacular language of our land" (Stroessner, 1972, cited in Gynan, 2001, p. 101). In 1971, the new Secondary Education Plan was established with Guaraní as a subject of instruction during the first three years, which was incorporated into the curriculum in 1975. More recently, in 1983, a Transitional Bilingual Education model began being implemented at the primary level in order to improve Spanish teaching and learning for the monolingual Guaraní population (Corvalán, 1999, cited in Choi, 2004). Choi (2004) points out that "although this model resulted in low academic achievement and a high percentage of school desertion, it serves as a basis for a new and better plan for bilingual education" (p. 244).

Democratic Awakening and the New Constitution

After Stroessner's fall in 1989, bilingualism in Guaraní and Spanish was embraced as a symbol of national identity and democracy. Thus, in 1992, Guaraní was recognized as an official language, along with Spanish, in the new democratic constitution (Choi, 2003; Gynan, 2001; Steckbauer, 2000; Villagra-Batoux, 2002). Villagra-Batoux (2003) calls this act a "conquered right" (p. 78). Article

140 establishes that "Paraguay is a multicultural and bilingual country. Spanish and Guaraní are official languages. Legislation will establish the ways in which each shall be used" (Convención Nacional Constituyente, 1992, pp. 140). At the same time, Article 77 of the 1992 constitution, "On instruction in the mother tongue," stipulates that

> *Instruction at the outset of the school experience shall be conducted in the official mother tongue of the pupil. Also, students will be instructed in the knowledge and use of both official languages of the Republic. In the case of ethnic minorities whose mother tongue is not Guaraní, one of the two official languages will be elected. (Convención Nacional Constituyente, 1992, pp. 41-2)*

Conversely, more than a decade after this historic event, legislation regulating these constitutional articles is yet to be promulgated (Corvalán, 2005; Moles, 2005; Trinidad Sanabria, 2005). Legislation was proposed in the late 1990s (Rojas Lopez & Escurra, 2000), and recently a group of Guaraní lobbyists finished a draft and planned to present it to Congress. The latter appears to be a revamped version of the initial proposal and would include dispositions regarding language policy and planning, such as language rights, public use of official languages, standardization of Guaraní, and the creation of official organizations in charge of these issues (National Office of Linguistic Policy, National Institute for the Standardization of Guaraní, and the National Assembly of Guaraní Speakers). Moreover, it is notable that after the passing of the new constitution, language policy and planning has remained primarily in the hands of the Ministry of Education (Corvalán, 2000).

Impact on Curriculum: Bilingual Education and Guaraní

Shortly after the passing of the new constitution in 1992, the teaching of both official languages was approved for the educational curriculum across the entire country (Choi, 2005) within the context of education reform. This reform was launched by the Paraguayan Ministry of Education (MEC) in 1994 and bilingual education was initiated for about 10,000 students. Modalities were instituted in both Guaraní and Spanish. The first one incorporated Guaraní as medium of instruction for Guaraní primary speakers, and the second modality had Guaraní as a second language to Spanish speakers (Gynan, 2001; Steckbauer, 2000). This program design included theoretical input from the fields of applied psycholinguistics and sociolinguistics, operating on the premise that first language literacy is essential for successful development of cognitive academic linguistic proficiency in the second language (Gynan, 2001).

In order to make this policy a reality, many issues needed to be considered, which included corpus, status, and acquisition planning (Kaplan & Baldaulf, 1997), and because historically Spanish has been the language of official business and education, many challenges were presented and are still present in this process. Despite the fact that about 50,000 students enter the school system each year as primary Guaraní speakers, schools in the Guaraní modality are scarce and have, in fact, decreased in the last several years (Pic Gillard, 2000). According to Mello-Walter (2004), there were 235 Guaraní-medium schools out of 5,671 elementary public schools in 2004. More recently, however, a third modality was started for those students who entered the system as bilinguals, which incorporates both languages as languages of instruction from the start (Benítez, 2005). The Ministry of Education's reform, implemented since 1994, also stipulates the teaching of Guaraní as a subject through high school.

According to documents released by the Ministry of Education and Cutlure (MEC, 2004), many challenges arise in the implementation of formal education in Guaraní, especially in relation to corpus planning, including those related to lexical, graphic, semantic, and pragmatic issues. Other challenges involve discourse and language use. Mello-Walter (2004) indicates that some of the debated issues include not only the type of Guaraní to be used for instruction, teachers' attitudes and training, and the lack of theoretical and methodological tools to carry out bilingual teaching, but also the ability of the nation to allocate funds to provide for the most urgent needs of each term. Issues of authenticity and language purism have been, and continue to be, controversial, especially in relation to the phenomenon of *Jopara* (Guaraní-Spanish code-mixing) and its use in the classroom. In regard to this, Gynan (2001) argues that corpus planning in Paraguay was initially characterized by purist tendencies. These were not highlighted in language planning documents, however, but were expressed as an objective of bilingual education, which entailed the production of "coordinate bilinguals capable of using Guaraní and Spanish in any context with equal ability, but maintaining the codes of the systems separate" (Paraguay, 1994, cited in Gynan, 2001, p. 97). According to the same author, these tendencies correspond to the nationalist agenda inherent in the language policy design.

Over 10 years after the adoption of Guaraní as an official language and its implementation as language of schooling, disagreements as to what type of Guaraní should be taught in schools remain, especially in the area of vocabulary and spelling. In the absence of a normative institution or "academy," the MEC acts as the main *de facto* corpus planning institution. In response to research that found a discrepancy between the Guaraní taught in schools and the Guaraní used in the homes and in communities (Centro Paraguayo de Estudios Sociológicos [CEPES], 1998; Ministerio de Educación y Cultura, 2001), the MEC published new guidelines for the teaching of Guaraní in 2004. According to this document, the purpose of these guidelines is "to facilitate learning and to more efficiently respond to the communicative needs of students" (p. 40). For this reason, the variety adopted for the texts published by MEC is that of Paraguayan (or popular) Guaraní. The document summarizes the criteria adopted for the inclusion of this variety in education and for the borrowing of "integrated" lexical terms to be used in education.

The document identifies six areas that need to be considered for the teaching of written Guaraní, including: 1) acceptable texts—those that include Paraguayan cultural elements through a minimal use of lexical borrowings, and those that go beyond the local culture using Guaraní as a specialized language, and admitting lexical borrowings or lexical innovations; 2) characteristics of Guaraní discourse in texts—including enunciation patterns and the avoidance of grammatical calques; 3) lexical creation—semantic precision (avoiding ambiguity), semantic independence, semantic value, and standard orthography; 4) "integrated" lexical borrowings—respecting Guaraní orthography, phonology, and morphology; 5) other lexical borrowings—proper names and un-integrated terms using original orthography, in cursive; 6) orthography—the alphabet to be used and the norms for using it.

These guidelines have been very controversial and contested from a variety of interest groups and authors. The most criticized aspects are the inclusion of "integrated" borrowings and certain non-Guaraní graphemes, that are associated with the teaching of *Jopara*, or mixed Guaraní. What most opponents of these guidelines argue is that they are detrimental to the development of Guaraní and that they will result in the corruption and loss of Guaraní. They also argue that by doing this, MEC is granting a lower status to Guaraní, as Spanish is taught in its "standard" form. These critics point out that according to the 1992 constitution, the use of Spanish and Guaraní needs to be legislated, but this has not yet happened. They call for the creation of an academy that would take the task of standardizing Guaraní in order to avoid all the controversies and disagreements that continue to plague the educational arena in regards to Guaraní. While some of them are not completely against the incorporation of lexical borrowings, they advocate the development of *Guaraní Porã*—"pretty" or "good" Guaraní (Mansfeld, 2004; Moles, 2005; Thun, 2004; Trinidad Sanabria, 2004).

On the other hand, Melià (2001) argues that in Paraguay there is a cohesive Guaraní, spoken by the majority of the people, and there is a divisive Guaraní, which is the one that causes disputes with regard to spelling, grammar, and lexical terminology. He points out that what could be observed in Paraguay in the teaching of Guaraní at schools was a clash between the "popular" Guaraní and the "unpopular" Guaraní. He advocates the use of a form of Guaraní that is more similar to what people use, without resorting to the indiscriminate use of either lexical borrowings or neologisms.

These issues are similar to other contexts in which education is launched in a language that had previously oral traditions, as is the case of Guaraní. For example, Quechua in the Andean countries and Hawaiian have undergone similar debates. These debates bring to the forefront issues of standardization and authenticity (King, 2001), and finding an agreeable solution is not always easy.

Scheduling and Time

In regard to the time allotted to the teaching of Guaraní in schools, MEC establishes two modalities: *Guaraní Hablante* (for speakers of Guaraní) and *Hispano Hablante* (for speakers of Spanish). In the first modality, students receive literacy and content instruction in Guaraní for the first three years of schooling, while receiving instruction of Spanish as a second language. The opposite occurs in the Spanish modality. In grades 4-6, L1 is used for literacy and as a medium of instruction in all areas, while L2 is used for literacy and as medium of instruction in some areas of study (70% students' first language, or L1; 30% students' second or additional language, or L2). In grades 7-9, both Spanish and Guaraní are used for literacy and as a medium of instruction (100% for communication; 80/20 for math, 60/40 for science, and 50/50 for social studies, the arts, and physical education). For grades 10-12 (non-mandatory), Guaraní is taught only as a literary language for two hours a week (MEC, 2004).

While this is the model proposed by the MEC, the reality does not always reflect this design, especially because the most widely used model is the Spanish modality, even in regions where children are monolingual Guaraní speakers. Schools that use other languages as media of instruction (e.g., English, French, Chinese, etc.) do not follow this model. They are limited to teaching Guaraní as a second language throughout elementary and middle school and as a literary language in high school. Furthermore, Pic Gillard (2000) notes that the teaching of Guaraní in the Spanish modality resembles more the teaching of a foreign language than a national language. She concludes that "the teaching in the Guaraní modality takes into account bilingualism, while the teaching in the Spanish modality does not. This is in complete contradiction to the linguistic reality, since Spanish monolinguals only represent 6% of the population, while Guaraní monolinguals represent 47%" (p. 177). Because of this, Gynan (2003) advocates for a more widespread use of the Guaraní modality since, according to studies conducted by students under his guidance, Guaraní-speaking students in this modality performed significantly better in language tests of reading and writing. While there are many challenges, most researchers and practitioners agree that the inclusion of Guaraní in the curriculum is a positive step toward the valorization of the language.

Teacher Training

In addition to issues of status and corpus planning, issues of acquisition planning and implementation are crucial to the success of a campaign, such as the Paraguayan Education Reform and Bilingual Education. Many challenges are presented in the area of implementation. Despite the great possibilities and optimism, particularly from the perspective of the Ministry of Education, many challenges still remain. Teaching methodologies and materials are still weak; thus, better teaching training is a must and more materials are needed (Corvalán, 2005). Currently, a more traditional grammar paradigm is followed as opposed to a more communicative approach, adversely affecting interest in Guaraní, as well as Spanish, in schools. In this regard, Melià (2001) criticizes a very rigid way of schooling, especially when the language used is not the one used in the family or even in the community. Moreover, Pic Gillard (2000, 2004) observes that the impact of the bilingual program in Paraguay is significant and has created needs, especially, to reiterate, in the area of teaching methodology. Finally, she points out that there is a difference between the enthusiasm displayed by teachers and the slow change in conditions in which they have to teach (four hours of class, several shifts, tired students, poor infrastructure). In short, the Ministry of Education and teacher training institutes have some great challenges to ensure that teachers are well-trained in order to engage students in more meaningful learning environments, relative to the teaching of Guaraní and Spanish.

Advances, Challenges, and Prospects of Guaraní in Education

Villagra Batoux (2002) summarizes the advances made in Paraguay for Guaraní since its adoption as an official language in 1992. As mentioned previously, this act restructured the whole education system in Paraguay, while creating a rich field for research and study. The increased status allowed for the language to become more visible in the media and in literature. It also contributed to an increased awareness of other languages and their utility, especially within the context of a globalized economy. Furthermore, Guaraní has been declared the "historic" language of Mercosur (a regional trade agreement in South America, including Paraguay, Brazil, Argentina, Uruguay, Chile, and Bolivia), and may become an official language of this regional block if the proposal of Paraguayan Guaraní advocates is accepted.

Despite these gains, many challenges remain, in educational and official contexts as well as in other domains. Throughout this chapter, I have addressed many of these challenges, especially in educational contexts. Furthermore, Gynan (2001) reminds us that "there are huge challenges to be faced beyond language contact: disease, hunger, exhaustion among the children for whom these programs have been developed, as well as a complex linguistic ecology that a centralized dual-modality approach is not flexible enough to serve" (p. 109). Other challenges include the normalization of Guaraní, which, despite much debate and controversy, has not yet taken place, as well as the formal inclusion of the language in government and official contexts. As Choi (2003) notes, "Education is a key component in language maintenance, especially for a minority language. However, education cannot be the sole tool, and it definitely cannot be entirely responsible for the revitalization and maintenance of a language" (p. 91).

Membership in Mercosur presents another challenge not only to Paraguay, which is the least modern and industrial country of that regional bloc, but also to its national language, vis-à-vis the bloc's official status given to Spanish and Portuguese. Along the border with Brazil, the contact among these three languages is strongly felt and has serious repercussions for both the linguistic ecology as well as education in that region, especially because of Brazil's economic and technological superiority (Corvalán, 2005; Hamel, 2003). A phenomenon encountered in this zone of language contact is the mix not only between Spanish and Guaraní or Spanish and Portuguese, but also between Guaraní and Portuguese in rural areas and all three (*Tripara* or *Portuguarañol*).

Despite all the challenges, most authors and educators are optimistic with regard to the effects of education on the future of Guaraní. None of the educators interviewed in the context of a study of Guaraní and education in Paraguay expressed the idea that the inclusion of Guaraní in the education system would be detrimental to the language's survival. Furthermore, most of them viewed this inclusion in a positive light and with having many potential benefits (Canese, 2008). Most researchers and educators view the inclusion of Guaraní in education as a positive step in the valorization of the language. The following quotation summarizes this view:

> The last three decades of the 20th century have been the most crucial period in the history of the Guaraní language. A language that was spoken only in familial and informal circles is now an academic language, taught and learned in all formal educational institutions. It is hoped that the efforts and political decisions directed towards the expansion, enrichment and maintenance of Guaraní will help to change the negative image of the native language and will promote its unfettered use in all linguistic domains. (Choi, 2005, p. 237)

With respect to the prospects of Guaraní, researchers present divergent views. Solé (1995) predicted that in Paraguay, as in other countries, the long-range situation would be one of "slow but progressive displacement of the ethnic mother tongue, with the likelihood of sharp increases in the next generation due to the age profile of their respective subpopulations" (pp. 130-131). Gynan (2001) agrees with this prediction in regard to the urban sector, but he notes that "the rural population presents patterns of increasing Guaraní vitality, some of which are related to language maintenance and shift, while others are purely demographic" (p. 106), he also predicts that "Guaraní monolingualism will remain vital, even while Spanish increases at high rates" (p. 106). He argues, however, that Spanish monolingualism will continue to be confined to a very small minority of the population. He concludes that even though it is problematic to apply a national profile to the country, given the difference in regions, "there is every indication that the country will not abandon the language that has come to symbolize Paraguay's uniqueness as a nation" (p. 109).

On the other hand, both Pic Gillard (2000, 2004) and Solé (2000) argue that the situation might be very different for the future of Guaraní. Pic Gillard (2000) questions the role of literacy and methodology in "reducing" the cultural content of the oral language and the future of Guaraní if all Paraguayans become bilingual. She argues that the Bilingual Education Program is a project of planned acculturation in the long term. On the other hand, according to Solé (2000), "losing Guaraní, from the outside, would be not only to lose a language, but a culture that has contributed to the molding of Paraguayans and distinguished them from others" (p. 166). She argues that the survival of Guaraní can only be ensured in the long term insofar as the people and society at large disidentify the rural from Guaraní and reidentify it with the urban, and redefine its values and functions. "Otherwise, Guaraní could become, in fact, a historic relic," she concludes (p. 166).

These two views can be brought together in the wise words of one Paraguayan educator. He argued that

> *The future of Guaraní depends exclusively on its speakers and the linguistic policy that the government seriously implements. Both corpus and status planning are also in the hands of the media and education. The media can greatly assist the process by airing radio and television programs and writing in a real and comprehensible Guaraní. Schools need to motivate students providing appropriate materials and methodologies used by teachers trained in the teaching of language. (Canese, 2008, p. 63)*

This view is shared by several authors, including Choi (2003), who argues that "the future of minority languages depends to a large degree on the individuals that speak these languages and the efforts of the entire community" (p. 91). Similarly, Palacios Alcaine (2004) argues that only the valorization of Guaraní in social, political, and educational contexts will guarantee the equality of all Paraguayan citizens. Corvalán (2005) agrees and notes that the maintenance and expansion of the bilingual process depends to a large extent on the enrichment and prestige, including the social and official status that is given to Guaraní by the state, including education, public administration, and local and central governments. This prestige needs to be in all contexts of use—not just historical or cultural, but also social, educational, and economic—as evidenced by its widespread visibility in all contexts of society (Choi, 2003; Corvalán, 2005; Moles, 2005). Villagra-Batoux (2003) is optimistic in asserting that as part of the Paraguayan education system, Guaraní is ready to face the challenges in more favorable conditions, which will guarantee a creative and instrumental bilingualism as well as promote the cultural values represented by the language.

As noted throughout the discussion, the linguistic and educational situation in Paraguay does not present a simple "either/or" dichotomy; as in many other multilingual contexts, it encompasses a very complex range of linguistic proficiency, variation, and use. Gynan (2001) observes that "Guaraní has survived despite formal language policy favoring the spread of Spanish since Paraguay's colonial period. Cultural, socioeconomic and political forces are more significant contributors to the current language situation" (p. 78). Furthermore, he emphasizes the instrumental role that language policy and education reform play in safeguarding the linguistic rights of all, which derive "from a commitment to the physical and economic well-being of Paraguay's youngest citizens" (p. 110).

Note

[1] All quotations originally in Spanish have been translated by the author.

References

Benítez, N. (2005). Personal communication with Director of Curriculum, Ministerio de Educación y Cultura, Paraguay. December 15, 2005.

Canese, V. (2008). *When policy becomes practice: Teachers' perspectives on the teaching of Guaraní as a second language.* Unpublised doctoral dissertation. Arizona State University, Tempe, Arizona.

Centro Paraguayo de Estudios Sociológicos. (1998). *Investigación sobre escuelas bilingües con la modalidad Guaraní-hablante.* Asunción, Paraguay: Author.

Choi, J. (2003). Language attitudes and the future of bilingualism: The case of Paraguay. *International Journal of Bilingual Education and Bilingualism,* 6(2).

Choi, J. (2004). La planificación lingüística y la revaloración del guaraní en el Paraguay: Comparación, evaluación e implicación. *Language Problems & Language Planning,* 28(3), 241-259.

Choi, J. (2005). Bilingualism in Paraguay: Forty years after Rubin's study. *Journal of Multilingual and Multicultural Development,* 26(3).

Convención Nacional Constituyente. (1992). *Constitución nacional de la República del Paraguay.* Asunción, Paraguay: Author.

Corvalán, G. (1981). *Paraguay, una nación bilingüe.* Asunción, Paraguay: Centro Paraguayo de Estudios Sociológicos.

Corvalán, G. (2000). Consideraciones para las políticas lingüísticas del Paraguay. *Revista Paraguaya de Sociología,* 37(109), 137-154.

Corvalán, G. (2005). *La vitalidad de la lengua guaraní en el tercer milenio en Paraguay.* Retrieved November 30, 2005, from www.datamex.com.py/guarani/opambae_rei/tembihai/Corvalán_vitalidad_del_guarani. html on.

Corvalán, G., & Krivoshein de Canese, N. (1987). *El Español del Paraguay en contacto con el Guaraní.* Asunción, Paraguay: Centro Paraguayo de Estudios Sociológicos.

Dirección General de Estadística, Encuestas y Censo. (2005). *Trípticos de los resultados finales del censo nacional de población y viviendas 2002.* Retrieved on September 10, 2005, from www.dgeec.gov.py/

Granda, G. (1988). *Sociedad, historia y lengua en el Paraguay.* Bogotá: Publicaciones del Instituto Caro y Cuervo, LXXX.

Gynan, S. (1998). El futuro del bilingüismo Paraguayo. *Ñemity: Revista Bilingüe de Cultura,* N° 36.

Gynan, S. (2001). Language planning and policy in Paraguay. *Current Issues in Language Planning,* 2(1).

Gynan, S. (2003). *El bilingüismo Paraguayo: Aspectos sociolingüísticos* (2nd ed.). Asunción, Paraguay: Etigraf.

Gynan, S. (2004). Paraguayan attitudes toward standard Guaraní and Spanish. *Internet Journal for Cultural Sciences,* No. 15. Retrieved from www.inst.at/trans/15Nr/06_1/gynan15.htm

Gynan, S. (2005). Official bilingualism in Paraguay, 1995-2001: An analysis of the impact of language policy on attitudinal change. In L. Sayahi & M. Westmoreland (Ed.), *Selected proceedings of the second workshop on Spanish sociolinguistic*s (pp. 24-40). Somerville, MA: Cascadilla Proceedings Project.

Kaplan, R., & Baldauf, Jr., R. (1997). *Language planning.* Clevedon, UK: Multilingual Matters.

King, K. (2001). *Language revitalization processes and prospects: Quichua in the Ecuadorian Andes.* Clevedon, UK: Multilingual Matters.

Krivoshein de Canese, N. (2001). Cultura y bilingüismo en el Paraguay. In *Ñemity: Revista Bilingüe de Cultura,* N° 42, ISSN: 0254-8178

Lustig, W. (2004). *Mbaé'ichapa oiko la Guaraní. Guaraní y jopara en el Paraguay.* Mainz University. Retrieved on December 13, 2004, from www.uni-mainz.de/~lustig/Guaraní/

Mansfeld, M. E. (2004). La lengua Guaraní y las nuevas normativas del MEC. Retrieved on November 30, 2005, from www.datamex.com.py/guarani/opambae_rei/tembihai/mec_mansfeld_guarani_y_nuevas_normativas.html on.

Melià, B. (1995). *Elogio de la lengua Guaraní: Contextos para una educación bBilingüe en el Paraguay.* Asunción, Paraguay: Centro de Estudios Paraguayos "Antonio Guasch."

Melià, B. (1997). *El Paraguay inventado.* Asunción, Paraguay: Centro de Estudios Paraguayos "Antonio Guasch."

Melià, B. (2001). El Guaraní popular y el Guaraní impopular. In *Ñemity: Revista Bilingüe de Cultura,* N°

41, ISSN: 0254-8178

Melià, B. (2003). *La lengua Guaraní en el Paraguay colonial.* Asunción, Paraguay: Centro de Estudios Paraguayos "Antonio Guasch."

Melià, B. (2004). Vitalidad y dolencias de la lengua Guaraní en el Paraguay. In A. Lluís I Vidal-Folch & A. Palacios Alcaine (Eds.), *Lenguas vivas en América Latina, IV. Jornadas internacionales sobre indigenismo Americano* (pp. 269-282). Madrid, Barcelona, España: Universidad Autónoma de Madrid, Institut Català de Cooperació Iberoamericana.

Mello-Walter, R. M. (2004). Política lingüística y realidad educativa en la República del Paraguay. In A. Lluís I Vidal-Folch & A. Palacios Alcaine (Eds.), *Lenguas vivas en América Latina, IV. Jornadas internacionales sobre indigenismo Americano* (pp. 257-268). Madrid, Barcelona, España: Universidad Autónoma de Madrid, Institut Català de Cooperació Iberoamericana.

Ministerio de Educación y Cultura. (1999). La lengua Guaraní y los procesos de planificación lingüística. In *Ñemity: Revista Bilingüe de Cultura,* N° 37, ISSN: 0254-8178

Ministerio de Educación y Cultura. (1999). Enseñanza de las lenguas en el 3er ciclo de la educación media. In *Ñemity: Revista Bilingüe de Cultura,* N° 38, ISSN: 0254-8178

Ministerio de Educación y Cultura. (2001). *El Guaraní mirado por sus hablantes.* Asunción, Paraguay: Author.

Ministerio de Educación y Cultura. (2004). *La educación bilingüe en la reforma educativa Paraguaya.* Asunción, Paraguay: Author.

Ministerio de Educación y Cultura. (2004). *Estrategias para el mejoramiento y fortalecimiento de la educación bilingüe: Foros regionales de consulta sobre educación bilingüe.* Asunción, Paraguay: Author.

Ministerio de Educación y Cultura. (2004). *Desarrollo de la educación: Informe nacional de Paraguay.* Reunión de la Conferencia Internacional de Educación. Asunción, Paraguay: Author.

Moles, J. (2005). *Ñamopu'ã avañe'ẽ (paraguaiñe'ẽ) oñondivepa! Cooperación internacional al desarrollo lingüístico, nuevo tema de la agenda política mundial. El caso del Paraguay.* Retrieved on December 5, 2005, from www.datamex.com.py/guarani/opambae_rei/tembihai/moles_namopua_avanee_onondivepa.html.

Organización de Estados Iberoamericanos para la Educación la Ciencia y la Cultura. (1997). *Sistema educativo nacional del Paraguay.* Madrid: Author.

Palacios Alcaine, A. (2004). Políticas educativas en Paraguay: Revisión y Balance. In A. Lluís I Vidal-Folch & A. Palacios Alcaine (Eds.), *Lenguas vivas en América Latina, IV. Jornadas internacionales sobre indigenismo Americano* (pp. 213-223). Madrid, Barcelona, España: Universidad Autónoma de Madrid, Institut Català de Cooperació Iberoamericana.

Paraguay. (1992). *Constitución Nacional de la República del Paraguay.* Asunción: Convención Nacional Constituyente.

Paraguayan Congress. (2000). Proyecto de ley que reglamenta los Artículos 77 y 140 de la Constitución Nacional y crea la Dirección Nacional de Política Lingüística. *Ñemity: Revista Bilingüe de Cultura,* N° 40, ISSN: 0254-8178.

Pic Gillard, C. (2000). La transformación de un país plurilingüe en un país bilingüe. Un caso ejemplar: el Paraguay. *Revista Paraguaya de Sociología, 37*(109) 155-183.

Pic Gillard, C. (2004). *El plan de educación bilingüe en en Paraguay: Incidencias sociolingüísticas.* Asunción, Paraguay: Servilibro.

Reiter, F. J. (1995). *They built utopia (The Jesuit missions in Paraguay, 1610-1768).* Potomac, Maryland: Scripta Humanistica.

Rojas Lopez, D., & Escurra, M. C. (2000). Proyecto de ley que reglamenta los articulos 77 y 40 de la constitución nacional y crea the Dirección de Political Lingüística. *Revista Ñemity,* No. 40, pp. 8-19.

Romero, R. (1998). *Protagonismo histórico del idioma Guaraní* (2nd ed.). Asunción, Paraguay: Arte Final.

Roulet, F. (1993). *La resistencia de los Guarní del Paraguay a la conquista (1537-1556).* Misiones, Argentina: Editorial Universitaria, Universidad Nacional de Misiones.

Rubin, J. (1968). *National bilingualism in Paraguay.* The Hague: Mouton.

Solé, Y. R. (1995). Language, nationalism, and ethnicity in the Americas. *International Journal of the Sociology of Language, 116,* 111-137.

Solé, Y. R. (2000). *Valores comunicativos y emblemáticos del Español y del Guaraní.* Bogotá: Publicaciones del Instituto Caro y Cuervo, CIV.

Spolsky, B. (2004). *Language policy: Key topics in sociolinguistics.* Cambridge, UK: Cambridge University

Press.

Steckbauer, S. (2000). *Historia y presente del Guaraní en el Paraguay.* Ñemity: *Revista Bilingüe de Cultura,* N° 39, ISSN: 0254-8178

Thun, H. (2004). Reflexiones sobre las "Orientaciones Prácticas" del MEC. In *Guaraní Renda.* Retrieved December 15, 2004, from www. datamex.com/py/guarani/opambae_rei/tembihai/mec_thun_reflexiones_sobre_orientaciones.htm.

Trinidad, S. (2005). El Guaraní y la clase política. *ABC Color.* Retrieved on May 29, 2005, from www.abc.com.py.

UNESCO. (2002). El universo cultural Guaraní como patrimonio oral e intangible de la humanidad. In Ñemity: *Revista Bilingüe de Cultura,* N° 43 & 44, ISSN: 0254-8178.

U.S. Department of State. (2005). *Background note: Paraguay.* Retrieved on November 29, 2005, from www.state.gov/r/pa/ei/bgn/1841.htm.

Villagra-Batoux, D. (2002). *El Guaraní Paraguayo: de la oralidad a la lengua literaria.* Asunción, Paraguay: Expolibro.

Villagra-Batoux (2003). El bilingüismo Paraguayo: ¿Una apuesta o una utopía? In *Guaraguao,* 7(17), 71-82.

Zanardini, J. (2004). *Educación indígena.* Asunción, Paraguay: Consejo Nacional de Educación y Cultura.

Zajíková, L. (2004). Actitudes y usos del Guaraní en Paraguay. In A. Lluís I Vidal-Folch & A. Palacios Alcaine (Eds.), *Lenguas vivas en América Latina, IV. Jornadas internacionales sobre indigenismo Americano* (pp. 223-237). Madrid, Barcelona, España: Universidad Autónoma de Madrid, Institut Català de Cooperació Iberoamericana.

Zuccolillo, G. (2000). Paraguay "PLURICULTURAL Y BILINGÜE" (o ¿cómo se dice mestizo en guaraní?). In *Revista Paraguaya de Sociología, 37*(109), 1185-202.

About the Author

Valentina Canese is a professor of English as a Foreign Language at the National University of Asunción, Paraguay. She graduated with a Ph.D. in Curriculum and Instruction with an emphasis in language and literacy from Arizona State University in 2008 and her research focuses on educational linguistics, including language policy and planning, language ideologies, ESOL, and minority language education. She teaches courses related to bilingual education, second language development, second language teaching methodologies, and qualitative research methods. E-mail: Valentina.Canese@asu.edu

The History of Education and Curriculum Development in Poland

Agnieszka Gutthy

Education in Poland spans the distance from its medieval roots and simple curriculum development to more turbulent times in recent centuries. In these later periods, the education system has assumed the additional responsibilities of preserving the national identity; defending the language from Germanization and Russification; and, during the Nazi occupation, safeguarding Polish culture from annihilation. The curricula over these thousand years have reflected various goals: general education; an emphasis on church- or trade-related topics; the importance of nationalism through such subjects as Polish history and literature; and, under communism, instruction devised for political indoctrination.

Medieval Poland: The Role of Education

With the acceptance of Christianity in 966, Poland became part of the cultural, political, and social world of the Medieval West. The monastic orders as well as the secular clergy fostered the new Christian culture. Soon, Poland had created ties with present-day Italy, France, and Belgium. Monasteries did not restrict their activities to the religious field, contributing as well to the country's economic and artistic development. Monks were brought from France and the region of Silesia to teach modern methods of agriculture to Polish peasants. Soon, the first collegiate and cathedral schools appeared. With the increasing "Polonization" of clergy, the number of schools grew; by the middle of the 13th century, there were 14 collegiate and 13 "cathedral" schools preparing students for priesthood (Kurdybacha, 1967a). These students often continued their education at universities abroad and, upon their return to Poland, held high civil or church offices.

Medieval Poland also had a system of parochial schools largely independent of the church. They were organized and supported by the growing urban middle class to meet the needs of commerce in the cities. The cur-

Poland

riculum in these schools included Latin, dialectics, and rhetoric. More advanced schools taught basic law, the methods of drafting official documents, and other skills necessary for becoming educated notaries and clerks in the city halls, churches, and court.

The church-based portion of the parochial school curriculum included mathematics, astronomy, and music. The first two subjects related to the Roman Catholic Church's needs for calculating the calendar and determining the dates of church holidays and moveable feasts. "Textbooks" included the classical works of Roman and medieval writers, the latter mostly religious works. Teachers were usually priests and city clerks. Students came from the wealthy urban class, the rising tradesman class, and occasionally even the peasantry.

In general, education in medieval Poland was subject to the methods employed by the Church. Latin was the language of instruction, and learning was accomplished through repetition and memorization. Corporal punishment was common.

Casimir the Great founded the first university in Poland at Cracow in 1364, although it did not begin its continuous existence until 1400, when Queen Jadwiga donated her jewels for this cause. Cracow Academy, known later as Jagiellonian University, became one of Europe's most distinguished universities and a center of intellectual tolerance. It embraced the faculties common to the medieval institutions of higher learning: theology, medicine, law, and liberal arts. By the end of the 15th century, Cracow Academy was known as an important center of astrology and astronomy. And it boasted a very gifted student, Nicolaus Copernicus.

Humanistic Thought

Poland slowly began to feel the influence of the new humanistic thought of the Renaissance. The number of students in the country was growing and the number of schools increased. Latin remained the most important subject, but teachers were now being educated at Cracow University, which contributed to a higher level of education.

New ideas for curriculum soon appeared, including those of the influential Polish author Mikolaj Rej, who saw the need for teaching Polish history, Polish law, and the geography of foreign countries. By the end of the 15th century, almost every town, and often the richer villages, had their own schools.

With the new economic growth, the role of nobility became more prominent. Among the aristocrats it became fashionable to educate children with private tutors who emphasized the study of classical authors. The knighthood, who had come from the modest ranks of society, were rewarded for their gallantry and became landed aristocracy. These men sought to educate their sons in topics more aligned with the newer times, rather than in theology and classical philosophy. Subjects like history, moral science, politics, and, above all, rhetoric, were becoming widespread.

The invention of print and the resulting access to books were slowly chipping away at the clergy's monopoly of knowledge. New humanistic schools appeared. In 1519, Lubranski Academy in Poznan was founded. This was a five-year high school which, in addition to offering classes in Greek, Latin, and rhetoric, also taught geography, history, moral science, and Roman and Polish law. Around this time, studying abroad also became fashionable.

The spirit of humanistic culture and religious tolerance promoted the appearance of institutions whose affiliations were as diverse as Calvinist, Lutheran, Arian, Jesuit, and Piarist. In 17th-century Poland, there were already 1,500 schools, both Catholic and Protestant (Kurdybacha, 1967, vol. 1).

Lutheran high schools were founded in the regions of Pomerania and Wielkopolska: in Elblag (1530), Gdansk (1558), and Torun (1568). By the early 17th century, the curriculum included Copernican theory, Latin, rhetoric, Polish culture and literature, and modern European languages (Kurdybacha, 1967, vol. 1).

In the 17th and 18th centuries, a Gdansk Lutheran school became known for its superior level of medical studies. Gdansk doctors were widely respected as anatomists, performing some of the first medically supervised dissections of the human body. They also gained renown for introducing smallpox vaccinations, researching the means of disease prevention, and fighting epidemics.

Calvinist gymnasia were founded in Pinczow (1551), followed by others in Cracow, Lancut, Bychawa, Kock, Belzyce, Chmielnik, Vilnius, Kiejdany, and Sluck. Their existence was brief, however. German was their language of instruction, which most Poles did not know, and most of the Calvinist clergy did not understand Polish. Moreover, the coming dominance of the Jesuits strengthened the Catholic identity of Poland.

The Arians, a quasi-Christian order, founded a school in Lewartow (1588) and, instead of focusing on religion, taught rhetoric as it related to social and political topics. It also taught secular moral science, politics, economics, and Latin, along with Polish and German. The five-year Arian gymnasium in Rakow (1603-1638) taught Latin, rhetoric, economics, politics, moral science, mathematics, and geometry. In addition to these fundamentals, it taught the history of Poland, biological sciences, and the works of Aristotle and Francis Bacon. This school, in particular, promoted religious tolerance.

A gymnasium in Sierakow (1650-1656) was open to all students, both noble and plebeian. It taught Polish and Latin grammar, Polish and world history, astronomy, geology, biological sciences, anatomy, and law. Although students were free to attend church, the school was strictly secular and never held religion classes. These schools usually had their own libraries, print shops, and textbooks.

There was, as yet, no uniform system of national education offering guidelines or requirements for school programs. Thus, each school created its own curricula specific to the school's orientation, whether it be Catholic or Protestant. Many schools were now being founded by nobility. Some of these schools were progressive and excelled in academics. Many others varied widely in the quality of their education. Most schools admitted, in theory, children from all social groups. In practice, however, only the sons of the nobility attended them.

Since the early Renaissance, Poland had been a haven for intellectuals who were not tolerated in neighboring countries as a result of their nonconformist thought. These refugees founded schools that promoted a wealth of new ideas, notably in the field of natural sciences—not always a friendly area to the Church. The Catholic Church was disturbed by such studies; in 1564, King Stanislaw August deemed it politic to bring Jesuits into Poland.

The Jesuits opened their first high school in Braniewo, then established high schools in Jaroslaw, Plock, Ryga, and Lublin. In 1579, they established a university in Vilnius; by 1600, they had already founded 26 schools (Kurdybacha, 1967).

Jesuit schools offered a solid education within comfortable and spacious new buildings. Above all, the Jesuits brought a very high level of excellence to the teaching profession. Instructors were carefully selected from among the priests and were well-qualified. The purpose of their schools was to educate secular young men, usually the sons of nobility. The Jesuits introduced a uniform school system, emphasizing not only academics, but also physical education and personal hygiene. Open-air courts were even constructed for lessons in competitive sports.

In addition to the fundamentals of Latin, Greek, syntax, and rhetoric, the curriculum included swimming, fencing, equitation, and sometimes music and dancing. Unfortunately, the texts were devoid of any reference to current times. The Polish language was admitted only for writing speeches, letters, or panegyrics, and even then it was freighted with Latin expressions and quotations. However, the program of a Jesuit school was well-organized and class material was systematically recycled and reviewed. The school year ended with exams, which, as today, determined who would pass to the next level.

When it appeared the Jesuits were monopolizing the education of the Polish nobility and even attempting to exert a Jesuitical influence over the university in Cracow, the institution decided to open its own high school of humanistic orientation. This school, open to students from all social backgrounds, taught mathematics, the history of Poland, and rhetoric based on progressive social ideas. The university founded similar school colonies—in effect, extended campuses—in over 10 other Polish cities. It supervised and coordinated the curricula and programs, and appointed teachers and principals.

In 1593, Jan Zamoyski opened a progressive academy in Zamosc. His school taught the sons of noblemen from the age of 7. They first learned to read and write in Polish. Next, came Latin and

Greek, which included readings from Cicero and Demosthenes. This was followed by philosophy and rhetoric. Students in more advanced classes could study mathematics, geometry, logic, metaphysics, natural science, medicine, geography, astronomy, physics, politics, economics, and law.

The Zamosc academy, however, did not manage to lessen the Jesuit control over education. This situation began to change only in the second half of the 17th century when, in 1642, King Wladyslaw IV brought the religious order of Piarists to Poland. They opened collegiate schools and academies and very soon assumed a large responsibility for quality secondary education in Poland, second only to the Jesuits in influence.

By the mid-18th century, however, the school system in Poland was decaying. Most of the Protestant schools had closed. The Jesuit high schools persisted in offering outdated philological studies. They propagated religious intolerance, hostility to new ideas, and were graduating students who were ill-prepared for the modern world.

The Enlightenment

The Enlightenment, dawning in western Europe in the late 1600s, spread new intellectual life throughout Western civilization. Horace's call of *Sapere aude* ("dare to know" or "dare to be wise") became the motto of the times. New pedagogical ideas from John Locke to Rousseau and Basedow (an 18th-century German educational theorist) were changing the ways in which education was understood. Educational theories promoted teaching in the spirit of eclectic pragmatism. The concepts of learning and teaching began to occupy a prominent place in the minds of political reformers.

At the inception of the Enlightenment, education in Poland, as in most other European countries, was in the hands of religious orders, primarily Jesuit and Piarist. Innovative teachers were required to spread the secular ideals of the new times. But this was not swiftly accomplished in Poland, and the Enlightenment was not fully felt in the schools until the late 18th century.

It was a Piarist, the Reverend Stanislaw Konarski, who played a key role in the revival of school curriculum. He also positively influenced the philosophy of education within his own order. (It is worth noting that the Piarists favored a more progressive form of education than the Jesuits.) In 1740, Konarski founded the Collegium Nobilium in Warsaw, which, as the name suggests, was for sons of nobility. The school not only reduced the number of classes dedicated to the study of Latin grammar, but also included mathematics, modern languages, Polish and world history, Polish literature, geography, physics, biological science, and the new philosophical ideas of Descartes, Spinoza, and Francis Bacon. Students were encouraged to read current newspapers and journals, especially those of France and Germany. The Collegium even had its own theater, where students performed works from Polish literature and other European authors. Soon, the reforms began to affect other Piarist schools. Emphasis was also placed on the appropriate training of teachers.

The Commission on National Education

It was the year 1773, however, that brought changes on a broader scale. This was the year of the expulsion of the Jesuits from Poland after Pope Clement XIV suppressed the order. It was also the year in which the Commission on National Education was created, the first secular state authority on education in Europe. The commission was created by the order of the Polish parliament and King Stanislaw August Poniatowski on October, 14, 1773, and functioned until 1794. It was funded by confiscated Jesuit property, whose well-planned educational buildings furnished the backbone of the new system. Many members of the Commission had lived in France or England for prolonged periods and brought back to Poland new pedagogical, philosophical, and scientific ideas.

The commission, which enjoyed full legal, administrative, and financial independence, began to organize a uniform national system of public education, open to all social groups. During the approximately 20 years of its existence, the commission organized two universities, 74 secondary schools, 1,600 parochial schools, and several secular colleges for training teachers (Davies, 2005b). It also reorganized existing schools and established a new system of high school education. The three universities, in Warsaw, Cracow, and Vilnius, were granted the rights of curatorship over secondary and elementary schools, including those that remained under the influence of the Church.

The Commission on National Education introduced a secular, Enlightenment-based school curriculum and textbooks. With Polish mandated to replace Latin as the language of instruction, the commission faced the problem of an almost complete lack of textbooks in Polish. Accordingly, it created the Society of Elementary Books, which prepared and published in Polish 27 textbooks in mathematics, logic, botany, ethics, grammar, as well as the first anthology of Polish poetry. Authors of new scientific books had the additional challenge of creating lexicons of specialized terms in Polish. Books and methodological guides for teachers accompanied these new textbooks.

School curricula now introduced subjects ranging from modern languages to natural sciences, and emphasized physical activity and hygiene as much as academics. Beyond the new programs, new methods of teaching were implemented. Analytical thinking now replaced mechanical memorization. Schools used various teaching aids, such as maps and current newspapers. Field trips were organized, and schools introduced a system of rewards and medals to recognize students' scholarly achievements.

Arguably, it was owing to the efforts of the commission that the Polish culture and language survived the coming national partitions and the long years of Germanization and Russification. The Commission on National Education managed to introduce modern changes in the Polish education system and to destroy its feudal structure. The longevity of these new ideas was significant and its principles continued to be applied to education (although limited by the effects of Poland's partitioning) until the 1830s.

Poland's partitioning lasted from 1773 to 1918, and none of the three partitioning powers, Russia, Prussia, and Austria, had the least interest in protecting Polish culture. The policies of Germanization and Russification during this period severely limited the use of the Polish language and threatened to destroy the Polish national consciousness. Large pockets of resistance, however, continued teaching and even publishing in Polish.

The spirit of the Commission of National Education endured in the Russian sector of Polish territory for some time. Polish schools in Lithuania, Byelorussia (now Belarus), and Ukraine, founded before the partitions, continued to function. The Polish lyceum in Krzemieniec, established in 1805, offered university-level courses. In the Vilnius school district, administered by Adam Czartoryski, Polish elementary and secondary schools continued to function, as did the University of Vilnius. With Cracow in Austrian hands and Warsaw in Prussian, and both subjected to a policy of Germanization, Vilnius, in the Russian sector, became an outpost of Polish culture, indeed the only center of higher learning where Poles were free to promote Polish national tradition and culture (Hans, 1959).

From 1807-1815 and 1815-1830, Polish schools actually developed without serious interruption. The first period was that of the Duchy of Warsaw, created from lands ceded by Prussia, a result of Napoleon's conquests and friendship with the stateless Polish nation. The second period of uninterrupted school growth occurred in the early part of the Congress Kingdom, a semi-independent state in central Poland created upon Napoleon's defeat, with the tsar of Russia assuming its crown. This 15-year period of relative freedom came to an end with the Polish uprising of 1830.

In the Russian sector, provisions were made for universal primary and higher education. By 1820, over 1,200 elementary and 35 secondary schools were operating, along with technical and vocational colleges (Davies, 2005a). The lyceum in Krzemieniec was one of the most progressive schools in Europe. At this time, Polish education was more advanced than in any of the schools in central Russia (Hans, 1959).

The nontraditional areas of education grew in this sector. Boarding schools for girls were becoming more common. Special education schools arose. In 1817, a school for deaf children opened; in 1842, the Institute for Blind Children opened. Specialized colleges were established to prepare teachers for educating children with special needs. In 1830, a special "Institute for Morally Neglected Children," the first juvenile correctional institution, was established in Warsaw. Vocational education was becoming more specialized, with schools established for veterinary and pharmaceutical sciences. In addition, an Institute of Forestry and Farming was founded. Sunday schools for craftsmen educated them in reading, writing, arithmetic, and subjects related to their trade (Kurdybacha, 1967, vol. 2).

Russification and Germanization

The November 1830 uprising resulted in alarming swings in education policy within the Russian sector. From that point came an intensifying trend toward Russification, and the rather small area encompassing the Congress Kingdom—the last portion of Poland with a semblance of freedom—lost its semi-independent status. The ensuing repressions resulted in the closing of Warsaw University, the Lyceum in Krzemieniec, and other Polish elementary and secondary schools. Many teachers lost their jobs, and some were even exiled to Siberia.

Soon, however, a system of secret schools developed in the Russian sector that offered classes of 10 to 15 students a basic education in Polish: reading, writing, history, and geography. Students formed secret study groups and read Polish literature from clandestine libraries. They also read censored Russian literature—Bielinski, Niekrasov, Herzen—and, in these writings, they found inspiration for protest and rebellion.

In general, Poland's Austrian sector had the least developed education system. Austrian authorities commandeered Polish gymnasia and high schools. Curricula were modified to comply with the requirements of the policies of Germanization. Once again, learning was based on memorization and the languages of instruction were Latin and German. In the region of Galicia, education remained in the hands of the Church, its curriculum including Latin, religion, and German. Subjects like mathematics, history, and geography were given only minor importance in the Austrian sector. After all, the objective now was to Germanize, not to educate. Schools were largely preparing students for church, trade, or office work. Instruction in Polish was allowed in the more remote elementary and parochial schools, but instruction in the cities was only in German. By 1819, physics was removed from the curricula, and more classes were devoted to teaching German culture. The Jagiellonian University in Cracow became a completely Germanized institution. Faced with the repressive policies of Germanization, Polish students and teachers reacted just as they had under the oppression of the Russian sector: they formed underground study groups. These included secret youth associations, which promoted Polish language and culture.

From the beginning, the third sector of Poland, the Prussian, was intent on teaching German culture only. Separate Polish schools were not supported, nor was there a Polish university in this sector. Parochial schools offered a scant elementary education consisting of reading, writing, mathematics, and church singing. Elementary education was compulsory and sanctions were imposed on parents who did not send their children to school. The purpose of a Polish student's education was, as in the Austrian sector, to learn the German language and obedience to Prussian authorities.

The Germanizing efforts, however, were not very effective. In the region of Silesia, only the nobility and part of the wealthier middle class knew German. So in 1821, parochial country schools in Silesia were granted the right to use Polish as their language of instruction. In order to integrate and Germanize Polish children, a system of "simultaneous" schools taught both German and Polish children. Many schools, especially in the cities, taught in both languages for early instruction, but only German was allowed in the more advanced years.

In Warsaw, The Society of Friends of Science, after great effort, received permission from Prussian authorities to establish a high school with an expanded curriculum. In 1804, the Royal Warsaw Lyceum was founded. The first two years of classes were taught in both Polish and German. Later, German was the only language of instruction. The school offered humanistic education and taught five languages: Polish, German, French, Latin, and Greek. There were four optional languages: English, Hebrew, Russian, and Italian. The curriculum also included mathematics, physics, chemistry, and geography, as well as classes in dance, music, and horsemanship. The level of education was quite high; in 1805, the school became the curator for the entire Warsaw school system. But in the mid-19th century, under Bismarck, anti-Polish politics strengthened and, among the new restrictions, the Polish language was banned from all schools.

Resistance

In all three sectors, underground study groups continued to thrive, led by Polish schoolteachers who formed the foundation of the national movement. Thanks to their clandestine classes, the Polish language and culture were not forgotten. Nor should one forget the role of parents in the promulgation and protection of national culture. They were home-schooling their children in the spirit of Polish national values and patriotism. These were the children who were not afraid to rebel years later, when the German language was imposed on religious instruction in the parochial schools.

This first large-scale rebellion of pupils took place in 1901, in a school in Wrzesc, when children were handed catechisms written in German. In spite of receiving severe corporal punishment, children refused to participate in classes conducted in German. Students also refused German language texts in the Pomeranian and Poznan regions, where roughly 90% of the schools went on strike (Kurdybacha, 1967, vol. 2). The Polish education system persevered with the help of students, teachers, parents, and the many underground Polish cultural movements.

The year 1918 brought a short 20-year period of independence, during which a new Poland was faced with the daunting task of devising a uniform national education system out of the three separate systems. Immediately, the minister of education, Ksawery Prauss, prepared a program of educational policy. According to this declaration, the systems from the three former sectors were to be placed under one secular authority. The program established a free and obligatory seven-year elementary education for all children, and provided for a continuity of school programs from elementary through secondary school.

In April 1919, the Congress of the Polish Teachers Associations met in Warsaw. It formally rejected the previous practice of making secondary education accessible only to privileged children, while peasant and working-class children were offered only very basic education. In the new system, the curricula were to progress from lower to upper schools and even on to vocational schools. Great emphasis also was placed on teachers' education, and special five-year schools were established to prepare teachers for their profession.

In practice, however, secondary schools were not directly tied to elementary schools but remained a separate area for the privileged as well as a path to their university education. The seven years of compulsory elementary school comprised three levels: four years of elementary education, two years of preparatory education, and a seventh year, which, for peasant and working-class children, was their final year of school. For the privileged children, however, the seventh year would entail studies in an exclusive secondary school, and this then would lead to university study.

During the 1920s, Poland established various specialized secondary schools and vocational schools, as well as a system of kindergarten education. The Polish Academy of Learning and the state universities in Warsaw, Vilnius, and Poznan were founded. The illiteracy rate was lowered considerably, from 33 to 18% (Davies, 2005b).

Nazi Occupation and the Underground

With the German invasion of 1939, organized attempts again were made to annihilate the Polish culture. Following the capitulation of Warsaw on 28 September, Poland was once more dismembered: the western regions of Pomerania, Silesia, and Poznan were annexed by Germany. The portion of Poland east to the Bug river became Germany's occupation zone, with its capital in Cracow, and was administered by the Nazi Governor-General, Hans Frank. Lands east of this were seized by the Soviet Union. Hans Frank's method of enforcing Nazi domination was to remind Poles of the helplessness of their situation. In an October 1939 interview, he said,

> *Poland can only be administered by utilizing the country through means of ruthless exploitation, deportation of all supplies, raw materials, machines, factory installations, etc., which are important for the German war economy . . . reduction of the entire Polish economy to absolute minimum necessary for bare existence of*

the population, closing of all educational institutions, especially technical schools and colleges in order to prevent the growth of the new Polish intelligentsia. ("Nazi Conspiracy and Aggression," 1946, p. 649)

Teachers, priests, university professors, artists, and the nobility—intelligentsia in general—were considered dangerous. They were persecuted: imprisoned, tortured, and, in many instances, sent to concentrations camps and murdered. Among the teachers murdered by the Nazis in Poland was Andrzej Zielinski, an elementary school teacher and principal in the town of Swaty, and the great-grandfather of the author of this chapter. He was deported to Auschwitz in 1941. There, he fainted during a morning formation of inmates and was taken immediately to the crematorium.

On December, 6, 1939, professors from Jagiellonian University were invited for a lecture, ostensibly about the future of the university. After the lecture, all of them were arrested and sent to concentration camps. All universities, secondary schools, and vocational schools were closed to Poles. Only the elementary schools remained open, but their curricula were stripped of all national content and reduced to basic arithmetic, reading, and writing. Devastation and theft of Polish cultural property began. Two-thirds of valuable Polish library collections were destroyed. Poles were to be reduced to a mere labor force. In Governor-General Hans Frank's words, "Poland shall be treated as a colony; the Poles shall be the slaves of the Greater German World Empire" ("Nazi Conspiracy and Aggression," 1946, p. 649).

The Polish educators' response was immediate: In October 1939, the Polish Teachers' Association was changed into a secret organization. The clandestine Committee for Public Education was formed; in cooperation with the secret teachers' organizations, they developed an extensive system of underground teaching. In the territories under the Government-General of Germany, elementary and vocational schools remained legally opened to Poles, but only for the purpose of preparing a workforce for Nazi interests. Teachers, however, were secretly teaching forbidden topics: Polish history, literature, and geography. And the vocational schools were also clandestinely following the program of the prewar gymnasia, secondary schools, and lycea. This secret teaching would sometimes involve entire classes, or just selected groups of students.

There were no Polish schools at all in the western territory annexed by Germany. Yet, secret study enabled students to follow the pre-war elementary and secondary school curricula. The number of school hours was limited for obvious reasons. In private homes, clandestine study groups of five or six students met with their teachers, studying math, Polish history, and literature. Surviving university professors and schoolteachers, including those who had retired before the war, risked their lives to participate in underground teaching. Clandestine print shops were producing Polish books and textbooks. By 1941, these underground print shops had published an estimated 12,000 books (Wroczynski, 1996b). Secret higher education classes began at Warsaw University in 1940 and Jagiellonian University in 1942. Students studied Polish philology, Polish history, and law. Due to the increased fighting on the war front, Germans agreed to open a medical school, which was intended to train only auxiliary medical personnel. Instead, the school was secretly educating students to become doctors. Soon, there were nearly 1,000 students secretly studying medicine (Wroczynski, 1996, vol. 2).

Underground teaching and studying became a massive movement involving the entire country and was unprecedented in the history of education. It was a fight for survival, of a nation facing the threat of literal annihilation. While it is difficult to give exact numbers, it is estimated that in the German-occupied territory during 1940-41, there were 27,000 teachers involved in the secret education of one million students (Wroczynski, 1996, vol. 2).

In August 1944, with the war and the German occupation coming to an end, the newly created Polish Committee of National Liberation (PKWN) passed a law recognizing the validity of all school diplomas achieved during the Nazi occupation. The Department of Education prepared schools in the liberated territory for reopening in the academic year of 1944-45 and classes began on September, 1, 1944.

Marxist-Leninist Ideology

By early 1945, the last of the German forces had been driven from Polish territory. Once again, Poland was faced with the massive task of education reconstruction. Now, however, the education system was to be state-controlled and subjugated to Marxist-Leninist ideology.

In accordance with these new principles, all citizens had a constitutional right to learn and education was free and widely available. The first eight years of elementary education were compulsory. Schools were secular but, through an unusual concession, the Church was allowed to establish a network of separate religious education centers. The Ministry of Education was now the chief organ of state administration. It determined curricula and textbooks and defined the principles of operation, including procedures for admission and the awarding of scholarships. The Ministry also established methods for examinations as well as criteria for awarding titles and diplomas. At the local level, school superintendents determined personnel policy, hired and trained teachers, and periodically visited schools to evaluate teachers.

At the age of 6, children were required to attend a special preliminary "0" ("zero") class, which prepared them for the following eight years of primary school. After graduating from primary school, pupils had three choices, pending their entrance examination results and grades achieved in primary school. They could attend a four-year lyceum (which prepared them for the university), a secondary technical school, or a shortened three-year vocational school, after which the students would become skilled workers.

Students who graduated from lycea and the secondary vocational schools were expected, although not required, to continue their education. After the fourth year of the lyceum or secondary technical school, students took a national exit exam. Upon passing, they received a certificate of secondary education, which gave them the right to take the entrance examination to the university.

Schools were generally very traditional and knowledge-oriented. Order, discipline, and distance were maintained between students and teachers. Structurally, it was a formal classroom and lesson system. Schools provided a sound education and imparted a vast body of knowledge.

Curricula being centralized, teachers were required to present interpretations in agreement with Marxist-Leninist ideology, particularly in history, literature, and social science. Elements of this indoctrination were introduced to schools quite rigorously in the early 1950s while Stalin was alive, but this had tapered off significantly by the 1980s.

Ideological distortions in the syllabi appeared early, especially in the humanities and social studies subjects. Andrzej Janowski (1992) divides these distortions into two categories: those that changed facts, and those that changed the meaning of notions or concepts. Certain topics were not allowed in schools, such as any discussion of the 1939 division of Poland between Nazi Germany and the Soviet Union. Some historical facts, especially of recent times, were altered or entirely omitted. For instance, the 1940 Soviet massacre of 4,321 Polish army reserve officers (most of whom were university graduates and thus intelligentsia) at Katyn, and certain clauses of the German-Soviet Nonaggression Pact of 1939.

The ideological distortions of the second category, concerning concepts, altered the meaning of certain terms. The word "democracy," for instance, was applied to socialist and communist countries only. Western countries were referred to as "pseudo" or "bourgeois democracies." The resulting "contamination of meaning" allowed a repressive, totalitarian dictatorship to be called "liberal, progressive, parliamentary, and peaceful" (Janowski, 1992, pp. 44-45).

Standard curriculum for grades 1 through 4 included such subjects as Polish, mathematics, social and natural environment, fine arts, music, and physical education. Grades 5 through 8 gradually incorporated other subjects, like physics and chemistry. Russian, a requirement for all pupils, regardless of the school, was introduced in the 5th grade as the main foreign language. Few schools offered optional classes in such Western European languages as English, German, and French. These were only taught as an obligatory subject in college preparatory schools. Many parents and students, especially in the larger cities, believed in the value of knowing a Western European language. As a result, a large number of private tutors in English and, to a lesser degree, French emerged.

It is important to emphasize the educational impact of the Catholic Church. The Church was the only non-state institution with an independent social structure and a real power in society, and this arrangement was indeed unusual for a Soviet-dominated country. The Church played an important role in philosophy and cultural life, and in simply keeping up morale in society. And merely attending church on Sunday or taking religion classes were forms of passive disobedience to the official materialist ideology.

There was also a form of underground community education, a "hidden" curriculum that emerged, particularly in the 1980s. This took the form of alternative cultural life: student theater groups, dialogue and self-education within discussion groups, and the circulation of underground publications.

Andrzej Janowski (1992) makes an interesting observation regarding one of the effects of state organized, propaganda-laden education. He refers to the two faces of the system: one repressive and one protective. As a protector, the state promised full employment and offered inexpensive holidays, free health care, free education, and practically free housing. Although these promises were never carried out entirely, they created a common attitude toward the state as a generous giver. He concludes that the product of such education was "extended immaturity": viewing the state authorities as parents who must give, and against whom one can also rebel (Janowski, 1992).

Solidarity Movement and Beyond

During the Solidarity movement of the 1980s, students and teachers called for an overhaul of the state-controlled education system. As a result, various placating committees were formed but no real changes were made. However, Solidarity's momentum grew and with the communists voted out of power in 1989, tangible change could occur.

The postwar public school structures were left intact by the new government of Poland. The eight-year primary schools continued to be free and compulsory. The first stage of public education remained kindergarten, followed by the special "0" class at age 6. The eight-year primary school was followed by either a preparatory lyceum, which continued to a university, or the two types of secondary technical schools.

A system of new private schools developed, some of them affiliated with the Catholic Church. These featured classes of a dozen or so students, boasted higher teacher salaries, and allowed freedom for educational innovation. These schools were regarded as models of inspiration for future public schools.

In 1990, national minimum curriculum requirements were established. Teachers also were given greater autonomy in their methods of instruction. The earliest curriculum reforms were in the areas of civics, history, and foreign languages. Political dogma was removed. Ideological distortions were rectified and certain omitted facts were reintroduced into the history curriculum. English, French, and German replaced Russian. Slowly, the ponderous, knowledge-based curricula were reduced as the obligatory minimum was defined. This abridgement provided more opportunities for teacher innovation. Now, teachers were expected to provide a learning content that met the local interests and demands.

Although the new reforms encouraged teacher innovations, these were not fully realized. Teachers felt unprepared to make their own curriculum decisions or to prepare their own syllabi. So they were unable to make creative changes in their classrooms. Most of them safely followed the old curricula and traditional methods of teaching.

In 1991, a new law amended the education system to its present form. It commences, as it did before, with the introductory "0" class for 6-year-old children; this is followed, however, by a six-year primary school, as opposed to the previous system of eight years. Primary school ends with a test that allows pupils to enter a three-year gymnasium. The gymnasium ends with an exam focusing on humanities, mathematics, and science. On the basis of the results—as in the previous system—students then select one of three secondary schools: a three-year college preparatory lyceum, a four-year technical secondary school, or a two- to three-year vocational school.

The college-preparatory lycea and technical secondary schools end with exit exams. These are graded by external examining boards following a national set of criteria. Students who graduate from lycea and technical secondary schools may continue to the university level after passing the entrance exams.

Prior to 1989, basic vocational schools that provided training for a specific occupation attracted between 50 and 60% of elementary schools' graduates (MEN, 1995). Jobs were easily available and wages were comparatively high. The enrollment in those schools, however, fell considerably, with the collapse of much of Poland's state-subsidized industry and the resulting changes in the employment opportunities.

Private schools in Poland are becoming more popular at all levels, from elementary to higher education. They must meet the standards set by the Ministry of Education in order to operate and issue diplomas. There are also various international schools in major cities, where education is provided in English, French, and other languages. Special education is an integral part of the Polish education system. Depending on their specific needs, most of these children are taught in special schools or integrated into classes in general public schools.

The transformations of the education system have now made schools responsible for devising and following certain educational "paths." A "path" is a way to gain meaning from a subject by applying to its study themes belonging to a completely different discipline. For example, the themes or goals of the "philosophical path" (which include critical and abstract thinking) may be applied to the study of history. This integrative or holistic understanding is more apt to result in a practical marriage of both knowledge and skills. It assists students in understanding processes, rather than forcing them to half-consciously consume encyclopedic facts. With their interdisciplinary benefit, paths can even enable the earlier study of foreign languages, which are now introduced to the very young "0" class.

The new educational paths are followed in both the six-year primary schools and the three-year gymnasia.

Primary schools pursue the paths of:
1. Reading and media
2. Ecology, health, and hygiene
3. Preparation for life in a family.
In the gymnasia, three more educational paths are required:
4. The philosophical path
5. The European path
6. The regional and cultural heritage path.
The goals of the philosophical path are to:
1. Stimulate critical thinking and require participation in discussions, thus facilitating the students' own points of view
2. Require understanding of specific philosophical problems: their origins, development, and role in culture
3. Develop abstract thinking
4. Raise students' awareness of existential and morally important issues.

Here is an example of the philosophical path in action. Polish literature students might discuss the ethical dilemmas of the protagonist in "The Dismissal of the Grecian Envoys," a drama by the Renaissance author, Jan Kochanowski. This work recounts the events leading to the Trojan War. The implicit issues in this work—honesty, personal responsibility, and sound statesmanship—can all be better understood by invoking the above goals.

Following the philosophical path in a history class might lead to discussions of various aspects and influence of logic, or absence thereof, during the course of history. And if the philosophical path is invoked for a mathematics class, the principles of logical thinking and problem-solving would be introduced, involving concepts like negation, conjunction, alternative, implication, and equipoise.

The goals of the European education path are to:
1. Learn and understand the history, goals, and purpose of the European Union in the context of the globalization of the contemporary world
2. Understand European integration in the context of global geo-political changes
3. Understand Poland and the European Union: the issues of mutual sovereignty and interdependence among the countries within the Union.

If applied in a history class, the European path would involve discussing key events in the prehistory of the European Union and the understanding of Poland's involvement in creating a unified Europe. In a religion class, Christianity would be presented as a unifying and integrating force in Medieval Europe, and Poland's Pope John Paul II would be portrayed as one who promoted the ideal of a unified Europe. A social studies class invoking the European goals would discuss the role of Polish citizens in constructing the new European unity.

Realizing these paths requires cooperation among teachers to maintain continuity and coherence at all levels of education. Teachers are expected to be familiar with the paths of the lower levels of education to avoid repetition. Since there was no tradition of teachers integrating their efforts and cooperating in teams, training a new generation of teachers has been problematic. This is, indeed, the first generation to prepare and teach inter-subject curricula.

With the decentralization of Polish education, the emphasis has shifted to the individual schools, now regarded as communities of students, teachers, and parents, whose involvement in the old system had been minimal. There is an obvious movement away from the mere dissemination of facts to providing cognitive and problem-solving instruction.

Some controversy, however, has resulted from the new reforms. Many of the teachers and parents prefer a more traditional education offering students a broad and deep body of knowledge. Another problem is the continuing lack of adequately trained teachers and the serious shortage of classroom space. Limited space has often required two shifts of classes and rooms of 30 to 40 students in most primary schools. Hence, private schools, with their smaller classes and individual attention, are becoming more popular, despite the high tuition costs.

Religion classes in public schools, although embraced initially with enthusiasm, have caused some concern. Many regard the 1991 directive from the Ministry of National Education requiring every student to receive a grade in religion or ethics to be an infringement on their convictions. Some parents, on the other hand, believe that prohibiting religious studies from the public schools would smack too much of the old communist system.

While Poland's admission to the European Union was not made official until 2004, the educational principles of the Union were beginning to influence the education sector in Poland as early as 1995, when the country agreed to participate in the European programs. The Union's objective is to make Europe the world leader in the quality of its education and training systems. A number of programs have been established to encourage the mobility of students, teachers, and researchers. These programs offer grants to study or teach in other European countries, and they offer institutions the opportunity to establish networks and exchange ideas.

Through these programs, European countries are working toward the convergence of a single education system. There are also programs of cooperation between universities and high schools, which have contributed to a higher mobility of students. In the 1999-2000 academic year, over 3,000 Polish students were studying at institutions in other European countries.

Once again, the Polish education system faces challenges, thankfully less daunting than those from the past. But there are now the tasks of maintaining a well-grounded path to democracy and preparing students adequately for the free market economy. And, of course, continuing to strengthen Poland's partnership with its new European partners.

References

Curtis, G. E. (Ed.). (1992). *Poland: A country study.* Washington, DC: Government Printing Office for the Library of Congress.

Davies, N. (2005a). *God's playground. A history of Poland* (Vol. 1). New York: Columbia University Press.

Davies, N. (2005b). *God's playground. A history of Poland* (Vol. 2). New York: Columbia University Press.

Hans, N. (1959). Polish schools in Russia, 1772-1831. *The Slavonic Review, XXXVIII,* 394-414.

Janowski, A. (1992). Polish education: Changes and prospects. *Oxford Studies in Comparative Education,* 2(1), 41-55.

Kurdybacha, L. (Ed). (1967a). *Historia wychowania* (Vol. 1). Warsaw: Panstwowe Wydawnictwo Naukowe.

Kurdybacha, L. (Ed). (1967b). *Historia wychowania* (Vol. 2). Warsaw: Panstwowe Wydawnictwo Naukowe.

Lojek, J. (2003). *Sciezki edukacyjne w szkole ponadgimnazjalnej.* Warsaw: Wydawnictwo Szkolne i Pedagogiczne.

MEN (Ministry of National Education). (1995). *Poland: Education in a changing society. Background Report for the OECD Review.* Warsaw: Author.

Nazi Conspiracy and Aggression. (1946). Washington, DC: US Government Printing Office. Retrieved September 28, 2007, from www.ess.uwe.ac.uk/genocide/Frank.htm

Wroczynski, R. (1996a). *Dzieje oswiaty polskiej* (Vol. 1). Warsaw: Wydawnictwo Zak.

Wroczynski, R. (1996b). *Dzieje oswiaty polskiej* (Vol. 2). Warsaw: Wydawnictwo Zak.

About the Author

Agnieszka Gutthy holds an M.A. in English Philology from Maria Curie-Sklodowska University, Lublin, Poland, and an M.A. in Spanish Philology from Warsaw University, Poland. She earned her Ph.D. at Temple University, Philadelphia. Currently, she is a professor of Spanish language and literature at Southeastern Louisiana University.

From Pearls to Petroleum to Reform: Curriculum Development in Qatar

Allen J. Fromherz and Robin E. Fromherz

Qatar is a country open to the sea. It is nearly surrounded by the Persian Gulf. Once primarily populated by fishermen, pearl divers, nomads, and merchants, Qatar recently has become a country open to the sea of information and new ideas that define the era of globalization. Instead of catching fish or searching for pearls, modern Qataris are searching for new ideas. One of the most important of these new ideas adopted by Qatar is that educational curriculum should be focused on developing the individual student, on individualized learning styles, and on creating critical thinking skills, not simply on the transmission or memorization of information. This chapter will examine how the small State of Qatar has developed this remarkable blending of ideas and how it may come to have profound implications for the future of the country and the future of education in the region.

Historically, Qatar has had an influence greater than its relatively small population and small area would suggest. Centuries ago, long before the rise of modern oil production, Qatar was a center for the ship building and pearl trades. Qatari ships were said to sail with the first rulers of Islam as they conquered new lands for the faith. Merchants and nomadic traders from Qatar regularly traveled to India and the Arabian Sea. The influence of these industrious people of early Qatar reached far and wide.

Characteristics of Qatar Today

While the State of Qatar is a small, compact area only about the size of Connecticut in the United States, the country has a per capita gross domestic product approaching that of Switzerland. Nearly surrounded by water, Qatar sticks out of the Arabian Peninsula and into the Persian Gulf like a thumb or a droplet. Qatar shares its southern border with the large Kingdom of Saudi Arabia and has been heavily influenced by conservative Saudi standards. The renowned international, jet-setting city of Dubai in the separate gulf state of the United Arab Emirates is only a one-hour plane flight

Qatar

away. While Dubai has most of the glitz, Doha, the capital of Qatar, has attracted international attention as a center for world diplomacy, international trade, innovative media (the Arabic Cable news channel al-Jazeera is headquartered in Doha) and, most recently, for education development and education reform.

Education Reform Development

As the enterprising spirit of Qataris is bolstered by vast petroleum wealth, a wealth affording the state ample resources for experimentation and development in education, the State of Qatar has rapidly become a remarkable model of education and curriculum reform in the Arab and Islamic world. Yet it is not simply because of its oil wealth that Qatar has embarked on new educational initiatives. In many Arab states, some with even more oil wealth, education reform lags far behind the Qatari system. Saudi Arabia only reluctantly changed a small portion of its official educational policy, and it is likely that the Kingdom of Saudi Arabia would be less than willing to implement the systematic reforms being adopted in Qatar. Many other states in the region are hesitant to cede control over the education of new citizens. Loyalty to the regime is, for some countries, more important than creating an effective, knowledge-based workforce. The Middle East North African region from Morocco to Iraq has experienced something of a demographic explosion in recent decades, making official government access and control of youth education paramount for most states in the region. Reform, if it is adopted at all, is often implemented very slowly or in controlled and isolated experimental schools. Qatar is an exception to this slow-moving trend.

The impressive and direct involvement of Qatar's ruling elite, and their specific interest and investment, in curriculum reform, in the loosening of Qatar's education bureaucracy, in the adaptation of religious curriculum, and in the introduction of new science, history, and liberal arts courses taught only in English has made Qatar a special and important case study of reform.[1] Qatari citizens, students, and parents are actively embracing the reforms, despite some resistance from more conservative sectors of society. Many of these conservative elements are concerned that curriculum reform will not allow students to be properly exposed to their own culture, history, and religion, and that education reform will lead to a loss of identity.[2] Reformers in Qatar have, however, generally prevailed with the argument that reforms will not be meant to expel a Qatari model and replace it with a Western one, but rather to modify and strengthen education along international standards. It is believed that a stronger education system will benefit Qataris while not threatening their sense of identity. In this sense, Qatar certainly contradicts the common assumption of some editorialists and commentators in the Western world that reform and change can only happen slowly in the Arab world and that the Arab world has historically rejected fundamental changes to its society. Change in the Qatari education system has been so rapid that new developments now often occur on a monthly basis.

Qatari Awareness of Education Changes

Qataris are aware of the revolutionary nature of recent changes; they are also aware of a special responsibility to show how modern education reform can be effectively implemented while maintaining Arab cultural and religious norms. In a *Washington Post* article, Darwish Emadi (2003), who was chosen to spearhead the implementation of the RAND corporation's suggestions for curriculum reforms, said, "The reform in this country [Qatar] is something you won't see anywhere else in the Middle East" (Glasser, 2003, p. A20). Indeed, Qatar aspires to be a model for education reform. As many reports on curriculum development and education systems in the Middle East attest, curriculum reform, textbook renewal, updated teaching methodologies, and critical thinking skills are highly needed, especially as the region wrestles with the pros and cons of more fundamental democratic reforms (Nonneman, 2006).

Qatari education and curriculum reform are, in many ways, still in the beginning stages, and some of the information provided here will change as Qatari education continues to move forward.

While there is not enough space to discuss every detail of Qatar's remarkable education and curriculum reform, this chapter will show how Qatar is becoming an almost unique trailblazer for curriculum development in the Arabic-speaking world. Although Qatar is a small state, the actions and experiences of this wealthy and progressive, but also solidly Islamic, country should be an essential reference and model for curriculum reform throughout the region.

Brief History of Education in Qatar

Before the exploitation of oil in the 1950s, education in Qatar was based on highly traditional methods. The educational curriculum for most boys meant teaching them the basics of reading and writing and having students recite and memorize the Qur'an. Girls learned to read and write at home. Only the very wealthiest were able to send their children overseas to private schools, usually in Britain. Most education in Qatar's pre-petroleum-boom era occurred within the family. Pearl farmers would teach their sons how to find the perfect oysters and how to sail the *dhow*, the traditional Arabian boat. Mothers and grandmothers of Bedouin girls would teach girls the essential skills of surviving as nomads in harsh desert conditions. Oil exploitation in the 1950s, however, rapidly transformed Qatari society and educational expectations. The first school in Qatar opened in 1952.

The Sheikh Khalifa bin Hamad al-Thani built the foundations of Qatar's education system almost from scratch. Nevertheless, for decades, the educational curriculum retained much of its traditional, religious focus under the centralized rule of Sheikh Khalifa. Yet even under the rule of Sheikh Khalifa, enterprising reformers began to consider the possibility of changing and modernizing the curriculum. Two leading woman were especially important in planting the early seeds of curriculum development in Qatar: Sheikha Ahmad al-Mahmoud and Sheikha Abdullah al-Misnad. Currently, president of Qatar University and author of important studies and evaluations of Qatar's education system, Sheikha al-Misnad was instrumental in creating the basic foundations of a systematic and modernizing curriculum structure in the State of Qatar (Misnad, 1985). Sheikha Ahmad al-Mahmoud, minister of education, created the foundation of assessment and evaluation procedures for Qatar, encouraging the movement of Qatar toward modern pedagogical techniques in the early 1990s. She also spearheaded the inclusion of women in the highest levels of Qatar's education system. Although these systems provided the initial roots for systematic evaluation of student learning and teaching supervision and assessment, they were often not fully implemented because of bureaucratic hurdles. Education and society entered a new era of rapid modernization with the assumption of power by Sheikh Hamid al-Thani, the son of Sheikh Khalifa, in 1995. Almost immediately, Sheikh Hamid and his wife, Sheikha Mozah, who has taken a personal interest in education reform in Qatar, set up the "Qatar Foundation" to reform the state's science, arts, and language programs. The Foundation started with higher education, including reforms of the University of Qatar and the establishment of satellite campuses of American universities, such as Cornell and Georgetown, in Qatar.

Education for a New Qatari Era

Education reform is overseen by the newly reformed Qatar Supreme Education Council, founded in November 2002 with the Emiri Decree Number 37, and by its three institutes. The three institutes of the Supreme Education Council are: the Education Institute, which directly oversees the independent schools and supports them with professional development for teachers and a wide range of educational resources; the Evaluation Institute, which develops and conducts periodic assessments of student learning and evaluates school performance; and the Higher Education Institute, which advises individuals on opportunities for higher education and careers and administers a scholarship program.

Primary, middle, and secondary education transformed less rapidly than did higher education. Qatari children must attend six years of primary school, three years of middle school, and three years of secondary schooling. Children start school at age 4 and finish when they are 17 or 18. Boys and girls attend separate schools. Schools are open Sunday to Thursday to allow for religious services, and classes usually begin by 7:00 a.m. and finish at 1:00 p.m. In the summer months, schools may start and end earlier due to the heat. The school year is divided into three terms: Autumn (September to December), Spring (January to April), and Summer (April to July).

Nursery and preschools are not usually registered with the Ministry of Education. Nursery schools, which may accept children from birth to two years, usually have no waiting lists. Not all nursery school teachers are qualified and certified, however. Preschools are often attached to nurseries and will take children starting at 3 years of age. There is one Montessori nursery/preschool in Doha, a testament to the more open educational philosophy of the Qatar system.

At the secondary level, students can specialize in business training, technical education, religious studies, or teacher training (Willis, 2004). Until only a few years ago, students in Qatari primary and secondary schools studied from officially written and approved textbooks. All educational curricula were reviewed and approved and supervised by the centralized Qatari ministry of higher education. Now, however, students and parents choose their schools. Schools now have much more independence in setting their curriculum and choosing texts. Teachers, schools, parents, and students can choose their own courses and have more freedom in establishing the climate of their schools.

Special education in Qatar advocates for the rights of children with special needs to obtain an appropriate education within the system of schools. Programs have been developed to address the special educational needs of children. Until 2001, education services for children with special needs were provided in separate schools and/or separate classrooms in regular schools. The Qatari Ministry of Education started providing services in 1921 (Al Said, 2002) by setting up a classroom for boys with hearing loss in a regular primary school. Then, in 1981, a separate school for boys with hearing loss/deafness was established, followed by the founding of a school for girls with hearing loss/deafness in 1982. In 1984, the Ministry of Education, established separate schools for boys and girls with developmental disabilities. A co-educational, hospital-based school for children with physical disabilities has been operational since 1984. A speech therapy and counseling/psychology was developed in 1992 to work with children with learning and emotional problems. An English language-based co-educational school for children with learning disabilities was established in 1996. Children with visual impairments were often sent to other Gulf countries by the Qatari government. Some were kept at home until a school for children with visual impairments was opened in 1998. In 1999, a co-educational school for children with autism spectrum disorders came into being. In 2006, the schools for serving the children with developmental disabilities were closed down and the children were sent to this new center.

Teachers and staff for the Qatari special education schools are recruited from both Arabic-speaking and Western countries. Little or no inclusion of special needs children in regular classrooms existed until 2001, when the Special Needs Committee of the Supreme Council for Family Affairs set up a task force to begin the process of identifying a means to include children with physical disabilities in regular classrooms (Yossef, 2002). As in systems throughout the world, the greatest barrier to this idea was the lack of accessible schools. The Qatari government helped two schools to become handicapped accessible; consequently, a pilot inclusion program was started. Staff received additional training in educating children with special needs, especially those with physical handicaps, and specialists were hired to construct curriculum and spearhead the project. This beginning project is indicative of the new education reform system in Qatar. The project was initiated, studied, and implemented with all parties, families, schools, and government participating equally to discover ways to investigate the potential of inclusive special education in Qatar. This pilot project was well received by the group and led to the appointment of a committee to develop a full inclusion strategy for the Ministry of Education and the Supreme Family Council (al Attiyah & Lazarus, 2007).

Motivations for Recent Curriculum Reform

Referring to the establishment of the Qatar Foundation for Education, His Highness Sheikh Hamad Bin Khalifa Al-Thani (2007), the Emir (ruler) of Qatar, said, "Let us be resolved and look forward to the future with trust and boldness in order to be among the active and influential and to provide our coming generations with the best opportunities to meet their future and overcome its challenges" (¶ 1). As the Emir so clearly acknowledges, education reform in Qatar is linked not only with the advancement of learning, but also with the advancement of Qatari society, leading to a more progressive state that holds true to its Islamic identity. But education reform is not viewed as a purely internal, state-controlled exercise. Qatar has reached out with remarkable speed and agility to educators and educational institutions throughout the world, especially Europe and America, in search of consultants, teachers, and new ideas. For example, RAND corporation, a major research institution based in the United States, was commissioned by the State of Qatar in 2001 to analyze and help overhaul the educational bureaucracy.

An essential part of this internationalization of Qatari education is a new emphasis on English language learning. While Arabic is still the official language and is taught along with Islamic studies, English has become the de facto language of learning, and is now taught from 1st grade. Qatar's rulers are promoting education reform as an essential way to connect Qatar and Qatar's citizens with a rapidly globalizing world. As Her Highness Sheikha Mozah Bint Nasser Al-Misnad, the second wife of the Emir, and a very vigorous proponent of education reform, recently said, "The sharing of knowledge, ideas and values is the noblest way to transcend barriers. In this sense, globalization is the architect, which constructs academic bridges across cultural and geographical landscapes" (2007, ¶ 2).

Education reform in Qatar is itself a product of globalization. As the quote from Sheikha Mozah indicates, the vision for education and curriculum reform has certainly been set by Qatar's rulers. The specific implementation of these reforms has required the combined effort of Qatar's educational establishment, parents, students, and the extensive use of international consultants, teachers, and practitioners for advice and ideas. As Qatar and the Qatar government reforms its education curriculum, it is also opening itself up to the world.

Evolution of Curriculum Development: Challenges and Opportunities

Curriculum development in Qatar has faced several opportunities and challenges since the creation of the Qatar Foundation for education in 1995. Compared with neighboring countries, the number of school children in Qatar's K-12 government education system is relatively small: 88,502 students as of May 2007, with 9,381 teachers and 231 ministry of education, private Arabic, and independent schools.[3] This has allowed for a more flexible and rapid adaptation than would be possible in larger populations. This small population of students, however, also makes potential over-centralization and top-down control of schools easier. The existence of long-standing bureaucratic structures meant that teachers at the ground level were, and sometimes still are, often faced with difficult barriers to creativity and adaptation of the curriculum, particularly with respect to meeting individual student needs.

In the past, one of the main barriers to adaptation and creativity in the classroom was the lack of any real flexibility or accountability for teachers in the traditional system. The development of new teaching methodologies and standards is a primary part of Qatar's education reforms. Embedded in these reforms is a dedicated emphasis on modeling the constructivist theory of teacher-directed, yet student-emphasized, learning. The teacher asks, activates, and assesses the learning of the student. The student interacts with other students, the teacher, and the classroom environment to associate and apply the learning process. This allows for the learning to become more internal to the students and helps to build a learning foundation that will allow the student to reach out of the classroom walls to see how ideas and change can occur through collective thought and educational sharing of views and ideas.

Whether or not a school is independent or still under Ministry of Education oversight, curriculum standards are being implemented across the educational spectrum in Qatar. Arabic language, math, science, and English have been standardized for all grades. The standards implemented by the Supreme Education Council are deemed by RAND Corporation to be comparable with the most successful international education systems. The teaching of Arabic language, in particular, has undergone revolutionary changes with an emphasis on literature, creative writing, and the use of diverse resources. Arabic used to be taught according to a set of memorized texts and routines, often tied to specifically religious texts. The new standards for Arabic language learning, however, have allowed students to express and model new and creative ideas in their own language. Indeed, many of the Arabic language standards are among the first in the region to be implemented.

The development of these Arabic-specific standards and curriculum reforms, not only in language courses, but in other courses taught in Arabic, is perhaps the most important curriculum change so far. It is a curriculum model that could be rapidly adopted by other Arabic-speaking countries. Also, unlike specifically English language-oriented reforms, where there are significant language barriers for many students, Arabic language reforms allow for the immediate implementation of new curriculum goals across the board. These reforms, of course, allow for greater involvement by parents, who often are not trained in English.

The actual subjects taught and the curriculum standards for Qatar's schools are in the process of being shaped and standardized by the Supreme Educational Council. Previously, under the Education Ministry, most standards were in Arabic and based on traditional or religious expectations. One of the first curriculum standards developed was in English teaching. Grade 10 standards in English reading, comprehension, writing, and analysis for Qatari students were published in 2004.[4] The Supreme Education Council also has developed standards in math, science, and Arabic. Other subjects will vary from school to school.[5]

Teaching Methodologies

In traditional Qatari education, teaching methodology was dominated by rote memorization and recitation, not only of religious texts like the Qur'an, but also of famous poems and songs and the best places to catch fish or herd nomadic animals. Rote memorization is valuable in a society where paper and books are scarce and remains an essential part of Qatari culture and identity. New curriculum reforms in Qatar, while not completely abandoning traditional models and methods, are emphasizing creative learning and the use of constructivist theory, allowing for more student-teacher interaction and more flexible class management. Qatar's New National Professional Standards for Teachers and School Leaders, instituted in April 2007, for example, generally follow the constructivist approach to teaching and student-centered learning.[6]

Yet before this new emphasis on constructivist methods could occur, laying the groundwork for a change in standards and evaluation procedures was necessary. Traditional teaching methodology included almost no performance indicators, evaluations, or standards. Only a few ways of knowing how much the students had actually learned or of gauging the effectiveness of various teaching methodologies were available. After receiving recommendations from RAND corporation reports, the Ministry of Education created a Supreme Education Council and Evaluation Institute to provide this vital information about the performance of schools, teachers, and students. The first report of the Evaluation Institute came out in 2004. This basic reporting and evaluation structure has allowed parents a better choice in deciding the location of schools for their children, even as it has prodded schools and teachers to rapidly adopt new curriculum strategies to meet more rigorous standards. Autonomy, especially teacher and principal autonomy in deciding and implementing teaching methodology, is an essential part of the RAND report recommendation. According to RAND (2007), "It is particularly important to emphasize the principles of decentralized autonomy and accountability for results." RAND recommends the gradual reorganization of a centralized ministry of education schools into so-called "independent schools," or charter-style schools.

Cultural, Gender, and Ethnic Influences on School-Age Youngsters

With almost no exception, all education in Qatar has been and continues to be gender-segregated. Most parents will agree to send their college-age sons overseas for education, but are not willing to allow their daughters to leave Qatar unsupervised. The issue of gender-segregated classrooms at all educational levels will continue to be contentious as many Qatari parents attempt to preserve these traditional values. However, beginning a few years ago, universities in the Education City, including Georgetown, Cornell, and others, have integrated men and women in classrooms.

The presence of large, expatriate, non-citizen communities in Qatar, especially from India, Pakistan, and Europe, has created a parallel education system of private schools, not a combined Qatari, mixed cultural-based school system. Thus, although Qatari society has become incredibly diverse since the oil boom, the education of Qatari nationals has remained fairly separated from the rest of society. Now, at the university level at least, the beginnings of change have started to flow. Young college-age women will be on campus with college-age men and will learn from professors from other countries. This innovative, unique blending of gender differences will create a more diverse foundation for the earlier years of education. Changes in a cultural belief cannot happen successfully overnight. The education reform system of Qatar appears to be aware of the challenges and seemingly has created the beginnings of a workable system. One of the most important challenges still facing Qatar today is the reform of the teacher education system.

Teacher Education

Hessa Sadiq, Dean of the Qatar University School of Education and leader of a new era of teacher education reform, has attempted to completely integrate its curriculum with the new, independent schools, as suggested by the RAND report. In 2006, the school of education received a license to run a prestigious independent (not government-controlled) school. This laboratory school will be a model for education reform and will provide direct experiences in independent school teaching for student teachers. The courses and programs of the school of education were based on the standards of accreditation institutions in the United States, such as NCATE (National Council for Accreditation of Teacher Education). Reform is not limited to teacher training; the promotion of independent research by faculty also is encouraged. The school of education has committed itself to a long-term development and reform plan to accommodate and encourage the growth of more independent schools; more independent teachers; and, most important, more independent, creative, and productive students.

Conclusion:
A Bright Future, Despite Social, Political, and Religious Dilemmas

Qatari education often seems precariously balanced between traditional, religious expectations, promoted by religious scholars (the official religious doctrine in Qatar, like Saudi Arabia, is Sunni Wahhabism), and free-thinking modernity, as represented by new media, economic development, and influences from expatriates. While the Sheikh, influenced by his own British education, has ultimate control over the government and education system, the influences of traditional religious expectations remain strong. Also, in the long term, high expectations for education as the ultimate source of economic development after the oil runs out may compromise the less immediately pragmatic and economic aspects of the educational curriculum.

Nevertheless, there are several reasons to predict a positive forecast for the future of Qatar's education reform. First, as discussed in this chapter, not only is Qatar's leadership fully behind the process of reform, but so is Qatari society in general. Also, in the hypercompetitive environment of gulf development, Qatar is determined to find a specific niche in education. The government has devoted tremendous resources and capital to the development of independent schools and a modernized curriculum at every level. Although some fear that the change will happen too fast, the relatively small and flexible state of Qatar's education system make it an ideal candidate for successful reform. As Qatar makes a name in education reform, other states in the region have already begun to take notice. Abu Dhabi in the United Arab Emirates, for example, has begun its own educational city and has encouraged the cooperation of international pedagogical techniques. If Qatar's education reform is a success, it is possible that even Qatar's neighbor Saudi Arabia, a highly traditional country, could eventually follow suit with substantial education reforms.

Notes:

[1] In Arab and Islamic society, the often exclusive, or at least dominant, use of Arabic in primary school has been seen as an essential way to maintain core Arab and Islamic values. According to Muslims, the only true and accurate copies of the Qur'an are in Arabic. Memorization of parts of the Qur'an, Arabic poetry, and sayings of the Prophet is an essential part of traditional Islamic learning. Translating the Qur'an into other languages or emphasizing other languages, even within the school curriculum, can potentially be seen as a challenge to traditional Islamic values. For these reasons, the introduction of significant amounts of English instruction in the early, primary levels, despite potential challenges from a religious point of view, is a special step forward even as Arabic and religious instruction is, of course, strictly maintained.

[2] In her book *The Development of Modern Education in the Gulf* (1985), Sheikha Misnad, the current President of Qatar University, discusses the many conservative challenges to Qatari education reform. These challenges come mainly from tribal and religious groups concerned with maintaining a patriarchal moral system.

[3] This number does not include international or community schools operating in Qatar. International and community schools are used mainly by the children of expatriate workers and have an independent structure. They are not subject to the same curriculum reforms or developments as schools under Supreme Education Council oversight (Sayed, 2007).

[4] For current English Standards, see the pdf download at this Supreme Education Council Address: www.education.gov.qa/CS/en/10f.pdf.

[5] According to Dr. Aliaa Al Khulaifi, director of the office of Curriculum Standards, "The Supreme Education Council's Education Institute has developed curriculum standards in four subjects: Arabic, English, mathematics, and science. Other subjects will also be taught at the Independent Schools but may vary from one school to another." www.english.education.gov.qa/section/sec/education_institute/cso/curriculum_standards

[6] See the Supreme Education Council Press Release on New National Professional Standards, www.english.education.gov.qa/content/resources/detail/5045

References and Resources

Al Attiyah, A., & Lazarus, B. (2007). "Hope in the life": The children of Qatar speak about inclusion. *Childhood Education, 83*, 366-369.

Al Said, M. (2002). *The State of Qatar's experience in the special needs field.* Doha, Qatar: Special Needs Committee, Supreme Council for Family Affairs.

Al-Thani, Sheikh Hamid bin Khalifa. (1999). *The opening of the 28th Ordinary Session of the Advisory Council*, 9 Nov. 1999. Retrieved from www.diwan.gov/qa/english/the_amir/the_amir_speeche_1.htm

Glaser, S. (2003, Feb. 2). Qatar reshapes its schools, putting English over Islam. *The Washington Post*, p. A20.

Misnad, Sheikha. (1985). *The development of modern education in the Gulf.* London: Ithaca Press.

Mozah, Sheikha Bint Nasser Al-Misnad. (2007). *Who are we?* www.qf.edu.qa/output/page295.asp

Nonneman, G. (June 2006). Political reform in the Gulf monarchies: From liberalisation to democratisation? A comparative Perspective. *Durham Middle East Papers*, No. 80, Sir William Luce Fellowship Paper No. 6.

Rand-Qatar Policy Institute. (2007). *Research brief: A new system for K-12 education in Qatar.* Santa Monica, CA: Author. Available at www.rand.org.

Sayed, A. (Ed.). (May 2007). *Schools and schooling in Qatar 2005-2006: A statistical overview.* Doha, Qatar: Evaluation Institutue of the Supreme Education Council.

Willis, T. (2004). *Qatar.* New York: Scholastic.

Yossef, A. (2002). *Inclusion: Students with special needs in general education. A report of the Social Education Unit, Ministry of Education.* Doha, Qatar: Ministry of Education.

About the Authors

Allen Fromherz is currently a professor at Georgia State University, teaching Middle Eastern and Mediterranean history. He can be reached at afromherz@gsu.edu.

Robin Wright Fromherz, Ph.D., is Coordinator of Early Childhood and Elementary Education at Willamette University School of Education MAT Program in Salem, Oregon. She can be reached at rfromher@willamette.edu

Overview of Curriculum Development in the Russian Federation

Elizabeth J. Sandell, Olga V. Klippa, and Maria S. Taratukhina

An old Russian parable tells the story of Alyosha, a boarding school student, who rescued a little black hen from a future as the main course at dinner. The hen belonged to an underground kingdom. The king rewarded Alyosha for his good deed with a magic seed of corn that enabled him to know his school lessons without having to study. Alyosha was sent back to his regular life with a warning from the underground king: "If you tell anyone about our underground kingdom, you will destroy our happiness and bring us much hardship." Alyosha was confident in his lessons, with the magic seed in his pocket, but he betrayed the kingdom. Eventually, Alyosha learned his life lessons about the importance of studying to learn and of treating others well. Alyosha returned to school and was determined to set a fine example in the future (Pogorelsky, 1829/2003).

During the past 200 years, Russian society (and therefore, education) has gone through many changes that are similar to those of American society: living in urban environments instead of rural settings, working with knowledge more than with one's hands, and using computers and media more than pianos or farm tools. Russians have learned the lesson of the Little Black Hen very well and are careful to study hard and get along with others.

Russia is geographically the largest nation in the world. It spans more than 11 time zones. The government is organized into 89 regions (known, variously, as *raions, oblasts, krais*, or *okrugs*). Since the fall of the Soviet structures, education programs and schools in the Russian Federation are making transitions from the systems and practices that existed during periods of centralized decision-making. These practices were honed throughout more than 300 years of tsarist rule and more than 70 years of Soviet authoritarianism.

For purposes of this chapter, some vocabulary is quite specific to the Russian education system. For example, "children," used for the Russian дети (dyet-ee), refers to youngsters between birth and age 6 years old. "Pu-

Russian Federation

pil," based on the Russian ученик (uch-en-ik), refers to those who are between 7 and 15 years old. "Student," for the Russian студент (stood-yent), refers to young adults attending post-secondary institutes and universities. When other Russian words or phrases are used, the pronunciation based on the English alphabet will be provided, as well as the English translation.

History of Education and Curriculum Development

Pre-Tsarist Period (prior to 1547)

Throughout early Russian history, there was little structure or consistency to educational opportunities throughout the Russian territories. Education in the pre-tsarist period was generally about surviving life through military skills, merchant trade, and agriculture resources. These skills were taught informally through the Russian мир (meer), or community-based village government, and passed along from parent to child or from master to apprentice. The Russian мир, besides its direct meanings in English of "peace" and "world," was used to denote the local self-government of peasant communities. More specifically, мир referred to the village or community, with the idea that all community members must work together to ensure mutual survival (such as by sharing work, food, shelter, and heat) (Richmond, 2003).

Mongol-Tatar invasions often interrupted social structures, including educational opportunities. The conquerors destroyed many old cities and their resources and values (Klypa, 2007).

Imperial Period (1547 to 1917)

Imperial leaders regarded education as one means to preserve and maintain society, but education was available only to a very small portion of the population. Schools for upper-class, male pupils taught a variety of academic subjects, as well as moral and character education, known as воспитание (vos-pit-an-ee-yeh), or upbringing. Teachers taught pupils, using such languages as Slavonic, Latin, and Greek, how to behave and get along with other people according to their status in society (Richmond, 2003).

The first private kindergarten was opened in St. Petersburg in 1863. Shortly thereafter (in 1866), the journal *Detsky Sad* (*Kindergarten*) began to be published. The 1870s saw the establishment of Ye. N. Vodovozova's publishing company, which produced books on teaching and popular science, as well as children's books. The teaching journals *Uchitel Vospitanie* (*Teacher Education*) and *Zhurnal Ministerstva Narodnogo Prosveshcheniya* (*Journal of the Ministry of Public Education*) published numerous articles about the system of early education created by Friedrich Froebel (Taratukhina et al., 2006).

In 1763, the first residential educational "house" for children between birth and 14 years of age was established in Moscow (Klypa, 2007). Often, more than 1,000 children lived in these houses, where they were trained for future work. Some children were prepared as manual laborers and some as skilled craftsmen, while others continued to university education.

In the early 19th century, the first Russian gymnasia were established in major provincial centers as secondary schools for boys and young men. Pupils often attended schools in provinces other than those in which their parents lived. Many schools, such as the Imperial Lyceum near Saint Petersburg, were founded by the Emperor Alexander I. For 44 years, the Imperial Lyceum educated noble youths (including the famous Russian poet Alexandr Pushkin) so that they would grow up to occupy important positions in the Imperial service (Viltchkovsky, 1910).

Throughout the 19th century, the Russian Empire had a small number of schools (categorized as "chapel school communities" by Gromyko and St. Maurice, 2000) that were similar to the common or one-room schools of the United States. In Russia, the curriculum of these communities included uniform teaching and learning activities (such as memorization and recitation) conducted for small groups of pupils from among the nobility and social elite. The history of the empire's expansion was an important part of the curriculum. The textbooks did not often refer to cultural, language, or ethnic groups among the broader population (Klypa, 2007; Loskoutova, 2002; Manning, 1982).

After the abolition of serfdom in 1861, the Russian economy became increasingly industrialized and urbanized. There were a variety of reforms and adaptations in all elements of education, including re-organization of schools, expansion of the school networks, and new curricula and textbooks. Shortly after 1860, progressive educators experimented with new themes and methodologies, including the concept of kindergarten, translated into детский сад (dyet-sky sod), literally "children's garden," in Russian (Kirschenbaum, 2000). The first kindergartens were private, tuition-based, and unavailable to poor families. The curriculum included games, gymnastics, excursions, stories, the alphabet, and reading. In 1896, there were 66 registered kindergartens throughout European Russia (Klypa, 2007).

Schools increasingly became places to shape the character of pupils through teacher instruction and correction (Klypa, 2007). Studitskii (1843, cited in Loskoutova, 2002) reported that the daily lives of pupils (their intellectual capacities, their family and community environments, etc.) became the very objects of their study and exploration. Teachers were trained in observation of individual children in order to plan for their optimum development (Klypa, 2007). The curriculum was planned in ways that guided the pupil from studying the familiar to studying the strange and unknown.

Education came to be regarded as a means to promote the efficient social progress needed for working in the industrial plants and factories. Learning opportunities expanded through the establishment of more schools (categorized as "production school communities" by Gromyko and St. Maurice, 2000). Until that period, according to Vesin (1877, cited in Loskoutova, 2002), there were only about 230 different published learning materials and games in Russia. Schools became divided into efficient, regimented, age-specific, and subject-specific learning environments. The result of all this activity, according to the 1897 census, was that only 28.4% of the population was literate (Klypa, 2007; Loskoutova, 2002).

In the early 20th century, alternative schools were established, often organized in an "underground" fashion and in opposition to schools sponsored by the government for the more elite. The curriculum in this type of school community included values formation through strong social and spiritual traditions. In 1900, the first kindergarten home for deaf children opened, followed by others in St. Petersburg (1902) and Kiev (1904) (Klypa, 2007).

Teacher training became more systematic. In 1909, a one-year training program was started in Moscow. The program included human physiology, psychology, pedagogical psychology, preschool education, outdoor games and gymnastics, hygiene, children's literature, drawing, singing, and manual skills. In 1911, a magazine known as *Preschool Education* was started. By 1917, there were approximately 250 kindergartens that were provided free of charge (Klypa, 2007).

Soviet Period (1917 to 1991)

The Soviet revolution of 1917 led to a complete overhaul of the education system, in order to incorporate the new political and economic assumptions. The Soviet Period was characterized by a totalitarian society, in which decisions were made centrally by a single authoritarian party based in Moscow. Soviet leaders regarded education as the means to put ideological, economic, and social changes into practice throughout the country (Matyash, 1991; Richmond, 2003).

The state took very seriously the way future leaders were shaped and used education as a way to ensure that children and youth developed "right" ways of thinking and working. Children as young as kindergarten age started their lifelong process of indoctrination into Soviet political and social values (Klypa, 2007; Richmond, 2003; Valkanova & Brehony, 2006).

According to Heller and Nekrich (1986), the Soviet approach to education may be attributed to Anton Makarenko, who had worked with homeless and delinquent youth for many years. Makarenko believed that education should be organized as if it were a labor collective and operated according to military discipline. Important distinctions of the Soviet approach included school uniforms, large classes, rote learning and memorization, authoritarian methods, oral examinations, rigid funding and budgeting, and centrally controlled curriculum (Eklof & Dneprov, 1993). Pearson (1990) even observed that pupils in schools as far apart as Moscow and Novosibirsk were likely to be on the same page in the same geography book on the same day.

The Soviet education system between 1924 and 1991 also was characterized by its equity and access. The Soviet decision-makers instituted universal compulsory education intended to lift the population out of illiteracy and into training for success at work. Millions of illiterate people all over the country, including residents of small towns and villages, were enrolled in special literacy schools. A huge network of so-called "national schools" was established by the 1930s, and this network continued to increase enrollments throughout the Soviet period. The literacy rate rose to 56.6% of the population in 1926 and grew to 87.4% in 1939 (population census data) (Anderson & Silver, 1984).

Education at all levels was free to all students who qualified. Girls were encouraged to secure an education and pursue a career in the factory or the office. Communal nurseries were set up for the care of small children, and efforts were made to shift the center of people's social life from the home to educational and recreational groups. The education systems followed the Soviet ideas of "collectives," in which teachers were grouped into teams of workers that were responsible for the production of educated citizens according to the definitions and curriculum of the central authorities.

Teachers and assistants in Soviet kindergartens, детских садов (dyet-sky sod-of), took care of very young children (between birth and age 5 or 6 years) while their parents worked. Elementary schools were the "beginning" level, начальное (nah-chal-noh-ye), for formal education, and lasted for three or four years. Secondary schools included the next six or seven years of school and were called "incomplete secondary education," неполное среднее образование (neh-pol-no-ye sredne-ye ob-raz-ah-van-i-yeh). Since 1958, this level was compulsory for all pupils and optional for under-educated adults (who could study in so-called "evening schools"). After 1981, taking two or three additional years to complete the "secondary education" level became compulsory. These years could be completed in a secondary education, vocational institute, or college setting (Richmond, 2003).

The Soviet education collectives incorporated elements of the "production school communities" and characteristics of "club school communities" (categorized by Gromyko & St. Maurice, 2000) in order to achieve social and cultural goals as well as educational aims. Richmond (2003) described how, as they entered primary school, pupils were first organized into the "Octobrists." Their educational program included "work," such as cleaning up their school rooms, evaluating the viewpoints and performance of other pupils, and learning about Comrade Josef Stalin, Lenin, and the Soviet Motherland. During their third year of school, pupils were organized into the "Young Pioneers." Their group indoctrination was correspondingly increased. Later, at about age 14, pupils were pressured to join the Young Communist League, important for their future membership in the Communist Party.

Eklof and Dneprov (1993) concluded that schools during the Soviet period actually fostered Communist orthodoxy and squelched individual invention and enterprise. Pupils were in school for up to six hours a day and for five or six days each week. Youngsters were usually grouped by ability and performance levels, and segregated by curricula specializations (e.g., sciences, arts and humanities, and industries and trades).

Reform Period or Transition Period (1991 to 2001)

Efim Kogan, Head of the Education Department of Samara Oblast, described the Reform Period (also called the Transition or post-Soviet Period) as the time of change from a dictatorial society to a pluralistic society based on a market-driven, liberal economy in which people "have a right to think what they want to think" (Fishman, 1999, p. 370). The Soviet Ministry of Education lost its centralized power and control. Local and regional educators, parents, and administrators were given a previously unknown level of autonomy.

In 1998, the State Education Standard document was designed to provide equivalent educational standards and academic qualifications across Russia. Beginning in 2007, national pupil assessment at the conclusion of secondary school has provided outcome assessment regarding pupil achievement, rather than assessment of input (required content) and process (e.g., length of course, hours of class, etc.) (Zajda, 2003).

In 2000, two major education policy papers were adopted: the *National Doctrine on Education Growth* and the *Federal Program on Developments in Education to 2010* (Ministry of General and Professional Education, 2000). The Basic Curriculum Plan (known as the Moscow Basic Curriculum) prescribed a 12-year model of public education.

According to Zajda (2003), the Reform Period was characterized by three popular slogans: democracy, humanization, and individuation. Slogans, however, have not necessarily translated well to implementation strategies in teacher education and in pupil learning experiences. (See the chapter section on Dilemmas.) Several authors (Kogan, cited in Fishman, 1999, and Zajda, 2003) maintain that there are still two basic problems in education in the Russian Federation: inadequate financing of education and out-of-date decision-making processes.

CURRENT EDUCATION

Introduction

Following the Reform Period, the Russian government has started to pass laws to set the stage with regulations and financing for regional education authorities to implement the required reforms. However, the transition and changes in regulations are not complete. Kogan described some examples of changes in one oblast (or state) that included implementation of curriculum standards for the region's schools; changes in categories of certification for teachers, administrative leaders, and schools; reformation in teachers' work situations; and overhaul in the financing of education programs. Other changes have included revised curricula, decentralized decision-making, the addition of elective courses, and official permission to allow private schools (Fishman, 1999). There was an additional year of secondary education added in 2007, to make a total of 12 years of compulsory education.

Gromyko and St. Maurice (2000) categorized some efforts as "experimental school communities," similar to "charter schools" in the United States. Social organizations or religious groups, as well as regional governments, were allowed to sponsor such schools. The curriculum and specific civic focus are determined by the sponsors. Such schools illustrate the increased freedom being given to teachers to try out new teaching techniques.

As technology in Russian education advances, some learning experiences are organized into "network school communities" (Gromyko & St. Maurice, 2000). These virtual communities exist in cyberspace through television networks or Internet connections. The learning groups are characterized by a lack of face-to-face personal contact and exist only online or through interactive video programs. Schools in Russia, as in the United States, may turn to networking to maintain learning opportunities in times of declining population and decreasing financial resources.

Definition of Curriculum

The Basic Curriculum Plan (also known as the Moscow Basic Curriculum) has called for a 12-year model of public education, generally from age 6 years to 18 years (Federal Institute for Education Planning, 1997). The key objectives of Russian education are to 1) develop the individual, 2) provide necessary knowledge and skills, and 3) contribute to social change and society. The curriculum now includes many new subjects, such as ecology, economics, and foreign languages. Many decision-makers perceive that a "good" education leads to the best jobs, with income, social status, and privilege; consequently, economic goals receive much attention (Zajda, 2003).

Curriculum is viewed as transforming teacher behavior and student knowledge for the future Russian democracy and market economy. Cuban (1993) noted that decision-makers often mistakenly assume that curriculum can directly and independently impact understanding and behavior in terms of government and economics. Zajda (2003) suggests that this may certainly be the case in Russia, where decision-makers have had the time or inclination to discuss only the "official curriculum," that which governmental authorities define about what teachers are supposed to teach and what pupils should learn. Russian reformers are still attending to centralized decisions about educational content and about school efficiency. The other three types of curriculum (i.e., that which is actually taught in the classroom, that which is actually learned by the pupils, and that which is tested on the exams and assessments) have not received much attention.

Curriculum and Teaching Methods: Kindergarten and Early Childhood Education

Some children attend kindergarten, which refers to the Russian child care system for children between birth and age 6 or 7 years old. These programs are less common in recent times because of financial issues. When children attend kindergarten today, their families usually pay some tuition and fees.

According to Taratukhina (2006), kindergartens are organized into one or more of the following categories of curriculum:

- Kindergartens that emphasize one or several directions of child development (e.g., intellectual, artistic and aesthetic, physical, etc.)
- Kindergartens that emphasize compensation and skilled correction of abnormalities in children's physical or psychological development
- Kindergartens that emphasize health improvement, including sanitation, hygiene, and prophylaxis measures and procedures
- Kindergartens that emphasize general development, compensation, and health improvements in various combinations
- Child development centers that emphasize physical and psychological development, as well as correction and health improvement of all children who attend.

According to Melnik and Sidlovskaja (2002), a typical kindergarten may include more than 150 children who meet in a large school building. Each class is grouped together by age level. The environments are especially designed for small children and may include an art room, a gymnasium, a music room, a game room, a television or theater room, bedrooms, cloakrooms, bathrooms, kitchen, and display areas for exhibits of teachers' and children's works.

Kindergarten staff members include: administrators and secretaries, teachers (two for each group), helpers (to make meals, keep things clean, and assist teachers during lessons), a sports coordinator, a music teacher, speech and language teachers, a nurse, and a cook. Once a week, the psychologist may give advice on child-raising issues during a parents meeting.

Kindergartens may open early, about 7:00 a.m., and children may arrive between then and 9:00 a.m. Children have morning exercises, wash their faces, brush their teeth, and eat their breakfast. At about 9:00 a.m., formal group lessons begin. Young children may have only one lesson each day, while older children may have two to three lessons. Lessons may include math and communication skills, as well as ecology, music, drama, drawing, modeling, appliqué work, sports, and language lessons.

Outdoor activities are important year-round. During warm weather, children go outside to play and ride tricycles. During cold weather, children go outside to skate and ski. Children go on supervised walks to observe nature and to play. They also go on excursions to theaters, museums, and expositions.

At midday, children have lunch and take a long nap (between 1-1/2 to 3 hours). Then children have breathing and health-improvement exercises, as well as gymnastics. During the afternoon, children might play or have special organized activities, such as arts and craft class, dancing club, etc. Children often eat dinner at kindergarten. Parents arrive between 5:00 p.m. and 6:30 p.m. to pick up their children.

General Elementary Education

According to the Russian Federation Constitution, six years of general elementary education is compulsory and open to the public. The Moscow Basic Curriculum (Federal Institute for Education Planning, 1997) outlines the required curriculum goals for general elementary education:

- Progress of the pupil's personality, creative abilities, interest in studies, and will and ability to learn
- Development of moral and aesthetic senses, system of values and emotions, and positive attitude towards the pupil's self and the surrounding world
- Assimilation of the system of knowledge, skills, abilities, and experience of performing various activities
- Development of the pupil's physical and mental health
- Sustainable development of the pupil's personality.

The Moscow Basic Curriculum is built on the idea that the development of pupils' personality and abilities occurs during various activities, such as studying and learning, and practical and social activities. The general elementary education curriculum acknowledges that pupils come to school with different training, different social experience, and varied psychological and physiological backgrounds. So, the mission of general elementary education is to help every pupil to realize his or her abilities and to provide necessary conditions for each individual's development.

The Moscow Basic Curriculum lists the following compulsory core subjects for general elementary education: Russian language, literature and reading, foreign language, mathematics, world environment, arts, music, technology, physical education. Schools may teach in Russian or in a native, non-Russian ethnic language. When available, computer practice is provided.

Pupils who successfully complete general elementary education may continue into general secondary education.

General Secondary Education

According to the Russian Federation Constitution, general secondary education is also compulsory and open to the public. The Moscow Basic Curriculum outlines the required curriculum goals for general secondary education:

- Formation of an integral world view, based on acquired knowledge, skills, experience, and work methods
- Gaining experience in various activities (personal and collective), cognition, and self-actualization
- Preparations for conscious choice of personal learning or professional direction.

The Moscow Basic Curriculum is based on the idea that general secondary education will be adjusted in content for age-specific characteristics of teenagers, with activities that are applicable to real-life situations, self-awareness, and recognition of their world surroundings. The standard is knowledge-oriented and activity-oriented, which helps to increase learning motivation and realize child's abilities, potentials, requirements, and interests to the fullest extent. The specific character of secondary school teaching goals is linked more with the pupil's personal development, than with his or her learning progress.

One of the major requirements for this educational stage is achieving functional literacy in mathematics and natural sciences, as well as in sociology and culture. Another of the main aims of secondary school is preparing pupils to make informed decisions about their future lives (such as career choices). According to the Moscow Basic Curriculum, the basic requirement for this step is consistency, individualized instruction, and pre-professional training.

The Moscow Basic Curriculum lists the following compulsory core subjects for general secondary education: Russian language, literature, foreign language, mathematics, information and communication technologies, history, social studies (including economics and law), geography, nature studies, physics, chemistry, biology, arts (fine arts and music), technology, safety of living, and physical education. Schools may teach in Russian or in a native, non-Russian ethnic language.

Around 1991, military education was removed from school curricula. It returned, however, in 2000 to prepare boys, especially, for their mandatory service in the armed forces. Girls are now trained in basic nursing techniques so they can assist with medical care of soldiers (Richmond, 2003). Administrators are finding that pupils, after grade nine, often actually leave the school building and enroll in экстернат (ek-ster-nat), an off-campus, correspondence type of program (Zajda, 2003).

The level of general secondary education ends with compulsory final state examinations. The examinations are developed on the basis of state standard requirements for the pupil's level of training.

Senior Secondary Education

Senior secondary education is the final stage of general education in the Russian Federation, and is open to the public according to the Russian Federation Laws.

The Moscow Basic Curriculum outlines the approach of senior secondary education as one that provides for individual educational needs and interests, and that cultivates the importance of making right choices with respect to professional growth and engagement in meaningful social circles. Moreover, the program supports pupils in their understanding of citizenship and civil rights. The required curriculum goals for senior secondary education include:

- Formation of an individual's civil responsibility and legal consciousness, spirituality and culture, self-dependence, creativity, and ability for successful socialization in the society
- Differentiated education with broad and flexible opportunities for developing individual educational programs for high school students, based on their abilities, needs, and affections
- Providing students with equal opportunities for further professional education and career, considering actual labor market demands.

Educational courses have two levels: basic and subject. The basic level of the educational course standard focuses on the formation of a common culture and is linked mostly to the socialization tasks of general education (e.g., view of the world, education, and progress). The subject level of the educational course standard is chosen according to the personal preferences and affections of a pupil and is oriented on the pupil's preparations for further professional education or professional occupation.

The law gives senior secondary education institutions the responsibility to consider their resources and the educational requirements of pupils and their parents (or a pupil's legal representatives), thus forming their own education plans (e.g., the certain set of subjects, whether taught at the basic or subjects level of education).

The Moscow Basic Curriculum lists the following core subjects for senior secondary education: Russian language, literature, foreign language, mathematics, informatics and information and communication technologies, history, social studies, economics, law, geography, biology, physics, chemistry, natural studies, world art and culture, technology, safety of living, and physical education.

The level of senior secondary education ends with compulsory final state examinations. The examinations are developed on the base of state standard requirements for the pupils' level of training. The pupils who finish senior secondary education and fit specific requirements have a right to continue their training in educational institutions of primary, secondary, and higher professional education.

FACTORS THAT INFLUENCE CURRICULUM DEVELOPMENT

Culture, Ethnicity, and Language

The Russian Federation reportedly includes approximately 160 different ethnic groups (*Goskomstat,* 2002). Twenty percent of the members of the Russian population do not consider themselves Russians (Aklaev, 1997). According to Obidovskii (1844, cited in Loskoutova, 2002), early school curricula ignored the history and ethnic composition of regional populations. Later, Soviet educators built education around a policy of "indigenization," from the mid-1920s to the late 1930s. The development and use of non-Russian languages in education was viewed as the fastest way to increase the educational levels of younger generations. Soviet native-language and bilingual education resulted in widespread literacy in dozens of languages among the indigenous people groups, accompanied by widespread and growing bilingualism (Anderson & Silver, 1984).

Economic conditions have made equal access to education a serious issue in post-communist Russia. As noted in this chapter, a lack of resources is beginning to hinder pupil enrollment in schools. Decentralized decision-making allows some schools to discourage pupil enrollment on grounds of ethnicity, religion, language, and gender. Zajda (2003) reports that administrators at schools in some provinces have discouraged Muslim girls from completing their secondary education.

Disabilities and Giftedness

Another aspect of the Soviet inflexibility was the high rate at which pupils were held back and required to repeat a year of school. In the early 1950s, typically 8 to 10% of the pupils in elementary grades were held back a year. This was partly attributable to the pedagogical style of teachers, and partly to the fact that many of these children had disabilities that impeded their performance.

In the latter part of the 1950s, however, the Ministry of Education began to promote the creation of a wide variety of special schools for children with physical or mental disabilities. Once those children were taken out of the mainstream schools, and once teachers began to be held accountable for the repeat rates of their pupils, the retention rates fell sharply. By the mid-1960s, the repeat rates in the general primary schools declined to about 2%, and to less than 1% by the late 1970s (Anderson, Silver, & Velkoff, 1987). Today, children who are gifted and talented still are able to enroll in special schools that emphasize mathematics, science, the arts, or foreign languages.

DILEMMAS IN CURRICULUM DEVELOPMENT AND PEDAGOGY

Social (Transitions in Individual Decision-making and Responsibility)

Social transitions toward more individual and community-based decision-making and responsibility are challenging the previous centralized, authoritarian approach to determining educational curricula and programming. Some school districts are organizing "guardianship counsels," similar to local school district boards of education in the United States. These counsels may eventually have the responsibility to determine educational programs and curricula. Kogan (cited in Fishman, 1999) noted that the country does not yet have a tradition of civic boards that would prepare the citizenry for this process, so this development may prove challenging.

Political (Transitions in Power and Authority)

Educational curricula are caught among the transitions in political power and authority. Some, such as Kogan (in Fishman, 1999), see the federal government's authority as determining the key tasks or goals of education, along with the main general strategies. However, in the chaos of the Reform

Period, the national system of educational regulations has not been revised fast enough to adapt to new ways of thinking. Proposed but not-yet-implemented reforms have included standardized assessments at the end of secondary education, which would evaluate education in terms of outputs (student achievement and learning) rather than inputs (such as numbers of courses and hours of instruction).

Even during a period of transition to individual choice and decision-making, some leaders, such as Kogan (in Fishman, 1999), view the worth of an individual in his or her value to the state. Kogan declared the government's main goal or aim is to "organize life in a way that allows the individual's interests to work for the benefit of the State and of society and to use these interests with maximum efficiency." Kogan and others see education as an investment in an individual that assumes future reimbursement from the individual through service to the society by a life well-lived.

Economic (Transition to Market Economy)

In the Soviet Union, education at all levels was free for anybody who could pass entrance exams. The downside of that system was that institutions had to be funded entirely from the federal and regional budgets; therefore, after the collapse of the Soviet Union, expenditures for education were reduced to general block grants to regional authorities; institutions found themselves unable to provide adequate teachers' salaries, to subsidize students' scholarships, and to maintain their school facilities. Zajda (2003) reported that some wealthy regions were able to spend four to six times as much on education as the poorer regions.

Until this time, Kogan suggests, educational leaders have only been concerned with keeping school costs low, often by hiring teachers with low credentials. However, school financial strategies are emerging that are based on student enrollment. Therefore, educational leaders face actual competition for students to enroll in their educational institutions.

The free market economy has mystified many Russians, who are only familiar and comfortable with the old Soviet-style system of assignments. Meanwhile, one result, according to Zajda (2003), is that students from wealthy families will increasingly be able to afford and to access the high-demand courses at highly selective schools, школах лицеях (shkol-ah lit sey yah), while students from poor families will find limited opportunities at state-run schools. School enrollment statistics seem to support this observation. Upper secondary education has experienced declines in enrollment rates from 66% in the early 1990s to 59% in 1998. Analysts report that this may be due to students dropping out of school to seek employment (Zajda, 2003).

Kogan (in Fishman, 1999) advocates the idea that educational leaders implement programs that carefully consider the needs of the student, the student's family, and the community. In turn, this will encourage more students to attend specific schools and therefore generate more funding for those schools.

Religious (State and Individual Religion)

During the Imperial Period, schools and academies were often sponsored by the Russian Orthodox Church. Being "Russian" was synonymous with being "Russian Orthodox." During the Communist Period, the central government provided financial support for schools and academies. The religious content of education changed from Russian Orthodox to almost literal worship of Communism. Young people in Russian today can remember singing songs of devotion and praise to Comrade Lenin during their kindergarten years (Morison, 1987).

During the Transition Period, educators scrambled to find curriculum for history classes that would address cultural values and history in ways that avoided repeating Communist ideology. Pending new curriculum, teachers taught enthusiastically about the pre-Communist Russian (i.e., Orthodox) religious heritage and culture. In 1989, the State Committee for Public Education decided that there should be more emphasis on the humanities and that teaching was to become more "humanized." Sutherland (1999) pointed out that this actually meant that teachers were to show more respect for the child and the child's human spirit and individual skills and interests.

Educators increasingly discuss this humanization as a subject that, as translated into English, is the "spiritual development" of children and the impact of their school experience on that development. In actuality, this topic in Russia is related to ethical values and moral behavior, rather than religious beliefs (Husband, 1994; Klypa, 2007).

Education (Transitions in Local Decision-making and Autonomy)

Regional and local governments and education leaders are assuming responsibility for the implementation of federal goals and tasks for education. However, each of the 89 regions has its own special characteristics based on culture, traditions, levels of education, and economics, as well as the personalities of its leaders. Some regions have accomplished changes in regional regulations, regional organizational structures, and school finance. One of the main challenges to educational leaders, according to Kogan (cited in Fishman, 1999), is to make changes that avoid a "mess," so there is still room to make changes to meet future challenges and regulations.

In reality, as observed by Zajda (2003), regional administrators are making difficult decisions, such as using limited resources to pay for heat and medical personnel to keep hospitals open and warm in the winter or to pay for heat and teacher salaries to keep schools open in the winter. Zajda (2003) reports that rural schools make up more than two-thirds of the total schools in Russia. Approximately 1% of the rural schools closed between 1996 and 1998 due to lack of economic resources. More than 17% of the rural schools have two shifts of students, often taught by the same group of teachers. Only about half the rural school buildings have water and almost two-thirds have no sewer system. Class size is about 35 pupils, compared to the recommended maximum of 24 pupils.

CONCLUSION

Teachers in the Russian Federation are going through tremendous changes in their political, social, and economic situations. Education reform requires fundamental shifts in philosophies, values, and goals throughout the entire education system and even throughout the entire society.

In spite of serious economic issues, teachers are creatively addressing their challenges and maintaining their commitment to rethinking and redesigning curriculum and instruction. Teachers and teacher educators are beginning to consider ways of reasoning, questioning, and talking about assumptions of knowledge and culture. These discussions are difficult when decisions cause stress, loss of faith in the government, and alienation from the community among teachers.

Education curriculum in the Russian Federation, as elsewhere in the world, may benefit from international partnerships for action research in the real-world of teaching and learning. Collaborative field studies will help educators engage in self-examination and mutual exchange of best practices that consider the social, economic, and political dimensions of education in the next period.

References

Aklaev, A. (1997). *Interethnic conflict and political change in Russia and former Soviet Union: An annotated bibliography of Russian articles (1993-1995).* Airat Aklaev, Compiler, with contributions by Nadezhda Lebedeva. Dundas, Ontario, Canada: Peace Research Institute-Dundas.

Anderson, B. A., & Silver, B. D. (1984, December). Equality, efficiency, and politics in Soviet bilingual education policy: 1934-1980. *American Political Science Review, 78,* 1019-1039.

Anderson, B. A., Silver, B. D., & Velkoff, V. A. (1987). Education of the handicapped in the USSR: Exploration of the statistical picture. *Soviet Studies, 39,* 468-488.

Cuban, S. (1993). The lure of curriculum reform and its pitiful history. *Phi Delta Kappan, 75*(2), 182-185.

Eklof, B., & Dneprov, E. (Eds.). (1993). *Democracy in the Russian school: The reform movement in education since 1984.* Boulder, CO: Westview Press.

Federal Institute for Education Planning. (1997). *Osnovnye polozheniia kontseptsii ocherednogo etapa reformirovaniia sistemy obrazovaniia Rossiiskoi Federatsii* [Basic propositions: Conceptions of the next step in reforming the system of education of the Russian Federation]. Moscow: Federal'nyi institut planirovaniia obrazovaniia.

Fishman, L. (1999). "To implement reforms in education means first of all understanding expected outcomes." An interview with Dr. Efrim Kogan (Samara, Russia). *International Journal of Leadership in Education: Theory and Practice, 2*(4), 369-376.

Goskomstat. State Committee on Statistics of the Russian Federation. (n.d.). *Itogi vserossiskoi perepisi naseleniia 2002 goda.* [All-Russia Population Census.] Moscow. Retrieved July 19, 2007, from *http://udbstat. eastview.com, Eastview Information Services.*

Gromyko, Y., & St. Maurice, H. (2000). Constructions of community: Aspects of cultural historical study of school curriculum. *Discourse: Studies in the Cultural Politics of Education, 21*(2), 193-204.

Heller, M., & Nekrich, A. M. (1986). *Utopia in power: The history of the Soviet Union from 1917 to the present* (P. B. Carlos, Trans.). New York: Summit Books.

Husband, W. B. (1994). History education and historiography in Soviet and post-Soviet Russia. In A. Jones (Ed.), *Education and society in the new Russia* (pp. 119-139). Armonk, NY: Sharp Publishers.

Kirschenbaum, L. (2000). The kindergarten and the revolutionary tradition in Russia. In R. Wollons (Ed.), *Kindergartens and cultures: The global diffusion of an idea* (pp. 195-213). New Haven, CT: Yale University Press.

Klypa, O. V. (2007). (unpublished manuscript). *History of kindergarten education in Russia.* Magadan, RU: Northern International University.

Loskoutova, M. V. (2002). A motherland with a radius of 300 miles: Regional identity in Russian secondary and post-elementary education from the early nineteenth century to the war and revolution. *European Review of History—Revue européenne d'histoire, 9*(1), 7-22.

Manning, R. (1982). *The crisis of the old order in Russia: Gentry and government.* Princeton, NJ: Princeton University Press.

Matyash, O. (1991). Social values and aims in Soviet education. *Journal of Education for Teaching, 17*(1), 5- 9.

Melnik, O., & Sidlovskaja, O. (2002). Daily life in a regular Russian kindergarten. *Childhood Education, 78,* 341. Retrieved July 19, 2007, from FindArticles.com http://findarticles.com/p/articles/mi_qa3614/is_200201/ai_n9060121.

Ministry of General and Professional Education. (2000, August 29). *Uchitelskaia gazeta (Teachers' Journal),* 10.

Morison, J. (1987). Recent developments in political education in the Soviet Union. In G. Avis (Ed.), *The making of the Soviet citizen. Character formation and civic training in Soviet education* (pp. 123-149). New York: Croom Helm.

Obidovskii, A. (1844). *Kratkaia geografia Rossiiskoi Imperii* (2nd ed.). St. Petersburg, Russia: Imperial Academy of Sciences.

Federal Institute for Education Planning. (1997). *Osnovnye polozheniia kontseptsii ocherednogo etapa reformirovaniia sistemy obrazovaniia Rossiiskoi Federatsii* [Basic propositions: Conceptions of the next step in reforming the system of education of the Russian Federation]. Moscow: Federal'nyi institut planirovaniia obrazovaniia.

Pearson, L. (1990). *Children of glasnost: Growing up Soviet.* Seattle, WA: University of Washington Press.

Pogorelsky, A. (2003). *The little black hen*. (Retold by E. James). Verona, NJ: Simply Read Books. (Original work published 1829)

Richmond, Y. (2003). *From nyet to da: Understanding the Russians*. Yarmouth, ME: Intercultural Press.

Sutherland, J. (1999). *Schooling in the new Russia: Innovation and change 1984-1995*. London: Macmillan.

Taratukhina, M., & others. (2006). *Early childhood care and education in the Russian Federation. Paper commissioned for the EFP Global Monitoring Report 2007, Strong foundations: Early childhood care and education*. Paris, France: UNESCO.

Valkanova, Y., & Brehony, K. J. (2006). The gifts and "contributions": Friedrich Froebel and Russian education (1850-1929). *History of Education, 35*(2), 189-207.

Viltchkovsky, S. N. (1910). *Tsarskoe Selo: 1710-1910*. Saint Petersburg: Palace Administration of Tsarskoe Selo. Retrieved July 12, 2007, from www.alexanderpalace.org/tsarskoe/lyceum.html.

Zajda, J. (2003). Educational reform and transformation in Russia: Why education reforms fail. *European Education, 35*(1), 58-88.

About the Authors

Elizabeth J. Sandell, Ph.D., Educational Studies, College of Education, Minnesota State University, Mankato, Minnesota. Contact: 507-389-5713; elizabeth.sandell@mnsu.edu.

Olga Victorovna Klypa, Ph.D., Educational Studies, North-Eastern State University, Magadan, Russian Federation. Contact: 4132-63-07-71; ovk61@mail.ru.

Maria S. Taratukhina, Ph.D., Pedagogical Faculty, A. I. Hertzen Institute of Childhood, Russian State Pedagogical University, St. Petersburg, Russian Federation. Contact: maria_013@mail.ru.

Curriculum Development in Scotland

Kevin Kelman and June Mitchell

According to many commentators on the history and development of the Scottish education system, two significant myths form the background to descriptions of both the past and the present.[1] These foundational myths concern social egalitarianism (McCrone, 2001) and educational democracy (Paterson, 2003). Both are predicated on aspirations to provide opportunities for all learners to succeed through common provision of neighborhood schooling and a broad and general education. The legislation behind the myths and the aspirations has been well-documented and may be familiar to many readers, as Scotland has enjoyed a reputation for having established universal education very early—during the 16th and 17th centuries. With a history of legislative support for the establishment of a national education system, there are continuing perceptions that Scotland was a significant influence on the development of formal education in worldwide terms. According to Anderson (2003), the Scottish lowlands were among the more literate areas of Europe during the early stages of the industrial revolution. Herman (2002) is struck by the combination of poverty and high levels of learning. Despite the country's relative poverty and small population, Scottish culture had a built-in bias towards reading, learning, and education in general.

What might be the reasons for this early and successful implementation of educational provision, which seems to have transcended economic wealth and social status? Herman (2002) argues that there was a cultural disposition toward valuing learning and toward honoring the right of individuals as members of Scottish society to become literate. Literacy skills were supported by both church and secular agencies and were valued for the contribution made to the education of artisans, merchants, and farmers. Literacy was also at the core of traditions of self-improvement and self-education, particularly significant for the working classes. It was considered to be a distinctive feature of Scottish education that able children from parish schools have opportunities to access bursaries and to enter university level education, returning to their communities as ministers of religion or school

Scotland

teachers.

From 1901 until the 1960s, the basic curriculum in the post-elementary sector concentrated on history, geography, elementary science, physical training, and some craft skills, as well as English and mathematics. However, state schooling in both elementary and post-elementary sectors also was used to promote social welfare with statutory school meals and medical inspections.

Further significant developments in relation to the curriculum relate to a move in the 1960s from the selection of pupils for senior or junior secondary schooling to comprehensive schools and an extension of national certification of academic attainment in the secondary and tertiary sectors. In 1965, the selective system in the state sector was abolished, and mixed comprehensive schools were made available to all pupils. Currently, 96% of pupils in Scotland attend local comprehensive primary and secondary schools.

As a broad generalization, a standardization and uniformity of approach emanated from policy initiatives during the period of the 1960s until the late 1990s, as local education authorities sought to implement national guidelines for curriculum and assessment. It may be worth noting here that legislation in Scottish education focuses on organization and administration, and curricula decisions are based on the recommendations from the Scottish Executive Education Department. Education acts require adherence, and the acts are supplemented by regulations and circulars that local education authorities develop as policies and recommended practices.

In 2000, five National Priorities were established that constitute the aspirations for parents, pupils, and educators working in partnership (www.nationalpriorities.org.uk/) to further develop an education system in which democratic and egalitarian principles are core values. Additionally, a consultation exercise, *The National Debate on Education* (2002), invited all citizens to offer their views on a long-term vision for education in Scotland. The debate started a process of further legislation and curriculum reform, which is being implemented during this decade. A *Curriculum for Excellence* (2004) is the significant development that might be considered the outcome of these initiatives.

The themes indicated in this lightly sketched overview of the establishment of the education system in Scotland continue to have impact on the state provision of schooling and on how the curriculum enacts the aspirations. The rest of this chapter offers a more detailed examination of the curricula of primary/elementary and secondary levels of the national system.

History of Elementary Curriculum Structure

Elementary schooling was placed on a fully statutory basis for the first time in 1872 in Scotland. As its name suggests, the elementary school's function was to teach the elements, often referred to as the "three Rs." The 1872 Act made schooling compulsory, although children could be exempted if they could demonstrate a satisfactory ability in reading, writing, and arithmetic. In addition to the three Rs, the most commonly taught subject in schools before the 1872 Act was religious education.

At the end of the 19th century, the Scottish Education Department (SED), as it was known, determined the grants that they issued to schools on the basis of pupils' results in tests of the *Six Standards*. The progression of the curriculum in reading, writing, and arithmetic, at that time, can be seen from the basic *Standard I* through to the much more complex *Standard VI*.[2]

These *Standards* influenced the structure of the curriculum and were designed to indicate the progress through the stages of elementary education. The grants, which were effectively payments by results, were abolished in Scotland in the late 1880s, a decision that was widely welcomed by teachers. Further significant changes occurred in the 1890s when the tests in the *Standards*, and then the *Standards* themselves, were abolished, too.

After the abolition of the *Standards*, schools were being encouraged to develop their own curricula. However, as Anderson (1995) observes, the flexibility was not an easy process for teachers to respond to: "The habit of uniformity being now deeply ingrained, teachers continued to think in terms of the *Standards* long after they had been officially abolished" (p. 208). Slowly, other subjects became part of the curriculum—for example, dancing, needlework, and singing for younger pupils. Older pupils were involved in a range of subjects, such as geography, history, science, and English literature.

In 1917, the Scottish Education Reform Committee suggested that the curriculum included too many subjects. Paterson (2003, p. 47) notes that the process of reducing the number of subjects in the curriculum became known as "getting rid of the lumber." Interestingly, a similar phenomenon exists in the current Scottish educational context and is being referred to as "decluttering" the curriculum.

Debate raged during the 1920s and 1930s concerning the curriculum and pedagogy. Child-centered education was first promoted in the 1920s, and Scotland's leading voice in this arena was A. S. Neill, a well-known and controversial educationist.

Paterson (2003, p. 109) goes on to observe that, in 1941, there were discussions in the field of education around eroding the distinction of subjects and the adoption of cross-curricular project work. A report presented by the Advisory Council in Education in Scotland, *Primary Education* (1946), listed the subjects of a primary school as: physical education, handwork, arithmetic, art, spoken English, nature study, geography and history, reading and writing, singing, written composition, spelling and dictation, and religion.

In 1965, the Scottish Education Department published *Primary Education in Scotland* (1965). This publication is more commonly known as the *Primary Memorandum* and is widely recognized as the publication that helped teachers come to terms with child-centered learning. The publication set out a philosophy for primary education that had the needs of the children at the center and was responsive to the needs of the child. The value of continuity in a pupil's education, the differences in pupils' rates of development, and the significance of creating links between subjects so that they were not treated as separate entities were reinforced. The report (1965) clearly stated that:

> the curriculum is not to be thought of as a number of discrete subjects, each requiring a specific allocation of time each week or each month. Indeed, it is quite impossible to treat the subjects of the curriculum in isolation from one another if education is to be meaningful to the child. (p. 37)

Hunter (1971) suggests that the approach did not sit well with Scottish teachers, at the time, nor, some may argue, with present-day teachers. He attributes the professional discourse to the traditional Scottish emphasis on teachers teaching rather than on children learning.

Although some teachers harbored resentment, the report eventually produced major changes, in that it demanded that primary school curriculum should integrate different subjects—history, geography, science, technology, health, and expressive arts. Teachers at that time had little experience in teaching an integrated study. Again, this is a theme that is at the forefront of the professional debate in current education reform in Scotland.

Twenty years later, the consultative paper *Curriculum and Assessment in Scotland: A Policy for the 90s*, published by the Scottish Education Department in 1987, suggested that there were weaknesses in the curricular and assessment practices of primary and early secondary schools. It also identified a lack of definition of curriculum as well as poor school policies for the curriculum. The paper went on to suggest a strategy that would improve on those weaknesses, which, in effect, was to produce detailed guidelines on the aims, objectives, and content for each aspect of the curriculum.

This paper resulted in a pendulum swing to a centralized curriculum framework. Unlike other countries that developed a national curriculum in the late 1980s and early 1990s, Scotland developed curricular guidelines developed by groups of professionals in working parties of teachers and educationists involved in work in the schools. Eventually, guidelines were created for the following curricular areas: expressive arts, English language, mathematics, social subjects, personal and social development, and religious and moral education.

The implementation of the 5-14 guidelines[3] led to subjects again being separated out in many primary schools. A time-tabled week showing periods of separate aspects of the 5-14 curriculum became commonplace in schools. Many schools developed programs of study to ensure continuity and progression in the children's learning in each of the 5-14 curricular areas. These programs of study were often developed by local education authorities (districts) and resulted in common programs for schools across the authority (district). A teacher in the 1990s could find these programs to be rather prescriptive and in many ways restrictive of teachers' creativity in curriculum delivery. In most schools, there was as an expectation that all teachers followed, to the letter, the programs of study that had been developed for the curricular areas and that each curricular area was delivered as a discrete subject.

Interestingly, in 2002, the Scottish Executive embarked on an extensive consultation exercise on the state of school education in Scotland. This consultation exercise was known as the *National Debate on Education*. The debate confirmed that a number of features present within the Scottish curriculum were highly valued. However, it also highlighted that a number of aspects needed to be reviewed. The main recommendations were to:

- Reduce overcrowding in the curriculum
- Make learning more enjoyable
- Make better connections between the stages in the curriculum from the ages of 3 to 18
- Achieve a better balance between "academic" and "vocational" subjects
- Broaden the range of learning experiences for young people
- Equip young people with the skills they need now and in future employment
- Make sure that approaches to assessment and certification support learning
- Offer more choice to meet the needs of individual young people.

Teaching Methodologies in Elementary Education

As early as 1936, there had been debate about the importance of schools helping to develop critical, thoughtful, and self-reliant citizens in a democracy (Paterson, 2003). McClelland (1936, cited in Paterson, 2003) suggests that,

> *One of the social dangers of our time is the prevalence of certain qualities, for whose propagation our schools are not exempt from a measure of responsibility – qualities like submissiveness, blind receptiveness, taking one's views on trust or from tradition, susceptibility to suggestion. (p. 78)*

Teaching methodology in many Scottish primary schools was very traditional well into the 1940s and beyond. The children would be sitting silently, focused on the teacher's words. All the children would be sitting in rows of desks facing the teacher, there would be little discussion among the pupils, and there would be limited activity in the classroom. The teacher would ask questions and these would be answered by the pupils, who would raise their hands to let the teacher know that they could answer the question. Hunter (1971) summarizes this sort of methodology succinctly:

> *Everything is planned, orderly, under control. The teacher knows what she wants, and generally gets it. She is there to teach, the pupils are there to learn. The emphasis is on the individual, rather than the group; on competition rather than co-operation. (p. 88)*

Reading aloud was commonplace and much of the arithmetic was working through complicated, repetitive examples. Other than the blackboard, few teaching aids found their way into Scottish classrooms.

In the 1950s and 1960s, the principles and methodologies of progressive nursery schools or kindergartens started to influence the teaching approaches used in the early stages of primary schools. There was a slow liberating of the classroom atmosphere. Project work and group work started to be used by teachers in the "infant" classes of primary schools. By the late 1950s, school inspectors noted that group work was becoming a more common feature of primary classrooms.

When *Primary Education in Scotland* was issued by the Scottish Education Department in 1965, many educationists thought that its contents were revolutionary (Osborne, 1966). The *Primary Memorandum*, as this document became more widely called, helped take forward some of the developments that would make primary classrooms less rigid in Scotland. The emphasis in the document on the pupil can be seen in this short excerpt:

> *Where children have an active part in their own learning, where they feel secure in the knowledge that they can achieve success and have a particular place in class and school activities, where they understand the routine and rules which order their lives, where the school is an interesting place to come to and they can accept the teachers as their friends, they readily develop not only the qualities of character which they need as individuals but also the qualities of conduct which living with others demands. (SED, 1965, p. 90)*

There has been much debate (Paterson, 2003) about the impact of the *Primary Memorandum* on teachers moving away from traditional teaching methods to child-centered methodology. Bone and Morrow (1975) suggest that in Scotland many teachers adopted a third style, which included aspects of traditional and child-centered methodologies in primary schools.

In the late 1980s, the government introduced more prescriptive curriculum guidelines and at the same time introduced standard tests. The document that launched the 5-14 curriculum, *Curriculum and Assessment in Scotland: A Policy for the 1990s* (1987), did not criticize teaching methods. Paterson (2003) suggests that one of the main changes in the 1980s and 1990s was that more attention was given to children's emotional development, which meant that teachers were more sympathetic in their treatment of children. The use of television broadcasts and computers added to the variety of teaching materials available in the primary school. The use of the Internet also is a regular feature in primary schools nowadays.

During this period, Scottish primary teachers have used a range of methodologies in their classroom that have involved children in mixed-ability groups, ability groups, whole-class task, and individual tasks. Most teachers have been teaching math and language in ability groups to ensure that children can progress through programs of study at different rates, depending on their ability. Other curricular areas have been taught in mixed-ability groupings or as class lessons.

Generally, you would find three or four mathematics groups and perhaps one or two individuals with their own program of work in a primary classroom. Each of these groups may be working on quite different aspects of mathematics, and each group would progress through the program at quite different paces. A similar structure of groupings would be found in most primary classrooms for language work, too. Other curricular areas, like physical education, art, music, and religious and moral education, would be taught as a class lesson, and pupils may participate in mixed-ability group tasks as part of the lesson.

Assessment, particularly testing, was a significant element in the 5-14 Program in Scotland in the 1990s and 2000s. The publication of *Inside the Black Box* (Black & Wiliam, 1998) indicated that the concerns raised in Scotland regarding assessment were held elsewhere. In particular, the authors argued that if the government, its agencies, and the teaching profession were seriously concerned about raising standards, there were a number of aspects of current practice that needed to be rethought, particularly the role of assessment and, more specifically, formative assessment—"when the evidence is actually used to adapt the teaching work to meet the needs [of pupils]" (p. 2).

The development of formative assessment strategies in schools has been taken forward under the umbrella of the Assessment is for Learning (AifL) program in Scotland. This approach to developing classroom methodology has been novel, in that it has combined top-down and bottom-up development. Individual projects have been determined at the national level and developed within a national framework, but the precise nature of the work undertaken within individual schools or school clusters has, in large part, been determined by the staff in the schools, working with local authority personnel. Participating schools have been given financial support to use the program in ways they see fit (e.g., supply cover, material resources, staff development). Most classroom-based projects have been undertaken in ways that resembled action research, with planning, reviewing, reflecting, and modifying phases, culminating in a case study report. The overall impact of the AifL developments in Scottish primary classrooms continues to be evaluated, especially to monitor the impact it is having on children's learning.

History of Secondary Curriculum Structure

In Scotland, the use of the term "secondary," to indicate the post-elementary sector of schooling, dates from the 1860s; by 1892, there was what Anderson (2003) describes as an effective national network, able to prepare both for the universities and for business careers. These two strands of the academic and vocational purposes may offer useful distinctions to hold in mind as the following description of secondary schooling in the 19th and 20th centuries develops.

Historically, Scotland had made significant contributions to learning, having founded universities in the 15th and 16th centuries and forming "an integral part of the European community of scholars since medieval times" with 17 or 18 Scottish rectors of the University of Paris (Devine, 1999, p. 71). The Scottish Enlightenment movement in the 18th century gave further evidence of the leadership role of Scottish scholars. The core curriculum of philosophy, science, economics, arts, and theology offered in the universities had an impact on what was offered as the curriculum in the parish schools, to aspiring ministers and schoolmasters, and in the royal burgh schools training pupils for university or commercial careers. Furthermore, according to Devine (1999), the economic growth of the country in the 19th century and developments in curricular provision were distinctively intertwined in Scotland: "The curriculum was broadening even further to include subjects of direct vocational relevance, which were also becoming more important in the burgh schools and central to the teaching of the new academies" (p. 96).

The Impact of Selection

The Education (Scotland) Act of 1918 extended free secondary education to all, and the legislation of the Education Act of 1936 consolidated the post-elementary sector with divisions into a five-year senior secondary and a three-year junior secondary system to cater, respectively, to academic and vocational education. The selection of pupils for senior or junior schools was made on the basis of a test of academic ability, "the qualifying examination."

The two tiers of this system, however, led to fewer actual distinctions between the curricula offered in the post-elementary sectors. The Leaving Certificate was what granted entry to university courses. It was initially a Group Certificate offered as the Higher Certificate, and it identified particular subjects and levels as required: Higher English; Higher or Lower Mathematics; either two languages, one of which had to be Latin; or a science and a language. In 1950, the grouping of subjects and requirement of levels were abandoned and replaced by the record of results for individual subjects. In other post-elementary provision, it had been the expectation that the curriculum would offer a general liberal education that, in many cases, involved instruction in English, history and geography, mathematics, science, and French, with a few studying technical subjects, as well as commercial and domestic subjects. The Lower Certificate courses suffered from a lack of focused curriculum development and "tended not to be well-defined, but rather to be the first two years of a three-year or five-year course" (Wade, 1939, p. 227). Paterson (2003) sums up the direction of Scottish education prior to this time as "educational democracy was in the process of being defined as gaining wide access to the academic tradition" (p. 68).

From the 1950s until the mid-1960s, the certification systems were possibly the main drivers of the secondary curricula. Beginning in 1962, the Scottish Education Department acted on arguments based on statistical evidence gathered over a period of time that the selection structures and assessments leading to certification were not promoting educational mobility or supporting the aspiration of educational meritocracy. Changes to examinations and certification led to a new Ordinary Grade certificate, to be taken at about age 16; the Higher Grade would be taken one or two years later. These examinations recorded achievement in individual subjects, rather than as group certificates. At this point, the central subjects of the secondary curriculum continued to be English, mathematics, geography, history, science, art, music, and physical education—a course design that provided a broad general education.

These changes to the systems of certification and the end of selection procedures in state schools had an impact on arrangements within schools for grouping pupils by ability levels. A Scottish Education Department survey (1972) shows evidence that mixed-ability classes were operating in two-thirds of comprehensive schools at that time.

The Influence of Policymaking

Boyd (1997) has described Scottish education as having "a largely consensual approach to educational policy-making" with secondary schooling having "evolved in a more uniform fashion than elsewhere in the United Kingdom" (p. 52). Subject teaching, which is delivered by an all-graduate and subject specialist profession, drives the post-elementary sector and, in general throughout the period from the mid-1960s until the late 1990s, developments in curriculum and in assessment structures were managed with references to stages—the first two years, the middle two years, and the final years of secondary schooling—rather than from an overall sector perspective. During the 1970s, 1980s, and 1990s, the processes of change and development were driven by the continuing reviews of these stages within post-elementary education in Scotland. These reviews were dealt with piecemeal, with little reference to the stages before and after and were undertaken at different points during these decades. Therefore, discontinuities that existed before the reviews were amplified to the point where the secondary stage operates currently under three quite disparate approaches to curriculum, assessment, and certification of attainment.

The following paragraphs describe developments in terms of the chronology of the reviews, in order to indicate the gaps and disparities in the development of a coherent secondary structure.

The Middle Stages of Secondary Schooling

The first review process relates to the middle stages of the secondary school. Between 1974 and 1977, the curriculum structure of the middle stages of the secondary school was reviewed and significantly altered. Even the adjustments to the certification and examination systems of the 1960s did not aim to take into account the needs of all learners in the secondary sector; by the 1970s, it was clear that, to some extent, most comprehensive schools were offering separate provision for "certificate" and "non-certificate" classes. As a result, a large proportion of pupils left school with no certification of their learning, even after 11 years of schooling. Three committees were established by the Scottish Education Department to consider the structure of the curriculum (Munn Committee), the assessment and certification of learning (Dunning Committee), and issues of truancy and indiscipline in secondary school (Pack Committee).

After extensive consultation and an extended implementation period, a new and more integrated structure was put into place, with a mixture of internal and external assessment. Also included were the subjects that had been part of the secondary curriculum for many years, which were now offered as Standard Grades certificates at three levels (Foundation, General, and Credit) to accommodate the needs of all learners. It was hoped that the whole population of the secondary school sector might be motivated by being provided with short-term goals in internally assessed elements, and that they would engage in an education process that had the final outcome of a certificate. The policy changes did make a difference to the assessment and certification of learning. However, the curriculum of the secondary school was not altered very much, and pupils were offered limited choice between history or geography or modern studies (social subjects); from among art, drama, music, or physical education (creative and aesthetic subjects); between computing or technological studies or home economics (technology subjects). English and mathematics, religious and moral education, physical education, and social education are core elements. The aim of providing a broad liberal education underpins this subject structure, with little opportunity for individualization of the curriculum available to pupils in the compulsory stages of education in Scotland.

One initiative that aimed to support flexibility and diversity in curriculum structure in the 1980s was the Technical and Vocational Education Initiative, a United Kingdom program, from which local education authorities could access Department of Employment funding to support preparation for pupils' work lives beyond school. This initiative had the potential to extend the curriculum with its concentration on technology, problem-solving, communication skills, work experience placements, enterprise education, and personal and social skills development. Development teams were set up to support secondary schools in participating local education authorities to encourage flexible learning, pupil-centered approaches, action planning, and differentiation strategies. The business and technology communities were encouraged to form partnerships with education institutions and became, discursively at least, stakeholders in education.

The Upper Secondary Stages

Further changes in assessment and certification systems also affected the curriculum for the final stages of secondary schooling, but without radically altering the broad and general base of Scottish schooling. In 1984, the Scottish Vocational Education Council (SCOTVEC) offered a catalogue of modular National Certificates; initially, these were taken up in the further education colleges on behalf of students who had left secondary schools and who were pursuing either general courses or preparatory vocational training after the leaving age of 16. However, with the pressure to retain pupils in schools during the post-compulsory education stages, secondary schools began to enroll pupils in fifth and sixth years for the SCOTVEC modules. The modules were assessed internally and assessments moderated by external verifiers at a national level.

The modules in secondary schools were often used to provide courses for those who were "non-certificate" with respect to Higher Grade levels of attainment. As a result, course design for these pupils tended to lack planning and structure. While there was some impact on the general curriculum and some new certificated programs of study, such as work experience, media studies, and social and vocational skills, became embedded in secondary schools, this was a period of considerable unrest in Scottish education, stemming from a lengthy dispute and industrial action over pay and conditions of service. In the late 1980s and early 1990s, the Howie Committee consulted on the provision of courses in fifth and sixth year and on the kinds of reforms of curriculum, assessment, and certification that might lead to courses that were fit for purpose in respect of the pupil population. By 1994, what was put in place for secondary schools and further education colleges was a new, structured, coherent, and progressive program, "Higher Still," proceeding at five levels from Access through Intermediate 1, Intermediate 2, and Higher to Advanced Higher and incorporating both academic and vocational education. This program was meant to combine internally assessed components and externally examined features. Eventually, a new examining body, the Scottish Qualifications Authority, was formed. For some, the principles of general liberal education were being set aside in the interests of incorporating vocational qualifications into the secondary school provision, while others had concerns that the traditional academic standards would be diluted.

Two national policy statements were issued by agencies of policy development, one in 1994 (Scottish Consultative Council on the Curriculum, 1994) and the other in 2000 (Her Majesty's Inspectorate [HMI], 2000), relating specifically to links between education and the world of work. These initiatives have had a variable impact on the secondary school curriculum. The Scottish Executive has endorsed Education for Work as a priority so that young people are prepared to take up employment. In some schools the outcome has been the integration into the curriculum of such programs as enterprise projects, work experience/work shadowing schemes, and joint projects with industry and commerce extending specific subject courses. In others, however, there has been limited impact across the ranges of pupils in the school populations, with lower academic attainment tending to be associated with more work-related study.

The Early Secondary Years

Before the mid-1980s, the initial two years of secondary school were viewed by most teachers, parents, and pupils as a new beginning, a new phase of the experience of schooling. With serious concerns expressed explicitly by the Consultative Council on the Curriculum (1986) and Her Majesty's Inspectorate (1993) about progression and continuity of learning, a review was undertaken. A series of changes to curriculum, pedagogy, and assessment was explicated in a discussion paper produced by the Council followed by "guidelines" produced by the Scottish Education Department between 1987 and 1993. These guidelines applied to the primary phase and the first years of the secondary (ages 5-14), covered all areas of the curriculum with a common assessment structure, and encouraged learning and teaching approaches that would create continuities across the two sectors. What did not change in secondary practice was the very wide range of subjects faced by pupils moving into this phase of schooling. The 5-14 Guidelines are described in some detail in earlier sections of this chapter.

Recent Policy Changes in the Secondary Phase

Until 2003, it was the expectation that pupils in first and second years would be engaged in 5-14 Program studies, that the Standard Grade course would be the course delivered in all subjects to pupils in third and fourth years, and that the Higher Still program was the course for fifth- and sixth-year pupils. The assessments associated with these year groups were those that related to the courses. These restrictions were lifted, and many state schools took the opportunity to begin Higher Grade study programs at earlier stages of the secondary school phase in order to prepare pupils for the highest levels of academic certification by the end of the school career. This has resulted in considerable alteration to the course content, methodologies, and assessment practices being used in schools. For Bryce and Humes (2003), "Curricular influences are top-down; what goes on in S1 is determined more by what goes on in S5 than by what goes on in P7" (p. 41).

This recent change may be a continuing driver of the subject-focused, rather than learner-centered, curriculum in secondary schools, and it is a very interesting prospect to engage with the principles of *Curriculum for Excellence* at the point where secondary schools are developing higher courses in the early and middle stages of the secondary sector.

Such initiatives as the *National Priorities in Education, Enterprise Education, Health Promoting Schools,* and *Curriculum for Excellence* apply to preschool, primary school, and secondary school, and the current drive to see formal education as a continuous process from ages 3 to 18 presents particular challenges in the secondary school sector.

Teaching Methodologies in Secondary Education

The assessment-driven and subject-focused curriculum has constrained a diversity of methodologies to a considerable degree. Before the implementation of the National Tests (*Framework for National Testing,* SEB, 1993), schools had the freedom to interpret the 5-14 Guidelines and to integrate the strands within approaches that incorporated individual, group, and whole-class activities and direct teaching or investigation work. However, as an outcome of the results of tests being collated and published at the school, local education authority, and national levels, and with departmental and school effectiveness being judged in relation to achievement in the highest levels of awards, the methodologies employed tended toward a narrower approach. In addition, during the decade of the 1990s, Her Majesty's Inspectorate used the observations and evaluations gathered during inspection visits to propose that grouping pupils by ability was an important strategy for the raising of attainment in the early years of secondary schooling. This support from a powerful policy agency and pressure from the academic attainment agenda had the effect of homogenizing methodology in the secondary school toward what was perceived to be the most effective route to academic success.

In the middle and upper stages of the secondary school, as has been described, there had been a focus for some considerable time on matching classroom teaching and learning to the requirements of the national assessment systems. Although group activities and investigations and problem-solving approaches were featured parts in the curriculum arrangements of the Standard Grade and Higher courses, the emphasis continued to be on developing the knowledge, understanding, and skills of the individual pupil. Consequently, the certification of pupil attainment offers a record of attainment in academic subjects, rather than on process skills, cross-curricular elements, and social learning. For Bryce and Humes (2003), "Scottish educators remain fairly one-dimensional in their outlook. . . . The emphasis in Scottish Education is and always has been upon subject ability" (p. 42). Subject ability tends to be recorded and reported in relation to the assessment criteria applied in the systems of national qualifications. Despite these evaluations of how learning is managed in secondary schools, descriptions of individual subject areas indicate aspirations, whether or not practices, toward what might be termed social constructivist methodologies.

English language group activities are utilized to support learning, but group talk and listening in groups are also areas for formal assessment and grading of individual pupil work in the early and middle, though not the final, stages of secondary schooling. Similarly there is formal assessment of reading and writing, and grades are part of the reporting systems that record the achievement of individual pupils. The national assessments of reading and writing at all stages give evidence of the attainment of the individual pupil, and there is no recording of achievement of collaborative or cooperative working skills in the areas of literacy. For learners in other languages, whether Gaelic or other "first/home languages," modern foreign, or classical, the same tensions exist between social constructivist approaches to developing literacies and the rather more behaviorist assessment methods. The extension of formative assessment approaches in all Scottish schools by 2007 has yet to be seen to have effected change in the formal assessment practices—or arguably on the modes of operation of most secondary school teachers—although there is much optimism that the Assessment is for Learning initiatives will have a significant impact on methodologies in all subjects.

The advice given by Her Majesty's Inspectorate (1997, 1999) to teachers of mathematics refers to effective teaching in high-performing Third International Mathematics and Science Study (TIMSS) schools and advises the use of whole-class teaching and ability-set organization more than the more interactive or collaborative approaches. The use of investigation activities as a component of the assessable areas of the mathematics curriculum is lessening, and there is little evidence that the cross-curricular linkages that the subject might offer are supported in many secondary schools.

The broad category of Environmental Studies—one that incorporates history, geography, and science—in the earlier stages and becoming differentiated as social studies, including modern studies, and scientific studies in the middle stages of the secondary schools, is another area of the curriculum in which student-centered learning is an aspiration of many teachers. Practitioners list such inquiry approaches as the use of ICT, investigatory and problem-solving activities, field trips, and collaborative group work as methods that should be central to their practice. However, with these approaches come resourcing implications and the need for differentiation strategies that impose heavier requirements on teacher time and classroom management skills. Of particular concern in these subject areas, from the early to the final stages of secondary schooling, is overreliance on "worksheet learning," which is often used instead of a range of methods to match pupil learning readiness to the subject content to be covered at any particular curricular stage.

The creative/aesthetic or expressive arts subjects include art and design, drama, music, and physical education in the earlier and middle stages of the secondary school. As with the environmental studies subject grouping, there is plenty of evidence of the use of paired and small-group collaboration, interdepartmental joint working, out-of-school visits, and invitations to visiting specialists or experts. In the creative/aesthetic areas, performances and exhibitions and the interlinking of curricular and extracurricular initiatives are common. However, for the subjects represented within these groupings, there remains a tension between teaching of theory, required in national qualifications assessments, and the desire to promote artistic and creative expression as part of the wider conceptualization of the education project.

The technological subjects generally are taken as including computing, business education, craft and design, technological studies, sometimes annexing home economics or art and design. In the implementation of the Munn Report (1977), the subject groupings were more rigidly defined within the 8-mode model, but subsequent curriculum reforms and reorganization of management structures towards a "faculty" model in the secondary school sector (McCrone Agreement, 2000) have blurred the boundaries between the modes. There are often structural, traditional, workload, or assessment system barriers to teachers using active, practical, or skills-based, interactive approaches to learning, and these result in the same variations in actual (rather than aspirational) practice in this subject grouping, as in others.

Religious and moral education, personal and social education, and physical education are compulsory elements of the curricular provision. These subjects may hold a greater potential for creative and experimental learning activities.

Cross-curricular and embedded features, such as process skills and values education, are difficult to discern in such a subject-focused system, and so recent developments by the education agencies have sought to produce evaluation tool kits for teachers, subject departments, and schools. Much work has been done by Her Majesty's Inspectorate of Education and Learning, and by Teaching Scotland, to prepare materials that might identify characteristics of good practice and support educators in implementing learning and teaching strategies in subject departments, and in the embedded and permeating elements of the secondary school curriculum.

Scotland's Future: Curriculum for Excellence

Scotland is currently undertaking an education reform program under the Scottish Government's *Ambitious, Excellent Schools'* agenda. Like many other countries, we are facing new influences, which means that we must look differently at the curriculum. These have been described in the *Purposes and Principles for the Curriculum 3-18* (2004) as the

> global, social, political and economic changes, and the particular challenges facing Scotland: the need to increase the economic performance of the nation; reflect its growing diversity; improve health; and reduce poverty. In addition, we can expect more changes in the patterns and demands of employment, and the likelihood of new and quite different jobs during an individual's working life. (p. 10)

The current curriculum reform agenda in Scotland, known as *Curriculum for Excellence*, is a program of work that aims to provide:

- More freedom for teachers
- Greater choice and opportunity for pupils
- A single coherent curriculum for all young people ages 3-18.

Curriculum for Excellence developments are encouraging educators to think differently about the curriculum. It is anticipated by the Scottish Government that the implementation of *Curriculum for Excellence* will go beyond the provision of guidance on curriculum content and that it will have implications for:

- The teaching profession and other staff
- The organization of the curriculum in schools and centers
- The qualifications system
- The recognition of wider achievement
- The improvement framework.

The Scottish Government is seeking to achieve the following outcomes through this program of reform:

- For the first time ever, a single 3-18 curriculum, supported by a simple and effective structure of assessment and qualifications; this will allow the right pace and challenge for young people, particularly at critical points, like the move from nursery to primary and from primary to secondary
- Greater choice and opportunity, earlier, for young people, to help them realize their individual talents and to help close the opportunity gap by better engaging those who currently switch off from formal education too young
- More skills-for-work options for young people, robustly assessed and helping them to progress into further qualifications or work
- More space in the curriculum for in-depth work, and to ensure that young people develop the literacy, numeracy, and other essential skills and knowledge they will need for life and work
- Young people achieving the broad outcomes that we look for from school education, both through subject teaching and more cross-subject activity
- More space for sport, music, dance, drama, art, learning about health, sustainable development and enterprise, and other activities that broaden the life experiences—and life chances—of young people.

The current curriculum reforms are not suggesting a particular curriculum design for all schools in Scotland to follow. Instead, a new phenomenon in Scottish education has evolved as part of the reforms and is being described as *Curriculum Architecture*. Educators are being encouraged to *build* a revised curriculum in schools, and this process is being supported with documentation that encourages practitioners to reflect on their practice and review it to fit with the principles of *Curriculum for Excellence*.

A literature review of *Curriculum Architecture,* published by Boyd (2007) found that the concept was first found in tertiary sectors in the United States. The review states that:

> *Curriculum architecture is not simply about structural issues but the extent to which the underlying aims of the curriculum are reflected in the pedagogies in classrooms. (p. 8)*

Two recent documents, *Building the Curriculum 1* and *Building the Curriculum 2,* have helped educators focus their thinking about the current curriculum reform developments. The key messages in Scotland's curriculum reform to date suggest that, in Scotland, we should be focusing on *how* children learn as well as *what* they learn. Indeed, *Curriculum for Excellence* developments want educators to embrace a wider definition of how and what children should learn, and not to focus on a single curriculum's content.

In summary, the aspirations of Scotland's reforms in many ways mirror some of the work of Hawkins and Graham's (1994) publication *Curriculum Architecture: Creating a Place of Our Own.* In their work, Hawkins and Graham suggest that each school must create its own curriculum, based on its own study of its students, its community, its faculty, and with the real involvement of the students themselves—namely, a "learner-centered" approach to curriculum planning. This is a wonderful aspiration for our education system to have for all 3- to 18-year-olds!

Notes:

[1] While Scotland is a part of the United Kingdom, it has its own unique curricular needs and challenges. For more information on the United Kingdom, please see chapter 26.

[2] **Standard I**: Reading—One of the narratives next in order after monosyllables in an elementary reading book used in the school; Writing—Copy in manuscript character a line of print, and write from dictation a few common words; Arithmetic—Simple addition and subtraction of numbers of not more than four figures, and the multiplication table to multiplication by six.

   Standard VI: Reading—To read with fluency and expression; Writing—A short theme or letter, or an easy paraphrase; Arithmetic—Proportion and fractions (vulgar and decimal).

[3] The 5-14 guidelines for Scottish local authorities and schools cover the structure, content, and assessment of the curriculum in primary schools and in the first two years of secondary education. Schools are not legally required to follow the guidelines. The 5-14 curriculum is divided into five broad curricular areas: language, mathematics, environmental studies, expressive arts, and religious and moral education. Each curricular area includes broad attainment outcomes, each with a number of strands or aspects of learning that pupils experience. Most strands have attainment targets at five or six levels: A-E or A-F. The aim of the 5-14 program has been to promote the teaching of a broad, coherent, and balanced curriculum that offers all pupils continuity and progression as they move through school.

References

Advisory Council in Education in Scotland. (1946). *Primary education*. Edinburgh: Author.

Anderson, R. D. (1995). *Education and the Scottish people, 1750-1918*. Oxford: Clarendon.

Anderson, R. D. (2003). *The history of Scottish education, pre-1980*. In T. G. K. Bryce & W. M. Humes (Eds.), *Scottish education, second edition, post-devolution* (pp. 219-228). Edinburgh: Edinburgh University Press.

Black, P., & Wiliam W. (1998). *Inside the black box. London: NFERNelson*.

Bone, T. R., & Morrow, T. D. (1975, February 28). Training teachers for a new-style primary education. *Times Educational Supplement* (Scotland), p. 18.

Boyd, B. (1997). *The statutory years of secondary education: Change and progress*. In M. M. Clark & P. Munn (Eds.), *Education in Scotland: Policy and practice from pre-school to secondary* (pp. 52-66). London: Routledge.

Boyd, B. (2007). *Curriculum architecture –A literature review*. Glasgow: University of Strathclyde.

Bryce, T. G. K., & Humes, W. M. (2003). *Scottish secondary education: Philosophy and practice*. In T. G. K. Bryce & W. M. Humes (Eds.), *Scottish education, second edition, post-devolution* (pp. 37-48). Edinburgh: Edinburgh University Press.

Consultative Committee on the Curriculum. (1986). *Education 10-14 in Scotland*. Edinburgh. Author.

Devine, T. M. (1999). *The Scottish nation 1700-2000*. London: Penguin Press.

Hawkins, M., & Graham, M. (1994). Curriculum architecture: Creating a place of our own. Westerville, OH: National Middle School Association.

Her Majesty's Inspectorate. (1997). *Improving mathematics education 5-14*. Edinburgh: SOEID.

Her Majesty's Inspectorate. (1999). *Standards and quality in secondary schools 1995-1999: Mathematics*. Edinburgh: SOEID.

Herman, A. (2002). The Scottish enlightenment. London: Fourth Estate.

McCrone, D. (2001). *Understanding Scotland: The sociology of a nation*. London: Routledge.

McIntosh, D. M., & Walker, D. A. (1970). The O-grade of the Scottish certificate of education. *British Journal of Educational Psychology, 40*, 179-199.

Osborne, G. S. (1966). *Scottish and English schools: A comparative survey of the past fifty years*. Pittsburgh, PA: University of Pittsburgh Press.

Paterson, L. (2003). *Scottish education in the twentieth century*. Edinburgh: Edinburgh University Press.

Scottish Consultative Council on the Curriculum. (1994). *Education for work: Education industry links in Scotland*. Dundee: Author.

Scottish Education Department. (1965). *Primary education in Scotland*. Edinburgh: Her Majesty's Stationery Office.

Scottish Education Department. (1987). *Curriculum and assessment in Scotland: A policy for the 1990s.* Edinburgh: Author.

Scottish Education Department. (1977). *The structure of the curriculum in the third and fourth years of the Scottish secondary school (the Munn report).* Edinburgh: HMSO.

Scottish Education Department. (1972). Scottish education statistics, secondary schools staffing survey 1970. Edinburgh: Author.

Scottish Examination Board. (1993). *The framework for national testing.* Dalkeith: Author.

Scottish Executive. (2000). *Education for work in schools, a report by HMI Inspectors of Schools.* Edinburgh: Author.

Scottish Executive Education Department. (2001). *A teaching profession for the 21st century. Agreement reached following recommendation made in the McCrone report.* Edinburgh: Author.

Scottish Executive Education Department. (2002). *The national debate on education.* Edinburgh: Author.

Scottish Executive Education Department. (2004). *A curriculum for excellence.* Edinburgh: Author.

Scottish Executive Education Department. (2004). *Purposes and principles for the curriculum 3-18.* Edinburgh: Author.

Wade N. A. (1939). *Post-primary education in the primary schools of Scotland, 1872-1936.* London: University of London Press

About the Authors

Kevin Kelman is Head Teacher (Principal) at Burnside Primary in South Lanarkshire, Scotland. Currently, Kevin is on secondment as an Associate Senior University Teacher within the Faculty of Education at the University of Glasgow. He is also a part-time doctoral student at the University of Strathclyde in Glasgow. His post-graduate studies include a Diploma in Educational Leadership and Management as well as the Scottish Qualification for Headship awarded by the Scottish Executive. Kevin's current research interests concern the transition from early childhood education to primary education.

June Mitchell, M.A., B.A. (Hons.), M.Litt., MSc., Ph.D. is a lecturer in the Department of Educational and Professional Studies at the University of Strathclyde. After teaching English in secondary schools for over 30 years, she joined the Faculty of Education in 2005 and is course director of the Doctor of Education programs. June's current research interests are in citizenship and marginalized groupings in secondary schools and in professional doctorate studies in higher education.

Curriculum Development:
Perspectives From Swaziland

Betty T. Dlamini

A̲s I thought about this chapter, I was reminded of an old story of the "saber-toothed curriculum," which was said to have dominated prehistoric education in one prehistoric civilization. The following version is adapted from Solomon and Aikenhead (1994):

THE STORY OF THE SABER-TOOTHED CURRICULUM

Stone Age people survived by catching fish with bare hands, clubbing tiny horses to death, and scaring the saber-toothed tigers with a torch. Therefore, the Stone Age school curriculum was about teaching these skills. However, changes occurred in the environment, resulting in muddied streams making it impossible to see fish (therefore, no catching fish with bare hands), the tiny horses fled and antelopes replaced them, and the saber-toothed tigers died of pneumonia and big ice bears replaced them.

So to survive, Stone Age people developed nets to catch fish, invented antelope snares, and dug pits to trap the bears. These activities had become essentials for life of that time.

BUT the schools continued to teach fish-catching with bare hands, horse-clubbing, and tiger-scaring. When some liberals wanted to teach net-making, twisting antelope snares, and digging bear pits, they were met with opposition. The argument was that the old skills were culturally valuable to teach, even though they were useless.

This curriculum, it is said, was practical and meant to equip learners of the time with skills to deal with imminent personal and national issues, such as safety, food, and leisure. When environmental conditions changed, resulting in a change in the source of danger and food, however, the saber-toothed curriculum remained unchanged, because it was revered as fundamentally "good." Although the story of the saber-toothed curriculum is often used in education to illustrate a parallel situation of resistance to change that is often found to occur in practice, I have used it in this context to underline the functions of a curriculum.

Current curricula have a function to deal with issues that, incidentally, continue to grow both in diversity and sophistication. It is meant to equip individuals with skills and knowledge to function both within the confines of their context and beyond. Curriculum design and development are thus a function of translating elements of that context into teachable units of enabling content. Ideally, when

Swaziland

those elements change, the curriculum is expected to respond to those changes. It is no news that current curricula are faced with rapid development in technological and scientific knowledge; the adverse impact of these technologies on the environment, and thus on life; and the advent of such life-threatening diseases as the HIV/AIDS pandemic, malaria etc. Curriculum development is, therefore, under pressure not only to ensure relevance in those terms, but also to adhere to quality and respond to current local and global trends. This chapter attempts to show how attempts to break away from the saber-toothed curriculum situation have been made, and the extent to which curriculum in Swaziland has responded to the inherent needs. I will present government views as stated in official documents, the current curriculum development situation, and views from curriculum developers.

BACKGROUND OF CURRICULUM DEVELOPMENT IN SWAZILAND

Contemporary education reached Swaziland as a result of the European colonization of Africa. When South Africa was colonized, it received education in its contemporary format, which was then developed to suit the South African context. Education spread to Swaziland from South Africa as the European settlers invaded more of the African territory. By 1907, Swaziland had become a British Protectorate. Prior to that period, education, both in Swaziland and in South Africa, was mainly parallel to the saber-toothed curriculum in that it had the sole aim to deal with practical issues of survival, leisure, and safety. It was characterized by an oral tradition by which generations acquired knowledge pertinent to their cultural and socio-political practices. Elders were considered the sole custodians of knowledge, and thus no records of the traditional schools or curriculum content were kept or preserved at the time.

Upon colonization, Swaziland adopted a curriculum that was mainly the South African version of a western curriculum, in combination with the curriculum that was designed and developed in Britain for British citizens. Such teaching materials as books and assessment practices, were all prescribed from these countries. I recall that as a primary school pupil prior to independence, my classmates and I used to read English language and literature books written in Oxford, England. We read about Big Ben, the Thames, and Westminster Abbey. As children in the primary school, we were quite happy to learn about structures from a land that, to us, existed only in our imaginations, and we had very little or no conceptions that rivers, palaces, and town structures existed in Swaziland. Nobody had written about Swaziland in that way to enable us to learn about things that existed in, and made sense in, our immediate environment. Meanwhile, the African languages and literature books, history books, and some general knowledge books were all South African. While nothing appeared to be wrong with learning of Big Ben or South African contexts, it became clear at independence that there was something substantially wrong with the absence of local content from the prescribed curriculum. Thus, upon gaining its independence in 1968, Swaziland turned to Britain for its curriculum redefining. It was at this time that Swaziland borrowed ideas and learning materials in the form of books from Great Britain. For example, Secondary Mathematics Project (SMP) books, as well as the integrated science program from Scotland, were used as the basis for producing local materials. However, the resultant curriculum was said to be highly academic, geared towards white-collar jobs, and irrelevant to the needs of the individual Swazi and the nation at large (Magagula, 1988).

Around the time of independence, Swaziland started a process of redefining its national agenda and policy for all sectors. The first policy document to address issues of education was a thesis of the political leadership of the time called the Imbhokodvo Manifesto of 1972. Among the statements set for education in the document are the following:

- The purpose of education is to produce an enlightened and participant citizenry
- The content of education must be work-oriented from primary to the highest levels
- It is a policy of the Imbhokodvo that all education shall be designed to inculcate love for our land, loyalty to our king and country, self-respect, self-discipline, respect for law, accompanied by the highest degree of knowledge and building of character. (p. 27)

Note the socio-cultural-political tone, which characterizes the typical, ideal Swazi person (love for the country and king, and respect and discipline) in the statement of aims for education. This document, complete with its biases, has guided subsequent curriculum design and development to the present day. To operationalize the aims stated above, the government of Swaziland produced a series of national development plans (NDPs) that attempted to unpack broad aims of education into implementable units. According to Magagula (1988), the initial concern for education was to increase access to education in order to address the need for social development and to improve the condition of all Swazi people.

The first NDP for the period 1969 to 1973 spelled out the broad aims of education according to the statements in the Imbhokodvo manifesto. This plan was described by Magagula as a program of socio-economic action, aimed primarily at improving the living conditions of the mass of the people of Swaziland. Therefore, this plan focused mainly on access, equity, and quality of education. It mandated school inspectors be responsible for curriculum development, which at the time was restricted to drafting and disseminating syllabi. To this end, having locally written teaching/learning materials with a socio-cultural bias was seen as necessary. Toward the end of the plan period, it became clear that consultation was a necessary factor in accomplishing the stated goals and aims of education in the country for a relevant curriculum. In response to this concern, the government of Swaziland set up a commission to define, with consultation, the country's desired curriculum.

Thus, the First National Education Commission was set up in 1972 (Magagula, 1988). According to Magagula, among the terms of reference for this commission was that it should consult widely among Swazi nationals and make recommendations to the government on the desired curriculum. In a discussion paper prepared for the World Bank, Magagula states that recommendations from this commission culminated in the establishment of the primary curriculum development unit (PCU) at the end of the first national development plan period in 1973 (Magagula, 1988). This unit defined the first step towards institutionalization of curriculum development in Swaziland. Mandates for the PCU included the responsibility to develop a curriculum that responds to the national goals and objectives. The proposed structure of the education system was to broaden the curriculum at the primary school level, gradually moving towards specialization at high school or senior secondary school level. According to the commission's report, this curriculum was meant to be geared towards the development of practical and self-employment skills while preparing learners for higher academic experiences.

The second NDP for the period 1973 to 1977 linked students' poor performance, particularly in science and mathematics, to the overall non-technological bias of the school curriculum, which dated back to pre-independence days (2nd National Development Plan, 1973). It was felt at this time that the curriculum still placed more emphasis on non-science subjects at the expense of science and technical subjects. The plan emphasised the need to match the school curriculum to the economic opportunities likely to be available to school leavers. To do this, it suggested that science and technical subjects (e.g., woodwork, home economics, and agriculture), although considered to be expensive, should be given more weight. Therefore, the plan set out to:

- Revise existing syllabi and introduce more local content in the non-science syllabus.
- Introduce new practical and self employment-oriented subjects. These new syllabi were to be drawn up with local situations in mind and to be practical and oriented to self-employment as well as to further academic life.
- Ensure that agriculture and home economics be taught ultimately in all schools at the junior secondary school level. At the time, only one school offered agriculture at that level. At the high school or senior secondary school level, these subjects were to be offered by some schools to prepare learners for academic careers in these areas.
- Introduce development studies at the junior secondary school level.
  During the time of the second NDP, subject panels were given responsibilities for drawing the syllabi.

Subject panels were set up at the time as a means to improve the curriculum and achieve the policy of diversification. Subject panels act as the Ministry of Education's professional advisory body. They are made up of representatives from all subject stakeholders from educational institutions (such as the Teacher Training Colleges [TTC], the National Curriculum Centre [NCC], and the University of Swaziland [UNISWA]); teachers; and the inspectorate. Panels are chaired by the senior inspector for that subject. Subject panels took over syllabi development, and thus the definition of what should be incorporated in the school curricula.

In 1978, by the end of this period, a secondary school curriculum unit (SCU) was established (Mabuza, n.d.) to speed up the process of addressing concerns for diversification from the previous plan and to complement the PCU. To further improve the designing and delivery of the curriculum, four teacher innovation and development centers were completed in 1977, and they served as resource centers for teachers.

The third development plan for the period 1978 to 1983 decried the mismatch, in the previous plan, between the provision for secondary school and the actual development of secondary schools. Schools were developing faster than the provisions made for them, in terms of resources and teacher training. As a result, many schools were poorly resourced and many teachers at both primary and junior secondary school levels were untrained. This mismatch was said to place the curriculum reform process, and thus the quality of education, in jeopardy. The plan set out to reiterate the curriculum description and purposes outlined in the previous plans. By the end of this plan period, the current National Curriculum Centre (NCC) was established to consolidate curriculum development. The NCC is a result of the merger in 1983 of the two units: the PCU, which developed materials for primary school level, and the SCU, which developed materials for the junior secondary school level (Mabuza, n.d.).

The main goal of the fourth and last NDP was to address the issue of curriculum quality and relevance and to strengthen and consolidate the newly established NCC. It specifically indicates its interest in developing a curriculum that would be in keeping with the social and cultural norms of the country. It is the first to spell out plans for curriculum development in a separate section. According the NDP (1983), the NCC was given the task to:

- Coordinate all curriculum development activities. This involves soliciting comments and opinions on curriculum suitability from stakeholders, and designing, completing, and distributing curriculum materials in the form of teachers' guides and pupils' work books. It was also tasked to develop materials for pre-vocational education.
- Explain the curriculum to teachers to ensure adequate implementation.
- Cooperate more closely with TTCs and subject panels, and associate with regional education resource centers. It was also expected to establish a system for information exchange and interchange within the center to ensure quality.
- Establish a scheme for continuous assessment (CA).
- Incorporate Swazi culture, traditions, and values in the content of the national curriculum.

To achieve these aims, a second National Education Review Commission (NERCOM) was set up to consult widely, redefine the curriculum, and make recommendations to the Ministry of Education. The NERCOM report was tabled to and adopted by the cabinet in March 1984 (Magagula, 1988). Its main trust with regard to curriculum development was to strengthen the work of the NCC by emphasizing the research element. It proposed the following recommendations for the NCC:

- Carry out research and develop draft materials, and submit these to the review committee of panel for input and approval. Materials are then circulated to pilot schools for trial testing. These pilot schools give continuous feedback to the teacher education component of the NCC.
- Have materials refined and approved by panels before they are submitted to the Ministry of Education (MOE) for approval through a body called the Curriculum Coordinating Committee (CCC),

which was set up to give its final approval of curriculum materials before these are distributed to all schools for implementation. The first nationwide implementation of primary subject teaching materials was in 1985, and it gradually progressed through the classes.

The NERCOM report identified a number of problems that slowed down the education reform process with respect to curriculum development, as follows:

- Unclear guidelines or education policy to guide curriculum development
- Inadequate staff at NCC
- Insufficient funds for infusion workshops
- Unsatisfactory teamwork in materials production
- Lack of evaluation mechanism for infused materials
- Absence of CA and evaluation of the curriculum system
- Insufficient involvement of TTCs and other trainers in the curriculum reform process.

Based on the recommendations of the NERCOM report, curriculum development has, to some extent, involved participation from teacher education institutions and the UNISWA.

THE NATIONAL CURRICULUM CENTRE (NCC)

Before describing the processes that take place in the NCC, I would like to present a geographical, personnel, and organizational context of the NCC. The NCC is situated in the premises allocated to one of the TTCs called William Pitcher College in Manzini city (Manzini is also a name for the central district of the small country of Swaziland). The physical structure of the NCC consists of four buildings: two office block spaces, plus a conference room, one work room, and one conference and materials storage space. It has four departments that work in coordination to ensure efficient and successful designing, writing, trial testing, distribution, and evaluation of curriculum material.

Design and Preparation: responsible for designing and developing curriculum materials. It is organized by subject area as follows: language arts, mathematics and science, social studies, and practical arts.

Teacher Education: responsible for dissemination of curriculum.

Evaluation: collect feedback on teaching materials and produce reports on effectiveness of the materials.

Continuous Assessment: affects the recommendation of the NDS on the necessity to improve assessment practices to include school-based assessment. Its aim is to ensure that competency-based learning occurs.

Production: once the draft materials have gone through the approval system and have been finalized, it is produced for trial testing and piloting by this department of the NCC.

Using the syllabus prepared by the subject panels, they produce a teachers' guide, pupils' book, and something like a pupil's workbook. It is the responsibility of the teacher education department to see to running infusion workshops in conjunction with the inservice department.

Personnel at NCC

The NCC has a complement of 28 professional staff from all departments, two administrators, and 12 support staff. Each area of specialization is held by at least one staff member, from among whom chief designers for each of the four departments are chosen. According to one staff member, the current staff complement is not adequate as designer staff, but could be considered adequate as coordinators of curriculum design process. In the latter case, the NCC staff may obtain expert services of specialists to carry out the design process while NCC staff organize, facilitate, and, at times, participate as co-designers. As the staff indicated, staffing tends to lag behind development and diversification of programs.

In addition to staff at the NCC, a number of partners, such as a consultant, subject panels, teachers, and learners, play a pivotal role in curriculum development. A consultant is identified by the publisher Macmillan to work with designers by providing professional advice, ensuring relevance of materials to global trends, guiding selection and sequencing of content, ensuring quality and appropriateness of the level of materials, and preparing finished books for publication. Subject panels initiate and approve changes in the curriculum. Subject panels are mandated by government policy to define development and review syllabi in collaboration with the NCC. Panels also receive and approve reports from NCC and thus guide the direction of the curriculum. Teachers use materials at the pilot stage and provide feedback on workability, level of content, relevance, and appropriateness of time allocations.

The basic qualification requirement for curriculum developers is at least a first degree in the relevant subject area. Once inside the system, the NCC has a program for staff development. Currently, the majority of the staff are master's degree holders. While this is considered a strength for curriculum development, it has been described as a drawback in some cases, since replacing staff-in-training is not normally possible. In one case, a whole review process was derailed by the absence of the incumbent developer, who was on training leave. As mandated by the national policies, the NCC staff's responsibility is twofold: to design the country's curriculum materials and to coordinate the entire curriculum design process in the country.

The Curriculum Development Process

As indicated in the government documents presented earlier, the tasks for the NCC include the following:

- Developing syllabi in collaboration with members of subject panels. In so doing, the NCC is instrumental in defining the national curriculum.
- Conducting research, developing, trial testing, and evaluating instructional materials.
- Conducting workshops for pilot teachers and monitoring the pilot process of the draft materials.
- Conducting infusion workshops for teachers on the use of new instructional materials. This task is done in collaboration with the inservice unit of the MOE and the inspectorate.
- Continually assessing pupils' achievement of curricular objectives and diagnosing learning difficulties, thus developing curricula that respond to learners' developmental and academic needs.
- Designing and developing remedial and enrichment materials in line with curriculum objectives. This process is done by the continuous assessment unit.
- Providing continued formative evaluation for use in revising existing school teaching/learning materials.
- Working with the Examination Office to develop and mark pilot examinations.

According to the staff at NCC, the curriculum development process follows a combination of models of curriculum development but is mainly an adaptation of Hilda Taba's model. It features 10 stages, as shown in Figure 1. Each stage connects to other stages, as shown by the arrows. The formative evaluation stage does not fit in the cycle because each stage undergoes this stage to ensure that effectiveness.

Situational Analysis. This step consists of two parts: needs assessment and survey of government policies. It defines the research considered necessary for the development of relevant local curriculua. It is carried out periodically to enable the curriculum to respond to the ever-changing societal needs, problems, and issues. The needs assessment is carried out to discern the needs, concerns, and aspirations of the Swazi society. It normally takes the form of public meetings, interviews, questionnaires, and observations. Opinions are sought from various institutions, which include such professional associations as the Swaziland National Association of Teachers (SNAT); "Tinkhundla," which are local governments and represent public opinion; the Swazi National Council (SNC), which is the custodian of the Swazi culture; and church organizations. Meanwhile, the document analysis is done to find out the government's view of education and the currculum. Much of this exercise is carried out on documents, such as the National Development Plans, policy statements, the constitution, education commission reports, and relevant institutional reports. Furthermore, this search seeks to find out the resource-based position for the proposed curriculum: the manpower resource (i.e., the skill situation of curriculum planners, developers, and implementers); the financial resource implications for the new curriculum, which includes funding for curriculum development and implementation activities, equipment, and supplies; and the logistical support of the new curriculum.

Selection and Statement of Objectives. Objectives are formed according to the identified needs, with consideration for the resource needs mentioned above. Objectives are normally an interpretation of the national education aims stated in government documents.

Selection and Development of Content, Methods, and Evaluation Devices. Content is selected and methods are suggested based on stated objectives. The criteria for selecting content is based on Hilda Taba's writings (NCC document, undated). Curriculum developers often cite Taba (1992), who wrote that "if the curriculum is to be useful . . . its content and outcomes it pursues need to be in tune with social and cultural realities of the time" (quoted in an NCC working document, undated). This statement connotes that the curriculum responds to the needs of a dynamic society. Other principles governing the selection of content are that it should be within the developmental capabilities of the learners, relate to learners' environment and contemporary society, be scientifically valid, and have transfer value.

Organization of Content and Learning Activities. Selected content is then written into units, based on findings from the consultative research mentioned earlier. The evaluation department is responsible for checking and rechecking each step of the curriculum development process, including

The Main Steps in Curriculum Development Process
(Source: an unpublished NCC working document)

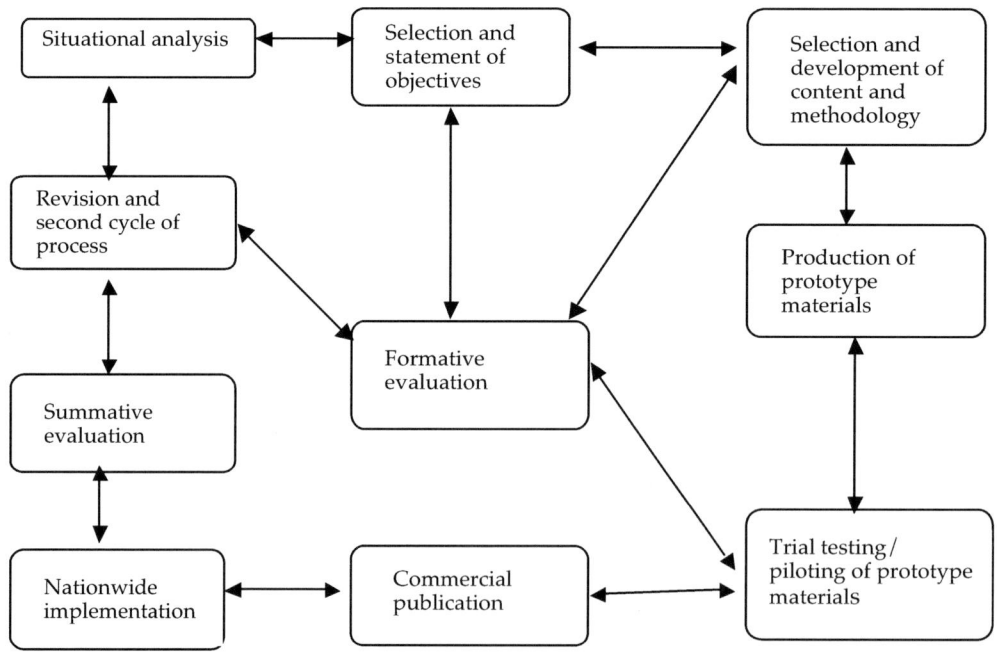

Figure 1

drafts, through trials and consultations. These coordinators work in an integrative manner across subject areas. When the NCC restructured, they introduced posts for senior designers in each subject area. These designers took over the responsibility of the coordinator, whose post was then phased out. Drafts are then sent to the MOE professional body, the subject panels, for further input and/or review. At this point, working drafts are ready for the next stage.

Trial Testing. Two forms of trial testing are used: "lab-testing" and piloting. Lab-testing refers to a process that ensures that suggested units are meaningful and understandable to learners by giving a unit or lesson to a class of learners during the drafting period. Lab-testing can be done as a one-shot exercise or as one that extends over a short period of one or several weeks, depending on the length of the lesson/unit. This exercise helps curriculum developers produce realistic units of currciulum materials.

According to the NCC staff, the pilot is done over a period of two years. All lessons and units are taught during this time. Feedback is obtained from the pilot school by submission of the pilot teachers, as well as from activities of the NCC evaluating team. They have a mandate to:

• Test content validity, language level, and scope and sequence of the materials
• Evaluate the availabilty of suggested learning aids
• Evaluate the effectiveness of suggested methods and evaluation devices
• Gauge the impact of the news curriculum materials over those in current use by giving the same tests to a pilot and a non pilot group and then comparing the performance of the the the two groups.

Final Approval by the Ministry of Education (MOE). After incorporating the pilot findings, the NCC sends the final draft materials to a committee of the MOE called the Curriculum Coordinating Committee (CCC) for final approval. The CCC consists of members from all MOE departments and such units as the Teaching Service Commission, Faculty of Education (UNISWA), NCC, Examinations Council, Guidance and Counselling, Inspectorate, Regional Education Offices (REO), TTCs, and the Swaziland National Teachers' Association (SNAT). This body makes its own input into the materials before they are prepared for mass commercial pulication and nationwide implementation.

Revision and Second Cycle Process. After appropriate summative evaluation, the material undergoes another cycle of revision, when innovations are introduced. In the case of Swaziland primary curriculum, this period encompasses seven years, corresponding to the primary schooling period, plus an additional two years of planning and syllabus review. This period defines the curriculum development cycle. The most recent development in curriculum change is toward context-based teaching materials. Contextualized teaching materials, at least in science and mathematics, are now at the Grade 7 level. It is expected that appropriate evaluation of the new approach will lead to further changes in the syllabi and curriculum materials; thus, this period marks the beginning of a fresh review of the contextualized curriculum at the primary school level.

At the junior secondary school level, the curriculum development followed is slightly different from the model described above. Subject panels tend to be much more involved in the development of curriculum materials across the subject areas. The Ministry of Education or donors normally run writers' workshops for the writing teams. At this level, the NCC assumes the coordinating role. According to staff at NCC, at this level they are sometimes side-stepped if a top-down change is introduced.

At the senior secondary or high school level, the curriculum is still imported from the United Kingdom. Until 2006, the country used the Cambridge "O Level curriculum"; the General Certificate of Education (GCE). Since then, the country has moved toward using the International General Certificate of Secondary Education (IGCSE/HIGCSE). The latest change of curriculum is a step towards localization of the high school curriculum. With the exception of materials for instruction on the SiSwati language and literature, which have always been designed and produced locally, teaching materials and textbooks for this level of schooling also are imported.

The School Curriculum

In the context of curriculum development in Swaziland, the school curriculum refers to the organized experiences for learners in the form of formal subjects appearing in the school time table, and other school activities (such as singing for competitions, sport, and community service) that have no written curriculum, but are formal school activities and appear in the school timetable. At the end of each cycle of schooling, all students take the same national examination. These examinations are the responsibility of the national examinations council, which is responsible for setting, dissemination, marking, compiling, and publishing results at primary and junior secondary school level. The process of localizing high school examinations is still in progress.

As stated earlier, the school curriculum in the country was defined in terms of its desired impact on the individual. One such stated impact is to develop problem solvers as well as participants in national development. This includes issues of participation in poverty reduction, unemployment, and managing the impact of disease and natural disaster as well as coping with scientific and technological development. According to the Ministry of Education (2004), challenges faced by the country are aggravated by the impact of the HIV/AIDS pandemic and high levels of unemployment, both of which contribute to high poverty rates. For this reason, current curriculum reform means a shift from the white collar curriculum to one that promotes a sense of entrepreneurship among children. To this end, pre-vocational studies are now part of the primary school curriculum. The curriculum is the same in all schools, with the exception of a few private school.

Subject Areas
Primary School Level

1980s	**New (current)**
SiSwati	SiSwati
English	English
Social Studies	Social Studies
Religious Education	Religious education
Mathematics	Mathematics
Science	Science
Home Economics	Home Economics
Agriculture	Agriculture
	Practical arts
	Computer education
	Technology
	Physical education

The national goals of education have always required a curriculum that is relevant to the needs of society by being skills-based and practical. Until the 1980s, however, primary school subjects were mainly traditional academic subjects, with only home economics and agriculture as formal practical subjects. According to Mabuza (n.d.), attempts at introducing other practical subjects (such as carpentry) were made occasionally, but were limited to a few schools because of no clear guidelines and support for these subjects. Staff at NCC concurred with Mabuza regarding the stagnation of some programs due to lack of guidelines and support. Recently, however, there has been an increase in subjects of a more practical and relevant nature for which a formal curriculum is needed. The introduction of such subjects as computer science and technology is in response to developments in these areas, while practical arts is a wide area that includes a number of skills-based subjects, such as drawing and woodwork. Children's experiences should include proficiency in the use of computers, which would lead to national development. Furthermore, contemporary issues, such as HIV/AIDS, child abuse, health education, environmental education, road safety, and gender studies, are increasingly incorporated as chapters or themes within existing subjects.

Secondary and High School Level. The NCC is also responsible for developing teaching materials for the three years of the junior secondary school level in the following subjects currently offered in all public schools. Currently, the NCC develops curriculum materials for all subjects except those marked with asterisk.

English language
English literature
French*
SiSwati
Afrikaans*
Mathematics
Commercial arithmetic*
Human and social biology
Integrated science
Agriculture
Additional mathematics

Bookkeeping and commerce
Development studies
Geography
History
Metalwork
Religious knowledge
Technical drawing
Typewriting*
Woodwork
Home economics

Approach of Curriculum Materials

The NCC materials adopt a spiral approach to content organization. Both the old and new materials feature recurrent themes in the form of units. To illustrate this point, the science curriculum is used to illustrate the style of learning materials; however, this trend is not limited to science. Beginning in the 1980s, until about 2000, the science learning materials featured the following units: plants, animals, health and the human body, matter, atmosphere and weather, and the Earth's crust. Units are recurrent over the seven levels, with some units introduced at higher levels. Table 1 illustrates this situation.

Each unit grows in incremental complexity at each level. Since 2000, a new approach to curriculum materials in all subject areas has been developed, starting from the Grade 1 level. In science, the current contextualized materials have units that cover all content relating to all the units presented above. Table 2 represents the structure of the current science curriculum.

The Old Primary Science Curriculum for Grades 1 to 7

Unit	Grade 1	Grade 2	Grade 3	Grade 4	Grade 5	Grade 6	Grade 7
1	Plants	Plants	Plants	Plants	Plants	Plants	Plants
2	Animals	Animals	Animals	Animals	Animals	Animals	Animals
3	Health & the Human Body	Health & the Human Body	Health & the Human Body	Health & the Human Body	Health & the Human Body	Health & the Human Body	Health & the Human Body
4	Matter	Matter	Matter	Matter	Matter	Matter	Matter
5	Atmosphere & Weather	Atmosphere & Weather	Atmosphere & Weather	Atmosphere & Weather	Atmosphere & Weather	Atmosphere & Weather	Atmosphere & Weather
6	The Earth's Crust	The Earth's Crust	The Earth's Crust	The Earth's Crust	The Earth's Crust	The Earth's Crust	The Earth's Crust
7	Astronomy	Astronomy	Astronomy	Astronomy	Astronomy	Astronomy	Astronomy
8	-	-	-	-	-	Ecology & conservation	Ecology & conservation

Table 1

New unit names signify a shift in focus toward using content areas to teach issues relating to the learner's experiences. This came about because of the change in education policy towards context-based teaching.

The NCC Materials Presentation

The NCC product consists of the following:

- *Teacher's Guide:* presents the aims of the science program and a description of the scientific process skills, objectives of each unit, background information on each unit, suggestions for lesson activities and assessment procedure.
- *Pupils' Activity Book:* presents lesson activities for learners in a colorful presentation. Pictures are gradually replaced by text at the upper levels.
- *Pupils' Workbook:* a new addition prevalent in mathematics. It contains exercises for learners.

VIEW FROM THE NCC STAFF

A brief survey of the NCC personnel was carried out to find out about current practices and developments, cultural and socio-political influences, success stories, constraints, and future directions of curriculum development. Questionnaire and interview schedules were used for the purpose. Data captured were used to enrich the foregoing discussion and are summarized below.

The Story of Curriculum Development

According to those members of staff consulted, the NCC has developed over the years both in scope and focus. Initially, curriculum development was done only for traditional subjects. More subjects were introduced as the personnel base for curriculum development increased. This process was said to have been gradual and often halted by a lack of support. In terms of focus, the initial curriculum development process was guided by foreign ideas; it has gradually shifted to represent more original Swazi views and contexts. As consultations with the Swazi community increases, the material base for curriculum development has increased and the resultant materials have become more relevant to the Swazi society.

More affordable curricula, which use readily available examples and materials, are produced, as per the dictates of education policy (The Government of Swaziland, 1999). The current curriculum utilizes presentations that children can easily relate to without diminishing its value in the development of more global competencies.

The Current Primary Science Curriculum

Unit	Grade 1	Grade 2	Grade 3	Grade 4	Grade 5	Grade 6	Grade 7
1	Health & the Human Body	Health & the Human Body	Health & the Human Body	Health & the Human Body	Life Science	Life Science	Life Science
2	The Environment Around Us	The Environment Around Us	The Environment Around Us	The Environment Around Us	Physical Science	Physical Science	Physical Science
3	-	-	-	-	Earth Science	Earth Science	Earth Science
4	-	-	-	-	Technology Awareness	Technology Awareness	Technology Awareness

Table 2

Strengths and Success Stories

The major strength of the NCC is based on the collaborative effort of curriculum developers. The NCC has personnel that promote mutual support in all areas of its mandates. Despite the fact that, in many cases, a department may be held by one individual, collaboration across subject areas is a common feature at NCC. It is in this context that coherence in managing changes is achieved.

NCC has, in general, managed to meet deadlines for producing draft manuscripts over the years. They also have managed to review materials in a seven-year cycle successfully in all but a few special cases, such as when the designer leaves for further training. The current review is now at Grade 7 level.

Concerns

The NCC personnel consulted for this chapter indicated that although NCC is able to meet its mandates, it does experience constraints. First, with regard to policy, they pointed out that although the mandate of the NCC is well articulated in some government documents, it is clear that in practice, these are not necessarily followed (The Government of Swaziland, 1996). For example, the NCC is responsible for coordination of all curriculum development; in practice, however, the NCC has been sometimes bypassed. They reiterated points made in a paper presented to a conference held by the Association for Educational Assessment in Africa (AEAA) in Swaziland in 2006, in which members of the NCC complained that it has been difficult to fully influence the curriculum, primarily because the MOE policy on education and the curriculum is not coherent. This resulted, they say, in interference in the execution of their duties.

Second, it is said that, because of the lack of coherent policies, the pilot process is adversely affected, particularly at the high school level. As a result, the current IGCSE program now in use was neither piloted nor adequately infused before implementation.

Third, they point out a lack of internal evaluation of projects and external evaluation of programs. This was said to affect decision-making regarding appropriate implementation strategies.

Last, personnel point out that some programs, such as developmental studies, which have been in the education system for over 20 years, are still confined to only six schools. Had this program been adequately evaluated, the NCC would have been able to develop curriculum for high school education and implement it nationwide. In cases where programs face challenges, they either stagnate or are abandoned for lack of evaluative and corrective measures.

Socio-cultural and Political Influences

According to the members of the staff at NCC who were consulted, the Swazi culture plays a major role in setting up the content and method for teaching. While selecting content, examples, and activities, the curriculum developers seek relevant cultural and/or familial material. It is believed to be essential to propagate culture; thus, wherever, possible, curriculum materials incorporate appropriate cultural practices and norms in the curriculum content. Schools also engage in sport and culture, which does not have a written curriculum. Swaziland has an oral tradition by which knowledge is transmitted. The school curriculum includes this mode of knowledge transmission through an emphasis on telling folk tales. This oral culture accounts for the lack of documented information of cultural practices, knowledge, beliefs, and norms that could contribute to curriculum development. Thus, each time a new curriculum is introduced, fresh consultations are necessary, even when the data collected remain unchanged.

Meanwhile, although policies specify the mandate of the NCC to have sole responsibility for curriculum development, their experience demonstrates that political undertones interfere with that mandate. Many times, decisions are made at the political level and implemented without the input of the NCC. This is seen when a donor presents a program or materials to the MOE. An example of this was the continuous assessment program that eventually got handed over to the NCC. When it started, it did not go through the normal processes of curriculum development. Similarly, the high school programs have remained foreign because of political dictates. However, political does have a positive influence through legislating subsidised learning materials, making it possible for curriculum developers to produce quality books.

Future Trends

The NCC staff perceives a need for further diversification of the school curriculum. They feel that greater autonomy could improve the NCC's ability to move in this direction. In so doing, the NCC would develop all teaching/learning materials for all education, including early childhood and teacher education, without the current constraints. They also would ensure that the school curriculum dovetails with the tertiary education curriculum.

References and Resources

Imbhokodvo National Movement. (1972). *Imbhokodvo manifesto. The philosophy policies and objectives of the Imbhokodvo National Movement.* Mbabane, Swaziland: Author.

Mabuza, M. B. (n.d.). *History of curriculum development in Swaziland. A paper written for the Ministry of Education* (housed as part of a government collection of papers). Mbabane, Swaziland.

Magagula, C. M. (1988). *Educational reform in Swaziland. A discussion paper presented to the World Bank* (housed as part of a government collection of papers). Mbabane: Swaziland.

Solomon, J., & Aikenhead, G. (1994). (Eds.). *STS education. International perspectives on reform.* New York: Teachers' College Press.

The Government of Swaziland. (undated). *A 2022 national development strategy for Swaziland* (draft). Mbabane, Swaziland: Author.

The Government of Swaziland. (1969). *The National Development Plan (1969/1973).* Mbabane, Swaziland: Author.

The Government of Swaziland. (1973). *The National Development Plan (1973/1977).* Mbabane, Swaziland: Author.

The Government of Swaziland. (1978). *The National Development Plan (1978/1983).* Mbabane, Swaziland: Author.

The Government of Swaziland. (1983). *The National Development Plan (1984/1988).* Mbabane, Swaziland: Author.

The Government of Swaziland. (1996). *Education and training development strategy: Our children first.* A report prepared by the Educational and Training Sector Committee of the National Development Strategy. Mbabane, Swaziland: Author.

The Government of Swaziland. (1999). *National policy statements on education.* Ministry of Education. Mbabane, Swaziland: Author.

Ministry of Education. (2004). *The development of education. National report of the Kingdom of Swaziland.* Mbabane, Swaziland: Author. Available at www.ibe.unesco.org/international/ICE/instrap/Swaziland.pdf

Acknowledgment

I would like to acknowledge the contribution made by Ms. Makhosazana Madondo to this chapter. She read the draft, corrected the facts, and made suggestions to improve the accuracy of claims made in the chapter. Her dedication to this work is greatly appreciated.

About the Author

Betty T. Dlamini obtained a master's degree in science education from the University of Manitoba, Canada, and a Ph.D. (also in science education) from the University of the Witwatersrand, South Africa. She started the science education program for primary school teachers at the University of Swaziland, where she currently holds a senior lecturer position. She has been involved in research into contextualization in Swaziland since 1991. She has written various papers in the area and had a chapter published in a book on the role of professional organizations in professional development. She can be reached at University of Swaziland, Private Bag 4, Kwaluseni, Swaziland., Tel: +268 5184011, Fax: +268 5185276, E-mail: betty@uniswacc.uniswa.s

Special Education in Turkey: Curriculum, Policy, and Practice

Selda Ozdemir

During the past several decades, special education services have been undergoing a philosophical transformation in Turkey. In the past, best practices counseled that children with special needs should be educated in segregated classes, based on their disability, in segregated residential schools. However, with the Special Education Act 573 of 1997 and Special Education Law of 2005, effective implementation of inclusion, initiation of individualized education programs, importance of early intervention, and involvement of parents in educational provisions have been identified as critical priorities for the reestablishment of special education services in Turkey (Akkok, 2000). The Special Education Law 2005, the primary law governing education of students with disabilities, requires the provision of a free, appropriate public education in the least restrictive environment whereby individual student needs can be met.

Although considerable change has been achieved on the special education policy level, we can hardly see a significant impact in actual educational practices for children with special needs (Akkok, 2000). In other words, the realities in educational settings and attitudes and behaviors toward children with disabilities do not reflect that, in fact, societal and educational changes have been achieved with respect to inclusive education. The lack of culturally sensitive curriculum practices, effective instructional strategies, and inservice training opportunities are only a few of the critical issues facing those working with children with special needs in Turkey. These issues are further complicated by limited access and availability to curriculum specialists in the area of designing inclusive education.

This chapter will provide an understanding of special and general education practices in Turkey, with a special emphasis upon a new curriculum reform; examine critically how curriculum development has evolved over the years; and discuss the social, economic, and educational dilemmas of curriculum implementations in inclusive education practices. More important, although Turkey has made

Turkey

progress in developing a new policy and legislative framework in building an inclusive education system, several core problems in current practices remain that must be examined critically to improve future reform and implementation efforts. For this purpose, this chapter will discuss three major topics: 1) the historical side of general and special education in Turkey; 2) the new curriculum reform and social, economic, and educational dilemmas in implementations; and 3) inclusive multilevel curriculum and a need for a transformative change agenda in inclusive education practices.

Turkish Educational System: A Brief Overview

The Turkish education system is centralized with respect to a wide range of matters, including policy decisions, curriculum, approval of textbooks and other instructional materials, governance and inspection of schools, and inservice training of teachers. Elementary education covers eight years of compulsory education and is divided into two cycles. The first five years (primary level) are mainly taught by classroom teachers, while subject area teachers teach the last three years. The ministry of national education governs all public kindergartens, elementary schools, and secondary schools covering K-11 education throughout the country. A uniform curriculum is carried out in all public and private schools. In order to meet the goals and objectives of the curriculum, the textbooks or related materials, which are approved by the Milli Egitim Bakanligi (Ministry of National Education), are selected each year by committees for each subject area. The teachers and schools can only use the textbooks and teaching materials approved by the Ministry. A prerequisite for approval of a textbook or teaching material is that it must reflect or possess qualities of the national curriculum. While daily plans are prepared by individual teachers, the yearly content outline is pretty much determined by the scope and sequence provided by the Ministry of National Education. Thus, classroom teaching is highly prescribed and leaves little room for creativity.

The elementary school curriculum is divided into seven major subjects: mathematics, science, social studies, Turkish, music, art, and physical education. Major emphasis is given to the development of communication skills in Turkish, including reading/writing and speaking/listening. All elementary schools operate on the semester system, and frequent short tests are given to provide periodic checks of student mastery in all subjects. Midterm and final examinations are typically given each semester. Semester grades at the elementary school level are customarily on a five-point scale. In addition to the standardized assessment techniques, the new curriculum introduces alternative assessment strategies, such as portfolios, checklists, and performance-based projects. Thus, the new curriculum takes a radical approach, improving the ongoing assessment system by employing both traditional and alternative assessment strategies (Koc, Isiksal, & Bulut, 2007).

Historical Context

In Turkey, education is uniform for people in all parts of the country, and the transmission and advancement of the Turkish culture is an integral part of this education. To understand the education system in Turkey and the magnitude of the current reforms, it is important to provide a brief historical context of educational services. Following the foundation of the young Turkish Republic in 1923, Mustafa Kemal Ataturk, the founder of modern Turkey, started an educational revolution, with systematic innovations in curriculum development studies, by introducing a new Turkish Latin alphabet to replace the Arabic script, as well as a Western-style education system. In 1924, with the Law of Common Education, the Ministry of National Education became the only authority responsible for the operation of all education institutions (Gozutok, 2003). Considering the needs of the newly established republic, initial curriculum development studies were conducted, with a special emphasis upon the importance of Europe for Turkey's modernization (Koc et al., 2007).

The national curriculum aimed to make Turks more conscious of their original identity and their unique cultural heritage and pre-Islamic past, and to develop a society of individuals, rather than servants or subjects of an empire or emperor. According to Massials (1971), "The emphasis on Turkish language and culture in the curriculum was necessary because the reform of Kemalist revolution intended to Turkicize the people by providing a new set of Turkish ideals (not Ottoman), by eliminating religion from state-related activity" (p. 283). Early education efforts, successive national policies, and plans had been directed towards establishing universal primary education and eradicating illiteracy, particularly in rural areas.

Many factors influence the education systems of a country, one of the greatest in Turkey being the political regimes and regime transitions. In fact, democracy in the young Turkish Republic has experienced many military interventions in its short history. These interventions have changed Turkish society, including the education system, and have resulted in the creation of new policies in education. After the last military intervention of 1980, the military regarded education as a tool designed to reshape society and legitimize the control of government. Both the Turkish constitution and the educational implementations can be viewed as instruments through which the military made efforts to establish a new society and implement a predetermined policy. In the 1980s, the military's supremacy over education was thereby reaffirmed, and a military-ordered educational structure was revived (Guven, 2004). While the generals of the 1980 military intervention are today long gone, their effects on the education system and quality of education are still prominent. With a program model presented by the Ministry of National Education in 1982, encouraging thinking and discussion became strictly off-limits (Guven, 2004). However, the rapidly changing nature of Turkish society and greater democratization efforts resulted in a new wave of curriculum change in the early 1990s under the guidance of the National Education Development Project. This project aimed to increase the efficiency and effectiveness of elementary and secondary level education by improving the quality of teaching in various subject areas.

Although various debates on its status of democratization, human rights, and fundamental freedoms are still ongoing, Turkey aims to transform itself into a knowledge society with a highly competitive economy capable of sustainable development and eventually to become a member of the European Union. Since January 2004, the Turkish Ministry of National Education has been in the process of a massive change in school curricula, especially at the elementary level. The reform has been initiated by a grant from the European Union. Elementary school curricula in five different subject areas—mathematics, science, social science, life science, and Turkish—have been completely redeveloped and were implemented in the 2005-06 school year. The basic idea behind the reform was to change the curriculum from a subject-centered to a learner-centered one, and to change the pedagogies from behaviorist to constructivist (Babadogan & Olkun, 2006).

The purpose of student-centered instruction is to replace rote memorization with learning for understanding. Thus, the whole trend moves from a static, passive view of knowledge toward a more adaptive and active one. The teacher's role becomes one of purposeful instruction, a mediator of activities and substantial experiences, allowing the learner to attain his or her zone of proximal development (Blanton, 1998). A constructivist approach focuses on how children learn and the nature of the knowledge to be learned, and it provides the starting point for developing curriculum. For example, a constructivist teacher begins with what is known about the child and the child's way of knowing, rather than from curriculum or national standards. Constructivist curriculum highlights the ways that teachers consider the processes by which children learn, address problem-solving, organize materials, take an active role throughout the day, and relate curriculum to the context in which they teach (Osterman, 1998). Therefore, the Turkish curriculum reform may be perceived as a paradigm shift in putting a considerable amount of emphasis on individuality, considering the fact that the dynamics of the Turkish socio-cultural system do not encourage individual development as much as social development (Koc et al., 2007).

A Brief History of Special Education in Turkey

The beginning of formal special education in Turkey can be traced to the 1880s, with the establishment of two schools for individuals with visual and hearing impairments (Akkok, 2000). At the time of Turkey's creation in 1923, the government's efforts were channeled toward nation-building;

consequently, educational provisions for children with special needs were limited (Ozyurek, 2004). Services for children with special needs continued to be inadequate or non-existent in many areas until the 1950s, when a department was established in the Ministry of National Education to serve a small group of children with special needs (Akcamete & Kaner, 1999; Ozyurek, 2004). The formalization of special education in Turkey was instituted through adding a series of items to the Turkish Constitution in 1961 to establish an administrative and organizational special education system. When special education was regulated in 1961, a segregated system was created through the establishment of special schools and special classes in general education schools. The primary objective of the formalization of special education was to provide an education for the many children with special needs still being excluded from schooling.

The 1983 Act was the first document that sought to avoid segregation and facilitate integration of students with special needs into regular classrooms. This act not only tried to promote the integration of students with special needs previously assigned to special schools, but also sought to change Turkey's schools by modifying educational conditions and providing support for the many students with learning difficulties (Batu & Kircaali-Iftar, 2005). However, the proposed integration of individuals with disabilities into the regular education system remained only on paper and in political rhetoric. Although the 1983 Act showed that Turkey was not ignorant of the inclusive education approaches developed in the United States and Europe, the new ideas did not crystallize into an adequate system for meeting the needs of children with special needs (Ataman, 2003).

Public funds continued to be directed toward educational services provided in segregated private institutions, rather than the integration of individuals with special needs into the regular education system. This approach was not much criticized, even though many of the individuals in these institutions could be integrated into regular schools. Many parents argued that, compared to ordinary schools, these segregated institutions provided human and material resources that were more efficient for their children's development. However, such an argument clearly ignored the value of integration that takes place between typically developing and impaired individuals as a means to stimulate social, intellectual, and affective development in both groups. Furthermore, although this argument was mainly based on the idea that general education teachers were not prepared to meet the needs of students with disabilities in inclusive settings, the funds used by private institutions could have been used to prepare teachers and provide material resources in public schools in order to facilitate the inclusion of individuals with special needs into regular education settings.

In 1997, the government introduced the landmark Special Education Act 573, which ushered in a new era for special and general education alike (Milli Egitim Bakanligi, 2000). For the first time, Turkish children with special needs were going to enjoy free public education and access to specialized services. Special Education Act 573 requires the provision of a free, appropriate public education in the least restrictive environment in which a student's needs can be met (Ataman, 2003). The least restrictive environment means that students with disabilities must be educated in the setting least removed from the general education classroom. To the greatest extent possible, students with disabilities are not to be restricted to special education schools or special classrooms, but rather should have access to the same settings to which students without disabilities have access (Mastropieri & Scruggs, 2000).

It is important to highlight that this act also requires that students with special needs participate in general education curricula and assessment activities with supplementary aids and services and specially designed instruction, as appropriate. Special Education Act 573 was the first attempt by the Ministry of Education to indicate that special education was part of the global context of education for all (Kargin, 2004). However, the methodology adopted for the special education curriculum was merely a diluted version of the regular curriculum, and the qualitative changes necessary to address specific disabilities were not considered. In other words, there was clearly ambiguity in the legislation regarding how to implement inclusive education. This ambiguity was mainly resolved with the acceptance of the 2005 Special Education Law. The regulations contemplate special education becoming integrated with basic education and sharing the same broadened curriculum, albeit flexible and optional in many of its parts.

Overall, special education in Turkey, in keeping with international trends, is in the process of transformation. Beginning in 1997, Turkey's plans and policies had a different vision of special education; today, special education is considered part of regular education. The current tendency is to include students with disabilities in regular school classrooms, with the exception of students whose needs require placement in a special school or classroom. However, 10 years after the launch, policy developers and implementers have arrived at the realization that there are both challenges and possibilities associated with the implementation of inclusive education in Turkey (Eripek, 2004; Kargin, 2004; Kaya, 2003). While there is enough reason to be highly optimistic about the future of inclusive education in Turkey, the caveat is not to underestimate the challenges and complexities of developing a single education system for all learners.

Curriculum Reform:
Social, Economic, and Educational Dilemmas in Implementation

Meeting the challenges associated with the educational integration of students with special needs begins with the development of a broad-based and flexible curriculum that is sensitive to the special needs of all students. However, basic curriculum in Turkey traditionally excluded and segregated many students based on their learning differences, until the acceptance of a new approach, the constructivist curriculum, in 2005. The new constructivist curriculum provided the basis for the development of inclusive education through more rigorous and relevant school subjects and by emphasizing the way in which teachers consider the processes by which children learn, address problem-solving, organize materials, take an active role throughout the day, and relate curriculum to the context in which they teach. This transformation has sought to reach the ideal of international standards of education implemented in Europe (Koc et al., 2007). Moreover, the transformation has aimed to minimize the impact of learning difficulties exhibited by students with mild and moderate disabilities and to make general education responsible for meeting their educational needs. To date, this has only been moderately successful, since most public schools have maintained their inflexible and rigid curricular objectives and goals, as well as their traditional school organizational structures and practices.

While the new curriculum reform intended to improve learning outcomes for children with special needs, certain sociocultural and sociopolitical forces blurred the visions of meeting the needs of these children in an effective, equitable, and democratic manner. These forces included economics, systemic constraints, and negative beliefs about the educability and worth of people with disabilities in Turkish society. Turkish society's overreliance on a deficit perspective, coupled with cultural, sociopolitical, and economic forces, negatively affected early inclusive education efforts. Not only teachers, but many parents of typically developing children have difficulty in viewing inclusion as a civic right for all students with disabilities. Even though some parents and teachers agree on the philosophy of inclusive education, many are skeptical about inclusive practice in the light of the inadequacy of existing resources in the school system (Batu, Kircaali-Iftar, & Uzuner, 2004). Thus, it is critical that teachers develop a non-discriminative disability perspective that not only focuses on deficits, but also focuses explicitly on student strengths and the importance of instructional contexts. The new definition of disability will expand our understanding of people with disabilities and encourage teachers to take active roles in promoting the learning experiences of these children in inclusive environments.

Often, developing a new definition of disability in order to create an inclusive classroom for students with disabilities is inconsistent with the current cultural attitudes, beliefs, and practices of many schools. Unfortunately, a human rights ethic is not a defining characteristic of most schools in Turkey, and the culture of competition prevails. Each year, over 1 million high school graduates in Turkey take a national university entrance exam. Thus, schools feel pressure to have their students do well on the exam, and to align their instruction with the exam and to engage in more exam preparation. Most families have generally concluded that in order for their children to be successful in this era of competition, schools must prepare the students to meet the demands of the education system. However, due in part to concerns over poor outcomes and low expectations for students with disabilities, many families are concerned that children with disabilities in inclusive classrooms will demand too much teacher time for individualized instruction and lower the academic achievement levels of classrooms (Ozbaba, 2000). Even the elementary school teachers are reported to be pressured by many parents, who want their children to be successful at school and ultimately gain a good score on the national university entrance exam.

The interplay between inclusive education reform and its implicit pursuit of a cultural agenda that privileges dominant groups has generated continuing debates among teachers, parents, policymakers, and researchers about best practices for inclusive education. Many special education teachers and researchers are concerned that the new inclusive education reform—without enough preparation—will shortchange students with disabilities, as teachers feel compelled to cover content and promote more sophisticated forms of learning, thus leaving less time to support students with disabilities. Special education teachers and researchers are also concerned that through improper interpretation and implementation of inclusion, general education classes will be used as "dumping grounds" for students with disabilities, with no additional support, planning, or training for the teachers and students (Eripek, 2004). A proof of this failure can be found in the large number of students who are enrolled in special education institutions or special education classrooms without a clear reason for being there.

On the other hand, general education teachers have reported being overwhelmed with the responsibility of working with large numbers of typically developing students and students with disabilities with no in-class support, no assistance in adapting instruction to meet the special needs of students, and no time to plan and coordinate in-class activities with the special education teachers who may have worked with the students in the past (Batu, Kircaali-Iftar, & Uzuner, 2004; Baykoc-Donmez, Avci, & Aslan, 1997). Often, they fear that the students with disabilities will take too much of their time and effort, and that their regular education students' learning will suffer. Important to this issue is the recognition that general educators' willingness to include students with special needs in their classes is critical to the successful implementation of inclusive educational practices (Soodak, Podell, & Lehman, 1998).

From the available findings, it appears that Turkish teachers' attitudes toward inclusive education are highly related to the perceived ability of teachers to instruct students with special needs (Gozun & Yikmis, 2004; Kaya, 2005). That is, Turkish teachers often find themselves in a state of transition between traditional ways of teaching and new approaches that may be inconsistent with what they have believed to be true for most of their teaching careers. As most of the general education teachers in Turkey are educated in their undergraduate programs, which are based on strong behaviorist theory, and learned to use direct instruction to teach their students, many teachers are unable to see the commonalities extant between two paradigms and feel that they are not prepared well enough to address the needs of students with disabilities in inclusive education environments. It is not surprising, then, that planned inclusion efforts have posed a serious challenge to schools, given the strong tradition of teacher-directed, whole-class, age-graded instruction, with little instructional variability across relatively homogeneous groups of children (Goodlad, 1983). Furthermore, the majority of general education teachers in Turkey are skeptical about inclusive education, because new curriculum provides only vague descriptions about instruction to students with disabilities based on constructivist principles (Batu, Kircaali-Iftar, & Uzuner, 2004). Without detailed descriptions, general education teachers find it difficult to comprehend how children with disabilities, through student-centered activities facilitated by a teacher, can construct knowledge that will enhance student performance in their zones of proximal development.

Thus, it is important to recognize for Turkish policymakers that if the new curriculum fails to provide explicit rationales and descriptions of practices that are guided by a constructivist curriculum approach, they will have done little to advance the value of the inclusive education paradigm and the emergence of widespread, improved learning outcomes for children with disabilities. Because a good understanding of change and a clear conception of curriculum are necessary conditions for improved implementation of new curriculum practice, learning about educational change and its key features should become integral elements of any serious curriculum reform process.

In addition, teacher educators in Turkey have to transcend extreme views about certain curriculum approaches and should develop teacher education programs that will enable teachers to understand how common threads run across various instructional models and paradigms. Thus, it is critical that university-level education programs develop a much broader curriculum approach with respect to diversity in learning. Research suggests that effective teachers learn to integrate strategically instructional models based on the needs and strengths of their students (Teddlie, Kirby, & Stringfield, 1989). Therefore, teaching techniques representative of many learning styles and various curriculum approaches must be incorporated into the teacher training curriculum in Turkey. Furthermore, a variety of methods, including collaborative, cooperative, teaming, and consultative styles, must be adequately addressed in teacher training programs.

Bringing Special and General Education Closer Together

In addition to transforming general education, special education will need to become more flexible in how it provides services, and will have to establish a professional development program to update special education personnel regarding the new realities of a common school for all students. Current education reform in Turkey will continue to require strong reciprocity and collaborative planning between general and special education teachers, since changing the way that teachers teach and students learn requires specific approaches (Kargin, 2004). In fact, helping teachers to create professional learning communities and schools to learn from each other is essential for successful inclusion. This collaboration occurs when educators work together and support each other to provide the highest quality curriculum and instruction for all the students they serve. However, it is important to consider that many general and special education teachers would consider that the radical changes in the Turkish education system would mean giving up some of the power and control inherent in the teacher's role as an authority figure in the traditional classroom.

The change that results from systematic reform efforts raises hope, because it offers growth and progress. It also stirs fear, however, because it challenges competence and power, creates confusion, and risks the loss of continuity and meaning (Evans, 1993). A possible answer to this dilemma may have to do with the concepts of teacher efficacy and educational change. Hence, special and general education teachers are encouraged to develop an understanding of the rationale for changing what they do and what they think. Through collaboration, ideas can be shared, new and better strategies can be developed, problems can be solved, students' progress can be better monitored, and their outcomes can be evaluated effectively (Mastropieri & Scruggs, 2000). Through the process of combining separate expertise and skills to achieve a common goal, a collaborative team is able to accomplish much more together than the individuals could accomplish working alone (Falvey, 1995).

Successful inclusion of students with disabilities largely depends on the willingness of general education teachers to accept the concept in principle. It is hypothesized in the literature that the teacher's attitude has a significant impact on the success of any inclusion effort, since it appears to be related to the willingness of teachers to instruct students with disabilities. In a survey study, Weiner (2003) found that 74% of inclusion teachers "felt that the teacher's attitude towards students was the first or second most important condition needed for successful inclusion" (p. 16). For 33% of teachers, the most important condition was having teachers see students as valued members of the class, and 36% of teachers saw a teacher taking a personal interest in a child as an important condition. Overall, Weiner's survey indicates that teachers who implement inclusive teaching practices acknowledge the importance of positive teacher attitudes and beliefs toward students. Policymakers and teacher educators often disregard the beliefs and attitudes of teachers toward inclusive education and teaching students with diverse needs. Thus, in order to facilitate systematic reform, a change model must be developed to help teachers become aware of their implicit beliefs about inclusive education and provide them with the information and skills that would allow them to engage in teaching practices that are more responsive to the diverse needs of all students.

Many general education teachers in Turkey are overly concerned about not being trained in techniques and strategies to meet the needs of students with disabilities. Helping teachers recognize the relationship that exists between their beliefs and attitudes about their teaching practices and students with special needs is a critical factor in developing teachers' willingness to consider and experiment with inclusive education practices. Through incorporating guidelines from systematic reform into staff development programs, Turkish educators may be able to recognize how this relationship impacts the planning and execution of curricular activities that address the needs of all students in their classrooms.

Inclusive Multilevel Curriculum and a Need for a Change Agenda

Designing curriculum at the onset so that all students can meaningfully participate has been hailed as a powerful alternative to modifying previously planned instructional lessons in an effort to accommodate diverse learners (Jorgensen, 1998; Udvari-Solner, 1995). Creating and enacting accessible curriculum demands that the teacher be an active participant who facilitates, mediates, and reconstructs understanding in the interactive learning event as it occurs. Rather than adding modifications and adaptations onto already established lesson plans, the teacher instead creates instructional events at the planning stage so that all learners can actively participate in the curriculum experience (Falvey, 1995; Falvey, Givner, & Kimm, 1996). Multilevel curriculum selection has occurred in regular education as an adaptation of Bloom's Taxonomy of Educational Objectives (1956), including knowledge, comprehension, application, analysis, synthesis, and evaluation goals for students with different abilities, disabilities, strengths, and needs. For example, in a lesson on money, one student might be learning at the knowledge level (e.g., identifying money), another at the comprehension level (e.g., understanding the uses of money), and others might be applying their knowledge and comprehension by making purchases and budgeting (Giangreco & Putnam, 1991).

Creating a multilevel curriculum provides support and access to the general education curriculum for students identified with different learning needs. This approach, derived from a constructivist perspective, recognizes that knowledge and meaning are composed through socially mediated interactions (Udvari-Solner & Thousand, 1996). Multilevel curricula recognize that learning takes place when the students and teacher engage in curriculum experiences whereby new and previously established understandings come together in a dynamic context. Knowledge in this sense is not obtained, but rather constructed through socially mediated interactions, and it is always evolving in light of new experiences. This whole process requires that curriculum orientation shift from a curriculum as product model to a curriculum as process model. Re-conceptualizing curriculum also would transform the role of the curriculum from an overloaded and confusing document into a more comprehensive idea that also serves as a guideline for successful inclusion.

Multilevel curriculum, from a social constructivist, critical disability studies lens, is potentially transformative; reflective of students' talents, interests, and voices; and values all individuals as contributing and cherished members of the community. Multilevel curriculum occurs when a student with disabilities and typically developing peers participate together in a shared activity and students have individually appropriate learning outcomes at multiple levels, but all within the same curriculum area (Giangreco, 1996; Sapon-Shevin, 1996). The teacher may teach a curricular content: 1) with a functional application to daily routines of life, 2) at a less complex level, 3) with reduction in the performance standards, and 4) at a slower pace. Teachers become the deliberate decision-makers when composing authentically meaningful curriculum experiences in which all learners are challenged and supported. Looking at curriculum from this angle challenges the dominant roles, responsibilities, and social images of teachers often promoted in our schools.

Available studies on the preferred teaching practices of Turkish teachers suggest that undifferentiated large-group instruction, teacher lecture, and independently completed question-answer assignments remain prevalent in most of Turkey's schools. ·In observing classroom practice in Turkey, Kahveci and Cakmak (in preparation) concluded that Turkish teachers appeared to be more concerned with maintaining routine in classrooms than with matching instruction to individual differences. Findings from the study suggest that while educators in Turkey understand that not all learners are the same, and that their needs are diverse, few teachers accommodate these differences in their classrooms. Uniformity, rather than attending to diversity, dominates the culture of many contemporary classrooms in Turkey. The reality of today's schools in Turkey is disconnecting and requires that we question how to best reform our education systems. The crucial dimension of change is affecting the culture of school simultaneously with improving individuals' knowledge and skills. In fact, the ways in which the curricula and inclusive education are implemented depend on our perspectives of change and the meaning and intent of the curriculum. Thus, learning about educational change and its key features should become integral parts of the education reform process in Turkey (Sucuoglu, 2004).

Conclusion

Reform and restructuring of the Turkish education system have long been topics of discussion within the field of education and political organizations. Beginning in 1997, some reforms in both special and general education have been moving toward a unified, inclusive system of education, so that the education of all students will become the concern of the entire school system. After the release of Special Education Act 573 in 1997, education reformists intensified their efforts to enact a series of laws that formalized the different phases of the development of inclusive education in Turkey and introduced a new constructivist curriculum, particularly in response to the modern developments and changes in educational practices in Europe. The education reforms have received attention, both positive and negative, from educators, parents, faculty members, administrators, and policymakers. Although still controversial, such attention to the education reforms has been credited with leading to more functional and more applied curriculum, as well as to instruction that is more diverse and responsive to student needs. In addition to a focus on curriculum, reform efforts also have targeted the style of instruction. Designing instructional procedures that are compatible with students' learning styles and needs is of value for students for developing the skills of critical thinking and decision-making, and thus to apply information taught at school to everyday life.

Although many important reforms have been achieved to overcome the challenges facing special and general education in Turkey, many issues remain unresolved with regard to implementing inclusive education. Obviously, Turkey is a developing country intent on becoming a member of the European Union, working to construct a unified education system that is capable of meeting the needs of both special and general education. Indeed, Turkey's current laws, which are both advanced and innovative, include all of the requirements needed for supporting effective educational programs for students with disabilities and for integrating them into the regular education system. However, even though these laws are not far from being put into practice, Turkey's current special and general education practices suggest that such a broad-based reform requires thoughtful restructuring of beliefs and practices at school and classroom levels, involving teachers, parents, administrators, and students. Policymakers, faculty members, and educators need to know more about the drivers of successful change in education systems. Small steps are being accomplished that can create highly powerful changes in the education of students with disabilities. Larger steps that will support a national change for all students are sure to follow. The ultimate goal is creating a unified system of education in which all students, including students with disabilities, have equal access to quality educational experiences and become active members of their community.

References

Akcamete, G., & Kaner, S. (1999). *Cumhuriyetin 75. yilinda cocuga yonelik ozel egitim calismalari* [Special education studies at the 75th anniversary of Republic of Turkey]. 2. Proceedings of Ulusal Cocuk Kulturu Kongresi: Cumhuriyet ve Cocuk. Ankara: Ankara Universitesi Cocuk Kulturu Arastirma ve Uygulama Merkezi, 2, 395-405.

Akkok, F. (2000). Special education research: A Turkish perspective. *Exceptionality, 8*(4), 273-279.

Ataman, A. (2003). *Ozel egitime giris* [Introduction to special education]. Gunduz Egitim ve Yayincilik, Ankara.

Babadogan, C., & Olkun, S. (2006). Program development models and reform in Turkish primary school mathematics curriculum [Electronic version]. *International Journal for Mathematics Teaching and Learning,* April. Available at www.ejmste.com/v3n3/EJMSTE_v3n3_Bulut.pdf

Batu, S., & Kircaali-Iftar, G. (2005). *Kaynastirma* [Inclusion]. Kok Yayincilik, Ankara.

Batu, S., Kircaali-Iftar, G., & Uzuner, Y. (2004). Ozel gereksinimli ogrencilerin kaynastirildigi bir kiz meslek lisesindeki ogretmenlerin kaynastirmaya iliskin gorus ve onerileri [Teachers' perceptions and suggestions on the inclusive education in an inclusive vocational high school for girls]. *Ankara Universitesi Egitim Bilimleri Fakultesi Ozel Egitim Dergisi, 5*(2), 33-50.

Baykoc-Donmez, N., Avci, N., & Aslan, N. (1997, September). *Ilk ve ortaogretim kurum ogretmenlerinin engellilere ve kaynastirmaya iliskin bilgi ve gorusleri* [Elementary and secondary school teachers' knowledge and perceptions about inclusion and disability]. Paper presented at the meeting of 4. Ulusal Egitim Bilimleri Kogresi, Eskisehir.

Blanton, M. L. (1998). *Prospective teachers emerging pedagogical content knowledge during the professional semester.* Unpublished doctoral dissertation, North Carolina State University, Raleigh.

Bloom, B. S. (1956). *Taxonomy of educational objectives: Handbook I. Cognitive domain.* New York: David McCay Co.

Eripek, S. (2004). Turkiye'de zihin engelli cocuklarin kaynastirilmalarina iliskin olarak yapilan arastirmalarin gozden gecirilmesi [An overview of studies conducted on the inclusion of children with mental retardation in Turkey]. *Ankara Universitesi Egitim Bilimleri Fakultesi Ozel Egitim Dergisi, 5*(2), 25-32.

Evans, R. (1993). The human face of reform. *Educational Leadership, 51*(2), 19-23.

Falvey, M. A. (Ed.). (1995). *Inclusive and heterogeneous schooling: Assessment, curriculum, and instruction.* Baltimore: Paul H. Brookes.

Falvey, M. A., Givner, C. C., & Kimm, C. (1996). What do I do Monday morning? In S. B. Stainback & W. C. Stainback (Eds.), *Inclusion: A guide for educators* (pp. 117-138). Baltimore: Paul H. Brookes.

Giangreco, M. F. (1996). Choosing options and accommodations for children (COACH): Curriculum planning for students with disabilities in general education. In W. Stainback & S. Stainback (Eds.), *Inclusion: A guide for educators* (pp. 237-254). Baltimore: Paul H. Brookes.

Giangreco, M. F., & Putnam, J. (1991). Supporting the education of students with severe disabilities in regular education environments. In L. H. Meyer, C. Peck, & L. Brown (Eds.), *Critical issues in the lives of people with severe disabilities* (pp. 245-270). Baltimore: Paul H. Brookes.

Goodlad, J. (1983). A study of schooling: Some findings and hypotheses. *Phi Delta Kappan, 64*, 462-470.

Gozun, O., & Yikmis, A. (2004). Ogretmen adaylarinin kaynastirma konusunda bilgilendirilmelerinin kaynastirmaya yonelik tutumlarinin degisimindeki etkililigi [Effectiveness of teacher training on teachers' attitudes towards inclusion]. *Ankara Universitesi Egitim Bilimleri Fakultesi Ozel Egitim Dergisi, 5*(2), 65-77.

Gozutok, F. D. (2003). Curriculum development in Turkey. In W. F. Pinar (Ed.), *International handbook of curriculum research* (pp. 607-622). London: Lawrence Erlbaum.

Guven, I. (2004). Education, the military, and politics in Turkey. In K. Mutaa & C. S. Sunal (Vol. Eds.), *Research on education in Africa, the Caribbean and the Middle East* (4th ed., pp. 243-265). Greenwich, CT: Information Age Publishing.

Jorgensen, C. M. (1998). *Restructuring high schools for all students: Taking inclusion to the next level.* Baltimore: Paul H. Brookes.

Kahveci, G., & Cakmak, S. (2007). Ogretmenlerinin siniflarinda yapisalci mufredata yer verme duzeyleri [The level of teachers' constructivist teaching practices in their classrooms]. Manuscript submitted for publication.

Kargin, T. (2004). Kaynastirma: Tanimi, gelisimi ve ilkeleri [Inclusion: Definition, development and principles]. *Ankara Universitesi Egitim Bilimleri Fakultesi Ozel Egitim Dergisi, 5*(2), 1-13.

Kaya, I. (2005). *Anasinifi Ogretmenlerinin Kaynastirma Egitimi uygulamalarinda yeterlilik duzeylerinin incelenmesi* [Examination of kindergarten teachers' competency on inclusive education implementations]. Unpublished master's thesis, Selcuk University, Konya.

Kaya, U. (2003). *Ilkogretim okulu yoneticilerinin, sinif ogretmenlerinin ve rehber ogretmenlerin kaynastirma ile ilgili bilgi, tutum ve uygulamalarinin incelenmesi* [Examination of elementary school teachers' knowledge, attitudes, and implementations of inclusive education]. Unpublished master's thesis, Gazi University, Ankara

Koc, Y., Isiksal, M., & Bulut, S. (2007). Elementary school curriculum reform in Turkey. *International Educational Reform, 8*(1), 30-39.

Massials, B. G. (1971). Turkey. In L. C. Deighton (Ed.), *Encyclopedia of education* (pp. 280-285). New York: The MacMillan Company & The Free Press.

Mastropieri, M. A., & Scruggs, T. E. (2000). *The inclusive classroom: Strategies for effective instruction.* Upper Saddle River, NJ: Merill.

Milli Egitim Bakanligi. (2000). *Ozel egitim hakkinda kanun hukmunde kararname ve ozel egitim hizmetleri yonetmeligi* [Legal decisions on inclusive education and regulations for implementations]. Ankara: Author.

Osterman, K. F. (1998, April). *Reflective practice: Linking professional development and school reform.* Paper presented at the annual meeting of the American Educational Research Association, San Diego, CA.

Ozbaba, N. (2000). *Normal cocuk annelerinin kaynastirma uygulamasina iliskin gorusleri* [Perceptions of mothers of normally developing children on inclusion]. Unpublished master's thesis, Marmara Universitesi, Istanbul.

Ozyurek, M. (2004). *Bireysellestirilmis egitim programi: Temelleri ve gelistirilmesi* [Individualized education program: Principles and development]. Ankara: Kok Yayincilik.

Sapon-Shevin, M. (1996). Full inclusion as disclosing tablet: Revealing the flaws in our present system. *Theory Into Practice, 35*(1), 35-41.

Soodak, L., Podell, D., & Lehman, L. (1998). Teacher, student, and school attributes as predictors of teachers' responses to inclusion. *The Journal of Special Education, 31*(1), 480-497.

Sucuoglu, B. (2004). Turkiye'de kaynastirma uygulamalari: Yayinlar/Arastirmalar (1980-2005) [Inclusive education practices in Turkey: Publications/Research (1980-2005)]. *Ankara Universitesi Egitim Bilimleri Fakultesi Ozel Egitim Dergisi, 5*(2), 15-23.

Teddlie, C., Kirby, P. G., & Stringfield, S. (1989). Effective versus ineffective schools: Observable differences in the classroom. *American Journal of Education, 97,* 221-236.

Udvari-Solner, A. (1995). A process for adapting curriculum in inclusive classrooms. In R. Villa & J. Thousands (Eds.), *Creating an inclusive school* (pp. 100-124). Alexandria, VA: Association for Supervision and Curriculum Development.

Udvari-Solner, A., & Thousand, J. S. (1996). Creating a responsive curriculum for inclusive schools. *Remedial & Special Education, 17*(3), 182-193.

Weiner, H. M. (2003). Effective inclusion: Professional development in the context of the classroom. *Teaching Exceptional Children, 35*(6), 12-18.

About the Author

Selda Ozdemir earned a B.S. in psychology from Ankara University, an M.S. in moderate and severe disabilities from Syracuse University, and a Ph.D. in early childhood special education from Arizona State University. Ozdemir worked with the full spectrum of disability categories and children with AD/HD in a variety of educational settings. As an assistant professor, she currently teaches in the special education program at Gazi University in Turkey. Her research examines social skills and emotion regulation problems of children with attention deficit/hyperactivity disorder. Ozdemir can be reached at seldaozdemir@gazi.edu.tr, Gazi University, Egitim Fakultesi, Ozel Egitim Bolumu, L Blok, Teknik okullar, Ankara, Turkey.

Curriculum Development in the United Kingdom: Themes, Trends, and Tensions

Martin Braund

Curriculum development in the United Kingdom (UK) is inseparable from the politics and cultural milieu of the times. It is perhaps astonishing to readers in other countries that in the UK, almost every aspect of the school system today (except for the statutory age ranges of schooling) would be almost unrecognizable to a teacher from 20 years ago. That this amount of change has been possible and achieved through legislation and statute, often with minimum amounts of consultation, research, and teacher involvement, is unprecedented and says much about the political psyche of the key players in curriculum development and about the rather loose and anarchic situation that existed for much of the 20th century. This chapter inevitably has its limits. It deals with the curriculum bounded by the compulsory age range of the school system, which is currently from age 5 to 16 (though some reference is made to the post-16 curriculum, where relevant), and what is discussed applies mainly to the situation in England.[1] Analysis and reflection are limited to the post-1944 period.

Curriculum is an elusive concept in the UK setting. For Goodson (1988), it is a complex, interacting matrix that includes: schools in the state and private sectors, teachers and how they are trained, resources available, and, of course, the subjects taught. It is interesting to note that the word "curriculum" hardly enters the educational language in the UK until the 1970s (Bourdillon & Storey, 2002). Philip Taylor, writing for an Open University course book on curriculum development in 1971, commented that only one book on curriculum theory and practice in the UK appeared in the literature at this time (Taylor, 1971); by contrast, since the 1980s, there have been hundreds. For many in the UK, curriculum development has become synonymous with the post-1989 National Curriculum and also, wrongly in the author's opinion, with "imposed change" rather than the more voluntary, less coercive term "development."

United Kingdom

To understand curriculum development in the UK, it is necessary to consider two triadic relationships, one determining students' experience of learning and the other the key players whose policies and actions shape experiences in the school system. These relationships are shown diagrammatically (see Figure 1).

Triad A shows that learning experiences are shaped by what is taught (*curriculum*) and the ways in which it is taught (*pedagogy*), and that both are affected by the practices through which we *assess* learning (Bennett et al., 2006). In the history of recent change in the UK, much has been done by government to define and control curriculum content and assessment methods. Until recently, however, pedagogy has been left largely to those who have to engage with it on a daily basis—namely, teachers (although even this is beginning to change).

Triad B shows the partners (key actors) in curriculum development. It has been the tradition in the UK that central government devises macro policy on curriculum. Local Education Authorities organize for it regionally, while local delivery is left to schools operating with broad consensus, support, and approval among all three partners. These relationships held sway for most of the 20th century—from the Education Act of 1904 to what is commonly called the Education Reform Act (ERA) of 1988 (DES, 1988a), which established a National Curriculum (Goodson, 1988; Kelly, 2004). Figure 2 summarizes key trends in the UK curriculum for each of the three interacting aspects of triad A. In the bulk of this chapter, each aspect is considered in turn, using a broad historical-political-sociological perspective, before considering currrent directions for curriculum development.

CURRICULUM CONTENT, POLICY, AND PRACTICE

Before the National Curriculum

The 1944 Education Act established statutory schooling for all between the ages of 5 and 13 and a tripartite secondary school system of grammar, technical, and vocational/modern schools. It did little, however, to change the content of a curriculum that had existed for much of the first half of the 20th century. The secondary school curriculum devised by the Board of Education in 1904 comprised subjects taught in the (selective and private) public and grammar schools of the day, the classics or a "modern" foreign language, English literature, history and geography, science, drawing

Two Crucial Triads in UK Curriculum Development

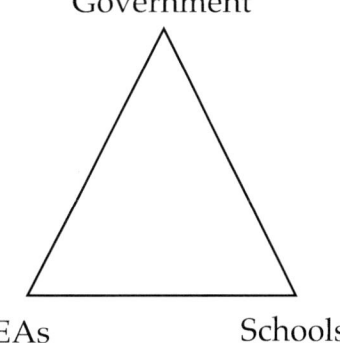

Triad A: Learning experiences

Curriculum

Pedagogy   Assessment

Triad B: Partnerships

Government

LEAs   Schools

Figure 1

(art), and either manual work (for boys) or housewifery (for girls). This subject-based framework has changed little and is mostly still in place. Some see the 1904 subject list as a clear attempt at social division, preserving a privileged education for an elite ruling and bureaucratic class, while creating something different for the blue- and white-collar workers of the lower-middle and working classes who served the nation's factories and offices (Goodson, 1988; Kelly, 2004). Hence, the foundations of a vocational-academic divide were laid, something that has bedeviled curriculum development to this day.

As was done for the 1904 curriculum, the state recommended subjects in the 1944 act, but they were not prescribed or controlled by the state, with the exception of religious education. This left schools and teachers, in partnership with their local education authorities (LEAs), a remarkable degree of freedom to determine the precise nature of what could be included and how it should be taught, within certain limitations imposed by examination boards. Grace (1987) considers this decentralized autonomy in curriculum and pedagogy as reflecting a unique British sense of democracy in attitudes to schooling and a certain degree of faith in the professional integrity of teachers. It also may have been that the alternative—a prescriptive, state-controlled system—smacked of totalitarianism, which was anathema to the post-war Labour government of the time (Bourdillon & Storey, 2002).

By the 1960s, the tripartite system of secondary schooling based on selecting students at age 11

Key Trends in UK Education, 1944-2008, As They Affect Curriculum, Assessment, and Pedagogy

1944-1980	2008
Curriculum	
Subject matter suggested centrally, but refined locally and largely decided by schools and teachers (except for RE). →	Subject matter decided and controlled by central government and its delivery policed by school inspections.
Assessment	
System limited to examinations at school-leaving ages (16+ and 18+) and controlled by examination boards with substantial involvement of teachers. →	Centrally controlled examination and testing systems, administered by examination boards with national testing at preschool, 7, 11, 14, 16+, 17, and 18+. Minimal involvement of teachers.
Pedagogy	
Teaching methods, distribution of teaching time, lesson sequences, and detailed approaches left to teachers to decide. →	Methods, organization, lesson sequences and precise methods, though not statutory, all heavily promoted by government strategies, training programs and publications and monitored through school inspections.

Figure 2

on the basis of psychometric tests (the 11 plus) and allocating them to either grammar, technical, or secondary modern schools was coming under fire. The selection process was seen as inefficient, unfair, and biased (Trowler, 2003), and the incoming Labour government of 1964 was determined to end it. By 1982, well over 80% of all state schools had become "comprehensives" admitting pupils of all abilities, without recourse to selection. The evolution of comprehensive schools offered new opportunities for curriculum development, including some innovative organization. For example, there were attempts to break down the subject-dominated grammar school curriculum by integrating and combining subject content. This occurred most notably in the humanities, where history, geography, religious education, and sometimes English were combined to form "integrated," "combined," or "liberal" studies, as well as in the sciences, where physics, chemistry, and biology were combined into themes taught as "integrated science." The uptake of these more innovative schemes, however, was rare, and the curriculum of the new comprehensive schools, in reality, became a version of that provided by the old grammar schools, with notable additions of such subjects as "rural science" for those students of whom it was thought might benefit from a more practically based curriculum (Goodson, 1988). Thus, the old divisions between a curriculum for an academic elite and the lower classes, enshrined in the pre-1944 era, continued and were exacerbated when the school-leaving age was raised from 14 to 16 in 1972. Now, a new cohort of students less inclined to academic subjects but also likely to stay on in schools or colleges beyond 16 had to be catered to, as unemployment in the mid-late 1970s rose, leading to worries about a new generation whose job opportunities might be blighted by educational inequality.

During the 1970s, a feeling developed that the education system was beginning to stagnate, that standards of achievement at every level were depressed, and that the curriculum was inadequate to fulfill the needs of an increasingly diverse and technologically based workplace (Convey & Merritt, 2000). Hence, the status of vocational subjects was revisited (as we shall see in the section on assessment). It is in this context that James Callaghan, the Labour Prime Minister of the time, gave what is widely regarded as one of the most important speeches to affect education in the UK, at Ruskin College, Oxford, in 1976 (Callaghan, 1976). The speech and the white paper *Better Schools* that followed (DES, 1985) stressed the government's intention to raise standards through legislation, thus paving the way for the most fundamental change to affect British education since 1944 and ending forever the balanced tripartite relationship between state, LEAs, and schools that had determined the curriculum for nearly 80 years.

The National Curriculum

The pre-national curriculum period of curriculum development is regarded by some as a sort of relative "golden age" during which teachers could effectively decide what they wanted to teach (Lawton, 1980). The truth of the matter is that this degree of "curricular autonomy" was already being eroded by a succession of government initiatives. In 1982, for example, in response to a perceived need to modernize the curriculum of secondary schools and again to address the vocational-academic divide, the government introduced the Technical and Vocational Education Initiative (TVEI). Substantial sums of money were on offer for schools to invest in curriculum innovation in the sciences, craft and technical subjects, and in information technology. At first, schools and teachers were suspicious of TVEI as it challenged their professionalism and represented a major shift toward centralized control of the curriculum. In effect, research has shown that initiatives at the local level were often vehicles for innovative and creative teachers to engage in professional growth and develop high-risk teaching (Harland, 1987). Harland describes some of these "TVEI-warm" teachers as "released prisoners" (p. 47) able to shake off complacency about their teaching and to begin developing into what Schön has called reflective practitioners (Schön, 1987).

The 1988 Education Reform Act (ERA), which introduced the National Curriculum for all state-run schools in England and Wales, required schools to provide pupils with a balanced and broadly based curriculum that included a core (English, maths, and science) and foundation subjects (design technology, information technology, history, geography, art, physical education, music, and, in secondary schools, a modern foreign language). The content of each subject to be taught was statutory, devised by subject working groups, and framed as age-related programs of study (DES, 1989). Programs of study were defined for each of four age groups, or "Key Stages" (5-7, 7-11, 11-14, 14-16). Content for advanced study beyond 16 was not part of the National Curriculum, and so this remained a contested area. A statutory assessment system was developed and appeared for core subjects as a series of "Attainment Targets," each containing criterion-referenced statements of expected knowledge, understanding, and skills, all assessed on a 10-level scale. In science, for example, the 1989 version of the National Curriculum contained 17 Attainment Targets (ATs) and over 460 statements of attainment (SoAs). The introduction of such a massive statutory edifice was viewed suspiciously by some, who saw little educational value in it, but rather plenty of political and ideological motives as an attempt by a Conservative government to rein in the power of (mainly) Labour-controlled LEAs (Arnot, 1992; Burton & Weiner, 1990).

Problems soon emerged in the primary schools as few teachers had sufficient knowledge or training to teach a subject-based curriculum, especially one that clashed with preferred notions of child-centered teaching (see section on pedagogy). Hence, fears were expressed over diminution of professionalism through having to teach a prescribed curriculum that teachers were obliged by law to implement and test (Gilroy, 1991). Concurrently, the language and landscape of education changed fundamentally. The rise of the "New Right," as it became known, meant the language of the market, rather than of education, was used; hence, the curriculum was seen as being "delivered," teachers were "accountable" and set "targets" to be achieved by their students.[2] James (2000) quotes a study in which teachers' language was observed to change from "a moral concept of responsibility for children to the managerial concept of accountability" (p. 349). According to a study by Broadfoot (1996), "Some teachers expressed fragmented identities . . . torn between a discourse which emphasised technical and managerial skills and values which continued to emphasise the importance of an emotional and affective dimension to teaching" (p. 127).

However, the idea of teachers, particularly in the primary schools, being de-skilled, passive recipients of a centrally imposed curriculum or acting as counter-revolutionaries, opposing its every nuance and therefore incapable of developing their teaching and pupils' learning, has been challenged. For example, Osborn et al. (1997) present evidence from a longitudinal study, the Primary Assessment, Curriculum and Experience (PACE) study, showing that as teachers got used to requirements of the National Curriculum, they accepted and internalized the programs of study, working them in ways that suited their beliefs about best practice. In some cases, they did so very creatively—a process that Osborn et al. call "creative mediation." Thus, crucial differences evolved between the *formal* curriculum (as devised by government and represented in official documentation) and the *perceived* curriculum (as interpreted and mediated by teachers), which resulted in an *experiential* curriculum (the learning experiences of the school students) that could often be highly variable, a process that has been well-documented, particularly for science (Van den Akker, 1998).

Perhaps inevitably, the weight of so much subject detail and a cumbersome and unworkable assessment system (see next section) resulted in "reviews" of the National Curriculum. With each review, the assessment system was pruned and requirements for subjects to be studied were relaxed. James (2000) notes that the original intentions of a broad and balanced curriculum (e.g., the ambitious subject list from the original National Curriculum of 1989) were substantially reduced in these revisions. For example, by 2000, the requirement to study design and technology, and, more controversially, a foreign language, to the end of Key Stage 4 (age 16) were removed, thereby stripping the required subjects almost to the core. The most fundamental review of the curriculum since 1988 was published in 2004 (The Tomlinson Review: DfES, 2005; see recommended website). Tomlinson recommended the most radical changes yet, effectively reconceiving the post-14 curriculum as a continuum, integrating academic and vocational strands and qualifications up to the age of 19.

Assessing the Curriculum

The Public Examination System and Curriculum Development pre-1988

The assessment system set up after the 1944 Act introduced examinations at age 16 (ordinary or "O-level" General Certificate of Education [GCE]) and at age 18 (the advanced or "A-level" GCE). These examinations were designed to certificate traditional academic subjects taught in grammar schools. It soon became apparent, however, that a means of recognizing the achievement of students who had failed the 11-plus tests and were taught in modern and vocational schools was needed. Thus, the Certificate of Secondary Education (CSE) examination was devised. After raising the school-exit age to 16 in 1972, the number of CSE syllabi proliferated. Some were based on content solely devised, examined, and moderated by teachers with minimal involvement of examination boards. Therefore, the teacher-controlled CSE system was different in that it developed in response to curriculum need, rather than as a measure to control and constrain it.

By the mid-1970s, however, as comprehensive education became the norm, tensions arose between the two parallel systems of examination: the GCE, designed to assess predominantly academically more able students, and the CSE, for those who were seen as more suited to vocational or practically based subjects. This was further evidence of a continuing academic-vocational divide. In reality, since top grades were only available via the "O-level" examinations, the watered-down, grammar school-dominated curriculum continued and was one that most schools and parents aspired to. By the mid-1970s, pilot programs for a 16-plus examination combining CSE and GCE were in place but it took another decade before this common system, the General Certificate of Secondary Education (GCSE), became statutory for all state schools. At first, the new examinations retained a significant proportion of assessment under teacher control. In science, for example, assessment of practical skills and project work might constitute up to 50% of the total marks and one scheme, Suffolk Science (Dobson, 1991), was wholly assessed by teachers.

Gradually, concerns about reliability of different assessment schemes and the difficulties and expense of moderating teacher assessment resulted in massive decreases in the amount of assessment under teacher control. So, as was the case for curriculum content, assessment moved inexorably towards centralized government control. The agency controlling assessment (The Schools Examinations and Assessment Council [SEAC]) progressively limited the flexibility and control exerted by examination boards and, as a consequence, the extent to which teachers and schools could exploit the system, as previously, to match and assess a curriculum they wanted to teach.

National Curriculum Assessment and Testing, and Its Effects on Curriculum

The Education Reform Act in 1988 (DES, 1988a) made clear that government wanted, in addition to the GCSE, a system to judge students' achievement at each of the "Key Stages" defined in the National Curriculum (i.e., at ages 7, 11, and 14). This was to be done through a combination of teacher judgments and externally set assessment tasks. The Task Group on Assessment and Testing (TGAT), chaired by Paul Black at Kings College, London, was set up with the purpose of designing a system to achieve this (DES, 1988b). TGAT strongly supported teacher assessment for formative and diagnostic purposes while also designing a 10-level scale of criterion-referenced assessment to measure and report on students' progress. By applying a common scheme across all four Key Stages, TGAT provided a radically different solution to assessment—one offering progression and continuity through a common language of educational outcomes recognizing knowledge, skill, and understanding, and applied across the entire age range of statutory schooling. The system was clearly meritocratic, with the potential to be understood by many different users—students, parents, school inspectors, and so on.

The TGAT report had broad appeal across the teaching community, but Black always conceded his report was a design brief, not a total solution (Black & Wiliam, 2005). TGAT envisaged that the preparation and piloting of new methods for such a radically new system would take at least five years. Some novel methods using assessment tasks in formative and diagnostic ways did emerge, including some creative applications of tasks to assess students' collaborative and problem-solving skills. Despite early signs that TGAT might win political acceptance, the prime minister of the time, Margaret Thatcher, saw its approaches rather as a subversive invention of a left-wing educational establishment, stating that the fact that the TGAT report was "welcomed by the Labour party, the National Union of Teachers and the Times Educational Supplement was enough to confirm for me that its approach was suspect" (Thatcher, 1993, p. 595).

The academic establishment was suspicious (rightly so, as it turned out) and saw TGAT as a "Trojan horse of the political right" (Black, quoted in James, 2000, p. 353). Black himself got a hostile reception at a conference of the British Educational Research Association (BERA), as academics claimed that TGAT would lead to crude performance indicators and increased summative testing. The conservative government dominated by the New Right in education were determined to do even more than BERA had warned and wanted judgments of "performance" at the end of each Key Stage, so that schools would be forced to publish results and parents could judge which schools were performing best, thereby reinforcing the education marketplace. As a result, "tasks" became end-of-Key Stage "tests"; by the time of the Dearing review of the curriculum (NCC/SEAC, 1993), nothing remained of TGAT's rhetoric on formative and diagnostic purposes for assessment of the National Curriculum.

After initial attempts at mediating the effects of tests, particularly by teachers in primary schools, where tasks might be played as games and questions as quizzes (James, 2000), a myriad of complex assessment, recording, and reporting systems evolved that, while providing a mass of summative information on attainment, were ill-suited to support student learning (Black & Wiliam, 2005). Although the Dearing review reduced assessment loading by combining hundreds of criterion-referenced statements into general paragraphs describing performance, the test-dominated regime continued. Teacher assessment, though still required to be reported and published alongside test data and given equal weighting by Dearing, was effectively downgraded.

The post-Dearing level system survives to this day, but successive reviews produced poorly defined, confused criteria that clouded comparability of levels across the age ranges, so that the opportunities to improve progression and continuity envisaged by TGAT, particularly between primary and secondary schools, were consequently made more difficult. For example, in a study of transition in science in England, about half of primary and secondary teachers said they doubted that common criteria could be applied to learning outcomes in both primary and secondary schools in any consistent or meaningful way (Braund & Hames, 2005). Additionally, secondary teachers tend to distrust assessment information received from primary schools, and science work is needlessly repeated with consequent demotivation for students, who see their efforts from primary school devalued. This lack of confidence in end-of-Key Stage 2 assessment has resulted in many secondary schools using their own tests of cognitive ability to place students in appropriate teaching groups—this just a few months after the same pupils have taken national (end-of-Key Stage 2) tests. It seems that many teachers have become so accustomed to the national testing regime that they cannot break out of its influences. This supposition is supported by the large number of schools (80%) that choose to use optional additional test materials to assess students in year groups in primary schools not covered by statutory assessment (Slater, 2000).

Tony Blair's "New Labour" government published *Qualifying for Success* (DfEE, 1999a), which paved the way for yet another revision of the National Curriculum and the introduction of new Advanced Supplementary (AS) examinations at the mid-point of advanced studies in sixth forms—that is, at age 17. Taken together, these changes in assessment over the last 20 years have resulted in England having the dubious distinction of having the world's most-assessed school students and of spending the most money in achieving this (Whetton, 1999).

If schools and teachers thought that New Labour government would relax the market-driven and assessment-led approaches of the Thatcher years, when they came to power after 18 years of conservative government in 1997, they were in for a shock. In its white paper *Excellence in Schools* (DfEE, 1997), New Labour set out that it would use the national test system to ratchet up standards, particularly in what it called "literacy" and "numeracy," by setting national targets based on the 10-level TGAT/Dearing scale. Ambitious national targets were set (to be achieved by 2002): at least 80% of 11-year-old students were required to reach the level 4 target in English (literacy) and 75% in maths (numeracy). This effectively set in motion a plethora of government-led initiatives to make sure that schools achieved the targets and hence that the Labour government could show it was raising standards to a greater degree than its conservative predecessors did. While there was some year-on-year improvement, the targets were never met. In recent years, particular pedagogical practices, enshrined in what are known as "strategies" (see the following section on pedagogy), have been used in an attempt to hike annual cohort percentages toward the government's targets (Boyle & Bragg, 2005).

The effect on the curriculum of national, local, and school target setting, combined with the often obsessive fear of personal criticism and failure felt by teachers whose students did not meet the targets, has had a very harmful effect on the curriculum, especially in primary schools. For example, studies have shown that science, a core subject, is now taught mainly in short afternoon time slots and in a vastly reduced total of curriculum time (Boyle & Bragg, 2005; Galton & MacBeath, 2002). Moreover, the very nature of science teaching has changed. Practical work, which always formed an essential core of primary school science, has all but disappeared in the teaching year of the national tests (age 11) (Braund & Driver, 2005). There is a real fear that as pupils become more target- and test-oriented, their attitudes to learning will decline and deep-rooted disaffection with school, and so poorer behavior, will set in (Connor, 2003). The PACE project, referred to earlier, has indeed shown that primary school students have become performance- rather than learning-oriented (Pollard & Triggs, 2000). In a study on attitudes to practical work in science in the first year of secondary school, Braund and Driver (2005) found students who believed the only reason for doing practical work was to prepare them to take GCSE examinations—still five years away.

It seems that rather than assessment being the servant of curriculum and a fair reflection of the "broad and balanced" curriculum that was intended by the 1988 Education Reform Act and TGAT, the very reverse has occurred.

Pedagogy—Last Corner of the "Secret Garden"?

So, to the final element of the triadic relationship governing students' learning experiences (Triad A, Figure 1)—pedagogy, or the way in which curriculum is translated through teaching as student learning experiences. To what extent has the education establishment (particularly teachers) been able to cling to any vestige of control in the drive to increased centralism that characterized much of the 1980s and 1990s? The answer is a rather guarded and qualified—to a certain extent. Attempts by government to influence and change pedagogy in schools have been more subtle, compared with the legislative changes used to influence organization, structure, content, and assessment of the curriculum. Development has been undertaken through a process of persuasion, sometimes attrition, typically by publication of government reports and political pamphlets, each seeking to open up public debate on what has been termed the "secret garden" in British education.[3] Pressure for change has been increased through the combined use of highly persuasive (though not statutory) government "strategies," funding incentives, inservice training, and school inspection. Each has attempted to influence (sometimes to criticize) teaching methods.

As noted earlier, in the section on curriculum content, policy, and practice, significant shifts in the ways in which schools were organized with creation of non-selective comprehensive schools and the raising of the school-leaving age paved the way for significant curriculum development in the late 1960s and early 1970s. Integration of subjects and more liberal approaches to teaching resulted in more problem-solving, pattern-seeking, and individualized learning (Kelly, 2004). The Plowden report (Central Advisory Council for Education, 1967) was highly influential in changing practice in primary schools, away from whole-class methods that depended on drill and practice and rote learning and toward more child-centered approaches and informal activity-based learning. Post-Plowden, the "integrated day" became a common sight in primary schools. Typically, children were placed into different activity-focused groups, each pursuing work related to one or more curriculum area within a common topic, such as Romans and toys, acting as organizing frameworks for learning (Kerry & Eggleston, 1994). At the same time, the developmental stage-related work of Jean Piaget was made available to teachers and taught in teacher training colleges. Perhaps inevitably, such liberalizing moves in both primary and secondary sectors elicited a response from the political right; in 1969, several educational "Black Papers" were published (Cox & Dyson, 1969a, 1969b). These papers attacked the progressive curriculum, the organization of schools, and teaching methods. Comprehensive schools were viewed as inferior to grammar schools, mixed-ability classes as being unproductive to learning, and the primary school integrated day as little more than unstructured play. A central thesis of these "Black Papers" was that developments were lowering standards. The debate, if it can be called that, in effect created the standards agenda central to Callaghan's 1976 Ruskin College speech and that later emerged in the rhetoric of the National Curriculum. Kelly (2004) criticized the "Black Papers" for creating assertions without recourse to research or evidence:

> In general . . . the claim [that standards were declining] was asserted with no apparent recognition of the need for evidence to support such a claim, for some conceptual clarification of notions such as that of "standards," or even of an acknowledgement of the research evidence which had led to those innovations in the first place. (p. 171)

A further attack on the pedagogy of primary schools, a critique of progressive teaching, child-centered methods, and integration of subject matter, occurred early after the introduction of the National Curriculum in 1992. Concerned about so-called standards in primary schools, John Major's Conservative government, in 1991, established a review group comprising three eminent educators of the time to report on best practice in primary school organization and teaching (the so-called *Three Wise Men Report* by Alexander, Rose, & Woodhead, 1992). This time, criticisms leveled at the "Black Papers" for their lack of an evidence base could not be applied, as the work was essentially a review of existing research on primary practice. The report argued that the integrated topic-based day and, particularly, the use of group work were ineffective in promoting the necessary degree of cognitive challenge required for children to progress. The premise that such subjects as science, geography, and particularly English and maths could contain suitable and sufficiently identifiable subject content (and so maintain their integrity) when constrained by and contained in a topic such as "Romans" or "toys" came in for particular criticism. The report promoted teaching of separate subjects using whole-class methods. Since the critique appeared to reinforce the subject-based National Curriculum (although organization and teaching methods were never specified in NC documents), itself supported by the New Right, the *Three Wise Men Report* represented yet another nail in the coffin for those supporting a liberalizing agenda decided by teachers who knew best how to teach (Acker, 1997). Ball (1990) went further, claiming that the report represented a discourse of derision. Whether it was the *Three Wise Men* report or a combination of a subject-focused curriculum, an assessment and testing system, and school inspections reported by subjects is unclear, but by 2000 it seemed that subject-based teaching had become the norm especially in the older classes of primary schools (Galton & MacBeath, 2002; Webb & Vulliamy, 2006).

In 1997, New Labour introduced strategies that took an even more interventionist approach on pedagogy, particularly in English and mathematics. On the back of observations of teaching in other countries (notably Pacific Rim states, such as Taiwan and Singapore, in the case of mathematics) and of teaching methods and research in Australia (in the case of English), the Blair government set about introducing what it termed "National Strategies" to raise standards in primary schools. The National Literacy Strategy (NLS) was launched in 1998 and, for the first time in British education, specific teaching methods were set out. A three-part lesson starter, main activity, and plenary was suggested, content for each year group was specified, and organization of lessons into episodes of whole-class, individual, and group work (with exact time limits apportioned to each) were suggested (DfEE, 1998). Although the NLS was never made statutory, schools were effectively coerced through school inspections and pressure from LEAs into adopting it. Few declined to do so. The National Numeracy Strategy (NNS) followed a year later (DfEE, 1999b). While it defined teaching content and methods, however, it was widely regarded as being much less prescriptive than the NLS. There was initial hostility to both strategies, seen by teachers as a further attempt at yet more centralized control, but after an intiation period whereby many of the more draconian suggestions of the NLS were moderated by teachers, key elements of both strategies appear to have been assimilated and accepted as good practice by many primary schools (Webb & Vulliamy, 2006). As was the case for content of the curriculum, mediation by teachers, especially in the primary schools, seems to have played a key role in development and change in the curriculum.

Pressures to change pedagogy had been focused for almost three decades on primary schools. In 2000, however, faced with successes of the NLS and NNS but also criticism that standards in secondary schools were still woefully behind the targets set in 1997, the Blair government decided finally to intervene in the pedagogy of secondary schools, the final corner of the secret garden. The Key Stage Three (KS3) strategy (see recommended websites) extended ideas seen as successful in primary schools, such as the three-part lesson, clear objective setting, collaborative group work, and more effective whole-class teaching, using ICT to secondary schools. The strategy was delivered through an extensively funded, locally organized scheme of inservice training supported by "Strategy Consultants" appointed to work with schools in each LEA. The model of development was therefore shifted more to one of persuasion through teacher development rather than by central dictate, coercion, and control. Evaluations of the KS3 strategy show that teachers largely have been warm toward the methods and approaches promoted by training, and glad for the high quality of ideas and materials provided, which are based on significant amounts of educational research into best practices (OfSTED, 2004). The Key Stage 3 strategy, now known as the National Strategy, has been extended to all curriculum subjects and across the entire statutory age range of secondary schools.

Toward a Curriculum for the 21st Century

The pace and quantity of legislation and initiatives driving curriculum development over the last 20 years might seem implausible to those from outside the UK system, but perhaps there is now a general acceptance that there is no going back to a presumed "Golden Age," if indeed there ever was one. That changes have been for the better is debatable and dependent on what is valued and used to evidence benefits of change. While it is true that results in national end-of-Key Stage tests and GCSE and "A-level" examinations have improved, there are also worrying signs of decline in pupils' attitudes to school life and increased incidences of poor behavior that have been attributed to the overloaded curriculum and its testing regime (National Union of Teachers, 2005). In science, for example, there has been a year-on-year decline in uptake of science subjects at "A-level," coupled with a sustained decline in students' enjoyment of and liking for the subject (Bennett et al., 2006). Efforts to address the situation include the introduction of new courses that concentrate on social debates about sciences as well as content knowledge (Millar, 2006). Indeed, the move toward considering science as a socially constructed body of knowledge requiring assessment of risk and evidence as essential in becoming more scientifically literate has led to calls for substantial changes to the National Curriculum for science (Bennett et al., 2006).

There is now, at last, recognition that the curriculum of the past, with its 19th-century, industrialist, nationalistic, classical, and class-divided ethics and origins, is no longer relevant to the needs of young people in the post-industrialized world of the 21st century (Morris, 2007). The radical re-conceptualization of the curriculum in the 14-19 age range envisaged by the Tomlinson Review, and the changes to many subjects in the National Curriculum for 2008 (along the lines of those for science), represent a new appetite for greater equality and access in the school curriculum as well as a new greater push to address the academic-vocational divide that has remained an obstacle in UK curriculum development for so long. As discussed earlier, the assessment system has had a markedly negative impact on the breadth of curriculum and pedagogy, but signs are emerging of a shifting climate here, too. In Wales, end-of-Key Stage tests have already been ditched in favor of a teacher-controlled system along the lines of one that already exists in Scotland (see recommended websites). Whether assessment regulations in England will be relaxed remains to be seen. In England and Wales, school inspections are now shorter and require schools to provide evidence of impact of curriculum innovation. The requirement for schools to provide evidence on which key decisions about curriculum and teaching are made is an interesting one, reflecting shifts in education policy toward approaches used for some time in the health service. The Department for Education and Skills (DfES) has funded a center for evidence-based practice, thus providing systematic reviews of international research in many areas of curriculum, assessment, and pedagogy (see the website of the EPPI Centre). Thus, schools, curriculum developers, teacher trainers, and policymakers now have much improved access to a high-quality evidence base that should result in a better relationship among research, innovation, and practice.

As was shown earlier in the section on pedagogical content and practice, the curriculum as *experienced* by students is not always as closely related to the *intended* curriculum as some politicians and policymakers might imagine or would like. Some of the attempts in science education to move student learning toward a greater appreciation of risk and evidence have been slow to take root, and so there have been attempts to drive curriculum change in schools by influencing the next generation of teachers through methods used in their initial training (Braund et al., 2005). The problem with this approach has been that when new entrants trained in the new pedagogical approaches enter their first posts, the new methods are often overshadowed by the more traditional approaches, entrenched attitudes, or requirements for assessment that already exist in these schools (Braund et al., 2006). Therefore, their teaching is regarded as being against the grain of current practice and it is difficult to make inroads.

In the final analysis, perhaps, curriculum development in the UK has become a typical example of a British compromise among competing interests, values, and approaches. At least at the beginning of the 21st century, there seems to be a more moderate consensus than in the Thatcher era, when the National Curriculum was introduced—even one that touches some deeply entrenched political convictions. At the time of this writing, the Conservative Party Leader, David Cameron, has announced that his party will no longer push for the construction of more grammar schools—a change in policy unimaginable 20 years ago. Perhaps, then, in this new age of convergent politics, the old arguments about elitism and choice, vocational and academic "Gold Standards" or unification, and so on, will become less important than discussions about a more holistically based and challenging curriculum more suited to a shifting world demography and a globally based economy.

Notes:

[1] The education system in Scotland differs most from other parts of the UK, since the country has powers to decide legislation and raise local taxes to fund it. The websites recommended at the end of the chapter provide details of the current curriculum in each of the countries of the UK.

[2] The "New Right" was an informal alliance of right wing pressure groups and others, seeking to guide, shape, or influence the Conservative Party policy. In the mid-1980s, the most prominent of these were: The Centre for Policy Studies, The Hillgate Group, The Adam Smith Institute, and the Campaign for Real Education.

[3] In the 1960s, the metaphor of a "secret garden" was used to critique the lack of transparency on content and teaching methods in state schools at the time. In 1996, Anthea Millett reprised the term in speeches given on behalf of the government agency for training teachers. She referred, in these lectures, to the government's attempts to influence pedagogy being the "last corner of the secret garden" (Millett, 1996).

References

Acker, S. (1997). Primary school teachers' work: The response to educational reform. In G. Helsby & G. McCulloch (Eds.), *Teachers and the national curriculum* (pp. 34-51). London: Cassell.

Alexander, R. J., Rose, A. J., & Woodhead, C. (1992). *Curriculum organisation and classroom practice in primary schools. A discussion paper.* London: Department of Education and Science.

Arnot, M. (1992). Feminism, education and the New Right. In M. Arnot & L. Baron (Eds.), *Voicing concerns: Sociological perspectives on contemporary education reforms* (pp. 41-65). Oxford: Triangle.

Ball, S. J. (1990). *Politics and policy making in education.* London: Routledge.

Bennett, J., Burden, J., Campbell, P., Millar, R., Osborne, J., & Swinbank, E. (2006). *Looking forward: Making Key Stage 3 science work.* York, UK: Centre for Innovation and Research in Science Education, University of York.

Black, P., & Wiliam, D. (2005). Lessons from around the world: How policies, politics and cultures constrain and afford assessment practices. *The Curriculum Journal, 16,* 249-261.

Bourdillon, H., & Storey, A. (2002). *Aspects of teaching and learning in secondary schools, perspectives on practice.* London: RoutledgeFalmer for the Open University.

Boyle, B., & Bragg, J. (2005). No science today—the demise of primary science. *The Curriculum Journal, 16,* 423-437.

Braund, M., & Driver, M. (2005). Pupils' attitudes to practical science around the KS2/3 transition. *Education 3-13, 33*(2), 20-26.

Braund, M., & Hames, V. (2005). Improving progression and continuity from primary to secondary science: Pupils' reactions to bridging work. *International Journal of Science Education, 27,* 781-801.

Braund, M., Erduran, S., Simon, S., Taber, K., & Tweats, R. (2005). Teaching ideas and evidence in science at key stage 3. *Science Teacher Education, 41,* 12-13.

Braund, M., Campbell, B., Cook, H., Ladds, J., & Walkington, A. (2006). A community of practice to learn to teach about ideas and evidence in science. *School Science Review, 87*(321), 83-90.

Broadfoot, P. (1996). *Education assessment and society.* Buckingham, UK: Open University Press.

Burton, L., & Weiner, G. (1990). Social justice and the national curriculum. *Research Papers in Education, 5,* 203-227.

Callaghan, J. (1976, October). *Towards a national debate.* Speech given at a foundation stone laying ceremony at Ruskin College, Oxford, on October 18, 1976. Reprinted in *The Guardian,* Monday, January 15, 2001. Available online at http://education.guardian.co.uk/thegreatdebate/story/0,9860,574645,00.html

Central Advisory Council for Education. (1967). *Children and their primary schools (the Plowden Report).* London: Her Majesty's Stationery Office.

Connor, M. (2003). Pupil stress and standard assessment tasks (SATs)—an update. *Emotional and Behavioural Difficulties, 8*(2), 101-107.

Convey, A., & Merrit, A. (2000). The United Kingdom. In C. Brock & W. Tulasiewicz (Eds.), *Education in a single Europe* (2nd ed., pp. 377-403). London: Routledge.

Cox, C. B., & Dyson, A. E. (Eds.). (1969a). *Fight for education: A black paper.* Manchester, UK: Critical Quarterly Society.

Cox, C. B., & Dyson, A. E. (Eds.). (1969b). *Black paper 2: The crisis in education.* Manchester, UK: Critical Quarterly Society.

Department for Education and Science (DES). (1985). *Better schools.* London: Her Majesty's Stationery

Office.

Department for Education and Science (DES). (1988a). *Education reform act.* London: Department of Education and Science and the Welsh Office.

Department for Education and Science (DES). (1988b). *Task group on assessment and testing: A report.* London: Department of Education and Science and the Welsh Office.

Department for Education and Science (DES). (1989). *The national curriculum: From policy to practice.* London: Her Majesty's Stationery Office.

Department for Education and Employment (DfEE). (1997). *Excellence in schools.* London: Her Majesty's Stationery Office.

Department for Education and Employment (DfEE). (1998). *The national literacy strategy: Framework for teaching.* London: Author.

Department for Education and Employment (DfEE). (1999a). *Qualifying for success: A consultation paper on the future of post-16 qualifications.* London: Author.

Department for Education and Employment (DfEE). (1999b). *The national numeracy strategy: Framework for teaching mathematics from reception to year 6.* London: Author.

Department for Education and Skills (DfES). (2005). *14-19 education and skills* (The Tomlinson Review). Nottingham, UK: Author.

Dobson, K. (Ed.). (1991). *Co-ordinated science—the Suffolk approach.* Suffolk, UK: HarperCollins and Suffolk County Council.

Galton, M., & MacBeath, J. (2002). *A life in teaching? The impact of change on primary teachers' working lives.* Cambridge: Faculty of Education, University of Cambridge.

Gilroy, P. (1991). The loss of professional autonomy. *Journal of Education for Teaching, 17,* 1-5.

Goodson, I. F. (1988). *The making of the curriculum. Collected essays.* London: Falmer Press.

Grace, G. (1987). Teachers and the state in Britain: A challenging relationship. In M. Lawn & G. Grace (Eds.), *Teachers: The culture and politics of work* (pp. 193-228). London: Falmer Press.

Harland, J. (1987). The TVEI experience: Issues of control, response and the professional role of teachers. In D. Gleeson (Ed.), *The TVEI and secondary education: A critical appraisal* (pp. 38-54). Milton Keynes, UK: Open University Press.

James, M. (2000). Measured lives: The rise of assessment as the engine of change in English schools. *The Curriculum Journal, 11,* 343-364.

Kelly, A. V. (2004). *The curriculum theory and practice.* London: Sage.

Kerry, T., & Eggleston, J. (1994). The evolution of the topic. In A. Bourne & J. Bourne (Eds.), *Teaching and learning in the primary school* (pp. 188-193). London: Routledge.

Lawton, D. (1980). *The politics of the school curriculum.* London: Routledge and Kegan Paul.

Millar, R. (2006). Twenty-first century science: Insights from the design and implementation of a scientific literacy approach in school science. *International Journal of Science Education, 28,* 1499-1522.

Millett, A. (1996). *Pedagogy—last corner of the secret garden.* Invitation lecture. London: Kings College.

Morris, E. (2007, 27 February). *What next for schools after two decades of change?* The Annual York Education Lecture, York.

National Curriculum Council (NCC) and School Examinations and Assessment Council (SEAC). (1993). *The National Curriculum and its assessment* (The Dearing Review). London: Authors.

National Union of Teachers (NUT). (2005). *Learning to behave. A charter for schools.* London: Membership and Communications Department of the National Union of Teachers.

Office for Standards in Education (OfSTED). (2004). *The Key Stage 3 Strategy: Evaluation of the third year.* London: Author.

Osborn, M., Croll, P., Broadfoot, P., Pollard, A., McNess, E., & Triggs, P. (1997). Policy into practice and practice into policy: creative mediation in the primary classroom. In G. Helsby & G. McCulloch (Eds.), *Teachers and the national curriculum* (pp. 52-65). London: Cassell.

Pollard, A., & Triggs, P. (2000). *Policy, practice and pupil experience.* London: Continuum International Publishing Group.

Schön, D. (1987). *Educating the reflective practitioner.* San Francisco: Jossey-Bass.

Slater, J. (2000, 5 May). Generation stress. *The Times Educational Supplement,* 24.

Taylor, P. (1971). Purpose and structure in the curriculum. In R. Hopper (Ed.), *The curriculum: Context, design and development* (pp. 153-177). Edinburgh, UK: Oliver and Boyd.

Thatcher, M. (1993). *The Downing Street years*. London: HarperCollins.

Trowler, P. (2003). *Education policy* (2nd ed.). London: Routledge.

Van den Akker, J. (1998). The science curriculum: Between ideals and outcomes. In B. J. Fraser & K. Tobin (Eds.), *International handbook of science education* (pp. 421-447). Dordrecht, Netherlands: Kluwer Academic Publishers.

Webb, R., & Vulliamy, G. (2006). *Coming full circle? The impact of New Labour's education policies on primary school teachers' work*. London: Association of Teachers and Lecturers.

Whetton, C. (1999, May). *Attempting to find the true cost of assessment systems*. Paper presented at the IAEA conference, Bled, Slovenia.

Useful Websites

The following websites give details about the current curriculum in each of the component countries of the UK:

For Scotland: www.ltscotland.org.uk/

For Wales: http://new.wales.gov.uk/topics/educationandskills/curriculum_and_assessment/?lang=en

For Northern Ireland: www.deni.gov.uk/index/80-curriculumandassessment_pg.htm

For England: www.qca.org.uk/

Other Websites Mentioned in the Chapter

Evidence Based Policy and Practice Initiative (EPPI) Centre: http://eppi.ioe.ac.uk/cms/

National Strategy and the Key Stage Three Strategy: www.standards.dfes.gov.uk/secondary/keystage3/

Office for Standards in Education (OfSTED) Framework for School Inspections: www.ofsted.gov.uk/publications/

The Tomlinson Review, 14-19 Education and Skills: www.dfes.gov.uk/publications/14-19educationandskills/

About the Author

Martin Braund is Senior Lecturer in Science Education at the University of York, England, and is an Adjunct Professor in Education and Social Sciences, Cape Peninsula University of Technology, Cape Town, South Africa. He has a B.Sc. in zoology and geology and a M.Ed. in science education and has worked in curriculum development and research for over 20 years. He directs master's degrees in science education and is Deputy Director of Undergraduate Programmes in Educational Studies at York. He is the author of over 70 publications in the fields of research, policy, and curriculum. He can be reached at mb40@york.ac.uk, Tel: +44(0)1904433465

Curriculum in the United States: A Work in Progress

Susan P. Santoli, Rebecca McMahon Giles, and Edward L. Shaw, Jr.

In the book *School: The Story of American Public Education*, 20th-century statesman Adlai Stevenson is quoted as saying: "The free common school system is the most American thing about America" (Tyack, 2001, p. 1). Although an educated citizenry was considered desirable from the nation's beginning, the idea of educating every citizen through public funds emerged gradually from social, political, and economic factors that led to the development of a unique education system. In this chapter, the authors will introduce some of these factors, as well as the people who shaped, and continue to shape, education and curriculum in the United States.

It is not possible to find one commonly agreed-upon definition of the word "curriculum." Curriculum means many different things to different people and has been interchangeably used with "program," "model," "framework," "approach," or "guidelines" (Hyun, 2000). Before the early decades of the 20th century, curriculum typically referred to the subject matter, or to the courses of study that were offered by a school. Since that time, however, more complex definitions of curriculum have been debated. This chapter uses the definition of curriculum that "curriculum is concerned with what is taught and how it is taught, in organic relationship to the learner and society" (Tanner & Tanner, 1990, p. 2). Since the concept of curriculum is continually evolving, it is impossible to separate its evolution from the historical, social, political, and technological forces of each era. In this chapter, the authors have attempted to address the effect of these forces on the development of curriculum in the United States, from the English settlement of the country through the present.

Curriculum in Colonial America

Education in the United States actually began with the establishment of Jamestown, Virginia, in 1607. The early settlers brought with them the values and ideas of their original communities, religions, and homelands, all of which influenced the organization of the

American education system. While the settlers brought some books, most early colonists could not read or write. Despite the high degree of illiteracy, many settlers were interested in education. The only model with which they were familiar was that used in Europe, which meant that America's first schools were reserved for only the most affluent. Even though the settlers wanted to escape the problems of their homelands and sought greater rights and opportunities, they originally imitated many of the European traditions, including those pertaining to schools and curriculum.

As the population of the colonies increased, so did the diversity of occupations and the need for skilled workers. While not all trades (e.g., field work, textile spinning, and fishing) required a formal education, some did (e.g., navigation, surveying, and conducting business). Providing adequate educational opportunities was complicated by the diverse immigrant population and by the locations of settlements. Rural settlers, farmers in particular, could be miles apart with limited transportation and communication. These factors contributed to the appearance of the one-room schoolhouse, in which all children in an area were educated in one classroom by one teacher. Often, rural school had terms lasting only three to four months, no established curriculum, few teachers with any formal training, and erratic student attendance; however, in urban areas, large private or parochial schools eventually provided more reliable educational opportunities.

In every society, education is affected by occupations and domestic arrangements (Good & Teller, 1973). In colonial America, the economic survival of the family often depended on children working in adult jobs. Children assuming adult occupations had little time for education. In 1642, Massachusetts passed a law requiring parents to teach their children to read and write (Good & Teller, 1973). It was difficult to comply with this education law, however, as the lack of public education meant that many parents were themselves unable to read and write. In 1647, Massachusetts passed a second law requiring that all towns with over 50 households employ a teacher of reading and writing and that towns with over 100 households establish a Latin grammar school (Tanner & Tanner, 1990).

Many schools used the horn book, considered by many as the first teaching device. The horn book was a piece of wood on which an alphabet and prayer were printed and covered with cow horn (Kaestle, 2001). The horn book was followed by the primer. Benjamin Harris' *New England Primer,* from 1690, contained a rhyming alphabet to aid in memorization and used Scripture to teach reading and pronunciation. The educational process was dull and boring, with memorization used as the main pedagogical technique. This oral method of instruction resulted in most children being able to read passages but, unfortunately, unable to comprehend what was read. So-called dame schools, which were conducted in the kitchens of older women, taught children basic literacy. Other schools operated in public buildings and were taught by men, but both types included rote tasks completed independently, harsh means of ensuring obedience, and a view of the teacher as the ultimate authority. These common practices reflected the negative view of childhood found in the early Puritan churches: that humanity was inherently evil and that teachers were to abolish students' sinful ways through religious-based lessons and strict discipline (Nourot, 2005).

Before 1775, education was mentioned in six of the newly written colonial constitutions. This suggested the states believed they "should supplement private facilities" but that the idea of "universal public schooling" had not yet developed (Good, 1962, p. 89). During the Revolutionary War (1775-1789), education came to a standstill and literacy rates declined drastically (Tanner & Tanner, 1990). After the war, concern over education began in earnest, as many, such as Thomas Jefferson and Benjamin Franklin, articulated that the success of the newly formed republic hinged on an educated citizenry and the development of a sense of American nationalism (Tanner & Tanner, 2007). Noah Webster aided in the formulation of both ideals with the publication of the *Blueback Speller.* "The *Speller* promoted a new national language to be spelled and pronounced differently from British English" (Tyack, 2001, p. 22) and provided the means to combine many cultures, languages, religions, and backgrounds into an American identity (Tanner & Tanner, 1990).

Pre-Revolutionary education laws did not include girls. Most girls attended the dame schools and learned basic reading and writing, but it was assumed that they needed little education beyond that.

Some girls did receive private educations and the Quaker schools offered the same curriculum to boys and girls. Quakers also believed that blacks and Indians should receive the same education as the European children. Within a few decades after the Revolution, girls were allowed to attend school in most communities. Still, until the mid-19th century, schools varied greatly from community to community, attendance was very erratic, and little teacher training or supervision existed (Tanner & Tanner, 1990).

Early childhood education began in 1816 with infant schools in Boston. The infant schools were an early preschool preparation program and a "forerunner of primary grades in elementary school" (Tanner & Tanner, 1990, p. 47). The younger children were taught by the same memorization-based methods as were the older children. A curricular problem, which became even more pronounced after the war, was that the Latin grammar schools were not offering such subjects as navigation, bookkeeping, or surveying (Tanner & Tanner, 1990). Proficiency in Latin and Greek was not necessary for many of the new occupations, nor for those students not intending to pursue high education. What resulted was not a reform of the public-supported grammar school, but the establishment of a new vehicle of education, the private academy. While all students were eligible to attend, the schools were not free. Because they were not bound by college entrance requirements, the academies offered subjects that the Latin schools did not, and "by 1820, the tuition academy had all but replaced the tax supported grammar school" (Tanner & Tanner, 1990, p. 32). Besides an expanded curriculum, the academies also offered teaching methods and instructional materials that differed from those of the Latin schools. One problem that arose was a huge variance in curricular offerings among academies, and academies that had a large number of courses being taught and added to the curriculum. One way of dealing with the large number of poor children who wanted to attend school was to use a system that was developed in Europe, called the monitorial or Latin system. In theory, one teacher taught a certain number of bright students, who then taught other students. The idea was that this method allowed one teacher to supervise large numbers of students (Ornstein & Hunkins, 1998). The same aspect—bright students as teachers—that made this model both economical and efficient also caused its demise, as students, who actually knew little, taught others who knew even less (Ornstein & Hunkins, 1998).

Education developed differently in each region of the country. In the middle-Atlantic colonies, many schools and colleges were established and maintained by churches, groups of individuals, and even early boards of education. According to Good and Teller (1973), this was called "the region of the parochial or church schools" (p. 14). Although the southern colonies were called "the region of the private school" (p. 14), many church schools existed there as well. The curriculum of the church school emphasized the views of the church, with the main goal being the perpetuation of the religion and church.

During the early part of the 19th century, the United States entered an era of tremendous expansion, industrial growth, and urban migration. Juvenile crime was on the rise, and education was considered a means to promote nationalism, prevent crime, and teach morals. Two educators, Horace Mann (1796-1859) of Massachusetts and Henry Barnard (1811-1900) of Connecticut, were essential in reviving and reforming public education in the United States. Both men set out to examine as many schools in their states as they could, traveled widely, and reported what they found. Mann publicized his findings and proposed a new system of schools, which he called the "common school." These schools would be free to all students and the education the students received would be "of the highest quality" (Kaestle, 2001, p. 29). He recommended the implementation of state standards, supervision, and funding of the system through tax dollars. Mann's ideas were implemented in the northern states prior to the Civil War (Gutek, 1988), and these ideas spread throughout the southern states after the war. The common school movement was considered by many to be the true beginning of the American public school system. The common schools helped to assimilate immigrant children into the American society by incorporating American nationalism. Additionally, the values esteemed by industries, such as hard work and punctuality, were stressed. As a result of the common school movement, states enacted legislation that: 1) allowed voters to tax themselves to support their local schools, 2) encouraged monies from the general school fund to be used by districts that supported the establishment and continuation of public schools, 3) required that school districts be formed, and 4) provided elementary education through local taxes (Gutek, p. 24). Unfortunately, teaching methods and philosophies remained the same, with rote memorization being equated with learning.

While many of the immigrants from Europe were Catholic, most public schools stressed Protestant, and sometimes anti-Catholic, ideas. One result of these circumstances was the development of privately funded Catholic schools in many U.S. cities. As well, some schools became more secular by removing religious references from textbooks (Tyack, 2001). Although African Americans were legally allowed to attend public schools in the North, they were often prohibited from doing so, and segregated schools began to develop. In 1855, however, court cases filed by African Americans in Boston led Massachusetts to become the first state to pass a law outlawing segregation. In the South, little education of African Americans occurred until after the Civil War (Kaestle, 2001).

As Americans moved West, so did education. William McGuffey contributed to the establishment of a feeling of nationalism and morality through his five *Readers,* which were written for children of the West (Kaestle, 2001). It is estimated that over 120 million copies were produced and distributed before the beginning of the 20th century (Good & Teller, 1973).

Although most students left school after finishing the elementary grades, there was a need to extend learning opportunities to non-college-bound students, in order to provide for more advanced practical educations. An 1827 Massachusetts law required that each town of 500 households establish a public high school. These high schools focused on practical, rather than classical, studies and were supported by public taxes. This was truly an American innovation in education (Tanner & Tanner, 1990). "The high school represented an institutional response to the educational needs of modern society" (Gutek, 1988, p. 28). American children could now attend both publicly funded elementary and secondary schools. The tremendous expansion of the American high school after 1875 eventually caused the academies to disappear. Along with these new high schools, a new secondary curriculum was developed. Course offerings expanded and greater choice was given to students to find subjects they were interested in studying.

Although the development of the high school was a departure from the European influences on U.S. curriculum, early childhood and elementary education continued to be tremendously influenced by some non-traditional European educational practitioners. Swiss philosopher Johann Heinrich Pestalozzi, writing in the early 1800s, urged that the physical and mental development of children should guide the curriculum. The integration of science, music, and art into elementary schools had its basis in Pestalozzi's philosophies (Tanner & Tanner, 1990).

German educator Friedrich Froebel focused his attention on working with 5-year-old children and was known as the father of kindergarten. The first U.S. kindergarten, which was German-speaking, opened in Watertown, Wisconsin, in 1855. Froebel outlined his original approach to teaching young children in his book *Education of Man.* This 1886 publication described his teaching materials and techniques, emphasizing the benefits of childhood play, the importance of mothers as a child's first teacher, and the valuable role of singing and music as enjoyable learning tools (Henniger, 2005). Froebel was credited with creating the first curriculum specifically for young children, which he deemed "gifts" and "occupations." Pestalozzi and Froebel influenced U.S. curriculum in the late 19th and early 20th century, but were often met with "opposition and a call to return to the traditional methods of education" (Tanner & Tanner, 2007, p. 16).

By the final decades of the 19th century, the numbers of children being educated in public schools had greatly expanded. In 1870, 7.6 million children were in public schools; by 1890, the numbers had increased to 12.7 million. Most of the enrollment increase was in elementary schools, as comparatively few students attended high schools or colleges and universities (Marsh & Willis, 2007). When high schools began, they served the dual purpose of providing higher education to both students who would attend college and those who would not. Throughout the century, the high school's curriculum increased as the needs of society changed; "by 1900, the number of parallel courses of study offered in the high schools had grown to 36" (Tanner & Tanner, 1990, p. 66).

Because of the variance among high school course offerings, three National Education Association committees evaluated the content and purpose of elementary and high school curricula in the late 1800s. All three reinforced the notion of strong mental discipline as the basis for the curriculum at both levels (Ornstein & Hunkins, 1998). The prevailing notions reflected much of the philosophy of laissez-faire, which placed the factor of student success on the student's effort rather than on any teaching methods or course offerings. Additionally, schools were considered sorting systems, as they were in Europe, to identify those who were intellectually able to benefit from further education. A "one-size-fits-all" approach that ignored individual differences (Tanner & Tanner, 2007, p. 83).

The report of the Committee of Ten on Secondary School Studies (1893) was probably the most influential of the three reports from the various committees. It identified nine academic subjects that should be taught in high school. Additionally, it suggested four different tracks of study: classical, Latin scientific, modern languages, and English (Orstein & Hunkins, 1998). The committee identified the first two tracks as being rigorous ones and, as a result, linked them to college prep curricula. In these tracks, art, music, and physical and vocational education were ignored. The committee further insisted that the nine academic subjects, with the exceptions of Latin and Greek, be taught at the elementary level. Throughout the 20th century and into the 21st, the debate over the superiority of college prep curricula to vocational curricula has continued (Tanner & Tanner, 2007).

The Committee of Fifteen (1895) recommended "the number, length, and—in some cases—type of lessons to be given in each subject" (Marsh & Willis, 2007, p. 40) in elementary schools. Members resisted adding newer subjects to the curriculum, refused to consider the reformed pedagogy advocated by many European educators, were against the establishment of kindergartens, and advocated separate, rather than interdisciplinary, subjects or curricula (Ornstein & Hunkins, 1998). The compartmentalization of today's elementary curricula can be attributed to the report issued by this committee.

The Committee on College Entrance Requirements (1895) had a lasting impact through its suggestion that high schools "strengthen the college preparatory aspect of the high school curriculum" (Ornstein & Hutchins, p. 80). It established the Carnegie Unit (CU) credit evaluation for college admission that continues to be used today.

Although these three committees tended to endorse the status quo, there certainly were some instances of experimental programs and curricula in the late 1800s. The fact that curriculum was being examined at all indicated the disequilibrium that would come to full fruition in the early years of the 20th century.

1900-1950: Progressivism

It is difficult to find a phrase encompassing the monumental social, political, and economic changes that took place during the 20th century; however, "improving access" is quite appropriate (Tanner & Tanner, 2007, p. 3). Throughout the 20th century, increasing opportunities, throughout many areas, were extended to formerly excluded populations. Nowhere was this more true than in the area of education. When the 20th century began, only 50% of American children were enrolled in schools, and they attended for an average of five years (Bernard & Mondale, 2001b). Eleven percent of 14- to 17-year-olds were enrolled in secondary schools, and of that percentage, only 6.5% graduated from high school. Within 20 years, these percentages had more than doubled (Ornstein & Hunkins, 1998, p. 75).

At the beginning of the 20th century, elementary and secondary curricula had changed very little from those of the past century. The primary teaching methods, at both levels, were whole-group, teacher-directed instruction (Cuban, cited in Pinar, Reynolds, Slattery, & Taubman, 1995). These methods correlated student success to student effort rather than to teaching methods or course offerings. The primary goal of the secondary curriculum was to prepare students to go to college; however, only a very small percentage of students did so.

The United States was emerging as a world industrial power in the early 1900s, and the industrial growth was partially responsible for a shift in urban and rural populations. The number of immigrants pouring into the United States also significantly affected the size and composition of the population. Most immigrants settled in cities. Thus, preparing workers for industrial work and acculturating immigrant children, whose English was poor, became prime concerns for society and for the schools (Ravitch, 2001).

These and other societal changes impacted education. Diverse reform movements, known collectively as Progressivism, focused on "improving the quality of life" and, as such, provided the "needed momentum to change the purpose of the school" (Tanner & Tanner, 2007, p. 125). The belief of some Progressives that education should focus on the individual student, rather than just on subject matter, came from sources both outside of and within education. With the expansion and development of the natural and behavioral sciences, during the late 1800s, came a growing distrust of beliefs that were accepted just for the sake of tradition, even curriculum, without proof that there was a factual basis behind the belief. Psychologist Edward Thorndike argued, in his 1901 theory of learning transfer, that the classics were no more valuable than other curricula that students might study, and that the idea of mental discipline, based on rote memorization, was not conducive to the development of critical, inductive thinking (Ornstein & Hunkins, 1998; Pinar et al., 1995). Thorndike's work paved the way for those who sought to quantify student potential through psychological measurement and would greatly influence the emerging social efficiency movement (Pinar et al., 1995).

It is impossible to speak of curriculum development without a discussion of John Dewey's contributions. Dewey's ideas had profound effects on curriculum, not only in the early 20th century but through to the present as well. Dewey believed "that schools should focus on the needs of individual students" (Armstrong, 2003, p. 10) rather than on the curriculum content (Bernard & Mondale, 2001b). Dewey envisioned schools where students and teachers would learn together and teachers would serve as guides for the students. Because of his belief that the world was constantly changing, he opposed the idea that there was a body of knowledge that all students needed to know, focusing instead on helping students develop learning skills and identify learning tools. According to Dewey, academics were "resource[s], not the center of the curriculum" (Pinar et al, 1995, p. 107). Dewey also proposed that the purpose for the curriculum should be democracy. To Dewey, the classroom exemplified the democratic process, allowing students to actively participate in real-life activities that would prepare them to effectively promote social changes, rather than just accepting the status quo (Tanner & Tanner, 2007).

William Heard Kilpatrick's work with project learning grew out of Dewey's ideas about children engaging in activities. Kilpatrick proposed the idea of units or projects, which would replace separate subjects and would give students the opportunity to probe more deeply into topics of their interest (Marsh & Willis, 2007; Pinar et al., 1995). A contemporary extension and elaboration of these early in-depth investigative projects, now referred to as the Project Approach, has been adopted in many preschool and primary classrooms (Katz & Chard, 2000).

It is understandable that in a society so infused with new technology and industrial development, the world of business would have such an influence on curriculum from. In contrast to Dewey's child-centered approach, the idea of the student as a product developed from the principles of scientific management. Franklin Bobbitt, of the University of Chicago, urged the development of standards against which students could be measured. Bobbitt encouraged "scientifically determined job specifications, scales of measurement, and standards of attainment," for what he viewed as a "scientific curriculum for education worthy of our age of science" (Tanner & Tanner, 2007, p. 49). In 1918, Bobbitt's *The Curriculum* was published. This work has been evaluated by some as marking the "birth of curriculum as a field of study" (Pinar et al., 1995, p. 70). In this work, Bobbitt argued that education should be organized around a business model, and advocated that curriculum reforms be based on "scientific notions of organization and measurement" (Pinar et al., p 70).

The business model of education contributed to the creation of the National Education Association's Committee on Economy of Time in 1911. Using scientific methods, the committee investigated what was being taught and how much time was being spent on each subject in school districts throughout the country. In its reports, the committee averaged the time spent on the different subject areas and used those figures as the recommendations for the times that should be used in all schools. The committee defined "the goals of education in terms of life, as it was," and proposed "a curriculum that would accommodate youngsters to existing conditions with little emphasis on improving them" (Tanner & Tanner, 2007, p. 51).

The idea of quantification in education was supported by others as well. Just as the new field of psychology focused on the behavior of the individual, so sociology focused on the behavior of groups. The I.Q. test that had been developed in France by Alfred Binet, in 1905, came into wide use with the development of the multiple choice test format, in 1914. This test was used to determine students' potentials for success as well as a way to test the products of the schools (Armstrong, 2003).

The idea of who should attend school and what kind of schools they should attend became a major issue in the early 1900s. This distinction previously had not been a problem, because college preparation was the goal of all secondary public schools. Students who could not achieve academically or who needed to work simply dropped out. In the early years of the 20th century, secondary education faced many new challenges, in addition to some remaining from the last century: few students attended high school, many who began high school did not graduate, instruction was based on preparing students for college admission, and curriculum did not take into account the role of student development. Some Progressives blamed high schools and their lack of vocational courses for the prevalence of child labor (Tanner & Tanner, 1990).

Businesses and industries began demanding better educated and skilled workers, and so more students began to enter high school. The question of what curriculum should be offered became paramount (Ravitch, 2001). Some school districts created separate vocational high schools, but there was no consensus on the best way to offer vocational training to large numbers of students. Some urged the adoption of the European model, which was to create two different types of schools. Others, such as John Dewey, argued passionately for the creation of a new type of high school, a comprehensive high school, where all students would be educated in a way that was more appropriate in a democracy (Tanner & Tanner, 2007).

The decision on what pattern U.S. secondary education would take was greatly aided by the demands of World War I for skilled workers, and by a report published by the National Educational Association (NEA) in 1918. Increasing demand for skilled war time workers prompted President Wilson to sign the Smith-Hughes Act of 1917, which required states to match federal funds for technical and vocational education for students over 14 in non-college settings.

A second factor influencing the establishment of a comprehensive high school, was the 1918 NEA committee report, the *Cardinal Principles of Secondary Education,* which some evaluate as the most influential curriculum report ever issued in the United States (Marsh & Willis, 2007). Cremin (cited in Pinar et al., 1995) lauded the report, commenting that "most of the important and influential movements in the field since 1918 have simply been footnotes to the classic itself" (p. 99). This one report changed the entire direction of education in the United States and was a complete break from the focus and methods of education in the 19th century. The overriding idea was that within a single, comprehensive high school, students would have a variety of experiences that would better prepare them for effective citizenship in a democratic society (Marsh & Willis, 2007; Pinar et al., 1995). The committee's recommendations stressed the idea of whole child development rather than merely academic development (Ornstein & Hunkins, 1998). Many issues raised by the 1918 report continue to have a profound impact on curriculum practices within the United States today, as industrialists, politicians, and educators continue to debate whether or not one high school can truly serve the needs of all students.

An additional effect of the 1918 committee was the support for and the reorganization of junior high schools. The first junior high schools were established in 1909. Prior to this time, students spent eight years in elementary school, but were required to attend school until age 14, which often occurred in the 9th grade. Studies on human development identified the period of late adolescence as having very different needs and characteristics than those of younger children (Tanner & Tanner, 2007). In addition, some high school educators did not believe that the elementary students who came to them were academically prepared. By 1930, there were some 4,000 junior high schools (Tanner & Tanner, 1990). Some of the "notable accomplishments" (Tanner & Tanner, p. 236) of the junior high were that curriculum redesign was possible in the 9th grade, since it was no longer a part of the high school. Students were exposed to a greater variety of courses than could be provided in elementary schools. More male teachers were attracted to teaching in junior high schools. As well, over time, the junior high contributed new curriculum ideas, such as "block-time and correlated and integrated core classes for general education" (Tanner & Tanner, p. 236). Unlike most elementary schools, most junior high schools were organized around separate subject matter courses and teachers were content-oriented, as they were in high schools (Gutek, 1988). By the 1950s, most K-12 systems contained junior high schools, with an overall 6-3-3 or 6-2-4 organization (Gutek, p. 202).

While the philosophy of the junior high was exploration and the philosophy of the comprehensive high school was helping all students achieve individual goals, in reality, curriculum often served as a means of tracking students. Students who performed poorly on standardized tests were not given the opportunity to experience the academic track of classes. I.Q. tests were administered to more than one million children by the 1920s. Designed to measure "mental aptitude rather than academic achievement" (Bernard & Mondale, 2001b, p. 102), these tests often discriminated against those students who did not speak English well or who had received a poor elementary education. Commenting on the tendency to put certain students into vocational courses, historian James Anderson (2001) commented, "When you look at the curricula that was [sic] developed—domestic science for women, industrial education for African Americans, boarding schools for Native Americans—much of what developed under the guise of a democratic and differentiated curriculum was in fact a way to reinforce the kind of class, gender, and race prejudice that existed in society" (p. 113).

The 1920s were an age of experimentation and battling curriculum theories. In the early years of the decade, the business-driven efficiency model had the stronger influence. However, after the stock market crash and economic problems that followed, business lost much of its influence and a focus on social reform and child-centered education began to take hold (Pinar et al., 1995). "New curriculum structures and arrangements" were implemented and many educators attempted to apply the "findings of child development to the organization, placement and articulation of studies" (Tanner & Tanner, 2007, p. 81). Some schools developed curriculum structures that differed greatly from the traditional subject-centered schools. One example of these was in Winnetka, Illinois, where all elementary school "children were allowed to work on achievement-skills units as long as needed for mastery" (Tanner & Tanner, 2007, p. 81).

Many university lab schools were organized around the principle of child centeredness. Dewey began the first of these schools at the University of Chicago in the late 1800s. In the early decades of the 1900s, other lab schools were established, such as The Lincoln School of Teachers College, Columbia University, and the lab school at the Bank Street College of Education. In these environments, teachers tried teaching methods and materials, documented their findings, and then used what they learned in other schools (Cuffaro, Nager, & Shapiro, 2005; Ornstein & Hunkins, 1998; Pinar et al., 1995).

The 1930s brought challenges for those who wished to see the expansion of the dramatic changes that were occurring in some schools. The Great Depression marked the federal government's first involvement with early childhood education through the establishment of Works Progress Administration (WPA) nurseries, which were created to employ out-of-work teachers and make it possible for mothers to enter the workforce (Graves, Gargiulo, Sluder, & Holmes, 1996). During the Great Depression, the federal government passed laws outlawing child labor, and many states passed laws requiring students to stay in school until age 16. These laws often resulted in overcrowded schools. Faced with more students, tracking was increasingly used, often to the detriment of minority students (Anderson, 2001). "By the 1930s, two thirds of Mexican American students in Los Angeles were classified as slow learners and even mentally retarded, on the basis of IQ tests given as early as kindergarten" (Anderson, 2001, p. 104). Although there was a national increase in students attending high school (51.4%), this was not true in all areas of the country (Ornstein & Hunkins, 1998). In the south, only "two of every 10 African American children of high school age were enrolled" (Anderson, 2001, p. 126). Nor were minority experiences included in most curricula (Gutek, 1998).

Many educators and researchers doubted the validity of the Progressive curricula and clung to the traditional subjects and teaching methods. One factor greatly influencing the supporters of traditional education was the college admissions process, which dictated most high school college preparatory curricula (Tanner & Tanner, 2007). Continued support for Progressive reforms was still evident in such works as Harold Rugg's and Ann Shumaker's *The Child Centered School* (1928), which promoted child-centered education, and Rugg's elementary social studies series, *Man and His Changing Society*, which became among the "most widely adopted school texts in a Progressive vein" (cited in Pinar et al., 1995, p. 132).

In 1931, the Progressive Education Association began its Eight Year Study, attempting to determine whether college success was related to a specific high school curriculum (Ornstein & Hunkins, 1998). Tanner and Tanner (2007) characterize this study as "the most important and comprehensive curriculum experiment ever carried on in the United States" (p. 85). Thirty schools willing to make curriculum changes were matched with 30 traditional schools. Three hundred colleges agreed to waive entrance requirements for students in those schools, beginning in 1936. Evaluations were ongoing during the time that the students were in high school, and then their performance in college was examined as well. The results overwhelmingly revealed that students who participated in the experimental programs "had higher grade point averages, received more academic honors, and were found to be more precise, systematic, and objective thinkers" in both high school and college (Tanner & Tanner, 2007, p. 87). In fact, the more experimental the curriculum, the higher the student achievement.

Ironically, by 1950, only one experimental school, which had been part of the study, still retained its curriculum (Tanner & Tanner, 2007). The results of the Eight Year Study were reported in 1942 and had little initial impact because of World War II (Marsh & Willis, 2007). As thinking in many arenas became more conservative during and after the war, the idea of experimentation in education fell into disfavor and more traditional programs were once again promoted (Tanner & Tanner, 1990). The study was not without substantial impact, however. While the experimental programs were being designed, Ralph Tyler created the concept of behavioral objectives, against which student performance was measured (Pinar et al., 1995), and implemented the inservice teacher workshop, as a way to help teachers who were struggling with developing new curricula (Tanner & Tanner, 2007). In addition to using behavioral objectives, teachers were asked to use the results of the evaluations to evaluate and modify what and how they were teaching, which currently remains a significant part of curriculum development and revision (Tanner & Tanner, 2007). Tyler's best-known work, *Basic Principles of Curriculum and Design,* originally written as a college syllabus in 1949, is often still used in planning curriculum (Ornstein & Hunkins, 1998). He proposed four basic steps in planning any curriculum: "identifying objectives, selecting the means for attainment of these objectives, organizing these means, and evaluating the outcome" (Tanner & Tanner, 2007, p. 135). Pinar et al. (1995) pronounced this work "the single most influential curriculum text ever written" (p. 148).

It was during the 1930s that curriculum began to develop as an integrated field, combining instruction and content, previously viewed as two different processes (Tanner & Tanner, 1990). Before this time, curriculum changes had been implemented on a school-by-school or city-by-city basis. In the 1930s, "state departments of education had become actively interested in comprehensive programs of curriculum development" (Tanner & Tanner, 1990, p. 236). This change was very significant, because the idea developed that the "revision of the curriculum should have as its central purpose the improvement of instruction" (Caswell, cited in Tanner & Tanner, 1990, p. 236), rather than merely listing objectives to be taught. Also, in 1938, the first department of curriculum and teaching in the United States was established at Columbia Teachers College (Tanner & Tanner, 2007). This marked an important milestone in the establishment of curriculum as a field of study, as previously those academics working in curriculum were primarily in departments of educational administration (Pinar et al., 1995).

Although some experimentation in teaching methods continued during the 1920s and 1930s, traditional methods were predominant in both elementary and secondary schools (Cuban in Pinar et al., 1995). There were some instances of progressive teaching in elementary schools, but only "mere traces" in secondary settings (Cuban in Pinar et al., 1995, pp. 753-754). By the 1940s, "common patterns of instruction included the following (a) employing the entire class as the primary teaching vehicle, (b) the use of the question-answer format, (c) a teacher monopoly of classroom talk, and (d) a general reliance upon the textbook" (Pinar et al., 1995, p. 754).

During the 1940s, World War II and its aftermath dominated most aspects of American life, and education was no exception. As had occurred during the Great Depression, the need for women workers brought the federal government into education. The 1942 Lanham Act provided almost 2,000 nurseries in 41 states, which provided early childhood education and child care (Osburn, cited in Graves et al., 1996). Debates continued over what courses and what school structures were needed in order to best prepare students for vocations or academics, and which would strengthen American democracy. Three developments continued to support the idea of comprehensive education at a time when the concept was under sharp attacks. In 1944, the Educational Policies Commission (EPC) of the NEA-issued *Education for All American Youth.* This document was truly revolutionary, calling not only for the continuation of the comprehensive high school, but also for extending education from nursery school through the first two years of community college. Students at all grade levels would take a "common learnings course which would be geared to effective citizenship" (Tanner & Tanner, 2007, p. 284). They also would be given time to explore personal interests. Upon entering high school, they would then add vocational and academic training. All courses would be open to all students (Tanner & Tanner, 2007).

Another concept, known as "life adjustment" education, also entered the curriculum arena in the mid-1940s. Developed because of concern over the high school drop-out rate and the number of high school graduates not going on to college, proponents of this curriculum called for more meaningful education for the general track student. The life adjustment curriculum had little impact on high school curricula, but protests against it as anti-intellectual unified those opposing Progressive reforms to demand a return to a "mental disciplinarian and classical curriculum orientation," a position that had not been commonly expressed in many decades (Pinar et al., 1995, p. 147).

In 1948, the Report of the Harvard Committee called for educators and policymakers to combine the best practices from traditional and Progressive education. Definite courses in subject areas would remain, but all students would take a common group of courses. Other courses or activities, whether vocational or academic, would be recognized as equally valuable (Ornstein & Hunkins, 1998). The Committee believed that the general education courses "would help produce an educated citizenry capable of making wise decisions in a democratic society" (Pinar et al., 1995, p. 145).

As attacks mounted against Progressive education, James Conant became the mid-century voice in support of the comprehensive high school. Conant, a scientist, Harvard president, and U.S. ambassador, asserted that "the strengthening of comprehensive secondary education [was] the best assurance of a 'classless' and free society (Tanner & Tanner, 2007, p. 68). In *The American High School Today*, published in 1959, Conant proposed curriculum requirements for high schools—"4 years of English, 3 or 4 years of social studies . . ., one year of math, and one year of science" (Pinar et al., 1995, p. 158)—that became widely used in high schools across the country. By 1950, 60% of school-age students graduated from high school and nearly half of them attended college (Bernard & Mondale, 2001a). This was not true of school-age minority and disabled students, however, as "Mexican Americans attended school an average of 5.6 years and 72% of disabled school age children were not enrolled" (Bernard & Mondale, p. 133). African American students were segregated by law in many states and by custom in others. Concluding a four-year study of race relations in America, Gunnar Myrdals wrote, in 1944, that "civil rights reforms and expanding educational opportunities to all regardless of color" would improve the situation for racial minorities (Tanner & Tanner, 1990, p. 261).

African American servicemen, having made some gains toward equality in the military, were determined to fight the discrimination they faced upon returning home. In 1954, their cause was realized when the U.S. Supreme Court decision *Brown v. the Board of Education of Topeka* reversed the 1896 doctrine of "separate but equal" ruling in *Plessy v. Ferguson* and ended racial segregation in schools. This was "an historic first step in the long and still unfinished journey toward equality in U.S. education" (*American Educational History Timeline*, n.d.).

1950s-Present

Although 1950-1975 were years of turmoil, violence, and uncertainty, they were also years of progress. The decision that separating educational facilities by race was unconstitutional placed government on the side of desegregation and inspired the move for equitable education of minority groups. The 1974 court ruling in *Lau v. Nichols* directed school districts to establish special language programs for non-English-speaking children. Funding for such programs was provided the same year, when Congress passed the Bilingual Education Act (Wortham, 1992).

The Soviet launching of Sputnik in 1957 led Americans to question existing educational practices, resulting in the implementation of numerous national curriculum projects (Ryan & Cooper, 2001), many of which were financed by the National Defense Education Act (NDEA). Passed by Congress in 1968, the NDEA provided assistance to both private and public schools for the primary purpose of advancing areas considered crucial for national defense—science, mathematics, and foreign languages (National Defense Education Act, 2001-04). Additionally, educational advancements for the gifted resulted from the nation's general sense of urgency to educate its more advanced students (Hearne & Maurer, 2000).

As part of President Lyndon Johnson's "War on Poverty," the Elementary and Secondary Education Act (ESEA) of 1965 significantly improved educational opportunities for the disadvantaged. ESEA authorized funds for the educationally disadvantaged child, library resources, efforts to advance creativity, educational research, and state departments of education (Jeffrey, 1978). Head Start, an eight-week summer program designed to increase the chances of school success for poor children, was created under the Economic Opportunity Act of 1965. The original program soon became a year-long school-readiness program providing comprehensive services to enrolled children and families. The creation of Head Start resulted in an instantaneous and large-scale need for curriculum designed specifically for young children identified as disadvantaged. Several curricula models, including behaviorist, play-based, Montessori, and cognitive interactionists, were implemented and systematically assessed as part of the general evaluation of Head Start's effectiveness. Initial results showed significant gains for all children in Head Start programs, regardless of curriculum model, compared with those not enrolled, and the long-term positive effects of Head Start were confirmed with longitudinal data from the Perry Preschool Project, published in 1981 (Nourot, 2005).

Despite such federally funded educational efforts to compensate for differences between affluent and underprivileged students, the achievement gap continued to widen, contributing to heavy enrollment growth in vocational education programs. Congress responded by enacting the Manpower Development and Training Act of 1961 (MDTA), followed by the Vocational Education Act of 1963 (VEA). These two pieces of legislation, along with the Applied Technology Act (1984), have helped to upgrade the nation's workforce and ensure that vocational training was available for economically or physically challenged young people ("Vocational Education," 2007).

The Education for All Handicapped Children Act, commonly known as Public Law 94-142, was passed under the Ford Administration in 1975. This law, which extended and amended the ESEA of

1965, improved the access to education for handicapped children through provision of a free appropriate education, established the concept of least restrictive environment, and mandated the use of an Individualized Education Plan (IEP) for all students eligible for special education services. A 1986 amendment (Public Law 94-457) established early intervention services for special needs children ages 3-5, and the law itself was renamed as the Individuals With Disabilities Education Act (IDEA). Seven years later, significant amendments to IDEA expanded the definition of disabled and provided procedures for mediating parental disputes. In 2004, in an effort to align with the No Child Left Behind Act of 2001, the law was again amended and became known as the Individuals With Disabilities Education Improvement Act (IDEIA). As of 2006, more than 6 million children in the United States had received special education services through IDEA (*IDEA Parent Guide*, 2006).

The strong religious influence found in early American schools had all but disappeared from the curriculum by the 1960s. In 1962, the U.S. Supreme Court's *Engel v. Vitale* decision found that prayer in schools violated the First Amendment. This ruling was reaffirmed in the 1963 cases *School District of Abington Township, PA v. Schempp* and *Murray v. Curlett,* and in the 1985 case of *Wallace v. Jaffre* (Sass, 2007).

The Progressive education era of the 1920s-1940s emphasized a child-centered curriculum, stressing development of the individual rather than mastery of fixed subject matter. By the 1950s, curriculum had been broadened to accommodate the need for vocational preparation and personal development. By the 1960s, however, the curriculum had become more subject matter-centered, focusing on academic disciplines, particularly science and mathematics. The actual approach to teaching specific disciplines underwent significant change during the 1960s and 1970s, largely as a response to Jerome Bruner's 1960 publication of *The Process of Education*, in which he advocated a method called discovery learning. Rather than learning random facts associated with a discipline's content, Bruner proposed that students learn *how* to learn by discovering meaning for themselves (Ryan & Cooper, 2001).

The federally funded intervention and compensation programs of the 1960s and 1970s were undoubtedly influenced by the trends in educational thinking and psychology of their time. The behavioral formulation of objectives, however, has been linked to the federal funding of these curricula initiatives (Pinar et al., 1995). Behavioral objectives established measurable goals and outcomes for curriculum, making it quantifiable and, as a result, accountable. Benjamin S. Bloom established the system for classifying educational goals and objectives in his 1956 publication of *Taxonomy of Educational Objectives: The Classification of Educational Goals,* and later contributed to the development of the concepts, now known as Mastery Learning, an instructional strategy based on the principle that all students can learn a set of reasonable objectives with appropriate instruction and sufficient time to learn (Forehand, 2005).

The period from 1960-1980 has been characterized as a time of educational optimism and enthusiasm for improving the learning of all students (Wortham, 1992). One innovation was that many junior high schools were replaced by "middle schools" for grades 6, 7, and 8. In an effort to provide more developmentally appropriate education for young adolescents, the middle school movement is now the most common school type between elementary and high school. The middle school has yet to fulfill the expectations of its founders in terms of improving academic performance of 11- to 14-year-olds. The National Forum to Accelerate Middle Grades Reform, developed in 1997, continues to search for evidence that middle schools are implementing academically excellent, developmentally responsive, and socially equitable practices (The National Forum to Accelerate Middle Grades Reform, n.d.).

Back-to-Basics

The inability of schools to eliminate poverty and solve societal problems produced a perceived decline in educational excellence. This disenchantment with public schools triggered a back-to-basics movement in the late 1970s and early 1980s, which gained national attention with the December 8, 1975, *Newsweek* cover story titled, "Why Johnny Can't Write" (Shells, 1975). Movement leaders viewed numerous elective courses at the secondary level as weakening academic expectations and advocated for more demanding curriculum, not only emphasizing the fundamental subjects of reading, writing, and arithmetic, but also including science, history, geography, and grammar (Ryan & Cooper, 2001). At the elementary level, "Outdoor play, the creative arts, social studies and science became secondary to the basics of reading, writing and mathematics" (Ryan & Cooper, 2001, p. 67). In an almost opposite reaction to the personal freedom movement of the 1960s and early 1970s, the back-to-basics movement wanted schools to once again address the basics of morality, including the virtue of patriotism. Curriculum became more centralized as statewide curriculum objectives were mandated for preschool through 12th grade (Wortham, 1992). Further, attention was first given to the unintended, but real, outcomes and features that result from participation in the schooling process, the "hidden curriculum" (Pinar et al., 1995).

From 1960 to the present, the work of Jean Piaget and his early contemporary Lev Vygotsky has influenced theories of child development and teaching. During the last decades of the 20th century, Piaget's 1929 book *The Child's Conception of the World* became an important factor in developing cognitive views of learning and teaching (Sass, 2007). Both Piaget's theory of cognitive development and Vygotsky's sociocultural theory emphasized play's value to intellectual development and stressed the need for children to interact with objects and peers in their environment. These theories had a significant impact on educational theory and practice, leading to the perspective known as constructivism.

Constructivists believe that learners construct, or create, their own knowledge rather than passively receiving it; thus, they require an active learning process incorporating hands-on experimentation, with the teacher's role being to guide and facilitate the learning process. While behaviorist teachers are sometimes criticized for assuming too much control of learning, critics of the constructivist approach claim that its student-centered nature leads to a decline both in academic learning and classroom discipline.

The back-to-basics movement brought pressure for more academic learning at an earlier age, resulting in a conflict between accepted theories of child development and pedagogy. By the late 1980s, curriculum and instruction designed for older students were being used with young children (Nourot, 2005). This "academic pushdown" (Nourot, 2005, p. 28) became an issue of major concern, as opposing views of development and learning arose in preschools, kindergartens, and primary grade classrooms (Wortham, 1992). The National Association for the Education of Young Children (NAEYC) urged educators to consider not only age and individual appropriateness, but also the social and cultural appropriateness of materials and activities (Bredekamp & Copple, 1997).

Within the civil rights context of the 1960s, educators began to reexamine educational trends to either suppress or fuse cultural diversity. An increasing awareness of the cultural and linguistic diversity of children living within the United States produced a deeper understanding of multicultural education, defined by Banks and Banks (1995) as a "field of study and an emerging discipline whose major aim is to create equal educational opportunities for students from diverse racial, ethnic, social-class, and cultural groups" (p. xi). As a result, a more comprehensive approach emerged under the heading "anti-biased," acknowledging gender, social class, religion, sexual orientation, and disabilities, in addition to racial and cultural groups (Derman-Sparks & the ABC Task Force, 1989). This perspective advocated an inclusive approach that integrated the contributions of all traditionally underrepresented groups throughout the curriculum.

By the end of the 20th century, U.S. society experienced significant changes affecting schools and the curriculum, such as the need for job skills related to the dramatic increase in service industry employment, the availability of microcomputers for business and home use, and the surge of Asian and Latin American immigrants.

Curriculum patterns in high schools shifted considerably between the Civil War and World War I; however, most of the same subjects offered during World War I are still present (Ryan & Cooper, 2001). High school graduation requirements outlined in the 1959 publication of James Conant's influential work *The American High School Today* were common practice in secondary schools across the United States from 1960 to the early 1980s (Pinar et al., 1995). In 1983, the National Commission on Excellence in Education published its report *A Nation at Risk: The Imperative for Educational Reform*, which declared that American educational achievement was being matched and even surpassed by other nations. The report, claiming that the nation was threatened by "a rising tide of mediocrity," primarily focused on secondary education. Recommendations for improvement were concentrated in the following five areas: content, standards and expectations, time, teaching, and leadership and fiscal support. The report's authors recommended that all students complete four years of English, three years of math, three years of science, three years of social studies, and half a year of computer science, while college-bound students also would complete two years of foreign language (*A Nation at Risk*, 1983; Tanner & Tanner, 1990).

In 1989, President George H. W. Bush and the nation's governors convened for a bipartisan education summit that laid the groundwork for the 1994 law known as The Goals 2000: Educate America Act. In an effort to restructure schools and radically increase expectations for student performance (National Education Goals Panel, 1991), six national goals were identified to guide future educational initiatives and establish national standards in various subject areas that would measure the output of education systems throughout the country. By 1996, these centralized efforts had lessened, leaving virtually every state to establish its own standards for student learning, many of which were accompanied by rigorous testing in an attempt to hold both students and educators accountable for performance levels (Ryan & Cooper, 2001).

An Era of Accountability

The noticeable contribution of the back-to-basic movement evident in more recent reform efforts is a revived interest in the primary mission of schools—helping children become productive, contributing members of society (Ryan & Cooper, 2001). The No Child Left Behind (NCLB) Act of 2001, signed into law on January 8, 2002, by President George W. Bush, reauthorized the ESEA of 1965 and greatly increased the standards of accountability for states, school districts, and schools. Aimed at improving the performance of elementary and secondary schools and closing the achievement gap between minority and white students, NCLB promoted an increased focus on reading and, to a lesser extent, math, and mandated standardized testing. NCLB has been controversial since its inception; criticisms about NCLB have ranged from failure to fund the act to violation of states' rights, allegations of corruption, and claims of a narrow curriculum (McKenzie, 2007).

The 21st-century curriculum of American schools has been significantly influenced by the federal government's involvement in education. Today's curriculum is a product of landmark legislation and groundbreaking court rulings over the past 50 years, which have resulted in a process of continuous evolution as schools attempt to implement momentous changes outlined by lawmakers and judges. However, there are many voices calling for a return to more local, site-based control of schools, more teacher control over curriculum, and less emphasis on standardized testing as a measure of a school's success. For more than two centuries, public schools have both responded to and helped to shape American society and culture. Throughout these years, schools have been confronted with tremendous challenges, many of which persist today. Schools are still confronted with figuring out how to provide the best education to immigrant children and to those with disabilities, how to address the high drop-out rate, and how to provide meaningful vocational and college preparatory training in one high school. At the heart of these issues lies the curriculum—what is taught, how is it taught, and the relationship between what is taught to the students and to society (Tanner & Tanner, 2007). Curriculum must constantly be renewed and schools must "take advantage of changing conditions and in addressing emerging problems, recognize them for the opportunities they are" (Tanner & Tanner, 2007, p. 476). To this end, curriculum in the United States remains a work in progress.

References

A nation at risk: The imperative for educational reform. (1983, April). Retrieved August 8, 2007, from www.ed.gov/pubs/NatAtRisk/recomm.html

American educational history timeline. (n.d.). Retrieved July 27, 2007, from www.cloudnet.com/~edrbsass/educationhistorytimeline.html

Anderson, J. D. (2001). Introduction. In S. Mondale & S. B. Patton (Eds.), *School: The story of American education* (pp. 123-130). Boston: Beacon Press.

Armstrong, D. G. (2003). *Curriculum today.* Upper Saddle River, NJ: Merrill Prentice Hall.

Banks, J. A., & Banks, C. A. M. (Eds.). (1995). *Handbook of research on multicultural education.* New York: Simon & Schuster/MacMillan.

Bernard, S. C., & Mondale, S. (2001a). Why don't you go to school with us? In S. Mondale & S. B. Patton (Eds.), *School: The story of American education* (pp. 132-170). Boston: Beacon Press.

Bernard, S. C., & Mondale, S. (2001b). You are an American. In S. Mondale & S. B. Patton (Eds.), *School: The story of American education* (pp. 71-119). Boston: Beacon Press.

Bredekamp, S., & Copple, C. (Eds.). (1997). *Developmentally appropriate practice in early childhood programs.* Washington, DC: National Association for the Education of Young Children.

Cuffaro, H. K., Nager, N., & Shapiro, E. K. (2005). The developmental-interaction approach at Bank Street College of Education. In J. L. Roopnarine & J. E. Johnson (Eds), *Approaches to early childhood education* (pp. 280-295). Upper Saddle River, NJ: Prentice-Hall.

Derman-Sparks, L., & the ABC Task Force. (1989). *Anti-bias curriculum: Tools for empowering young children.* Washington, DC: National Association for the Education of Young Children.

Forehand, M. (2005). Bloom's taxonomy: Original and revised. In M. Orey (Ed.), *Emerging perspectives on learning, teaching, and technology.* Retrieved September 4, 2007, from http://projects.coe.uga.edu/epltt/index.php?title=Bloom%27s_Taxonomy

Good, H. (1962). *A history of American education.* New York: Macmillan.

Good, H. G., & Teller, J. D. (1973). *A history of American education.* New York: Macmillan.

Graves, S. B., Gargiulo, R. M., Sluder, L. C., & Holmes, P. (1996). *Young children: An introduction to early childhood education.* Minneapolis, MN: West Publishing.

Gutek, G. L. (1988). *Education and schooling in America.* Englewood Cliffs, NJ: Prentice Hall.

Hearne, J., & Maurer, B. (2000). Gifted education: A primer. *New Horizons for Learning.* Retrieved August 12, 2007, from www.newhorizons.org/spneeds/gifted/hearne.htm

Henninger, M. L. (2005). *Teaching young children: An introduction.* Upper Saddle River, NJ: Pearson/Merrill/Prentice Hall.

Hyun, E. (2000, April). *Critical examination of U.S. curriculum in early childhood education.* Paper presented at the Annual Meeting of the American Educational Research Association, New Orleans, LA.

Jeffrey, J. R. (1978). *Education for the children of the poor: A study of the origins and implementation of the Elementary and Secondary Education Act of 1965.* Columbus, OH: State University Press.

Kaestle, C. F. (2001). Introduction. In S. Mondale & S. B. Patton (Eds.), *School: The story of American education* (pp. 11-60). Boston: Beacon Press.

Katz, L. G., & Chard, S. C. (2000). *Engaging children's minds: The project approach.* Stamford, CT: Ablex.

Marsh C. J., & Willis, G. (2007). *Curriculum: Alternative approaches, ongoing issues.* Upper Saddle River, NJ: Pearson.

McKenzie, J. (2007). *Beginning of the end of NCLB.* Retrieved September 4, 2007, from http://nochildleft.com/2007/mar07begin.html

National Center for Learning Disabilities. (2006). *IDEA parent guide.* Retrieved June 16, 2007, from www.ncld.org/images/stories/downloads/parent_center/idea2004 parentguide.pdf

National Defense Education Act (2001-2004). *The Columbia Encyclopedia, 6.* Retrieved August 12, 2007, from www.bartleby.com/65/

National Education Goals Panel. (1991). *Executive summary: The National Education Goals Report.* Washington, DC: Author.

National Forum to Accelerate Middle Grades Reform. (n.d.). *Our vision statement.* Retrieved September 4, 2007, from www.mgforum.org/about.vision.asp

Nourot, P. M. (2005). Historical perspectives on early childhood education. In J. L. Roopnarine & J. E. Johnson (Eds.), *Approaches to early childhood education* (pp. 3-43). Upper Saddle River, NJ: Prentice-Hall.

Ornstein, A. C., & Hunkins, F. P. (1998). *Curriculum foundations, principles and issues.* Boston: Allyn and Bacon.

Pinar, W. F., Reynolds, W. M., Slattery, P., & Taubman, P. (1995). *Understanding curriculum: An introduction to historical and contemporary discourses.* New York: Peter Lang.

Ravitch, D. (2001). Introduction. In S. Mondale & S. B. Patton (Eds.), *School: The story of American education* (pp. 62-70). Boston: Beacon Press.

Ryan, K., & Cooper, J. M. (2001). *Those who can teach.* Boston: Houghton Mifflin.

Sass, E. (2007). *American educational history: A hypertext timeline.* Retrieved August 17, 2007, from www.cloudnet.com/~edrbsass/educationhistorytimeline.html

Shells, M. (1975). Why Johnny can't write. *Newsweek, 92*(23), 58-65.

Tanner, D., & Tanner, L. (1990). *History of the school curriculum.* New York: Macmillan.

Tanner, D., & Tanner, L. (2007). *Curriculum development: Theory into practice.* Upper Saddle River, NJ: Pearson.

Tyack, D. (2001). Introduction. In S. Mondale & S. B. Patton (Eds.), *School: The story of American education* (pp. 1-8). Boston: Beacon Press.

Vocational Education. (2007). *The Columbia encyclopedia, 6.* Retrieved August 12, 2007, from http://columbia.thefreedictionary.com/vocational+education

Wortham, S. C. (1992). *Childhood 1892-1992.* Olney, MD: Association for Childhood Education International.

About the Authors

Susan Santoli, Ph.D., teaches courses in secondary education and social studies methods.

Rebecca M. Giles, Ph.D., teaches courses in elementary and early childhood education and is the co-author of *Write Now! Publishing With Young Authors, Pre-K Through Grade 2* (Heinemann, 2007).

Edward. L. Shaw, Jr., Ed.D., teaches courses in elementary science education.

The authors are faculty in the Department of Leadership and Teacher Education at the University of South Alabama, Mobile, AL.

Epilogue:
Pulling It All Together

Jerry Aldridge, Lois Christensen, and L. Kay Emfinger

James Kirylo and Ann Nauman are to be commended for gathering these perspectives on curriculum development from around the world. In this volume, we see the incredible similarities and differences in curriculum. Here, we have the difficult job of trying to pull it all together. What do these curriculum development perspectives actually have in common, and where are the points at which these different national ideas diverge? There are virtually hundreds of ways to answer this question. For example, Ryder (2008) has approached curriculum from an instructional design models paradigm. He provides a list of over 100 websites that address modern prescriptive models and postmodern phenomenological models. Ryder also lists web-based resources that deal with comparative summaries. If all of the resources were printed from Ryder's website, this would result in thousands of pages of just introductory material concerning curriculum and instructional models. Indeed, the task of pulling together the perspectives in this volume is a daunting one.

Another issue in pulling together curriculum perspectives from around the world has to do with interpretation. Most epilogues that we read are somewhat patronizing. The authors tell us what all of the preceding material means from their own perspective, but usually fail to suggest tools with which the reader can come to his or her own conclusions. We have decided the best approach for us is to provide three major ways in which the reader can consider the multiple perspectives found in this book. As we have stated, there are hundreds of ways to look at curriculum. Therefore, we have chosen three that we believe provide broad lenses through which the meaning of these different curriculum perspectives can be viewed: 1) Fraser's Model of Social Justice (Fraser, 1997), 2) Jungck and Marshall's (1992) curriculum perspectives, and 3) Aldridge, Emfinger, and Martin's (2006) frameworks, approaches, and models ideas concerning curriculum differentiation. So, the purpose of this epilogue is to propose three ways that you, the reader, can analyze each of the curriculum development perspectives presented in this volume.

Epilogue

Fraser's Model of Social Justice

Most of the perspectives presented in this text consider social justice, either explicitly or implicitly, to be one of the cornerstones of curriculum. "Social justice" is a term that has been used extensively with regard to curriculum development over the past two decades. However, "the conceptual underpinnings of this catchphrase frequently remain tacit and underexplored" (North, 2006, p. 507). When we begin to examine what a social justice curriculum means to different populations, we immediately notice tensions and collisions among different ideologies. Fraser (1997) describes many of these tensions, and North (2006) elaborates on Fraser's three-sphere model of social justice. This section explores three major tensions surrounding social justice beliefs and resulting practices with regard to curriculum development.

Sameness/Difference

The issue of how to promote equal access and equity is the first tension put forth by Fraser. Is equality achieved by working for **sameness** or is it accomplished by valuing **difference**? This tension is found in many of the curriculum perspectives from around the world. One example is curriculum development in Australia. In chapter 2, Pannizon suggests that "it would seem that a national focus [**sameness**] on curriculum provides many valuable educational outcomes as part of an integrated and coordinated approach. However, of equal significance for educationalists in Australia is the loss of autonomy for individual jurisdictions in terms of being able to develop and implement a curriculum that addresses the needs of students by using an established infrastructure and process that is relevant within a particular educational context" [**difference**].

Another example of this **sameness/difference** conflict can be found in the United States. For example, the No Child Left Behind Act of 2001 was created to close the gap between low-income and middle-income schools by creating **sameness**. Students in special groups, such as English language learners or children in special education, are expected to meet the **same** standards as everyone else. Contrast this with the Individuals With Disabilities Education Improvement Act of 2004 (IDEA). IDEA was created to promote social justice and equity in curriculum by emphasizing **difference**. Students with special needs receive an individual education plan to meet their unique needs because they are **different**. Accommodations or modifications are made based on how different a student is from his or her peers.

Many of the authors of the different perspectives presented in this book would argue that curriculum development involves a balance between sameness and difference. While this is true, most curriculum perspectives lean toward one or the other. We encourage the reader to examine the curriculum ideas presented in this volume from the tension resulting from sameness/difference. Which countries tend to promote sameness through a national curriculum, and which ones focus more on the individual autonomy and differences promoted by local or regional groups?

Redistribution/Recognition

The second of Fraser's social justice tensions revolves around **redistribution** versus **recognition** (North, 2006). In capitalist societies, curriculum tends to be framed as a commodity to be distributed or redistributed. Social benefits and burdens are entities that must be distributed for social justice. "These benefits include material resources, such as income, but also nonmaterial goods, such as rights and self-respect. When employed in social justice discussions, the distributive paradigm frequently fails to examine social structures and institutional contexts, such as the division of labor and the organization of decision-making bodies" (North, 2006, p. 510).

Rawls (2001) describes two conditions necessary for redistribution. One is that everyone has the right to an education, to work for the "good life," and to determine what this means. People also should have the opportunity to change their minds or plans as they choose, as long as they work within the rules of society. The second condition is that those with disadvantages or disabilities should have equal opportunity and be given special opportunities to succeed, since this initial inequity was not of their choosing (Kymlicka, 1989). However, most of the discussion about redistribution has centered on the political economy and class structures. Limited discussions concerning redistribution have been made concerning curricula.

Considering the curriculum perspectives presented in this book, readers are encouraged to consider how redistribution of the curriculum for social justice has occurred, or is currently happening, in different countries. A good place to start would be the chapter on Brazil (chapter 4). Historically, it appears that Brazil has grappled with issues of curriculum redistribution since the beginning of its educational programs. Similarly, Kenya (chapter 13) has been dealing with redistribution since its independence.

Not everyone supports the **redistribution** model as it relates to curriculum. Many pedagogists instead believe that the **recognition** model should prevail. "The politics of recognition, emphasized by various feminist, communitarian, cultural studies, queer, (dis)ability, postcolonial, psychoanalytical, and poststructuralist theories, take issue with the presuppositions put forth by this redistributive vision of social justice" (North, 2006, p. 513). Redistribution can take the form of redistributing mainstream knowledge that is biased and favors dominant groups. This happens often in countries that have heterogeneous and distinctly diverse populations. The notion that knowledge must be distributed so that minorities, new language learners, and special education students succeed on standardized tests does nothing to recognize unique abilities and potential contributions of the marginalized populations—not to mention that this distribution or redistribution of knowledge is usually based on the dominant cultural view, producing a biased curriculum.

Those who support a **recognition** model of social justice emphasize marginalized cultural knowledge—knowledge that is not determined by what the dominant culture values. In the past, many students did not see themselves reflected in the curriculum, in books, or anywhere else in school. To a great extent, this is still the case. It is as if their stories and what is important to them and their families do not exist or are invisible. Marginalization, exclusion, and silencing are used to intimidate cultural knowledge that is not sanctioned by the government through the curriculum. Recognition "locates the core of all experiences of injustice in the withdrawal of social recognition, in the phenomena of humiliation and disrespect" (Honneth, 2003, p. 134).

With regard to any curriculum, recognition requires valuing differences, reading about them, discussing them, and teaching in ways that accept and promote difference. We suggest that you consider the curriculum perspectives of each country related to how the curriculum promotes or denies recognition. A good place to start would be to consider the integrated education in Northern Ireland (chapter 18) as it relates to peace education, or the bilingual education and curriculum development found in Paraguay (chapter 19).

Micro Level/Macro Level

A third conflict related to curriculum involves a **micro level** focus (such as what goes on in an individual classroom) versus a **macro level** emphasis (such as what occurs at the national debate level). In reality, curriculum cannot be achieved without focusing on both. Most government mandates are dependent on teachers, who are expected to stay in their classrooms and teach to the microsystem. In some countries, this micro level edict from the government is not encouraged for social justice, but is used to perpetuate the dominant structures of the society that are already in place. For example, if teachers' job security is based on the test scores of their students, then they must attend to their individual classroom students, leaving them no time or energy to work beyond the micro level of their classrooms (Aldridge & Goldman, 2007).

At the micro level, teachers can teach for equity and social justice. They can recognize their students' individual learning styles, cultures, interests, and use these as tools to bring about the full potential of their students. They also can work to make sure that children of poverty, those with special needs, and children with different language, ethnic, or racial backgrounds are fully included in the classroom through attitude, curricula, and any other means within their power (Wink, 2005). In short, teachers at the micro level possess the power to make a preferential option for those students who have been historically marginalized (Kirylo, 2006). However, the challenge is that some countries encourage teaching toward diversity at the micro level more than others do. The reader is encouraged to consider each chapter presented here with regard to how curriculum perspectives support or discourage autonomy at the micro level of the classroom. The chapters on New Zealand (chapter 17), Poland (chapter 20), Russia (chapter 22), Turkey (chapter 25), the United Kingdom (chapter 26), and the United States (chapter 27) would be good places to address how curriculum is implemented at the micro level.

Then there is the **macro level**. Education cannot be achieved through micro level participation alone. When we move beyond each individual classroom, the question must be asked, "Who is in charge of the curriculum?" Does the power reside within the local community, the state, or the province, or is the power administered top-down from the national level? Many of the countries presented here have developed and are implementing a national curriculum. For those with a national curriculum, is the power all top-down or is there room for local and regional variations? The reader is encouraged to examine the curriculum in this volume from a macro level perspective. The chapters on Australia (chapter 2), Botswana (chapter 3), Korea (chapter 14), Malawi (chapter 16), Qatar (chapter 21), and Swaziland (Chapter 24) are suggested places to start.

Jungck and Marshall's Curriculum Perspectives

How curriculum is implemented is largely the responsibility of classroom teachers. Still, when curriculum guides are developed, there is either an implicit or explicit imperative as to how to carry out the curriculum. According to Jungck and Marshall (1992), there are basically three ways a curriculum can be implemented: 1) transmission, 2) transaction, and 3) transformation. Essentially, all forms of curriculum implementation fall under one of these three categories (Aldridge & Goldman, 2007). We will describe each as we encourage the reader to look at the curricula presented in this book from these three perspectives.

Transmission

"Without question, transmission teaching is the most common form of teaching" (Aldridge & Goldman, 2007). Transmission teaching is what many people refer to as traditional teaching. With transmission, the instructor figuratively pours the knowledge into the students' heads. A teacher's manual or guide provides the words for the teacher to say verbatim. Transmission is necessary for teaching social conventions. One example is the alphabet or characters of any language. The smartest students in the world will not know the names of the letters or characters unless some form of transmission occurs. While transmission is necessary, most educators agree that transmission is not the ultimate goal of the curriculum or education.

The teacher's role in transmission is often direct instruction. Transmission is closely aligned with the mechanistic paradigm and behavioral approaches (Thomas, 2005). Learning usually occurs in discrete steps of providing information fragments. A scope and sequence chart is usually provided to show the range and order in which the skills are to be taught. The instructor is considered a technician more than a reflective decision-maker, because most teaching decisions already have been made for the teacher by the developers of the curriculum materials.

Students, in a transmission curriculum, are the receivers of knowledge. Their job is to sit quietly, pay attention to the teacher, and respond appropriately to the teacher's direct instruction. Often there is only one correct answer. Students progress through workbooks, worksheets, computer-generated instruction, or through oral recitation of "correct answers." Instruction is often a one-way street and is non-negotiable.

Through assessment, students are placed in their appropriate levels of instruction and are then expected to move through the materials in a lock-step fashion. The materials supposedly have been sequenced from simple to complex or in ever-increasing difficulty. Students are to move through the curriculum in this linear order.

Which curriculum perspectives presented in this book are focused predominantly on transmission? This is a challenging question to answer. The reader is encouraged to consider which curricula focus more on the transmission of facts rather than on how these facts are used.

Transaction

Transaction is quite different from transmission. In transaction, "Knowledge is seen as constructed and reconstructed by those participating in the teaching-learning act" (Jungck & Marshall, 1992, p. 94). Teachers still follow curriculum guides but have more choices and a greater decision-making role in transaction. Students work in groups, share ideas, and work on activities that are "more open-ended and promote higher level thinking. Students can choose among various ways to represent what they have learned" (Aldridge & Goldman, p. 19). The transaction curriculum also has been referred to as the "generative model" (Wink, 2005). Constructivist teaching also is associated with transaction (Kamii, 2000).

While the teacher's role in transaction is to teach the prescribed curriculum, she also has the responsibility of promoting social interaction, selecting materials for students' research, and encouraging students to represent what they have learned in novel or interesting ways. The teacher also encourages students to share this information with the class. Teachers who are pressured to cover a plethora of material in a short amount of time find transaction difficult to implement. If a curriculum focuses more on covering a large amount of content, then transaction teaching is impeded.

Students are required to work with others as they prepare for a common goal. While the process is often considered more important than the product in transaction, groups are still required to represent and present what they have learned. Students also are involved in researching and planning. Learners take a more active role in transaction than they do in transmission.

Materials used in transaction are more authentic than those used in transmission. This means that resources used in transaction classrooms are similar to what we would experience outside the classroom or in everyday life. For example, we read real books, magazines, and newspapers instead of scripted direct instruction books. With transaction, real literature, periodicals, and the Internet are all used to learn the prescribed curriculum.

Materials also are used for representation. Instead of relying on worksheets, workbooks, or standardized tests, students show what they have learned through representation. There are hundreds of ways students can choose to represent what they have learned. They can make a mural, a mobile, a fact sheet, an overhead, a web page, or a game, or choose numerous other ways to show what they have learned (Aldridge & Goldman, 2007).

Which curriculum perspectives presented in this resource encourage transaction? Some researchers have suggested that transaction curricula are more popular in western countries and cultures, but is this actually the case? The reader is encouraged to consider whether transaction is a western phenomenon, or whether other countries promote transaction.

Transformation

Transformation is defined as curricula that encourage students to care for others and make a difference in the world (Aldridge & Goldman, 2007). A transformative curriculum can be controversial, because one person's idea of transformation is another person's notion of ideology.

The teacher's first task in transformation is to work to make a difference in the world and then instill in her students ways to make a difference. A transformative curriculum does not neglect accountability or research-based programs; rather, the teacher recognizes that there is more to curriculum than working to improve standardized test scores.

A transformational teacher carefully considers the context in which she teaches and is sensitive to the land mines associated with some forms of transformation. While seeking to help students transform their school, neighborhood, or community, the teacher carefully considers these values and beliefs.

Students are expected to take an active role in developing the transformative curriculum. Students are asked to suggest ways of making a difference in the school, neighborhood, or community, often based on the topics promoted through the traditional curriculum. For example, if the students are studying the conservation of energy, they are asked to think of ways to promote and implement conservation of energy in their school and community. Transformative projects develop from students' suggestions.

Materials are used to explore ways to make a difference in the world. Materials are used to develop projects and plans to implement change, and to support and document whole-class, small-group, and individual transformational projects. However, the word "materials" is too limiting for transformation. Teachers and children seek a wide variety of resources that go beyond the use of traditional classroom materials. Individuals and human resources are used to inspire and support transformational activities (Ostrow, 1995).

A transformational curriculum can be difficult to implement. Aldridge and Goldman (2007) have suggested four questions that should be asked of any transformational attempts in the classroom:

1. **Whose transformation is it?** What is chosen for transformational topics should not intentionally be controversial or confrontational.

2. **What about the imposition of well-intentioned, impractical, or harmful ideas?** Extensive research must be involved in transformational projects so that well-intentioned but harmful ideas are not imposed on others.

3. **Who and what are transformed by the project**? This question should be answered before a transformative idea is implemented.

4. **What are unintended consequences of transformation?** Sometimes individuals are marginalized by a transformational curriculum. For example, if students are selected for a gifted program in which a transformative curriculum is implemented, then the other students who are not part of the "gifted program" are discriminated against and not encouraged to participate in transformative projects.

We believe that many developers of curriculum would consider their ideas to be transformational. After all, the curriculum is designed to improve the educational level and lives of the students. However, how many curricula presented in this resource focus on helping students to make a difference in the world? Is it simply implied or expected? Or, is it a primary focus of the curriculum? The reader is encouraged to examine each chapter for curricula that explicitly encourage students to make a difference in the world.

Frameworks, Approaches, and Models

Aldridge, Emfinger, and Martin (2006) suggest that curriculum terminology is often vague—specifically, the terms "framework," "approach," and "model." All of these terms have been used interchangeably but actually have different meanings. This section provides a third way to consider international curriculum perspectives by focusing on frameworks, approaches, and models.

Frameworks

A framework is a general set of guidelines proposed by a professional organization or group of associates that describes the most basic ways to deliver instruction. While content may be addressed in a framework, the focus of a framework is on the "process" of instruction. An example of a framework is *Best Practices* (Zemelman, Daniels, & Hyde, 1998).

Approaches

Approaches are more specific than frameworks, providing more explicit guidelines with regard to both content and instruction. However, an approach is not meant to be replicated exactly from one context to the next. For example, the *Bank Street Approach* (Nager & Shaprio, 2007) is a progressive education approach that should be adapted from context to context.

Models

Although the term "model" typically encompasses frameworks and approaches, a model is quite distinct with regard to one very important requirement. That is, a model involves a "script" from which teachers should not vary. An example would be most scientifically based research "models" in the United States approved by the national government under No Child Left Behind. In most cases, models are scripted and teachers are not allowed to add additional instruction or modify the script in any way, as doing so would influence the fidelity of treatment. Direct instruction is one of the best examples of a model.

All of the curriculum perspectives of the countries provided in this volume promote either a framework, an approach, or a model for the curriculum. The reader is encouraged to consider and classify each in terms of curriculum frameworks, approaches, or models. By doing so, the reader gains a better understanding of who owns the power and how to implement the curriculum.

Conclusions

Kirylo and Nauman have provided an extensive look at curriculum perspectives from around the world. There are hundreds of ways to evaluate each curriculum. All of these ways are biased, because the reader cannot possibly understand the historical, political, and cultural contexts of each country. However, we have proposed three broad ways to examine each curriculum: 1) Fraser's Model of Social Justice (Fraser, 1997), 2) Jungck and Marshall's (1992) curriculum perspectives, and 3) Aldridge, Emfinger, and Martin's (2006) frameworks, approaches, and models. We encourage you to think of other ways to consider curriculum perspectives and to apply those that you believe are most appropriate.

References

Aldridge, J., Emfinger, K., & Martin, K. (2006). Curriculum frameworks, approaches, and models in early childhood education: What's the difference? *Focus on Teacher Education, 7*(2), 3-7.

Aldridge, J., & Goldman, R. (2007). *Moving toward transformation. Teaching and learning in inclusive classrooms.* Washington, DC: U.S. Department of Education; Birmingham, AL: Seacoast.

Fraser, N. (1997). *Justice interruptus: Critical reflections on the "postsocialist" condition.* New York: Routledge.

Honneth, A. (2003). *Redistribution or recognition? A political-philosophical exchange.* New York: Verso.

Individuals With Disabilities Education Act of 2004 (IDEA 2004). Public Law 108-446, 108th Congress. Dec. 3, 2004. Available at http://idea.ed.gov/explore/home

Jungck, S., & Marshall, J. D. (1992). Curricular perspectives on one great debate. In S. Kessler & B. B. Swadener (Eds.), *Reconceptualizing the early childhood curriculum: Beginning the dialogue* (pp. 19-37). New York: Teachers College Press.

Kamii, C. (2000). *Young children reinvent arithmetic: Implications of Piaget's theory* (2nd ed.). New York: Teachers College Press.

Kirylo, J. (2006). Preferential option for the poor: Making a pedagogical choice. *Childhood Education, 82,* 266-270.

Kymlicka, W. (1989). Liberal individualism and liberal neutrality. *Ethics, 99*(4), 883-905.

Nager, N., & Shapiro, E. (2007). *A progressive approach to the education of teachers: Some principles from Bank Street College of Education.* New York: Bank Street College of Education.

No Child Left Behind Act of 2001, P.L. 107-110, 11. U.S. Department of Education.

North, C. (2006). More than words? Delving into the substantive meaning(s) of "social justice" in education. *Review of Educational Research, 76*(4), 507-535.

Ostrow, J. (1995). *Room with a difference view: First through third graders build community and create curriculum.* Portland, ME: Stenhouse.

Rawls, J. (2001). *Justice as fairness: A restatement.* Cambridge, MA: Belknap Press of Harvard University Press.

Ryder, M. (2008). *Instructional design models.* [Online]. Available at http://carbon.cudenver.edu/-mryder/itc_data/idmodels.html

Thomas, R. M. (2005). *Comparing theories of child development* (6th ed.). Belmont, CA: Wadsworth.

Wink, J. (2005). *Critical pedagogy: Notes from the real world* (3rd ed.). Boston: Allyn and Bacon.

Zemelman, S., Daniels, H., & Hyde, A. (1998). *Best practice: New standards for teaching and learning in America's schools* (2nd ed.). Portsmouth, NH: Heinemann.

About the Authors

Jerry Aldridge is professor and coordinator of the Ph.D. program in early childhood education at the University of Alabama at Birmingham. He has published over 200 articles and authored or co-authored 12 books. He is the former president of the United States National Committee for the World Organization for Early Childhood Education (OMEP), and serves on the publications committee for the Association for Childhood Education International. He has appeared on CNN Headline News, The Health News Network, and has been quoted in *USA Today* and the *Chicago Sun Times.* He can be reached at jta@uab.edu.

Lois McFadyen Christensen is an associate professor of curriculum and instruction at the University of Alabama at Birmingham. She specializes in teaching and researching elementary social studies methods at the undergraduate and graduate levels. She teaches research methods and critical theory, and participates in a collaborative endeavor to educate graduate students about the civil rights movement. Technology is infused into all of her work. She is co-author of a Sage publication, *Integrating Teaching and Learning, and Action Research: Enhancing Instruction in the K-12 Classroom.* She can be reached at lmchrist@uab.edu

L. Kay Emfinger is an assistant professor of early childhood education at the University of Alabama at Birmingham. She specializes in constructivist teaching and gay, lesbian, bisexual, and transgender literature. She has published numerous articles, books, and book chapters. She also serves on several state advisory boards for early childhood education. She can be reached at emfinger@uab.edu